FROM BONDAGE

TO LIBERATION

FROM BONDAGE TO LIBERATION

Writings by and about
Afro-Americans from
1700 to 1918

Edited and Narrated by

FAITH BERRY

CONTINUUM

NEW YORK · LONDON

2001

The Continuum International Publishing Group Inc
370 Lexington Avenue, New York, NY 10017

The Continuum International Publishing Group Ltd
The Tower Building, 11 York Road, London SE1 7NX

Printed in the United States of America

Library of Congress Cataloging-in-Publication Data

From bondage to liberation : writings by and about Afro-Americans
from 1700 to 1918 / edited and narrated by Faith Berry.
p.   cm.
Includes bibliographical references (p.   ) and index.
ISBN 0-8264-1370-6 (alk. paper) — ISBN 0-8264-1345-5 (pbk. : alk. paper)
1. Afro-Americans—Literary collections.   2. American literature—
—Afro-American authors.   3. Afro-Americans—Civilization.
I. Berry, Faith.
PS509.N4F76   2001
810.8′0896073—dc20   93-31913
CIP

Dedicated to my ancestors
both black and white

CONTENTS

Preface   15

Acknowledgments   19

PART 1: FROM SLAVERY TO THE CIVIL WAR

Samuel Sewall (1652–1730)   23
From *The Selling of Joseph* (1700)   24

John Woolman (1720–72)   26
From *Some Considerations on the Keeping Negroes: Part Second* (1762)   27

Thomas Paine (1737–1809)   30
"African Slavery in America" (1775)   31

Thomas Jefferson (1743–1826)   35
From *Notes on the State of Virginia* (1785)   39
Letter to Marquis de Chastellux (1785)   43

Benjamin Banneker (1731–1806)   45
A Letter to Thomas Jefferson (1791)   46

Jupiter Hammon (1711–ca. 1806?)   50
An Address to the Negroes in The State of New York (1787)   51

Olaudah Equiano [Gustavus Vassa] (ca. 1745–ca. 1797)   60
From *The Interesting Narrative of the Life* . . . (1789)   61

Benjamin Franklin (1706–90)   69
An Address to the Public: . . . *for Promoting the Abolition
of Slavery, and the Relief of Free Negroes* . . . (1789)   70

Absalom Jones (1746–1818)   72
From A *Thanksgiving Sermon on Abolition of the Slave Trade* (1808)   73

Samuel E. Cornish (1795–1858) and John B. Russwurm (1799–1851)   77
"To Our Patrons"—Opening Editorial of *Freedom's Journal* (1827)   79

James Fenimore Cooper (1789–1851)   83
"On Slavery" (1838)   84
"On American Slavery" (1838)   85

David Walker (1785–1830)   87
From Article IV of *David Walker's Appeal in Four Articles* (1829–30)   88

William Lloyd Garrison (1805–79)   92
"To the Public"—the *Liberator*'s First Editorial (1831)   94

Maria W. Stewart (1803–79)   96
From *Religion and the Pure Principles of Morality* . . . (1831)   98

Nat Turner (1800–1831)   102
From *The Confessions of Nat Turner, the leader of the late insurrection in Southampton, Va.* (1831)   103

Frances Milton Trollope (1780–1863)   108
From *Domestic Manners of the Americans* (1832)   109

John Pendleton Kennedy (1795–1870)   111
From *Swallow Barn; or, A Sojourn in the Old Dominion* (1832)   112

Lydia Maria Francis Child (1802–80)   119
From *An Appeal in Favor of Americans Called Africans* (1833)   120

John Greenleaf Whittier (1807–92)   122
From *Justice and Expediency*. . . (1833)   123

Alexis de Tocqueville (1805–59)   127
From *Democracy in America* (1835)   128

James Kirke Paulding (1778–1860)   130
From *Slavery in the United States* (1836)   131

Angelina Grimké (1805–79)   134
From *Appeal to the Christian Women of the Southern States* (1836)   135

Theodore Dwight Weld (1803–95)   137
From *American Slavery as It Is* (1839)   139

Sarah Mapps Douglass (1806–82)   141
A Letter to Brother Garrison [w/ Grace Douglass] (1839)   142

William Whipper (1804?–76)   144
On "Colorophobia"—from a Letter in the *Colored American* (1841)   145

Henry Highland Garnet (1815–82)   146
"An Address to the Slaves of the United States" (1843)   148

Frederick Douglass (1818?–95)   155
"The Rights of Women" (1848)   158

Harriet Beecher Stowe (1811–96)   160
From *Key to Uncle Tom's Cabin:* "Poor White Trash" (1853)   162

George Fitzhugh (1806–81)   166
From *Sociology of the South* (1854)   167

William Gilmore Simms (1806–70)   169
From *Woodcraft; or, Hawks about the Dovecote* . . . (1854)   170

Martin Robison Delany (1812–85)   173
From *The Political Destiny of the Colored Race* (1854)   175

William Wells Brown (ca. 1816–84)   179
From *Sketches of Places and People Abroad: The American Fugitive
in Europe* (1854)   181

William Cooper Nell (ca. 1814–74)   185
From *The Colored Patriots of the American Revolution* (1855)   186

Roger Brooke Taney (1777–1864)   190
From *Dred Scott Decision: Opinion of the Court* (1857)   192

Walt Whitman (1819–92)   200
Slavery (1857)   202

Josiah Henson (1789–1883)   204
From *Truth Stranger Than Fiction: Father Henson's
Story of His Own Life* (1858)   206

John Brown (1800–1859)   208
Last Speech to the Virginia Court (November 2, 1859)   210

Charles Howard Langston (1817–92)   212
A Black Abolitionist in Defense of John Brown (November 18, 1859)   213

Henry David Thoreau (1817–62)   217
From *A Plea for John Brown* (1859)   219

Sarah Parker Remond (1826–1894)   223
An Exchange of Letters on American Citizenship (1859)   224

Robert Purvis (1810–98)   227
From *Your Government—It Is Not Mine* (1860)   228

Ellen Craft (ca. 1826–97) and William Craft (1827–1900)   232
From *Running a Thousand Miles for Freedom* (1860)   234

Frederick Law Olmsted (1822–1903)   237
From *The Cotton Kingdom: A Traveller's Observations on
Cotton and Slavery in the American Slave States* (1861)   238

Mary Boykin Chesnut (1823–86)   241
From *A Diary from Dixie* (1861)   243

Harriet Jacobs [Linda Brent] (1813–97)   247
From *Incidents in the Life of a Slave girl* . . . (1861)   249

Nathaniel Hawthorne (1804–64)   252
From *Chiefly about War Matters* (1862)   254

Abraham Lincoln (1809–65)   255
Address on Colonization . . . (1862)   258
Meditation on the Divine Will (1862)   262

Isabella Van Wagenen [Sojourner Truth] (1797–1883) 263
Letter after a Visit to President Lincoln (1864) 266

Charlotte L. Forten Grimké (1837–1914) 268
From *The Journal of Charlotte L. Forten* (1863) 270

Thomas Wentworth Higginson (1823–1911) 272
From *Army Life in a Black Regiment* (1870) 274

PART 2: FROM RADICAL RECONSTRUCTION TO THE DAWN OF THE HARLEM RENAISSANCE

Frances Ellen Watkins Harper (1825–1911) 281
From Speech to Eleventh National Women's Rights Convention (1866) 283

Joel Chandler Harris (1848–1908) 286
The Old Plantation (1877) 288

Alexander Crummell (1819–98) 291
From *The Black Woman of the South: Her Neglects and Her Needs* (1883) 293

T. Thomas Fortune (1856–1928) 294
From *Black and White: Land, Labor, and Politics in the South* (1884) 297

Albion W. Tourgée (1838–1905) 302
From An Appeal to Caesar (1884) 305

George Washington Cable (1844–1925) 308
From The Freedman's Case in Equity (1885) 311

Booker T. Washington (1856–1915) 316
The South as an Opening for a Career (1888) 319

James Weldon Johnson (1871–1938) 324
Best Methods of Removing the Disabilities of Caste from the Negro (1892) 327

William Dean Howells (1837–1920) 331
From *An Imperative Duty* (1892) 334

Anna Julia Cooper (1858–1964)   342
From *A Voice from the South* (1892)   344

Fannie Barrier Williams (1855–1944)   346
From The Present Status and Intellectual Progress
of Colored Women (1893)   348

Samuel L. Clemens [Mark Twain] (1835–1910)   358
From *The Tragedy of Pudd'nhead Wilson* (1894)   361

Paul Laurence Dunbar (1872–1906)   370
The Intervention of Peter (1898)   374

Sutton Griggs (1872–1930)   379
From *Imperium in Imperio* (1899)   381

Caroline Hollingsworth Pemberton (186?–1927)   384
From *Stephen the Black* (1899)   386

George Henry White (1852–1918)   390
From *The Negroes' Temporary Farewell to Congress* (1901)   392

Charles W. Chesnutt (1858–1932)   393
White Weeds (ca. 1903)   397

Pauline Elizabeth Hopkins (1859–1930)   412
From As the Lord Lives, He Is One of Our
Mother's Children (1903)   416

William Monroe Trotter (1872–1934)   418
Has the Race the Element of Self-Salvation in It? (1903)   423

The Niagara Movement: The Men and Ideas behind It   425
From The Niagara Movement "Declaration of Principles" (1905)   427

Kelly Miller (1863–1939)   430
An Open Letter to Thomas Dixon, Jr. (1905)   432

Ida B. Wells-Barnett (1869–1931)   443
"Brutal Burnt Offerings" (1909)   447

Oswald Garrison Villard (1872–1949)   451
"A Call to Action"—the Advent of the NAACP (1909)   455

William Pickens (1881–1954)   458
From *The New Negro* (1916)   462

Carter G. Woodson (1875–1950)   465
From A *Century of Negro Migration* (1918)   467

Index   473

PREFACE

Many of the authors in this collection have never been assembled together before. They represent both black and white voices from different cultural backgrounds, from the beginnings of American history through World War I. All provide insights into the development of American racial thought through more than two centuries. Side by side, their divergent views reveal how attitudes on race, gender, and class evolved and helped form our culture.

Until the late 1960s, the traditional American academic literary canon was segregated. Before that time, finding a nonwhite author represented in a mainstream text was as unlikely as seeing the moon at noon. Moreover, writings of widely anthologized authors rarely touched on race in survey courses. Academicians selected and anthologized such works for various publishers. But the contents were almost all identical, as if chosen by chefs planning the same menu. Not until the 1970s and 1980s did college curricula and texts begin to reflect the multicultural diversity of the United States. But while mainstream anthologies became more inclusive and integrated, Afro-American literature collections concentrated on black authors excluded from the traditional Anglo-American canon.

From Bondage to Liberation attempts a literary and cultural dialogue across the racial divide, to show the roots of our present situation. The polarized status of American literature makes a collection with black and white on common ground almost an anomaly. But it is an idea whose time is overdue. The focus in these pages is on a historic relationship that reveals the two races—Afro-American and Anglo-American—both as adversaries and as allies.

The works are interdisciplinary in nature, with selections arranged chronologically, each a sequel to an unfolding documentary. All selections are in prose, including fiction and nonfiction. It is important to point out this work is not intended as an American literature survey but as a companion volume for courses on related subjects, and as a resource for American Studies.

Among the seventy-five selections are those from microfilm and out-of-print publications. Reexamining them together in their literary and social context allows an understanding of the *Zeitgeist* that produced them. Each author's writing illuminates aspects of our literary and social history through the early part of the twentieth century. The book is in two parts to reflect significant periods of American history: "From Slavery to the Civil War" and "From Radical Reconstruction to the Dawn of the Harlem Renaissance." I conclude with Carter G. Woodson, who is rightly called "The Father of Negro History."

For reasons discussed in the biographical narratives—which are intended both as introduction to respective pieces as well as a general guide to the times and conditions under which they were written—some of the works have been previously ignored or suppressed. In this way, it is hoped this book will not only be of use to students and general readers, but also to scholars. Above all, the purpose of this work is to offer an integrated panorama of significant American writers who helped form our national heritage and consciousness. Together, they reveal the saga of a nation that began on a separate and unequal footing. Their words and deeds show what is required of us now and in the future. A companion volume, from the Harlem Renaissance to the Present, is planned. It will take readers into a new millennium with the hope that we may learn and thus avoid the racial mistakes, mistrust, and misunderstandings of the past.

With the historic foundation of the writers who follow, it is hoped that we may better understand our conflicts as well as what we, as a people from all parts of the world, have in common.

FAITH BERRY

Managing Editor's Foreword

Several years ago, we were approached by an attorney named Theodore M. Berry who was representing another project that was written by the editor and narrator of this book. It was only later that I came to learn this was Ted Berry, former mayor of Cincinnati and himself a pioneer: the first Afro-American mayor of a large North American city. His client, Faith, was one of his daughters. (Although I never met Mayor Berry, over the years I felt I came to know him through a familiarity with his words and deeds. It is sad that the Mayor recently passed away, not to see the publication of this work which he had first set in motion.)

For some time, we had searched for the right person to anthologize black American voices for a new generation. Faith Berry had a slightly different, and better, vision. These voices—some famous, some neglected with the passage of time—actually form a debate on perhaps the most important and complicated subject that faces each of us in our daily lives: race relations. We believe this book features new and important views, through the lens of Dr. Berry's narratives, on such well-known figures as Harriet Beecher Stowe, Mark Twain, Abraham Lincoln, Frederick Douglass, and many others. As has been remarked about great writing, this is news that stays news.

From Bondage to Liberation presents an unflinching, multifaceted view of the literary history of race relations in the United States. It is a fascinating story. The purpose of the book is to give us a better understanding of ourselves: where we have come from spiritually, socially, and economically, and where we may be going. Because of its nature, this volume will be unusually controversial for a collection of writers who principally precede the modern (and postmodern) eras. We need to take a good look at ourselves in the mirror this book holds up. Upon the planned publication of a sequel and companion, taking readers into the twenty-first century—also under the direction of Dr. Berry—we may yet see ourselves more clearly.

EVANDER LOMKE
CONTINUUM INTERNATIONAL

ACKNOWLEDGMENTS

As the author–editor of this volume, I wish to express a debt of gratitude to all those who have helped me at various times during the project, notably my father, Attorney Theodore M. Berry, for his unflinching moral and legal support before his recent death. I also owe much appreciation to my editor at Continuum International, Evander Lomke, as well as to Bruce Cassiday. I likewise have much gratitude for the love and encouragement of my mother and the support of my sister, Gail Berry West, who during my recent illness motivated me to complete this project.

F. B.

PART 1

From Slavery
to the
Civil War

SAMUEL SEWALL

(1652–1730)

The *Selling of Joseph*, one of the earliest tracts on slavery and the first written by a New England Puritan, was printed in Boston on June 12, 1700. It condemned slavery as immoral and inhumane, but Sewall's own prejudices about African inferiority precluded his call for abolition.

His representation of Joseph is from a biblical parable in the Book of Genesis—37:20–28, where the sons of Jacob, for twenty pieces of silver, sold their brother Joseph to Ishmaelite merchants, who sold him into slavery. Sewall argued that "Joseph was rightfully no more a slave to his brethren than they were to him" and lamented, " 'Tis a pity there should be more Caution used in buying a horse, . . . than there is in purchasing Men and Women."

Born in England, reared in Massachusetts colony, trained at the Harvard Divinity School, where he graduated in 1671 intending to enter the ministry, he instead chose a business career and later became one of the wealthiest men in Boston. Appointed to several judicial posts, including judge of the General Court in 1692, and chief justice of the superior court from 1718 to 1728, he was influential as a magistrate and member of the mercantile class. The most celebrated event of his public career was a penitent apology—before a church congregation—for his role as a commissioner and one of seven judges in the Salem witchcraft trial persecutions of 1692–93.

His famous *Diary*, a private record covering fifty years of New England colonial social history, was not published until the late nineteenth century. The *Diary* chronicled his family life and his transition from religious cleric to secular businessman, identifying piety, thrift, and hard work as keys to economic progress. The American exemplification of the Puritan ethic and glorification of business acumen can be traced in part to the ideas and example of Samuel Sewall. His avowed belief that New England was divinely appointed, and its white inhabitants spiritually anointed, was central to his apocalyptic book, *The New Heaven and New Earth* in 1697. His vision for New World Puritans did not include a holy alliance or social contract with Africans or Indians. He opposed a colony council bill on "Marriage of White Men with Negroes or Indians" but supported Puritan missionary work among dispossessed Indian groups.

The Selling of Joseph, called by scholars one of the first antislavery tracts, resists definition as "antislavery," in comparison to later pieces aimed not only at denouncing slavery but ending it.

The following excerpt from the 1700 document is reprinted from *Proceedings of the Massachusetts Historical Society, 1863–1864,* vol. 7 (Boston, 1864).

From *The Selling of Joseph* (1700)

. . . And all things considered, it would conduce more to the Welfare of the Province, to have White Servants for a Term of Years,[1] than to have Slaves for Life. Few can endure to hear of a Negro's being made free; and indeed they can seldom use their freedom well; yet their continual aspiring after their forbidden Liberty, renders them Unwilling Servants. And there is such a disparity in their Conditions, Colour & Hair, that they can never embody with us, and grow up into orderly Families, to the Peopling of the Land: but still remain in our Body Politick as a kind of extravasat Blood. As many Negro men as there are among us, so many empty places there are in our Train Bands, and the places taken up of Men that might make Husbands for our Daughters. And the Sons and Daughters of *New England* would become more like *Jacob,* and *Rachel,* if this Slavery were thrust quite out of doors. Moreover it is too well-known what Temptations Masters are under, to connive at the Fornication of their Slaves; lest they should be obligated to find them Wives, or pay their Fines. It seems to be practically pleaded that they might be Lawless; 'tis thought much of, that the Law should have Satisfaction for their Thefts, and other Immoralities; by which means, *Holiness to the Lord,* is more rarely engraven upon this sort of Servitude. It is likewise most lamentable to think, how in taking Negros out of *Africa,* and Selling of them here, That which GOD has joined together men do boldly rend asunder; Men from their Country, Husbands from their Wives, Parents from their Children. How horrible is the Uncleanness, Mortality, if not Murder, that the Ships are guilty of that bring great crowds of these miserable Men, and Women. Methinks, when we are bemoaning the barbarous usage of

---

[1] "White Servants for a Term of Years" referred to white indentured servants, who worked in the early colonies for five to six years in exchange for free boat passage, food, clothing, and a temporary contract or "indenture." After service, they were released as freemen and, in some colonies, entitled to land and supplies to begin farming or a trade. This barter system was a means of increasing population and apprentice labor.

our Friends and Kinsfolk in *Africa*: it might not be unseasonable to enquire whether we are not culpable in forcing the *Africans* to become Slaves amongst our selves. And it may be a question whether all the Benefit received by *Negro* Slaves, will balance the Accompt of Cash laid out upon them; and for the Redemption of our own enslaved Friends out of *Africa*. Besides all the Persons and Estates that have perished there. . . .

JOHN WOOLMAN

(1720–72)

The writings of John Woolman, an ascetic Quaker abolitionist, reflected the major differences between most colonial Quakers and Puritans on the issue of slavery.[1] In theology and literature, the Puritans considered history, nations, people shaped by a divine plan—and themselves preordained and justified in their roles and purposes. Their precepts were antithetical to beliefs and practices of the Quakers, whose meditative, soul-searching ways forced them to flee Puritan intolerance and persecution in New England. Woolman blamed exploitation of Negroes and Indians on English Puritans who practiced "the Spreading of a Wrong Spirit."

Quaker "seekers" or the "Society of friends" as they called themselves, believed in the spiritual force of the "inner light" of God guiding them in actions of Christian charity—without traditional preachers, rituals, sacraments, liturgy, and fire-and-brimstone sermons on sin, salvation, heaven and hell. Quaker principles and faith in the "inner light" directed John Woolman, of New Jersey,[2] to take a step as the first abolitionist Quaker to crusade against slavery.

In his public career, he chose the inverse path of the Puritan Samuel Sewall, who disapproved of Quakers but never knew Woolman, whose life began on a Northampton, New Jersey farm only ten years before Sewall's death. Whereas the latter had altered his career from clergyman to merchant, Woolman switched his own from business to religion. Reared in the Quaker community of Mount Holly, in the colonial province of West Jersey, near Philadelphia, he was trained as a farmer, bookkeeper, tailor, and notary public but abandoned those trades after deciding his income exceeded his needs. From 1743 until his death of smallpox during a tour of England in 1772, he devoted twenty-nine

---

[1] Woolman was not the earliest Quaker voice against slavery, but he was the first to exert influence without public rebuke from the Quaker Society of Friends. Earlier colonial eighteenth-century Quaker antislavery tracts included: John Hepburn, *The American Defense of the Golden Rule* (1715); Ralph Sandiford, *A Brief Examination of the Practices of the Times* (1729); and Elihu Coleman, *A Testimony against the Antichristian Practice of Making Slaves of Men* (1733); and Benjamin Lay, *All Slave-Keepers, That Keep the Innocent in Bondage, Apostates* (1737).

[2] Colonial New Jersey was divided into the provinces of East and West Jersey. The Woolman family was from West Jersey. The author was born in Rancocas, Burlington County.

years of his life to the Quaker ministry. In his religious duties, he was best known as a benevolent reformer; his reputation grew posthumously with publication of the *Journal of the Life and Travels of John Woolman in the Service of the Gospel,* in 1774. Commenting on the *Journal* in the nineteenth century, Ralph Waldo Emerson noted, "I find more wisdom in these pages than in any other book written since the days of the Apostles."

Woolman's personal experiences, study of Quaker doctrines, his abhorrence of slavery, and his commitment to justice were an impetus for his spiritual journey South—by foot and buggy—to urge Quakers who held slaves to free them. During those travels, he refused lodging "with People who lived in Ease on the hard labour of their slaves." Many Quaker "Friends" heeded his persuasion for emancipation, convinced that bondage was inconsistent with the humane tenets of their religion. During this time, he began writing the antislavery anecdotes that were published in his *Journal* two years after his death. But in his lifetime, he was able to summon more Quaker converts with publication and wide distribution of the abolitionist essays in his book, *Some Considerations on the Keeping of Negroes,* printed in two parts: the first in 1754, and a sequel in 1762.[3]

The following selection is excerpted from "Part Second."

From *Some Considerations on the Keeping of Negroes: Part Second* (1762)

. . . While we have no right to keep men as servants for term of life but that of superior power, to do this with design by their labour to profit ourselves and our families I believe is wrong. But I do not believe that all who have kept slaves have therefore been chargeable with guilt. If their motives thereto were free from selfishness and their slaves content, they were a sort of freemen, which I believe hath sometimes been the case.

Whatever a man does in the spirit of charity, to him it is not sin; and while he lives and acts in this spirit, he learns all things essential to his happiness as

---

[3] Woolman's manuscript, *Some Considerations on the Keeping of Negroes: Recommended to the Professors of Christianity,* was completed in 1747 but not published until 1754. The first published part included the word *Some* in the title; in the 1762 sequel, subtitled *Part Second* (printed by Benjamin Franklin and David Hall), *Some* was dropped from the title.

an individual. And if he doth not see that any injury or injustice to any other person is necessarily promoted by any part of his form of government, I believe the merciful Judge will not lay iniquity to his charge. Yet others who live in the same spirit of charity from a clear convincement may see the relation of one thing to another and the necessary tendency of each; and hence it may be absolutely binding on them to desist from some parts of conduct which some good men have been in.

As some in most religious Societies amongst the English are concerned in importing or purchasing the inhabitants of Africa as slaves, and as the professors of Christianity of several other nations do the like, these circumstances tend to make people less apt to examine the practice so closely as they would if such a thing had not been, but was now proposed to be entered upon. It is, however, our duty and what concerns us individually, as creatures accountable to our Creator, to employ rightly the understanding which he hath given us, in humbly endeavouring to be acquainted with his will concerning us and with the nature and tendency of those things which we practice. For as justice remains to be justice, so many people of reputation in the world joining with wrong things do not excuse others in joining with them nor make the consequence of their proceedings less dreadful in the final issue than it would be otherwise.

Where unrighteousness is justified from one age to another, it is like dark matter gathering into clouds over us. We may know that this gloom will remain till the cause be removed by a reformation or change of times and may feel a desire, from a love of equity, to speak on the occasion; yet where error is so strong that it may not be spoken against without some prospect of inconvenience to the speaker, this difficulty is likely to operate on our weakness and quench the good desires in us, except we dwell so steadily under the weight of it as to be made willing to endure hardness on that account.

Where men exert their talents against vices generally accounted such, the ill effects whereof are presently perceived in a government, all men who regard their own temporal good are likely to approve the work. But when that which is inconsistent with perfect equity hath the law or countenance of the great in its favour, though the tendency thereof be quite contrary to the true happiness of mankind in an equal, if not greater, degree than many things accounted reproachful to Christians, yet as these ill effects are not generally perceived, they who labour to dissuade from such things which people believe accord with their interest have many difficulties to encounter.

The repeated charges which God gave to his prophets imply the danger they were in of erring on this hand: "Be not afraid of their faces; for I am with thee to deliver thee, saith the Lord." Jer. 1:8. "Speak . . . all the words that I command thee to speak to them; diminish not a word." Jer. 26:2. "And thou son of man, be not afraid of them . . . nor dismayed at their looks. Speak my words to them, whether they will bear or forebear." Ezek. 2:6[–7].

Under an apprehension of duty, I offer some further considerations on this subject, having endeavoured some years to consider it candidly. I have observed people of our own colour whose abilities have been inferior of the affairs which relate to their convenient subsistence, who have been taken care of by others, and the profit of such work as they could do applied toward their support. I believe there are such amongst Negroes and that some people in whose hands they are keep them with no view of outward profit, do not consider them as black men who, as such, ought to serve white men, but account them persons who have need of guardians, and as such take care of them. Yet where equal care is taken in all parts of education, I do not apprehend cases of this sort are likely to occur more frequently amongst one sort of people than another.

It looks to me that the slave trade was founded and hath generally been carried on in a wrong spirit, that the effects of it are detrimental to the real prosperity of our country, and will be more so except we cease from the common motives of keeping them and treat them in future agreeable to Truth and pure justice.

Negroes may be imported who, for their cruelty to their countrymen and the evil disposition of their minds, may be unfit to be at liberty; and if we, as lovers of righteousness, undertake the management of them, we should have a full and clear knowledge of their crimes and of those circumstances which might operate in their favour; but the difficulty of obtaining this is so great that we have great reason to be cautious therein. But should it plainly appear that absolute subjection were a condition the most proper for the person who is purchased, yet the innocent children ought not to be made slaves because their parents sinned. . . .

THOMAS PAINE

(1737–1809)

Born of a Quaker father and an Anglican mother at Thetford, Norfolk, England, Thomas Paine never joined the Quaker Society nor advocated its pacifism, yet he often credited Quaker influence on his egalitarian thought.

He arrived in colonial America on November 30, 1774, a thirty-seven-year-old unknown author of two letters and an obscure pamphlet published in London. His encounter with the New World led to his campaign for separation from Great Britain and to some of his most popular writings: *Common Sense* (1777); and *The American Crisis* (1777–83). Those titles, however, were preceded by an uncelebrated essay denouncing slavery and the slave trade—a system that he deemed as tyrannical as British political domination. Written a few weeks after his arrival, his plea was published March 8, 1775, under the nom de plume "Justice and Humanity" in the *Philadelphia Journal* and the *Weekly Advertiser*. It took the form of an open letter entitled "To Americans."[1]

The crusading and persuasive tract, printed one year before the Declaration of Independence, dared to challenge what America's historic document would not: the situation of half a million slaves in the colonies. A month after publication of the essay, the first antislavery society in America began in Philadelphia—with Thomas Paine as a member.

Although he is best known as a pamphleteer who defended not only the American Revolution but the French Revolution—in *The Rights of Man*—and brought a new political philosophy with deistic religious principles to the common man—in *The Age of Reason*—he combined the essential concepts of a humanist and internationalist with a fighting spirit in defending the rights of the downtrodden everywhere.

His eighteenth-century text is reprinted here with modernized spelling, punctuation, and the title under which it appears in *The Complete Writings of Thomas Paine*, collected and edited in two volumes by Philip S. Foner.

---

[1] In the 1775 publication—now on microfilm—the text signed "Justice and Humanity" is printed on p. 5, minus Paine's name.

African Slavery in America (1775)

To Americans: That some desperate wretches should be willing to steal and enslave men by violence and murder for gain, is rather lamentable than strange. But that many civilized, nay, Christianized people should approve, and be concerned in the savage practice, is surprising; and still persist, though it has been so often proved contrary to the light of nature, to every principle of justice and humanity, and even good policy, by a succession of eminent men,[2] and several late publications.

Our traders in MEN (*an unnatural commodity!*) must know the wickedness of that SLAVE-TRADE, if they attend to reasoning, or the dictates of their own hearts; and such as shun and stifle all these, willfully sacrifice conscience, and the character of integrity to that golden idol.

The managers of that trade themselves, and others, testify, that many of these African nations inhabit fertile countries, are industrious farmers, enjoy plenty, and lived quietly, averse to war, before the Europeans debauched them with liquors, and bribing them against one another; and that these inoffensive people are brought into slavery, by stealing them, tempting kings to sell subjects, which they can have no right to do, and hiring one tribe to war against another, in order to catch prisoners. By such wicked and inhuman ways the English are said to enslave towards one hundred thousand yearly; of which thirty thousand are supposed to die by barbarous treatment in the first year; besides all that are slain in the unnatural wars excited to take them. So much innocent blood have the managers and supporters of this inhuman trade to answer for to the common Lord of all!

Many of these were not prisoners of war, and redeemed from savage conquerors, as some plead; and they who were such prisoners, the English, who promote the war for that every end, are the guilty authors of their being so; and if they were redeemed, as is alleged, they would owe nothing to the redeemer but what he paid for them.

They show as little reason as conscience who put the matter by with saying—"Men, in some cases, are lawfully made slaves, and why may not these?" So men, in some cases, are lawfully put to death, deprived of their goods, without their consent; may any man, therefore, be treated so, without any

---

[2] Dr. Ames, Baxter, Durham, Locke, Carmichael, Hutcheson, Montesquieu, and Blackstone, Wallis, etc., etc. Bishop of Gloucester. [Author's note.]

conviction of desert? Nor is this plea mended by adding—"They are set forth to us as slaves, and we buy them without farther inquiry, let the sellers see to it." Such men may as well join with a known band of robbers, buy their ill-got goods, and help on the trade; ignorance is no more pleadable in one case than the other; the sellers plainly own how they obtain them. But none can lawfully buy without evidence that they are not concurring with men-stealers; and as the true owner has a right to reclaim his goods that were stolen, and sold; so the slave, who is proper owner of his freedom, has a right to reclaim it, however often sold.

Most shocking of all is alleging the sacred Scriptures to favor this wicked practice. One would have thought none but infidel cavillers would endeavor to make them appear contrary to the plain dictates of natural light, and conscience, in a matter of common justice and humanity; which they cannot be. Such worthy men, as referred to before, judged otherways; Mr. Baxter declared, *the slave-traders should be called devils, rather than Christians; and that it is a heinous crime to buy them.* But some say, "the practice was permitted to the Jews." To which may be replied.

1. The example of the Jews, in many things, may not be imitated by us; they had not only orders to cut off several nations altogether, but if they were obliged to war with others, and conquered them, to cut off every male; they were suffered to use polygamy and divorces, and other things utterly unlawful to us under clearer light.

2. The plea is, in a great measure, false; they had no permission to catch and enslave people who never injured them.

3. Such arguments ill become us, *since the time of reformation came,* under gospel light. All distinctions of nations, and privileges of one above others, are ceased; Christians are taught to *account all men their neighbors; and love their neighbors as themselves; and do to all men as they would be done by; to do good to all men; and man stealing is ranked with enormous crimes.* Is the barbarous enslaving our inoffensive neighbors, and treating them like wild beasts subdued by force, reconcilable with all these *divine precepts?* Is this doing to them as we would desire they should do to us? If they could carry off and enslave some thousands of us, would we think it just?—One would almost wish they could for once; it might convince more than reason, or the Bible.

As much in vain, perhaps, will they search ancient history for examples of the modern slave trade. Too many nations enslaved the prisoners they took in war. But to go to nations with whom there is no war, who have no way provoked, without farther design of conquest, purely to catch inoffensive people, like wild beasts, for slaves, is a height of outrage against humanity and justice, that seems left by heathen nations to be practiced by pretended Christians. How shameful are all attempts to color and excuse it!

As these people are not convicted of forfeiting freedom, they have still a natural, perfect right to it; and the governments whenever they come should, in justice set them free, and punish those who hold them in slavery.

So monstrous is the making and keeping them slaves at all, abstracted from the barbarous usage they suffer, and the many evils attending the practice; as selling husbands away from wives, children from parents, and from each other, in violation of sacred and natural ties; and opening the way for adulteries, incests, and many shocking consequences, for all of which the guilty masters must answer to the final Judge.

If the slavery of the parents be unjust, much more is their children's; if the parents were justly slaves, yet the children are born free; this is the natural, perfect right of all mankind; they are nothing but a just recompense to those who bring them up: And as much less is commonly spent on them than others, they have a right, in justice, to be proportionably sooner free.

Certainly one may, with as much reason and decency, plead for murder, robbery, lewdness, and barbarity, as for this practice. They are not more contrary to the natural dictates of conscience, and feelings of humanity; nay, they are all comprehended in it.

But the chief design of this paper is not to disprove it, which many have sufficiently done; but to entreat Americans to consider.

1. With that consistency, or decency they complain so loudly of attempts to enslave them, while they hold so many hundred thousands in slavery; and annually enslave many thousands more, without any pretence of authority, or claim upon them?

2. How just, how suitable to our crime is the punishment with which providence threatens us? We have enslaved multitudes, and shed much innocent blood in doing it; and now are threatened with the same. And while others evils are confessed, and bewailed, why not this especially, and publicly; than which no other vice, if all others, has brought so much guilt on the land?

3. Whether, then, all ought not immediately to discontinue and renounce it, with grief and abhorrence? Should not every society bear testimony against it, and account obstinate persisters in it bad men, enemies to their country, and exclude them from fellowship; as they often do for much lesser faults?

4. The great question may be—What should be done with those who are enslaved already? To turn the old and infirm free, would be injustice and cruelty; they who enjoyed the labors of their better days should keep, and treat them humanely. As to the rest, let prudent men, with the assistance of legislatures, determine what is practicable for masters, and best for them. Perhaps

some could give them lands upon reasonable rent, some, employing them in their labor still, might give them some reasonable allowances for it; so as all may have some property, and fruits of their labors at their own disposal, and be encouraged to industry; the family may live together, and enjoy the natural satisfaction of exercising relative affections and duties, with civil protection, and other advantages, like fellow men. Perhaps they might sometime form useful barrier settlements on the frontiers. Thus they may become interested in the public welfare, and assist in promoting it; instead of being dangerous, as now they are, should any enemy promise them a better condition.

5. The past treatment of Africans must naturally fill them with abhorrence of Christians; lead them to think our religion would make them more inhuman savages, if they embraced it; thus the gain of that trade has been pursued in opposition to the Redeemer's cause, and the happiness of men. Are we not, therefore, bound in duty to him and to them to repair these injuries, as far as possible, by taking some proper measures to instruct, not only the slaves here, but the Africans in their own countries? Primitive Christians labored always to spread their *divine religion*; and this is equally our duty while there is a heathen nation. But what singular obligations are we under to these injured people!

These are the sentiments of—

JUSTICE AND HUMANITY.

THOMAS JEFFERSON

(1743–1826)

It was Jefferson's destiny to have a leading role in an unfolding national drama until the day he died. His death, as fate would have it, came on July 4, 1826—the fiftieth anniversary of the Declaration of Independence, the historic document that he had written and signed in 1776. Enshrined in the history of the American colonial era and early Republic, his public career for nearly thirty years led from one high political post to another: member of the Virginia House of Burgesses, delegate to the Continental Congress, governor of Virginia, ambassador to France, first American Secretary of State, second Vice President, and third President of a developing new nation. Shaped by the intellectual climate of the eighteenth-century enlightenment, his interests were as broad as the territory he helped to develop.

Provincial and traditional, yet unconventional and complex, Jefferson's character is reflected in the discourse of his first and only full-length book, *Notes on the State of Virginia.* Undertaken in 1780–81 in response to a French government questionnaire on the American states, it was written over a three-year period during Jefferson's temporary retirement—amidst conflict following the British invasion of Virginia in the Revolutionary War.

His knowledge of his native state—for which he served two years as governor from 1779 to 1781—is corroborated in the twenty-three commentaries he wrote on Virginia's resources, inhabitants, institutions, and geography. The book excerpts included here on slavery are from his chapter on "Laws" (Query XIV) and the full text of "Manners" (Query XVIII).

He did not envision publication of the work; it was originally intended only as a communication to François de Marbois, secretary of the French legation in Philadelphia. When a privately printed edition of two hundred copies appeared in Paris in 1785—during his diplomatic service in France—he permitted only his initial on the title page. If his attitudes on race and emancipation made him reluctant to be quoted, he had good reason. His personal views represent the contradictions of a slave owner in a democratic society, fighting for the embattled ideals of a conservative, emerging nation in conflict with itself.

Although he authorized English publication of an expanded and "corrected" edition of his *Notes* in 1787—from which excerpts are reprinted here—neither edition included his more positive sentiments about blacks in a letter dated June 7, 1785, to the Marquis François-Jean de Chastellux.

Excerpted in this section are those epistolary comments to the marquis, a French aristocrat who visited Jefferson at Monticello in 1780 and 1782. Their exchange of correspondence in France in June 1785 pivots around *Notes on the State of Virginia*. After reading the Paris edition, de Chastellux penned a letter (in French, dated June 2, 1785) seeking clarification of Jefferson's disagreements with the scientific theories of Georges-Louis Leclerc de Buffon,[1] the leading French naturalist of the day. In his lengthy response, Jefferson added new suppositions on the differences in the mental and physical abilities of whites, Indians, and blacks. The Frenchman's letter[2] hardly evoked such a reply, but Jefferson's comments amplify those in his book.

As a diplomat abroad, Jefferson was less prejudicial about Africans than he was at home; nevertheless, he failed to do anything to destroy slavery once he returned to America, where invention of the cotton gin in 1793 ended efforts of slaveholders inclined toward emancipation.

Notes on the State of Virginia does not acknowledge that the author was a slave owner. But his text is unequivocal on what to do with the manumitted slave: "When freed he is to be removed beyond the reach of mixture." Jefferson publicly opposed miscegenation, interracial mating, the social sin of the South, though it was an accepted practice of white men with slave concubines. The rumor that he later engaged in the practice himself—after the 1782 death of his wife—is now public knowledge. The fact that he never remarried, after becoming a widower at age thirty-nine, was perhaps not only to keep a death-bed promise to his wife not to wed again. His last will and testament documents manumission of five slaves with the surname Hemings—but not Sally

---

[1] Some of the theories of de Buffon (1707–88) in his multivolume *Histoire naturelle* were refuted in the *Notes* by Jefferson, who disagreed with the Frenchman that domestic and wild animals and aboriginal "savages" and "lower class" transplanted Europeans in the New World climate were smaller in physical size, less informed, and subject to greater degeneration in comparison with their European counterparts.

[2] Only obliquely does de Chastellux's letter touch on race: in his reaction to theories of Spanish author and explorer Don Ulloa [Antonio de Ulloa, 1716–95] whose descriptions of South American Indians in his *Noticias Americanas* (1772) Jefferson respected but did not fully agree with; de Chastellux comments that he himself was moved by Don Ulloa's assertion that "les motifs venant d'une négresse et d'un espagnol, ont plus de force et d'industrie que ceux qui naisssent d'une indienne et d'un espagnol." (the expectations emanating from the union of a Negress and a Spaniard bode more strength and skill than those born of an Indian woman and a Spaniard).

De Chastellux's handwritten letter was interlineally transcribed by Jefferson, who misinterpreted or omitted words or variant spellings he could not decipher in the penmanship. The transcribed letter is in *The Papers of Thomas Jefferson*.

Hemings, his quadroon servant with whom he allegedly had a thirty-eight-year liaison and seven children born at Monticello, from 1790–1808. When the taboo relationship with Sally—thirty years his junior and a half sister of his dead wife—made news in the *Richmond Recorder*, creating a scandal in 1802 (during Jefferson's Presidency), he neither publicly disavowed nor admitted the affair. But for over 160 years the rumor was either denied, repudiated, deleted, or uninvestigated by Jeffersonian heirs, scholars, and biographers—until several books surfaced during the 1960s and 1970s to highlight the concealed events.[3]

Notes on the State of Virginia, written when Sally Hemings was a small child growing up on Jefferson's plantation, cannot directly be linked to their intimacy. However, when writing the book, Jefferson had among the slave population at Monticello 135 slaves inherited by his wife, after the death of her father, John Wayles, who with his third slave mistress, Betty Hemings, sired Sally, born in 1773. The legacy of mixed blood in the offspring of his father-in-law was compounded by Wayles's dealing in the slave trade, the same profession of Jefferson's own grandfather. That heritage is behind the corrosive but controlled anguish in the contradictory prose on race in *Notes on the State of Virginia*. The curtain over the hidden domestic scene at Monticello, with its chiaroscuro of light and dark, of master and slave, the family legacy of passion, chattel, conflict, subjugation, and guilt is drawn in Jefferson's chapters on "Laws" and "Manners."

Jefferson was unsuccessful in winning adoption of his moderate antislavery proposals in the Virginia Assembly or in a draft of the Declaration of Independence. However, his declaration draft absolved American colonists for being slaveholders and blamed British King George III "for capturing and carrying [Africans] into slavery in another hemisphere."

Believing slavery and the slave trade a moral wrong while he himself owned chattel was a contradiction Jefferson never resolved. However, records of his *Farm Book* indicate humane treatment of slaves on his own plantations. In his *Autobiography*, undertaken when he was seventy-seven—with caution to conceal his private life after 1790—he wrote: "Nothing is more certainly written in the book of fate than that these people should be free."

Blacks were not on the national agenda of his Presidency and only reluctantly the focus of a private letter he wrote in Washington, February 25,

[3] On Sally Hemings, see the chapter by Winthrop Jordan on Jefferson in *White over Black: American Attitudes toward the Negro, 1550–1812* (1968), a chapter reprinted in his abridged and modified book, *The White Man's Burden: Historical Origins of Racism in the United States* (1974); the Hemings-Jefferson relationship is illuminated and documented in the late Fawn M. Brodie's biography, *Thomas Jefferson: An Intimate History* (1974); and the focus of a novel, *Sally Hemings* (1979) by Barbara Chase-Riboud, an Afro-American writer who includes French research into the two years Sally spent in Paris with Jefferson and his daughter.

1809—to Abbé Henri Grégoire, a French bishop, senator, and writer. Thanking Grégoire for a copy of his 1808 anthology, *De la Littérature des nègres*—in which some two hundred authors, eight of African descent, "pleaded the cause of unfortunate blacks and mixed bloods," and showed those who "distinguished themselves in the sciences, art or literature"—Jefferson replied, "Whatever be their degree of talent, it is no measure of their rights." Eight months later, perturbed anew with Grégoire for having pushed a 1795 decree to abolish slavery in the French colony of St. Domingo (later Haiti), where the French Revolution caused slaves to rise up, resist Napoleon's forces, and proclaim independence in 1804, Jefferson communicated his dismay to American diplomat and poet Joel Barlow:

> [Grégoire] wrote to me also on the doubts I had expressed five or six and twenty years ago, in the Notes of Virginia, as to the grade of understanding of the negroes, and he sent me his book on the literature of the negroes. His credulity has made him gather up every story he could find of men of color, (without distinguishing whether black, or of what degree of mixture,) however slight the mention, or light the authority on which they are quoted. . . . St. Domingo will, in time, throw light on the question.[4]

In his final years, he modified his earlier belief that emancipation be followed by deportation and colonization. But when abolitionism was gathering momentum, he showed no inclination to become involved in it—or to be aroused enough from his apathy to free his own slaves at Monticello.

The following passages from *Notes on the State of Virginia* reveal his ideas about slavery, colonization, and race to be biased, paternalistic, and insensitive. But in eighteenth-century Virginia, he represented the more enlightened Southern agrarian.

---

[4] Jefferson letter written at Monticello, October 8, 1809, to Joel Barlow (1754–1812), a writer who began his literary and political career as more conservative than Jefferson and ended as a radical friend of Thomas Paine; spent seventeen years abroad and returned to Washington from 1804 until 1811; died in 1812 while an emissary in Poland, where he is buried. In the same Letter to Barlow, Jefferson mentioned Benjamin Banneker; see his remarks in the Banneker biographical introduction in this volume, pages 45–46.

From *Notes on the State of Virginia*[5]

Laws

. . . To emancipate all slaves born after passing the act.[6] The bill reported by the revisors does not itself contain this proposition; but an amendment containing it was prepared, to be offered to the legislature whenever the bill should be taken up, and further directing, that they should continue with their parents to a certain age, then be brought up, at the public expense, to tillage, arts or sciences, according to their geniusses, till the females should be eighteen, and the males twenty-one years of age, when they should be colonized to such place as the circumstances of the time should render most proper, sending them out with arms, implements of household and of the handicraft arts, seeds, pairs of the useful domestic animals, &c. to declare them a free and independent people, and extend to them our alliance and protection, till they shall have acquired strength; and to send vessels at the same time to other parts of the world for an equal number of white inhabitants; to induce whom to migrate hither, proper encouragements were to be proposed. It will probably be asked, Why not retain and incorporate the blacks into the state, and thus save the expense of supplying, by importation of white settlers, the vacancies they will leave? Deep-rooted prejudices entertained by the whites; ten thousand recollections, by the blacks, of the injuries they have sustained; new provocations; the real distinctions which nature has made; and many other circumstances, will divide us into parties, and produce convulsions which will probably never end but in the extermination of the one or the other race.—To these objections, which are political, may be added others, which are physical and moral. The first difference which strikes us is that of colour. Whether the black of the negro resides in the reticular membrane between the skin and scarfskin, or in the scarfskin itself; whether it proceeds from the colour of the blood, the colour of the bile, or from that of some other secretion, the difference is fixed in

---

[5] First draft completed 1781; revisions 1783–84; printed privately, 1785, Paris; first authorized edition, 1787, London; first American edition, 1788, Philadelphia.

Excerpted from the authentic text (London: John Stockdale, 1787). William Peden, ed., *Notes on the State of Virginia*. Institute of Early American History and Culture, Williamsburg, Virginia (Chapel Hill: University of North Carolina Press, 1955).

[6] The proposed emancipation act was never passed. Jefferson and a committee introduced the proposals in the Virginia Assembly in 1779. See Julian P. Boyd, ed., *The Papers of Thomas Jefferson*, 2:470–73 (Princeton: Princeton University Press, 1950–72).

nature, and is as real as if its seat and cause were better known to us. And is this difference of no importance? Is it not the foundation of a greater or less share of beauty in the two races? Are not the fine mixtures of red and white, the expressions of every passion by greater or less suffusions of colour in the one, preferable to that eternal monotony, which reigns in the countenances, that immovable veil of black which covers all the emotions of the other race? Add to these, flowing hair, a more elegant symmetry of form, their own judgment in favour of the whites, declared by their preference of them, as uniformly as is the preference of the Oran-ootan for the black women over those of his own species. The circumstance of superior beauty, is thought worthy attention in the propagation of our horses, dogs, and other domestic animals; why not in that of man? Besides those of colour, figure, and hair, there are other physical distinctions proving a difference of race. They have less hair on the face and body. They secrete less by the kidnies, [sic] and more by the glands of the skin, which gives them a very strong and disagreeable odor. This greater degree of transpiration renders them more tolerant of heat, and less so of cold, than the whites. Perhaps too a difference of structure in the pulmonary apparatus, which a late ingenius experimentalist has discovered to be the principal regulator of animal heat, may have disabled them from extricating, in the act of inspiration, so much of that fluid from the outer air, or obliged them in expiration, to part with more of it. They seem to require less sleep. A black, after hard labour through the day, will be induced by the slightest amusements to sit up till midnight, or later, though knowing he must be out with the first dawn of the morning. They are at least as brave, and more adventuresome. But this may perhaps proceed from a want of forethought, which prevents their seeing a danger till it be present. When present, they do not go through it with more coolness or steadiness than the whites. They are more ardent after their female: but love seems with them to be more an eager desire, than a tender delicate mixture of sentiment and sensation. Their griefs are transient. Those numberless afflictions, which render it doubtful whether heaven has given life to us in mercy or in wrath, are less felt, and sooner forgotten with them. In general, their existence appears to participate more of sensation than reflection. To this must be ascribed their disposition to sleep when abstracted from their diversions, and unemployed in labour. An animal whose body is at rest, and who does not reflect, must be disposed to sleep of course. Comparing them by their faculties of memory, reason, and imagination, it appears to me, that in memory they are equal to the whites; in reason much inferior, as I think one could scarcely be found capable of tracing and comprehending the investigations of Euclid; and that in imagination they are dull, tasteless, and anomalous. It would be unfair to follow them to Africa for this investigation. We will consider them here, on the same stage with the whites, and where the facts are not apocryphal on which a judgment is to be formed. It will be right to make great allowances for the difference of condition, of education, of conversation, of the sphere in which they move. Many millions of them have been brought to, and born in America. Most of them indeed have been confined to tillage, to their own homes, and their own society: yet many have been so situated, that they might have availed themselves of the conversation of their masters; many have been brought up to the handicraft arts, and from that circumstance have always been associated with the whites. Some have been liberally educated, and all have lived in countries where the arts and sciences are cultivated to a considerable degree, and have had before their eyes samples of the best works from abroad. The Indians, with no advantages of this kind, will often carve figures on their pipes not destitute of design and merit. They will crayon out an animal, a plant, or a country, so as to prove the existence of a germ in their minds which only wants cultivation. They astonish you with strokes of the most sublime oratory; such as prove their reason and sentiment strong, their imagination glowing and elevated. But never yet could I find that a black had uttered a thought above the level of plain narration; never see even an elementary trait of painting or sculpture. In music they are more generally gifted than the whites with accurate ears for tune and time, and they have been found capable of imagining a small catch. Whether they will be equal to the composition of a more extensive run of melody, or of complicated harmony, is yet to be proved. Misery is often the parent of the most affecting touches in poetry.—Among the blacks is misery enough, God knows, but no poetry. Love is the peculiar œstrum of the poet. Their love is ardent, but it kindles the senses only, not the imagination. Religion indeed has produced a Phyllis Whately; [sic][7] but it could not produce a poet. The compositions published under her name are below the dignity of criticism. . . .

Manners

The particular customs and manners that may happen to be received in that state?

It is difficult to determine on the standard by which the manners of a nation may be tried, whether *catholic,* or *particular.* It is more difficult for a native to

---

[7] Phillis Wheatley (ca. 1753–84) female African poet, who began writing verses within seven years of her arrival as a child in Colonial America in 1761, after being purchased as a servant by a prosperous Boston family that tutored her to read and write; published first poem in 1770, and her only book, *Poems on Various Subjects, Religious and Moral,* in 1773; left forty-six known poems—almost all sentimental elegies and panegyrics inspired by the poetic model of Alexander Pope.

bring to that standard the manners of his own nation, familiarized to him by habit. There must doubtless be an unhappy influence on the manners of our people produced by the existence of slavery among us. The whole commerce between master and slave is a perpetual exercise of the most boisterous passions, the most unremitting despotism on the one part, and degrading submissions on the other. Our children see this, and learn to imitate it; for man is an imitative animal. This quality is the germ of all education in him. From his cradle to his grave he is learning to do what he sees others do. If a parent could find no motive either in his philanthropy or his self-love, for restraining the intemperance of passion towards his slave, it should always be a sufficient one that his child is present. But generally it is not sufficient. The parent storms, the child looks on, catches the lineaments of wrath, puts on the same airs in the circle of smaller slaves, gives a loose to his worst of passions, and thus nursed, educated, and daily exercised in tyranny, cannot but be stamped by it with odious peculiarities. The man must be a prodigy who can retain his manners and morals undepraved by such circumstances. And with what execration should the statesman be loaded, who permitting one half the citizens thus to trample on the rights of the other, transforms those into despots, and these into enemies, destroys the morals of the one part, and the amor patriæ of the other. For if a slave can have a country in this world, it must be any other in preference to that in which he is born to live and labour for another: in which he must lock up the faculties of his nature, contribute as far as depends on his individual endeavours to the evanishment of the human race, or entail his own miserable condition on the endless generations proceeding from him. With the morals of the people, their industry also is destroyed. For in a warm climate, no man will labour for himself who can make another labour for him. This is so true, that of the proprietors of slaves a very small proportion indeed are ever seen to labour. And can the liberties of a nation be thought secure when we have removed their only firm basis, a conviction in the minds of the people that these liberties are of the gift of God? That they are not to be violated but with his wrath? Indeed I tremble for my country when I reflect that God is just: that his justice cannot sleep for ever: that considering numbers, nature and natural means only, a revolution of the wheel of fortune, an exchange of situation, is among possible events: that it may become probable by supernatural interference! The Almighty has no attribute which can take side with us in such a contest.—But it is impossible to be temperate and to pursue this subject through the various considerations of policy, of morals, of history natural and civil. We must be contented to hope they will force their way into every one's mind. I think a change already perceptible, since the origin of the present revolution. The spirit of the master is abating, that of the slave rising from the dust, his condition mollifying, the way I hope preparing, under the auspices of heaven, for a total emancipation, and that this is disposed, in the order of events, to be with the consent of the masters, rather than by their extirpation.

Letter to Marquis de Chastellux[8]

DEAR SIR   Paris June 7, 1785
I have been honoured with the receipt of your letter of the 2d. instant, and am to thank you, as I do sincerely for the partiality with which you receive the copy of the *Notes* on my country. As I can answer for the facts therein reported on my own observation, and have admitted none on the report of others which were not supported by evidence sufficient to command my own assent, I am not afraid that you should make any extracts you please for the *Journal de physique* which come within their plan of publication. The strictures on slavery and on the constitution of Virginia are not of that kind, and they are the parts which I do not wish to have made public, at least till I know whether their publication would do most harm or good. It is possible that in my own country these strictures might produce an irritation which would indispose the people towards the two great objects I have in view, that is the emancipation of their slaves, and the settlement of their constitution on a firmer and more permanent basis. If I learn from thence, that they will not produce that effect, I have printed and reserved just copies enough to be able to give one to every young man at the College. It is to them I look, to the rising generation, and not to the one now in power for these great reformations. The other copy delivered at your hotel was for Monsr. De Buffon. . . .

I am safe in affirming that the proofs of genius given by the Indians of N. America, place them on a level with whites in the same uncultivated state. The North of Europe furnishes subjects enough for comparison with them, and for a proof of their equality. I have seen some thousands myself, and conversed much with them, and have found in them a male, sound understanding. I have had much information from men who had lived among them, and whose veracity and good sense were so far known to me as to establish a reliance on their information. They have all agreed in bearing witness in favour of the genius of

---

[8] François-Jean de Chastellux (1734–88). French general and author of *Travels in North America in the Years 1780, 1781, 1782*. Introduction and notes by Howard C. Rice, Jr. (Chapel Hill: University of North Carolina Press, 1963).

this people. As to their bodily strength, their manners rendering it disgraceful to labour, those muscles employed in labour will be weaker with them than with the European labourer: but those which are exerted in the chase and those faculties which are employed in the tracing an enemy or a wild beast, in contriving ambuscades for him, and in carrying them through their execution, are much stronger than with us, because they are more exercised. I believe the Indian then to be in body and mind equal to the white man. I have supposed the black man, in his present state, might not be so. But it would be hazardous to affirm that, equally cultivated for a few generations, he would not become so. 3. As to the inferiority of the other animals of America, without more facts I can add nothing to what I have said in my *Notes*. . . .

BENJAMIN BANNEKER

(1731–1806)

Never a slave, Benjamin Banneker represented what a free black man could attain in colonial America, given equal opportunity to exercise his ability. His achievements were later cited as supporting evidence in antislavery debates.

Born in Baltimore County, Maryland, the son of emancipated slaves, Banneker grew up on a hundred-acre tobacco farm purchased by his maternal grandmother, an Englishwoman and former indentured servant. Instructed by her to read and write, he had little formal schooling but demonstrated a boyhood talent for mathematical calculations and experiments.

A farmer and self-taught clock maker and scientist, he helped in 1791 to survey the Federal Territory—now the District of Columbia. He was then sixty years old when he joined the land-surveying team of Major Andrew Ellicott, appointed by General George Washington to plan the site of the national capital. That same year, Banneker completed calculations for an astronomical almanac; Ellicott and his cousins (Maryland Quaker neighbors of Banneker) helped him publish it through a printer in Baltimore in 1792.

On August 19, 1791, he sent a copy of the unpublished almanac with a personal letter to Thomas Jefferson, then secretary of state in Philadelphia. Jefferson replied to him within ten days: "I have taken the liberty of sending your Almanac to Monsieur de Condorcet, Secretary of the Academy of Sciences in Paris." The correspondence to France arrived amid turmoil of the French Revolution; the Marquis Antoine Nicolas de Condorcet, philosopher-scientist and moderate Girondist republican in the revolution, was in hiding. He died of unknown causes in captivity of extremist Jacobins in 1794, with no extant correspondence to Banneker.

The 1791 exchange of letters with Jefferson appeared in the second published edition of Banneker's 1793 almanac.[1] Success and sales of various edi-

---

[1] History proved Jefferson insincere in his August 30, 1791, correspondence to Banneker who, dead by 1806, never knew that the man who had signed his letter, "I am with great esteem, Sir, Your most humble Servant, Thomas Jefferson," wrote eighteen years later—October 8, 1809—to Joel Barlow: "We know he had spherical trigonometry enough to make almanacs, but not without the suspicion of aid from Ellicott, who was his neighbor and friend, and never missed an opportunity of puffing him. I have a long letter from Banneker, which shows him to have had a mind of very common stature indeed." See also note on other content of letter to Barlow in Jefferson biographical introduction in this volume, p. 38.

tions of his ephemeris continued in the colonies and England until 1797, when publication ceased due to Banneker's declining health. His efforts on astronomical calculations lasted until 1804.

He was able to live independently on a modest income from manuscript earnings and land parcels sold from the Banneker farm, until he died—one month before his seventy-fifth birthday. His death—in the log house his father had built—signaled a fateful end to a rich legacy; the house mysteriously caught fire during his last rites at the family burial plot. Many of his possessions, inventions, and journals of natural phenomena were lost in the flames. His record as the first black American of science survives in letters and manuscripts now in historical societies.

Reprinted here is his only letter to Thomas Jefferson. Written before Banneker's international recognition, it reveals his reflective nature and the persecution felt by his race—despite his own personal isolation from racial discrimination during most of his long and productive life.

A Letter to Thomas Jefferson (1791)

I am fully sensible of that freedom, which I take with you in the present occasion; a liberty which seemed to me scarcely allowable, when I reflected on that distinguished and dignified station in which you stand, and the almost general prejudice and prepossession, which is so prevalent in the world against those of my complexion.

I suppose it is a truth too well attested to you, to need a proof here, that we are a race of beings, who have long labored under the abuse and censure of the world; that we have long been looked upon with an eye of contempt; and that we have long been considered rather as brutish than human, and scarcely capable of mental endowments.

Sir, I hope I may safely admit, in consequence of that report which hath reached me, that you are a man less inflexible in sentiments of this nature, than many others; that you are measurably friendly, and well disposed towards us; and that you are willing and ready to lend your aid and assistance to our relief, from those many distresses, and numerous calamities, to which we are reduced.

Now Sir, if this is founded in truth, I apprehend you will embrace every opportunity, to eradicate that train of absurd and false ideas and opinions, which so generally prevails with respect to us; and that your sentiments are concurrent with mine, which are, that one universal Father hath given being to us all; and that he hath not only made us all of one flesh, but that he hath also, without partiality, afforded us all the same sensations and endowed us all with the same faculties; and that however variable we may be in society or religion, however diversified in situation or color, we are all in the same family and stand in the same relation to him.

Sir, if these are sentiments of which you are fully persuaded, I hope you cannot but acknowledge, that it is the indispensable duty of those, who maintain for themselves the rights of human nature, and who possess the obligations of Christianity, to extend their power and influence to the relief of every part of the human race, from whatever burden or oppression they may unjustly labor under; and this, I apprehend, a full conviction of the truth and obligation of these principles should lead all to.

Sir, I have long been convinced, that if your love for yourselves, and for those inestimable laws, which preserved to you the rights of human nature, was founded on sincerity, you could not but be solicitous, that every individual, of whatever rank or distinction, might with you equally enjoy the blessings thereof; neither could you rest satisfied short of the most active effusion of your exertions, in order to the promotion from any state of degradation, to which the unjustifiable cruelty and barbarism of men may have reduced them.

Sir, I freely and cheerfully acknowledge, that I am of the African race, and in that color which is natural to them of the deepest dye; and it is under a sense of the most profound gratitude to the Supreme Ruler of the Universe, that I now confess to you, that I am not under that state of tyrannical thraldom, and inhuman captivity, to which too many of my brethren are doomed, but that I have abundantly tasted of the fruition of those blessings, which proceed from that free and unequaled liberty with which you are favored; and which, I hope, you will willingly allow you have mercifully received, from the immediate hand of that Being, from whom proceedeth every good and perfect Gift.

Sir, suffer me to recall to your mind that time, in which the arms and tyranny of the British crown were exerted, with every powerful effort, in order to reduce you to a state of servitude: look back, I entreat you, on the variety of dangers to which you were exposed; reflect on that time, in which ever human aid appeared unavailable, and in which even hope and fortitude wore the aspect of inability to the conflict, and you cannot but be led to a serious and grateful sense of your miraculous and providential preservation; you cannot but acknowledge, that the present freedom and tranquility which you enjoy you have mercifully received, and that it is the peculiar blessing of Heaven.

This, Sir, was a time when you clearly saw into the injustice of a state of slavery, and in which you had just apprehensions of the horror of its condition. It was now that your abhorrence thereof was so excited, that you publicly held forth this true and invaluable doctrine, which is worthy to be recorded and remembered in all succeeding ages: "We hold these truths to be self-evident, that all men are created equal; that they are endowed by their Creator with certain unalienable rights, and that among these are, life, liberty, and the pursuit of happiness."

Here was a time, in which your tender feelings for yourselves had engaged you thus to declare, you were then impressed with proper ideas of the great violation of liberty, and the free possession of those blessings, to which you were entitled by nature; but, Sir, how pitiable is it to reflect, that although you were so fully convinced of the benevolence of the Father of Mankind, and of his equal and impartial distribution of these rights and privileges, which he hath conferred upon them, that you should at the same time counteract his mercies, in detaining by fraud and violence so numerous a part of my brethren, under groaning captivity, and cruel oppression, that you should at the same time be found guilty of that most criminal act, which you professedly detested in others, with respect to yourselves.

I suppose that your knowledge of the situation of my brethren, is too extensive to need a recital here; neither shall I presume to prescribe methods by which they may be relieved, otherwise than by recommending to you and all others, to wean yourselves from those narrow prejudices which you have imbibed with respect to them, and as Job proposed to his friends, "put your soul in their souls' stead"; thus shall your hearts be enlarged with kindness and benevolence towards them; and thus shall you need neither the direction of myself or others, in what manner to proceed herein.

And now, Sir, although my sympathy and affection for my brethren hath caused my enlargement thus far, I ardently hope, that your candor and generosity will plead with you in my behalf, when I make known to you, that it was not originally my design; but having taken up my pen in order for the succeeding year, I was unexpectedly and unavoidably led thereto.

This calculation is the product of my arduous study, in this most advanced stage of life; for having long had unbounded desires to become acquainted with the secrets of nature, I have had to gratify my curiosity herein through my own assiduous application to Astronomical Study, in which I need not recount to you the many difficulties and disadvantages which I have had to encounter.

And although I had almost declined to make my calculation for the ensuing year, in consequence of that time which I had allotted therefor, being taken up at the Federal Territory, by the request of Mr. Andrew Ellicott, yet finding myself under several engagements to Printers of this State, to whom I had communicated my design, on my return to my place of residence, I industriously applied myself thereto, which I hope I have accomplished with correctness and accuracy; a copy of which I have taken the liberty to direct to you, and which I humbly request you will favorably receive; and although you may have the opportunity of perusing it after its publication; yet I choose to send it to you in manuscript previous thereto, that thereby you might not only have an earlier inspection, but that you might also view it in my own handwriting.

JUPITER HAMMON

(1711–ca. 1806?)

Jupiter Hammon lived and died the property of a family he obediently served for three generations: the Lloyds of Long Island, New York, and Hartford, Connecticut. An atypical slave who willingly conformed to slavery, in turn he had unconventional owners who permitted him a rudimentary education and encouraged publication of his writings. On Christmas Day 1760, he penned his earliest known poem, "An Evening Thought. Salvation by Christ, with Penitential Cries." Its printing early the next year made him the first black male poet published in North America. He was forty-nine.

Not until eighteen years later, in 1778, did his next poem appear in print. In the context of literary history, its significance was that it was a dedicatory poem to the *second*[1] *published* African-American poet: "An Address to Miss Phillis Wheatly [sic], Ethiopian Poetess in Boston." Wheatley (who was not Ethiopian but West African from the region of Senegal and Gambia) was Hammon's spiritual soul mate in human bondage, a servant and poet over forty years his junior, whom he would never meet except through the printed elegies that had made her a curiosity and celebrity in the colonies since 1770.

By 1782, the aging Hammon, a pious Calvinist, wrote and published a pliant poetical dialogue, "The Kind Master and Dutiful Servant," setting the tone evident four years later in "An Address to the Negroes in the State of New York." In that prose work, he turned preacher with a sermon, urging his brethren to obey a heavenly and earthly master, exhorting from Scripture about "salvation" from "sin," with evangelistic echoes of his white New England contemporary Jonathan Edwards, whose apocalyptic sermons had roused the Eastern seaboard for four decades. Although Edwards did not make a reputation addressing the slavery issue, by 1791 he would write "The Justice and Impolicy of the Slave Trade, and the Slavery of Africans"—an explicit condemnation that the Lloyds' loyal servant never expressed in his own writing.

Hammon's conviction that slavery was unlawful did not mitigate his meek acceptance of it. He is the first "contented slave" in Afro-American literature.

---

[1] The first Afro-American female poet was Lucy Terry, whose "Bars Fight" was composed as an oral ballad in 1746, but not published until 1893.

Like the devout poet Phillis Wheatley, he barely spoke of the tyranny of servitude; and they both seemed identical twins in defining Africa as a "dark abode."[2]

His total canon, consisting of only eight published works, includes four in verse and four in prose—all primarily religious in content. He created no literary landmarks, but he remains of social and historical importance for "An Address to the Negroes in The State of New York." The piece, dedicated in September 1786 "To Members of the African Society of New York City," and published there in 1787 by Caroll and Patterson Printers, was his last work— and one that revealed his lifelong remoteness from his people. Separated from the New York African Society by laws that sequestered slaves and freemen, Hammon nevertheless expressed no desire for personal freedom. "I take the liberty to dedicate an address to my poor brethren to you," he wrote.

His "Address" was later ignored by white proslavery strategists, who shared a belief that slavery was a benign institution that some slaves had no desire to end. The piece was reprinted in 1806 but unresurrected by nineteenth-century abolitionists. He died in quiet ignominy, his work buried and forgotten until the early twentieth century.

An Address to the Negroes in The
State of New York[3] (1787)

When I am writing to you with a design to say something to you for your good, and with a view to promote your happiness, I can with truth and sincerity join with the apostle Paul, when speaking of his own nation the Jews, and say that "I have great heaviness and continual sorrow in my heart for my brethren, my kinsmen according to the flesh." Yes my dear brethren, when I think of you, which is very often, and of the poor, despised and miserable state you are in, as to the things of this world, and when I think of your ignorance and stupidity,

---

[2] See note on Phillis Wheatley, p. 41. For the only antislavery passage in Wheatley's verse, see "To the Right Honorable William, Earl of Dartmouth, His Majesty's Secretary of State for North America." On her sentiments about her adopted land compared to her native land, see "On Being Brought from Africa to America," and "To the University of Cambridge." The latter expresses thoughts similar to those in Hammon's 1778 poem dedicated to her.

[3] The title of this piece has been reprinted in various sources with the preposition *of* rather than *in The State of New York. In* appeared as part of the original title in the first printing.

and the great wickedness of the most of you, I am pained to the heart. It is at times almost too much for human nature to bear, and I am obliged to turn my thoughts from the subject or endeavour to still my mind, by considering that it is permitted thus to be by that God who governs all things, who seteth up one and pulleth down another. While I have been thinking on this subject, I have frequently had great struggles in my own mind, and have been at a loss to know what to do. I have wanted exceedingly to say something to you, to call upon you with the tenderness of a father and friend, and to give you the last, and I may say dying advice, of an old man, who wishes your best good in this world, and in the world to come. But while I have had such desires, a sense of my own ignorance and unfitness to teach others has frequently discouraged me from attempting to say anything to you; yet when I thought of your situation, I could not rest easy.

When I was at Hartford in Connecticut, where I lived during the war, I published several pieces which were well received, not only by those of my own colour, but by a number of the white people, who thought they might do good among their servants. This is one consideration, among others, that emboldens me now to publish what I have written to you. Another is, I think you will be more likely to listen to what is said, when you know it comes from a Negro, one your own nation and colour, and therefore can have no interest in deceiving you, or in saying anything to you, but what he really thinks is your interest and duty to comply with. My age, I think, gives me some right to speak to you, and reason to expect you will hearken to my advice. I am now upwards of seventy years old, and cannot expect, though I am well, and able to do almost any kind of business, to live much longer. I have passed the common bounds set for man, and must soon go the way of all the earth. I have had more experience in the world than the most of you, and I have seen a great deal of the vanity and wickedness of it. I have great reason to be thankful that my lot has been so much better than most slaves have had. I suppose I have had more advantages and privileges than most of you who are slaves have ever known, and I believe more than many white people have enjoyed, for which I desire to bless God, and pray that he may bless those who have given them to me. I do not, my dear friends, say these things about myself to make you think that I am wiser or better than others; but that you might hearken, without prejudice, to what I have to say to you on the following particulars.

1st. Respecting obedience to matters. Now whether it is right, and lawful, in the sight of God, for them to make slaves of us or not, I am certain that while we are slaves, it is our duty to obey our masters, in all their lawful commands, and mind them unless we are bid to do that which we know to be sin, or forbidden in God's word. The apostle Paul says, "Servants be obedient to them that are your masters according to the flesh, with fear and trembling in single-ness in your heart as unto Christ: Not with eye service, as men pleasers, but as the servants of Christ doing the will of God from the heart: With goodwill doing service to the Lord, and not to men: Knowing that whatever thing a man doeth the same shall he receive of the Lord, whether he be bond or free."— Here is a plain command of God for us to obey our masters. It may seem hard for us, if we think our masters wrong in holding us slaves, to obey in all things, but who of us dare dispute with God! He has commanded us to obey, and we ought to do it cheerfully, and freely. This should be done by us, not only be-cause God commands, but because our own peace and comfort depend upon it. As we depend upon our masters, for what we eat and drink and wear, and for all our comfortable things in this world, we cannot be happy, unless we please them. This we cannot do without obeying them freely, without mutter-ing or finding fault. If a servant strives to please his master and studies and takes pains to do it, I believe there are but few masters who would use such a servant cruelly. Good servants frequently make good masters. If your master is really hard, unreasonable and cruel, there is no way so likely for you to convince him of it, as always to obey his commands, and try to serve him, and take care of his interest, and try to promote it all in your power. If you are proud and stubborn and always finding fault, your master will think the fault lies wholly on your side, but if you are humble, and meek, and bear all things patiently, your master may think he is wrong, if he does not, his neighbours will be apt to see it, and will befriend you, and try to alter his conduct. If this does not do, you must cry to him, who has the hearts of all men in his hands, and turneth them as the rivers of waters are turned.

2d. The particular I would mention, is honesty and faithfulness. You must suffer me now to deal plainly with you, my dear brethren, for I do not mean to flatter, or omit speaking the truth, whether it is for you, or against you. How many of you are there who allow yourselves in stealing from your masters. It is very wicked for you not to take care of your masters' goods, but how much worse is it to pilfer and steal from them, whenever you think you shall not be found out. This you must know is very wicked and provoking to God. There are none of you so ignorant, but that you must know that this is wrong. Though you may try to excuse yourselves, by saying that your masters are unjust to you, and though you may try to quiet your consciences in this way, yet if you are honest in owning the truth you must think it is as wicked, and on some ac-counts more wicked to steal from your masters, than from others.

We cannot certainly, have any excuse either for taking anything that belongs to our masters without their leave, or for being unfaithful in their business. It is our duty to be faithful, *not with eye service as men pleasers.* We have no right to stay when we are sent on errands, any longer than to do the business we were sent upon. All the time spent idly, is spent wickedly, and is unfaithfulness to our masters. In these things I must say, that I think many of you are guilty. I know that many of you endeavour to excuse yourselves, and say that you have nothing that you can call your own, and that you are under great temptations to be unfaithful and take from your masters. But this will not do, God will certainly punish you for stealing and for being unfaithful. All that we have to mind is our own duty. If God has put us in bad circumstances, that is not our fault and he will not punish us for it. If any are wicked in keeping us so, we cannot help it, they must answer to God for it. Nothing will serve as an excuse to us for not doing our duty. The same God will judge both them and us. Pray then my dear friends, fear to offend in this way, but be faithful to God, to your masters, and to your own souls.

The next thing I would mention, and warn you against, is profaneness. This you know is forbidden by God. Christ tells us, "swear not at all," and again it is said "thou shalt not take the name of the Lord thy God in vain, for the Lord will not hold him guiltless, that taketh his name in vain." Now though the great God has forbidden it, yet how dreadfully profane are many, and I don't know but I may say the most of you? How common is it to hear you take the terrible and awful name of the great God in vain?—To swear by it, and by Jesus Christ, his Son—How common is it to hear you wish damnation to your companions, and to your own souls—and to sport with in the name of Heaven and Hell, as if there were no such places for you to hope for, or to fear. Oh my friends, be warned to forsake this dreadful sin of profaneness. Pray my dear friends, believe and realize, that there is a God—that he is great and terrible beyond what you can think—that he keeps you in life every moment—and that he can send you to that awful Hell, that you laugh at, in an instant, and confine you there forever, and that he will certainly do it, if you do not repent. You certainly do not believe, that there is a God, or that there is a Heaven or Hell, or you would never trifle with them. It would make you shudder, if you heard others do it, if you believe them as much, as you believe anything you see with your bodily eyes.

I have heard some learned and good men say, that the heathen, and all that worshiped false Gods, never spoke lightly or irreverently of their Gods, they never took their names in vain, or jested with those things which they held sacred. Now why should the true God, who made all things, be treated worse in this respect, than those false Gods, that were made of wood and stone. I believe it is because Satan tempts men to do it. He tried to make them love their false Gods, and to speak well of them, but he wishes to have men think lightly of the true God, to take his holy name in vain, and to scoff at, and make a jest of all things that are really good. You may think that Satan has not power to do so much, and have so great influence on the minds of men: But the Scripture says, "he goeth about like a roaring Lion, seeking whom he may devour—That he is the prince of the power of the air—and that he rules in the hearts of the children of disobedience,—and that wicked men are led captive by him, to do his will." All those of you who are profane, are serving the Devil. You are doing what he tempts and desires you to do. If you could see him with your bodily eyes, would you like to make an agreement with him, to serve him, and do as he bid you? I believe most of you would be shocked at this, but you may be certain that all of you who allow yourselves in this sin, are as really serving him, and to just as good purpose, as if you met him, and promised to dishonor God, and serve him with all your might. Do you believe this? It is true whether you believe it or not. Some of you to excuse yourselves, may plead the example of others, and say that you hear a great many white people, who know more than such poor ignorant Negroes as you are, and some who are rich and great gentlemen, swear, and talk profanely, and some of you may say this of your masters, and say no more than is true. But all this is not a sufficient excuse for you. You know that murder is wicked. If you saw your master kill a man, do you suppose this would be any excuse for you, if you should commit the same crime? You must know it would not; nor will your hearing him curse and swear, and take the name of God in vain, or any other man, be he ever so great or rich, excuse you. God is greater than all other beings, and him we are bound to obey. To him we must give an account for every idle word that we speak. He will bring us all, rich and poor, white and black, to his judgment seat. If we are found among those who *feared his name*, and *trembled at his word*, we shall be called good and faithful servants. Our slavery will be at an end, and though ever so mean, low, and despised in this world, we shall sit with God in his kingdom as Kings and Priests, and rejoice for ever, and ever. Do not then, my dear friends, take God's holy name in vain, or speak profanely in any way. Let not the example of others lead you into the sin, but reverence and fear that great and fearful name, the Lord our God.

I might now caution you against other sins to which you are exposed, but as I meant only to mention those you were exposed to, more than others, by your being slaves, I will conclude what I have to say to you, by advising you to become religious, and to make religion the great business of your lives.

Now I acknowledge that liberty is a great thing, and worth seeking for, if we can get it honestly, and by our good conduct, prevail on our masters to set us free. Though for my own part I do not wish to be free, yet I should be glad if others, especially the young Negroes, were to be free, for many of us, who are grown up slaves, and have always had masters to take care of us, should hardly know how to take care of ourselves, and it may be more for our own comfort to remain as we are. That liberty is a great thing we may know from our own feelings, and we may likewise judge so from the conduct of the white people, in the late war. How much money has been spent, and how many lives has been lost, to defend their liberty? I must say that I have hoped that God would open their eyes, when they were so much engaged for liberty, to think of the state of the poor blacks, and to pity us. He has done it in some measure, and has raised us up many friends, for which we have reason to be thankful, and to hope in his mercy. What may be done further, he only knows, for *known unto God are all his ways from the beginning.* But this, my dear brethren, is by no means the greatest thing we have to be concerned about. Getting our liberty in this world, is nothing to our having the liberty of the children of God. Now the Bible tells us that we are all by nature, sinners, that we are slaves to sin and Satan, and that unless we are converted, or born again, we must be miserable forever. Christ says, except a man be born again, he cannot see the kingdom of God, and all that do not see the kingdom of God, must be in the kingdom of darkness. There are but two places where all go after death, white and black, rich and poor; those places are Heaven and Hell. Heaven is a place made for those who are born again, and who love God, and it is a place where they will be happy forever. Hell is a place made for those who hate God, and are his enemies, and where they will be miserable to all eternity. Now you may think you are not enemies to God, and do not hate him. But if your heart has not been changed, and you have not become true Christians, you certainly are enemies to God, and have been opposed to him ever since you were born. Many of you, I suppose, never think of this, and are almost as ignorant as the beasts that perish. Those of you who can read I must beg you to read the Bible, and whenever you can get time, study the Bible, and if you can get no other time, spare some of your time from sleep, and learn what the mind and will of God is. But what shall I say to them who cannot read? This lay with great weight on my mind, when I thought of writing to my poor brethren, but I hope that those who can read will take pity on them and read what I have to say to them. In hopes of this I will beg of you to spare no pains in trying to learn to read. If you are once engaged you may learn. Let all the time you can get be spent in trying to learn to read. Get those who can read to learn you, but remember, that what you learn for, is to read the Bible. If there was no Bible, it would be no matter whether you could read or not. Reading other books would do you no good. But the Bible is the word of God, and tells you what you must do to please God; it tells you how you may escape misery, and be happy forever. If you see most people neglect the Bible, and many that can read never look into it, let it not harden you and make you think lightly of it, and that it is a book of no worth. All those who are really good, love the Bible, and meditate on it day and night. In the Bible God has told us everything it is necessary we should know in order to be happy here and hereafter. The Bible is a revelation of the mind and will of God to men. Therein we may learn what God is. That he made all things by the power of his word; and that he made all things for his own glory, and not for our glory. That he is over all, and above all his creatures, and more above them that we can think or conceive—that they can do nothing without him—that he upholds them all, and will overrule all things for his own glory. In the Bible likewise we are told what man is. That he was at first made holy, in the image of God, that he fell from that state of holiness, and became an enemy to God, and that since the fall, all the imaginations of the thoughts of his heart, are evil and only evil, and that continually. That the carnal mind is not subject to the law of God, neither indeed can be. And that all mankind, were under the wrath and curse of God, and must have been for ever miserable, if they had been left to suffer what their sins deserved. It tells us that God, to save some of mankind, sent his Son into this world to die, in the room and stead of sinners, and that now God can save from eternal misery all that believe in his Son, and take him for their saviour, and that all are called upon to repent, and believe in Jesus Christ. It tells us that those who do repent, and believe, and are friends to Christ, shall have many trials and sufferings in this world, but that they shall be happy forever, after death, and reign with Christ to all eternity. The Bible tells us that this world is a place of trial, and that there is no other time or place for us to alter, but in this life. If we are Christians when we die, we shall awake to the resurrection of life; if not, we shall awake to the resurrection of damnation. It tells us, we must all live in Heaven or Hell, be happy or miserable, and that without end. The Bible does not tell us of but two places, for all to go to. There is no place for innocent folks that are not Christians. There is no place for ignorant folks, that did not know how to be Christians. What I mean is, that there is no place besides Heaven or Hell. These two places will receive all mankind, for Christ says, there are but two sorts, *he is not with me is against me, and he that gathereth not with me, scattereth abroad.* The Bible likewise tells us that this world, and all things in it shall be burnt up—and that "God has appointed a day in which he will judge the world, and that he will bring every secret thing whether it be good or bad into judgment—that which is done in secret shall be declared on the house top." I do not know, nor do I think any can tell, but that the day of judgment may last a thousand years. God could tell the state of all his creatures in a moment, but then everything that everyone has done, through his whole life is to be told, before the whole world of angels and men. There, Oh how solemn is the thought! You and I must stand, and hear everything we have thought or done, however secret, however wicked and vile, told before all the men and women that ever have been, or ever will be, and before all the angels, good and bad.

Now my dear friends seeing the Bible is the word of God, and everything in it is true, and it reveals such awful and glorious things, what can be more important than that you should learn to read it; and when you have learned to read, that you should study it day and night. There are some things very encouraging in God's word for such ignorant creatures as we are; for God hath not chosen the rich of this world. Not many rich, not many noble are called, but God hath chosen the weak things of this world, and things which are not, to confound the things that are: And when the great and the rich refused coming to the gospel feast, the servant was told, to go into the highways, and hedges, and compel those poor creatures that he found there to come in. Now my brethren it seems to me, that there are no people that ought to attend to the hope of happiness in another world so much as we do. Most of us are cut off from comfort and happiness here in this world, and can expect nothing from it. Now seeing this is the case, why should we not take care to be happy after death? Why should we spend our whole lives in sinning against God, and be miserable in this world, and in the world to come? If we do thus, we shall certainly be the greatest fools. We shall be slaves here, and slaves forever. We cannot plead so great temptations to neglect religion as others. Riches and honours which drown the greater part of mankind, who have the gospel, in perdition, can be little or no temptations to us.

We live so little time in this world that it is no matter how wretched and miserable we are, if it prepares us for heaven. What is forty, fifty, or sixty years, when compared to eternity? When thousands and millions of years have rolled away, this eternity will be no nigher coming to an end. Oh how glorious is an eternal life of happiness! And how dreadful, an eternity of misery. Those of us who have had religious masters, and have been taught to read the Bible, and have been brought by their example and teaching to a sense of divine things, how happy shall we be to meet them in heaven, where we shall join them in praising God forever. But if any of us have had such masters, and yet have lived and died wicked, how will it add to our misery to think of our folly. If any of us who have wicked and profane masters should become religious, how will our estates be changed in another world. Oh my friends, let me intreat of you to think on these things, and to live as if you believed them to be true. If you become Christians you will have reason to bless God forever, that you have been brought into a land where you have heard the gospel, though you have been slaves. If we should ever get to Heaven, we shall find nobody to reproach us for being black, or for being slaves. Let me beg of you my dear African brethren, to think very little of your bondage in this life, for your thinking of it will do you no good. If God designs to set us free, he will do it, in his own time, and way; but think of your bondage to sin and Satan, and do not rest, until you are delivered from it.

We cannot be happy, if we are ever so free or ever so rich, while we are servants of sin, and slaves to Satan. We must be miserable here, and to all eternity.

I will conclude what I have to say with a few words to those Negroes who have their liberty. The most of what I have said to those who are slaves may be of use to you, but you have more advantages, on some accounts, if you will improve your freedom, as you may do, than they. You have more time to read God's holy word, and to take care of the salvation of your souls. Let me beg of you to spend your time in this way, or it will be better for you, if you had always been slaves. If you think seriously of the matter, you must conclude, that if you do not use your freedom, to promote the salvation of your souls, it will not be of any lasting good to you. Besides all this, if you are idle, and take to bad courses, you will hurt those of your brethren who are slaves, and do all in your power to prevent their being free. One great reason that is given by some for not freeing us, I understand, is that we should not know how to take care of ourselves, and should take to bad courses. That we should be lazy and idle, and get drunk and steal. Now all those of you, who follow any bad courses, and who do not take care to get an honest living by your labour and industry, are doing more to prevent our being free, than anybody else. Let me beg of you then for the sake of your own good and happiness, in time, and for eternity, and for the sake of your poor brethren, who are still in bondage to lead quiet and peaceable lives in all Godliness and honesty, and may God bless you, and bring you to his kingdom, for Christ's sake, Amen.

OLAUDAH EQUIANO [GUSTAVUS VASSA]

(ca. 1745–ca. 1797)

Captured in boyhood from his village near the ancient West African empire of Benin (now Nigeria), Olaudah Equiano later wrote one of the first accounts of the black experience in the diaspora. The autobiographical memoir—of his background, kidnapping, journey from Africa, enslavement, and release—was published in London in 1789, under the lengthy title *The Interesting Narrative of the Life of Olaudah Equiano; or, Gustavus Vassa, the African, Written by Himself.* The book saw eight editions in Britain and one in America during the author's life, plus posthumous printings and foreign translations, making it the first best-seller by a black man in the Western world.

Although he spent less time as a slave in the American colonies than in England—where he obtained basic schooling—he was one of the few eighteenth-century Africans to write and publish an autobiography. Son of a tribal chief, he lost his African name in slavery and acquired the name of a royal Swedish and Polish dynasty, Gustavus Vassa. It was given him by a British naval officer whom he served as a slave-steward on voyages to the Mediterranean and Canada. From another master, a Philadelphia Quaker merchant, who permitted him to earn income on journeys to the West Indies, he purchased his freedom in 1766, at age twenty-one.

After travels as a seaman between ports in the Caribbean, Europe, the Arctic, and Central America, he settled in England and converted to Methodism. With memories of ferrying manacled slaves against his will, he became an active abolitionist lecturer and writer. In 1787, he completed his book and assisted the first expedition of freed slaves to settle in Sierra Leone. His plan to travel there as a Methodist missionary was thwarted by agents opposed to his speeches to abolish the slave trade.

According to a British periodical, the *Gentleman's* magazine, Gustavus Vassa died in London in April 1797. Subsequent dates were also printed elsewhere. Hence the exact year remains as uncertain as the date of his birth.

The following excerpt of his autobiographical narrative is from chapter 1, "The Author's Account of His Country, Their Manners, and Customs," reprinted with modern spelling and punctuation, from the first American edition of 1791.

From *The Interesting Narrative of the Life of Olaudah Equiano; or, Gustavus Vassa, the African, Written by Himself* (1789)

That part of Africa known by the name of Guinea to which the trade for slaves is carried on extends along the coast above 3,400 miles, from the Senegal to Angola, and includes a variety of kingdoms. Of these the most considerable is the kingdom of Benin, both as to extent and wealth, the richness and cultivation of the soil, the power of its king, and the number and warlike disposition of the inhabitants. It is situated nearly under the line and extends along the coast about 170 miles, but runs back into the interior part of Africa to a distance hitherto I believe unexplored by any traveler, and seems only terminated at length by the empire of Abyssinia, near 1,500 miles from its beginning. This kingdom is divided into many provinces or districts, in one of the most remote and fertile of which, called Eboe, I was born in the year 1745, situated in a charming fruitful vale, named Essaka. The distance of this province from the capital of Benin and the seacoast must be very considerable, for I had never heard of white men or Europeans, nor of the sea, and our subjection to the king of Benin was little more than nominal; for every transaction of the government, as far as my slender observation extended, was conducted by the chiefs or elders of the place. The manners and government of a people who have little commerce with other countries are generally very simple, and the history of what passes in one family or village may serve as a specimen of a nation. My father was one of those elders or chiefs I have spoken of and was styled Embrenché, a term as I remember importing the highest distinction, and signifying in our language a *mark* of grandeur. This mark is conferred on the person entitled to it by cutting the skin across at the top of the forehead and drawing it down to the eyebrows, and while it is in this situation applying a warm hand and rubbing it until it shrinks up into a thick *weal* across the lower part of the forehead. Most of the judges and senators were thus marked; my father had long borne it. I had seen it conferred on one of my brothers, and I was also *destined* to receive it by my parents. Those Embrenché or chief men decided disputes and punished crimes, for which purpose they always assembled together. The proceedings were generally short, and in most cases the law of retaliation prevailed. I remember a man was brought before my father and the other judges for kidnapping a boy, and although he was the son of a chief or senator, he was condemned to make recompense by a man or woman slave. Adultery, however, was sometimes punished with slavery or death, a punishment which I believe is inflicted on it throughout most of the nations of Africa, so sacred among them is the honour of the marriage bed and so jealous are they of the fidelity of their wives. Of this I recollect an instance—a woman was convicted before the judges of adultery, and delivered over, as the custom was, to her husband, to be punished. Accordingly he determined to put her to death: but it being found just before her execution that she had an infant at her breast, and no woman being prevailed on to perform the part of a nurse, she was spared on account of the child. The men however do not preserve the same constancy to their wives which they expect from them, for they indulge in a plurality, though seldom in more than two. Their mode of marriage is thus: both parties are usually betrothed when young by their parents, (though I have known the males to betroth themselves). On this occasion a feast is prepared, and the bride and bridegroom stand up in the midst of all their friends who are assembled for the purpose, while he declares she is thenceforth to be looked upon as his wife, and that no other person is to pay any addresses to her. This is also immediately proclaimed in the vicinity, on which the bride retires from the assembly. Some time after she is brought home to her husband, and then another feast is made to which the relations of both parties are invited: her parents then deliver her to the bridegroom accompanied with a number of blessings, and at the same time they tie round her waist a cotton string of the thickness of a goose-quill, which none but married women are permitted to wear: she is now considered as completely his wife, and at this time the dowry is given to the new married pair, which generally consists of portions of land, slaves, and cattle, household goods, and implements of husbandry. These are offered by the friends of both parties, besides which the parents of the bride-groom present gifts to those of the bride, whose property she is looked upon before marriage; but after it she is esteemed the sole property of her husband. The ceremony being now ended, the festival begins, which is celebrated with bonfires and loud acclamations of joy accompanied with music and dancing.

We are almost a nation of dancers, musicians, and poets. Thus every great event such as a triumphant return from battle or other cause of public rejoicing is celebrated in public dances, which are accompanied with songs and music suited to the occasion. The assembly is separated into four divisions, which dance either apart or in succession, and each with a character peculiar to itself. The first division contains the married men, who in their dances frequently exhibit feats of arms and the representation of a battle. To these succeed the married women, who dance in the second division. The young men occupy the third and the maidens the fourth. Each represents some interesting scene of real life, such as a great achievement, domestic employment, a pathetic story, or some rural sport, and as the subject is generally founded on some recent event it is therefore ever new. This gives our dances a spirit and variety which I have scarcely seen elsewhere. We have many musical instruments, particularly drums of different kinds, a piece of music which resembles a guitar, and another much like a stickado. These last are chiefly used by betrothed virgins who play on them on all grand festivals.

As our manners are simple, our luxuries are few. The dress of both sexes is nearly the same. It generally consists of a long piece of calico or muslin, wrapped loosely round the body somewhat in the form of a highland plaid. This is usually dyed blue, which is our favourite colour. It is extracted from a berry and is brighter and richer than any I have seen in Europe. Besides this our women of distinction wear golden ornaments, which they dispose with some profusion on their arms and legs. When our women are not employed with the men in tillage, their usual occupation is spinning and weaving cotton, which they afterwards dye and make into garments. They also manufacture earthen vessels, of which we have many kinds. Among the rest tobacco pipes, made after the same fashion and used in the same manner, as those in Turkey.

Our manner of living is entirely plain, for as yet the natives are unacquainted with those refinements in cookery which debauch the taste: bullocks, goats, and poultry, supply the greatest part of their food. These constitute likewise the principal wealth of the country and the chief articles of its commerce. The flesh is usually stewed in a pan; to make it savory we sometimes use also pepper and other spices, and we have salt made of wood ashes. Our vegetables are mostly plantains, eadas, yams, beans, and Indian corn. The head of the family usually eats alone; his wives and slaves have also their separate tables. Before we taste food we always wash our hands: indeed our cleanliness on all occasions is extreme, but on this it is an indispensable ceremony. After washing, libation is made by pouring out a small portion of the drink on the floor, and tossing a small quantity of the food in a certain place for the spirits of departed relations, which the natives suppose to preside over their conduct and guard them from evil. They are totally unacquainted with strong or spirituous liquors, and their principal beverage is palm wine. This is got from a tree of that name by tapping it at the top and fastening a large gourd to it, and sometimes one tree will yield three or four gallons in a night. When just drawn it is of a most delicious sweetness, but in a few days it acquires a tartish and more spirituous flavour, though I never saw anyone intoxicated by it. The same tree also produces nuts and oil. Our principal luxury is in perfumes; one sort of these is an odoriferous wood of delicious fragrance, the other a kind of earth, a small portion of which thrown into the fire diffuses a more powerful odor. We beat this wood into powder and mix it with palm oil, with which both men and women perfume themselves.

In our buildings we study convenience rather than ornament. Each master of a family has a large square piece of ground, surrounded with a moat or fence or enclosed with a wall made of red earth tempered, which when dry is as hard as brick. Within this are his houses to accommodate his family and slaves which if numerous frequently present the appearance of a village. In the middle stands the principal building, appropriated to the sole use of the master and consisting of two apartments, in one of which he sits in the day with his family. The other is left apart for the reception of his friends. He has besides these a distinct apartment in which he sleeps, together with his male children. On each side are the apartments of his wives, who have also their separate day and night houses. The habitations of the slaves and their families are distributed throughout the rest of the enclosure. These houses never exceed one storey in height: they are always built of wood or stakes driven into the ground, crossed with wattles, and neatly plastered within and without. The roof is thatched with reeds. Our day houses are left open at the sides, but those in which we sleep are always covered, and plastered in the inside with a composition mixed with cow dung to keep off the different insects which annoy us during the night. The walls and floors also of these are generally covered with mats. Our beds consist of a platform raised three or four feet from the ground, on which are laid skins and different parts of a spongy tree called plantain. Our covering is calico or muslin, the same as our dress. The usual seats are a few logs of wood, but we have benches, which are generally perfumed to accommodate strangers: these compose the greater part of our household furniture. Houses so constructed and furnished require but little skill to erect them. Every man is a sufficient architect for the purpose. The whole neighbourhood afford their unanimous assistance in building them and in return receive and expect no other recompense than a feast.

As we live in a country where nature is prodigal of her favours, our wants are few and easily supplied; of course we have few manufactures. They consist for the most part of calicoes, earthenware, ornaments, and instruments of war and husbandry. But these make no part of our commerce, the principal articles of which, as I have observed, are provisions. In such a state money is of little use; however we have some small pieces of coin, if I may call them such. They are made something like an anchor, but I do not remember either their value or denomination. We have also markets, at which I have been frequently with my mother. These are sometimes visited by stout mahogany-coloured men from the southwest of us: we call them *Oye-Eboe*, which term signifies red men living at a distance. They generally bring us firearms, gunpowder, hats, beads, and dried fish. The last we esteemed a great rarity as our waters were only brooks and springs. These articles they barter with us for odoriferous woods and earth, and our salt of wood ashes. They always carry slaves through our land, but the strictest account is exacted of their manner of procuring them before they are suffered to pass. Sometimes indeed we sold slaves to them, but they were only prisoners of war, or such among us as had been convicted of kidnapping, or adultery, and some other crimes which we esteemed heinous. This practice of kidnapping induces me to think that, notwithstanding all our strictness, their principal business among us was to trepan our people. I remember too they carried great sacks along with them, which not long after I had an opportunity of fatally seeing applied to that infamous purpose.

Our land is uncommonly rich and fruitful, and produces all kinds of vegetables in great abundance. We have plenty of Indian corn, and vast quantities of cotton and tobacco. Our pineapples grow without culture; they are about the size of the largest sugarloaf and finely flavoured. We have also spices of different kinds, particularly pepper, and a variety of delicious fruits which I have never seen in Europe, together with gums of various kinds and honey in abundance. All our industry is exerted to improve those blessings of nature. Agriculture is our chief employment, and everyone, even the children and women, are engaged in it. Thus we are all habituated to labour from our earliest years. Everyone contributes something to the common stock, and as we are unacquainted with idleness we have no beggars. The benefits of such a mode of living are obvious. The West India planters prefer the slaves of Benin or Eboe to those of any other part of Guinea for their hardiness, intelligence, integrity, and zeal. Those benefits are felt by us in the general healthiness of the people, and in their vigour and activity; I might have added too in their comeliness. Deformity is indeed unknown amongst us, I mean that of shape. Numbers of the natives of Eboe now in London might be brought in support of this assertion, for in regard to complexion, ideas of beauty are wholly relative. I remember while in Africa to have seen three negro children who were tawny, and another quite white, who were universally regarded by myself and the natives in general, as far as related to their complexions, as deformed. Our women too were in my eyes at least uncommonly graceful, alert, and modest to a degree of bashfulness; nor do I remember to have ever heard of an instance of incontinence amongst them before marriage. They are also remarkably cheerful. Indeed cheerfulness and affability are two of the leading characteristics of our nation.

Our tillage is exercised in a large plain or common, some hours walk from our dwellings, and all the neighbours resort thither in a body. They use no beasts of husbandry, and their only instruments are hoes, axes, shovels, and beaks, or pointed iron to dig with. Sometimes we are visited by locusts, which come in large clouds so as to darken the air and destroy our harvest. This however happens rarely, but when it does a famine is produced by it. I remember an instance or two wherein this happened. This common is often the theater of war, and therefore when our people go out to till their land they not only go in a body but generally take their arms with them for fear of a surprise, and when they apprehend an invasion they guard the avenues to their dwellings by driving sticks into the ground, which are so sharp at one end as to pierce the foot and are generally dipped in poison. From what I can recollect of these battles, they appear to have been irruptions of one little state or district on the other to obtain prisoners or booty. Perhaps they were incited to this by those traders who brought the European goods I mentioned amongst us. Such a mode of obtaining slaves in Africa is common, and I believe more are procured this way and by kidnapping than any other. When a trader wants slaves he applies to a chief for them and tempts him with his wares. It is not extraordinary if on this occasion he yields to the temptation with as little firmness, and accepts the price of his fellow creatures liberty with as little reluctance as the enlightened merchant. Accordingly he falls on his neighbours and a desperate battle ensues. If he prevails and takes prisoners, he gratifies his avarice by selling them; but if his party be vanquished and he falls into the hands of the enemy, he is put to death: for as he has been known to foment their quarrels it is thought dangerous to let him survive, and no ransom can save him, though all other prisoners may be redeemed. We have firearms, bows and arrows, broad two-edged swords and javelins: we have shields also which cover a man from head to foot. All are taught the use of these weapons; even our women are warriors and march boldly out to fight along with the men. Our whole district is a kind of militia: on a certain signal given, such as the firing of a gun at night, they all rise in arms and rush upon their enemy. It is perhaps something remarkable that when our people march to the field a red flag or banner is borne before them. I was once a witness to a battle in our common. We had been all at work in it one day as usual, when our people were suddenly attacked. I climbed a tree at some distance, from which I beheld the fight. There were many women as well as men on both sides; among others my mother was there, and armed with a broad sword. After fighting for a considerable time with great fury and after many had been killed, our people obtained the victory and took their enemy's Chief prisoner. He was carried off in great triumph, and though he offered a large ransom for his life he was put to death. A virgin of note among our enemies had been slain in the battle, and her arm was exposed in our marketplace where our trophies were always exhibited. The spoils were divided according to the merit of the warriors. Those prisoners which were not sold or redeemed we kept as slaves: but how different was their condition from that of the slaves in the West Indies! With us they do no more work than other members of the community, even their master; their food, clothing and lodging were nearly the same as theirs, (except that they were not permitted to eat with those who were freeborn), and there was scarce any other difference between them than a superior degree of importance which the head of a family possesses in our state, and that authority which, as such, he exercises over every part of his household. Some of these slaves have even slaves under them as their own property and for their own use.

As to religion, the natives believe that there is one Creator of all things and that he lives in the sun and is girded round with a belt that he may never eat or drink; but according to some he smokes a pipe, which is our own favourite luxury. They believe he governs events, especially our deaths or captivity, but as for the doctrine of eternity, I do not remember to have ever heard of it: some however believe in the transmigration of souls in a certain degree. Those spirits which are not transmigrated, such as their dear friends or relations, they believe always attend them and guard them from the bad spirits or their foes. For this reason they always before eating, as I have observed, put some small portion of the meat and pour some of their drink, on the ground for them, and they often make oblations of the blood of beasts or fowls at their graves. I was very fond of my mother and almost constantly with her. When she went to make these oblations at her mother's tomb, which was a kind of small solitary thatched house, I sometimes attended her. There she made her libations and spent most of the night in cries and lamentations. I have been often extremely terrified on these occasions. The loneliness of the place, the darkness of the night, and the ceremony of libation, naturally awful and gloomy, were heightened by my mother's lamentations; and these, concurring with the doleful cries of birds by which these places were frequented, gave an inexpressible terror to the scene.

We compute the year from the day on which the sun crosses the line, and on its setting that evening there is a general shout throughout the land; at least I can speak from my own knowledge throughout our vicinity. The people at the same time make a great noise with rattles, not unlike the basket rattles used by children here, though much larger, and hold up their hands to heaven for a blessing. It is then the greatest offerings are made, and those children whom our wise men foretell will be fortunate are then presented to different people. I remember many used to come to see me, and I was carried about to others for that purpose. They have many offerings, particularly at full moons;

generally two at harvest before the fruits are taken out of the ground, and when any young animals are killed sometimes they offer up part of them as a sacrifice. These offerings when made by one of the heads of a family serve for the whole. I remember we often had them at my father's and my uncle's, and their families have been present. Some of our offerings are eaten with bitter herbs. We had a saying among us to anyone of a cross temper, "That if they were to be eaten, they should be eaten with bitter herbs."

We practiced circumcision like the Jews and made offerings and feasts on that occasion in the same manner as they did. Like them also, our children were named from some event, some circumstance, our fancied foreboding at the time of their birth. I was named *Olaudah,* which in our language signifies vicissitude or fortunate. . . .

BENJAMIN FRANKLIN

(1706–90)

Benjamin Franklin's antislavery posture was one of paradox. His complete writings reveal mercurial views on race and social class, making him appear as changeable as the weather and currency predictions in his annual *Poor Richard's Almanack.* During different phases of his diverse career, his economic, political, scientific, diplomatic, and philanthropic interests overlapped and often converged with his ideas about democracy and justice toward Indians and Africans.

The same Franklin who could ask, "Why increase the Sons of Africa by planting them in America?" could also say slavery was an "atrocious debasement of human nature." In his 1751 "Observations Concerning the Increase of Mankind and the Peopling of Countries," his chief concern was that white men were deprived of jobs by importing blacks. Over three decades later, his emphasis was different when he was chosen president of an abolitionist organization whose name was probably the longest in the history of the movement: "The Pennsylvania Society for Promoting the Abolition of Slavery, for the Relief of Free Negroes Unlawfully Held in Bondage, and for Improving the Condition of the African Race." Yet, Franklin's last literary work was a satirical defense of slavery—in the persona of an Algerian pirate. During his long and productive life, he cast himself in a succession of sometimes contradictory roles: an inventor who conveniently reinvented himself with the times.

In eighteenth-century America, he was a double, embodying the ideals and dogmas of the Age of Reason and the Age of Revolution. A purveyor of doctrines of freedom, equality, hard work, progress, wealth, success, civic concern and public duty, he was unable to apply them to all people. A Deist and one of the great inquiring minds of his day, with interests as broad as they were eclectic, he undertook numerous projects including establishing a library, a philosophical society, an academy (later the University of Pennsylvania), a post office, a fire department, and a hospital; experimenting with bifocals, stoves, kites, electricity, and lightning. He was as theoretical and scientific as he was skeptical and mystical—an American original who stood apart from orthodoxy.

Some of the miscalculated judgments of his youth about people of color were tempered by moderation in the benevolent acts of his old age. "Moral self-improvement is possible," he once wrote in his *Almanack,* and he often tried to prove it. In American cultural history, he is revered by many as a colonial Horatio Alger: the industrious, rags-to-riches printer, editor, and self-educated entrepreneur, whose frugal "Way to Wealth" allowed him to retire from commerce at age forty-two. That he devoted his remaining career to government, arts and letters, education, science, and international diplomacy increased his legend. Abolitionist activities are not usually listed in his biographical highlights, but in the final analysis, they belong there—even if such involvement came late rather than soon.

After having been a colonial agent in England, a delegate to the Continental Congress, a framer of the Declaration of Independence, and American negotiator and minister in France from 1776 to 1784, he retired from public life in 1788. A final act before his death in April 1790 was to sign a petition to Congress to abolish slavery. The first national census of the newly independent republic was taken that year, and he perhaps recognized what the figures told: in a total U.S. population of 3,929,214, nearly 700,000 were slaves and almost 60,000 were free but disempowered persons of African descent. On their behalf, as president of a Pennsylvania abolitionist society, he signed the following document in Philadelphia five months before he died, an elder statesman approaching age eighty-four.

An Address to the Public

From *The Pennsylvania Society for Promoting the Abolition of Slavery, and the Relief of Free Negroes Unlawfully Held in Bondage* (1789)

It is with peculiar satisfaction we assure the friends of humanity, that, in prosecuting the design of our association, our endeavours have proved successful, far beyond our most sanguine expectations.

Encouraged by this success, and by the daily progress of that luminous and benign spirit of liberty, which is diffusing itself throughout the world, and humbly hoping for the continuance of the divine blessing on our labours, we have ventured to make an important addition to our original plan, and do therefore earnestly solicit the support and assistance of all who can feel the tender emotions of sympathy and compassion, or relish the exalted pleasure of beneficence.

Slavery is such an atrocious debasement of human nature, that its very extirpation, if not performed with solicitous care, may sometimes open a source of serious evils.

The unhappy man, who has long been treated as a brute animal, too frequently sinks beneath the common standard of the human species. The galling chains, that bind his body, do also fetter his intellectual faculties, and impair the social affections of his heart. Accustomed to move like a mere machine, by the will of a master, reflection is suspended; he has not the power of choice; and reason and conscience have but little influence over his conduct, because he is chiefly governed by the passion of fear. He is poor and friendless; perhaps worn out by extreme labour, age, and disease.

Under such circumstances, freedom may often prove a misfortune to himself, and prejudicial to society.

Attention to emancipated black people, it is therefore to be hoped, will become a branch for our national policy; but, as far as we contribute to promote this emancipation, so far that attention is evidently a serious duty incumbent on us, and which we mean to discharge to the best of our judgment and abilities.

To instruct, to advise, to qualify those, who have been restored to freedom, for the exercise and enjoyment of civil liberty, to promote in them habits of industry, to furnish them with employments suited to their age, sex, talents, and other circumstances, and to procure their children an education calculated for their future situation in life; these are the great outlines of the annexed plan, which we have adopted, and which we conceive will essentially promote the public good, and the happiness of these our hitherto too much neglected fellow creatures.

A plan so extensive cannot be carried into execution without considerable pecuniary resources, beyond the present ordinary funds of the Society. We hope much from the generosity of enlightened and benevolent freemen, and will gratefully receive any donations or subscriptions for this purpose, which may be made to our treasurer, James Starr, or to James Pemberton, chairman of our committee of correspondence.

Signed, by order of the Society,

B. FRANKLIN, *President.*

Philadelphia, 9th of
November, 1789.

ABSALOM JONES

(1746–1818)

Forty years separated the birth of Benjamin Franklin and Absalom Jones, who lived quite separate lives in the black and white worlds of Philadelphia. Jones arrived as a teenage slave from Delaware, apprenticed as a clerk and carpenter in his master's store, taught himself to read, and saved for twenty-two years to earn enough to purchase his freedom and a house in 1784. Three years later, he joined another former slave, Richard Allen, in organizing the African Free Society as a reform movement in the city. Through holding prayer meetings for free persons of color unwelcome in white churches, the two men became active lay preachers for the community. Allen the Methodist, and Jones the Episcopalian, helped lay the foundation in 1791 for what ultimately would become an influential and lasting national institution: the African Methodist Episcopal (A.M.E.) Church.

Meanwhile in 1793, a severe yellow fever epidemic in Philadelphia interrupted construction of their first parish. Allen and Jones galvanized their congregation to assist in nursing the sick and burying the dead. Accused by some local whites of profiteering, the two men were defended by Philadelphia's mayor, and they recorded their experience in A *Narrative of the Black People during the Late Awful Calamity in Philadelphia,* published in 1794. Later the same year, they went their separate ways in the ministry, after indecision on whether Methodist or Episcopalian affiliation best suited their followers' needs. Jones remained as titular head of their African church, which in 1794 became St. Thomas African Episcopal Church, where he was deacon and rector. Ordained in 1804 as the first black Episcopal priest in the United States, but restricted in national participation by a conservative white hierarchy, he consecrated his Philadelphia church for worship and as a catalyst for social change.

He would later help ordain Allen as the first bishop of their consolidated A.M.E. church in 1816, but in intervening years the two friends continued as coworkers in community enterprises and as petitioners to the state legislature and to Congress for the immediate abolition of slavery.

On New Year's Day, January 1, 1808, the Slave Trade Act of 1807 became law of the land. Theoretically it abolished the importation of African slaves but continued slavery as an institution. Absalom Jones, from the pulpit of his St. Thomas Episcopal Church, responded with "A Thanksgiving Sermon on Account of the Abolition of the African Slave Trade by the Congress of the United States." His message is excerpted here from the text printed for his congregation.

Although best remembered for this sermon, he left a legacy as a respected preacher, educator, and pathfinder in the early organized black American church. During an era when white religious institutions closed their doors to blacks for worship, sacrament, baptism, marriage, last rites, and burial, Jones offered them a refuge, and the St. Thomas Church School, which he founded the year of his ordination as a priest.

From A Thanksgiving Sermon on Abolition of the Slave Trade by the Congress of the United States (1808)

. . . The history of the world shows us that the deliverance of the children of Israel from their bondage is not the only instance in which it has pleased God to appear in behalf of oppressed and distressed nations, as the deliverer of the innocent, and of those who call upon his name. He is as unchangeable in his nature and character as he is in his wisdom and power. The great and blessed event, which we have this day met to celebrate, is a striking proof that the God of heaven and earth is *the same, yesterday, and today, and forever.* Yes, my brethren, the nations from which most of us have descended, and the country in which some of us were born, have been visited by the tender mercy of the Common Father of the human race. He has seen the affliction of our countrymen, with an eye of pity. He has seen the wicked arts, by which wars have been fomented among the different tribes of the Africans, in order to procure captives, for the purpose of selling them for slaves. He has seen ships fitted out from different ports in Europe and America, and freighted with trinkets to be exchanged for the bodies and souls of men. He has seen the anguish which has taken place when parents have been torn from their children, and children from their parents, and conveyed, with their hands and feet bound in fetters, on board of ships prepared to receive them. He has seen them thrust in crowds into the holds of those ships, where many of them have perished from the want of air. He has seen such of them as have escaped from that noxious place of confinement, leap into the ocean, with a faint hope of swimming back to their native shore, or a determination to seek an early retreat from their impending misery, in a watery grave. He has seen them exposed for sale, like horses and cattle, upon the wharves; or, like bales of goods, in warehouses of West India and American seaports. He has seen the pangs of separation between members of the same family. He has seen them driven into the sugar, the rice, and the tobacco fields, and compelled to work—in spite of the habits of ease which they derived from the natural fertility of their own country—in the open air, beneath a burning sun, with scarcely as much clothing upon them as modesty required. He has seen them faint beneath the pressure of their labours. He has seen them return to their smoky huts in the evening, with nothing to satisfy their hunger but a scanty allowance of roots; and these, cultivated for them-selves, on that day only, which God ordained as a day of rest for man and beast. He has seen the neglect with which their masters have treated their immortal souls; not only in withholding religious instruction from them, but, in some instances, depriving them of access to the means of obtaining it. He has seen all the different modes of torture, by means of the whip, the screw, the pincers, and the red-hot iron, which have been exercised upon their bodies, by inhuman overseers, did I say? Yes: but not by these only. Our God has seen masters and mistresses, educated in fashionable life, sometimes take the instruments of torture into their own hands, and, deaf to the cries and shrieks of their agoniz-ing slaves, exceed even their overseers in cruelty. Inhuman wretches! though You have been deaf to their cries and shrieks, they have been heard in Heaven. The ears of Jehovah have been constantly open to them: He has heard the prayers that have ascended from the hearts of his people; and he has, as in the case of his ancient and chosen people the Jews, *come down to deliver* our suffer-ing countrymen from the hands of their oppressors. He *came down* into the United States, when they declared, in the constitution which they framed in 1788, that the trade in our African fellowmen should cease in the year 1808: He *came down* into the British Parliament, when they passed a law to put an end to the same iniquitous trade in May, 1807: He *came down* into the Con-gress of the United States, the last winter, when they passed a similar law, the operation of which commences on this happy day. Dear land of our ancestors! thou shalt no more be stained with the blood of thy children, shed by British and American hands: the ocean shall no more afford a refuge to their bodies, from impending slavery: nor shall the shores of the British West India islands, and of the United States, any more witness the anguish of families, parted for ever by a publick sale. For this signal interposition of the God of mercies, in behalf of our brethren, it becomes us this day to offer up our united thanks. Let the song of angels, which was first heard in the air at the birth of our

Saviour, be heard this day in our assembly: *Glory to God in the highest,* for these first fruits of *peace upon earth, and goodwill to man:* O! let us *give thanks unto the Lord:* let us *call upon his name,* and *make known his deeds among the people.* Let us *sing psalms unto him and talk of all his wondrous works.*

Having enumerated the mercies of God to our nation, it becomes us to ask, What shall we render unto the Lord for them? Sacrifices and burnt offerings are no longer pleasing to him: the pomp of public worship, and the ceremonies of a festive day, will find no acceptance with him, unless they are accompanied with actions that correspond with them. The duties which are inculcated upon us, by the event we are now celebrating, divide themselves into five heads.

In the first place, Let not our expressions of gratitude to God for his late goodness and mercy to our countrymen, be confined to this day, nor to this house: let us carry grateful hearts with us to our places of abode, and to our daily occupations; and let praise and thanksgivings ascend daily to the throne of grace, in our families, and in our closets, for what God has done for our African brethren. Let us not forget to praise him for his mercies to such of our colour as are inhabitants of this country; particularly, for disposing the hearts of the rulers of many of the states to pass laws for the abolition of slavery; for the number and zeal of the friends he has raised up to plead our cause; and for the privileges we enjoy, of worshiping God agreeably to our consciences, in churches of our own. This comely building, erected chiefly by the generosity of our friends, is a monument of God's goodness to us, and calls for our gratitude with all the other blessings that have been mentioned.

Secondly, Let us unite, with our thanksgiving, prayer to Almighty God, for the completion of his begun goodness to our brethren in Africa. Let us beseech him to extend to all the nations in Europe, the same humane and just spirit towards them, which he has imparted to the British and American nations. Let us, further, implore the influence of his divine and holy Spirit, to dispose the hearts of our legislatures to pass laws, to ameliorate the condition of our brethren who are still in bondage; also, to dispose their masters to treat them with kindness and humanity; and, above all things, to favour them with the means of acquiring such parts of human knowledge, as will enable them to read the holy scriptures, and understand the doctrines of the Christian religion, whereby they may become, even while they are the slaves of men, the freemen of the Lord.

Thirdly, Let us conduct ourselves in such a manner as to furnish no cause of regret to the deliverers of our nation, for their kindness to us. Let us constantly *remember the rock whence we were hewn, and the pit whence we were digged. Pride was not made for man,* in any situation; and, still less, for persons who have recently emerged from bondage. The Jews, after they entered the promised land, were commanded, when they offered sacrifices to the Lord, never to forget their humble origin; and hence, part of the worship that accompanied their sacrifices consisted in acknowledging, *that a Syrian, ready to perish, was their father:* in like manner, it becomes us, publicly and privately, to acknowledge, that an African slave, ready to perish, was our father or our grandfather. Let our conduct be regulated by the precepts of the gospel; let us be sober-minded, humble, peaceable, temperate in our meats and drinks, frugal in our apparel and in the furniture of our houses, industrious in our occupations, just in all our dealings, and ever ready to honour all men. Let us teach our children the rudiments of the English language, in order to enable them to acquire a knowledge of useful trades; and, above all things, let us instruct them in the principles of the gospel of Jesus Christ, whereby they may become *wise unto salvation.* It has always been a mystery, why the impartial Father of the human race should have permitted the transportation of so many millions of our fellow creatures to this country, to endure all the miseries of slavery. Perhaps his design was that a knowledge of the gospel might be acquired by some of their descendants, in order that they might become qualified to be the messengers of it, to the land of their fathers. Let this thought animate us, when we are teaching our children to love and adore the name of our Redeemer. Who knows but that a Joseph may rise up among them, who shall be the instrument of feeding the African nations with the bread of life, and of saving them, not from earthly bondage, but from the more galling yoke of sin and Satan.

Fourthly, Let us be grateful to our benefactors, who, by enlightening the minds of the rulers of the earth, by means of their publications and remonstrances against the trade in our countrymen, have produced the great event we are this day celebrating. Abolition societies and individuals have equal claims to our gratitude. It would be difficult to mention the names of any of our benefactors, without offending many whom we do not know. Some of them are gone to heaven, to receive the reward of their labours of love towards us; and the kindness and benevolence of the survivors, we hope, are recorded in the book of life, to be mentioned with honour when our Lord shall come to reward his faithful servants before an assembled world.

Fifthly, and lastly, Let the first of January, the day of the abolition of the slave trade in our country, be set apart in every year, as a day of public thanksgiving for that mercy. Let the history of the sufferings of our brethren, and of their deliverance, descend by this means to our children to the remotest generations; and when they shall ask, in time to come, saying, What mean the lessons, the psalms, the prayers and the praises in the worship of this day? Let us answer them, by saying, the Lord, on the day of which this is the anniversary, abolished the trade which dragged your fathers from their native country, and sold them as bondmen in the United States of America. . . .

SAMUEL E. CORNISH

(1795–1858)

AND JOHN B. RUSSWURM

(1799–1851)

The black American press originated with Samuel Eli Cornish and John Brown Russwurm, editors and proprietors of *Freedom's Journal*, the first newspaper published by persons of African descent in the United States. Each man in his own way lived up to the pioneering weekly publication's motto: "Righteousness Exalteth a Nation."

In an opening editorial in 1827, the two editors remarked that the nation then included "FIVE HUNDRED THOUSAND free persons of colour—one-half of whom might peruse, and the whole be benefitted by the publication of the Journal; that no publication, as yet, has been devoted to their cause."

The editorial partnership of the two men lasted only six months—until September 27, 1827, when Cornish, a Presbyterian clergyman, resigned to devote full time to his ministry. The same issue revealed another significant new direction: *Freedom's Journal* would begin to examine and debate the idea of Emigration to Africa, through the American Colonization Society, with John Russwurm as the sole editor.

He was in his twenties, his foreign background unknown to most of his readers—and he did not boast of it. Born of mixed blood to the slave mistress of a wealthy white merchant in Jamaica, and sent by his father for formal education in Canada and Maine, Russwurm had made history as one of the first of his race to graduate from an American college. His alma mater was Bowdoin, where he earned his BA degree in 1826, one year after a later famous alumnus, Nathaniel Hawthorne; if the two students had ever known each other, their paths never crossed again. At Bowdoin, Russwurm had expressed a keen interest in perhaps living in Haiti; and by February 1829, in *Freedom's Journal*, he went further—shifting from ideas of abolitionism to black nationalism, embracing the then-not-popular idea of migration to Africa.

Although he and Cornish earlier had discouraged colonization—for the same reasons as David Walker[1] in his *Appeal*—Russwurm had now converted

---

[1] See biographical entry and text for David Walker, pages 87–91, below.

to it, an apostle of race solidarity and expatriation in a February 21, 1829, editorial:

> . . . The American Colonization Society has met with much opposition from us, but the mist which completely darkened our vision, having been dispelled, we now stand before the community a feeble advocate of the Society. We had generally wrong ideas of the Society, and the members thereof. It cannot be denied that our brethren mostly believe that Southern interest completely guides the plans of the Society—that all their movements tend to fetter more closely the chains of the enslaved—and that the removal of the free from among their slaves, is the ultimatum of their wishes. . . .
>
> [N]othing can be more simple, namely, the removal of those among the free coloured population of the United States, who are anxious to emigrate to Africa. We ask every man of colour can anything be more simple; here, is a land in which we cannot enjoy the privileges of citizens, for certain reasons known and felt daily; but there, is one where we may enjoy all the rights of freemen; where everything will tend to call forth our best and most generous feelings—in a word, where we may not only feel as men, but where we may also act as such . . . where the man of colour may not only act and feel as other responsible beings, but where all the energies of his mind, impelled by the most powerful motives, will put forth their best, and astonish the most prejudiced. . . .

By November 1829, Russwurm had moved to Liberia—the African nation founded in 1817 by the predominantly white American Colonization Society for freed slaves. There, until his death in June 1851, he worked zealously as an editor, educator, and public administrator. He had broken with the American Colonization Society by 1836, but he remained a strong advocate of migration to Africa—one of the first free men of color who saw Liberia as a promised land for fulfillment of their abilities and aspirations.

Samuel Cornish, Russwurm's cofounder of *Freedom's Journal*, born free in Delaware, determined to strive for emancipation and brotherhood, in 1829 resumed the editorship of the newspaper under a new name: *Rights of All*. Though the latter was short-lived, Cornish subsequently held other editorial positions and offices in missionary groups and antislavery societies. A foe of the American Colonization Society, in 1840 he coauthored with Theodore Wright a caustic pamphlet, *The Colonization Scheme Considered, in Its Rejection by the Coloured People—in Its Tendency to Uphold Cast—in Its Unfitness for Christianizing and Civilizing the Aborigines of Africa*. . . .

A pastor and reformer who preached race advancement through thrift, education, and work—from his pulpit as well as his pen—he served and organized parishes for Negroes in the Northeast, including Philadelphia, Newark, New York City, and Brooklyn, where he died in 1858, after a long illness.

The spirit of both Cornish and Russwurm endures in the pages of *Freedom's Journal*, which during a two-year existence struggled valiantly to survive. Published every Friday, at an annual subscription price of three dollars, it operated with little remuneration or encouragement to sustain the two editors; Russwurm, never one to withhold criticism to raise the consciousness of his people, summoned them to a higher calling in his farewell editorial on March 28, 1829: "Generally speaking, an editor's office is a thankless one," he wrote. "Prepared, we entered the lists; and unvanquished we retire, with the hope that the talent committed to our care, may yet be exerted under more favorable auspices, and upon minds more likely to appreciate its value."

The first *Freedom's Journal* editorial, reprinted here in full, set forth the hopes and purposes of the newspaper in its inaugural issue, March 16, 1827.

To Our Patrons—
—Opening Editorial[2] of *Freedom's Journal*
(March 16, 1827)

In presenting our first number to our Patrons, we feel all the diffidence of persons entering upon a new and untried line of business. But a moment's reflection upon the noble objects, which we have in view by the publication of this Journal; the expediency of its appearance at this time, when so many schemes are in action concerning our people—encourage us to come boldly before an enlightened publick. For we believe, that a paper devoted to the dissemination of useful knowledge among our brethren, and to their moral and religious improvement, must meet with the cordial approbation of every friend to humanity.

The peculiarities of this Journal, render it important that we should advertise to the world the motives by which we are actuated, and the objects which we contemplate.

---

[2] The original spelling, capitalization, and punctuation have been retained in this text.

We wish to plead our own cause. Too long have others spoken for us. Too long has the publick been deceived by misrepresentations, in things which concern us dearly, though in the estimation of some mere trifles; for though there are many in society who exercise towards us benevolent feelings; still (with sorrow we confess it) there are others who make it their business to enlarge upon the least trifle, which tends to the discredit of any person of colour; and pronounce anathemas and denounce our whole body for the misconduct of this guilty one. We are aware that there are many instances of vice among us, but we vow that it is because no one has taught its subjects to be virtuous: many instances of poverty, because no sufficient efforts accommodated to minds contracted by slavery, and deprived of early education have been made, to teach them how to husband their hard earnings, and to secure to themselves comforts.

Education being an object of the highest importance to the welfare of society, we shall endeavour to present just and adequate views of it, and to urge upon our brethren the necessity and expediency of training their children, while young, to habits of industry, and thus forming them for becoming useful members of society. It is surely time that we should awake from this lethargy of years, and make a concentrated effort for the education of our youth. We form a spoke in the human wheel, and it is necessary that we should understand our [de]pendence on the different parts, and theirs on us, in order to perform our part with propriety.

Though not desirous of dictating, we shall feel it our incumbent duty to dwell occasionally upon the general principles and rules of economy. The world has grown too enlightened, to estimate any man's character by his personal appearance. Though all men acknowledge the excellency of Franklin's maxims, yet comparatively few practise upon them. We may deplore when it is too late, the neglect of these self-evident truths, but it avails little to mourn. Ours will be the task of admonishing our brethren on these points.

The civil rights of a people being of the greatest value, it shall ever be our duty to vindicate our brethren, when oppressed, and to lay the case before the publick. We shall also urge upon our brethren (who are qualified by the laws of the different states) the expediency of using their elective franchise; and of making an independent use of the same. We wish them not to become the tools of party.

And as much time is frequently lost, and wrong principles instilled, by the perusal of works of trivial importance, we shall consider it a part of our duty to recommend to our young readers, such authors as will not only enlarge their stock of useful knowledge, but such as will also serve to stimulate them to higher attainments in science.

We trust also, that through the columns of the FREEDOM'S JOURNAL, many practical pieces, having for their bases, the improvement of our brethren, will be presented to them, from the pens of many of our respected friends, who have kindly promised their assistance.

It is our earnest wish to make our Journal a medium of intercourse between our brethren in the different states of this great confederacy; that through its columns an expression of our sentiments, on many interesting subjects which concern us, may be offered to the publick: that plans which apparently are beneficial may be candidly discussed and properly weighed; if worthy, receive our cordial approbation; if not, our marked disapprobation.

Useful knowledge of every kind, and every thing that relates to Africa, shall find a ready admission into our columns; and as that vast continent becomes daily more known, we trust that many things will come to light, proving that the natives of it are neither so ignorant nor stupid as they have generally been supposed to be.

And while these important subjects shall occupy the columns of the FREE-DOM'S JOURNAL, we would not be unmindful of our brethren who are still in the iron fetters of bondage. They are our kindred by all the ties of nature; and though but little can be effected by us, still let our sympathies be poured forth, and our prayers in their behalf, ascend to Him who is able to succour them.

From the press and the pulpit we have suffered much by being incorrectly represented. Men, whom we equally love and admire have not hesitated to represent us disadvantageously, without becoming personally acquainted with the true state of things, nor discerning between virtue and vice among us. The virtuous part of our people feel themselves sorely aggrieved under the existing state of things—they are not appreciated.

Our vices and our degradation are ever arrayed against us, but our virtues are passed by unnoticed. And what is still more lamentable, our friends, to whom we concede all the principles of humanity and religion, from these very causes seem to have fallen into the current of popular feeling and are imperceptibly floating on the stream—actually living in the practice of prejudice, while they abjure it in theory, and feel it not in their hearts. Is it not very desirable that such should know more of our actual condition, and of our efforts and feelings, that in forming or advocating plans for our amelioration, they may do it more understandingly? In the spirit of candor and humility we intend by a simple representation of facts to lay our case before the publick, with a view to arrest the progress of prejudice, and to shield ourselves against the consequent evils. We wish to conciliate all and to irritate none, yet we must be firm and unwavering in our principles, and persevering in our efforts.

If ignorance, poverty and degradation have hitherto been our unhappy lot, has the Eternal decree gone forth, that our race alone are to remain in this state, while knowledge and civilization are shedding their enlivening rays over the rest of the human family? The recent travels of Denham and Clapperton[3] in the interior of Africa, and the interesting narrative which they have published; the establishment of the republic of Hayti after years of sanguinary welfare; its subsequent progress in all the arts of civilization; and the advancement of liberal ideas in South America, where despotism has given place to free governments, and where many of our brethren now fill important civil and military station, prove the contrary.

The interesting fact that there are FIVE HUNDRED THOUSAND free persons of colour, one half of whom might peruse, and the whole be benefitted by the publication of the Journal; that no publication, as yet, has been devoted exclusively to their improvement—that many selections from approved standard authors, which are within the reach of few, may occasionally be made—and more important still, that this large body of our citizens have no public channel—all serve to prove the real necessity, at present, for the appearance of the FREEDOM'S JOURNAL.

It shall ever be our desire so to conduct the editorial department of our paper as to give offence to none of our patrons; as nothing is farther from us than to make it the advocate of any partial views, either in politics or religion. What few days we can number, have been devoted to the improvement of our brethren; and it is our earnest wish that the remainder may be spent in the same delightful service.

In conclusion, whatever concerns us as a people will ever find a ready admission into the FREEDOM'S JOURNAL, interwoven with all the principal news of the day.

And while every thing in our power shall be performed to support the character of our Journal, we would respectfully invite our numerous friends to assist by their communications, and our coloured brethren to strengthen our hands by their subscriptions, as our labour is one of common cause, and worthy of their consideration and support. And we do most earnestly solicit the latter, that if at any time we should seem to be zealous, or too pointed in the inculcation of any important lesson, they will remember, that they are equally interested in the cause in which we are engaged, and attribute our zeal to the peculiarities of our situation, and our earnest engagedness in their well-being.

THE EDITORS

---

[3] Hugh Clapperton (1778–1827); Major Dixon Denham (1786–1828). British explorers; collaborators on *Narratives of travel and discoveries in northern and central Africa in the Years 1822, 1823, 1824* (Boston and London: 1826).

JAMES FENIMORE COOPER

(1789–1851)

Cooper, the most prolific and famous American author of his generation, is best known for his epic novels of the frontier, the sea, and manners. He is identified and remembered less as a writer of social criticism. His two pieces here on slavery are from his 1838 volume of essays, *The American Democrat*,[1] which constitutes various ideas on American democracy delineated in his fiction.

Written during the second half of Cooper's long career, *The American Democrat* was one of several works in which he expressed disillusion with American society, after a seven-year sojourn in Europe (1826–33). Reared as a Federalist and man of property in rural New York, he returned from his trip inclined to be the aristocratic lord of the manor, disenchanted with the ungenteel era of Andrew Jackson (1829–37), whose new brand of democracy had taken hold in the United States during Cooper's residence abroad. His own definition of a democratic system was closer to one of the eighteenth century than to the nineteenth. A believer in individual political equality but not social egalitarianism, he disdained plutocracy as much as he detested mobocracy, and he considered enlightened conservatives—like himself—the best democrats. A decade earlier, he had defended his country in *Notions of the Americans* (1828), but he was motivated more toward defending traditional social hierarchy and rule of the few over the many in *The American Democrat*.

In the book, he is not an abolitionist nor a slavery advocate but a repatriated American observer. His early novels include a variety of characters of African descent in minor roles, notably in *The Spy* (1821), *The Pioneers* (1823), *The Last of the Mohicans* (1826), and *Red Rover* (1827). None is a slave, although one is a loyal servant; all are depicted without the demeaning stereotypical characteristics seen in fiction by some of Cooper's southern white contemporaries. Outside of his octoroon character, Cora Munro, in *The Last of the Mohicans*, his black characters are men with a predictable place in the social cosmos of his eighteenth- and nineteenth-century settings—like the various Indians in his *Leatherstocking Tales* and other novels of frontier life.

---

[1] Cooper subtitled the book *Or Hints on the Social and Civic Relations of the United States of America*.

His *American Democrat* essay, "On American Slavery," written as if he were abroad commenting to Europeans, looks backward more than forward. Yet, thirty-three years before the Civil War, he predicted danger signals to come. His other essay, titled "On Slavery," examines the institution in world history, reverberating notions about Africa also hinted by Thomas Jefferson, among others, who appear in this volume.

Cooper was not at home in a changing American society where a mythic past was disappearing and being replaced by new realities less idyllic than scenes of his imagination. Some of his opinions as a social critic were an anachronism, but seen through the lens of his time, they offer a composite picture of the forces that shaped his work for three decades.

On Slavery (1838)

Domestic slavery is an institution as old as human annals, and probably will continue, in its spirit, through different modifications, as long as man shall remain under the different degrees of civilization that mark his actual existence. Slavery is no more sinful, by the Christian code, than it is sinful to wear a whole coat, while another is in tatters, to eat a better meal than a neighbor, or otherwise to enjoy ease and plenty, while our fellow creatures are suffering and in want. According to the doctrines of Christ, we are "to do as we would be done by," but this law is not to be applied to slavery more than to any other interest of life. It is quite possible to be an excellent Christian and a slave-holder, and the relations of master and slave, may be a means of exhibiting some of the mildest graces of the character, as may those of king and subject, or principal and dependent, in any of the other modifications of human institutions.

In one sense, slavery may actually benefit a man, there being little doubt that the African is, in nearly all respects, better off in servitude in this country, than when living in a state of barbarism at home.

But, while slavery, in the abstract, can no more be considered a sin, than most human ordinances, it leads to sin in its consequences, in a way peculiarly its own, and may be set down as an impolitic and vicious institution. It encourages those faults of character that depend on an uncontrolled will, on the one side, and an abject submission, on the other. It usually limits the moral existence of the slave, too, as there is a necessity of keeping him ignorant, in order that he may be held in subjection.

Slavery is of two kinds; one in which the slave is a chattel, and can be disposed of as such, and one in which he is attached to the soil, like a fixture, and can only be sold with the land. The former is the condition of the American slave; the latter the condition of the European serf. All Europe, formerly, had serfs, or slaves, of the latter class, though their existence is now confined to a few countries in the north and east of that quarter of the world. Still, the consequences of the old system are, more or less, to be traced, in most European countries, and, though differing in degree, their people may as fairly be termed slaves in principle, as those of our own southern states.

On American Slavery (1838)

American slavery is of the most unqualified kind, considering the slave as a chattel, that is transferable at will, and in full property. The slave, however, is protected in his person to a certain extent, the power of the master to chastise and punish, amounting to no more than the parental power.

American slavery is distinguished from that of most other parts of the world, by the circumstance that the slave is a variety of the human species, and is marked by physical peculiarities so different from his master, as to render future amalgamation improbable. In ancient Rome, in modern Europe generally, and, in most other countries, the slave not being thus distinguished, on obtaining his freedom, was soon lost in the mass around him; but nature has made a stamp on the American slave that is likely to prevent this consummation, and which menaces much future ill to the country. The time must come when American slavery shall cease, and when that day shall arrive, (unless early and effectual means are devised to obviate it,) two races will exist in the same region, whose feelings will be embittered by inextinguishable hatred, and who carry on their faces, the respective stamps of their factions. The struggle that will follow, will necessarily be a war of extermination. The evil day may be delayed, but can scarcely be averted.

American slavery is mild, in its general features, and physical suffering cannot properly be enumerated among its evils. Neither is it just to lay too heavy stress on the personal restraints of the system, as it is a question whether men feel very keenly, if at all, privations of the amount of which they know nothing. In these respects, the slavery of this country is but one modification of the restraints that are imposed on the majority, even, throughout most of Europe. It is an evil, certainly, but in a comparative sense, not as great an evil as it is usually imagined. There is scarcely a nation of Europe that does not possess institutions that inflict as gross personal privations and wrongs, as the slavery of America. Thus the subject is compelled to bear arms in a quarrel in which he has no real concern, and to incur the risks of demoralization and death in camps and fleets, without any crime or agency of his own. From all this, the slave is exempt, as well as from the more ordinary cares of life.

Slavery in America, is an institution purely of the states, and over which the United States has no absolute control. The pretense, however, that congress has no right to entertain the subject, is unsound, and cannot be maintained. Observing the prescribed forms, slavery can be legally abolished, by amending the constitution, and congress has power, by a vote of two-thirds of both houses, to propose amendments to that instrument. Now, whatever congress has power to do, it has power to discuss; by the same rule, that it is a moral innovation on the rights of the states to discuss matters in congress, on which congress has no authority to legislate. A constitutional right, and expediency, however, are very different things. Congress has full power to declare war against all the nations of the earth, but it would be madness to declare war against even one of them, without sufficient cause. It would be equal madness for congress, in the present state of the country, to attempt to propose an amendment of the constitution, to abolish slavery altogether, as it would infal-libly fail, thereby raising an irritating question without an object.

DAVID WALKER

(1785–1830)

Too militant for moderate black and white abolitionists, he created his own mandate and manifesto: *David Walker's Appeal in Four Articles; Together with a Preamble, to the Coloured Citizens of the World, but in Particular, and Very Expressly, to Those of the United States of America.*

The controversial four-part tract began as a lecture in Boston, the autumn of 1828, when Walker stirred an audience of the General Coloured Association of Massachusetts. His new antislavery challenge reached a wider public that December 20 in the black abolitionist weekly, *Freedom's Journal,* for which he was Boston agent and editorial contributor. By September 1829, he had written and combined four articles into a pamphlet, printed and distributed at his own expense. With two more editions in quick succession—each more incendiary than the previous—his final *Appeal* was seventy-eight pages. Working as if his days were numbered, he was prescient that they were. After his text began circulating in the South to the anger of slaveholders and politicians, who wrote Boston's mayor to suppress it, rumors were rampant of a high financial reward for David Walker, dead or alive. He had violated no Massachusetts law, and his work could not legally be stifled. But for Southerners who resented Denmark Vesey's attempted 1822 slave revolt and Gabriel's bloody rebellion in 1800, Walker was considered seditious for challenging slaves to rise against oppressors. Shortly after the third edition of his *Appeal,* the forty-four-year-old author was found dead of uncertain causes in Boston on June 28, 1830, his mysterious death later attributed to poisoning.

Walker was born free in 1785 in Wilmington, North Carolina, the son of a slave father and free mother, whose status he inherited under North Carolina law. Little is known of his early life, except that he was a self-taught itinerant before settling in Boston, where he continued his education, opened a used clothing shop, married a fugitive slave, and joined the abolitionist movement. He found a growing and educated subculture of African descent in Boston, where slavery had been abolished by emancipation laws in Massachusetts—and elsewhere in New England—before 1800. But he had not forgotten what he called "the bloody land of the South" and his determination to "avenge the sorrows which my people have suffered." Nor could he forget "the American, having reduced us to the wretched state of *slavery*, treats us in that condition."

"Wretchedness" was in the title of all four articles of his *Appeal*: "Our Wretchedness in Consequence of our Slavery," "Our Wretchedness in Consequence of Our Ignorance," "Our Wretchedness in Consequence of the Preachers of the Religion of Jesus Christ," "Our Wretchedness in Consequence of the Colonizing Scheme." With frequent allusions to the Bible and antiquity, he attacked the hypocrisy of American society, directed righteous indignation at Thomas Jefferson's views on slavery in *Notes on the State of Virginia*, and Henry Clay's American Colonization Society.

Literate but denied fulfillment of his intellectual potential, disaffected over the plight of his people, David Walker was America's first revolutionary black writer. A foot soldier in the battle for justice, attacked on all sides by both blacks and whites, his ideas represented a departure from the abolitionist crusade of liberal white Quakers who set a moral tone of gentle persuasion. Walker was a symbol of resistance and social protest in which a black man spoke for his own people.

His militancy was continued by others, including his son, Edward Garrison Walker, who became a Boston lawyer and the first of his race elected to the Massachusetts legislature in 1866. Born shortly after his father's death, the younger Walker carried the middle name of another abolitionist crusader, William Lloyd Garrison—whose life and work are the subject of the next entry in this volume.

The following excerpt of David Walker's *Appeal* is from Article IV of his third and final 1830 edition.

From Article IV of *David Walker's Appeal in Four Articles* . . . (1829–30)

Our Wretchedness in Consequence of the Colonizing Scheme

. . . God will show the whites what we are, yet. I say, from the beginning, I do not think that we were natural enemies to each other. But the whites having made us so wretched, by subjecting us to slavery, and having murdered so many millions of us, in order to make us work for them, and out of devilishness—and they taking our wives, whom we love as we do ourselves—our mothers, who bore the pains of death to give us birth—our fathers and dear little children, and ourselves, and strip and beat us one before the other—chain, handcuff, and drag us about like rattlesnakes—shoot us down like wild bears, before each other's faces, to make us submissive to, and work to support them and their families. They (the whites) know well, if we are *men*—and there is a secret monitor in their hearts which tells them we are—they know, I say, if we *are* men, and see them treating us in the manner they do, that there can be nothing in our hearts but death alone, for them, notwithstanding we may appear cheerful, when we see them murdering our dear mothers and wives, because we cannot help ourselves. Man, in all ages and all nations of the earth, is the same. Man is a peculiar creature—he is the image of his God, though he may be subjected to the most wretched condition upon earth, yet the spirit and feeling which constitute the creature, man, can never be entirely erased from his breast, because the God who made him after his own image, planted it in his heart; he cannot get rid of it. The whites knowing this, they do not know what to do; they know that they have done us so much injury, they are afraid that we, being men, and not brutes, will retaliate, and woe will be to them; therefore, that dreadful fear, together with an avaricious spirit, and the natural love in them, to be called masters, (which term will yet honour them with to their sorrow) bring them to the resolve that they will keep us in ignorance and wretchedness, as long as they possibly can,[1] and make the best of their time, while it lasts. Consequently they, themselves, (and not us) render themselves our natural enemies, by treating us so cruel. They keep us miserable now, and call us their property, but some of them will have enough of us by and by—their stomachs shall run over with us; they want us for their slaves, and shall have us to their fill. We are all in the world together! !—I said above, because we cannot help ourselves, (viz. we cannot help the whites murdering our mothers and our wives) but this statement is incorrect—for we can help ourselves; for, if we lay aside abject servility, and be determined to act like men, and not brutes—the murderers among the whites would be afraid to show their cruel heads. But O,

---

[1] And still holds us up with indignity as being incapable of acquiring knowledge!!! See the inconsistency of the assertions of those wretches—they beat us inhumanely, sometimes almost to death, for attempting to inform ourselves, by reading the Word of our Maker, and at the same time tell us, that we are beings void of intellect!!! How admirably their practices agree with their professions in this case. Let me cry shame upon you Americans, for such outrages upon human nature!!! If it were possible for the whites always to keep us ignorant and miserable, and make us work to enrich them and their children, and insult our feelings by representing us as *talking Apes*, what would they do? But glory, honour and praise to Heaven's King, that the sons and daughters of Africa, will, in spite of all the opposition of their enemies, stand forth in all the dignity and glory that is granted by the Lord to his creature man. [Author's note.]

my God!—in sorrow I must say it, that my colour, all over the world, have a mean, servile spirit. They yield in a moment to the whites, let them be right or wrong—the reason they are able to keep their feet on our throats. Oh! my coloured brethren, all over the world, when shall we arise from this deathlike apathy?—And be men! ! You will notice, if ever we become men, (I mean *respectable* men, such as other people are,) we must exert ourselves to the full. For remember, that it is the greatest desire and object of the greater part of the whites, to keep us ignorant, and make us work to support them and their families.—Here now, in the Southern and Western sections of this country, there are at least three coloured persons for one white, why is it, that those few weak, good-for-nothing whites, are able to keep so many able men, one of whom, can put to flight a dozen whites, in wretchedness and misery? It shows at once, what the blacks are, we are ignorant, abject, servile and mean—and the whites know it—they know that we are too servile to assert our rights as men—or they would not fool with us as they do. Would they fool with any other peoples as they do with us? No, they know too well, that they would get themselves ruined. Why do they not bring the inhabitants of Asia to be body servants to them? They know they would get their bodies rent and torn from head to foot. Why do they not get the Aborigines of this country to be slaves to them and their children, to work their farms and dig their mines? They know well that the Aborigines of this country, or (Indians) would tear them from the earth. The Indians would not rest day or night, they would be up all times of night, cutting their cruel throats. But my colour, (some, not all,) are willing to stand still and be murdered by the cruel whites. In some of the West-Indies Islands, and over a large part of South America, there are six or eight coloured persons for one white.[2] Why do they not take possession of those places? Who

---

[2] For instance in the two States of Georgia, and South Carolina, there are, perhaps, not much short of six or seven hundred thousand persons of colour; and if I was a gambling character, I would not be afraid to stake down upon the board FIVE CENTS against TEN, that there are in the single State of Virginia, five or six hundred thousand Coloured persons. Four hundred and fifty thousand of whom (let them be well equipped for war) I would put against every white person on the whole continent of America. (Why? why because I know that the blacks, once they get involved in a war, had rather die than to live, they either kill or be killed.) The whites know this too, which make them quake and tremble. To show the world further, how servile the coloured people are, I will only hold up to view, the one Island of Jamaica, as a specimen of our meanness.

In that Island, there are three hundred and fifty thousand souls—of whom fifteen thousand are whites, the remainder, three hundred and thirty-five thousand are coloured people! and this Island is ruled by the white people!!!!!!!! (15,000) ruling and tyranizing over 335,000 persons!!!!!!!!—O! coloured men!! O! coloured men!!! O! coloured men!!!! Look!! look!!! at this!!!! and, tell me if we are not abject and servile enough, how long, O! how long my colour shall we be dupes and dogs to the cruel whites?—I only passed Jamaica, and its inhabitants, in review as a specimen to show the world, the condition of the blacks at this time, now coloured people of the whole world, I beg you to look at the (15000 white,) and (Three Hundred and Thirty-five Thousand coloured people) in that Island, and tell me how can the white tyrants of the world but say that we are not men, but

hinders them? It is not the avaricious whites—for they are too busily engaged in laying up money—derived from the blood and tears of the blacks. The fact is, they are too servile, they love to have Masters too well! ! Some of our brethren, too, who seeking more after self-aggrandizement, than the glory of God, and the welfare of their brethren, join in with our oppressors, to ridicule and say all manner of evils falsely against our Bishop. They think, that they are doing great things, when they can get in company with the whites, to ridicule and make sport of those who are labouring for their good. Poor ignorant creatures, they do not know that the sole aim and object of the whites, are only to make fools and slaves of them, and put the whip to them, and make them work to support them and their families. But I do say, that no man, can well be a despiser of Bishop Allen,[3] for his public labours among us, unless he is a despiser of God and of Righteousness. Thus, we see, my brethren, the two very opposite positions of those great men, who have written respecting this "Colonizing Plan." (Mr. Clay and his slaveholding party), men who are resolved to keep us in eternal wretchedness, are also bent upon sending us to Liberia. While the Reverend Bishop Allen, and his party, men who have the fear of God, and the welfare of their brethren at heart. The Bishop, in particular, whose labours for the salvation of his brethren, are well known to a large part of those, who dwell in the United States, are completely opposed to the plan— and advise us to stay where we are. Now we have to determine whose advice we will take respecting this all-important matter, whether we will adhere to Mr. Clay and his slave-holding party, who have always been our oppressors and murderers, and who are for colonizing us, more through apprehension than humanity, or to this godly man who has done so much for our benefit, together with the advice of all the good and wise among us and the whites. Will any of us leave our homes and go to Africa? I hope not.[4] Let them commence their attack upon us as they did on our brethren in Ohio, driving and beating us from our country, and my soul for theirs, they will have enough of it. Let no man of us budge one step, and let slaveholders come to beat us from our country. America is more our country, than it is the whites—we have enriched it with our *blood and tears.* . . .

---

were made to be slaves and Dogs to them and their children forever!!!!!!!—why my friend only look at the thing!!!! (15000) whites keeping in wretchedness and degradation (335000) viz. 22 coloured persons for one white !!!!!!! when at the same time, an equal number (15000) blacks, would almost take the whole of South America, because where they go as soldiers to fight death follows in their train. [Author's note.]

[3] Richard Allen (1760–1831). First bishop of the African Methodist Episcopal church in the United States. See also biographical notes on Absalom Jones in this volume, pp. pages 72–73.

[4] Those who are ignorant enough to go to Africa, the coloured people ought to be glad to have them go, for if they are ignorant enough to let the whites *fool* them off to Africa, they would be no small injury to us if they reside in this country. [Author's note.]

WILLIAM LLOYD GARRISON

(1805–79)

David Walker was deceased six months when a young white editor launched a four-page abolitionist weekly newspaper, the *Liberator*, on New Year's Day, 1831. Both the paper and the name William Lloyd Garrison would become synonymous—even after the final issue appeared on December 29, 1865. During more than three decades as an antislavery editor and lecturer, he was often called "liberator" by his followers and traitor by his enemies. Various other labels were attached to him then and later: rebel, reformer, martyr, fanatic, agitator, crusader, savior, romantic, emancipator, prophet, publicist. In the cause of abolition he was most of all an absolutist, driven by a principle of nonresistance.

Unlike some of his wealthy white Northeastern allies in the antislavery movement—including the family of his wife, Helen Benson—Garrison had no background of privilege. He was born in Newburyport, Massachusetts, the son of a merchant seaman whose alcoholism led to desertion of his wife and three children when William was a toddler. Reared in poverty, with little formal education except apprenticeships in printing and editing, he was a self-made man, determined, dependent on his inner resources, accountable only to himself and his conviction in the righteousness of his cause.

His rise as an abolitionist was a steady but rocky climb. By his early twenties, he had edited three quite different New England papers; in one, the *Journal of the Times* in Bennington, Vermont, he printed his first antislavery editorial on November 7, 1828. By Independence Day 1829, he was in Boston delivering his first abolitionist lecture, and two months later in Baltimore, working on an abolitionist paper, *Genius of Universal Emancipation*, which carried the front-page line: "EDITED AND PUBLISHED BY BENJAMIN LUNDY AND WM. LLOYD GARRISON." Within six months he had lost that position and entered a Baltimore jail, sued for libel by a slave trader. Publication with Lundy[1] was terminated, and the *Liberator* was started in partnership with Isaac Knapp.[2]

---

[1] See note 3 on Lundy with Garrison text, p. 94, below.

[2] Isaac Knapp (1804–43), a boyhood friend from Garrison's hometown, collaborated with him on various projects before and after they became copublishers of the *Liberator*. From late 1835 until 1838, Knapp was sole publisher and business manager, then printer until 1841, when his gambling debts caused Garrison's supporters to buy out Knapp's financial interest. He later claimed fraud and published one issue of *Knapp's Liberator*, attacking Garrison, on January 8, 1842.

More outspoken in the new weekly than in the *Genius* with Lundy—who was a Quaker supporter of gradual emancipation and the American Colonization Society—Garrison agitated then and later for immediate emancipation. He also argued against the colonizing concept in a 228-page pamphlet, *Thoughts on African Colonization* (1832). Determined to improve and empower the free colored population, he and fifteen abolitionists organized the New England Anti-Slavery Society in January 1832. Paradoxically no colored free persons were included in the nucleus—despite many who were Garrison's earliest subscribers, including the wealthy James Forten, a Philadelphia sail maker and financial patron of the *Liberator*.

Some of Garrison's actions contradicted his words; he condoned *David Walker's Appeal* but "publicly deprecated its spirit"—even while devoting the front page of his first three *Liberator* issues to debate on the pamphlet. Such pronouncements previewed his later reactions to John Brown, whose 1859 raid at Harper's Ferry Garrison called "well-intended but sadly misguided." Some would say his own actions were misguided when, during various periods of his career, he publicly denounced the clergy, burned the U.S. constitution in public, called for the North to secede from the Union, and shifted his allegiance almost weekly between abolitionists and Abraham Lincoln on the Civil War. He believed to his end that he was all he claimed in a January 1862 speech: "I am an original, uncompromising, irrepressible out-and-out unmistakable, Garrisonian Abolitionist."

He was also a women's rights advocate, who fought to include women on antislavery society councils, and who sat with female delegates in the balcony at an 1840 World Anti-Slavery Convention in London. But by 1870, he called suffragettes such as Susan B. Anthony "selfishly ambitious."

He was throughout his fifty-year public life a man of duality, who alienated friends and associates, but retained cordial relations with subordinates, spoke in biblical rhetoric but often argued with theologians. For most Afro-Americans he was revered and beloved as a self-sacrificing spirit and Christian martyr.

The following piece is his opening editorial reprinted from the first issue of the *Liberator*, January 1, 1831.

To the Public—the *Liberator's* First Editorial (1831)

In the month of August, I issued proposals for publishing "THE LIBERATOR" in Washington City; but the enterprise, though hailed in different sections of the country, was palsied by public indifference. Since that time, the removal of the *Genius of Universal Emancipation*[3] to the Seat of Government has rendered less imperious the establishment of a similar periodical in that quarter.

During my recent tour for the purpose of exciting the minds of the people by a series of discourses on the subject of slavery, every place that I visited gave fresh evidence of the fact, that a greater revolution in public sentiment was to be effected in the free states—*and particularly in New England*—than at the south. I found contempt more bitter, opposition more active, detraction more relentless, prejudice more stubborn, and apathy more frozen, than among slave owners themselves. Of course, there were individual exceptions to the contrary. This state of things afflicted, but did not dishearten me. I determined, at every hazard, to lift up the standard of emancipation in the eyes of the nation, *within sight of Bunker Hill and in the birth place of liberty*. That standard is now unfurled; and long may it float, unhurt by the spoliations of time or the missiles of a desperate foe—yea, till every chain be broken, and every bondman set free! Let Southern oppressors tremble—let their secret abettors tremble—let their Northern apologists tremble—let all the enemies of the persecuted blacks tremble.

I deem the publication of my original Prospectus unnecessary, as it has obtained a wide circulation. The principles therein inculcated will be steadily pursued in this paper, excepting that I shall not array myself as the political partisan of any man. In defending the great cause of human rights, I wish to derive the assistance of all religions and of all parties.

Assenting to the "self-evident truth" maintained in the American Declaration of Independence, "that all men are created equal, and endowed by their Creator with certain inalienable rights—among which are life, liberty and the

---

[3] Abolitionist newspaper (1821–35) founded and published by lifelong Quaker antislavery crusader Benjamin Lundy (1789–1839), who influenced William Lloyd Garrison and hired him as associate editor in 1829 in Baltimore, where Garrison worked some eight months until 1830. Equally as undaunted in his *Genius of Universal Emancipation* as Garrison in his *Liberator*, Lundy has been accorded less attention by American historians. The two abolitionists differed on matters of policy and were estranged at Lundy's death; Garrison eulogized him in a September 20, 1839, *Liberator* obituary editorial, "The Pioneer Fallen," and announced his intention to write a biography; the Lundy family denied him permission.

pursuit of happiness," I shall strenuously contend for the immediate enfranchisement of our slave population. In Park-Street Church, on the Fourth of July, 1829, in an address on slavery, I unreflectingly assented to the popular but pernicious doctrine of *gradual* abolition. I seize this opportunity to make a full and unequivocal recantation, and thus publicly to ask pardon of my God, of my country, and of my brethren the poor slaves, for having uttered a sentiment so full of timidity, injustice and absurdity. A similar recantation, from my pen, was published in the *Genius of Universal Emancipation* at Baltimore, in September, 1829. My conscience is now satisfied.

I am aware, that many object to the severity of my language; but is there not cause for severity? I *will be* as harsh as truth, and as uncompromising as justice. On this subject, I do not wish to think, or speak, or write, with moderation. No! No! Tell a man whose house is on fire, to give a moderate alarm; tell him to moderately rescue his wife from the hands of the ravisher; tell the mother to gradually extricate her babe from the fire into which it has fallen;—but urge me not to use moderation in a cause like the present. I am in earnest—I will not equivocate—I will not excuse—I will not retreat a single inch—*AND I WILL BE HEARD.* The apathy of the people is enough to make every statue leap from its pedestal, and to hasten the resurrection of the dead.

It is pretended, that I am retarding the cause of emancipation by the coarseness of my invective, and the precipitancy of my measures. *The charge is not true.* On this question my influence,—humble as it is,—is felt at this moment to a considerable extent, and shall be felt in coming years—not perniciously, but beneficially—not as a curse, but as a blessing; and posterity will bear testimony that I was right. I desire to thank God, that he enables me to disregard "the fear of man which bringeth a snare," and to speak his truth in its simplicity and power. . . .

WILLIAM LLOYD GARRISON
Boston, January 1, 1831

MARIA W. STEWART

(1803–79)

Militant abolitionism from 1831–50 was full of moral and religious arguments, and few were as persuasive as those of Maria Stewart—the first American woman, black or white, to lecture in public. In the historical annals of pioneering American women, however, she has been moved from center stage by some historians (including white feminists) who prefer top billing for the Grimké sisters as the first American women orators on racism and sexism. The Grimké sisters,[1] who did not speak in Boston until early 1838, were white Southern aristocrats. Maria Stewart, who presented her first speech to the Boston Afric-American Female Intelligence Society in the spring of 1832, was a black woman of humble origins. Her role then and later, however, is significant in the unfolding race drama of her time. Unlike Sojourner Truth,[2] the escaped slave appointed by some critics as a model of black antebellum feminism, Maria Stewart was literate, an intellect equal to her New England abolitionist contemporaries such as Maria Weston Chapman, Lucretia Mott, and Lydia Maria Francis Child[3]—all of whom are better known than she.

Implicit among reasons for historical neglect of Stewart by scholars was not only her race, class, or gender but her militancy. A disciple and protégée of David Walker, (mentioned in her text excerpted in this volume), she exceeded him by demanding an equal place for women in the vanguard of free black voices for political and social change.

She was born Maria Miller in 1803 in Hartford, orphaned at five, reared in a clergyman's family and later in "Sabbath schools." Signs of her early religious upbringing, readings in the Old Testament, and the classics, are in the biblical incantations and historic references in her prose. She had little other education when she became a widow at age twenty-six, after three years of marriage to a mulatto seaman and navy veteran, James Stewart, who died in December 1829. Domestic service was her only means of support after the inheritance her husband left was bilked by creditors in a will he wrote two days before his death.

[1,2,3] See entries on Grimké, Child, and Truth, in this volume, pages 134–36, 119–21, and 263–67, respectively.

Her feelings of remorse and bereavement led to a deep religious experience in 1830 and to writings she offered William Lloyd Garrison; he published her pamphlet, *Religion and Pure Principles of Morality, the Sure Foundation on Which We Must Build*, in 1831. Her written discourse is a union of defiance and prophecy, faith and doubt, authority and piety, with unrelenting evangelical exhortations to her community: "God uses means to bring about his purposes"; she announced to the Afric-American Female Intelligence Society in 1832, "and unless the rising generation manifests a different temper and disposition towards each other from what we have manifested, the generation following will never be an enlightened people." Some months later, she delivered her first public lecture to a racially integrated audience of women and men at Franklin Hall in Boston, September 21, 1832. Then, as in three other public lectures she gave in Boston, she was bold, challenging listeners with what they preferred not to hear. She admonished blacks for apathy: "It is useless for us any longer to sit with our hands folded, reproaching the whites, for that will never elevate us." She rebuked whites for paternalism: "As servants, we are respected; but let us presume to aspire any higher, our employer regards us no longer." She scoffed at male ego: "Man in his best estate is altogether vanity."

She recognized better than anyone that in the male-dominated society of the early 1830s, where most white American females were on a pedestal instead of a podium, an outspoken black woman like herself could have little impact among them—or great influence on most of her own people. On September 21, 1833—the anniversary of her first public lecture—she delivered "Mrs. Stewart's Farewell Address to Her Friends in Boston." She moved to New York, spending twenty years there, and several more in Baltimore, as a schoolteacher until after the Civil War, when she took up residency in Washington, DC. There, during Reconstruction, she became matron of the Freedmen's Hospital. In 1879, fifty years after her husband's death, she received a modest pension after a Congressional act rewarded widows of the War of 1812. She used the income for a return trip to Boston and a final edition of her collected works printed with tributes from friends—including William Lloyd Garrison, whose commendation dated April 4, 1879, came only seven weeks before his death. Stewart died at the end of the same year, without survivors.

The excerpt of her work reprinted here is from the 1831 pamphlet, *Religion and the Pure Principles of Morality. . . .*

From *Religion and the Pure Principles of Morality, the Sure Foundation on Which We Must Build* (1831)

. . . I am of a strong opinion that the day on which we unite, heart and soul, and turn our attention to knowledge and improvement, that day the hissing and reproach amongst the nations of the earth against us will cease. And even those who now point at us with the finger of scorn, will aid and befriend us. It is of no use for us to sit with our hands folded, hanging our heads like bulrushes, lamenting our wretched condition; but let us make a mighty effort, and arise; and if no one will promote or respect us, let us promote and respect ourselves.

The American ladies have the honor conferred on them, that by prudence and economy in their domestic concerns, and their unwearied attention in forming the minds and manners of their children, they laid the foundation of their becoming what they now are. The good women of Wethersfield, Connecticut, toiled in the blazing sun, year after year, weeding onions, then sold the seed and procured money enough to erect them a house of worship; and shall we not imitate their examples, as far as they are worthy of imitation? Why cannot we do something to distinguish ourselves, and contribute some of our hard earnings that would reflect honor upon our memories, and cause our children to arise and call us blessed? Shall it any longer be said of the daughters of Africa, they have no ambition, they have no force? By no means. Let every female heart become united, and let us raise a fund ourselves; and at the end of one year and a half, we might be able to lay the cornerstone for the building of a high school, that the higher branches of knowledge might be enjoyed by us; and God would raise us up, and enough to aid us in our laudable designs. Let each one strive to excel in good housewifery, knowing that prudence and economy are the road to wealth. Let us not say, we know this, or, we know that, and practise nothing; but let us practise what we do know.

How long shall the fair daughters of Africa be compelled to bury their minds and talents beneath a load of iron pots and kettles? Until union, knowledge and love begin to flow amongst us. How long shall a mean set of men flatter us with their smiles, and enrich themselves with our hard earnings,—their wives' fingers sparkling with rings, and they themselves laughing at our folly? Until we begin to promote and patronize each other. Shall we be a byword amongst the nations any longer? Shall they laugh us to scorn forever? Do you ask, What can we do? Unite, and build a store of your own, if you cannot procure a license. Fill one side with dry goods, and the other with groceries. Do you ask, where is the money? We have spent more than enough for nonsense, to do what building we should want. We have never had an opportunity of displaying our talents; therefore the world thinks we know nothing. And we have been possessed of by far too mean and cowardly a disposition, though I highly disapprove of an insolent or impertinent one. Do you ask the disposition I would have you possess? Possess the spirit of independence. The Americans do, and why should not you? Possess the spirit of men, bold and enterprising, fearless and undaunted. Sue for your rights and privileges. Know the reason that you cannot attain them. Weary them with your importunities. You can but die, if you make the attempt; and we shall certainly die if you do not. The Americans have practised nothing but head-work these 200 years, and we have done their drudgery. And is it not high time for us to imitate their examples, and practise head-work too, and keep what we have got, and get what we can? We need never to think that any body is going to feel interested for us, if we do not feel interested for ourselves. That day we, as a people, hearken unto the voice of the Lord our God, and walk in his ways and ordinances, and become distinguished for our ease, elegance and grace, combined with other virtues,—that day the Lord will raise us up, and enough to aid and befriend us, and we shall begin to flourish.

Did every gentleman in America realize, as one, that they had got to become bondmen, and their wives, their sons, and their daughters, servants forever to Great Britain, their very joints would become loosened, and tremblingly would smite one against another; their countenance would be filled with horror; every nerve and muscle would be forced into action; their souls would recoil at the very thought; their hearts would die within them, and death would be far more preferable. Then why have not Afric's sons a right to feel the same? Are not their wives, their sons, and their daughters, as dear to them as those of the white man's? Certainly, God has not deprived them of the divine influences of his Holy Spirit, which is the greatest of all blessings, if they ask him. Then why should man any longer deprive his fellowman of equal rights and privileges? Oh, America, America, foul and indelible is thy strain! Dark and dismal is the cloud that hangs over thee, for thy cruel wrongs and injuries to the fallen sons of Africa. The blood of her murdered ones cries to heaven for vengeance against thee. Thou art almost become drunken with the blood of her slain; thou hast enriched thyself through her toils and labours; and now thou refuseth to make even a small return. And thou hast caused the daughters of Africa to commit whoredoms and fornications; but upon thee be their curse.

O, ye great and mighty men of America, ye rich and powerful ones, many of you will call for the rocks and mountains to fall upon you, and to hide you from the wrath of the Lamb, and from him that sitteth upon the throne; whilst many of the sable-skinned Africans you now despise, will shine in the kingdom of heaven as the stars forever and ever. Charity begins at home, and those that provide not for their own, are worse than infidels. We know that you are raising contributions to aid the gallant Poles; we know that you have befriended Greece and Ireland; and you have rejoiced with France, for her heroic deeds of valor. You have acknowledged all the nations of the earth, except Hayti; and you may publish, as far as the east is from the west, that you have two millions of Negroes, who aspire no higher than to bow at your feet, and to court your smiles. You may kill, tyrannize, and oppress as much as you choose, until our cry shall come up before the throne of God; for I am firmly persuaded, that he will not suffer you to quell the proud, fearless and undaunted spirits of the Africans forever; for in his own time, he is able to plead our cause against you, and to pour out upon you the ten plagues of Egypt. We will not come out against you with swords and staves, as against a thief; but we will tell you that our souls are fired with the same love of liberty and independence with which your souls are fired. We will tell you that too much of your blood flows in our veins, and too much of your color in our skins, for us not to possess your spirits. We will tell you, that it is our gold that clothes you in fine linen and purple, and causes you to fare sumptuously every day; and it is the blood of our fathers and the tears of our brethren that have enriched your soils. AND WE CLAIM OUR RIGHTS. We will tell you that we are not afraid of them that kill the body, and after that can do no more; but we will tell you whom we do fear. We fear him who is able, after he hath killed, to destroy both soul and body in hell forever. Then, my brethren, sheathe your swords, and calm your angry passions. Stand still, and know that the Lord he is God. Vengeance is his, and he will repay. 'Til a long lane that has no turn. America has risen to her meridian. When you begin to thrive, she will begin to fall. God hath raised you up a Walker and a Garrison. Though Walker sleeps, yet he lives, and his name shall be had in everlasting remembrance. I, even I, who am but a child, inexperienced to many of you, am a living witness to testify unto you this day that I have seen the wicked in great power, spreading himself like a green bay tree, and lo, he passed away; yea, I diligently sought him, but he could not be found; and it is God alone that has inspired my heart to feel for Afric's woes. Then fret not yourselves because of evildoers. Fret not yourselves because of the men who bring wicked devices to pass; for they shall be cut down as the grass, and wither as the green herb. Trust in the Lord, and do good; so shalt thou dwell in the land, and verily thou shalt be fed. Encourage the noble-hearted Garrison. Prove to the world that you are neither orang-outangs,[4] nor a species of animals, but that you possess the same powers of intellect as those of the proudboasting American. . . .

I am sensible, my brethren and friends, that many of you have been deprived of advantages, kept in utter ignorance, and that your minds are now darkened; and if any of you have attempted to aspire after high and noble enterprises, you have met with so much opposition that your souls have become discouraged. For this very cause, a few of us have ventured to expose our lives in your behalf, to plead your cause against the great; and it will be of no use, unless you feel for yourselves and your little ones, and exhibit the spirits of men. Oh, then, turn your attention to knowledge and improvement; for knowledge is power. And God is able to fill you with wisdom and understanding, and to dispel your fears. Arm yourselves with the weapons of prayer. Put your trust in the living God. Persevere strictly in the paths of virtue. Let nothing be lacking on your part; and, in God's own time, and his time is certainly the best, he will surely deliver you with a mighty hand and with an outstretched arm.

I have never taken one step, my friend, with a design to raise myself in your esteem, or to gain applause. But what I have done, has been done with an eye single to the glory of God, and to promote the good of souls. I have neither kindred nor friends. I stand alone in your midst, exposed to the fiery darts of the devil, and to the assaults of wicked men. But though all the powers of earth and hell were to combine against me, though all nature should sink into decay, still would I trust in the Lord, and joy in the God of my salvation. For I am fully persuaded, that he will bring me off conqueror, yea, more than conqueror, through him who hath loved me and given himself for me.

---

[4] Stewart's allusion is to the word used by Thomas Jefferson in *Notes on the State of Virginia*, in which he wrote, ". . . the preference of the oran-ootan for the black women over those of his own species." His theory was considered an offense by antebellum black women and widely referred to in writings and speeches.

See Jefferson's "Laws" excerpt on pages 39–41, above.

For an explanation of Jefferson's derivation and use of the word *oran-ootan* see Fawn M. Brodie, *Thomas Jefferson: An Intimate History* (New York, 1974), pp. 232–33.

NAT TURNER

(1800–1831)

A slave from the Tidewater area of Southampton County Virginia, Nat Turner led what was later variously called "the Southampton Insurrection" or the "Nat Turner rebellion." On August 21–23, 1831, he and six followers, including several freemen, gathered rebel forces for a raid through the countryside, ransacking households for ammunition and guns forbidden them under Virginia law; within hours they had killed fifty-seven whites—men, women, and children—including the family of Turner's master. Repelled by a white militia that seized and shot some of his men, Turner survived two months, hiding in woods and swamps. Apprehended on October 30 near his dead master's farm, following a gubernatorial proclamation and five hundred dollars' reward for his capture, he was tried and sentenced in the County Courthouse—and two weeks later executed by hanging from a tree. He had turned thirty-one October 2, while a fugitive on the run.

In his jail "confession" dictated to Thomas R. Gray, a court-assigned lawyer, Turner cited a February 1831 solar eclipse as a divine signal for his act of rebellion. A slave preacher who had learned to read the Bible, he believed himself "ordained for some great purpose in the hands of the Almighty." To the Southern slaveocracy, he was a marauding villain with hallucinatory superstitions; to many blacks and some whites he was a tragic martyr and prophet of salvation.

Although Garrison in the *Liberator* warned that the Turner foray was "the first step of the earthquake, which is ultimately to shake down the fabric of oppression," it was not actually the first step. In the same year Turner was born, a twenty-four-year-old Virginia slave named Gabriel Prosser had organized a conspiracy of one thousand men, armed with bayonets and clubs, to sack Richmond. Their well-laid plans, betrayed when two men broke secrecy, ended with thunderstorms and rain; Gabriel was caught and hanged with fifteen rebels. In 1822, a similar fate befell Denmark Vesey, an ex-slave who had bought his freedom in South Carolina, where his revolt near Charleston failed when several slaves turned informant.

Eight years after Vesey, the Nat Turner conflict climaxed the major premeditated slave revolts of the nineteenth century, although other isolated uprisings persisted in the South until Emancipation. In turn, new measures of repression and patrol were enacted by slave owners, who defended their actions to prevent conspiracies.

Turner neither wrote nor read "The Confessions of Nat Turner," which Gray printed and sold as a pamphlet in 1831.[1] The following excerpt is adapted from the original edition, *The Confessions of Nat Turner, the leader of the late insurrection in Southampton, Va.; As Fully and Voluntarily Made to Thomas R. Gray* . . . (Baltimore, Md., 1831).

From *The Confessions of Nat Turner, the leader of the late insurrection in Southampton, Va.*[2] (1831)

. . . You have asked me to give a history of the motives which induced me to undertake the late insurrection, as you call it. To do so I must go back to the days of my infancy, and even before I was born. I was thirty-one years of age the 2nd of October last, and born the property of Benjamin Turner, of this county. In my childhood a circumstance occurred which made an indelible impression on my mind, and laid the groundwork of that enthusiasm, which has terminated so fatally to many, both white and black, and for which I am about to atone at the gallows. It is here necessary to relate this circumstance— trifling as it may seem, it was the commencement of that belief which has grown with time, and even now, sir, in this dungeon, helpless and forsaken as I am, I cannot divest myself of. Being at play with other children, when three or four years old, I was telling them something, which, my mother overhearing, said it had happened before I was born. I stuck to my story, however, and related some things which went, in her opinion to confirm it: Others called on were greatly astonished, knowing that these things had happened, and caused them to say in my hearing I surely would be a prophet, as the Lord had shown me things that had happened before my birth. And my father and mother strengthened me in this, my first impression, saying in my presence, I was intended for some great purpose, which they had always thought from certain marks on my head and breast. . . .

---

[1] The pamphlet received less attention than a 1967 novel of the same title by a white Southern author, William Styron, whose fiction took liberties with certain facts in the case.

[2] As told to Thomas R. Gray, ed. (Baltimore, 1831).

My grandmother, who was very religious, and to whom I was much attached; my master, who belonged to the church, and other religious persons who visited the house, and whom I often saw at prayers; noticing the singularity of my manners, I suppose, and my uncommon intelligence for a child, remarked I had too much sense to be raised, and if I was, I would never be of any service to any one as a slave. To a mind like mine, restless, inquisitive, and observant of everything that was passing, it is easy to suppose that religion was the subject to which it would be directed, and although this subject principally occupied my thoughts, there was nothing that I saw or heard of to which my attention was not directed. The manner in which I learned to read and write, not only had great influence on my own mind, (as I had acquired it with the most perfect ease, so much so, that I have no recollection whatever of learning the alphabet), but to the astonishment of the family, one day when a book was shown me to keep me from crying, I began spelling the names of the different objects. This was a source of wonder to all in the neighborhood, particularly the blacks, and this learning was constantly improved at all opportunities. When I got large enough to go to work, while employed, I was reflecting on many things that would present themselves to my imagination, and whenever an opportunity occurred of looking at a book, when the school children were getting their lessons, I would find many things that the fertility of my own imagination had depicted to me before. All my time, not devoted to my master's service, was spent either in prayer, or in making experiments in casting different things in moulds made of earth; in attempting to make paper, gunpowder, and many other experiments, that although I could not perfect, yet convinced me of its practicability if I had the means.[3] I was not addicted to stealing in my youth, nor have ever been, yet such was the confidence of the Negroes in the neighborhood even at this early period of my life, in my superior judgment that they would often carry me with them when they were going on any roguery, to plan for them. Growing up among them with this confidence in my superior judgment, and when this, in their opinions, was perfected by Divine inspiration, from the circumstances already alluded to in my infancy, and which belief was ever afterwards zealously inculcated by the austerity of my life and manners, which became the subject of remark by white and black, having soon discovered to be great, I must appear so, and therefore studiously avoided mixing in society, and wrapped myself in mystery, devoting my time to fasting and prayer.

By this time having arrived to man's estate and hearing the Scriptures commented on at meetings, I was struck with that particular passage which says:

---

[3] T. R. Gray footnote in the original edition reads: "When questioned as to the manner of manufacturing those different articles, he was found well-informed."

"Seek ye the Kingdom of Heaven and all things shall be added unto you." I reflected much on this passage, and prayed daily for light on this subject. As I was praying one day at my plough, the Spirit spoke to me, saying: "Seek ye the Kingdom of Heaven and all things shall be added unto you."

Question: What do you mean by the Spirit?

Answer: The Spirit that spoke to the Prophets in former days. And I was greatly astonished, and for two years prayed continually, whenever my duty would permit; and then, again, I had the same revelation, which fully confirmed me in the impression that I was ordained for some great purpose in the hands of the Almighty. Several years rolled round, in which many events occurred to strengthen me in this, my belief. At this time I reverted in my mind to the remarks made of me in my childhood, and the things that had been shown me, and as it had been said of me in my childhood by those by whom I had been taught to pray, both white and black, and in whom I had the greatest confidence, that I had too much sense to be raised, and if I was, I would never be of any use as a slave. Now, finding that I had arrived to man's estate, and was a slave, and these revelations being known to me, I began to direct my attention to this great object, to fulfill the purpose for which, by this time, I felt assured I was intended. Knowing the influence I had obtained over the minds of my fellow servants, (not by the means of conjuring and such like tricks, for to them I always spoke of such things with contempt), but by the communion of the Spirit, whose revelation I often communicated to them, and they believed and said my wisdom came from God. I now began to prepare them for my purpose by telling them something was about to happen that would terminate in fulfilling the great promise that had been made to me.

About this time I was placed under an overseer, from whom I ran away and after remaining in the woods thirty days I returned, to the astonishment of the Negroes on the plantation who thought I had made my escape to some other part of the country, as my father had done before. But the reason of my return was, that the Spirit appeared to me and said I had my wishes directed to the things of this world, and not to the Kingdom of Heaven, and that I should return to the service of my earthly master—"For he who knoweth his Master's will, and doeth it not, shall be beaten with many stripes, and thus have I chastened you." And the Negroes found fault and murmured against me, saying if they had my sense they would not serve any master in the world. And about this time I had a vision, and I saw white spirits and black spirits engaged in battle, and the sun was darkened—the thunder rolled in the Heavens, and blood flowed in streams—and I heard a voice saying, "Such is your luck, such you are called to see, and let it come rough or smooth, you must surely bear it."

I now withdrew myself as much as my situation would permit, from the intercourse of my fellow servants, for the avowed purpose of serving the Spirit more fully; and it appeared to me and reminded me of the things it had already shown me, and that it would then reveal to me the knowledge of the elements, the revolution of the planets, the operation of tides, and the changes of the seasons. After this revelation of the year 1825, and the knowledge of the elements being made known to me I sought more than ever to obtain true holiness before the great day of judgment should appear; and then I began to receive the true knowledge of faith. And from the first steps of righteousness until the last, was I made perfect; and the Holy Ghost was with me and said, "Behold me as I stand in the Heavens"; and I looked and saw the forms of men in different attitudes, and there were lights in the sky to which the children of darkness gave other names than what they really were, for they were the lights of the Saviour's hands, stretched forth from east to west, even as they were extended on the cross on Calvary for the redemption of sinners. And I wondered greatly at these miracles, and prayed to be informed of a certainty of the meaning thereof, and shortly afterwards, while labouring in the field, I discovered drops of blood on the corn, as though it was dew from heaven, and I communicated it to many, both white and black, in the neighborhood; and then I found on the leaves in the woods hieroglyphic characters and numbers, with the forms of men in different attitudes, portrayed in the blood, and representing the figures I had seen before in the Heavens. And now the Holy Ghost had revealed itself to me, for as the blood of Christ had been shed on this earth, and had ascended to Heaven for the salvation of sinners, and was now returning to earth again in the form of dew; and as the leaves on the trees bore the impression of figures I had seen in the Heavens, it was plain to me that the Saviour was about to lay down the yoke he had borne for the sins of men, and the great day of judgment was at hand.

About this time I told these things to a white man (Etheldred T. Brantley) on whom it had a wonderful effect, and he ceased from his wickedness and was attacked immediately with a cutaneous eruption, and blood oozed from the pores of his skin, and after praying and fasting nine days, he was healed; and the Spirit appeared to me again and said, "As the Saviour had been baptized so should we be also";—and when the white people would not let us be baptized by the church, we went down into water together, in the sight of many who reviled us, and were baptized by the Spirit. After this I rejoiced greatly, and gave thanks to God. And on the 12th of May, 1828, I heard a loud noise in the Heavens, and the Spirit instantly appeared to me and said the Serpent was loosened, and Christ had laid down the yoke he had borne for the sins of men, and that I should take it on and fight against the Serpent, for the time was fast approaching when the first should be last and the last should be first.

Question: Do you not find yourself mistaken now?

Answer: Was not Christ crucified?

And by signs in the Heavens that it would make known to me when I should commence the great work, and until the first sign appeared I should conceal it from the knowledge of men; and on the appearance of the sign (the eclipse of the sun last February), I should arise and prepare myself and slay my enemies with their own weapons. And immediately on the sign appearing in the Heavens the seal was removed from my lips, and I communicated the great work laid out for me to do, to four, in whom I had the greatest confidence, (Henry, Hark, Nelson, and Sam). It was intended by us to have begun the work of death on the 4th of July last. Many were the plans formed and rejected by us, and it affected my mind to such a degree that I felt sick, and the time passed without our coming to any determination how to commence. Still forming new schemes and rejecting them, when the sign appeared again, which determined me not to wait longer. . . .

FRANCES MILTON TROLLOPE

(1780–1863)

The antebellum South of the late 1820s seen by the English author Frances Trollope antedated the 1831 slave revolt of Nat Turner. Slave uprisings do not enter her 1832 book, *Domestic Manners of the Americans*, but few writers have so adroitly described the conduct of a slave-owning society. An outsider looking at the United States, she indicted almost all she saw, and in turn was lampooned and vilified by Americans sensitive and resentful of a foreigner's derogatory judgments.

Her criticisms of the new nation's values, morals, manners, and institutions grew from a three-year sojourn, which began on Christmas Eve, 1827. She disembarked at New Orleans with three of her children and Frances Wright, a Scottish-born heiress whose 1819 journey to the U.S. had resulted in a book, *Views of Society and Manners in America*, and a pamphlet, "A Plan for the Gradual Abolition of Slavery in the United States, without Danger of Loss to Citizens of the South." Frances Trollope came with no intent to write or to conduct a social experiment, such as Frances Wright's Nashoba Commune in rural Tennessee to educate and emancipate slaves. An emissary for her husband, Mrs. Trollope arrived to negotiate business affairs for his department store in Cincinnati but turned to writing when the emporium venture failed. Publication of her travel sketches about the American South, Midwest, and Northeast thrust her into the international limelight. Her prodigious literary career, which followed in England, influenced the later avocation of her sons, the novelists Thomas and Anthony Trollope.

The excerpt here of "Small Landed Proprietors, Slavery," is from Chapter XXII of *Domestic Manners of the Americans*.

From *Domestic Manners of the Americans* (1832)

. . . It is not among the higher classes that the possession of slaves produces the worst effects. Among the poorer class of landholders, who are often as profoundly ignorant as the Negroes they own, the effect of this plenary power over males and females is most demoralizing; and the kind of coarse, not to say brutal, authority which is exercised, furnishes the most disgusting moral spectacle I ever witnessed. In all ranks, however, it appeared to me that the greatest and best feelings of the human heart were paralyzed by the relative positions of slave and owner. The characters, the hearts of children, are irretrievably injured by it. In Virginia, we boarded for some time in a family consisting of a widow and her four daughters, and I there witnessed a scene strongly indicative of the effect I have mentioned. A young female slave, about eight years of age, had found on the shelf of a cupboard a biscuit, temptingly buttered, of which she had eaten a considerable portion before she was observed. The butter had been copiously sprinkled with arsenic for the destruction of rats, and had been thus most incautiously placed by one of the young ladies of the family. As soon as the circumstance was known, the lady of the house came to consult me as to what had best be done for the poor child; I immediately mixed a large cup of mustard and water (the most rapid of all emetics) and got the little girl to swallow it. The desired effect was instantly produced, but the poor child, partly from nausea, and partly from the terror of hearing her death proclaimed by half a dozen voices round her, trembled so violently that I thought she would fall. I sat down in the court where we were standing, and, as a matter of course, took the little sufferer in my lap. I observed a general titter among the white members of the family, while the black stood aloof, and looked stupified. The youngest of the family, a little girl about the age of the young slave, after gazing at me for a few moments in utter astonishment, exclaimed, "My! if Mrs. Trollope has not taken her in her lap, and wiped her nasty mouth! Why, I would not have touched her mouth for two hundred dollars!"

The little slave was laid on a bed, and I returned to my own apartments; some time afterward I sent to inquire for her, and learned that she was in great pain. I immediately went myself to inquire farther, when another young lady of the family, the one by whose imprudence the accident had occurred, met my anxious inquiries with ill-suppressed mirth—told me they had sent for the doctor—and then burst into uncontrollable laughter. The idea of really sympathizing in the sufferings of a slave, appeared to them as absurd as weeping over a calf that had been slaughtered by the butcher. The daughters of my hostess were as lovely as features and complexion could make them; but the neutralizing effect of this total want of feeling upon youth and beauty, must be witnessed to be conceived.

There seems in general a strong feeling throughout America, that none of the Negro race can be trusted, and as fear, according to their notions, is the only principle by which a slave can be actuated, it is not wonderful if the imputation be just. But I am persuaded that were a different mode of moral treatment pursued, most important and beneficial consequences would result from it. Negroes are very sensible to kindness, and might, I think, be rendered more profitably obedient by the practice of it towards them, than by any other mode of discipline whatever. To emancipate them entirely throughout the Union cannot, I conceive, be thought of, consistently with the safety of the country; but were the possibility of amelioration taken into the consideration of the legislature, with all the wisdom, justice, and mercy that could be brought to bear upon it, the Negro population of the Union might cease to be a terror, and their situation no longer be a subject either of indignation or of pity.

I observed everywhere throughout the slave states that all articles which can be taken and consumed are constantly locked up, and in large families, where the extent of the establishment multiplies the number of keys, these are deposited in a basket, and consigned to the care of a little Negress, who is constantly seen following her mistress's steps with this basket on her arm, and this, not only that the keys may be always at hand, but because should they be out of sight one moment, that moment would infallibly be employed for purposes of plunder. It seemed to me in this instance, as in many others, that the close personal attendance of these sable shadows must be very annoying; but whenever I mentioned it, I was assured that no such feeling existed, and that use rendered them almost unconscious of their presence.

I had, indeed, frequent opportunities of observing this habitual indifference to the presence of their slaves. They talk of them, of their condition, of their faculties, of their conduct, exactly as if they were incapable of hearing. I once saw a young lady, who, when seated at table between a male and a female, was induced by her modesty to intrude on the chair of her female neighbour to avoid the indelicacy of touching the elbow of *a man*. I once saw this very young lady lacing her stays with the most perfect composure before a Negro footman. A Virginian gentleman told me that ever since he had married, he had been accustomed to have a Negro girl sleep in the same chamber with himself and his wife. I asked for what purpose this nocturnal attendance was necessary? "Good heaven!" was the reply, "if I wanted a glass of water during the night, what would become of me?" . . .

JOHN PENDLETON KENNEDY

(1795–1870)

Lawyer, businessman, politician, journalist, and author, John Pendleton Kennedy is best known for his first novel, *Swallow Barn; or, A Sojourn in the Old Dominion.* A portrayal of antebellum Southern life from a proslavery viewpoint, it was first published in 1832, marking the earliest prototype of "the plantation novel" that emerged in more stereotypical and popular form in the postbellum period.

Born in Baltimore, where his Irish father settled, Kennedy's maternal family roots were in the Southern gentry of Virginia's Shenandoah Valley, where he spent his boyhood summers. His sentimental ties to the South, however, were severed when he denounced secession and sided with the Union during the Civil War. A political Whig,[1] his record as a politician was more notable than his literary achievements. Elected at age twenty-five to the Maryland legislature, he later served in Congress (1838–45), then as speaker of the Maryland House of Delegates (1846–47), and as Secretary of the Navy (1852–53).

His now forgotten prolix novels were on political subjects, including *Horse Shoe Robinson* (1835), a historical romance of the Revolution in South Carolina, and *Quodlibet* (1840), a satire on Andrew Jacksonian–era politics. The hybrid literary form of his better known novel *Swallow Barn* owes more to the style of Washington Irving's sketches in *Bracebridge Hall* (1822) than to his own originality.

Swallow Barn, published in two volumes in 1832, was revised in one volume (illustrated with pictures) in 1851. Titled for the fictional name of its Virginia Tidewater plantation setting, the narrative combines episodic sketches of nostalgia for provincial Southern life with a mocking burlesque of it. Chattel slavery, however, is not satirized but defended from a Southern planter position.

The narrator is a New Yorker, Mark Littleton, who visits the Swallow Barn estate owned by his relative, Frank Meriwether. Mark Littleton, Kennedy's pen name in the 1832 edition, is an interlocutor for his Southern host, who is

---

[1] Whig party, in the U.S. a national political party in the years 1824–55; represented conservative banking and property interests in the North and plantation owners in the South.

depicted as a benign slave master echoing arguments then prevalent among the Old Dominion aristocracy. His statements, such as Northern "interference is an unwarrantable and mischievous design to do us injury," and slaves are "a comparatively comfortable and contented race of people," are indicative of racist notions in various passages of the book.

Paternalism and prejudice in the 1832 edition became inexorable propaganda in the 1851 version, where Kennedy substantively revised a chapter entitled "The Quarter" to reflect his own antiabolitionist views. The following portions of that chapter are from the 1851 edition; excerpts are included also from chapter 31, "Summer Mornings," which reflect the Northern narrator's observations on slavery, during a stroll on the Swallow Barn plantation, where he is accompanied by a Southern country squire, Cousin Ned.

From *Swallow Barn; or, A Sojourn in the Old Dominion* (1832)

Chapter 31

Summer Mornings

. . . Ned and myself usually commence the morning with a stroll. If there happen to be visitors at Swallow Barn, this after-breakfast hour is famous for debates. We then all assemble in the porch, and fall into grave discussions upon agriculture, hunting, or horsemanship, in neither of which do I profess any great proficiency, though I take care not to let that appear. Some of the party amuse themselves with throwing pebbles picked from the gravel walk, or draw figures upon the earth with a cane, as if to assist their cogitations; and when our topics grow scarce, we saunter towards the bridge, and string ourselves out upon the rail, to watch the bubbles that float down the stream; and are sometimes a good deal perplexed to know what we shall do until dinner time.

There is a numerous herd of little negroes about the estate and these sometimes afford us a new diversion. A few mornings since, we encountered a horde of them, who were darting about the bushes like untamed monkeys. They are afraid of me, because I am a stranger, and take to their heels as soon as they see me. If I ever chance to get near enough to speak to one of them, he stares at me with a suspicious gaze; and, after a moment, makes off at full speed, very much frightened, towards the cabins at some distance from the house. They are almost all clad in a long coarse shirt which reaches below the knee, without any other garment: but one of the group we met on the morning I speak of, was oddly decked in a pair of ragged trousers, conspicuous for their ample dimensions in the seat. These had evidently belonged to some grown-up person, but were cut short in the legs to make them fit the wearer. A piece of twine across the shoulder of this grotesque imp, served for suspenders, and kept his habiliments from falling about his feet. Ned ordered this crew to prepare for a footrace, and proposed a reward of a piece of money to the winner. They were to run from a given point, about a hundred paces distant, to the margin of the brook. Our whole suite of dogs were in attendance, and seemed to understand our pastime. At the word, away went the bevy, accompanied by every dog of the pack, the negroes shouting and the dogs yelling in unison. The *shirts* ran with prodigious vehemence, their speed exposing their bare, black, and meager shanks, to the scandal of all beholders; and the strange baboon in trousers struggled close in their rear, with ludicrous earnestness, holding up his redundant and troublesome apparel with his hand. In a moment they reached the brook with unchecked speed; and, as the banks were muddy, and the dogs had become tangled with the racers in their path, two or three were percipitated into the water. This only increased the merriment, and they continued the contest in this new element, by floundering, kicking, and splashing about, like a brood of ducks in their first descent upon a pool. These young negroes have wonderfully flat noses, and the most oddly disproportioned mouths, which were now opened to their full dimensions, so as to display their white teeth in striking contrast with their complexions. They are a strange pack of antic and careless animals, and furnish the liveliest picture that is to be found in nature, of that race of swart fairies which, in the old time, were supposed to play their pranks in the forest at moonlight. Ned stood by, enjoying this scene like an amateur; encouraging the negroes in their gambols, and hallooing to the dogs, that by a kindred instinct entered tumultuously into the sport and kept up the confusion. It was difficult to decide the contest. So the money was thrown into the air, and as it fell to the ground, there was another rush, in which the hero of the trousers succeeded in getting the small coin from the ground in his teeth, somewhat to the prejudice of his finery. . . .

Ever since I have been at Swallow Barn, I have entertained a very philosophical longing for the calm and dignified retirement of the woods. I begin to grow moderate in my desires; that is, I only want a thousand acres of good land, an old manor house, on a pleasant site, a hundred negroes, a large library, a host of friends, and a reserve of a few thousands a year in the stocks,—in case of bad crops,—and, finally, a house full of pretty, intelligent, and docile children, with some few et ceteras not worth mentioning.

I doubt not, after this, I shall be considered a man of few wants, and great resources within myself.

Chapter 46

The Quarter

I came here a stranger, in great degree, to the negro character, knowing but little of the domestic history of these people, their duties, habits or temper, and somewhat disposed, indeed, from prepossessions, to look upon them as severely dealt with, and expecting to have my sympathies excited towards them as objects of commiseration. I have had, therefore, rather a special interest in observing them. The contrast between my preconceptions of their condition and the reality which I have witnessed, has brought me a most agreeable surprise. I will not say that, in a high state of cultivation and of such self-dependence as they might possibly attain in a separate national existence, sure they never could become a happier people than I find them here. Perhaps they are destined, ultimately, to that national existence, in the clime from which they derive their origin—that this is a transition state in which we see them in Virginia. If it be so, no tribe of people have ever passed from barbarism to civilization whose middle stage of progress has been more secure from harm, more genial to their character, or better supplied with mild and beneficent guardianship, adapted to the actual state of their intellectual feebleness, than the negroes of Swallow Barn. And, from what I can gather, it is pretty much the same on the other estates in this region. I hear of an unpleasant exception to this remark now and then; but under such conditions as warrant the opinion that the unfavorable case is not more common than that which may be found in a survey of any other department of society. The oppression of apprentices, of seamen, of soldiers, of subordinates, indeed, in every relation, may furnish elements of a bead roll of social grievances quite as striking, if they were diligently noted and brought to view.

What the negro is finally capable of, in the way of civilization, I am not philosopher enough to determine. In the present stage of his existence, he presents himself to my mind as essentially parasitical in his nature. I mean that he is, in his moral constitution, a dependent upon the white race; dependent for guidance and direction even to the procurement of his most indispensable necessaries. Apart from this protection he has the helplessness of a child,—

without foresight, without faculty of contrivance, without thrift of any kind. We have instances, in the neighborhood of this estate, of individuals of the tribe falling into the most deplorable destitution from the want of that constant supervision which the race seems to require. This helplessness may be the due and natural impression which two centuries of servitude have stamped upon the tribe. But it is not the less a present and insurmountable impediment to that most cruel of all projects—the direct, broad emancipation of these people;—an act of legislation in comparison with which the revocation of the edict of Nantes would be entitled to be ranked among political benefactions. Taking instruction from history, all organized slavery is inevitably but a temporary phase of human condition. Interest, necessity and instinct, all work to give progression to the relations of mankind, and finally to elevate each tribe or race to its maximum of refinement and power. We have no reason to suppose that the negro will be an exception to this law.

At present, I have said, he is parasitical. He grows upward, only as the vine to which nature has supplied the sturdy tree as a support. He is extravagantly imitative. The older negroes here have—with some spice of comic mixture in it—that formal, grave and ostentatious style of manners, which belonged to the gentlemen of former days; they are profuse of bows and compliments, and very aristocratic in their way. The younger ones are equally to be remarked for aping the style of the present time, and especially for such tags of dandyism in dress as come within their reach. Their fondness for music and dancing is a predominant passion. I never meet a negro man—unless he is quite old—that he is not whistling; and the women sing from morning till night. And as to dancing, the hardest day's work does not restrain their desire to indulge in such pastime. During the harvest, when their toil is pushed to its utmost—the time being one of recognized privileges—they dance almost the whole night. They are great sportsmen, too. They angle and haul the seine, and hunt and tend their traps, with a zest that never grows weary. Their gayety of heart is constitutional and perennial, and when they are together they are as voluble and noisy as so many blackbirds. In short, I think them the most good-natured, careless, lighthearted, and happily constructed human beings I have ever seen. Having but few and simple wants, they seem to me to be provided with every comfort which falls within the ordinary compass of their wishes; and, I might say, that they find even more enjoyment,—as that word may be applied to express positive pleasures scattered through the course of daily occupation—than any other laboring people I am acquainted with.

I took occasion to express these opinions to Meriwether, and to tell him how much I was struck by the mild and kindly aspect of this society at the Quarter.

This, as I expected, brought him into a discourse.

"The world," said he, "has begun very seriously to discuss the evils of slavery, and the debate has sometimes, unfortunately, been leveled to the comprehension of our negroes, and pains have even been taken that it should reach them. I believe there are but few men who may not be persuaded that they suffer some wrong in the organization of society—for society has many wrongs, both accidental and contrived, in its structure. Extreme poverty is, perhaps, always a wrong done to the individual upon whom it is cast. Society can have no honest excuse for starving a human being. I daresay you can follow out that train of thought and find numerous evils to complain of. Ingenious men, some of them not very honest, have found in these topics themes for agitation and popular appeal in all ages. How likely are they to find, in this question of slavery, a theme for the highest excitement; and, especially, how easy is it to inflame the passions of these untutored and unreckoning people, our black population, with this subject! For slavery, as an original question, is wholly without justification or defence. It is theoretically and morally wrong—and fanatical and one-sided thinkers will call its continuance, even for a day, a wrong, under any modification of it. But, surely, if these people are consigned to our care by the accident, or, what is worse, the premeditated policy which has put them upon our commonwealth, the great duty that is left to us is, to shape our conduct, in reference to them, by a wise and beneficent consideration of the case as it exists, and to administer wholesome laws for their government, making their servitude as tolerable to them as we can consistently with our own safety and their ultimate good. We should not be justified in taking the hazard of internal convulsions to get rid of them; nor have we a right, in the desire to free ourselves, to whelm them in greater evils than their present bondage. A violent removal of them, or a general emancipation, would assuredly produce one or the other of these calamities. Has any sensible man, who takes a different view of this subject, ever reflected upon the consequences of committing two or three millions of persons, born and bred in a state so completely dependent as that of slavery—so unfurnished, so unintellectual, so utterly helpless, I may say—to all the responsibilities, cares and labors of a state of freedom? Must he not acknowledge, that the utmost we could give them would be but a nominal freedom, in doing which we should be guilty of a cruel desertion of our trust—inevitably leading them to progressive debasement, penury, oppression, and finally to extermination? I would not argue with that man whose bigotry to a sentiment was so blind and so fatal as to insist on this expedient. When the time comes, as I apprehend it will come,—and all the sooner, if it be not delayed by these efforts to arouse something like a vindictive feeling between the disputants on both sides—in which the roots of slavery will begin to lose their hold in our soil; and when we shall have the means for providing these people a proper asylum, I shall be glad to see the State devote her thoughts to that enterprise, and, if I am alive, will cheerfully and gratefully assist in it. In the meantime, we owe it to justice and humanity to treat these people with the most considerate kindness. As to what are ordinarily imagined to be the evils or sufferings of their condition, I do not believe in them. The evil is generally felt on the side of the master. Less work is exacted of them than voluntary laborers choose to perform: they have as many privileges as are compatible with the nature of their occupations: they are subsisted, in general, as comfortably—nay, in their estimation of comforts, more comfortably, than the rural population of other countries. And as to the severities that are alleged to be practised upon them, there is much more malice or invention than truth in the accusation. The slaveholders in this region are, in the main, men of kind and humane tempers—as pliant to the touch of compassion, and as sensible of its duties, as the best men in any community, and as little disposed to inflict injury upon their dependents. Indeed, the owner of slaves is less apt to be harsh in his requisitions of labor than those who toil much themselves. I suspect it is invariably characteristic of those who are in the habit of severely tasking themselves, that they are inclined to regulate their demands upon others by their own standard. Our slaves are punished for misdemeanors, pretty much as disorderly persons are punished in all societies; and I am quite of opinion that our statistics of crime and punishment will compare favorably with those of any other population. But the punishment, on our side, is remarked as the personal act of the master; whilst, elsewhere, it goes free of ill-natured comment, because it is set down to the course of justice. We, therefore, suffer a reproach which other polities escape, and the conclusion is made an item of complaint against slavery.

"It has not escaped the attention of our legislation to provide against the ill-treatment of our negro population. I heartily concur in all effective laws to punish cruelty in masters. Public opinion on that subject, however, is even stronger than law, and no man can hold up his head in this community who is chargeable with maltreatment of his slaves.

"One thing I desire you specially to note: the question of emancipation is exclusively our own, and every intermeddling with it from abroad will but mar its chance of success. We cannot but regard such interference as an unwarrantable and mischievous design to do us injury, and, therefore, we resent it—sometimes, I am sorry to say, even to the point of involving the innocent negro in the rigor which it provokes. We think, and, indeed, we know, that we alone are able to deal properly with the subject; all others are misled by the feeling which the natural sentiment against slavery, in the abstract, excites. They act under imperfect knowledge and impulsive prejudices which are totally incompatible with wise action on any subject. We, on the contrary, have every motive to calm and prudent counsel. Our lives, fortunes, families—our commonwealth itself, are put at the hazard of this resolve. You gentlemen of the North greatly misapprehend us, if you suppose that we are in love with this slave institution—or that, for the most part, we even deem it profitable to us. . . .

LYDIA MARIA FRANCIS CHILD

(1802–80)

One of the most prolific and unconventional authors in nineteenth-century New England, Lydia Maria Child made her literary debut in 1824, with the first American fiction on racial intermarriage: *Hobomok*, a romance uniting a Puritan heroine and a noble Indian. Child's daring defense of Indians, repeated four years later in her nonfictional *The First Settlers of New England*, was equaled by *An Appeal in Favor of That Class of Americans Called Africans* (1833). However, the latter resulted in canceled subscriptions to her *Juvenile Miscellany*, forcing an end to her editorship of a periodical she founded for children in 1826.

A moralist, abolitionist, social reformer, and household name on domestic advice, her early literary career was a balancing act to sensitize nonfeminist readers and to caution moderation to radical abolitionists. Her husband, David Child, an impecunious lawyer-businessman, allied himself with William Lloyd Garrison in early 1833, and she followed, becoming active in the Boston Female Anti-Slavery Society, the New England Anti-Slavery Society, and its successor, the Massachusetts Antislavery Society. In late 1834, she collected works by her husband and some of their abolitionist friends together with her own pieces in a volume entitled *The Oasis*, for which her preface stated their main objective: "to familiarize the public with the idea that colored people are *human beings*— . . . ."

From 1841–43, she edited *The National Antislavery Standard*, weekly organ of the American Antislavery Society, and contributed prose sketches to the *Liberty Bell*, but broke with the formal abolitionist movement by January 1844. However, her commitment to racial justice never waned in the stories and books she produced over a thirty-year period, including *Antislavery Catechism* (1836), *The Evils of Slavery, and the Cure of Slavery* (1836), "The Kansas Immigrants" (1856); *Fact and Fiction: A Collection of Stories* (1857), *The Duty of Disobedience to the Fugitive Slave Act* (1860), *The Right Way, The Safe Way, Proved by Emancipation in The British West Indies and Elsewhere* (1860), *The Freedmen's Book* (1865), *A Romance of the Republic* (1867), and the editing and preface of *Incidents in the Life of a Slave Girl*, by Harriet Jacobs (1861).

Born into a Calvinist household in Medford, Massachusetts, the daughter of a well-to-do baker, she rejected orthodox Calvinism but revered the Bible. A contemporary of the transcendalists, but never their disciple, she was a complex and staunch individualist, who challenged the traditions of her nation, class, and gender at a time when female roles were circumscribed. For four decades her political and literary quest resulted in stories, articles, pamphlets, and novels on humanitarian subjects. She is conspicuously absent in a traditionally male-oriented American literary canon.

The following excerpt of her influential antislavery document, *An Appeal in Favor of That Class of Americans Called Africans*, is from Chapter One, "Brief History of Negro Slavery—Its Inevitable Effect upon All Concerned in It."

From *An Appeal in Favor of That Class of Americans Called Africans* (1833)

. . . We say the negroes are so ignorant that they must be slaves; and we insist upon keeping them ignorant, lest we spoil them for slaves. The same spirit that dictates this logic to the Arab, teaches it to the European and the American:—Call it what you please—it is certainly neither of heaven nor of earth.

When the slave ships are lying on the coast of Africa, canoes well armed are sent into the inland country, and after a few weeks they return with hundreds of negroes, tied fast with ropes. Sometimes the white men lurk among the bushes, and seize the wretched beings who incautiously venture from their homes; sometimes they paint their skins as black as their hearts, and by this deception suddenly surprise the unsuspecting natives; at other times the victims are decoyed on board the vessel, under some kind pretense or other, and then lashed to the mast, or chained in the hold. Is it not very natural for the Africans to say "devilish white?"

All along the shores of this devoted country, terror and distrust prevail. The natives never venture out without arms, when a vessel is in sight, and skulk through their own fields, as if watched by a panther. All their worst passions are called into full exercise, and all their kindlier feelings smothered. Treachery, fraud and violence desolate the country, rend asunder the dearest relations, and pollute the very fountains of justice. The history of the negro, whether national or domestic, is written in blood. Had half the skill and strength employed in the slave trade been engaged in honorable commerce, the native princes would long ago have directed their energies towards clearing the country, destroying wild beasts, and introducing the arts and refinements of civilized life. Under such influences, Africa might become an earthly paradise;—the white man's avarice has made it a den of wolves.

Having thus glanced at the miserable effects of this system on the condition of Africa, we will now follow the poor *slave* through his wretched wanderings, in order to give some idea of his physical suffering, his mental and moral degradation.

Husbands are torn from their wives, children from their parents, while the air is filled with the shrieks and lamentations of the bereaved. Sometimes they are brought from a remote country; obliged to wander over mountains and through deserts; chained together in herds; driven by the whip; scorched by a tropical sun; compelled to carry heavy bales of merchandise; suffering with hunger and thirst; worn down with fatigue; and often leaving their bones to whiten in the desert. A large troop of slaves, taken by the Sultan of Fezzan, died in the desert for want of food. In some places, travelers meet with fifty or sixty skeletons in a day, of which the largest proportion were no doubt slaves, on their way to European markets. Sometimes the poor creatures refuse to go a step further, and even the lacerating whip cannot goad them on; in such cases, they become the prey of wild beasts, more merciful than white men.

Those who arrive at the seacoast, are in a state of desperation and despair. Their purchasers are so well aware of this, and so fearful of the consequences, that they set sail in the night, lest the negroes should know when they depart from their native shores.

And here the scene becomes almost too harrowing to dwell upon. But we must not allow our nerves to be more tender than our consciences. The poor wretches are stowed by hundreds, like bales of goods, between the low decks, where filth and putrid air produce disease, madness and suicide. Unless they die in *great* numbers, the slave captain does not even concern himself enough to fret; his livestock cost nothing, and he is sure of such a high price for what remains at the end of the voyage, that he can afford to lose a good many.

JOHN GREENLEAF WHITTIER

(1807–92)

In the annals of antebellum American prose and poetry, few writers opposed slavery so consistently or celebrated emancipation so zealously as John Green-leaf Whittier. He enlisted in the abolitionist battle for three decades with his poems, editorials, letters, and essays but refused ever to compromise his Quaker principles of nonviolent resistance.

Born and educated in the seacoast town of Haverhill, Massachusetts, his name in American textbooks is linked often to an idyllic vision of a New England past sheltered in youthful innocence, rural simplicity, and moral rectitude. From his first published book of prose and poetry, *Legends of New England* (1831), until his death over sixty years later in 1892, he celebrated regional folklore in his varied volumes of verse. However, the frequency and sound of his call to action on slavery distinguished him as the preeminent abolitionist poet of his generation, exceeding his two worthy literary contemporaries, Ralph Waldo Emerson and William Cullen Bryant, on the subject.

In 1833, two essays signalized his antislavery position: "The Abolitionists: Their Sentiments and Objects," and "Justice and Expediency." The latter, first published that September in the *Anti-Slavery Reporter,* was reprinted as a pamphlet that he financed from his meager income. That December in Philadelphia he was delegate to a three-day organizing convention of the American Antislavery Society, about which he said, "I set a higher value on my name as appended to the Anti-Slavery Declaration of 1833 than on the title page of any book. Forty years later, in *The Atlantic Monthly,* he wrote a brief reminiscence of the convention's black abolitionist participants. Unmentioned were three women whose gender denied them admission to the Society but whose presence earned them an enduring tribute in a Whittier poem entitled "To the Daughters of James Forten."[1]

---

[1] The three Forten sisters of Philadelphia were Harriet, Sarah, and Margaretta, the well-educated daughters of a wealthy Afro-American freeman and sailmaker, James Forten, one of the most active abolitionists until his death in 1842. Whittier's poem was written December 7, 1833—a week before formation of the integrated Philadelphia Female Antislavery Society of which the three Forten sisters were charter members, with Margaretta elected the recording secretary. Harriet was the wife of another black abolitionist, Robert Purvis, and the aunt of writer Charlotte Forten—both of whom are represented in this volume.

In 1836 he became secretary of the Antislavery Society, and in 1838–39 edited *The Philadelphia Freeman*—until a mob burned the printing office. In the following decade, he was a frequent contributor to other abolitionist periodicals and a part-time editor of the *National Era* in Washington, DC. He was a close friend of Lydia Maria Child, and until the mid-1840s also close to Garrison, who two decades before as an apprentice editor had published Whittier's first poems in 1826 in the Newburyport *Free Press*. But as abolitionists, the two men disagreed when the pacifist Whittier publicly urged moderation in Garrison's quarrel with less radical elements in the movement, finally causing a once warm friendship to turn as frigid as a New England winter.

Whittier's abolitionist prose corresponded with his many crusading poems, notably "Massachusetts to Virginia" (1843), defending Boston's protection of a runaway slave named George Latimer, whose Norfolk owner attempted to reenslave; "A Sabbath Scare" (1850), attacking Northern clergy who claimed adherence to the Fugitive Slave Law a Christian duty; "The Proclamation" (1863), urging freedmen to forgive their oppressors, and "Laus Deo" (1865), praising ratification of the Thirteenth Amendment to the Constitution abolishing slavery. To the end of his long life, Whittier believed that America's past might be used to improve the future.

The following excerpt is from his well-argued essay, "Justice and Expediency; or, Slavery Considered with a View to Its Rightful and Effectual Remedy, ABOLITION."

From *Justice and Expediency; or, Slavery Considered with a View to Its Rightful and Effectual Remedy, ABOLITION*[2] (1833)

. . . What is this System which we are thus protecting and upholding?

A system which holds two millions of God's creatures in bondage—which leaves one million females without any protection save their own feeble strength, and which makes even the exercise of that strength in resistance to outrage, punishable with death!—which considers rational, immortal beings as articles of traffic—vendible commodities—merchantable property,—which

---

[2] From *Anti-Slavery Reporter*, vol. 1., no. 4, September 1833.

recognizes no social obligations—no natural relations—which tears without scruple the infant from the mother—the wife from the husband—the parent from the child. In the strong but just language of another—"It is the full measure of pure, unmixed, unsophisticated wickedness; and scorning all competition or comparison, it stands without a rival in the secure, undisputed possession of its detestable preeminence."

. . . .

I am not unaware that my remarks may be regarded by many as dangerous and exceptionable; that I may be regarded as a fanatic for quoting the language of eternal truth, and denounced as an incendiary for maintaining, in the spirit as well as the letter, the doctrines of American Independence. But if such are the consequences of a simple performance of duty, I shall not regard them. If my feeble appeal but reaches the hearts of any who are now slumbering in iniquity—if it shall have power given it to shake down one stone from the foul temple where the blood of human victims is offered to the Moloch of Slavery—if under Providence, it can break one fetter from off the image of God, and enable one suffering American

> ———To feel
> The weight of human misery less, and glide
> Ungroaning to the tomb,

I shall not have written in vain: my conscience will be satisfied.

Far be it from me to cast new bitterness into the gall and wormwood waters of sectional prejudice. No—I desire peace—the peace of universal love—of catholic sympathy—the peace of a common interest—a common feeling—a common humanity. But so long as Slavery is tolerated, no such peace can exist. Liberty and slavery cannot dwell in harmony together.

. . . .

The Slaveholding states are not free. The name of Liberty is there, but the *spirit* is wanting. They do not partake of its invaluable blessings. Wherever Slavery exists to any considerable extent, with the exception of some recently settled portions of the country, and which have not yet felt in a great degree the baneful and deteriorating influences of slave labor—we hear at this moment the cry of suffering. We are told of grass-grown streets—of crumbling mansions—of beggared planters and barren plantations—of fear from without—of terror within. The once-fertile fields are wasted and tenantless, for the curse of Slavery—the improvidence of that labor whose hire has been kept back by fraud—has been there, poisoning the very earth beyond the reviving influence of the early and the later rain. A moral mildew mingles as if the finger of the everlasting God had written upon the soil of the slaveholder the language of His displeasure.

Let the Slave-holding states consult their present interest by beginning without delay the work of emancipation. If they fear not, and mock at the fiery indignation of Him, to whom vengeance belongeth, let temporal interest persuade them. They know, they must know, that the present state of things cannot long continue. Mind is the same everywhere, no matter what may be the complexion of the frame which it animates: there is a love of liberty which scourge cannot eradicate—a hatred of oppression which centuries of degradation cannot extinguish. The slave will become conscious sooner or later of his strength—his physical superiority, and will exert it. His torch will be at the threshold and his knife at the throat of the planter. Horrible and indiscriminate will be this vengeance. Where then will be the pride—the beauty and the chivalry of the South? The smoke of her torment will rise upward like a thick cloud visible over the whole earth.

. . . .

Free labor is perfectly in accordance with the spirit of our institutions; slave labour is a relic of a barbarous, despotic age. . . .

Emancipation would reform this evil. The planter would no longer be under the necessity of a heavy expenditure for slaves. He would only pay a very moderate price for his labor; a price indeed far less than the cost of the maintenance of a promiscuous gang of slaves, which the present system requires.

In an old plantation of three hundred slaves, not more than one hundred effective laborers will be found. Children—the old and superannuated—the sick and decrepit—the idle and incorrigibly vicious—will be found to constitute two-thirds of the whole number. The remaining third perform only about one-third as much work, as the same number of free laborers.

Now disburden the master of this heavy load of maintenance; let him employ *free*, able, industrious laborers only, those who feel conscious of a personal interest in the fruits of their labor, and who does not see that such a system would be vastly more safe and economical than the present?

The slave states are learning this truth by fatal experience. Most of them are silently writhing under the great curse. Virginia has uttered her complaints aloud. As yet, however, nothing has been done even there, save a small annual appropriation for the purpose of colonizing the *free colored inhabitants of the State*. Is this a remedy?

. . . .

Dissemble as we may, it is impossible for us to believe, after fully considering the nature of slavery, that it can much longer maintain a peaceable existence among us. A day of revolution must come; and it is our duty to prepare for it.

Its threatened evil may be changed into a national blessing. The establishment of schools for the instruction of slave children; a general diffusion of the lights of Christianity; and the introduction of a sacred respect for social obligations of marriage, and for the relations between parents and children, among our black population, would render emancipation not only perfectly safe, but also the highest advantage to the country. Two million of freemen would be added to our population, upon whom in the hour of danger we could safely depend; "the domestic foe" would be changed into a firm friend, faithful, generous, and ready to encounter all dangers in our defense. It is well-known that during the last war with Great Britain, whenever the enemy touched upon our southern coast, the *slaves*, in multitudes hastened to join them. On the other hand, the *free blacks* were highly serviceable in repelling them. So warm was the zeal of the latter, so manifest their courage in defense of Louisiana, that the present Chief Magistrate of the United States publicly bestowed upon them one of the highest eulogiums ever offered by a commander to his soldiers.

Let no one seek an apology for silence on the subject of Slavery because the laws of the land tolerate and sanction it. But a short time ago the *Slave-Trade* was protected by laws and treaties, and sanctioned by the example of men eminent for the reputation of piety and integrity. Yet public opinion broke over those barriers; it lifted the curtain and revealed the horrors of that most abominable traffic; and unrighteous law, ancient custom, and avarice, and luxury, gave way before its irresistible authority. It should never be forgotten that human law cannot change the nature of human action in the pure eye of Infinite Justice; and that the ordinance of man cannot annul those of God. . . .

ALEXIS DE TOCQUEVILLE

(1805–59)

French political philosopher Alexis-Henri-Charles-Maurice Clerel de Tocqueville was not yet twenty-six when he landed in New York in May 1831 to study American prisons. A former magistrate at the court of Versailles, he was a member of the nobility, demoted with the fall of the Bourbon dynasty in the July 1830 revolution. Accompanying him to America was another French magistrate three years his senior, Gustave de Beaumont, an idealistic intellectual whose liberal political ideas influenced Tocqueville then and later. Their report on American prisons, with ideas for reform, was published in Paris and Philadelphia in 1833—*Du Système pénitentiare aux Etats-Unis et son application en France (The Penitentiary System in the United States and Its Application in France).*

Their interest in other aspects of the New World took the two men over seven thousand miles by stagecoach, steamer, and horseback, from New England to New Orleans, and east of the Mississippi, and into Quebec, before they embarked for Paris in February 1832. Their nine-month journey led to the 1835 publication of Tocqueville's acclaimed book, *De la Démocratie en Amérique (Democracy in America)*, and Beaumont's 1835 two-volume novel on American race relations, *Marie, ou l'esclavage aux Etats-Unis: Tableau des moeurs américaines.* Beaumont's text, one of the first on the "tragic mulatto" theme, contained a deliberate mélange of fiction and fact, and an appendix essay on "The Social and Political Condition of Negro Slaves and Freedmen." Untranslated into English for over a century,[1] it was destined to oblivion outside France, despite its revelations on racial attitudes of the 1830s.

The two friends had mutually agreed that Tocqueville would focus on American political institutions and Beaumont on the status of people of color in Anglo-American society. Thus Tocqueville's book notes—in various editions—include comments such as the following: "The chief aim of M. Gustave de Beaumont, my traveling-companion, was to inform Frenchmen of the position

---

[1] *Marie; or, Slavery in the United States: A Novel of Jacksonian America.* Translated from the French by Barbara Chapman (Stanford University Press, 1958).

of the Negroes among the white population in the United States. M. de Beaumont has plumbed the depths of a question that my subject has allowed me merely to touch upon." Consequently, in Tocqueville's cumulative two-volume appraisal of American laws and customs, the slavery issue is mentioned cursorily in Volume II, and discussed only in the last chapter of Volume I—in the context of the "Situation of the Black Population in the United States and Dangers with Which Its Presence Threatens Whites." He observed Africans enslaved in the South, and free persons of color despised in the North, and was aware of the American Colonization Society, but not the rising tide of the abolitionist movement. His perceptive observations are occasionally flawed by deductive reasoning based on assumptions and prophecies rather than facts. Nevertheless, his lucid text remains unparalleled in its penetrating look at American institutions in transition. The excerpt here from Volume I, Chapter XVIII, "The Present and Probable Future Condition of the Three Races That Inhabit the United States" is the 1862 translation by Francis Bowen, who retranslated Henry Reeve's 1835 English version of the French text.

From *Democracy in America* (1835)

. . . The human beings who are scattered over this space do not form, as in Europe, so many branches of the same stock. Three races, naturally distinct, and, I might almost say, hostile to each other, are discoverable among them at the first glance. Almost insurmountable barriers had been raised between them by education and law, as well as by their origin and outward characteristics; but fortune has brought them together on the same soil, where, although they are mixed, they do not amalgamate, and each race fulfills its destiny apart.

Among these widely differing families of men, the first that attracts attention, the superior in intelligence, in power, and in enjoyment, is the white, or European, the MAN preeminently so called; below him appear the Negro and the Indian. These two unhappy races have nothing in common, neither birth, nor features, nor language, nor habits. Their only resemblance lies in their misfortunes. Both of them occupy an equally inferior position in the country they inhabit; both suffer from tyranny; and if their wrongs are not the same, they originate from the same authors.

If we reason from what passes in the world, we should almost say that the European is to the other races of mankind what man himself is to the lower animals: he makes them subservient to his use, and when he cannot subdue he destroys them. Oppression has, at one stroke, deprived the descendants of the Africans of almost all the privileges of humanity. The Negro of the United States has lost even the remembrance of his country; the language which his forefathers spoke is never heard around him; he abjured their religion and forgot their customs when he ceased to belong to Africa, without acquiring any claim to European privileges. But he remains halfway between the two communities, isolated between two races; sold by the one, repulsed by the other; finding not a spot in the universe to call by the name of country, except the faint image of a home which the shelter of his master's roof affords.

The Negro has no family: woman is merely the temporary companion of his pleasures, and his children are on an equality with himself from the moment of their birth. Am I to call it a proof of God's mercy, or a visitation of his wrath, that man, in certain states, appears to be insensible to his extreme wretchedness and almost obtains a depraved taste for the cause of his misfortunes? The Negro, plunged in this abyss of evils, scarcely feels his own calamitous situation. Violence made him a slave, and the habit of servitude gives him the thoughts and desires of a slave; he admires his tyrants more than he hates them, and finds his joy and his pride in the servile imitation of those who oppress him. His understanding is degraded to the level of his soul.

The Negro enters upon slavery as soon as he is born; nay, he may have been purchased in the womb, and have begun his slavery before he began his existence. Equally devoid of wants and of enjoyment, and useless to himself, he learns, with his first notions of existence, that he is the property of another, who has an interest in preserving his life, and that the care of it does not devolve upon himself; even the power of thought appears to him a useless gift of Providence, and he quietly enjoys all the privileges of his debasement.

If he becomes free, independence is often felt by him to be a heavier burden than slavery; for, having learned in the course of his life to submit to everything except reason, he is too unacquainted with her dictates to obey them. A thousand new desires beset him, and he has not the knowledge and energy necessary to resist them: these are masters which it is necessary to contend with, and he has learned only to submit and obey. In short, he is sunk to such a depth of wretchedness that while servitude brutalizes, liberty destroys him. . . .

JAMES KIRKE PAULDING

(1778–1860)

Novelist, essayist, short story writer, playwright, and poet, Paulding was born in Dutchess County, New York, during the American Revolution. He usually is identified with the New York "Knickerbockers"—a group of writers who adopted their name from Washington Irving's *Knickerbocker History of New York*, and flourished from 1810 to 1840. A strong defender of a "national literature," but not of egalitarianism, Paulding's literary nationalism often waved the flag of propaganda. As a pro-slavery writer, some of his opinions resembled those of his younger contemporary, John Pendleton Kennedy, though the latter took a different last stand for the Union. Paulding's position on the side of slave owners grew more strident with the years, a Yankee who proudly supported Southern secession.

In 1817, he published a two-volume work entitled *Letters from the South, Written During an Excursion in the Summer of 1816*. Ostensibly penned to a Philadelphia college classmate by a Northerner traveling in Virginia, the fictional letters were personal essays that served the author's ideology. Letter XI, in particular, expressed his perspective toward the inequality of the races, with white agrarians depicted as virtuous and hardworking, and blacks as a "gay, harmless, and unthinking race," who are "well-treated by their masters."

Such viewpoints foreshadowed sentiments in Paulding's novel, *The Dutchman's Fireside*, with its claim that slaves "were all treated kindly, and as part of the family."

In a second edition of epistolary pieces, *Letters of a Northern Man* (1835), he deleted any hint that his earlier *Letters*—eighteen years before—had included the words, "Don't mistake and suppose that I am an advocate of slavery." His pro-slavery advocacy was unmistakable in writings he directed against abolitionists and slaves in the mid-1830s. Having also depicted Indians as savages and treacherous foes to heroic white backwoodsmen and noble pioneers—in novels such as *Koningsmarke* (1823), *The Dutchman's Fireside* (1831), and *Westward Ho!* (1836)—Paulding dipped his pen in vitriol against blacks, both slave and free, in a nonfiction volume of essays, *Slavery in the United States* (1836). The book, in an introduction and ten chapters, waged a campaign to vindicate the institution of slavery, with biblical quotes, threats of the consequences of emancipation, and arguments that "physiologists have classed the negro as the lowest in the scale of rational beings." Echoing the dogma of his time, he declared that "the government of the United States belongs . . . wholly and exclusively to the white man."

Paulding held federal government positions for four decades and was appointed Secretary of the Navy by President Martin Van Buren two years after publication of *Slavery in the United States*. At his death in 1860, he proudly repudiated the antislavery remarks of his earlier writings.

The following excerpt of *Slavery in the United States* is from Chapter IV, "Of Amalgamation and Community of Social Change and Political Rights"— revealing his antagonism toward abolitionism and an obsession with racial interbreeding.

From *Slavery in the United States* (1836)

The advocates of immediate emancipation, aware of the consequences sketched in the preceding chapter, have sought to obviate them by recommending amalgamation; that is, indiscriminate marriages, between the whites and blacks, accompanied of course by a communion of social and civil rights, as a remedy for all the evils which must necessarily result from the adoption of their first principle. The remedy is rather worse than the disease.

The project of intermarrying with the blacks, is a project for debasing the whites by a mixture of that blood, which, wherever it flows, carries with it the seeds of deterioration. It is a scheme for lowering the standard of our nature, by approximating the highest grade of human beings to the lowest, and is equivalent to enhancing the happiness of mankind by a process of debasement.

That the negro should relish the idea of thus improving his breed at the expense of the white race is quite natural; that there should be found among the latter, men who recommend and enforce such a plan, even from the pulpit, appears somewhat remarkable, as an example of extraordinary disinterestedness. But that there should be white women, well-educated and respectable females, supporting it by their money and their influence, their presence and cooperation; apparently willing, nay, anxious to barter their superiority for the badges of degradation; to become the mothers of mulattoes; voluntarily to entail upon their posterity a curse that seems coeval with the first existence of the negro, and cast away a portion of the divinity within them at the shrine of a mere abstract dogma, is one of the wonders which fanaticism alone can achieve.

That there are such men, and—shame on the sex—such women, is but too evident. But they are exceptions to the rest of their class, to the race to which they belong. They are traitors to the white skin, influenced by mad-brained fanaticism, or the victims of licentious and ungovernable passions, perverted into an unnatural taste by their own indulgence. The proposition has been everywhere received with indignant scorn.

Throughout the whole United States, with the single exception of little knots of raving fanatics in a few towns and villages, one chorus of disgust and abhorrence has met the odious project. In a country hitherto the most exemplary of any in the world for obedience to the laws, assemblages, not of idle and ignorant profligates, but of respectable citizens, have, in the absence of all statutes for repressing such outrageous attacks on the feelings of society and the established decorum of life, taken the law into their own hands, and dispersed or punished these aggressions. Nay, even the peaceable and orderly people of New England, celebrated for their cool self-possession, their habitual devotion to the peace and harmony of society, have everywhere risen against the monstrous indignity, and infringed upon the laws of the land, in vindication of the purity of their blood. The universal sentiment of our race stands arrayed against the disgraceful alliance; and whether it be natural instinct, inspired reason, or long-established prejudice, there exist no indications among us, to induce a belief that it will ever be eradicated from the hearts of the white people of the United States.

But, admitting it could, it is denied that such a consummation would be desirable, not only for the reasons just presented, but on the ground of other deep considerations. Such a mixture would at once destroy the homogeneous character of the people of the United States, on which is founded our union, and from which results nearly all those ties which constitute the cement of social life. A mongrel race would arise, of all shades and colours, each claiming under the new order of things equal social and civil rights, yet all enjoying real substantial consideration in proportion to the whiteness of their skin, and the absence of those indelible characteristics which mark the African race.

It could never become the climax of dignity to wear the black skin. The law of the land might declare it equal to the white, and confer on it equal social and political rights; but the law of nature, or what is equivalent to it in this inquiry, the long habits, and feelings, and thinking, and acting, which have descended from generation to generation, and become a part of our being, would declare against it with a force that nothing could resist. Instead of two factions, we should have a dozen, arrayed against each other on every occasion, animated, not like the parties subsisting among us at present, by certain known principles of action, which may be said to ennoble [sic] such contests, but by petty malignant jealousies, arising from different shades of colour, different conformations of the nose or the shin, each carrying with it a claim to more or less consideration. Does not every truehearted American shrink and scoff, at sharing, or rather surrendering his rights to factions animated by such considerations, instead of his own lofty preferences or dislikes, founded on the love of liberty and the fear of despotism? Let it also be borne in mind that all these varieties of shades and colours would, by a natural instinct, unite against the whites as the highest grade, and thus, by outvoting, strip them of their dominion, and place them at the foot of the ladder of degradation.

The idea of educating the children of the free white citizens of the United States to consider the blacks their equals, is founded on a total ignorance of nature, its affinities and antipathies. These antipathies may be for a moment overcome or forgotten in the madness of sensuality, but they return again with the greater force from their temporary suspension. White and black children never associate together on terms of perfect equality, from the moment the former begin to reason. There exist physical incongruities which cannot be permanently reconciled; and let us add, that we have a right to conclude, from all history and experience, that there is an equal disparity of mental organization. The difference seems more than skin-deep. The experience of thousands of years stands arrayed against the principle of equality between the white men and the blacks. . . .

ANGELINA GRIMKÉ

(1805–79)

Born into South Carolina's antebellum aristocracy, Angelina Emily Grimké broke with it to become an abolitionist. In February 1838 her petitions to a Committee of the Massachusetts legislature distinguished her as the first American-born woman to speak before a legislative body. She and her older sister, Sarah, known as the Grimké Sisters, were the first white Southern female antislavery agents.

Nearly thirteen years younger than Sarah, equally devout, less utopian, but more intrepid, Angelina was the thirteenth and last child of John and Mary Grimké—and the most radical. She questioned the traditions of Southern patriarchy that limited the roles of women; she resented the inhumane treatment of slaves, including those on the Grimké plantation, where some mulattos were the progeny of her father, John Faucheraud Grimké, a wealthy Charleston planter, lawyer, and judge, who died in 1819. A slaveholding society hostile to her ideas of Christian justice led her to join Sarah as a Quaker in Philadelphia in 1829, where she became a voice of the South in the emerging antislavery movement.

Sensitive to issues of both race and gender, she linked women's issues to abolition at a time when some Northern male abolitionists and feminists resented such advocacy. Convinced that part of her mission was to convert women of her class and region, she wrote in 1836 her evangelical *Appeal to the Christian Women of the Southern States*, urging them to petition their legislatures. A landmark pamphlet in antebellum literature, its impact was wider than Sarah's *An Epistle to the Clergy of the South*, also published in 1836. Angelina's first *Appeal* was followed in 1837 by *An Appeal to the Women of the Nominally Free States*, in which she beseeched them to identify with female slaves as sisters. In 1838 she published her *Letters to Catherine E. Beecher*, whose *Essay on Slavery and Abolitionism with Reference to the Duty of American Females* (1837) had attacked Angelina's views.

In 1835 her name had been launched in the *Liberator* when Garrison printed—without her foreknowledge—a supportive epistle Angelina wrote after his encounter with a Boston mob: "Slavery and the Boston Riot, a Letter to

William Lloyd Garrison." It attracted abolitionist and reformer Theodore Weld, who encouraged her to lecture for the American Antislavery Society in 1837; he married her a year later. Their wedding in Philadelphia, May 14, 1838, was attended by interracial guests, including Garrison, who had introduced the couple.

A new phase in her life began with domestic duties and periods of ill health during and after three pregnancies, but with Sarah's help she combined marriage and motherhood with teaching to help support the family. Her major writings had peaked by 1838, but during the Civil War she published one of her most passionate works, A *Declaration of War on Slavery*, (now lost), and "An Address to the Soldiers of our Second Revolution"—asking black and white Union soldiers to fight as brothers without prejudice. An exile from the Confederacy, she never witnessed the siege of Charleston, which brought financial ruin to the Grimké family and their Southern citadel. Until a stroke paralyzed her for six years before she died in 1879, she was active in her community near Boston, working toward equal rights for blacks and women.

The following, from her *Appeal to the Christian Women of the Southern States*, is representative of her forthright style.

From *Appeal to the Christian Women of the Southern States* (1836)

. . . But perhaps you will be ready to query, why appeal to *women* on this subject? *We* do not make the laws which perpetuate slavery. No legislative power is vested in *us*; *we* can do nothing to overthrow the system, even if we wished to do so. To this I reply, I know you do not make the laws, but I also know that *you are the wives and mothers, the sisters and daughters of those who do*; and if you really suppose *you* can do nothing to overthrow slavery, you are greatly mistaken. You can do much in every way: four things I will name. 1st. You can read on this subject. 2d. You can pray over this subject. 3d. You can speak on this subject. 4th. You can *act* on this subject. I have not placed reading before praying because I regard it more important, but because, in order to pray aright, we must understand what we are praying for; it is only then we can "pray with the understanding and the spirit also."

. . . .

The *women of the South can overthrow* this horrible system of oppression and cruelty, licentiousness and wrong. Such appeals to your legislatures would be irresistible, for there is something in the heart of man which *will bend under moral suasion*. There is a swift witness for truth in his bosom, which *will respond to truth* when it is uttered with calmness and dignity. If you could obtain but six signatures to such a petition in only one state, I would say, send up that petition, and be not in the least discouraged by the scoffs and jeers of the heartless, or the resolution of the house to lay it on the table. It will be a great thing if the subject can be introduced into your legislatures in any way, even by *women*, and *they* will be the most likely to introduce it there in the best possible manner, as a matter of *morals* and *religion*, not of expediency or politics. You may petition, too, the different ecclesiastical bodies of the slave states. Slavery must be attacked with the whole power of truth and the sword of the spirit. You must take it up on *Christian* ground, and fight against it with Christian weapons, whilst your feet are shod with the preparation of the gospel of peace. And *you are now* loudly called upon by the cries of the widow and the orphan, to arise and gird yourselves for this great moral conflict, with the whole armour of righteousness upon the right hand and on the left. . . .

THEODORE DWIGHT WELD

(1803–95)

Connecticut-born Theodore Weld was one of the great humanitarian reformers of the nineteenth century and a leading Christian soldier in the abolitionist movement. Before meeting Angelina Grimké in 1837 he had vowed to remain a bachelor until Emancipation. During their courtship, she wrote him: "We are the two halves of one whole, a twain one, two bodies animated by one soul . . . the Lord has given us to each other." Both divinely inspired, they devoted much of their married life of four decades urging the political freedom and social recognition of blacks as equals.[1] But by the Civil War, factions and changing realignments among abolitionists had exerted too great a toll on the health and finances of Theodore Weld for him to see Emancipation as a new stage of social struggle to engage him. The end of the war was the end of his radical activism, due to advancing age and the decision to return to teaching in a small community outside Boston.

In influence he had few equals among abolitionists—as editor, organizer, advisor, strategist, agent, and spell-binding orator. His powerful voice suffered the strain of years on the lecture circuit but galvanized a generation. Preferring obscurity to acclaim, he refused to include his name on his books and pamphlets, leaving posterity to search for the formidable legacy he left in the articles he published anonymously in newspapers and journals, and in the various annual *Antislavery-Slavery Almanacs* he edited. His unsigned *Bible Argument*

---

[1] The effort of Angelina Grimké and Theodore Weld to extend abolitionism to social equality was directed more personally to three ex-slave nephews Angelina discovered after the Civil War ended: Archibald Henry Grimké (b. 1849), Francis James Grimké (b. 1850), and John Grimké (b. 1853), sons of her brother Henry, a South Carolina lawyer, and his slave mistress, Nancy Weston. On Henry's death in 1852, he had bequeathed the three young boys to his eldest son, Montague, their white half brother, who kept them in servitude until they escaped after Lincoln's edict. The Welds and Sarah Grimké helped the youths complete their college education. Archibald and Francis graduated from Lincoln University in Pennsylvania in 1870; the latter went on to Princeton Theological Seminary, while the former earned a MA at Lincoln and became the second man of his race to earn a LLB from Harvard. Archibald achieved distinction as a lawyer and author, and Francis as a respected Presbyterian clergyman. Archibald named his only offspring Angelina Weld Grimké, in memory of the aunt who died four months before his daughter's February 1880 birth. Theodore Weld, in his will in 1889, bequeathed $850 to "my nephew, Archibald Grimké," for the daughter's education. She became a respected teacher, poet, and playwright.

against Slavery inspired hundreds of antislavery agents and won converts. As an antislavery agent himself, Weld was the messenger on horseback between villages and towns, lodging in the homes of free blacks and worshiping in their churches. He later directed the New York office of the New York Antislavery Society and lobbied against slavery to Congress in Washington, but he found American cities enemies of abolitionism, and he refused to accept roles of national authority or to address conventions.

His name as abolitionist advocate first became widely known after he encountered white hostility in Cincinnati in 1834, while a theology student at Lane Seminary, with his uncompromising arguments against the American Colonization Society in "Lane Debates" on slavery, and his defense of student projects to educate local free blacks. He and other Lane rebels soon left, turning their convictions into a crusade. For his power of moral suasion to others in the movement, Garrison called him "the luminary around which they all revolved," though the two men differed in their own tactics.

Like Garrison, Weld was a frequent target of proslavery mobs; he learned to resist by facing them with folded arms and a stern expression, as if he wore the whole armor of God. In spirit and mind, he was a millennialist, who believed in the second coming of Christ on earth, and a code of human conduct measured by humble and charitable deeds. Full of soul-searching and self-scrutiny, a determined reformer who had lectured on temperance and manual labor and worked his way through Phillips Academy, Hamilton College, Oneida Institute, and Lane Seminary, he was the son and grandson of New England clergymen. He had intended to be a minister himself before choosing antislavery work. At age twenty-eight, his spiritual life had deepened after his stagecoach overturned in a winter night storm, hurling him into the darkness beneath four frenzied horses in a flooded creek. Indebted for his rescue and survival, he pledged himself as "God's Instrument"—a pledge kept until he died at age ninety-one.

He combined farm labor with teaching to support his family during his years as reformer and abolitionist, living in rural simplicity in several Hudson River communities in New Jersey, before moving during the war to Massachusetts. After passage of the Thirteenth Amendment abolishing slavery, he led a reflective life, outliving other Massachusetts abolitionists who were companions during his final years: poets John Greenleaf Whittier and Henry Wadsworth Longfellow, and leaders William Lloyd Garrison and Wendell Phillips—both of whom he eulogized and served as honorary pallbearer.

Weld's own most lasting published works include a posthumous tribute to his wife—*In Memory, Angelina Grimké Weld* (1880)—and a controversial work they compiled together with Sarah Grimké, *American Slavery as It Is: Testimony of a Thousand Witnesses* (1839). Based on information from over twenty thousand Southern newspapers and many eye-witness accounts, the pioneering volume authenticated cruelties later fictionalized by Harriet Beecher Stowe in *Uncle Tom's Cabin.* In *Key to Uncle Tom's Cabin,* Stowe cited twenty references to the influence of *American Slavery as It Is* on her 1852 novel. Her sentiments were never expressed to Weld, who is mentioned twice in her *Key,* but the two never met after he shook up Lane Seminary, where her father, Lyman Beecher, was president.

Excerpted here is Weld's anonymous introduction to his book, first published by the American Antislavery Society.

From the introduction to *American Slavery as It Is* (1839)

. . . As slaveholders and their apologists are volunteer witnesses in their own cause, and are flooding the world with testimony that their slaves are kindly treated; that they are well fed, well clothed, well housed, well lodged, moderately worked, and bountifully provided with all things needful for their comfort, we propose,—first, to disprove their assertions by the testimony of a multitude of impartial witnesses, and then to put slaveholders themselves through a course of cross-questioning which will draw their condemnation out of their own mouths.

We will prove that the slaves in the United States are treated with barbarous inhumanity; that they are overworked, underfed, wretchedly clad and lodged, and have insufficient sleep; that they are often made to wear round their necks iron collars armed with prongs, to drag heavy chains and weights at their feet while working in the field, and to wear yokes and bells, and iron horns; that they are often kept confined in the stocks day and night for weeks together, made to wear gags in their mouths for hours or days, have some of their front teeth torn out or broken off, that they may be easily detected when they run away; that they are frequently flogged with terrible severity, have red pepper rubbed into their lacerated flesh, and hot brine, spirits of turpentine, &c., poured over the gashes to increase the torture; that they are often stripped naked, their backs and limbs cut with knives, bruised and mangled by scores and hundreds of blows with the paddle, and terribly torn by the claws of cats, drawn over them by their tormentors; that they are often hunted with bloodhounds and shot down like beasts, or torn in pieces by dogs; that they are often suspended by the arms and whipped and beaten till they faint, and when revived by restoratives, beaten again till they faint, and sometimes till they die; that their ears are often cut off, their eyes knocked out, their bones broken, their flesh branded with red-hot irons; that they are maimed, mutilated and burned to death, over slow fires. All these things, and more, and worse, we shall *prove.* . . .

We shall show, not merely that such deeds are committed, but that they are frequent; not done in corners, but before the sun; not in one of the slave states, but in all of them; not perpetrated by brutal overseers and drivers merely, but by magistrates, by legislators, by professors of religion, by preachers of the gospel, by governors of states, by "gentlemen of property and standing," and by delicate females moving in the "highest circles of society."

We know, full well, the outcry that will be made by multitudes, at these declarations; the multiform cavils, the flat denials, the charges of "exaggeration" and "falsehood" so often bandied, the sneers of affected contempt at the credulity that can believe such things, and the rage and imprecations against those who give them currency. We know, too, the threadbare sophistries by which slaveholders and their apologists seek to evade such testimony. If they admit that such deeds are committed, they tell us that they are exceedingly rare, and therefore furnish no grounds for judging of the general treatment of slaves; that occasionally a brutal wretch in the *free* states barbarously butchers his wife, but that no one thinks of inferring from that, the general treatment of wives at the North and West.

They tell us, also, that the slaveholders of the South are proverbially hospitable, kind, and generous, and it is incredible that they can perpetrate such enormities upon human beings; further, that it is absurd to suppose that they would thus injure their own property, that self-interest would prompt them to treat their slaves with kindness, as none but fools and madmen wantonly destroy their own property; further, that Northern visitors at the South come back testifying to the kind treatment of the slaves, and that the slaves themselves corroborate such representations. All these pleas, and scores of others, are bruited in every corner of the free States; and who that hath eyes to see, has not sickened at the blindness that saw not, at the palsy of heart that felt not, or at the cowardice and sycophancy that dared not expose such shallow fallacies. We are not to be turned from our purpose by such vapid babblings. In their appropriate places, we propose to consider these objections and various others, and to show their emptiness and folly. . . .

SARAH MAPPS DOUGLASS

(1806–82)

Born with the same surname as the man she married—Reverend William L. Douglass—Sarah Douglass was no relation to the later renowned Frederick Douglass, who was a decade younger than she. However, both were dedicated abolitionists who believed in what Frederick once called "the cause of human brotherhood as well as the cause of human sisterhood." An antebellum teacher, and a postbellum vice-chairperson of the Women's Pennsylvania Branch of the American Freedmen's Aid Association, Sarah Douglass was a trailblazer who devoted her career to improving black education and the status of women, in an era of disenfranchisement and discrimination.

Reared in a family of free, educated, and self-employed Philadelphians, her maternal grandfather was a member of the Free African Society and a Quaker who opened his own bakery, which was still thriving when he died in 1806—the year Sarah was born. Privately tutored by her mother, Grace Douglass, a Quaker and milliner, Sarah instilled Quaker beliefs at the academy she opened for black pupils in the 1820s. Much later, Philadelphia Quakers helped to finance the Institute for Colored Youth, where she was a teacher and principal.

During the 1820s, however, Sarah and Grace Douglass sadly witnessed a decline in Quaker antislavery activity, due in part to a growing schism between Orthodox leadership and reformist Hicksites, who boycotted slave-made products. The Douglasses remained faithful to the religion's doctrines of charity, despite being segregated on the "colored bench" at their Philadelphia Arch Street Meeting House, where some members were indifferent to their membership in Negro self-improvement associations or the Philadelphia Female Antislavery Society. The two women were also stoic, especially Grace, whose husband Robert helped organize Philadelphia's First African Presbyterian church, only to see the sanctuary damaged in 1834 by a mob bent on destroying it.

By 1855, Sarah would wed the rector of the city's venerated old St. Thomas Protestant Episcopal Church, whose pulpit by then forbade antislavery agitation, despite a history of social involvement. But in the 1830s, both Sarah and Grace remained in the American Society of Friends and close to the then–Quaker Grimké Sisters, who invited them to Angelina's nuptials in May

1838—to the scorn of the local white press. Angelina, banned by Quakers for marrying outside their faith, was chided by outsiders for an "amalgamated" wedding.

Two days after the Grimké–Weld ceremony, arsonists destroyed the city's new Pennsylvania Hall, abolitionist headquarters and site of the Second Anti-slavery Convention of American Women—for which Sarah Douglass was trea-surer. A year later, in May 1839, at the third and last women's antislavery convention, Sarah was reelected treasurer and Grace chosen vice-president, though soon thereafter females were allowed to join once all-male abolitionist societies. That same May, both Douglass women were among the black aboli-tionists who threw unanimous support to Garrison, after majority delegates at the Massachusetts Antislavery Society state convention accepted his plea for women to vote at sessions, while a disgruntled faction formed a rival group, the all-male Massachusetts Abolition Society. Black constituents from Boston to Philadelphia held meetings to impugn the schism and to rally around "Brother Garrison."

The following letter, cast in moral and religious probity, expresses the loyal support of Sarah and Grace Douglass.

A Letter to Brother Garrison [w/ Grace Douglass][1] (1839)

PHILADELPHIA, May 27th, 1839.

DEAR BROTHER GARRISON:

As our dearly beloved friends, _____, expect to meet you in a few days, we thought we would send you a line, expressive of our sympathy. We have felt much for you, and prayed God to sustain you and uphold you. Your enemies may say what they will of you: they can *never* convince us, that you are recreant to the cause of the crushed, degraded slave. No. Have you not endured impris-onment, scorn, contempt, and poverty, for our sakes—preferring to suffer af-fliction with the people of God, rather than enjoy the pleasures of sin for a season? Were you not the *first* who dared openly to ask for us equal rights with our fairer brethren. Yes, you were; and the memory of all you have done and suffered for us is traced upon our hearts as with an adamantine pen—never to

---

[1] The text of the letter, from microfilm, is reprinted exactly as it appeared in the *Liberator*, June 21, 1839.

be effaced. For this you are entitled to, (and shall have) our prayers, our love, our unceasing gratitude. We thank you, friend and brother, on behalf of our brethren in bonds, for your labors of love. Be encouraged—be strong—fear not! *Our* God, the God of the suffering slave, will be near you, to comfort and to bless.

O, the enemy of all good is busy, blinding the eyes and hardening the hearts of many. But those who are fixed on the rock Christ Jesus, need not fear force nor fraud.

We do not believe that the cause of the slave will be injured by the dissensions in the antislavery ranks; it is the cause of God, and he can get the victory by the few as well as by the many. I think of Gideon's three hundred men, and take courage.

* * * * * * You will please remember us affectionately to Mrs. Garrison—she is dear to us—we love her. Our family, father and brother, join us in love to you. Farewell!

May the blessing of heaven rest on you, now and forever.

GRACE & SARAH M. DOUGLASS.

WILLIAM WHIPPER

(1804?–76)

One of the wealthiest black entrepreneurs in the Northeast before or after the Civil War was William Whipper, whose purse and pen served to promote the reforms he espoused.

Free-born in Little Britain, Pennsylvania, he came to Philadelphia in the 1820s and by 1834 opened his own "free produce" grocery store, which sold no products made from slave labor. An advocate of self-improvement, education, and temperance as a way to repeal so-called black laws in the North and abolish slavery in the South, he stated those principles in various articles and in speeches to the Colored Reading Society for Mental Improvement, which he organized in 1828.

He generally opposed separatist Negro groups, believing that they reinforced segregation, but he was an active participant at state and national meetings of free men and women and a contributor to the *Colored American*. In 1835, he joined James Forten and other notable black Philadelphians as a founder of the American Moral Reform Society, whose monthly journal, the *National Reformer*, Whipper edited during its brief publication from September 1838 to December 1839.

Having then moved to Columbia, Pennsylvania, to become partner to Stephen Smith, an affluent black merchant in the lumber and coal business, Whipper amassed a fortune by 1845, and donated it generously to abolitionist sources. He turned his Columbia property into a station on the Underground Railroad to help escaped slaves to Canada, where he himself intended to emigrate until the outbreak of the Civil War. He supported Union troops with lumber and funds, and lobbied later for civil rights during Reconstruction. He relocated his business enterprises to New Brunswick, New Jersey, before returning to Philadelphia, where he died after a long illness.

On "Colorophobia"[1]—from a Letter in the *Colored American* (1841)

... There is no people on earth justly entitled to the commiseration of mankind on account of their peculiar situation until they are equally ready and willing to render the same justice to others.

As a people we are deeply afflicted with "colorophobia" (and notwithstanding there may have been causes sufficient to implant it into our minds), it is arrayed against the spirit of Christianity, republican freedom, and our common happiness, and ought once now and forever to be abolished. It is an evil that must be met, and we *must meet it now*. The holy cause of human freedom, the success and happiness of future generations depend upon it. We must throw off the distinctive features in the charters of our churches, and other institutions. We have refused to hear ministers preach from the pulpit, because they would not preach against slavery. We must pursue the same course respecting prejudice against complexion. I verily believe that no man ought to be employed as a pastor of any Christian Church, that would consent to preach to a congregation where the "negro pew" exists; and I also believe it to be a violation of Christian principles for any man to accept the pastoral charge of a Church under a charter based on complexional distinction. You now see my friend, that I am willing to accept the resolution in its catholic spirit. I trust that it will not be asking too much of you, and those that voted for it, to aid in promoting its faithful application to all existing institutions within your control.

I remain yours in the cause of liberty and equality.

WM. WHIPPER
Columbia, January 12, 1841

---

[1] From a letter in the *Colored American*, February 6, 1841, vol. 1, no. 49. The title is supplied by the editor of this volume.

HENRY HIGHLAND GARNET

(1815–82)

Among abolitionists in the early 1840s, a new phalanx emerged: educated fugitives. Their direct experience with slavery incited them to more radical proposals to end servitude in the South and injustice in the North. Leading this vocal new vanguard was Henry Highland Garnet.[1]

Born on a Kent County, Maryland, plantation, he had escaped at age nine with his family on the underground railway, settling in New York City, where he received formal instruction for two years at The New York African Free School. Unable to find employment after graduation, he was a cabin attendant on voyages to Cuba when, in 1829, slavehunters stalked his family, confiscated their belongings, and had his sister arrested and tried as a fugitive in New York. In 1835, another blow came when Garnet and several black clsssmates, including the later eminent Alexander Crummell, were forced out of Noyes Academy, a private white school that had opened the year before in Canaan, New Hampshire, soliciting "colored youth of good character on equal terms with whites of like character." Angry local citizens reacted by hauling in oxen to pull the schoolhouse from its foundation and dump it in a nearby swamp, while armed vigilantes harrassed the students.

That persecution in the North, plus segregated accommodations he encountered in travel, made a lasting impression on Garnet who was as black as sable and then nineteen. He was also lame—crippled at the knee from an earlier athletic mishap that forced him to limp on crutches then and after 1841, when his leg was amputated at the hip. His physical handicap, however, reinforced his determination to excel in a demanding curriculum of theological studies at Oneida Institute near Utica, New York, where he graduated in 1839. A year later, he established residence in nearby Troy, where he was soon licensed as

---

[1] In Garnet's own day, Frederick Douglass and William Lloyd Garrison spelled the name *Garnett* in their respective newspapers; it often has appeared misspelled ever since. No documentation exists that Garnet himself explained the origin or alternate spelling of his surname. Allegedly, it was a modification of the name *Garrett*, from Thomas Garrett, a Quaker, who aided the fugitive family in Wilmington, Delaware. Since the family could not read, write, or spell until later, uncertain orthography of their adopted name perhaps resulted.

clergyman of the town's Presbyterian church for a black congregation. His gospel became a social one and his pulpit a forum for issues of land reform, slave emancipation, and repeal of inequitable laws.

Garnet's militant posture as an abolitionist increased step by step from 1840 to 1843, leading him into confrontation with black and white Garrisonian abolitionists. The latter, mostly Boston- and Philadelphia-based, had directed their efforts since the 1830s to nonviolent antislavery societies, petitions, speeches, publications, boycotts of slave-made products, advocacy of full citizenship for free Negroes, and emancipation of slaves—but not for national political action or suffrage, since Garrison vowed never to vote as long as the government included slaveowners. Garnet encouraged another agenda by May 1840 when he and seven black clergymen–abolitionists helped found a rival antislavery group, the American and Foreign Antislavery Society, whose members were New York–based supporters of the dissenting Massachusetts Abolition Society, which broke with Garrison in 1839. In May 1841, Garnet was a featured speaker at the Massachusetts Abolition Society convention in Boston, supporting a resolution to combat slavery by organized political action. In 1842, he was the first black man to address and endorse the national convention of the new Liberty Party, formed in 1839 as an antislavery alternative to Whigs and Democrats. For the Liberty Party, he rejected violent measures to end slavery, but a year later, in 1843, he reversed himself at a convention of all-black men in Buffalo, where one of his most famous speeches, "An Address to the Slaves," called for civil disobedience, if not insurrection. Black Convention delegates voted twice against distribution of his "Address," which was also repudiated by Garrison's *Liberator*; Garnet's text was unprinted until 1848, when he published it with *David Walker's Appeal in Four Articles*.

Not until the 1850s would the impact of some of Garnet's 1840s strategies take hold and be adopted by many leading black abolitionists—including other fugitives. By then, he had more influence internationally than in the United States. In August 1850, he was delegate to the World Peace Congress in Germany, and a year later addressed antislavery societies in England and Scotland, thence in Jamaica, where he served three years as a Presbyterian pastor. After his return, he sanctioned voluntary emigration, became president of the African Civilization Society, and supported the American Colonization Society, further alienating Garrisonians, who also opposed his praise of John Brown's 1859 raid on Harper's Ferry. Although his own leadership declined by 1860, his militant ideas had gained a following among moderates, despite the ascendancy of his rival, Frederick Douglass.

Garnet supported the Republican party in the 1860s, and was the first black clergyman to deliver a sermon before the House of Representatives in 1865, while pastor of the Fifteenth Street Presbyterian Church in Washington. He continued his political organizing during the Civil War, and at its end worked among Southern freedmen for the American Home Missionary Society. During the 1870s, he lived mostly in semiretirement in New York, until January 1882 when the new republican President, Chester A. Arthur, ardent defender of fugitive slaves, appointed Garnet consul general to Liberia. A month later, he died there of tropical fever and was buried with ceremonial honors near the Liberian capital, Monrovia.

His significant career legacy is that of clergyman, civil rights activist, foreign emissary, and journalist, who edited three short-lived newspapers—the *Clarion,* the *National Watchman,* and the *Anglo-African,* and wrote several public lectures that documented his increasing militancy in public discourse: "The Past and Present Condition, and the Destiny, of the Colored Race" (1848); "Address of the Liberty Party to the Colored People of the Northern States" (1848)—both of which followed his controversial "An Address to the Slaves of the United States of America," which is reprinted here in full.

An Address to the Slaves of the United States of America (1843)

Brethren and Fellow Citizens: Your brethren of the North, East, and West have been accustomed to meet together in National Conventions, to sympathize with each other, and to weep over your unhappy condition. In these meetings we have addressed all classes of the free, but we have never, until this time, sent a word of consolation and advice to you. We have been contented in sitting still and mourning over your sorrows, earnestly hoping that before this day your sacred liberties would have been restored. But, we have hoped in vain. Years have rolled on, and tens of thousands have been borne on streams of blood and tears, to the shores of eternity. While you have been oppressed, we have also been partakers with you; nor can we be free while you are enslaved. We, therefore, write to you as being bound with you.

Many of you are bound to us, not only by the ties of a common humanity, but we are connected by the more tender relations of parents, wives, husbands, children, brothers, and sisters, and friends. As such we most affectionately address you.

Slavery has fixed a deep gulf between you and us, and while it shuts out from you the relief and consolation which your friends would willingly render, it afflicts and persecutes you with a fierceness which we might not expect to see in the fiends of hell. But still the Almighty Father of mercies has left to us a glimmering ray of hope, which shines out like a lone star in a cloudy sky. Mankind are becoming wiser, and better—the oppressor's power is fading, and you, every day, are becoming better informed, and more numerous. Your grievances, brethren, are many. We shall not attempt, in this short address, to present to the world all the dark catalogue of this nation's sins, which have been committed upon an innocent people. Nor is it indeed necessary, for you feel them from day to day, and all the civilized world look upon them with amazement.

Two hundred and twenty-seven years ago, the first of our injured race were brought to the shores of America. They came not with glad spirits to select their homes in the New World. They came not with their own consent, to find an unmolested enjoyment of the blessings of this fruitful soil. The first dealings they had with men calling themselves Christians, exhibited to them the worst features of corrupt and sordid hearts: and convinced them that no cruelty is too great, no villainy and no robbery too abhorrent for even enlightened men to perform, when influenced by avarice and lust. Neither did they come flying upon the wings of Liberty, to a land of freedom. But they came with broken hearts, from their beloved native land, and were doomed to unrequited toil and deep degradation. Nor did the evil of their bondage end at their emancipation by death. Succeeding generations inherited their chains, and millions have come from eternity into time, and have returned again to the world of spirits, cursed and ruined by American slavery.

The propagators of the system, or their immediate ancestors, very soon discovered its growing evil, and its tremendous wickedness, and secret promises were made to destroy it. The gross inconsistency of a people holding slaves, who had themselves "ferried o'er the wave" for freedom's sake, was too apparent to be entirely overlooked. The voice of Freedom cried, "Emancipate your slaves." Humanity supplicated with tears for the deliverance of the children of Africa. Wisdom urged her solemn plea. The bleeding captive plead his innocence, and pointed to Christianity who stood weeping at the cross. Jehovah frowned upon the nefarious institution, and thunderbolts, red with vengeance, struggled to leap forth to blast the guilty wretches who maintained it. But all was vain. Slavery had stretched its dark wings of death over the land, the Church stood silently by—the priests prophesied falsely, and the people loved to have it so. Its throne is established, and now it reigns triumphant.

Nearly three millions of your fellow citizens are prohibited by law and public opinion (which in this country is stronger than law), from reading the Book of Life. Your intellect has been destroyed as much as possible, and every ray of light they have attempted to shut out from your minds. The oppressors themselves have become involved in the ruin. They have become weak, sensual, and rapacious—they have cursed you—they have cursed themselves—they have cursed the earth which they have trod.

The colonists threw the blame upon England. They said that the mother country entailed the evil upon them, and that they would rid themselves of it if they could. The world thought they were sincere, and the philanthropic pitied them. But time soon tested their sincerity. In a few years the colonists grew strong, and severed themselves from the British Government. Their independence was declared, and they took their station among the sovereign powers of the earth. The declaration was a glorious document. Sages admired it, and the patriotic of every nation reverenced the God-like sentiments which it contained. When the power of Government returned to their hands, did they emancipate the slaves? No; they rather added new links to our chains. Were they ignorant of the principles of Liberty? Certainly they were not. The sentiments of their revolutionary orators fell in burning eloquence upon their hearts, and with one voice they cried, LIBERTY OR DEATH. Oh what a sentence was that! It ran from soul to soul like electric fire, and nerved the arm of thousands to fight in the holy cause of Freedom. Among the diversity of opinions that are entertained in regard to physical resistance, there are but a few found to gainsay that stern declaration. We are among those who do not.

SLAVERY! How much misery is comprehended in that single word. What mind is there that does not shrink from its direful effects? Unless the image of God be obliterated from the soul, all men cherish the love of Liberty. The nice discerning political economist does not regard the sacred right more than the untutored African who roams the wilds of Congo. Nor has the one more right to the full enjoyment of his freedom than the other. In every man's mind the good seeds of liberty are planted, and he who brings his fellow down so low, as to make him contented with a condition of slavery, commits the highest crime against God and man. Brethren, your oppressors aim to do this. They endeavor to make you as much like brutes as possible. When they have blinded the eyes of your mind—when they have embittered the sweet waters of life—when they have shut out the light which shines from the word of God—then, and not till then, has American slavery done its perfect work.

TO SUCH DEGREDATION IT IS SINFUL IN THE EXTREME FOR YOU TO MAKE VOLUNTARY SUBMISSION. The divine commandments you are in duty bound to reverence and obey. If you do not obey them, you will surely meet with the displeasure of the Almighty. He requires you to love him supremely, and your neighbor as yourself—to keep the Sabbath day holy—to search the Scriptures—and bring up your children with respect for his laws, and to worship no other God but him. But slavery sets all these at nought, and hurls defiance in the face of Jehovah. The forlorn condition in which you are placed, does not destroy your moral obligation to God. You are not certain of heaven, because you suffer yourselves to remain in a state of slavery, where you cannot obey the commandments of the Sovereign of the universe. If the ignorance of slavery is a passport to heaven, then it is a blessing, and no curse, and you should rather desire its perpetuity than its abolition. God will not receive slavery, nor ignorance, nor any other state of mind, for love and obedience to him. Your condition does not absolve you from your moral obligation. The diabolical injustice by which your liberties are cloven down, NEITHER GOD, NOR ANGELS, OR JUST MEN, COMMAND YOU TO SUFFER FOR A SINGLE MOMENT. THEREFORE IT IS YOUR SOLEMN AND IMPERATIVE DUTY TO USE EVERY MEANS, BOTH MORAL, INTELLECTUAL, AND PHYSICAL, THAT PROMISES SUCCESS. If a band of heathen men should attempt to enslave a race of Christians, and to place their children under the influence of some false religion, surely, Heaven would frown upon the men who would not resist such aggression, even to death. If, on the other hand, a band of Christians should attempt to enslave a race of heathen men, and to entail slavery upon them, and to keep them in heathenism in the midst of Christianity, the God of heaven would smile upon every effort which the injured might make to disenthral themselves.

Brethren, it is as wrong for your lordly oppressors to keep you in slavery, as it was for the man thief to steal our ancestors from the coast of Africa. You should therefore now use the same manner of resistance, as would have been just in our ancestors, when the bloody footprints of the first remorseless soul-thief was placed upon the shores of our fatherland. The humblest peasant is as free in the sight of God as the proudest monarch that ever swayed a scepter. Liberty is a spirit sent out from God, and like its great Author, is no respecter of persons.

Brethren, the time has come when you must act for yourselves. It is an old and true saying that, "if hereditary bondmen would be free, they must themselves strike the blow." You can plead your own cause, and do the work of emancipation better than any others. The nations of the old world are moving in the great cause of universal freedom, and some of them at least will, ere long, do you justice. The combined powers of Europe have placed their broad seal of disapprobation upon the African slave trade. But in the slaveholding parts of the United States, the trade is as brisk as ever. They buy and sell you as though you were brute beasts. The North has done much—her opinion of slavery in the abstract is known. But in regard to the South, we adopt the opinion of the *New York Evangelist*—"We have advanced so far, that the cause apparently waits for a more effectual door to be thrown open than has been yet." We are about to point you to that more effectual door. Look around you, and behold the bosoms of your loving wives heaving with untold agonies! Hear the cries of your poor children! Remember the stripes your fathers bore. Think of the torture and disgrace of your noble mothers. Think of your wretched sisters, loving virtue and purity, as they are driven into concubinage and are exposed to the unbridled lusts of incarnate devils. Think of the undying glory that hangs around the ancient name of Africa:—and forget not that you are native-born American citizens, and as such, you are justly entitled to all the rights that are granted to the freest. Think how many tears you have poured out upon the soil which you have cultivated with unrequited toil and enriched with your blood; and then go to your lordly enslavers and tell them plainly, that you *are determined to be free.* Appeal to their sense of justice, and tell them that they have no more right to oppress you, than you have to enslave them. Entreat them to remove the grievous burdens which they have imposed upon you, and to remunerate you for your labor. Promise them renewed diligence in the cultivation of the soil, if they will render to you an equivalent for your services. Point them to the increase of happiness and prosperity in the British West-Indies since the Act of Emancipation. Tell them in language which they cannot misunderstand, of the exceeding sinfulness of slavery, and of a future judgment, and of the righteous retributions of an indignant God. Inform them that all you desire is FREEDOM, and that nothing else will suffice. Do this, and for ever after cease to toil for the heartless tyrants, who give you no other reward but stripes and abuse. If they then commence the work of death, they, and not you, will be responsible for the consequences. You had far better all die—*die immediately,* than live slaves, and entail your wretchedness upon your posterity. If you would be free in this generation, here is your only hope. However much you and all of us may desire it, there is not much hope of redemption without the shedding of blood. If you must bleed, let it all come at once—rather *die freemen, than live to be the slaves.* It is impossible, like the children of Israel, to make a grand exodus from the land of bondage. The Pharoahs are on both sides of the bloodred waters! You cannot move *en masse,* to the dominions of the British Queen—nor can you pass through Florida and overrun Texas, and at last find peace in Mexico. The propagators of American slavery are spending their blood and treasure, that they may plant the black flag in the heart of Mexico and riot in the halls of the Montezumas. In the language of the Rev. Robert Hall, when addressing the volunteers of Bristol, who were rushing forth to repel the invasion of Napoleon, who threatened to lay waste the fair homes of England, "Religion is too much interested in your behalf, not to shed over you her most gracious influences."

You will not be compelled to spend much time in order to become inured to hardships. From the first moment that you breathed the air of heaven, you have been accustomed to nothing else but hardships. The heroes of the American Revolution were never put upon harder fare than a peck of corn and a few herrings per week. You have not become enervated by the luxuries of life. Your sternest energies have been beaten out upon the anvil of severe trial. Slavery has done this, to make you subservient to its own purposes; but it has done more than this, it has prepared you for any emergency. If you receive good treatment, it is what you could hardly expect; if you meet with pain, sorrow, and even death, these are the common lot of the slaves.

Fellowmen! patient sufferers! behold your dearest rights crushed to the earth! See your sons murdered, and your wives, mothers and sisters doomed to prostitution. In the name of the merciful God, and by all that life is worth, let it no longer be a debatable question, whether it is better to choose *Liberty* or *death*.

In 1822, Denmark Veazie [Vesey], of South Carolina, formed a plan for the liberation of his fellowmen. In the whole history of human efforts to overthrow slavery, a more complicated and tremendous plan was never formed. He was betrayed by the treachery of his own people, and died a martyr to freedom. Many a brave hero fell, but history, faithful to her high trust, will transcribe his name on the same monument with Moses, Hampden, Tell, Bruce and Wallace, Toussaint L'Ouverture, Lafayette and Washington. That tremendous movement shook the whole empire of slavery. The guilty soul-thieves were overwhelmed with fear. It is a matter of fact, that at that time, and in consequence of the threatened revolution, the slave States talked strongly of emancipation. But they blew but one blast of the trumpet of freedom, and then laid it aside. As these men became quiet, the slaveholders ceased to talk about emancipation: and now behold your condition today! Angels sigh over it, and humanity has long since exhausted her tears in weeping on your account!

The patriotic Nathaniel Turner followed Denmark Veazie [Vesey]. He was goaded to desperation by wrong and injustice. By despotism, his name has been recorded on the list of infamy, and future generations will remember him among the noble and brave.

Next arose the immortal Joseph Cinque, the hero of the *Amistad*. He was a native African, and by the help of God he emancipated a whole shipload of his fellowmen on the high seas. And he now sings of liberty on the sunny hills of Africa and beneath his native palm trees, where he hears the lion roar and feels himself as free as that king of the forest.

Next arose Madison Washington, that bright star of freedom, and took his station in the constellation of true heroism. He was a slave on board the brig *Creole*, of Richmond, bound to New Orleans, that great slave mart, with a hundred and four others. Nineteen struck for liberty or death. But one life was taken, and the whole were emancipated, and the vessel was carried into Nassau, New Providence.

Noble men! Those who have fallen in freedom's conflict, their memories will be cherished by the truehearted and the God-fearing in all future generations; those who are living, their names are surrounded by a halo of glory.

Brethren, arise, arise! Strike for your lives and liberties. Now is the day and the hour. Let every slave throughout the land do this, and the days of slavery are numbered. You cannot be more oppressed than you have been—you cannot suffer greater cruelties than you have already. *Rather die freemen than live to be slaves.* Remember that you are FOUR MILLIONS!

It is in your power so to torment the God-cursed slaveholders, that they will be glad to let you go free. If the scale was turned, and black men were the masters and white men the slaves, every destructive agent and element would be employed to lay the oppressor low. Danger and death would hang over their heads day and night. Yes, the tyrants would meet with plagues more terrible than those of Pharaoh. But you are a patient people. You act as though you were made for the special use of these devils. You act as though your daughters were born to pamper the lusts of your masters and overseers. And worse than all, you tamely submit while your lords tear your wives from your embraces and defile them before your eyes. In the name of God, we ask, are you men? Where is the blood of your fathers? Has it all run out of your veins? Awake, awake; millions of voices are calling you! Your dead fathers speak to you from their graves. Heaven, as with a voice of thunder, calls on you to arise from the dust.

Let your motto be resistance! *resistance!* RESISTANCE! No oppressed people have ever secured their liberty without resistance. What kind of resistance you had better make, you must decide by the circumstances that surround you, and according to the suggestion of expediency. Brethren, adieu! Trust in the living God. Labor for the peace of the human race, and remember that you are FOUR MILLIONS.

FREDERICK DOUGLASS

(1818?–95)

Like Henry Highland Garnet, Frederick Douglass knew bondage from experience. He had lived twenty years a slave and three years a fugitive when he delivered his first public speech to a Massachusetts Antislavery Society convention at Nantucket Island in August 1841. Then employed as a day laborer in New Bedford shipyards, he was soon hired by William Lloyd Garrison as antislavery lecturer and agent. Neither man anticipated the ideological differences that would divide them ten years later—in their interpretation of the Constitution, political action, and nonviolence. During the early 1840s, Douglass was a loyal Garrisonian, and Garrison in turn penned the preface to the personal story Douglass told from many Northern platforms and published as a book in May 1845: *Narrative of the Life of Frederick Douglass, An American Slave, Written by Himself.*

Three months after publication of the *Narrative*, Douglass sailed for the British Isles and remained there two years, aided by English abolitionists who purchased his freedom in 1846. Internationally known for powerful oratory less than a decade after his escape from slavery, he returned to the United States a free man, with manumission papers filed in Baltimore. Resettling in Rochester, New York, he launched his own newspaper, the *North Star*, December 3, 1847.

Measured by influence, he was one of the few black spokesmen to mobilize and sustain a power base outside the black church—then or later. His antebellum speeches were often eloquent political sermons, as were many of his editorials in the *North Star*—a journal he renamed *Frederick Douglass' Paper* in 1851 and *Douglass Monthly* in 1860—until publication ceased in 1863. More than any other abolitionist, he insisted that black and white, slave and free, male and female, must struggle *together* for progress. More than any black leader of his generation, he urged free people of color to take initiative for their own advancement, and to learn trades and skills to become self-sufficient, "that we may commence the battle of life with weapons commensurate with the exigencies of the conflict."

His message was neither black nationalism nor a return to Africa, and he frequently was at odds with those who supported colonization and emigration.

His protest against American injustice and religious hypocrisy was never a call to leave America, even in his defiant and famous speech "What to the Slave is the Fourth of July?" (1852). His little-known novella, *The Heroic Slave* (1853) portrayed the true story of Madison Washington, who led a mutiny aboard the slave ship *Creole* in 1841—a hero "who loved liberty as well as Patrick Henry." Douglass, in his own way, was a formidable Patrick Henry patriot. During the Civil War, few men traveled as widely to recruit black soldiers, including his own sons, for battle in Union regiments.

More militant black and white voices than his paved the way for him and advanced ideas that he modified for support. His public career began with a struggle to change the conscience of the nation on slavery and ended with a fifty-year record as a voice for social and political change. Much of that record is in two autobiographies published after the 1845 *Narrative: My Bondage and My Freedom* (1855) and *The Life and Times of Frederick Douglass* (1881, 1892)—minus some of his factional feuds and political compromises.

A self-declared "woman's rights man" in editorials and speeches, he participated in the first women's rights convention at Seneca Falls, New York, in 1848; but by 1868 he broke with feminist leaders who opposed a Fifteenth Amendment that denied women the vote granted to black freedmen. On other burning issues Douglass's fire often flickered as the winds changed. He sanctioned John Brown's raid on the federal arsenal at Harper's Ferry, but refused to join it and fled to England via Canada when federal marshals sought him as an accomplice. From 1856 onward, after experimenting with the Free Soil and Liberty parties, he became a loyal Republican, opposing then praising Lincoln for President in 1864, and campaigning in 1868 for Ulysses S. Grant. Three years later, Grant appointed him assistant secretary of commission to Santo Domingo, in exchange for support of a proposal to annex the island as a haven for ex-slaves.

In 1872, after suspected arsonists destroyed his Rochester, New York home, Douglass moved his family to Washington, DC. There, after a failed venture as owner–editor of *New National Era* newspaper, and president of Freedmen's Bank, he became entrenched as a Republican functionary in the Reconstruction era, appointed as U.S. Marshall to the District of Columbia by President Rutherford B. Hayes in 1876–77, and Recorder of Deeds by President James Garfield in 1881. Despite such post–Civil War roles, he was like a captain without a ship. Most white American historians, until the midtwentieth century, mentioned him only cursorily, and, in some cases, misspelled his surname.

He had adopted the surname Douglass after his escape from slavery in September 1838. Born Frederick Augustus Washington Bailey, on a farm in Tuckahoe, on Maryland's eastern shore, he never knew if his birth date was February

1817 or 1818. "I do not remember to have ever met a slave who could tell of his birthday," he wrote in his *Narrative*, which also voiced uncertainty about the name of his white father, who some whispered to be his master, Aaron Anthony. The latter died within a year of Frederick's mother, Harriet Bailey, who worked on a nearby plantation but rarely saw her son before her death when he was about seven. He and six of her other children were divided as property of Aaron Anthony's heirs; Douglass came of age on Maryland plantations and as a house servant in a Baltimore family, whose mistress, Sophia Auld, taught him the alphabet, until her husband convinced her "learning would spoil the best nigger in the world."

Thereafter, the young Frederick clandestinely taught himself to read and write, assisted by white youths in the street, while working as a mechanic and apprentice caulker on Baltimore docks. He fled to freedom, disguised as a sailor on a train to Philadelphia, aided by savings from his Baltimore fiancée, Anna Murray, a free domestic, whom he wed twelve days later in New York City. Officiating at their marriage was Reverend James W. C. Pennington, another Maryland ex-slave destined for international distinction.

The Douglass marriage lasted forty-four years, during which Anna reared five children but never learned to read or write. That legacy in the domestic life of Frederick Douglass is a paradox, given his public record of advocacy for women's equality and full participation in American society. After Anna died in August 1882, Douglass married a Mount Holyoke College graduate: his white former secretary, Helen Pitts. Their marriage in January 1884 was opposed by many blacks and whites, and the couple spent 1885–87 touring Europe, Egypt, and the Near East; from 1889 to 1891 Douglass was U.S. minister and consul general to Haiti; he lectured publicly until the year before his death of a heart attack at his Cedar Hill home in 1895.

The following editorial appeared in the *North Star* after the Seneca Falls Convention. It does not acknowledge his part in the proceedings, or that two weeks later he helped to ratify its resolutions at meetings sponsored by the Rochester Female Antislavery Society, which raised funds to found and sustain his paper. His supportive role at the Seneca Falls Convention was later commemorated on a plaque at the site:

ON THIS SPOT STOOD THE WESLEYAN CHAPEL
WHERE THE FIRST WOMAN'S RIGHTS CONVENTION IN THE WORLD'S
HISTORY WAS HELD JULY 19 AND 20, 1848
ELIZABETH CADY STANTON MOVED THIS RESOLUTION
WHICH WAS SECONDED BY FREDERICK DOUGLASS

THAT IT WAS THE DUTY OF THE WOMEN OF THIS COUNTRY
TO SECURE TO THEMSELVES THEIR SACRED RIGHT
TO THE ELECTIVE FRANCHISE.

The Rights of Women (1848)

One of the most interesting events of the past week, was the holding of what is technically styled a Woman's Rights Convention at Seneca Falls. The speaking, addresses, and resolutions of this extraordinary meeting was almost wholly conducted by women; and although they evidently felt themselves in a novel position, it is but simple justice to say that their whole proceedings were characterized by marked ability and dignity. No one present, we think, however much he might be disposed to differ from the views advanced by the leading speakers on that occasion, will fail to give them credit for brilliant talents and excellent dispositions. In this meeting, as in other deliberative assemblies, there were frequent differences of opinion and animated discussion; but in no case was there the slightest absence of good feeling and decorum. Several interesting documents setting forth the rights as well as the grievances of women were read. Among these was a Declaration of Sentiments, to be regarded as the basis of a grand movement for attaining the civil, social, political, and religious rights of women. We should not do justice to our own convictions, or to the excellent persons connected with this infant movement, if we did not in this connection offer a few remarks on the general subject which the Convention met to consider and the objects they seek to attain. In doing so, we are not insensible that the bare mention of this truly important subject in any other than terms of contemptuous ridicule and scornful disfavor, is likely to excite against us the fury of bigotry and the folly of prejudice. A discussion of the rights of animals would be regarded with far more complacency by many of what are called the *wise* and the *good* of our land, than would a discussion of the rights of women. It is, in their estimation, to be guilty of evil thoughts, to think that woman is entitled to equal rights with man. Many who have at last made the discovery that the Negroes have some rights as well as other members of the human family, have yet to be convinced that women are entitled to any. Eight years ago a number of persons of this description actually abandoned the antislavery cause, lest by giving their influence in that direction they might possibly be giving countenance to the dangerous heresy that woman, in respect to rights, stands on an equal footing with man. In the judgment of such persons the American slave system, with all its concomitant horrors, is less to be deplored than this *wicked* idea. It is perhaps needless to say, that we cherish little sympathy for such sentiments or respect for such prejudices. Standing as we do upon the watchtower of human freedom, we cannot be deterred from an expression of our approbation of any movement, however humble, to improve and elevate the character of any members of the human family. While it is impossible for us to go into this subject at length, and dispose of the various objections which are often urged against such a doctrine as that of female equality, we are free to say that in respect to political rights, we hold woman to be justly entitled to all we claim for man. We go farther, and express our conviction that all political rights which it is expedient for man to exercise, it is equally so for woman. All that distinguishes man as an intelligent and accountable being, is equally true of woman, and if that government only is just which governs by the free consent of the governed, there can be no reason in the world for denying to woman the exercise of the elective franchise, or a hand in making an administering the laws of the land. Our doctrine is that "right is of no sex." We therefore bid the women engaged in this movement our humble Godspeed.

North Star, July 28, 1848

HARRIET BEECHER STOWE

(1811–96)

To Frederick Douglass, *Uncle Tom's Cabin; or, The Man That Was a Thing* was "the *master book* of the nineteenth century." His praise was not shared by all black abolitionists, and least of all by white southern slaveholders—despite Stowe's effort to portray the latter as more cultivated and humane than her transplanted "Yankee" villain Simon Legree on his Louisiana plantation. When the two-volume novel was published in early 1852, "Uncle Tom" was already a household name, for Stowe's manuscript had begun appearing in serial form in the *National Era* newspaper on June 5, 1851, under the subtitle *Life among the Lowly*. The installments lasted nearly ten months, before the final chapter appeared April 1, 1852. It was no April Fool's Day joke that New England–born Harriet Beecher Stowe, then forty-one, wife of a college professor and mother of six children, had written a national best-seller about slavery, after only two brief trips to a slave state—namely Kentucky, across the river from Cincinnati, where the Beechers had moved in 1832, and where Harriet resided nearly eighteen years.

The novel was one of paradoxes that Douglass appeared to overlook. While composing her fiction, Stowe had written to him: "In the course of my story the scene will fall upon a cotton plantation. I am very desirous, therefore, to gain information from one who has been an actual laborer on one." It is uncertain what he provided about conditions on cotton plantations, but by March 1853 his newspaper printed an open letter to her: "My dear Mrs. Stowe, You kindly informed me, when at your house a fortnight ago, that you designed to do something which should permanently contribute to the improvement and elevation of the free colored people of the United States." Through fund-raising efforts in England, allegedly for "elevation of the African race," Stowe raised $20,000; she donated $500 of it toward a vocational school Douglass envisioned for freemen. No public record exists about dispensation of the remaining funds or her exact intentions. She believed that educated free blacks and fugitive slaves would be more useful by emigrating to the West African colony of Liberia, like her mulatto fugitive character George Harris, who studies and works as a mechanic, then decides at the end of *Uncle Tom's Cabin* that the "yearning of my soul is for an African *nationality*." In Stowe's fiction, no slave or fugitive is like Frederick Douglass, agitating for American citizenship.

Born in Litchfield, Connecticut, raised in Hartford, Boston, and Cincinnati, she lost her mother by age five and was reared by her father, Reverend Lyman Beecher, a renowned Congregationalist clergyman turned Presbyterian with strong Calvinist views; his racial attitudes were closer to the American Colonization Society than to abolitionists, whom he thought "misguided." He deeply influenced Harriet, as did her domineering older sister, Catharine, whose 1837 *Essay on Slavery and Abolitionism* chastised women who publicly crusaded against slavery—especially the Grimké sisters. Of Harriet's brothers, only Reverend Edward Beecher (and his wife) was an avowed abolitionist, but Harriet showed ambivalence toward emancipation in her writings on slavery, notably in the short story "Immediate Emancipation" (1845), and the novel *Dred: A Tale of the Great Dismal Swamp*, (1856)—a title she later changed to *Nina Gordon*, but restored again to *Dred*.

During the mid-1850s she lent her name to introductory prefaces of books by authors of color, William Cooper Nell, Frank J. Webb, and Josiah Henson (her prototype for "Uncle Tom"). After 1858, except for occasional editorials on the slavery issue, her fiction and nonfiction focused on themes related to oppressed womanhood, in books that included *The Minister's Wooing* (1859), *The Pearl of Orr's Island* (1862), *Oldtown Folks* (1869), *Lady Byron Vindicated* (1870), *Pink and White Tyranny* (1871), *Woman in Sacred History* (1874), and *Poganuc People* (1878). A travel book, *Palmetto Leaves* (1873), resulted from a winter spent in Florida, giving the nation early impressions about a state many Northerners had not seen, but also a view of her notions about the racial inferiority of blacks. Not atypical was her description that one man "might have been taken for a big baboon—the missing link of Darwin."

Active until senility set in during her early eighties, she published numerous articles, sketches, poems, and over thirty books, many about her native New England, where she died in 1896. Her pioneering New England novels, in the tradition of women's local color realism, are remembered less than *Uncle Tom's Cabin*, which spawned more translations, dramas, memorabilia, parodies, satires, polemics, and misconceptions about race than any novel in American culture.

The following piece is from Chapter X of *Key to Uncle Tom's Cabin: Presenting the Original Facts and Documents upon Which the Story Is Founded* (1853), written to offset critics.

From *Key to Uncle Tom's Cabin:*
"Poor White Trash" (1853)

When the public sentiment of Europe speaks in tones of indignation of the system of American slavery, the common reply has been, *"Look at your own lower classes."* The apologists of slavery have pointed England to *her own poor.* They have spoken of the heathenish ignorance, the vice, the darkness, of her crowded cities,—nay, even of her agricultural districts.

Now, in the first place, a country where the population is not crowded, where the resources of the soil are more than sufficient for the inhabitants,—a country of recent origin, not burdened with the worn-out institutions and clumsy lumber of past ages.—ought not to be satisfied to do *only* as well as countries which have to struggle against all these evils.

It is a poor defense for America to say to older countries, "We are no worse than you are." She ought to be infinitely better.

But it will appear that the institution of slavery has produced not only heathenish, degraded, miserable slaves, but it produces a class of white people who are, by universal admission, more heathenish, degraded, and miserable. The institution of slavery has accomplished the double feat, in America, not only of degrading and brutalizing her black working classes, but of producing, notwithstanding a fertile soil and abundant room, a poor white population as degraded and brutal as ever existed in any of the most crowded districts of Europe.

The way that it is done can be made apparent in a few words. 1. The distribution of the land into large plantations, and the consequent sparseness of settlement, make any system of common-school education impracticable. 2. The same cause operates with regard to the preaching of the gospel. 3. The degradation of the idea of labor, which results inevitably from enslaving the working class, operates to a great extent in preventing respectable working men of the middling classes from settling or remaining in slave states. Where carpenters, blacksmiths and masons, are advertised every week with their own tools, or in company with horses, hogs and other cattle, there is necessarily such an estimate of the laboring class that intelligent, self-respecting mechanics, such as abound in the free states, must find much that is annoying and disagreeable. They may endure it for a time, but with much uneasiness; and they are glad of the first opportunity of emigration.

Then, again, the filling up of all branches of mechanics and agriculture with slave labor necessarily depresses free labor. Suppose, now, a family of poor whites in Carolina or Virginia, and the same family in Vermont or Maine; how different the influences that come over them! In Vermont or Maine, the children have the means of education at hand in public schools, and they have all around them in society avenues of success that require only industry to make them available. The boys have their choice among all the different trades, for which the organization of free society makes a steady demand. The girls, animated by the spirit of the land in which they are born, think useful labor no disgrace, and find, with true female ingenuity, a hundred ways of adding to the family stock. If there be one member of a family in whom diviner gifts and higher longings seem a call for a more finished course of education, then cheerfully the whole family unites its productive industry to give that one the wider education which his wider genius demands; and thus have been given to the world such men as Roger Sherman and Daniel Webster.

But take this same family and plant them in South Carolina or Virginia—how different the result! No common school opens its doors to their children; the only church, perhaps, is fifteen miles off, over a bad road. The whole atmosphere of the country in which they are born associates degradation and slavery with useful labor; and the only standard of gentility is ability to live without work. What branch of useful labor opens a way to its sons? Would he be a blacksmith?—The planters around him prefer to *buy* their blacksmiths in Virginia. Would he be a carpenter?—Each planter in his neighborhood owns one or two now. And so coopers and masons. Would he be a shoemaker?—The plantation shoes are made in Lynn and Natick, towns of New England. In fact, between the free labor of the North and the slave labor of the South, there is nothing for a poor white to do. Without schools or churches, these miserable families grow up heathen on a Christian soil, in idleness, vice, dirt and discomfort of all sorts. They are the pest of the neighborhood, the scoff and contempt or pity even of the slaves. The expressive phrase, so common in the mouths of the negroes, of "poor white trash," says all for this luckless race of beings that can be said. From this class spring a tribe of keepers or small groggeries, and dealers, by a kind of contraband trade, with the negroes, in the stolen produce of plantations. Thriving and promising sons may perhaps hope to grow up into negro-traders, and thence be exalted into overseers of plantations. The utmost stretch of ambition is to compass money enough, by any of a variety of nondescript measures, to "buy a *nigger* or two," and begin to appear like other folks. Woe betide the unfortunate negro man or woman, carefully raised in some good religious family, when an execution or the death of their proprietors throws them into the market, and they are bought by a master and mistress of this class! Oftentimes the slave is infinitely the superior, in every respect,—in person, manners, education and morals; but, for all that, the law guards the despotic authority of the owner quite as jealously.

From all that would appear, in the case of Souther,[1] which we have recorded, he must have been one of this class. We have certain indications, in the evidence, that the two white witnesses, who spent the whole day in gaping, unresisting survey of his diabolical proceedings, were men of this order. It appears that the crime alleged against the poor victim was that of getting drunk and trading with these two very men, and that they were sent for probably by way of showing them "what a nigger would get by trading with them." This circumstance at once marks them out as belonging to that band of half-contraband traders who spring up among the mean whites, and occasional owners of slaves so much inconvenience by dealing with their hands. Can any words so forcibly show what sort of white men these are, as the idea of their standing in stupid, brutal curiosity, a whole day, as *witnesses* in such a hellish scene?

Conceive the misery of the slave who falls into the hands of such masters! A clergyman, now dead, communicated to the writer the following anecdote: In traveling in one of the Southern States, he put up for the night in a miserable log shanty, kept by a man of this class. All was dirt, discomfort and utter barbarism. The man, his wife, and their stock of wild, neglected children, drank whiskey, loafed and predominated over the miserable man and woman who did all the work and bore all the caprices of the whole establishment. He—the gentleman—was not long in discovering that these slaves were in person, language, and in every respect, superior to their owners; and all that he could get of comfort in this miserable abode was owing to their ministrations. Before he went away, they contrived to have a private interview, and begged him to buy them. They told him that they had been decently brought up in a respectable and refined family, and that their bondage was therefore the more inexpressibly galling. The poor creatures had waited on him with most assiduous care, tending his horse, brushing his boots, and anticipating all his wants, in the hope of inducing him to buy them. The clergyman said that he never so wished for money as when he saw the dejected visages with which they listened to his assurances that he was too poor to comply with their desires.

---

[1] Reference is to actual legal case of Simeon Souther, who was aided by two of his slaves in willfully whipping and torturing another slave to death in September 1849; he was indicted on fifteen counts of murder and sentenced to four years imprisonment by the Circuit Court of Hanover County, Virginia in October 1850. He moved for a new trial on manslaughter charges. Case was *Souther v. the Commonwealth.*

Souther's inhumane conduct toward his slave (named Sam) was reenacted through Stowe's fictional character, Simon Legree, whose Louisiana plantation slaves Sambo and Quimbo were accomplices in brutalizing Tom in *Uncle Tom's Cabin.*

This miserable class of whites form, in all the Southern States, a material for the most horrible and ferocious of mobs. Utterly ignorant, and inconceivably brutal, they are like some blind, savage monster, which, when aroused, tramples heedlessly over everything in its way.

Singular as it may appear, though slavery is the cause of the misery and degradation of this class, yet they are the most vehement and ferocious advocates of slavery.

The reason is this. They feel the scorn of the upper classes, and their only means of consolation is in having a class below them, whom they may scorn in turn. To set the negro at liberty would deprive them of this last comfort; and accordingly no class of men advocate slavery with such frantic and unreasoning violence, or hate abolitionists with such demoniac hatred. Let the reader conceive of a mob of men as brutal and callous as the two white witnesses of the Souther tragedy, led on by men like Souther himself, and he will have some idea of the materials which occur in the worst kind of Southern mobs.

The leaders of the community, those men who play on other men with as little care for them as a harper plays on a harp, keep this blind, furious monster of the MOB, very much as an overseer keeps plantation-dogs, as creatures to be set on to any man or thing whom they may choose to have put down.

These leading men have used the cry of *"abolitionism"* over the mob, much as a huntsman uses the "set on" to his dogs. Whenever they have a purpose to carry, a man to put down, they have only to raise this cry, and the monster is wide awake, ready to spring wherever they shall send him. . . .

GEORGE FITZHUGH

(1806–81)

Joining the pro-slavery outcries after publication of *Uncle Tom's Cabin* was George Fitzhugh, a Southern propagandist from Virginia. He considered fiction the domain of women and thought men better expressed ideas with facts and theories. He had already published a pamphlet, "Slavery Justified" (1849), and by the spring of 1854 he was a contributing editor to the *Richmond Examiner*, where he continued that influential newspaper's offensive against Northern abolitionists. Later that same year, he reprinted many of his articles in a book, *Sociology of the South; or, The Failure of Free Society*. Three years later, his second book, *Cannibals All! or, Slaves without Masters* appeared—its title and certain of its ideas borrowed from essays in *Latter Day Pamphlets* (1850), by Scottish-born prose writer Thomas Carlyle.

Fitzhugh's second book attacked labor practices of the industrial North, arguing that Northern exploitation of workers was worse than slavery "and little better than moral Cannibalism." His first book revived theories of Irish–born author Edmund Burke—an enemy of the French Revolution—who insisted the élite were best qualified to speak for the masses. He never abandoned his credo that "men are not born physically, morally or intellectually equal." But Fitzhugh thought the most expedient way for Southern planters to win solidarity with poor whites was to educate them, since the latter guarded Southern property, as militia and police.

Born into a once prosperous Virginia family that fell on hard times, Fitzhugh had no formal higher education, but he entered a legal apprenticeship and read enough political philosophy to be able to extrapolate ideas from European thinkers. He had his own sketchy interpretations of socialism, a word then bandied about on both sides of the Atlantic after publication of *The Communist Manifesto* (1848) by Karl Marx and Friedrich Engels. Fitzhugh ignored capitalistic exploitation in the plantation system and was one of the earliest Southerners to indict socialism in attacking Northern liberalism and industrialism. "Every abolitionist is either an agrarian, a socialist, an infidel" he wrote, "or in some way is trying to upset other institutions of society, as well as slavery in the South."

His polemical tracts brought irate reaction from Northern opponents of slavery such as Charles Sumner, a reformer and Senator from Massachusetts, who in a speech "The Barbarism of Slavery" in 1860 targeted George Fitzhugh as a purveyor of vigilante racial tensions in the South. When the Civil War broke out Fitzhugh was no secessionist, but he willingly worked in the Confederate Department of the Treasury, and two of his sons assisted Confederate troops. Following the war, he accepted Southern defeat and, in a paradox of his career, was appointed by the Freedmen's Bureau as a court associate to adjudicate labor cases for a year.

A race paternalist until his death in 1881, he was antagonistic to the idea of social equality during Racial Reconstruction, still believing as he had all his life that educating slaves was foolhardy and emancipating them amounted to class oppression rather than "true democracy" for all.

The following excerpt, in which he rationalizes slavery as a protective institution, comes from chapter 2 of *Sociology of the South*.

From *Sociology of the South* (1854)

. . . Slaves, too, have a valuable property in their masters. Abolitionists overlook this—overlook the protective influence of slavery, its distinguishing feature, and no doubt the cause of its origin and continuance, and abuse it as a mere engine of oppression. Infant negroes, sick, helpless, aged and infirm negroes, are simply a charge to their master; he has no property in them in the common sense of the term, for they are of no value for the time, but they have the most invaluable property in him. He is bound to support them, to supply all their wants, and relieve them of all care for the present or future. And well, and feelingly and faithfully does he discharge his duty. What a glorious thing to man is slavery, when want, misfortune, old age, debility and sickness overtake him. Free society, in its various forms of insurance, in its odd-fellow and temperance societies, in its social and communistic establishments, and in ten thousand other ways, is vainly attempting to attain this never-failing protective, caretaking and supporting feature of slavery. But it will blunder and flounder on in vain. It cannot put a heart and feeling into its societies and its corporations. God makes masters and gives them affections, feelings and interests that secure kindness to the sick, aged and dying slave. Man can never inspire his rickety institutions with those feelings, interests and affections. Say the Aboli-tionists—"Man ought not to have property in man." What a dreary, cold, bleak, inhospitable world this would be with such a doctrine carried into prac-tice. Men living to themselves, like owls and wolves and lions and birds and beasts of prey? No: "Love thy neighbor as thyself." And this can't be done till he has a property in your services as well as a place in your heart. *Homo sum, humani nihil a me alienum puto!* This, the noblest sentiment ever uttered by uninspired man, recognizes the great truth which lies at the foundation of all society—*that every man has property in his fellow man!* It is because that ade-quate provision is not made properly to enforce this great truth in free society, that men are driven to the necessity of attempting to remedy the defects of government by voluntary associations, that carry into definite and practical operation this great and glorious truth. It is because such defects do not exist in slave society, that we are not troubled with strikes, trade unions, phalansteries, communistic establishments, Mormonism, and the thousand other isms that deface and deform free society. . . .

WILLIAM GILMORE SIMMS

(1806–70)

The pro-slavery dogma in George Fitzhugh's nonfiction was echoed in the fiction of a contemporary from South Carolina: William Gilmore Simms, the most prolific Southern novelist, poet, essayist, and historian of the antebellum era.

Born and educated in Charleston, where he was reared in the modest home of a grandmother after his mother's death and father's departure to Mississippi, Simms was an avid reader who published his first book of verse at age nineteen and his first novel at twenty-seven. Self-taught in the law, he passed the bar and wrote for Southern periodicals. Proud of his Southern heritage, he justified plantation culture as a potentially "ideal" society, complete with chattel slaves—"so long as they remain the inferior beings which we find them now, and which they seem to have been from the beginning," he wrote in 1852—in an introduction to his essay, "The Morals of Slavery." That essay—initially a book review on Harriet Martineau—first appeared in 1837 in the *Southern Literary Messenger* and was reprinted in *The Pro-Slavery Argument as Maintained by the Most Distinguished Writers of the Southern States* (1852); the white supremacy attitude remained with Simms, who also wrote about Indians and frontiersmen, as well as merchants, planters, and slaves.

He aspired to be part of the wealthy mercantile-planter class he depicted in his fiction. His second marriage in 1836 brought his wish in the dowry of an eighteen-year-old bride whose family owned two plantations, numerous slaves, and a Charleston townhouse, satisfying his ambition for a life of ease, property, social and political influence, which he furthered by becoming a member of the state legislature.

He abhorred abolitionists as "annoyances" and "offenses" against the South's "peace and safety." He knew of the Denmark Vesey antislave conspiracy in Charleston in 1822, but as abolitionism heightened in the North, he defended his endangered South with increasing romanticism and nostalgia. His 1854 novel *Woodcraft; or, Hawks about the Dovecote: A Story of the South at the Close of the Revolution*, was the fourth in his series of seven novels on the colonial era; in it he pictured happy slaves loyal to their masters during the British occupation of Charleston in the Revolutionary War. First entitled

The Sword and the Distaff in an 1852 edition, the novel hid a reality that some slaves preferred to be kidnapped by Tories, who promised evacuation and freedom.

During the Civil War, Simms was a secessionist, whose fate was to lose all he cherished—including his wife, who died suddenly in 1863, after twenty-seven years of marriage and the birth of fifteen children, nine of whom they lost. By February 1865, when Charleston finally fell, Simms's favorite plantation, Woodlands, with his library of over ten thousand books, was burned to the ground by Sherman's army. It was the end of an era for a writer whose vision of a slavocracy never gave him foresight to see it was doomed. He lived five more years and wrote three more romances; his total canon was eighty-two books between 1825 and 1870.

The following excerpt is from a chapter of *Woodcraft*—"How a Supper May Take Away an Appetite"—in which an obedient slave, Tom, speaks in dialect, swearing loyalty to his "maussa" Captain Porgy, and overseer, Sargeant Millhouse.

From *Woodcraft; or, Hawks about the Dovecote: A Story of the South at the Close of the Revolution* (1854)

"Give you, Tom! Give you to anybody? No! no! old fellow! I will neither give you, nor sell you, nor suffer you to be taken from me in any way, by Saint Shadrach! who was your blessed father in the flesh, and from whom you inherit your peculiar genius for the kitchen! Nothing but death shall ever part us, and even death shall not if I can help it. When I die, you shall be buried with me. We have fought and fed too long together, Tom, and I trust we love each other quite too well, to submit to separation. When *your* kitchen fire grows cold, Tom, I shall cease to eat; and you, Tom, will not have breath enough to blow up the fire when mine is out! I shall fight for you to the last, Tom, and you, I know, would fight to the last for me, as I am very sure that neither of us can long outlast the other."

"Fight for you, maussa! Ha! Jes' le' dem tory try we, maussa!" responded Tom, quite excited, and shaking his head with a dire significance. But Tom did not exactly conceive the tenor of his master's speech, or the direction of his thoughts. He did not conjecture that the earnestness with which the latter spoke, had its origin in his recent meditations; and these had regard to civil rather than military dangers—to the claws of the sheriff, rather than tory weapons! Once on this track, Porgy found relief in continuing, and in making himself better understood.

"They shall take *none* of you negroes, if I can help it! But they shall take *all* before they touch a hair of your head, Tom!"

"Da's it, maussa! I know you nebber guine part wid Tom!"

"Before they shall tear you from me, Tom——"

"Day [they] can't begin to come it, maussa! I 'tick to you, maussa, so long as fire bu'n!"

"But, it might be, Tom; the time might come; circumstances might arise; events might happen; I might be absent, or unable; and then, you might fall into the clutches of some of these d——d harpies, who take a malignant pleasure in making people uncomfortable. You have heard, Tom, of such an animal as a sheriff, or sheriff's deputy?"

"Enty I know? He's a sort of warmint! I knows 'em well! He come into de henhouse, cut chicken t'roat, drink de blood, and suck all de eggs! I know 'em, for sartain! Da him?"

"Yes, they are bloodsuckers, and egg-suckers, and throat-cutters—that's true, Tom; vermin of the worst sort: but they still come in the shape of human beings. They are men after a fashion; men-weasels, verily, and they do the work of beasts! You will know them by their sly looks; their skulkings, peepings, watchings, and the snares they lay; by the great papers, with great seals, that they carry; and by their calling themselves sheriffs or constables, and speaking big about justice and the law. If any of you negroes happen to see any such lurking about the plantation, or within five miles, let me know. Don't let them lay hands on you, but make for the swamp, the moment they tell you 'stop.' You, Tom, in particular, beware of all such! Should they succeed in taking you, Tom—should I not be able to help you—should you find them carrying you off to the city or elsewhere, to sell you to some other master——"

"Gor-a-mighty! maussa, wha' for you scare me so, t'inking ob sich t'ings?"

"Tom! sooner than have you taken off by these vermin, I will shoot you!"

"Me! shoot me! me, Tom! Shoot me, maussa!"

"Yes, Tom! you shall never leave me. I will put a brace of bullets through your abdomen, Tom, sooner than lose you! But, it may be, that I shall not have the opportunity. They may take advantage of my absence—they may *steal* you away—coming on you by surprise. If they should do so, Tom, I rely upon you to put *yourself* to death, sooner than abandon me and become the slave of another. Kill yourself, Tom, rather than let them carry you off. Put your knife into your ribs, anywhere, three inches deep, and you will effectually baffle the bloodhounds!"

"Wha', me, maussa! kill mese'f! Me, Tom! 'Tick knife t'ree inch in me rib, and dead! Nebber, in dis worl' [world] maussa! I no want for dead! I always good for cook! I good for fight—good for heap o' t'ing in dis life! No good 'nough for dead, maussa! No want for dead so long as der's plenty ob bile, and brile, and bake, and fry, for go sleep . . . Don't talk ob sich t'ing, maussa, jis' now, when de time is 'mos [almost] come for me eat supper!"

"Tom!" exclaimed the captain of partisans, laying down his knife and fork, and looking solemnly and sternly at the negro—"I thought you were more of a man—that you had more affection for me. Is it possible that you could wish to live, if separated from me? Impossible, Tom! I will never believe it. No, boy, you shall never leave me. We shall never part. You shall be my cook, after death, in future worlds, even as you are here. Should you suffer yourself to survive me, Tom—should you be so hard-hearted—I will haunt you at mealtime always. Breakfast, dinner, supper—at every meal—you shall hear my voice. I will sit before you as soon as the broil is ready, and you shall always help me first!"

The negro looked aghast. Porgy nodded his head solemnly.

"Remember! It shall be as I have said. If you are not prepared to bury yourself in the same grave with me when I die, I shall be with you in spirit, if not in flesh; and I shall make you cook for me as now. At breakfast you will hear me call out for ham and eggs, or a steak; at dinner, perhaps, for a terrapin stew; at supper, Tom—when all is dark and dreary, and there is nobody but yourself beside the fire—I shall cry out, at your elbow, 'My coffee, Tom!' in a voice that shall shake the very house!"

"Oh, maussa! nebber say sich t'ing! Ef you promise sich t'ing, you hab for come!"

"To be sure;—so you see what you have to expect if you dare to survive me?"

Tom turned gloomily to the fire, not a little bewildered. The bravest negro is the slave of superstitious fancies, and Tom was a devout believer in ghosts, and quite famous in the kitchen for his own ghost experience.

"But to your own supper now, with what appetite you may, and see that you feed the other negroes. I see that *we* have all supped."

"Lor'-a-mighty, maussa, you tek' 'way all me appetite for supper."

"You will soon enough find it, I fancy," quoth Porgy, coolly, as he lighted his pipe. Millhouse followed the example, and, accompanied by Lieutenant Frampton, the two adjourned to the piazza, leaving the field to the negroes, who, at a given signal, rushed eagerly in to the feast. . . .

MARTIN ROBISON DELANY

(1812–85)

The Confederate William Gilmore Simms is not known to have crossed the Charleston path of a veteran abolitionist there at the end of the war: *Major* Martin Delany—the first commissioned black officer in the Union Army. Delany, then almost fifty-three-years old, had already distinguished himself as an author, medical doctor, antislavery orator, newspaper editor, and international explorer when he began recruiting freedom for the 104th and 105th Regiment of Colored Troops in South Carolina. In early February 1865, he had gone to Abraham Lincoln and said: "I propose, sir, an army of blacks commanded entirely of black officers, except such whites as may volunteer to serve . . . to penetrate through the heart of the South, and make conquests, with the banner of Emancipation unfurled, proclaiming freedom as they go. . . ."

Two months later, before Delany's troops had a chance to fire a shot, Richmond fell on April 2; General Robert E. Lee surrendered at Appomattox Court House April 9, and Lincoln was assassinated less than week later, ending a painful war to save the Union. For Delany and his occupation forces in Charleston, another battle was just beginning. In June 1865, he was abruptly transferred to Beaufort, South Carolina, and the Sea Islands, by a War Department then under President Andrew Johnson, who in May 1865 issued amnesty to white rebels—returning lands to them earlier granted to freedmen under an order of Union General W. T. Sherman.

Delany would stay in South Carolina, on and off, for over fourteen years: the first three-and-a-half under military command as subassistant commissioner in the Freedmen's Bureau, to aid newly freed slaves. When Andrew Johnson vetoed continuation of the Bureau after one year, Delany saw race tensions rising from feudal peonage instituted by some white landowners. He reentered civilian life in late 1868 and left South Carolina to rejoin his family in Xenia, Ohio, hoping the newly elected President Ulysses Grant might appoint him minister to Liberia, which he had visited while exploring the Niger Valley in 1859–60. When Grant ignored his overtures on Liberia, Delany answered pleas from black South Carolinians and returned in 1870 to Charleston, where he spent the next decade in a variety of political and nonpolitical roles, striving to maintain meager postwar gains. Despised by some white and black Southerners for his boldness, resiliency, candor, and self-reliance, he was nevertheless generally recognized for integrity in trying to accommodate both races during Radical Reconstruction.

But after a decade of dissent from machine politics, Northern influences, and ex-secessionists who were determined that so-called states rights could nullify black enfranchisement, a weary Delany left the state in 1880, still contemplating a move to Africa. He traveled North to lecture on his final book, *Principia of Ethnology: The Origin of Races with an Archeological Compendium of Ethiopian and Egyptian Civilization*, published in 1879—six years before he died in ill health at age seventy-three.

His South Carolina experience was not the first disappointment or challenge in a long, varied, and volatile career, which began in the Northeast. He once had been disappointed but resilient when the Harvard Medical School allowed him to complete only one term after white students protested his admission there in 1850. Having begun his first medical apprenticeship in 1833 in the office of a white physician in Pittsburgh, he would continue the study and practice of medicine as one of his life-long occupations. In the summer of 1839, he made his first journey South to investigate conditions among slaves in Mississippi, Louisiana, and Texas. The trip inspired notes for his first and only novel—*Blake; or, The Huts of America, a Tale of the Mississippi Valley, the Southern United States, and Cuba*, written and published serially during the 1850s. In 1843, he had launched a weekly abolitionist newspaper, the *Mystery*—with no previous experience as editor–publisher. His paper lasted five years, attracted the attention of Frederick Douglass, and widened Delany's influence. For several months, until June 1848, he co-edited the *North Star* with Douglass, before revenues failed to support two editors. By the early 1850s, both men quarreled on the emigration issue, after Delany advocated emigration in two controversial works: *The Condition, Elevation, and Destiny of the Colored People of the United States Politically Considered* (1852) and *Political Destiny of the Colored Race on the American Continent*—a report to a Cleveland Emigration Convention (1854).

Between his intermittent travels, Pittsburgh was his home for twenty-five years. There he married in 1843 and kept a residence until February 1856, when he emigrated with his growing family to Chatham, Canada West—the fugitive slave capital of Canada. He practiced medicine and continued abolitionist organizing there until the spring of 1859, when he undertook a nine-month exploratory tour of West Africa, where he hoped to establish a new self-governing colony. One of the first men to explore the Niger River Valley, his *Official Report of the Niger Valley Exploring Party* was published in 1861. Upon returning to the United States that year, he urged his people to emigrate but halted that plan after the Emancipation Proclamation. He then began officially recruiting for the Union's black military units. His attitute on emigration to Africa moved in cycles throughout his career, depending upon the American political climate. Both restlessness and brilliance characterized the actions of Delany, whose energy was as boundless as his hopes and plans.

Born free in Charles Town, Virginia (now West Virginia), the son of a slave and a free woman of color, who took her children to Chambersburg, Pennsylvania, for their early education, Delany was proud to be as "black as a full-blooded African." He boasted paternal descent from a Mandingo prince and named his six sons for black heroes, and his only daughter Ethiopia. Designated by some twentieth-century historians as America's first "black nationalist," he can also be credited as its first black *internationalist*. No one until W. E. B. Du Bois (1868–1963) went as far in vision or prophecy about the onslaught of Western imperialism on colored peoples of the world. Delany's prophetic outlook on that issue in the mid-nineteenth century is shown in the following excerpt.

From *The Political Destiny of the Colored Race* (1854)

. . . The truth is, we are not identical with the Anglo-Saxon, or any other race of the Caucasian or pure white type of the human family, and the sooner we know and acknowledge this truth the better for ourselves and posterity.

The English, French, Irish, German, Italian, Turk, Persian, Greek, Jew, and all other races, have their native or inherent peculiarities, and why not our race? We are not willing, therefore, at all times and under all circumstances to be moulded into various shapes of eccentricity, to suit the caprices and conveniences of every kind of people. We are not more suitable to everybody than everybody is suitable to us; therefore, no more like other people than others are like us.

We have, then, inherent traits, attributes, so to speak, and native characteristics, peculiar to our race, whether pure or mixed blood; and all that is required of us is to cultivate these, and develop them in their purity, to make them desirable and emulated by the rest of the world.

That the colored races have the highest traits of civilization, will not be disputed. They are civil, peaceable, and religious to a fault. In mathematics,

sculpture and architecture, as arts and sciences, commerce and internal im-
provements as enterprises, the white race may probably excel; but in languages,
oratory, poetry, music, and painting, as arts and sciences, and in ethics, metaphysics, theology, and legal jurisprudence—in plain language, in the true principles of morals, correctness of thought, religion, and law or civil government,
there is no doubt but the black race will yet instruct the world.

It would be duplicity longer to disguise the fact that the great issue, sooner
or later, upon which must be disputed the world's destiny, will be a question
of black and white, and every individual will be called upon for his identity
with one or the other. The blacks and colored races are four-sixths of all the
population of the world; and these people are fast tending to a common cause
with each other. The white races are but one-third of the population of the
globe—or one of them to two of us—and it cannot much longer continue that
two-thirds will passively submit to the universal domination of this one-third.
And it is notorious that the only progress made in territorial domain, in the
last three centuries, by the whites, has been a usurpation and encroachment
on the rights and native soil of some of the colored races.

The East Indies, Java, Sumatra, the Azores, Madeira, Canary, and Cape
Verde Islands; Socotra, Guardifui, and the Isle of France; Algiers, Tunis, Tripoli,
Barca, and Egypt in the North, Sierra Leone in the West, and Cape Colony in
the South of Africa; besides many other islands and possessions not herein
named; Australia, the Ladrone Islands, together with many others of Oceanica;
the seizure and appropriation of a great portion of the Western Continent,
with all its islands, were so many encroachments of the whites upon the rights
of the colored races. Nor are they yet content, but, intoxicated with the success
of their career, the Sandwich Islands are now marked out as the next booty to
be seized in the ravages of their exterminating crusade.

We regret the necessity of stating the fact, but duty compels us to the task,
that, for more than two thousand years, the determined aim of the whites has
been to crush the colored races wherever found. With a determined will they
have sought and pursued them in every quarter of the globe. The Anglo-Saxon
has taken the lead in this work of universal subjugation. But the Anglo-American stands preeminent for deeds of injustice and acts of oppression, unparalleled, perhaps, in the annals of modern history.

We admit the existence of great and good people in America, England,
France, and the rest of Europe, who desire a unity of interests among the whole
human family, of whatever origin or race.

But it is neither the moralist, Christian, nor philanthropist whom we now
have to meet and combat, but the politician, the civil engineer, and skillful
economist, who direct and control the machinery which moves forward, with

mighty impulse, the nations and powers of the earth. We must, therefore, if possible, meet them on vantage ground, or, at least, with adequate means for the conflict.

Should we encounter an enemy with artillery, a prayer will not stay the cannon shot, neither will the kind words nor smiles of philanthropy shield his spear from piercing us through the heart. We must meet mankind, then, as they meet us—prepared for the worst, though we may hope for the best. Our submission does not gain for us an increase of friends nor respectability, as the white race will only respect those who oppose their usurpation, and acknowledge as equals those who will not submit to their oppression. This may be no new discovery in political economy, but it certainly is a subject worthy the consideration of the black race.

After a due consideration of these facts, as herein recounted, shall we stand still and continue inactive—the passive observers of the great events of the times and age in which we live; submitting indifferently to the usurpation by the white race of every right belonging to the blacks? Shall the last vestige of an opportunity, outside of the continent of Africa, for the national development of our race, be permitted, in consequence of our slothfulness, to elude our grasp, and fall into the possession of the whites? This, may Heaven forbid. May the sturdy, intelligent Africo-American sons of the Western Continent forbid.

Longer to remain inactive, it should be borne in mind, may be to give an opportunity to dispoil us of every right and possession sacred to our existence, with which God has endowed us as a heritage on the earth. For let it not be forgotten that the white race—who numbers but *one* of them to *two* of us—originally located in Europe, besides possessing all of that continent, have now got hold of a large portion of Asia, Africa, all North America, a portion of South America, and all of the great islands of both hemispheres, except Paupau, or New Guinea, inhabited by negroes and Malays, in Oceanica; the Japanese Islands, peopled and ruled by the Japanese; Madagascar, peopled by negroes, near the coast of Africa; and the Island of Hayti, in the West Indies, peopled by as brave and noble descendants of Africa as they who laid the foundation of Thebias, or constructed the everlasting pyramids and catacombs of Egypt—a people who have freed themselves by the might of their own will, the force of their own power, the unfailing strength of their own right arms, and their unflinching determination to be free.

Let us, then, not survive the disgrace and ordeal of Almighty displeasure, of two to one, witnessing the universal possession and control by the whites of every habitable portion of the earth. For such must inevitably be the case, and that, too, at no distant day, if black men do not take advantage of the opportunity, by grasping hold of those places where chance is in their favor, and establishing the rights and power of the colored race.

We must make an issue, create an event, and establish for ourselves a position. This is essentially necessary for our effective elevation as a people, in shaping our national development, directing our destiny, and redeeming ourselves as a race. . . .

WILLIAM WELLS BROWN

(ca. 1816–84)

Like his contemporary Martin Delany, William Wells Brown was an abolitionist, author, orator, reformer—and, later in life, a physician. He was the first Afro-American to publish a book of foreign travels, a full-length drama, a compilation of slave songs, and among the first to publish a slave narrative, a novel, and several volumes of history.

Born the slave of a physician named John Young on a farm near Lexington, Kentucky, he had a mother who was a mulatto and a father who was a slave-holder as well as a blood relation of Young. In infancy he was taken as property of the John Young family to Missouri. There he grew up in the vicinity of St. Louis, where he worked as errand boy in Young's medical office and was "hired out" for various jobs to a succession of employers. Among them was Elijah P. Lovejoy, then a St. Louis editor, but later the first white American martyr to die in the antislavery cause.[1] Brown's slave narrative later credited Lovejoy as more humane than others, for as a boy he was mistreated by Mrs. Young, who resented her husband's quadroon kin, and he was abused by white men scornful that he could pass for white. Rejected also by black bondsmen, he would be the first Afro-American male author to fictionalize from experience the precarious existence of slaves of mixed blood.

Twice he tried to escape North—the first time with his mother, whom he encouraged to join him. Both were captured and she was immediately sold. He was bartered a few years later to a merchant, whom he often accompanied as servant on steamboat trips to Ohio—a free state. He escaped to freedom in Cincinnati, when they disembarked on New Year's Day, 1834. While traveling North as a fugitive, he adopted the name Wells Brown from a Quaker who saved him from cold and hunger. With a middle and surname, but no certain birth date—which he thought March 1815 or 1816—he set off to begin a new

---

[1] Elijah P. Lovejoy (1802–37), though not an active abolitionist, published antislavery editorials that caused mobs to destroy his printing press, first in St. Louis and later in nearby Alton, Illinois, where he was shot on November 1, 1837, defending his newspaper, the *Observer*, from a violent attack, which also killed two other men.

life in Cleveland. There he married, worked on Lake Erie steamboats, and became a father, before settling in Buffalo in 1836.

During nearly a decade in Buffalo, he educated himself, helped rear two young daughters, assisted slaves to Canada on the Underground Railroad, and lectured for the Western New York Anti-Slavery Society. Separated from his wife in 1847, he moved that year to Boston, joined William Lloyd Garrison and Wendell Philipps as an abolitionist lecturer, and published his first two major works: A *Lecture in Massachusetts Delivered before the Female Anti-Slavery Society at Salem Hall,* and an autobiography, *Narrative of William W. Brown, Fugitive Slave.* His *Narrative* had sold 10,000 copies in four American editions by 1849—a year in which he went abroad to stir antislavery advocates in Britain and address the International Peace Congress in Paris and Versailles.

During extended travels in France and the British Isles, he delivered numerous speeches, after the Fugitive Slave Act of 1850 caused him to postpone a return to the United States. Like Frederick Douglass before him, he risked capture on arrival for not being legally manumitted. And, like Douglass, his liberty was purchased by English friends. Free by 1854, he was the author of several new books published in London, a man transformed after nearly five years in Europe, where he met intellectuals such as Alexis de Tocqueville and Harriet Martineau, who had witnessed slavery in America. One of his London speeches, delivered at the Metropolitan Atheneum in May 1854—and seven months later in Philadelphia—was "St. Domingo: Its Revolutions and Its Patriots," which argued that the forceful overthrow of the French by slaves in St. Domingo (Haiti) led to Haitian independence in 1804, and was thus a paradigm for slaves in 1850s America. Brown's new call for more precipitous action by slaves marked a departure from the moral-suasion footsteps of Garrison and Phillips. Brown's metamorphosis was evident also in letters he sent from abroad to *Frederick Douglass' Paper*—most of which appeared in his 1852 travelogue, *Three Years in Europe; or, Places I Have Seen and People I Have Met.* Its final chapter hinted at his polemical novel published in England a year later: *Clotel; or, the President's Daughter: A Narrative of Slave Life in the United States.* In 1853 it was the first known novel written by an Afro-American abroad, but not the first published by an Afro-American in the United States.[2]

The 1853 version of *Clotel* caused none of the public controversy of Stowe's *Uncle Tom's Cabin* a year earlier, even though *Clotel* contained certain taboos

---

[2] It is believed that the first novel by an Afro-American published in the United States was *Our Nig; or, Sketches from the Life of a Free Black* . . . , written by Harriet E. Wilson, who printed it privately in Boston in 1859. Wilson had no known links to the abolitionist movement; her sentimental narrative condemned racism in the North and addressed a marginal black audience, but undoubtedly alienated a white Northern readership during the antebellum period. The novel was not reprinted until 1983.

that resulted in a suppression of the 1853 edition in America until 1969. The "President" in Brown's narrative was Thomas Jefferson, whose speeches were quoted, and whose fictional mulatto slave daughter was Clotel. After Brown's return to Boston in 1855, a serialization showed up in a (now lost) New York periodical: *Miralda; or, The Beautiful Quadroon, a Romance of American Slavery, Founded on Fact*. Nearly a decade later, in a less polemical American edition of 1864, Brown substituted an unnamed senator for Jefferson and altered the spelling of the heroine's name: *Clotelle: A Tale of Southern States* (1864). Yet another version was *Clotelle; or, the Southern Heroine: a Tale of the Southern States* (1867). Recurring patterns appear in Brown's antislavery fiction, nonfiction, and drama, including two extant plays written in 1856: *Experience; or, How to Give a Northern Man a Background*, and *The Escape; or, A Leap For Freedom*. The latter, by 1858, was the first drama in print by an Afro-American playwright.

During the Civil War, Brown resided in Boston and traveled to recruit black freemen for the Massachusetts Fifty-Fourth Regiment. He also apprenticed himself to a physician to study medicine, which led to a brief medical practice after the war. His writing continued with several groundbreaking books on Negro history: *The Black Man, His Antecedents, His Genius, and His Achievements*, followed by *The Negro in the American Rebellion: His Heroism and His Fidelity* (1867), and *The Rising Son; or, the Antecedents and Advancement of the Colored Race* (1874). His final book, in 1880—four years before his death— was *My Southern Home; or, The South and Its People*, sketches and reminiscences written after he toured several former slave states.

The following is taken from the American edition of his European travelogue, with the title and text emended for Boston publication in 1855.

From *Sketches of Places and People Abroad:*
The American Fugitive in Europe (1854)

. . . Most of the time I had resided in London. Its streets, parks, public buildings and its fog, had become "as familiar as household words." I had heard the deep, bass voice of the Bishop of London, in St. Paul's Cathedral. I had sat in Westminster Abbey, until I had lost all interest in the services, and then wandered about amongst the monuments, reading the epitaphs placed over the dead. Like others, I had been locked in the Temple Church, and compelled to wait till service was over, whether I liked it or not. I had spent days in the British Museum and National Gallery, and in all these I had been treated as a man. The "negro pew," which I had seen in the churches of America, was not to be found in the churches of London. There, too, were my daughters. They who had been denied education upon equal terms with children of a fairer complexion, in the United States, had been received in the London schools upon terms of perfect equality. They had accompanied me to most of the noted places in the metropolis. We had strolled through Regent Street, the Strand, Piccadilly and Oxford Street, so often, that sorrow came over me as the thought occurred to me that I should never behold them again.

Then the English manner of calling on friends before one's departure. I can meet an enemy with pleasure, but it is with regret that I part with a friend. As the time for me to leave drew near, I felt more clearly my identity with the English people. By and by the last hour arrived that I was to spend in London. The cab stood at the door, with my trunks on its top; and, bidding the household good-bye, I entered the vehicle, the driver raised his whip, and I looked for the last time on my old home in Cecil Street. As we turned into the Strand, Nelson's monument, in Trafalgar Square, greeted me on the left, and Somerset House on the right. I took a farewell look at Covent Garden Market, through whose walks I had often passed, and where I had spent many pleasant hours. My youngest daughter was in France, but the eldest met me at the depot, and after a few moments the bell rang, and away we went.

As the train was leaving the great metropolis of the world behind, I caught a last view of the dome of St. Paul's, and the old pile of Westminster Abbey.

In every town through which we passed on our way to Liverpool I could call to mind the name of some one whose acquaintance I had made, and whose hospitality I had shared. The steamer *City of Manchester* had her fires kindled when we arrived, and we went immediately on board. We found one hundred and seventy-five passengers in the cabin, and above five hundred in the steerage. After some delay, the ship weighed anchor, the machinery was put in motion, and, bidding Liverpool a long farewell, the vessel moved down the Mersey, and was in a short time out at sea. . . .

. . . .

After a long passage of twenty days we arrived at the mouth of the Delaware, and took a pilot on board. The passengers were now all life; the Irish were basking in the sun, the Germans were singing, and the Gypsies were dancing. Some fifteen miles below Philadelphia, the officers came on board, to see that no sickness was on the vessel; and, after being passed by the doctors, each person began to get his luggage on deck, and prepare to go on shore. About four o'clock, on the twenty-sixth day of September, 1854, the *City of Manchester* hauled alongside the Philadelphia wharf, and the passengers all on the move. . . .

At Philadelphia I met with a most cordial reception at the hands of the Motts,[3] J. M. M'Kim,[4] the Stills,[5] the Fortens,[6] and that distinguished gentleman and friend of the slave, Robert Purvis, Esq.[7] There is no colored man in this country to whom the antislavery cause is more indebted than to Mr. Purvis. Endowed with a capacious and reflective mind, he is ever in search after truth; and, consequently, all reforms find in him an able and devoted advocate. Inheriting a large fortune, he has had the means, as well as the will, to do good. Few men in this country, either colored or white, possess the rare accomplishments of Robert Purvis. In no city in the Free States does the antislavery movement have more bitter opponents than in Philadelphia. Close to two of our Southern States, and connected as it is in a commercial point of view, it could scarcely be otherwise. Colorphobia is more rampant there than in the proslavery, negro-hating city of New York. I was not destined to escape this unnatural and anti-Christian prejudice. While walking through Chestnut Street, in company with two of my fellow passengers, we hailed an omnibus going in the direction which we wished to go. It immediately stopped, and the white men were furnished with seats, but I was told that "We don't allow niggers to ride in here." It so happened that these two persons had rode in the same car with me from London to Liverpool. We had put up at the same hotel at the latter place, and had crossed the Atlantic in the same steamer. But as soon as we touch the soil of America we can no longer ride in the same conveyance, no longer eat at the same table, or be regarded with equal justice, by our thin-skinned democracy. During five years' residence in monarchical Europe I had enjoyed the rights allowed to all foreigners in the countries through which I passed; but on returning to my NATIVE LAND the influence of slavery meets me the first day that I am in the country. Had I been an escaped felon, like John Mitchell, no one would have questioned my right to a seat in a Philadelphia omnibus. Neither of the foreigners who were allowed to ride in this carriage had ever visited our country

---

[3] Family of Lucretia Coffin Mott (1793–1880) feminist and Quaker abolitionist; a founder of Philadelphia Female Antislavery Society; unseated U.S. female delegate to 1840 World Anti-Slavery Convention in London; co-organizer with Elizabeth Cady Stanton of First Women's Rights Convention in 1848 at Seneca Falls, New York.

[4] James Miller McKim (1810–74) Pennsylvania abolitionist lecturer; member of American Anti-Slavery Society; theologian whose liberal activities forced his resignation from Presbyterian ministry; coeditor of *Pennsylvania Freeman*; and later cofounder of *The Nation* in 1865.

[5] William Still (1821–1902) black freeman, clerk in office of Philadelphia Society for Abolition of Slavery, where his involvement in aiding fugitive slaves led him to keep records later published as *The Underground Railroad* (1872).

[6] See entry on Charlotte L. Forten Grimké, pages 268–71 below.

[7] See entry on Robert Purvis, pages 227–31, below.

before. The constitution of these United States was as a blank to them; the Declaration of Independence, in all probability, they had never seen,—much less, read. But what mattered it? They were white, and that was enough. The fact of my being an American by birth could not be denied; that I had read and understood the constitution and laws, the most proslavery, negro-hating professor of Christianity would admit; but I was colored, and that was enough. I had partaken of the hospitality of noblemen in England, had sat at the table of the French Minister of Foreign Affairs; I had looked from the strangers' gallery down upon the great legislators of England, as they sat in the House of Commons; I had stood in the House of Lords, when Her Britannic Majesty prorogued her Parliament; I had eaten at the same table with Sir Edward Bulwer-Lytton, Charles Dickens, Eliza Cook, Alfred Tennyson, and the son-in-law of Sir Walter Scott: the omnibuses of Paris, Edinburgh, Glasgow and Liverpool, had stopped to take me up; I had often entered the "Caledonia," "Bayswater," "Hammersmith," "Chelsea," "Bluebell," and other omnibuses that rattle over the pavements of Regent Street, Cheapside, and the west end of London,—but what mattered that? My face was not white, my hair was not straight; and, therefore, I must be excluded from a seat in a third-rate American omnibus. Slavery demanded that it should be so. I charge this prejudice to the proslavery pulpits of our land, which first set the example of proscription by erecting in their churches the "negro pew." I charge it to that hypocritical profession of democracy which will welcome fugitives from other countries, and drive its own into exile. I charge it to the recreant sons of the men who carried on the American revolutionary war, and who come together every fourth of July to boast of what their fathers did, while they, their sons, have become associated with bloodhounds, to be put at any moment on the track of the fugitive slave.

But I had returned to the country for the express purpose of joining in the glorious battle against slavery, of which this Negrophobia is a legitimate offspring. And why not meet it in its stronghold? I might have remained in a country where my manhood was never denied; I might have remained in ease in other climes; but what was ease and comfort abroad, while more than three millions of my countrymen were groaning in the prison house of slavery in the Southern States? Yes, I came back to the land of my nativity, not to be a spectator, but a soldier—a soldier in this moral warfare against the most cruel system of oppression that ever blackened the character or hardened the heart of man. And the smiles of my old associates, and the approval of my course while abroad by my colored fellow citizens, has amply compensated me for the twenty days' rough passage on my return.

WILLIAM COOPER NELL

(ca. 1814–74)

One of the contemporaries of William Wells Brown in Boston was the abolitionist lecturer, journalist, editor, and historian William Cooper Nell. His writings on the history of colored soldiers in early American wars became a blueprint for Brown's books on the subject over a decade later.

Nell's 1851 pamphlet, "The Services of Colored Americans in the Wars of 1776 and 1812," argued that his people deserved equal rights for their heroism shown in wars of national independence. Four years later, in a more comprehensive study, *The Colored Patriots of the American Revolution* (1855), he gained wider attention with an introduction by Harriet Beecher Stowe, who was then a household name. The book's success led him to initiate the first Crispus Attucks Day—March 5, 1858, in honor of the first man of African descent to fall in the Boston Massacre against the British in 1770. Some influential whites opposed the commemoration, but Nell found formidable allies such as the Harvard-educated lawyer and reformer, Wendell Phillips, who joined him at Boston's Faneuil Hall to inaugurate the event in 1858.

Better known for his writings on military history than for his antislavery activities and political oratory in his day, Nell ran unsuccessfully in 1850 for the Massachusetts legislature as a Free Soil Party candidate. By then, he was in open conflict with Frederick Douglass, although they had worked together on the *North Star*, before Douglass broke with Nell's editorial mentor, William Lloyd Garrison.

As journalist and abolitionist, Nell's ideological position was counterpoint to certain other black antislavery strategists of his generation—especially those who urged slave rebellions or racial identity with Africa. A zealous integrationist and assimilationist, his primary interest was in swaying unconverted whites toward recognition of the achievements and worthiness of blacks for freedom and citizenship. Faced with paternalistic prejudices of even well-intentioned white Boston abolitionists, such as the Unitarian minister Theodore Parker (1810–60), who once told an antislavery audience, "the African is the most docile and pliant of all the races of men," Nell felt a moral duty to impose a different message. In editorials and speeches, he waged a campaign against the

American Colonization Society, the Fugitive Slave Law of 1850, and the Dred Scott Decision of the Supreme Court in 1857.

Born free and educated in Boston but denied academic honors because of racial discrimination, he made equal educational opportunity and desegregation of Boston schools a banner issue of his early career. Later one of the first men of color appointed to a federal job, he held the position of postal clerk of Boston, from the outbreak of the Civil War until his death of a stroke in 1874. At his funeral he was eulogized by William Lloyd Garrison, in whose *Liberator* Nell had published his earliest articles.

The following excerpt on Crispus Attucks is from chapter 1 of *The Colored Patriots of the American Revolution*.

From *The Colored Patriots of the American Revolution* (1855)

On the 5th of March, 1851, the following petition was presented to the Massachusetts Legislature, asking an appropriation of $1,500, for the erection of a monument to the memory of CRISPUS ATTUCKS, the first martyr in the Boston Massacre of March 5th, 1770:—

To the Honorable the Senate and House of Representatives
of the State of Massachusetts, in General Court assembled:

The undersigned, citizens of Boston, respectfully ask that an appropriation of fifteen hundred dollars may be made by your Honorable Body, for a monument to be erected to the memory of CRISPUS ATTUCKS, the first martyr of the American Revolution.

> WILLIAM C. NELL,
> CHARLES LENOX REMOND,
> HENRY WEEDEN,
> LEWIS HAYDEN,
> FREDERICK G. BARBADOES,
> JOSHUA B. SMITH,
> LEMUEL BURR.

BOSTON, Feb. 22d, 1851.

This petition was referred to the Committee on Military Affairs, who granted a hearing to the petitioners, in whose behalf appeared Wendell Phillips, Esq., and William C. Nell, but finally submitted an adverse report, on the ground that a boy, Christopher Snyder, was previously killed. Admitting this fact, (which was the result of a very different scene from that in which Attucks fell), it does not offset the claims of Attucks, and those who made the 5th of March famous in our annals—the day which history selects as the dawn of the American Revolution.

Botta's History, and Hewes's Reminiscences (the tea party survivor), establish the fact that the colored man, ATTUCKS, was *of* and *with* the people, and was never regarded otherwise.

Botta, in speaking of the scenes of the 5th of March, says:—"The people were greatly exasperated. The multitude ran towards King Street, crying, *"Let us drive out these ribalds; they have no business here!"* The rioters rushed furiously towards the Custom House; "they approached the sentinel, crying, *"Kill him, kill him!"* They assaulted him with snowballs, pieces of ice, and whatever they could lay their hands upon. The guard were then called, and, in marching to the Custom House, "they encountered," continues Botta, "a band of the populace, led by a mulatto named ATTUCKS, who brandished their clubs, and pelted them with snowballs. The maledictions, the imprecations, the execrations of the multitude, were horrible. In the midst of a torrent of invective from every quarter, the military were challenged to fire. The populace advanced to the points of their bayonets. The soldiers appeared like statues; the cries, the howlings, the menaces, the violent din of bells still sounding the alarm, increased the confusion and the horrors of these moments; at length, the mulatto and twelve of his companions, pressing forward, environed the soldiers, and striking their muskets with their clubs, cried to the multitude: *"Be not afraid; they dare not fire: why do you hesitate, why do you not kill them, why not crush them at once?"* The mulatto lifted his arm against Capt. Preston, and having turned one of the muskets, he seized the bayonet with his left hand, as if he intended to execute his threat. At this moment, confused cries were heard: *"The wretches dare not fire!"* Firing succeeds. ATTUCKS is slain. The other discharges follow. Three were killed, five severely wounded, and several others slightly."

ATTUCKS had formed the patriots in Dock Square, from whence they marched up King Street, passing through the street up to the main guard, in order to make the attack.

ATTUCKS was killed by Montgomery, one of Capt. Preston's soldiers. He had been foremost in resisting, and was first slain. As proof of a front engagement, he received two balls, one in each breast.

John Adams, counsel for the soldiers, admitted that ATTUCKS appeared to have undertaken to be the hero of the night, and to lead the people. He and Caldwell, not being residents of Boston, were both buried from Faneuil Hall. The citizens generally participated in the solemnities.

The *Boston Transcript* of March 7, 1851, published an anonymous communication, disparaging the whole affair; denouncing CRISPUS ATTUCKS as a very firebrand of disorder and sedition, the most conspicuous, inflammatory, and uproarious of the misguided populace, and who, if he had not fallen a martyr, would richly have deserved hanging as an incendiary.[1] If the leader, ATTUCKS, deserved the epithets above applied, is it not a legitimate inference, that the citizens who followed on are included, and hence should swing in his company on the gallows? If the leader and his patriot band were *misguided*, the distinguished orators who, in after days, commemorated the 5th of March, must, indeed, have been misguided, and with them, the masses who were inspired by their eloquence; for John Hancock, in 1774, invokes the injured shades of *Maverick, Gray, Caldwell,* ATTUCKS, *Carr*; and Judge Dawes, in 1775, thus alludes to the band of "misguided incendiaries":—"The provocation of that night must be numbered among the master-springs which gave the first motion to a vast machinery,—a noble and comprehensive system of national independence."

Ramsay's *History of the American Revolution*, vol. 1, p. 22, says—"The anniversary of the 5th of March was observed with great solemnity; eloquent orators were successively employed to preserve the remembrance of it fresh in the mind. On these occasions, the blessings of liberty, *the horrors of slavery*, and the danger of a standing army, were presented to the public view. These annual orations administered fuel to the fire of liberty, and kept it burning with an irresistible flame."

The 5th of March continued to be celebrated for the above reasons, until the Anniversary of the Declaration of American Independence was substituted in its place; and its orators were expected to honor the feelings and principles of the former as having given birth to the latter.

On the 5th of March, 1776, Washington repaired to the intrenchments. "Remember," said he, "it is the 5th of March, and avenge the death of your brethren!"

In judging, then, of the merits of those who launched the American Revolution, we should not take counsel from the *Tories* of *that* or the *present* day, but rather heed the approving eulogy of Lovell, Hancock, and Warren.

Welcome, then, be every taunt that such correspondents may fling at ATTUCKS and his company, as the best evidence of their merits and their strong

---

[1] The *Transcript* of March 5, 1855, honorably alludes to CRISPUS ATTUCKS. [Author's footnote]

claim upon our gratitude! Envy and the foe do not labor to traduce any but prominent champions of a cause.

The rejection of the petition was to be expected, if we accept the axiom that a colored man never gets justice done him in the United States, except by mistake. The petitioners only asked for justice, and that the name of CRISPUS ATTUCKS might be honored as a grateful country honors other gallant Americans.

And yet, let it be recorded, the same session of the Legislature which had refused the ATTUCKS monument, granted one to ISAAC DAVIS, of Concord. Both were promoters of the American Revolution, but one was white, the other was *black*; and this is the only solution to the problem *why* justice was not fairly meted out.[2]

---

[2] Thirty-seven years later, in the autumn of 1888, a Crispus Attucks Monument was erected on the Boston Common to commemorate the Boston Massacre; it was done as a result of continued lobbying efforts from black and white public citizens, despite opposition from many prominent individuals and institutions in Massachusetts.

ROGER BROOKE TANEY

(1777–1864)

$\mathbf{T}$aney, the fourth Supreme Court Justice of the United States, was to some persons a name synonymous with injustice, due to his interpretation in the Dred Scott decision—the most controversial judicial ruling of the antebellum era.

The *Dred Scott* v. *Sandford*[1] case was heard before the Supreme Court in 1856–57 and raised the question of the constitutionality of slavery in nonslave territory. It concerned the status of Dred Scott, a slave who had served for several years in states and territories where slavery was prohibited.[2] In various venues Scott waged one of the longest and most complex battles in U.S. judicial history, but he ultimately lost it in the Supreme Court, which was then composed of five pro-slavery Southerners and four conservative Northerners. Only two of the high court justices—John McLean of Ohio and Benjamin Curtis of Massachusetts—dissented in the case. After a year of separate and often contradictory arguments from all nine members, Chief Justice Taney delivered what was ostensibly an "Opinion of the Court" in which he put forward his own opinion that the Missouri Compromise of 1820 was as unconstitutional as other laws of Congress inhibiting slavery in U.S. territories; he declared that

---

[1] During the litigation process in the case, a clerk misspelled *Sandford*, which led to subsequent misspellings in print. The defendant's actual name was John F. A. Sanford.

[2] Dred Scott, the plaintiff, was born a slave in Virginia at the end of the eighteenth century and owned for three decades by the John Blow family, which lived in various slave states. After Blow's death, one of his sons sold Scott as a valet in 1833 to a U.S. Army surgeon, Dr. John Emerson, whom he served at forts in Missouri, Illinois, and in the free federal territory of Minnesota and Wisconsin. After Emerson's death in 1843, Scott was hired out in Texas but returned to Missouri and tried to purchase his freedom from Mrs. Emerson, whose family refused; Scott sued in a St. Louis circuit court, where antislavery attorneys argued through provisions of the Missouri Compromise that Scott's residence in Illinois and free territory made him a free man. The jury ruled against him, and the case was retried in January 1850, with Scott winning a temporary reprieve until 1852, when the Missouri Supreme Court overturned the circuit court verdict. In November 1853, his lawyers went to federal court, by which time Mrs. Emerson had remarried; her brother, John Sanford, sued in Missouri that Scott was not a citizen with legal rights in federal district court. The jury declared Scott the property of Sanford, and Scott's lawyers moved for a writ of error to the U.S. Supreme Court, which heard the case twice before its March 6, 1857, ruling. With the Supreme Court decision, Scott and his wife were transferred to new owners, and he worked as a porter in a St. Louis hotel until his death of tuberculosis in September 1858.

Scott remained a slave according to Missouri law and was not a citizen, not free, and "had no rights which the white man was bound to respect."

Taney's opinion incensed some Northern legislators such as Massachusetts Senator Charles Sumner, who predicted the Chief Justice would be "hooted down the page of history." The Supreme Court decision, announced March 1857, was a political boost to pro-slavery forces, but it was opposed by Republicans who had pledged not to expand slavery into federal territory. In 1862, Congress prohibited territorial slavery, to the chagrin of Taney who, born and raised on a tobacco plantation in southern Maryland, believed in the sovereignty of states' rights. He had manumitted his own slaves but wanted them colonized outside the United States. A supporter of the American Colonization Society, his position on remanding slaves and free blacks to Africa was quiescent in his nondissent in the most controversial Supreme Court case related to slavery prior to the Dred Scott decision: *The United States v. The Libelants and Claimants of the Schooner Amistad.* Therein the court ruled in 1841 that the law favored freedom over slavery, though the opinion was delivered not by Chief Justice Taney but by Associate Justice Joseph Story from Massachusetts.[3]

A graduate of Dickinson College in 1792, Taney had no formal legal training, except several years of apprenticeship in the law office of an Annapolis judge. Admitted to practice law in Maryland in 1799, he held several state political positions before his career ascended during the Presidency of Andrew Jackson. In the latter's cabinet, Taney was U.S. Attorney General, then Secretary of the Treasury, before Jackson nominated him for the seat left vacant by the death

---

[3] Joseph Story (1779–1845) Associate Justice of the Supreme Court (1811–45). His "Opinion of the Court" in *U.S. v. Amistad,* freed Africans abducted from Sierra Leone and transported to Havana, where fifty-three were sold in violation of Spanish law and put aboard the Spanish schooner *Amistad.* En route from Havana for the Cuban port of Puerto Principe in June 1839, the Africans mutinied, killed the captain, took control of the *Amistad,* and ordered two Spanish slave owners to sail toward Africa. With no knowledge of navigation, the Africans were steered northwest, and the vessel ended up on New York's Long Island, where the mutineers were seized for salvage by a U.S. coast guard ship, accused of piracy and murder, and incarcerated in Connecticut. New York abolitionists financed a legal effort to defend the *Amistad* captives in the courts; after various appeals and decrees, former President John Quincy Adams, then a Congressman, argued their case before the Supreme Court, where Justice Joseph Story in February 1841 delivered an opinion that the appellants "are not slaves but are kidnapped Africans, who, by the law of Spain itself are entitled to their freedom, and were kidnapped and illegally carried to Cuba, and illegally detained and restrained on board of the *Amistad* . . . and that the said negroes be declared to be free, and be dismissed from the custody of the court." The Africans aided in fund-raising for their transport to Sierra Leone, where they returned in early 1842.

In the context of the *Amistad* case and other cases on slavery questions in which Judge Story wrote legal opinions, he was not an abolitionist but a moralist and gradualist who condemned the slave trade and extension of slavery; he was also a constitutionalist, and his interpretations, compromises, and conflicts with the Constitution appear in his *Commentaries on the Constitution* and *Conflict of Laws.*

of Chief Justice John Marshall. Confirmed as Chief Justice on March 15, 1836, he served for twenty-eight years, with much controversy over his decisions on sectional and regulatory issues.

At his death on October 12, 1864—the same day his home state of Maryland abolished slavery—some had scorned him as a Chief Justice unsupportive of the Union in the Civil War. He had preferred autonomy for the South, though Maryland had remained in the Union—torn between its past and its future, in antagonisms of regional conflict. Abraham Lincoln replaced the uncompromising Taney with an unyielding abolitionist lawyer and former U.S. Senator from Ohio—his Secretary of the Treasury, Salmon P. Chase, who became Chief Justice after 1864.

The following excerpt is from "Opinion of the Court" which Taney wrote and filed on the Dred Scott decision.

From *Dred Scott Decision:*
Opinion of the Court (1857)

. . . The question is simply this: Can a negro, whose ancestors were imported into this country, and sold as slaves, become a member of the political community formed and brought into existence by the Constitution of the United States, and as such become entitled to all the rights, and privileges, and immunities, guarantied by that instrument to the citizen? One of which rights is the privilege of suing in a court of the United States in the cases specified in the Constitution.

It will be observed, that the plea applies to that class of persons only whose ancestors were negroes of the African race, and imported into this country, and sold and held as slaves. The only matter in issue before the court, therefore, is, whether the descendants of such slaves, when they shall be emancipated, or who are born of parents who had become free before their birth, are citizens of a State, in the sense in which the word *citizen* is used in the Constitution of the United States. And this being the only matter in dispute on the pleadings, the court must be understood as speaking in this opinion of that class only, that is, of those persons who are the descendants of Africans who were imported into this country, and sold as slaves. . . .

We proceed to examine the case as presented by the pleadings.

The words *people of the United States* and *citizens* are synonymous terms, and mean the same thing. They both describe the political body who, according to our republican institutions, form the sovereignty, and who hold the power and conduct the Government through their representatives. They are what we familiarly call the "sovereign people," and every citizen is one of this people, and a constituent member of this sovereignty. The question before us is, whether the class of persons described in the plea in abatement compose a portion of this people, and are constituent members of this sovereignty? We think they are not, and that they are not included, and were not intended to be included, under the word *citizens* in the Constitution, and can therefore claim none of the rights and privileges which that instrument provides for and secures to citizens of the United States. On the contrary, they were at that time considered as a subordinate and inferior class of beings, who had been subjugated by the dominant race, and, whether emancipated or not, yet remained subject to their authority, and had no rights or privileges but such as those who held the power and the Government might choose to grant them.

It is not the province of the court to decide upon the justice or injustice, the policy or impolicy, of these laws. The decision of that question belonged to the political or law-making power; to those who formed the sovereignty and framed the Constitution. The duty of the court is to interpret the instrument they have framed, with the best lights we can obtain on the subject, and to administer it as we find it, according to its true intent and meaning when it was adopted.

In discussing this question, we must not confound the rights of citizenship which a State may confer within its own limits, and the rights of citizenship as a member of the Union. It does not by any means follow, because he has all the rights and privileges of a citizen of a State, that he must be a citizen of the United States. He may have all of the rights and privileges of the citizen of a State, and yet not be entitled to the rights and privileges of a citizen in any other State. . . .

It is very clear, therefore, that no State can, by any act or law of its own, passed since the adoption of the Constitution, introduce a new member into the political community created by the Constitution of the United States. It cannot make him a member of this community by making him a member of its own. And for the same reason it cannot introduce any person, or description of persons, who were not intended to be embraced in this new political family, which the Constitution brought into existence, but were intended to be excluded from it.

The question then arises, whether the provisions of the Constitution, in relation to the personal rights and privileges to which the citizen of a State should be entitled, embraced the negro African race, at that time in this country, or who might afterwards be imported, who had then or should afterwards be made free in any State; and to put it in the power of a single State to make him a citizen of the United States, and endue him with the full rights of citizenship in every other State without their consent? Does the Constitution of the United States act upon him whenever he shall be made free under the laws of a State, and raised there to the rank of a citizen, and immediately clothe him with all the privileges of a citizen in every other State, and in its own courts?

The court thinks the affirmative of these propositions cannot be maintained. And if it cannot, the plaintiff in error could not be a citizen of the State of Missouri, within the meaning of the Constitution of the United States, and, consequently, was not entitled to sue in its courts.

It is true, every person, and every class and description of persons, who were at the time of the adoption of the Constitution recognized as citizens in the several States, became also citizens of this new political body; but none other; it was formed by them, and for them and their posterity, but for no one else. And the personal rights and privileges guarantied to citizens of this new sovereignty were intended to embrace those only who were then members of the several State communities, or who should afterwards by birthright or otherwise become members, according to the provisions of the Constitution and the principles on which it was founded. It was the union of those who were at that time members of distinct and separate political communities into one political family, whose power, for certain specified purposes, was to extend over the whole territory of the United States. And it gave to each citizen rights and privileges outside of his State which he did not before possess, and placed him in every other State upon a perfect equality with its own citizens as to rights of person and rights of property; it made him a citizen of the United States.

It became necessary, therefore, to determine who were citizens of the several States when the Constitution was adopted. And in order to do this, we must recur to the Governments and institutions of the thirteen colonies, when they separated from Great Britain and formed new sovereignties, and took their places in the family of independent nations. We must inquire who, at that time, were recognized as the people or citizens of a State, whose rights and liberties had been outraged by the English Government; and who declared their independence, and assumed the powers of Government to defend their rights by force of arms.

In the opinion of the court, the legislation and histories of the times, and the language used in the Declaration of Independence, show, that neither the class of persons who had been imported as slaves, nor their descendants, whether they had become free or not, were then acknowledged as a part of the people, nor intended to be included in the general words used in that memorable instrument.

It is difficult at this day to realize the state of public opinion in relation to that unfortunate race, which prevailed in the civilized and enlightened portions of the world at the time of the Declaration of Independence, and when the Constitution of the United States was framed and adopted. But the public history of every European nation displays it in a manner too plain to be mistaken.

They had for more than a century before been regarded as beings of an inferior order, and altogether unfit to associate with the white race, either in social or political relations; and so far inferior, that they had no rights which the white man was bound to respect; and that the negro might justly and lawfully be reduced to slavery for his benefit. He was bought and sold, and treated as an ordinary article of merchandise and traffic, whenever a profit could be made by it. This opinion was at that time fixed and universal in the civilized portion of the white race. It was regarded as an axiom in morals as well as in politics, which no one thought of disputing, or supposed to be open to dispute; and men in every grade and position in society daily and habitually acted upon it in their private pursuits, as well as in matters of public concern, without doubting for a moment the correctness of this opinion.

And in no nation was this opinion more firmly fixed or more uniformly acted upon than by the English Government and English people. They not only seized them on the coast of Africa, and sold them or held them in slavery for their own use; but they took them as ordinary articles of merchandise to every country where they could make a profit on them, and were far more extensively engaged in this commerce than any other nation in the world.

The opinion thus entertained and acted upon in England was naturally impressed upon the colonies they founded on this side of the Atlantic. And, accordingly, a negro of the African race was regarded by them as an article of property, and held, and bought and sold as such, in every one of the thirteen colonies which united in the Declaration of Independence, and afterwards formed the Constitution of the United States. The slaves were more or less numerous in the different colonies, as slave labor was found more or less profitable. But no one seems to have doubted the correctness of the prevailing opinion of the time.

The legislation of the different colonies furnishes positive and indisputable proof of this fact. . . .

The language of the Declaration of Independence is equally conclusive:

It begins by declaring that, "when in the course of human events it becomes necessary for one people to dissolve the political bands which have connected them with another, and to assume among the powers of the earth the separate and equal station to which the laws of nature and nature's God entitle them, a decent respect for the opinions of mankind requires that they should declare the causes which impel them to the separation."

It then proceeds to say: "We hold these truths to be self-evident: that all men are created equal; that they are endowed by their Creator with certain unalienable rights; that among them is life, liberty, and the pursuit of happiness; that to secure these rights, Governments are instituted, deriving their just powers from the consent of the governed."

The general words above quoted would seem to embrace the whole human family, and if they were used in a similar instrument at this day would be so understood. But it is too clear for dispute, that the enslaved African race were not intended to be included, and formed no part of the people who framed and adopted this declaration; for if the language, as understood in that day, would embrace them, the conduct of the distinguished men who framed the Declaration of Independence would have been utterly and flagrantly inconsistent with the principles they asserted; and instead of the sympathy of mankind, to which they so confidently appealed, they would have deserved and received universal rebuke and reprobation.

Yet the men who framed this declaration were great men—high in literary acquirements—high in their sense of honor, and incapable of asserting principles inconsistent with those on which they were acting. They perfectly understood the meaning of the language they used, and how it would be understood by others; and they knew that it would not in any part of the civilized world be supposed to embrace the negro race, which, by common consent, had been excluded from civilized Governments and the family of nations, and doomed to slavery. They spoke and acted according to the then established doctrines and principles, and in the ordinary language of the day, and no one misunderstood them. The unhappy black race were separated from the white by indelible marks, and laws long before established, and were never thought of or spoken of except as property, and when the claims of the owner or the profit of the trader were supposed to need protection.

This state of public opinion had undergone no change when the Constitution was adopted, as is equally evident from its provisions and language.

The brief preamble sets forth by whom it was formed, for what purposes, and for whose benefit and protection. It declares that it is formed by the *people* of the United States; that is to say, by those who were members of the different political communities in the several States; and its great object is declared to be to secure the blessings of liberty to themselves and their posterity. It speaks in general terms of the *people* of the United States, and of *citizens* of the several States, when it is providing for the exercise of the powers granted or the privileges secured to the citizen. It does not define what description of persons are intended to be included under these terms, or who shall be regarded as a citizen and one of the people. It uses them as terms so well understood, that no further description or definition was necessary.

But there are two clauses in the Constitution which point directly and specifically to the negro race as a separate class of persons, and show clearly that they were not regarded as a portion of the people or citizens of the Government then formed.

One of these clauses reserves to each of the thirteen States the right to import slaves until the year 1808, if it thinks proper.[4] And the importation which it thus sanctions was unquestionably of persons of the race of which we are speaking, as the traffic in slaves in the United States had always been confined to them. And by the other provision[5] the States pledge themselves to each other to maintain the right of property of the master, by delivering up to him any slave who may have escaped from his service, and be found within their respective territories.

No one, we presume, supposes that any change in public opinion or feeling, in relation to this unfortunate race, in the civilized nations of Europe or in this country, should induce the court to give to the words of the Constitution a more liberal construction in their favor than they were intended to bear when the instrument was framed and adopted. Such an argument would be altogether inadmissible in any tribunal called on to interpret it. If any of its provisions are deemed unjust, there is a mode described in the instrument itself by which it may be amended; but while it remains unaltered, it must be construed now as it was understood at the time of its adoption. It is not only the same in words, but the same in meaning, and delegates the same powers to the Government, and reserves and secures the same rights and privileges to the citizen; and as long as it continues to exist in its present form, it speaks not only in the same words, but with the same meaning and intent with which it spoke when it came from the hands of its framers, and was voted on and adopted by the people of the United States. Any other rule of construction would abrogate the judicial character of this court, and make it the mere reflex of the popular opinion or passion of the day. This court was not created by the Constitution for such purposes. Higher and graver trusts have been confided to it, and it must not falter in the path of duty.

---

[4] Article I, section 9, U.S. Constitution.
[5] Article IV, section 2, U.S. Constitution. (This provision was superseded by the Thirteenth Amendment.)

What the construction was at that time, we think can hardly admit of doubt. We have the language of the Declaration of Independence and of the Articles of Confederation, in addition to the plain words of the Constitution itself; we have the legislation of the different States, before, about the time, and since, the Constitution was adopted; we have the legislation of Congress, from the time of its adoption to a recent period; and we have the constant and uniform action of the Executive Department, all concurring together, and leading to the same result. And if anything in relation to the construction of the Constitution can be regarded as settled, it is that which we now give to the word *citizen* and the word *people.*

And upon a full and careful consideration of the subject, the court is of opinion, that, upon the facts stated in the plea in abatement, Dred Scott was not a citizen of Missouri within the meaning of the Constitution of the United States, and not entitled as such to sue in its courts; and, consequently, that the Circuit Court had no jurisdiction of the case, and that the judgment on the plea in abatement is erroneous.

We arc aware that doubts are entertained by some of the members of the court, whether the plea in abatement is legally before the court upon this writ of error; but if that plea is regarded as waived, or out of the case upon any other ground, yet the question as to the jurisdiction of the Circuit Court is presented on the face of the bill of exception itself, taken by the plaintiff at the trial; for he admits that he and his wife were born slaves, but endeavors to make out his title to freedom and citizenship by showing that they were taken by their owner to certain places, hereinafter mentioned, where slavery could not by law exist, and that they thereby became free and upon their return to Missouri became citizens of that State.

Now, if the removal of which he speaks did not give them their freedom, then by his own admission he is still a slave; and whatever opinions may be entertained in favor of the citizenship of a free person of the African race, no one supposes that a slave is a citizen of the State or of the United States. If, therefore, the acts done by his owner did not make them free persons, he is still a slave, and certainly incapable of suing in the character of a citizen.

The principle of law is too well settled to be disputed, that a court can give no judgment for either party, where it has no jurisdiction; and if, upon the showing of Scott himself, it appeared that he was still a slave, the case ought to have been dismissed, and the judgment against him and in favor of the defendant for costs, is, like that on the plea in abatement, erroneous, and the suit ought to have been dismissed by the Circuit Court for want of jurisdiction in that court.

But, before we proceed to examine this part of the case, it may be proper to notice an objection taken to the judicial authority of this court to decide it; and it has been said, that as this court has decided against the jurisdiction of the Circuit Court on the plea in abatement, it has no right to examine any question presented by the exception; and that anything it may say upon that part of the case will be extrajudicial, and mere *obiter dicta*.[6]

This is a manifest mistake; there can be no doubt as to the jurisdiction of this court to revise the judgment of a Circuit Court, and to reverse it for any error apparent on the record, whether it be the error of giving judgment in a case over which it had no jurisdiction, or any other material error; and this, too, whether there is a plea in abatement or not.

---

[6] *Obiter dicta*: Latin plural for *incidental remarks*; a legal phrase designating passing statements made by a judge in conjunction with a judicial opinion; such remarks have no legal bearing, though they may have an effect on subsequent cases.

WALT WHITMAN

(1819–92)

In the same year that the Supreme Court issued the Dred Scott decision, Walt Whitman was writing pro-slavery editorials in New York newspapers. Such writings contradicted the image of the poet who jotted in his notebook in 1847: "I am the poet of slaves and of the masters of slaves." As a prose writer, his heart was with slave masters and white working-class "comrades" rather than with slaves.

In the century since his death, most critics have ignored or dismissed his voluminous prose writings as minor ramblings. According to one influential American literary historian, "it may be concluded that Whitman was a second-rate journalist whose products can scarcely be distinguished from those of others who wrote for the minor papers of the day." By readers and literary critics alike, Whitman has been judged almost solely by his poems in *Leaves of Grass*—a book that greatly changed and expanded between its first edition in July 1855 and the fifth and final edition in 1891–92. None of his editions, however, unveil the racist Whitman who emerges in his diaries, letters, sketches, fiction, essays, and journalism. His notebooks for *Leaves of Grass* reveal that he was calculating in self-admonitions, with an eye toward posterity: "Be careful to put in only what must be appropriate centuries hence," he wrote. "Be one whom all look toward with attention, respect, and love."

Yet his letters to his mother show the public poet was a different voice from the private man. Privately, he called slaves "darkeys" and black soldiers in the Union Army "niggers." His freelance writings—published between 1838–54 in small magazines and newspapers in New York—bring into sharper focus his attitudes on slavery, race, and abolition. He admonished Northern abolitionists for "mad fanaticism," and the "wicked wrong of 'abolitionist' interference with slavery in the southern states;" he derided British abolitionists for complaining of "the oppressed conditions of American negroes" and argued that slaves and their descendants were better off on American plantations than in Africa.

Racial stereotypes appear in his dime novelette on temperance, *Franklin Evans; or, The Inebriate—A Tale of the Times*, first published in 1842 and reprinted four years later as "Fortunes of a Country Boy: Incidents in Town—and his Adventures at the South." Whitman himself remained in various ways a "country boy"—the peasant born in a farmhouse on eastern Long Island, where his English and Dutch ancestors settled before moving to Brooklyn. In diary notes for his prose book *November Boughs*, he acknowledged, "I can myself almost remember negro slaves in New York state as my grandfather and great-grandfather (at West hills, Suffolk County) own'd a number. The hard labor of the farm was mostly done by them, and on the floor of the big kitchen, toward sundown, would be squatting a circle of twelve or fourteen 'pickaninnies' eating their supper of pudding (Indian corn mush) and milk."

His semi-illiterate father was a farmer and tradesman, who failed at nearly everything except being "addicted to alcohol." Young Walt himself stopped school around age twelve and began an apprenticeship in printing and newspaper offices in New York and Brooklyn, learning the basics of typesetting, writing, and editing at nine different periodicals in eight years. His working-class origins and economic hardships gave rise to a democratic stance in his poetry but to a reactionary posture in his prose.

His 1856 political tract, *The Eighteenth Presidency: Voice of Walt Whitman to Each Young Man in the Nation, North, South, East, and West,* was a direct response to the slavery controversy in the 1856 Presidential campaign, but his slant was the abolition of slavery for the sake of white laborers, who were "not willing to be put on the level of the negro slaves." Whitman had foreshadowed that message nine years earlier in a newspaper editorial.

In his later prose essays in *Democratic Vistas*—a tract first published privately in Washington in 1867—he railed against "the appalling dangers of universal suffrage," (before black men won a legal right to vote through the Fifteenth Amendment) and championed the idea of American empire and manifest destiny. "Long ere the second centennial arrives, there will be some forty to fifty states, among them, Canada and Cuba," he predicted. With a view of himself as large as the cosmos, Whitman had imperialistic notions of spread-eagleism and star-spangled nationalism, which he expounded further in his 1871 book, *Specimen Days*. At a time when America was both racist and expansionist, he was neither its conscience nor its egalitarian spirit, though he was romanticized as being the sage of his age at home and abroad. "I contradict myself" he wrote in the first edition of his poems. The contradictions become more evident in a comparative study of his poetry and prose.

Although he added many new poems to successive editions of *Leaves of Grass*, he omitted his late prose and his early journalism. Hubris blinded him to his prejudices and character flaws that led a publisher of the *Brooklyn Daily Eagle* to fire him as editor in 1848 and to tell readers that Whitman was "slow, indolent, heavy, discourteous and without steady principles. Mr. W. has no political principles, nor for that matter, principles of any sort."

A Free-Soiler nationalist who detested abolitionists but wanted to save the Union, Whitman revered Abraham Lincoln and wrote about him in several poems, but never penned a word about the Emancipation Proclamation. During the Civil War he served as volunteer nurse in military hospitals in the nation's capital, and made Washington, DC, his home for eight years after the war. His letters written during those years of Reconstruction reveal him to be as resentful toward black freemen as he was toward abolitionists before the war. Yet, he prided himself on earlier poems such as "Song of Myself" in which he identified with "the hounded slave" and the arrest of a fugitive slave in "A Boston Ballad" and with "a black divine-soul'd African, large, fine-headed, nobly form'd superbly destin'd on equal terms with me" in "Salut au Monde." But the voice behind the words masked a hypocritical soul beneath a towering ego, full of sound and fury.

In 1873 he suffered a paralytic stroke and moved to Camden, New Jersey, where he spent the remaining two decades of his life. Except for brief journeys to Colorado and Canada in 1879 and 1880, he saw little of the world beyond a trip in 1848 from New York to New Orleans.

The following is the full text of his newspaper article, "Slavery," from *The Brooklyn Daily Times* of July 17, 1857—two years after the first edition of *Leaves of Grass*.

Slavery (1857)

In their own country degraded, cruel, almost bestial, the victims of cruel chiefs, and of bloody religious rites—their lives never secure—no education, no refinement, no elevation, no political knowledge,—such is the general condition of the African tribes. From these things they are sold to the American plantations.

Would we then defend the slave trade? No; we would merely remind the reader that, in a large view of the case, the change is not one for the worse, to the victims of that trade. The blacks, mulattoes, &c., either in the Northern or Southern States, might bear in mind that had their forefathers remained in Africa, and their birth occurred there, they would now be roaming Krumen[1] or

---

[1] Whitman's obsolete spelling of the name of West African Kru people—fishermen, sailors, farmers, traders—inhabiting seaboard regions of Ivory Coast and Liberia.

Ashanteemen,[2] wild, filthy, paganistic—not residents of a land of light, and bearing their share, to some extent, in all its civilizations.

It is also to be remembered that no race ever can remain slaves if they have it in them to become free. Why do the slave ships go to Africa only?

The worst results of the slave trade are those mainly caused by attempts of the government to outlaw it. We speak of the horrors of the "middle passage,"—the wretched, suffocating, steaming, thirsty, dying crowds of black men, women and children, packed between decks in cutter-built ships, modeled not for space, but speed. This, we repeat, is not an inherent attribute of the slave trade, but of declaring it piracy.

The establishment of Liberia, and the deep interest felt in its welfare—the modern travelers in the old continent of the Nile and of the Desert—the almost morbid philanthropy of Europe and America—the opposition to slavery, so stern, so rapidly growing, more resolute in its defeat than in its triumph—these will before long tell fatally on the slave trade [by which slaves are imported to Cuba, the West Indies, and Brazil].

For the Brazils,[3] for Cuba, and it may be for some of the Southern States of this Confederacy, the infusion of slaves and the prevalent use of their labor are not objectionable on politico-economic grounds. Slaves are there because they must be—when the time arrives for them not to be proper there, they will leave.

For all that, America is not the land for slaves, on any grounds. The recorded theory of America denies slavery any existence in justice, law, or as a moral fact. The geography of the country, its interests, enterprise, labor, farmers, mechanics, commerce, agriculture, railroads, steamers—these with the rest disfavor slavery, and therefore the slave trade. The great heart and trunk of America is the West—and the West would be paralyzed by slavery. But Cuba and the Brazils are not the West.

---

[2] Ashanti or Asante people inhabiting modern Ghana, formerly called the Gold Coast during Whitman's lifetime; the Ashanti were known for resisting rule of the British, who colonized the country from 1820 until political independence in 1957. The Asante Empire was at its height in the eighteenth century.

[3] The United States of Brazil, not then an independent federal republic, was a group of provinces in 1857, when Whitman wrote this piece and referred to the region as "the Brazils."

JOSIAH HENSON

(1789–1883)

Josiah Henson's life began in slavery in Maryland and ended in freedom in Canada—his adopted home for over half a century. A self-taught Methodist preacher, he fled the South in 1830 with his wife and four children to Dawn, Upper Canada (later West Canada, renamed Ontario). The Hensons were among the earliest settlers in a community of fugitive slaves along the Detroit frontier of the British North American Provinces. Adjacent to the Dawn settlement, he organized a school near Dresden, West Canada, for vocational training and manual labor. With aid from white abolitionist missionaries and Quaker philanthropists, the school opened in 1842 as the British–American Institute for Fugitive Slaves, located on several hundred acres. Henson helped sustain the school by establishing a saw mill, which shipped lumber products to Boston. Meanwhile, he continued his work as a preacher and a volunteer conductor on the underground railroad.

Taught to read and write by one of his sons, he told his own life story in three autobiographical editions (the third an expanded version of the second). The first edition was a pamphlet in 1849, written by an editorial amanuensis. The last two editions have been called exaggerated, opportunistic and unreliable—notably by American critics preferential to narratives about slave experiences in the American South, rather than those glorifying black emigrationism. Henson's narratives, however, offer both perspectives: the perils of slaves in the United States and opportunities for fugitives in Canada—where settlers benefited from the British Parliament's Slavery Abolition Act of 1833, three decades before the Emancipation Proclamation.

Some literary critics have accused Henson of being a self-promoter who boasted of a bronze medal from Queen Victoria and private interviews with the Archbishop of Canterbury and the Prime Minister of England. He did attain public recognition during fund-raising trips to London, notably in 1851 at the Crystal Palace Exhibition, where he exhibited walnut lumber produced by his Canadian cooperative.

His activities and accomplishments have been overshadowed by tales that he was prototype for Harriet Beecher Stowe's fictional Uncle Tom. Stowe and

Henson met briefly in 1850 at the Boston home of her brother, Edward—after she read the 1849 pamphlet, "The Life of Josiah Henson, Formerly a Slave, Now an Inhabitant of Canada, as Narrated by Himself." But the ex-slave she met was not in flight from the 1850 Fugitive Slave Act but en route to England on business. It is likely that he told her stories about his former life in bondage: how his father was sold and not seen again by the eight-year-old Josiah, who himself was later flogged and maimed, but more loyal to his slavemasters than to fellow-slaves, before one of his owners betrayed a promise to let him purchase his liberty—whence Henson fled to Canada. Stowe recast the vicissitudes Henson endured in Kentucky and New Orleans into a fictional composite borrowed from other slave narratives for *Uncle Tom's Cabin*. In 1858, she also wrote the Introduction to *From Truth Stranger Than Fiction: Father Henson's Own Story of His Own Life*. Henson never claimed he was Stowe's "Uncle Tom," but he willingly accepted that identification. Unfortunately, his reputation as a leader in Canada is remembered less than the myth that he was Stowe's model for her famous antebellum novel.

His third and final autobiography, updated and published in 1879, appeared four years before he died of natural causes, at age ninety-four, in Dresden, Ontario. Due to his advancing age, it is uncertain how much of the book was an authentic recollection of dates and facts. He made accusations of unscrupulous financial mismanagement of his Canadian school and mill. However, he remained with the school until it officially closed in 1868.

He did not follow fugitives who returned to America after the Civil War. Though black Canadian settlements did not comprise more than 1 percent of the national population, Henson was unwavering in his belief that Canada, as part of the British Empire, offered black residents more economic opportunity and legal protection than the United States. A proponent of separatism and independent black Canadian institutions, his ideas were supported by settlers like author and lecturer Henry Bibb, editor of Canada's first black newspaper, *Voice of the Fugitive*. They were opposed by activists like Mary Ann Shadd Cary, educator and first black female newspaper editor, who advocated assimilation into Canadian society. (She eventually returned to the United States.)

Henson's vision of Canada as utopian refuge for permanent black residents is shown in the following selection—the final chapter of his 1858 autobiography.

From *From Truth Stranger Than Fiction: Father Henson's Story of His Own Life* (1858)

I have been requested by many friends in this country to devote a chapter of my book to the fugitive slaves in Canada; to a statement of their present numbers, condition, prospects for the future, etc. At the time of my first visit to Canada, in the year 1830, there were but a few hundred fugitive slaves in both Canadas; there are now not less than thirty-five thousand. At that time they were scattered in all directions, and for the most part miserably poor, subsisting not unfrequently on the roots and herbs of the fields; now many of them own large and valuable farms, and but few can be found in circumstances of destitution or want. In 1830 there were no schools among them, and no churches, and only occasional preaching. We have now numerous churches, and they are well filled from Sabbath to Sabbath with attentive listeners; our children attend the Sabbath School, and are being trained as we trust for Heaven. We depend principally upon our farms for subsistence, but some of our number are good mechanics—blacksmiths, carpenters, masons, shoemakers, etc., etc. We have found the raising of stock very profitable, and can show some of the finest specimens of horseflesh to be found on this continent, and we find a ready market for all our products. The soil is fertile and yields an abundant return for the husbandman's labor; and, although the season is short, yet ordinarily it is long enough to ripen corn, wheat, rye, oats, and the various productions of a Northern New England or New York farm. Of late considerable attention has been paid to the cultivation of fruit trees, apples, cherries, plums, peaches, quinces, currants, gooseberries, strawberries, etc., and they are doing well, and in a few years we doubt not will be quite profitable. It is a mistaken idea that many have, that fruit trees and vines cannot be cultivated to advantage on account of the severity of the climate; I have raised as delicious sweet potatoes on my farm as I ever saw in Kentucky, and as good a crop of tobacco and hemp.

We have at the present time a large number of settlements, and connected with these are schools at which our children are being taught the ordinary branches of an English education. We are a peaceable people, living at peace among ourselves and with our white neighbors, and I believe the day is not far distant when we shall take a very respectable rank among the subjects of her majesty, the excellent and most gracious Queen of England and the Canadas. Even now, the condition and prospects of a majority of the fugitive slaves in

Canada is vastly superior to that of most of the free people of color in the Northern States; and if thousands who are hanging about at the corners of streets waiting for a job, or who are mending old clothes, or blacking boots in damp cellars in Boston, New York, and other large cities, would but come among us and bring their little ones and settle down upon our fine lands, it would be but a few years before they would find themselves surrounded by a pleasant and profitable home, and their children growing up around them with every advantage for a good education, and fitting themselves for lives of usefulness and happiness. The climate is good, the soil is good, the laws protect us from molestation; each and all may sit under their own vine and fig tree with none to molest or make them afraid. We are a temperate people; it is a rare sight to see an intoxicated colored man in Canada.

My task is done, if what I have written shall inspire a deeper interest in my race, and shall lead to corresponding activity in their behalf I shall feel amply repaid.

JOHN BROWN

(1800–1859)

John Brown's historic antislavery attack on an ammunition arsenal at Harper's Ferry had a Canada connection. The spring of 1858, during a journey to West Canada to recruit fugitive slaves to join him, Brown visited the town of Chatham for a secret interracial meeting—known as the Chatham Convention. There he fortuitously met and enlisted for his Virginia raid a young black Canadian who had attended Oberlin College. He was Osborne P. Anderson, the sole survivor among the five Afro-American volunteers who attacked the government arsenal with Brown and sixteen white insurgents on October 16, 1859.[1] Anderson documented the experience in a book published in Canada in 1861: A Voice from Harper's Ferry: A Narrative of Events. . . . Anderson's book and public eulogy in Toronto hailed the moral principles of Brown, who then and later was traduced as a "fanatic" by many Americans. Even some abolitionists argued that it was folly to lead twenty-one young men in an onslaught that ended with seventeen corpses, including ten of Brown's recruits, plus many injuries, and his own capture within thirty-six hours. The act shook a nation and caused a debate to endure for decades.

Born the third of six children on a farm in Torrington, Connecticut, Brown grew up in the village of Hudson, Ohio, near Cleveland. Motherless at age eight, indifferent to school, he was reared by a father whose strong Calvinism and hatred of slavery he shared and passed to his own sons. Three of Brown's male offspring fought with him at Harper's Ferry; two—Oliver and Watson Brown—died from gunshot wounds; a third son, Owen, escaped. As husband and father, John Brown had experienced family tragedy and death before losing

---

[1] The four other Afro-Americans were twenty-three-year-old John A. Copeland who, like Anderson, attended Oberlin College; Copeland's uncle, Lewis Sheridan Leary; Shields Green, a fugitive introduced to Brown by Frederick Douglass; and Dangerfield Newby, an ex-slave and the only local resident. Leary and Newby were killed in combat; Copeland and Green were captured and later hung fourteen days after John Brown.

Besides Brown and his three sons, the other Caucasian insurgents were Jeremiah Anderson, John E. Cook, Barclay and Edwin Coppoc (brothers); Albert Hazlett, John H. Kagi, William E. Leeman, Francis J. Meriam, Aaron D. Stevens, Stewart Taylor, and Dauphin and William Thompson (brothers).

two sons to gunfire in Virginia. He fathered twenty children and lost over half to illnesses, bizarre accidents, or violence. Married at age twenty to an emotionally and physically ill wife who gave birth seven times before leaving him a widower with five youngsters, he remarried a woman half his age, who bore thirteen more children. As family breadwinner, his abolitionism was deferred and did not begin in earnest until he was of middle age.

In 1859, he was as strong in stamina as his grown sons, but stooped in gait with a graying beard and gaunt face, which made him look like their grandfather. Few men had toiled harder in small business ventures, which over the years included tanning leather, surveying land, raising cattle, herding sheep, selling wool—between moves in Ohio, Pennsylvania, Massachusetts, New York, and Kansas. Motivated by honesty in all his efforts, he shunned get-rich schemes, living in poverty amid mounting debts. The vocation of herding sheep perhaps best matched his spirit: the wandering shepherd who adopted as his flock the dispossessed slaves he was determined to free. In 1849 Brown moved his family from Springfield, Massachusetts, to North Elba, New York, to settle among a commune of freed slave farmers on a land grant of 120,000 acres from New York philanthropist, Gerrit Smith.

An abolitionist who believed in armed violence to end slavery, he proved it in 1856 in "bleeding Kansas" conflicts between free-state and antislavery forces; at Osawatomie, in Kansas Territory, he and less than fifty armed recruits fought off a band of over four hundred agitators, although he lost another son, Frederick. Elsewhere in Kansas, he and several of his elder sons were accused of murdering five proslavery men at the Pottawatomie Massacre. In late 1858, he led raids to help runaway slaves from Missouri to Canada.

His final foray as guerrilla fighter at Harper's Ferry was preplanned and subsidized by black freemen in Canada and affluent white Northeastern pacifists—known as the "Secret Six"—who supported his drive to instigate slave uprisings.[2] Although a military fiasco, Brown's violent attack to end slavery made his name immortal. Captured October 18 by federal troops in Virginia, he was hanged there on December 2, 1859, and buried near his home in North Elba, Essex County, New York, survived by his widow and eight children.

The following text is from his speech to the court in the village of Charlestown, Jefferson County, Virginia, where he was convicted November 2, nine miles from Harper's Ferry.

---

[2] The "Secret Six" were all prominent abolitionists: Thomas Wentworth Higginson, Samuel Gridley Howe, Theodore Parker, Franklin Benjamin Sanborn, Gerrit Smith, and George Luther Stearns. Only Higginson later refused to deny his link to Brown's raid.

Last Speech to the Virginia Court (November 2, 1859)

I have, may it please the Court, a few words to say.

In the first place, I deny everything but what I have all along admitted,—the design on my part to free the slaves. I intended certainly to have made a clean thing of that matter, as I did last winter, when I went into Missouri and there took slaves without the snapping of a gun on either side, moved them through the country, and finally left them in Canada. I designed to have done the same thing again, on a larger scale. That was all I intended. I never did intend murder, or treason, or the destruction of property, or to excite or incite slaves to rebellion, or to make insurrection.

I have another objection; and that is, it is unjust that I should suffer such a penalty. Had I interfered in the manner which I admit, and which I admit has been fairly proved (for I admire the truthfulness and candor of the greater portion of the witnesses who have testified in this case),—had I so interfered in behalf of the rich, the powerful, the intelligent, the so-called great, or in behalf of any of their friends,—either father, mother, brother, sister, wife, or children, or any of that class,—and suffered and sacrificed what I have in this interference, it would have been all right; and every man in this court would have deemed it an act worthy of reward rather than punishment.

This court acknowledges, as I suppose, the validity of the law of God. I see a book kissed here which I suppose to be the Bible, or at least the New Testament. That teaches me that all things whatsoever I would that men should do to me, I should do even so to them. It teaches me, further, to "remember them that are in bonds, as bound with them." I endeavored to act up to that instruction. I say, I am yet too young to understand that God is any respecter of persons. I believe that to have interfered as I have done—as I have always freely admitted I have done—in behalf of His despised poor, was not wrong, but right. Now, if it is deemed necessary that I should forfeit my life for the furtherance of the ends of justice, and mingle my blood further with the blood of my children and with the blood of millions in this slave country whose rights are disregarded by wicked, cruel, and unjust enactments,—I submit; so let it be done!

Let me say, also, a word in regard to the statements made by some of those connected with me. I hear it has been stated by some of them that I have induced them to join me. But the contrary is true. I do not say this to injure them, but as regretting their weakness. There is not one of them but joined me of his own accord, and the greater part of them at their own expense. A number of them I never saw, and never had a word of conversation with, till the day they came to me; and that was for the purpose I have stated.

Now I have done.

Let me say one word further.

I feel entirely satisfied with the treatment I have received on my trial. Considering all the circumstances, it has been more generous than I expected. But I feel no consciousness of guilt. I have stated from the first what was my intention, and what was not. I never have had any design against the life of any person, nor any disposition to commit treason, or excite slaves to rebel, or make any general insurrection. I never encouraged any man to do so, but always discouraged any idea of that kind.

CHARLES HOWARD LANGSTON

(1817–92)

Among those John Brown tried in vain to enlist for his insurrection at Harper's Ferry was Charles Howard Langston, one of the most committed and eloquent of black abolitionists. In the spring of 1859, Brown was in Cleveland shortly before the trial of Langston and thirty-six others, who had been indicted by a U.S. District Court for violating the Fugitive Slave Law. The daring act of aiding a Kentucky runaway slave named John Price put Charles Langston at the center of the "Oberlin–Wellington Rescue"—especially after he delivered an impassioned speech in court. Present in the courtroom was John Brown's clandestine "Secretary of War" John Henry Kagi, ostensibly covering the long trial as a newspaper reporter, but also in Ohio to enlist volunteers for Harper's Ferry. His belief that all blacks were ready for revolution seemed a reality after hearing Charles Langston boldly tell the court:

"We have, as a people, *consented* for two hundred years to be the *slaves* of whites. We have been scourged, crushed and cruelly oppressed, and have submitted to it all tamely, meekly, peaceably, I mean, as a people, with rare individual exceptions,—and today you see us thus meekly submitting to the penalties of an infamous law."

After being sentenced to twenty days in jail, and fined $100.00, plus court costs of $872.70, Langston was not disposed to join Brown's armed cadre, but Kagi succeeded in finding two recruits in nearby Oberlin: John Copeland, a college student, and his uncle Lewis Sheridan Leary, a harness maker, who left behind a wife and infant daughter.

Charles Langston, respected as a school teacher and participant at Ohio Anti-Slavery Society conventions of the 1840s and 1850s, was an older brother of John Mercer Langston, who in 1854 became the first American of mixed race admitted to the Ohio bar to practice law and the first elected to a town clerkship in the nation in 1855. John Brown sought to involve both Langston brothers in his Virginia conspiracy—without perhaps knowing their roots. Charles and John had been born in Louisa County, Virginia, and raised there until Charles was seventeen and John seven, the sons of a wealthy white planter, Ralph Quarles, whose half-Indian, half-African mistress was their mother, Lucy Langston. Quarles emancipated her by court order in 1806 and the couple lived together until both died in 1834, for reasons of the heart later explained in John Mercer Langston's memoir, *From The Virginia Plantation to the National Capitol.* Quarles's last will and testament in 1833 legally recognized his three sons and a daughter by Lucy and provided for their financial independence and education. The Langstons moved to Ohio, where the younger boys attended Oberlin and began their careers. As abolitionists, Charles was more militant than John, but neither dared risk gains by 1859 to attack Harper's Ferry. But, when Brown was captured, Charles Langston defended him, and when Brown died, he eulogized him at a Cleveland church.

A decade later Charles wed the Oberlin widow of Lewis Sheridan Leary, who was shot on the river rocks near Harper's Ferry. His widow, Mary Sampson Patterson Leary, received only his bullet-ridden shawl. In 1870, Charles and Mary joined the mass exodus to Kansas, settling in the Lawrence vicinity for the rest of their lives. Their daughter Carrie, born in 1873, would become mother of the poet Langston Hughes.

The following text is a letter Charles Langston wrote to a Cleveland newspaper, defending John Brown against the public outcry after the Harper's Ferry incident. His sentiments echoed those of many free blacks, slaves, and fugitives.

A Black Abolitionist in Defense of John Brown:
Letter to the Editor of
the *Cleveland Plain Dealer* (November 18, 1859)

Mr. Editor:

Card writing seems to be the order of the day, particularly with reference to Capt. John Brown and his insurrectionary movements at Harper's Ferry. We have heard through the public journals from many of the great men and some of the great women too who are said to be connected with the "bloody attempt to dissolve the Union," "to subvert and overturn the Government," "to push forward the irrepressible conflict," "and to incite the slaves of Virginia and

Maryland to cut their masters' throats." Giddings,[1] Hale,[2] Smith,[3] the Plumbs,[4] and others have denied any knowledge of, or connection with the "mad scheme or its crazy perpetrators." Why the hasty denial? Why all this hot haste to throw off the imaginary disgrace or danger, which may grow out of complicity with this daring friend of Liberty and lover of mercy? Were the noble old hero and his brave and faithful followers, engaged in a mean, selfish, and dastardly work? Were they "plotting crime" against the rights or liberties of any human being? Were they in Virginia to take the property or lives of men who respect the rights of life, liberty or property in others? Capt. Brown was engaged in no vile, base, sordid, malicious or selfish enterprise. His aims and ends were lofty, noble, generous, benevolent, humane and God-like. His actions were in perfect harmony with, and resulted from the teaching of the Bible, of our Revolutionary fathers and of every true and faithful antislavery man in this country and the world.

Does not the holy Bible teach that it is the duty of the strong and powerful to assist the weak and helpless, that the rich should succor the poor and needy? Does it not command us to remember those in bonds as being bound with them? Does it not tell us to loose the bonds of wickedness, undo the heavy burdens and let the oppressed go free? Does not the Bible plainly say, "whatsoever ye would that man shall do to you, do ye even so to them?" and further: "he that stealeth a man and selleth him or if he be found in his hand, he shall surely be put to death."

Did not Capt. Brown act in consonance with these biblical principles and injunctions? He went into Virginia to aid the afflicted and the helpless, to assist the weak and to relieve the poor and needy. To undo the heavy burdens, to let the oppressed go free, to do to others as he would have them to do to him. And above all to put to death, as the papers tell us, those who steal men and sell them, and in whose hands stolen men are found. His actions then are only the results of his faithfulness to the plain teaching of the word of God.

The renowned fathers of our celebrated revolution taught the world that "resistance to tyrants is obedience to God," that all men are created equal, and

---

[1] Joshua R. Giddings (1795–1864), antislavery advocate who, at the time of Langston's letter, had represented Ohio in the U.S. Congress for twenty years (1838–58), elected successively as a Whig, Free-Soiler, and Republican.

[2] John P. Hale, 1852 Free-Soil presidential candidate; active legal defender of fugitive slaves.

[3] Although several contemporaneous abolitionists were surnamed Smith, Langston's reference is to Gerrit Smith (1797–1874), a wealthy New Yorker who used his considerable fortune and influence in the antislavery cause and was accused of conspiring with his friend John Brown in the Harper's Ferry raid.

See: Ralph V. Harlow, *Gerrit Smith, Philanthropist and Reformer* (New York, 1939).

[4] Ralph Plumb—Oberlin, Ohio, attorney who assisted in helping fugitive slaves in underground railroad operations, including John Price in the Oberlin-Wellington Rescue.

have the inalienable right to life and liberty. They proclaim *death* but not *slavery*, or rather "give me liberty or give me death." They also ordained and established a constitution to secure the blessings of liberty to themselves and their *posterity*. (It is to be remembered that they have a large colored posterity in the Southern States.) And they further declared that when any government becomes destructive of these ends, namely, life, liberty, justice and happiness, it is the right of the people to abolish it and to institute a new government.—On these pure and holy principles they fearlessly entered into a seven-years' war against the most powerful nation of the earth, relying on a just God, whom they believed would raise up friends to fight their battles for them. Their belief was more than realized. The friends of freedom came to their assistance.

Did not Capt. Brown act in accordance with the foregoing revolutionary principles? Did not he obey God by resisting tyrants? Did he not in all things show his implicit faith in the equality of all men? and their unalienable right to life and liberty? When he saw that the governments of the South were destructive of these ends, did he not aim to abolish them and to institute a new government laying its foundation on such principles as to him seemed most likely to secure the happiness and safety of the people?

Some will say no doubt that the teaching of the renowned fathers had no reference to Negroes, for, says Judge Taney,[5] the prevalent opinion at the time of the revolution was that "black men had no rights which white men were bound to respect." In sober earnestness did the "great and good men of those days which tried men's souls," have no higher idea of liberty and the rights of man than that? Did they believe in one-sided, selfish, partial, sectarian freedom? Liberty for proud "Anglo-Saxon" and chains and fetters for "all the world and the rest of mankind." I think they must have had a higher, a nobler idea of man and his inalienable rights. But be this as it may, the Abolitionists, the true friends of God and humanity, are applying both the doctrines of the Bible and the teaching of the fathers to every human being, whether white or black, bond or free. We Abolitionists profess to propagate no new doctrines in politics or morals, but to urge all men to practice the old well-defined and immutable principles "of the fatherhood of God and the universal brotherhood of man." Liberty and equality belong naturally to the entire brotherhood; and the man who takes from his brother his liberty, becomes a tyrant and thus forfeits his rights to *live*.

Now it is plain to be seen that Capt. Brown only carried out in his actions the principles emanating from these three sources, viz: First—The Bible. Second—The Revolutionary Fathers. Third—All good Abolitionists.

---

[5] See excerpt of Judge Roger B. Taney, pages, 192–99, above.

If, then, Brown acted on these pure and righteous principles, why are the friends of justice, liberty and right so hasty in denying all connections with him or sympathy with his ends and aims? Perhaps they see the bloody gallows of the "affrighted chivalry" rising before them in awful horror. Or more probably they see a political grave yearning to receive them.

But to speak of myself I have no political prospects and therefore no political fears! for my black face and curly hair doom me in this land of equality to political damnation and that beyond the possibility of redemption. But I have a neck as dear to me as Smith's, Hale's or Giddings', and therefore I must like them publish a card of denial. So here it is. But what shall I deny? I cannot deny that I feel that the very deepest sympathy with the Immortal John Brown in his heroic and daring efforts to free the slaves.—To do this would be in my opinion more criminal than to urge the slaves to open rebellion. To deny any connection with the "daring and fiendish plot" would be worse than nonsense. The *fearless chivalry* of the old dominion would move me guilty without the least difficulty. For their heroic imaginations now convert every harmless pillow into an infernal machine, behold the veritable Capt. Brown in every peaceable nonresistant northern abolitionist, and see in every colored man the dusky ghost of Gen. Nat Turner, the hero of Southampton. So their testimony against me would be imaginary, their trial a farce, but their rope halter would be a stern and binding reality.

. . . With these explanations and denials, I hope the Marshal of the Northern District of Ohio, the Federal Administration generally, and all slaveholders and particularly all official "smelling committees," will be fully satisfied.

C. H. LANGSTON

Cleveland, November 1859.

HENRY DAVID THOREAU

(1817–62)

Thoreau was the first notable New England writer to plead John Brown's cause after the Harper's Ferry raid. Within two weeks of Brown's capture, Thoreau spoke at the Old Parish Church in Concord, defying local citizens who claimed his speech premature. In Worcester and Boston, he repeated his pleas, and on execution day delivered an encomium in Concord, and another in absentia at Brown's grave site in New York, July 4, 1861. By 1862, Thoreau himself was dead, at age forty-four, from tuberculosis. At his Concord funeral, he was eulogized by his mentor-friend, Ralph Waldo Emerson, who had previously joined him in homage to Brown.

Philosophical differences between Emerson and Thoreau echoed then and later in reaction to Brown's stand at Harper's Ferry. Privately, Emerson wrote in his journal that Brown was a "true hero, but he lost his head there." Publicly, he hailed him "a new saint . . . who, if he shall suffer, will make the gallows glorious like the cross." Those remarks by Emerson on November 8, 1859—in a Boston speech on "Courage"—were deleted a decade later when he revised his essays for publication.[1] Thoreau, fourteen years younger, died too soon to retract on Brown, but he gave no sign that his convictions about him would ever change.

Of Thoreau's New England colleagues who made Concord an intellectual center, he was the only one born and raised there. Two miles away, on property owned by Emerson, he built a one-room cabin, which became his spiritual home for two years—from 1845 to 1847—and the setting of his masterwork, *Walden Pond; or, Life in the Woods* (1854).

At his death, he had published only one other book, *A Week on the Concord and Merrimack Rivers* (1849), plus chapters from other projected books, and

---

[1] After his speech on "Courage," Emerson praised John Brown in three other public lectures: November 18, 1859, at a meeting in Boston's Tremont Temple to aid Brown's family; at a Concord service on execution day; and January 6, 1860, in Salem. No manuscripts of these last three speeches exist in Emerson's papers, but texts of them were printed in periodicals, and later in various compilations of his prose.

Brown visited Concord in March 1857, and May 1859, and both times met with Thoreau, who introduced him to Emerson.

various essays, including his now famous 1849 radical piece, "Resistance to Civil Government" (posthumously titled "Civil Disobedience"). That title would resound into the twentieth century, influencing passive resistance movements of Mohandas K. Gandhi and Martin Luther King, Jr. Equally incisive was his later essay, "Life without Principle," printed in the *Atlantic Monthly* a year after his death. Many of his voluminous unpublished writings were collected and printed posthumously in the 1860s: *Excursions* (1863), The *Maine Woods* (1864), *Cape Cod* (1864), *Letters to Various Persons* (1865), and *A Yankee in Canada, with Anti-Slavery and Reform Papers* (1866). Subsequent editions brought new volumes of his journals, poems, translations, correspondence, and essays.[2]

An introspective nonconformist, who preferred a Spartan and solitary life, he was indifferent to wealth, status, fame, marriage, and society—all of which put him at odds with a nation obsessed by manifest destiny, monetary profits, acquisitions, politics, race, and social position. In *Walden,* he wrote, "Rather than love, than money, than fame, give me truth." Emerson would say at Thoreau's funeral, "He chose to be rich by making his wants few, and supplying them himself."

The son of a pencil manufacturer, he considered taking up his father's vocation, but after graduation from Harvard in 1837 devoted himself to teaching school until 1841. Following the death of his older brother, John—with whom he had opened a private academy—he moved in with the Emerson family and worked as a handyman, editorial assistant, and a contributor for *The Dial,* which Emerson then edited.[3] Arrested briefly in 1844 for refusal to pay poll tax to a government that supported slavery, he held on to his undoctrinaire principles against such laws as the Fugitive Slave Act of 1850. He helped a slave escape to Canada in 1851, and voiced moral outrage at kidnappers of fugitives in "Slavery in Massachusetts: An Address Delivered at the Anti-Slavery Celebration at Framingham, July 4, 1854."

Not a political organizer or leader of abolitionist groups, he nonetheless took the lead in condoning John Brown when many abolitionists would not do so. Prophet, critic, lecturer, poet, author, and naturalist, he was a man for all sea-

---

[2] Since 1966, a group of scholars has worked with Princeton University Press to produce a complete annotated, definitive edition of Thoreau's writings, projected at thirty volumes.

[3] *The Dial,* a quarterly "Magazine for Literature, Philosophy and Religion," was founded in New England July 1, 1840, as an organ of the Transcendentalists, who included Bronson Allcott, Orestes Brownson, William Ellery Channing, Ralph Waldo Emerson, Margaret Fuller, Theodore Parker, and George Ripley. Thoreau did not identify himself as a Transcendentalist, though he continues to be identified with them; his early literary contributions were in *The Dial,* which was edited by Margaret Fuller from 1840 to 1842, and afterward by Emerson, with Thoreau's assistance, until 1844, when it ceased publication.

sons, a ubiquitous moral and social conscience who left a legacy deeper and wider than Walden Pond.

In the following excerpt, from his speech to Concord citizens, Sunday, October 30, 1859, he argues how and why John Brown's last stand at Harper's Ferry "distinguished him from all the reformers of the day."

From *A Plea for John Brown* (1859)

. . . I read all the newspapers I could get within a week after this event, and I do not remember in them a single expression of sympathy for these men. I have since seen one noble statement, in a Boston paper, not editorial. Some voluminous sheets decided not to print the full report of Brown's words to the exclusion of other matter. It was as if a publisher should reject the manuscript of the New Testament, and print Wilson's last speech. The same journal which contained this pregnant news, was chiefly filled, in parallel columns, with the reports of the political conventions that were being held. But the descent to them was too steep. They should have been spared this contrast, been printed in an extra at least. To turn from the voices and deeds of earnest men to the *cackling* of political conventions! Office-seekers and speech-makers, who do not so much as lay an honest egg, but wear their breasts bare upon an egg of chalk! Their great game is the game of straws, or rather that universal aboriginal game of the platter, at which the Indians cried *hub, bub!* Exclude the reports of religious and political conventions, and publish the words of a living man.

But I object not so much to what they have omitted, as to what they have inserted. Even the *Liberator* called it "a misguided, wild, and apparently insane—effort." As for the herd of newspapers and magazines, I do not chance to know an editor in the country who will deliberately print anything which he knows will ultimately and permanently reduce the number of his subscribers. They do not believe that it would be expedient. How then can they print truth? If we do not say pleasant things, they argue, nobody will attend to us. And so they do like some traveling auctioneers, who sing an obscene song in order to draw a crowd around them. Republican editors, obliged to get their sentences ready for the morning edition, and accustomed to look at everything by the twilight of politics, express no admiration, nor true sorrow even, but call these men "deluded fanatics"—"mistaken men"—"insane," or "crazed." It suggests what a *sane* set of editors we are blessed with, *not* "mistaken men"; who know very well on which side their bread is buttered, at least.

A man does a brave and humane deed, and at once, on all sides, we hear people and parties declaring, "I didn't do it, nor countenance *him* to do it, in any conceivable way. It can't be fairly inferred from my past career." I, for one, am not interested to hear you define your position. I don't know that I ever was, or ever shall be. I think it is mere egotism, or impertinent at this time. Ye needn't take so much pains to wash your skirts of him. No intelligent man will ever be convinced that he was any creature of yours. He went and came, as he himself informs us, "under the auspices of John Brown and nobody else." The Republican party does not perceive how many his *failure* will make to vote more correctly than they would have them. They have counted the votes of Pennsylvania & Co., but they have not correctly counted Captain Brown's vote. He has taken the wind out of their sails, the little wind they had, and they may as well lie to and repair.

What though he did not belong to your clique! Though you may not approve of his method or his principles, recognize his magnanimity. Would you not like to claim kindredship with him in that, though in no other thing he is like, or likely, to you? Do you think that you would lose your reputation so? What you lost at the spile, you would gain at the bung.

If they do not mean all this, then they do not speak the truth, and say what they mean. They are simply at their old tricks still.

"It was always conceded to him," *says one who calls him crazy*, "that he was a conscientious man, very modest in his demeanor, apparently inoffensive, until the subject of Slavery was introduced, when he would exhibit a feeling of indignation unparalleled."

The slave ship is on her way, crowded with its dying victims; new cargoes are being added in midocean; a small crew of slaveholders, countenanced by a large body of passengers, is smothering four millions under the hatches, and yet the politician asserts that the only proper way by which deliverance is to be obtained, is by "the quiet diffusion of the sentiments of humanity," without any "outbreak." As if the sentiments of humanity were ever found unaccompanied by its deeds, and you could disperse them, all finished to order, the pure article, as easily as water with a watering pot, and so lay the dust. What is that that I hear cast overboard? The bodies of the dead that have found deliverance. That is the way we are "diffusing" humanity, and its sentiments with it.

Prominent and influential editors, accustomed to deal with politicians, men of an infinitely lower grade, say, in their ignorance, that he acted "on the principle of revenge." They do not know the man. They must enlarge themselves to conceive of him. I have no doubt that the time will come when they will begin to see him as he was. They have got to conceive of a man of faith and of religious principle, and not a politician nor an Indian; of a man who did not wait till he was personally interfered with or thwarted in some harmless business before he gave his life to the cause of the oppressed.

If Walker[+] may be considered the representative of the South, I wish I could say that Brown was the representative of the North. He was a superior man. He did not value his bodily life in comparison with ideal things. He did not recognize unjust human laws, but resisted them as he was bid. For once we are lifted out of the trivialness and dust of politics into the region of truth and manhood. No man in America has ever stood up so persistently and effectively for the dignity of human nature, knowing himself for a man, and the equal of any and all governments. In that sense he was the most American of us all. He needed no babbling lawyer, making false issues, to defend him. He was more than a match for all the judges that American voters, or officeholders of whatever grade, can create. He could not have been tried by a jury of his peers, because his peers did not exist. When a man stands up serenely against the condemnation and vengeance of mankind, rising above them literally *by a whole body*— even though he were of late the vilest murderer, who has settled that matter with himself—the spectacle is a sublime one (didn't ye know it, ye Liberators, ye Tribunes, ye Republicans?), and we become criminal in comparison. Do yourselves the honor to recognize him. He needs none of your respect.

As for the Democratic journals, they are not human enough to affect me at all. I do not feel indignation at anything they may say.

I am aware that I anticipate a little, that he was still, at the last accounts, alive in the hands of his foes; but that being the case, I have all along found myself thinking & speaking of him as physically dead.

I do not believe in erecting statues to those who still live in our hearts, whose bones have not yet crumbled in the earth around us, but I would rather see the statue of Captain Brown in the Massachusetts Statehouse yard, than that of any other man whom I know. I rejoice that I live in this age—that I am his contemporary.

What a contrast, when we turn to that political party which is so anxiously shuffling him and his plot out of its way, and looking around for some available slaveholder, perhaps, to be its candidate, at least for one who will execute the

---

[+] Thoreau's reference is to Robert J. Walker (1801–69), also known as Robert James, the expansionist governor of Kansas Territory in 1857, then called "Bleeding Kansas" amid the guerrilla war following John Brown's 1856 Potawatomie Massacre, which Walker denounced. Earlier, as U.S. senator of Mississippi (1836–45), Walker was pro-slavery; as Secretary of the Treasury (1845–49), he originated the Walker Tariff of 1846, which was favorable to the South but not to the North in reducing tariff rates.

Fugitive Slave Law, and all those other unjust laws which he took up arms to annul!

Insane! A father and six sons, and one son-in-law, and several more men besides—as many at least as twelve disciples—all struck with insanity at once; while the sane tyrant holds with a firmer gripe than ever his four millions of slaves, and a thousand sane editors, his abettors, are saving their country and their bacon! Just as insane were his efforts in Kansas. Ask the tyrant who is his most dangerous foe, the sane man or the insane. Do the thousands who know him best, who have rejoiced at his deeds in Kansas, and have afforded him material aid there, think him insane? Such a use of this word is a mere trope with most who persist in using it, and I have no doubt that many of the rest have already in silence retracted their words. . . .

SARAH PARKER REMOND

(1826–94)

While the Harper's Ferry attack lingered in the national consciousness in late 1859, freeborn blacks battled discrimination unnoticed by most Americans. In that struggle was Sarah Remond, an articulate antislavery lecturer on two continents. Endowed with talents she could not fulfill in antebellum America, shackled by midnineteenth century barriers against her race and gender, it was her destiny to distinguish herself abroad.

Born and reared in Salem, Massachusetts, the daughter of a businessman from Curaçao who obtained American citizenship through a court, her early education was in Salem's integrated schools, which were then rare in New England. Influenced by her older brother, Charles Lenox Remond, an ally of Garrison, she began speaking for antislavery societies in the early 1840s. Charles, a riveting orator who was a role model for Frederick Douglass, was likewise a defender of women's rights. In 1840 he had joined Garrison to sit in with women in back seats at the 1840 World Anti-Slavery Convention in London, where American female delegates were denied equality with their male counterparts.

During their travels in the East, both Charles and Sarah endured racial hostility in boarding houses, railway cars, and steamships—conditions which he exposed in a speech in 1842 to the Massachusetts legislature on the "Rights of Colored Persons while Travelling." Sarah protested segregated churches, public exhibition halls, and theaters. In 1853, after she was ousted from an opera theater in Boston for presenting tickets she purchased for a box seat, she filed a civil suit against the theater and won. Her antislavery crusade revealed public prejudices in the North, and she linked both causes in her speeches and letters, some of which were printed in *The Liberator*, *National Anti-Slavery Standard*, *London Anti–Slavery Advocate*, and other periodicals.

In December 1859, during a lecture tour in the British Isles, she was turned away from the U.S. legation in London when she applied for a visa to travel to France. Informed that "an indispensable qualification of an American passport was United States citizenship," she petitioned an unrelenting U.S. Ambassador, before the British Foreign Secretary intervened to provide her with visa documents.

Her citizenship status resulted in an extended stay in London, where she studied at the Bedford College for Ladies until late 1866, then moved to Florence. There she pursued a course in paramedical studies at the Santa Maria Nuova Hospital until 1868 and was later certified as a practicing physician. Weary of racial obstacles to progress in America, she established permanent residence in Italy. In 1877, at age fifty-one, she married Lazzaro Pintor, an Italian. She never returned to the United States and, at her death in December 1894, was buried in Rome—one of the first Afro-American expatriates to have a successful career in Europe.[1]

The following texts are letters to and from the American legation in London, concerning her citizenship status in 1859.

An Exchange of Letters on American Citizenship (1859)[2]

No. 6 Grenville Street
Brunswick Square, . . .
[London,] December 12, 1859

Sir:

I beg to inform you that, a short time [ago], I went to the office of the American Embassy, to have my passport visaed for France.

I should remark that my passport is an American one, granted to me in the United States and signed by the Minister in due form. It states—what is the fact—that I am a citizen of the United States. I was born in Massachusetts.

Upon asking to have my passport visaed at the American Embassy, the person in the office refused to affix the visa, on the ground that I am a person of color.

Being a citizen of the United States, I respectfully demand, as my right, that my passport be visaed by the Minister of my country.

---

[1] The editor is indebted to Dorothy B. Porter, curator and archivist, for her pioneering research and previously printed documentation on Sarah Parker Remond in Europe.

Ira Aldrich (1807–67), a New York–born actor turned British citizen in 1863, was the first Afro-American expatriate to launch a celebrated career in Europe, after a London theater debut in Shakespeare's *Othello* in the 1820s.

[2] Title supplied by the editor of this volume.

As I am desirous of starting for the Continent, I must request an answer at your earliest convenience.

I remain, Sir, your obedient servant.

Sarah P. Remond

The Honorable George Mifflin Dallas
American Minister
No. 34 Portland Place
[London, England]

Legation of the United States
London, December 14, 1859

Miss Sarah P. Remond:

I am directed by the Minister to acknowledge the receipt of your note of the 12th . . . and to say, in reply, he must of course, be sorry if any of his country-women, irrespective of color or extraction, should think him frivolously disposed to withhold from facilities in his power to grant for traveling on the continent of Europe; but when the indispensable qualification for an American passport, that of "United States citizenship," does not exist—when, indeed, it is manifestly an impossibility by law that it should exist—a just sense of his official obligations, under instructions received from his Government as long ago as the 8th of July 1856, and since then strictly conformed to, constrains him to say that the demand of Miss Sarah P. Remond cannot be complied with.

Respectfully, your obedient servant,
Benjm [Benjamin] Moran
Assistant Secretary of Legation

A day later, Sarah P. Remond responded to Benjamin Moran's letter as follows:

Sir:

I have the honor to acknowledge the receipt of your letter of yesterday's date.

The purport of your communication is most extraordinary. You now lay down the rule that persons freeborn in the United States, and who have been subjected all their lives to the taxation and other burdens imposed upon American citizens, are to be deprived of their rights as such, merely because their complexions happen to be dark, and that they are to be refused the aid of Ministers of their country, whose salaries they continue to pay.

Sarah P. Remond

ROBERT PURVIS

(1810–98)

Freeborn, educated in private academies, heir to a family fortune, fair enough to pass for white, Robert Purvis bore the full burden of proof that ancestry, appearance, literacy, affluence, and refinement did not mitigate race prejudice or guarantee civil rights in antebellum America.

The son of an interracial marriage, he was born in 1810 in Charleston, South Carolina, where state law then allowed matrimony between the races. His English-born father, William Purvis, and half-Moroccan and half-German mother, Harriet Judah, moved to Philadelphia before their son was ten. When his father, a textile merchant, died in 1826, Robert, then sixteen, inherited $120,000 and used much of it in a long campaign to end slavery. Few nineteenth-century abolitionists of color equaled him in income or impact, or gave as much of themselves to help both slaves and freemen.

He was one of the earliest of his generation to lecture in England to antislavery societies, paving the way for his able successor and contemporary, Charles Lenox Remond. Purvis's first and only trip to the British Isles in the summer of 1834 was delayed by obstacles in obtaining an official U.S. passport (due to excuses similar to those heard by Sarah Remond over two decades later). But with letters of introduction from Garrison and others, the twenty-three-year-old leader was welcomed by influential British reformers.

Some months before, he had been a primary organizer of the American Anti-Slavery Society in December 1833, and one of the few men of his race at that historic first convention in Philadelphia. Later that same year, his first wife, Harriet Forten Purvis, cofounded the interracial Female Anti-Slavery Society, and Purvis himself urged women's rights in groups in which he was active for the next three decades, including the Pennsylvania Society for Promoting the Abolition of Slavery, and the Pennsylvania Anti-Slavery Society, which elected him President from 1845 to 1850.

With his financial inheritance and that of his wife—daughter of wealthy sailmaker and abolitionist James Forten, Jr.,—the couple moved in 1844 from Philadelphia to a rural estate in Byberry, Pennsylvania, where they raised poultry and livestock, in an effort to boycott slave-made products. Their large property was also home for their eight children and a station for fugitive slaves on the underground railway.

At annual conventions of free colored men in Northern states from 1830 until the Civil War, Purvis attended and advocated assimilationism over separatism and emigrationism. A dedicated integrationist reformer like William Whipper, he joined efforts to establish temperance unions, training centers, and libraries for freemen. He vigorously opposed Pennsylvania's legislative measures to bar them from settling in the state and threatened to refuse to pay his taxes if his race was denied the constitutional rights of American citizens.

During the Civil War, Purvis called for enlisting colored troops and officers in the Union Army. In 1863, at the thirtieth anniversary convention of the American Anti-Slavery Society, he pledged allegiance to a federal government that he had vilified three years earlier at the organization's twenty-seventh anniversary in New York City. The following text is from that militant speech of May 1860.

From *Your Government— It Is Not Mine* (1860)[1]

As one of your speakers today, I feel myself embarrassed by two opposite and conflicting feelings: one is a painful and distressing sense of my incapacity for the duty which you have imposed upon me, and the other is an irrepressible desire to do or say something effective for a cause which is dearer to me than my heart's blood. Sir, I need not say here that I belong to that class who, at the South, are bought, sold, leased, mortgaged, and in all respects treated as absolute property; I belong to the class who, here at the North, are declared, by the highest tribunal known to your government, to possess "no *rights* that a *white* man is bound to respect."[2]

I say *your* government—it is not mine. Thank God, I have no willing share in a government that deliberately before the world, and without a blush, declares one part of its people, and that for no crime or pretext of crime, disfranchised and outlawed. For such a government, I, as a man, can have no feeling but of *contempt, loathing,* and *unutterable abhorrence!* And, sir, I venture to

---

[1] Title supplied by the editor, from a sentence in the text.
[2] From a quote by Chief Justice Roger B. Taney in his "Opinion of the Court" on the Dred Scott Decision. See p. 195.

affirm that there is no man in this audience, who has a spark of manhood in him, who has a tittle of genuine self-respect in his bosom, that will not justify me in these feelings.

What are the facts in this case? What is the attitude of your boasting, braggart republic toward the six hundred thousand free people of color who swell its population and add to its wealth? I have already alluded to the dictum of Judge Taney in the notorious Dred Scott decision. That dictum reveals the animus of the whole government; it is a fair example of the cowardly and malignant spirit that pervades the entire policy of the country. The end of that policy is, undoubtedly, to destroy the colored man, as a man, to prevent him from having any existence in the land except as a "chattel personal to all intents, constructions and purposes whatsoever." With this view, it says a colored man shall not sue and recover his lawful property; he shall not bear arms and train in the militia; he shall not be a commander of a vessel, not even of the meanest craft that creeps along the creeks and bays of your Southern coast; he shall not carry a mailbag, or serve as a porter in a post office; and he shall not even put his face in a United States courtroom for any purpose, except by the sufferance of the white man.

I had occasion, a few days since, to go to the United States courtroom in the city of Philadelphia. My errand was a proper one; it was to go bail for one of the noble band of colored men who had so bravely risked their lives for the rescue of a brother man on his way to eternal bondage. As I was about entering the door, I was stopped, and ordered back. I demanded the reason. "I have my orders," was the reply. What orders? "To keep out all colored people." Now, sir, who was the man that offered me this indignity? It was Deputy-Marshal Jenkins, the notorious slave-catcher. And why did he do it? Because he had his orders from pious, praying, Christian Democrats, who hold and teach the damnable doctrine that the "black man has no rights that the white man is bound to respect." It is true that Marshal Yost, to whom I indignantly appealed, reversed this man's orders, and apologized to me, assuring me that I could go in and out at my pleasure. But, sir, the apology made the matter worse; for, mark you, it was not me personally that was objected to, *but the race* with which I stand identified. Great God! who can think of such outrages, such meanness, such dastardly, cowardly cruelty, without burning with indignation, and choking for want of words with which to denounce it? And in the case of the noble little band referred to, the men who generously, heroically risked their lives to rescue the man who was about being carried back to slavery; look at their conduct; you know the circumstances. We recently had a slave trial in Philadelphia—no new thing in the city of *"Brotherly Love."* A victim of Virginia tyranny, a fugitive from Southern injustice, had made good his escape from the land of whips and chains to Pennsylvania, and had taken up his abode near the capital of the State. The place of his retreat was discovered; the bloodhounds of the law scented him out, and caught him; they put him in chains and brought him before Judge Cadwallader—a man whose proslavery antecedents made him a fitting instrument for the execution of the accursed Fugitive Slave Law.

The sequel can easily be imagined. Brewster, a leading Democrat—the man, who, like your O'Conor of this city, has the unblushing hardihood to defend the enslavement of the black man upon principle—advocated his return. The man was sent into lifelong bondage. While the trial was going on, slaveholders, Southern students and proslavery Market Street salesmen were freely admitted; but the colored people, the class most interested, were carefully excluded. Prohibited from entering, they thronged around the door of the courthouse. At last the prisoner was brought out, handcuffed and guarded by his captors; he was put into a carriage which started off in the direction of the South. Some ten or twelve brave black men made a rush for the carriage, in hopes of effecting a rescue; they were overpowered, beaten, put under arrest and carried to prison, there to await their trial, before this same Judge Cadwallader, for violating the Fugitive Slave law! Mark you, they may go into the courtroom as *prisoners*, but not as *spectators!* They may not have an opportunity of hearing the law expounded, but they may be punished if they make themselves chargeable with violating it!

Sir, people talk of the bloody code of Draco, but I venture to assert, without fear of intelligent contradiction, that, all things considered, that code was mild, that code was a law of love, compared with the hellish laws and precedents that disgrace the statute books of this modern Democratic, Christian Republic! I said that a man of color might not be a commander of the humblest craft that sails in your American waters. There was a man in Philadelphia, the other day, who stated that he owned and sailed a schooner between that city and different ports in the State of Maryland—that his vessel had been seized in the town of Easton, (I believe it was), or some other town on the Eastern Shore, on the allegation that, contrary to law, there was no white man on board. The vessel constituted his entire property and sole means of supporting his family. He was advised to sue for its recovery, which he did, and, after a long and expensive litigation, the case was decided in his favor. But by this time the vessel had rotted and gone to wreck, and the man found himself reduced to beggary. His business in Philadelphia was to raise fifty dollars with which to take himself and family out of this cursed land, to a country where liberty is not a mockery, and freedom a mere idle name!

Sir, look for a moment at the detestable meanness of this country! What was the cause of your war of the Revolution? The tyrannical doctrine of taxation without representation! Who was the first martyr in your Revolutionary

War? Crispus Attucks, a Negro. It was a black man's blood that was the first to flow in behalf of American independence. In the War of 1812, what class of your inhabitants showed themselves more unselfishly loyal and patriotic than the free people of color? None sir. In Philadelphia the colored people organized themselves into companies, and vied with their more favored fellow citizens in the zeal of their efforts to guard and protect the city. In Louisiana their bravery and soldierlike behavior was such as to elicit the warmest encomiums from General Jackson, the commander in chief of the Southern army. . . .

But, sir, narrow and proscriptive as, in my opinion, is the spirit of what is called Native Americanism, there is another thing I regard as tenfold more base and contemptible, and that is your American Democracy—your piebald and rotten Democracy, that talks loudly about equal rights, and at the same time tramples one-sixth of the population of the country in the dust, and declares that they have "no rights which a white man is bound to respect." And, sir, while I repudiate your Native Americanism and your bogus Democracy, allow me to add, at the same time, that I am not a Republican. I could not be a member of the Republican party if I were so disposed; I am disfranchised; I have no vote; I am put out of the pale of political society. The time was in Pennsylvania, under the old Constitution, when I could go to the polls as other men do, but your modern Democracy have taken away from me that right. Your Reform Convention, your Pierce Butlers—the man who, a year ago, put up nearly four hundred human beings on the block in Georgia, and sold them to the highest bidder—your Pierce Butlers disfranchised me, and I am without any political rights whatever. I am taxed to support a government which takes my money and tramples on me. But, sir, I would not be a member of the Republican party if it were in my power. How could I, a colored man, join a party that styles itself emphatically the "white man's party!?" How could I, an Abolitionist, belong to a party that is and must of necessity be a proslavery party?[3] The Republicans may be, and doubtless are, opposed to the extension of slavery, but they are sworn to support, and they *will* support, slavery where it already exists.

The Liberator, May 18, 1860.

---

[3] At the time of Purvis's speech, May 8, 1860, the Republicans did not have as titular leader Abraham Lincoln, who later that same month was chosen the party's 1860 presidential nominee—on the third ballot—by delegates at the Republican National Convention in Chicago. Their convention platform advocated no slavery in the territories, but no interference in states where the institution existed. (The platform, adopted in Chicago May 18, 1860, coincided with the same date as publication of Purvis's speech in the *Liberator*. However, he and most other abolitionists, black and white, soon opposed the platform, which excluded them and repudiated John Brown.)

ELLEN CRAFT

(ca. 1826–97)

AND WILLIAM CRAFT

(1827–1900)

In one of the most daring and dramatic escapes by slaves from the American South, Ellen and William Craft also made literary history with a slave narrative of their heroic journey. Ellen, publicly hailed as heroine by most American abolitionists, was nevertheless overshadowed by her husband's dictated narration of their memoir published in London in 1860, and subsequently ignored by most historians. Late twentieth-century scholars, male and female, have since restored and illuminated her substantive role in the legend.

Born the daughter of a slave named Maria Smith and her slavemaster, Major James Smith, on a plantation in Clinton, Georgia, Ellen was reared a house servant, and at age eleven given as a "wedding present" to the Smiths' daughter Eliza and her husband, Dr. Robert Collins, who took her as their personal maid to Macon, Georgia, in 1837. In Macon, she met William Craft, a local slave hired out as a mechanic and cabinetmaker's apprentice, and both obtained their owners' consent to "marry" in 1846. In December 1848, four days before Christmas, with meager savings from William's work as carpenter-for-hire, and a short holiday pass granted slaves to travel in the countryside, the couple began their risky escape North. Ellen's skin color, hair, and features fit her disguise as a young, Southern male squire in an outfit she had sewn herself, while William, of darker hue, posed as valet; thus did the two journey as "Master William Johnson and slave." Under pretense of travel to Philadelphia for medical treatment, Ellen and William bound her right arm in a sling to avoid requests en route to sign papers or names.

The couple had not learned to read or write before their hazardous escape. By rail they traveled from Macon to Savannah, and on steamships to Charleston, South Carolina, Wilmington, North Carolina, and in more railcars to Richmond, Virginia, and Fredericksburg, Maryland, before a ferry ride up the Potomac River to Washington, DC, and a final train to Philadelphia. Arriving exhausted in the city on Christmas morning, slaves no more, they found in the strong abolitionist network of the underground railroad a boarding house and help from Robert Purvis and others. Purvis and his friends hid them with a Quaker farmer, Barclay Ivins, who led them to ex-fugitive William Wells Brown, who accompanied them safely to Boston. Brown penned the first news of the Crafts' escape in a jubilant letter printed in Garrison's *Liberator*, January 12, 1849. Ellen then twenty-two, and William twenty-four, were quickly the most famous fugitives in America.

In Boston, they were legally and ceremoniously married by abolitionist Unitarian clergyman Theodore Parker, and in no imminent danger until Congress passed the Fugitive Slave Act of 1850. The Act gave slavemasters legal right to recapture fugitives and forced Ellen and William to flee to Portland, Maine, thence by boat to Nova Scotia and to England, where they lived nineteen years in exile until after the Civil War. During their long odyssey abroad, husband and wife acquired both formal and industrial education at the Ockham School outside London, lectured to antislavery societies in the British Isles, published a narrative of their experience, bought a home in a London suburb, and reared five children. While William tried various occupations, including trips to Dahomey, West Africa, for British merchants in the early 1860s, Ellen kept the children and a transatlantic vigil on the war and emancipation in the American South. Her mother, Maria, was rescued by Union generals and reunited with her daughter in England in 1865. Before Maria's arrival, Ellen had known only one other American–born woman of color abroad: Sarah Parker Remond.

In 1868, the Craft family came full circle and returned to the United States: first to Boston, then in 1870 to their native Georgia, where they leased a plantation to manage an agricultural school for former slaves. When the property was burned by the Ku Klux Klan, the Crafts bought "Woodville" plantation near Savannah, where for the next two decades Ellen trained rural women and children and worked the land with tenant farmers; loss of Northern philanthropy forced her and William to give up the cooperative school and farm. She spent her final years in Charleston with her namesake-daughter, Ellen, a civic leader and wife of physician William Crum, an influential South Carolina Republican. Within a few years of his mother-in-law's death, Crum was appointed federal customs inspector for the Port of Charleston—a port where the Crafts boarded the first steamship on their historic journey North.

The following excerpt is from William's dictated memoir for the London edition in 1860, with his first-person narration of *Running a Thousand Miles for Freedom; or, The Escape of William and Ellen Craft from Slavery*.

From *Running a Thousand Miles for Freedom* (1860)

. . . My wife's first master was her father, and her mother his slave, and the latter is still the slave of his widow.

Notwithstanding my wife being of African extraction on her mother's side, she is almost white—in fact, she is so nearly so that the tyrannical old lady to whom she first belonged became so annoyed, at finding her frequently mistaken for a child of the family, that she gave her when eleven years of age to a daughter, as a wedding present. This separated my wife from her mother, and also from several other dear friends. But the incessant cruelty of her old mistress made the change of owners or treatment so desirable, that she did not grumble much at this cruel separation.

It may be remembered that slavery in America is not at all confined to persons of any particular complexion; there are a very large number of slaves as white as anyone; but as the evidence of a slave is not admitted in court against a free white person, it is almost impossible for a white child, after having been kidnapped and sold into or reduced to slavery, in a part of the country where it is not known (as often is the case), ever to recover its freedom.

I have myself conversed with several slaves who told me that their parents were white and free; but that they were stolen away from them and sold when quite young. As they could not tell their address, and also as the parents did not know what had become of their lost and dear little ones, of course all traces of each other were gone. . . .

. . . .

I have known worthless white people to sell their own free children into slavery; and, as there are good-for-nothing white as well as coloured persons everywhere, no one, perhaps, will wonder at such inhuman transactions: particularly in the Southern States of America, where I believe there is a greater want of humanity and high principle amongst the whites, than among any other civilized people in the world.

I know that those who are not familiar with the working of "the peculiar institution," can scarcely imagine any one so totally devoid of all natural affection as to sell his own offspring into returnless bondage. But Shakespeare, that great observer of human nature, says:—

> With caution judge of probabilities.
> Things deemed unlikely, e'en impossible,
> Experience often shows us to be true.

My wife's new mistress was decidedly more humane than the majority of her class. My wife has always given her credit for not exposing her to many of the worst features of slavery. For instance, it is a common practice in the slave States for ladies, when angry with their maids, to send them to the calaboose sugarhouse, or to some other place established for the purpose of punishing slaves, and have them severely flogged; and I am sorry it is a fact, that the villains to whom those defenseless creatures are sent, not only flog them as they are ordered, but frequently compel them to submit to the greatest indignity. Oh! if there is any one thing under the wide canopy of heaven, horrible enough to stir a man's soul, and to make his very blood boil, it is the thought of his dear wife, his unprotected sister, or his young and virtuous daughters, struggling to save themselves from falling a prey to such demons!

It always appears strange to me that anyone who was not born a slaveholder, and steeped to the very core in the demoralizing atmosphere of the Southern States, can in any way palliate slavery. It is still more surprising to see virtuous ladies looking with patience upon, and remaining indifferent to, the existence of a system that exposes nearly two millions of their own sex in the manner I have mentioned, and that too in a professedly free and Christian country. There is, however, great consolation in knowing that God is just, and will not let the oppressor of the weak, and the spoiler of the virtuous, escape unpunished here and hereafter.

I believe a similar retribution to that which destroyed Sodom is hanging over the slaveholders. My sincere prayer is that they may not provoke God, by persisting in a reckless course of wickedness, to pour out his consuming wrath upon them.

I must now return to our history.

My old master had the reputation of being a very humane and Christian man, but he thought nothing of selling my poor old father, and dear aged mother, at separate times, to different persons, to be dragged off never to behold each other again, till summoned to appear before the great tribunal of heaven. But, oh! what a happy meeting it will be on that great day for those faithful souls. I say a happy meeting, because I never saw persons more devoted to the service of God than they. But how will the case stand with those reckless traffickers in human flesh and blood, who plunged the poisonous dagger of separation into those loving hearts which God had for so many years closely joined together—nay, sealed as it were with his own hands for the eternal courts of heaven? It is not for me to say what will become of those heartless tyrants. I must leave them in the hands of an all-wise and just God, who will, in his own good time, and in his own way, avenge the wrongs of his oppressed people.

My old master also sold a dear brother and a sister, in the same manner as he did my father and mother. The reason he assigned for disposing of my parents, as well as of several other aged slaves, was, that "they were getting old, and would soon become valueless in the market, and therefore he intended to sell off all the old stock, and buy in a young lot." A most disgraceful conclusion for a man to come to, who made such great professions of religion!

This shameful conduct gave me a thorough hatred, not for true Christianity, but for slaveholding piety.

My old master, then, wishing to make the most of the rest of his slaves, apprenticed a brother and myself out to learn trades: he to a blacksmith, and myself to a cabinetmaker. If a slave has a good trade, he will let or sell for more than a person without one, and many slaveholders have their slaves taught trades on this account. But before our time expired, my old master wanted money; so he sold my brother, and then mortgaged my sister, a dear girl about fourteen years of age, and myself, then about sixteen, to one of the banks, to get money to speculate in cotton. This we knew nothing of at the moment; but time rolled on, the money became due, my master was unable to meet his payments; so the bank had us placed upon the auction stand and sold to the highest bidder. . . .

FREDERICK LAW OLMSTED

(1822–1903)

The 1850 Fugitive Slave Act, which reenslaved many escapees, so provoked Frederick Law Olmsted that he traveled South in 1852 to investigate for the *New York Daily Times*. He made two trips and published over seventy dispatches with the byline "Yeoman" in the *Times* between 1853 and 1854. His eyewitness accounts were luminous exposés on slavery in different Southern states: *A Journey in the Seaboard Slave States* (1856), *A Journey through Texas* (1857), and *A Journey in the Back Country* (1860). In 1861, his three volumes were the basis for a two-volume condensation: *The Cotton Kingdom: A Traveller's Observations on Cotton and Slavery in the American Slave States*. The "yeoman" journalist-author was a man of varied roles in American culture, and then beginning to be praised as the nation's premier urban landscape architect, after he was appointed engineer-superintendent of Manhattan's Central Park in 1857.

Olmsted's only previous book was *Walks and Talks of an American Farmer in England* (1852), about his walking trip through the British Isles, with ruminations on citizen responsibility to preserve the environment in a postindustrial world. By then, he had briefly tried being a farmer in Connecticut and Staten Island, a merchant seaman in China, manager of a mining company in California, and head of publishing house in New York—the latter with financial help from his wealthy father. Born into the gentry of Hartford, Connecticut, but often independent of it in his own quests, he was a gifted intellectual whose occupational setbacks were career discontinuities but also profound learning experiences that left him with both inner resources and inner conflicts.

He never graduated from high school, and only audited a few classes at Yale. Discontented in boarding schools from age seven to seventeen, his most indelible education came through his wide reading, travels, and spirit of inquiry. Both a social idealist and democratic pragmatist, he was politically a conservative Free-Soiler, who refused to join the abolitionist movement and expressed an ambivalence about slave emancipation in his travel book, *Walks and Talks*. He believed education a necessary prerequisite to the freedom of slaves, for the "amelioration, the improvement and the elevation of the Negro."

However, much of his writing on slavery expresses moral indignation at the institution.

The experimental projects most often identified with Olmsted came after the Civil War—and had little connection to his books about the slave states. His name looms largest as a creator of Eastern urban parks: Central Park in Manhattan, Prospect Park in Brooklyn, Franklin Park in Boston, the U.S. Capitol grounds, and in design proposals for other parks and planned American communities. He helped to civilize urban America, with his utilitarian vision for the future of its cityscapes during a period when the nation was recuperating from the Civil War. He accumulated notes for a book entitled *Civilization*, which he never completed, but his other works, in writing and in public art, are American cultural and historical landmarks of lasting value.

The following is excerpted from "The Rice District" in volume 1, chapter 6 of *The Cotton Kingdom*.

From *The Cotton Kingdom: A Traveller's Observations on Cotton and Slavery in the American Slave States* (1861)

. . . So far as I have observed, slaves show themselves worthy of trust most, where their masters are most considerate and liberal toward them. Far more so, for instance, on the small farms of North Carolina than on the plantations of Virginia and South Carolina. Mr. X's slaves are permitted to purchase firearms and ammunition, and to keep them in their cabins; and his wife and daughters reside with him, among them, the doors of the house never locked, or windows closed, perfectly defenseless, and miles distant from any other white family.

Another evidence that negroes, even in slavery, when trusted, may prove wonderfully reliable, I will subjoin, in a letter written by Mr. Alexander Smets, of Savannah, to a friend in New York, in 1853. It is hardly necessary to say, that the "servants" spoken of were negroes, and the "suspicious characters," providentially removed, were whites. The letter was not written for publication:—

> The epidemic which spread destruction and desolation through our city, and many other places in most of the Southern States, was, with the exception of that of 1820, the most deadly that was ever known here. Its appearance being sudden, the inhabitants were seized with a

panic, which caused an immediate *sauve qui peut* seldom witnessed before. I left, or rather fled, for the sake of my daughters, to Sparta, Hancock county. They were dreadfully frightened.

Of a population of fifteen thousand, six thousand, who could not get away, remained, nearly all of whom were more or less seized with the prevailing disease. The negroes, with very few exceptions, escaped.

Amidst the desolation and gloom pervading the deserted streets, there was a feature that showed our slaves in a favorable light. There were entire blocks of houses, which were either entirely deserted—the owners in many instances having, in their flight, forgotten to lock them up—or left in charge of the servants. A finer opportunity for plunder could not be desired by thieves; and yet the city was remarkable, during the time, for order and quietness. There were scarcely any robberies committed, and as regards fires, so common in the winter, none! Every householder, whose premises had escaped the fury of the late terrific storm, found them in the same condition he had left them. Had not the yellow fever scared away or killed those suspicious characters, whose existence is a problem, and who prowl about every city, I fear that our city might have been laid waste. Of the whole board of directors of five banks, three or four remained, and these at one time were sick. Several of the clerks were left, each in the possession of a single one. For several weeks it was difficult to get anything to eat; the bakers were either sick or dead. The markets closed, no countryman dared venture himself into the city with the usual supplies for the table, and the packets had discontinued their trips. I shall stop, otherwise I could fill a volume with the occurrences and incidents of the dismal period of the epidemic.

On most of the large rice plantations which I have seen in this vicinity, there is a small chapel, which the negroes call their prayerhouse. The owner of one of these told me that, having furnished the prayerhouse with seats having a back-rail, his negroes petitioned him to remove it, because it did not leave them *room enough to pray*. It was explained to me that it is their custom, in social worship, to work themselves up to a great pitch of excitement, in which they yell and cry aloud, and finally, shriek and leap up, clapping their hands and dancing, as it is done at heathen festivals. The back-rail they found to seriously impede this exercise.

Mr. X told me that he had endeavored, with but little success, to prevent this shouting and jumping of the negroes at their meetings on his plantation, from a conviction that there was not the slightest element of religious sentiment in it. He considered it to be engaged in more as an exciting amusement than from any really religious impulse. In the town churches, except, perhaps, those managed and conducted almost exclusively by negroes, the slaves are said to commonly engage in religious exercises in a sober and decorous manner; yet, a member of a Presbyterian church in a Southern city told me, that he had seen the negroes in his own house of worship, during "a season of revival," leap from their seats, throw their arms wildly in the air, shout vehemently and unintelligibly, cry, groan, rend their clothes, and fall into cataleptic trances.

On almost every large plantation, and in every neighborhood of small ones, there is one man who has come to be considered the head or pastor of the local church. The office among the negroes, as among all other people, confers a certain importance and power. A part of the reverence attaching to the duties is given to the person; vanity and self-confidence are cultivated, and a higher ambition aroused than can usually enter the mind of a slave. The self-respect of the preacher is also often increased by the consideration in which he is held by his master, as well as by his fellows; thus, the preachers generally have an air of superiority to other negroes; they acquire a remarkable memory of words, phrases, and forms; a curious sort of poetic talent is developed, and a habit is obtained of rhapsodizing and exciting furious emotions, to a great degree spurious and temporary, in themselves and others, through the imagination. I was introduced, the other day, to a preacher, who was represented to be quite distinguished among them. I took his hand, respectfully, and said I was happy to meet him. He seemed to take this for a joke, and laughed heartily. . . .

MARY BOYKIN CHESNUT

(1823–86)

The Civil War diaries written by Mary Boykin Chesnut from 1861 to 1865 sketched the end of Confederate society. A book edition first appeared nearly two decades after her death, entitled A *Diary from Dixie*—a title she never chose.[1] Nevertheless, her posthumous diary showed the rise and fall of an era, with more about the South's legacy of race and slavery than the public would see later in the celebrated novel of the Civil War and Reconstruction, *Gone with the Wind*.

No "Southern belle" in American fiction quite mirrors the mercurial and complex Mary Boykin Miller Chesnut. The outspoken daughter and wife of pro-slavery politicians in South Carolina, she made no case against slavery as an injustice to blacks, as Angelina and Sarah Grimké had done. "I *hate* the abolitionists for their cant and abuse of us," she wrote in a letter. Her disdain of the slave system was its disregard for Southern white wives powerless against the sexual immorality of their husbands with slave mistresses. Her diaries pointed implicitly at her dissolute father-in-law, James Chesnut, Sr., a wealthy slaveowner whose mix-blood offspring were numerous on his vast plantation near Camden, South Carolina, where Mary lived the first eight years of her marriage. "Like the patriarchs of old," she wrote, "our men live all in one house with their wives and their concubines."

Born in Statesburg, South Carolina, in 1823, she was the eldest child and namesake of Mary Boykin Miller and Stephen Decatur Miller, a lawyer and former U.S. Congressman. In an age when Southern women were not expected to acquire more than a boarding-school education or much knowledge of politics, Mary knew well the meaning of "Nullification"—the "states' rights" doctrine her father urged for South Carolina. During his rapid rise in electoral

---

[1] The title A *Diary from Dixie* was chosen by the *Saturday Evening Post*, which printed excerpts in 1905 prior to book publication that year; the first edition was compiled by Isabella D. Martin and Myrta L. Avary; a 1949 edition was prepared by Ben Ames Williams. For the unabridged text, see C. Vann Woodward and Elisabeth Muhlenfeld, eds. *The Private Mary Chesnut: The Unpublished Civil War Diaries*, (New York: Oxford University Press, 1984).

politics, after serving as Congressman, Miller was state legislator, governor, and U.S. Senator. At her father's death in 1838, Mary was fifteen.

In 1840, shortly after her seventeenth birthday, she married James Chesnut, Jr., a Princeton graduate eight years her senior. He, like her father, was a South Carolina lawyer and slaveowner, soon to become a state legislator and, in 1858, a U.S. Senator. She presided for nearly two years as a Washington political wife and hostess, until late 1860 when James Chesnut resigned from the Senate and returned to South Carolina to help draft an Ordinance of Secession; by late 1862, he was aide de camp and colonel to Jefferson Davis, the President of the Confederacy. Her diary was written in stops and starts during those war years, while she traveled with her husband between Camden, Columbia, Charleston, Montgomery, and Richmond. Few women were better positioned in the Confederacy to see what she called its "marvelous experiences" and to document its ultimate defeat. Her anecdotes and vignettes on the end of slavery and the war remain unsurpassed—if occasionally romanticized—evocations of that period. In 1865, the Chesnuts returned penniless to Camden, South Carolina, the fallen rulers of Mulberry, a war-ravaged plantation, where over five hundred slaves were then free, though in Mary's diary, "not one expressed the slightest pleasure at the *sudden* freedom."

Her generation encouraged women to be wives and mothers but not to be authors; she hoped to have children but had none; she aspired to write fiction but wrote little that equaled her wartime diaries. Her intended book of memoirs, *Mary Chesnut's Civil War*, was started in 1875 as a revision of her journals. Deferred due to family vicissitudes, the book was written between 1881 and 1884 but unpublished before Mary Chesnut's death of a heart attack in 1886.[2]

The following text is excerpted from A *Diary from Dixie*, as edited by Ben Ames Williams and published in 1949.

---

[2] See Elisabeth Muhlenfeld. *Mary Boykin Chesnut: A Biography* (Baton Rouge: Louisiana State University Press, 1981).

From *A Diary from Dixie* (1861)

MONTGOMERY, ALABAMA
MARCH 14TH 1861

. . . I wonder if it be a sin to think slavery a curse to any land. Men and women are punished when their masters and mistresses are brutes, not when they do wrong. Under slavery, we live surrounded by prostitutes, yet an abandoned woman is sent out of any decent house. Who thinks any worse of a Negro or mulatto woman for being a thing we can't name? God forgive us, but ours is a monstrous system, a wrong and an iniquity! Like the patriarchs of old, our men live all in one house with their wives and their concubines; and the mulattoes one sees in every family partly resemble the white children. Any lady is ready to tell you who is the father of all the mulatto children in everybody's household but her own. Those, she seems to think, drop from the clouds. My disgust sometimes is boiling over. Thank God for my countrywomen, but alas for the men! They are probably no worse than men everywhere, but the lower their mistresses, the more degraded they must be.

I think this journal will be disadvantageous for me, for I spend my time now like a spider spinning my own entrails, instead of reading as my habit was in all spare moments. . . .

CHARLESTON, SOUTH CAROLINA

April 13th 1861—Nobody hurt, after all. How gay we were last night. Reaction after the dread of all the slaughter we thought those dreadful cannons were making such a noise in doing. Not even a battery the worse for wear.

Fort Sumter has been on fire. He has not yet silenced any of our guns, or so the aids—still with swords and red sashes by way of uniform—tell us. But the sound of those guns makes regular meals impossible. None of us go to table, but tea trays pervade the corridors going everywhere. Some of the anxious hearts lie on their beds and moan in solitary misery. Mrs. Wigfall and I solace ourselves with tea in my room. These women have all a satisfying faith. "God is on our side," they cry. When we are shut in, we, Mrs. Wigfall and I, ask: "Why?" Answer: "Of course, He hates the Yankees! You'll think that well of Him."

Not by one word or look can we detect any change in the demeanor of these Negro servants. Lawrence sits at our door, as sleepy and as respectful and as profoundly indifferent. So are they all. They carry it too far. You could not tell that they even hear the awful noise that is going on in the bay, though it is dinning in their ears night and day. And people talk before them as if they were chairs and tables, and they make no sign. Are they stolidly stupid, or wiser than we are, silent and strong, biding their time. . . .

CAMDEN, SOUTH CAROLINA

OCTOBER 7TH 1861

. . . Mrs. Chesnut, who is their good angel, is and has always been afraid of Negroes. In her youth, the San Domingo stories were indelibly printed on her mind. She shows her dread now by treating everyone as if they were a black Prince Albert or Queen Victoria. We were beginning to forget Mrs. Cunningham, the only other woman we ever heard of who was murdered by her Negroes. Poor cousin Betsey was goodness itself. After years of freedom and indulgence and tender kindness, it was an awful mistake to threaten them like children. It was only threats. Everybody knew she would never do anything. Mr. Cunningham had been an old bachelor, and the Negroes had it all their own way till he married. Then they hated her. They took her from her room, just over one in which her son-in-law and her daughter slept. They smothered her, dressed her, and carried her out—all without the slightest noise—and hung her by the neck to an apple tree, as if she had committed suicide. If they want to kill us, they can do it when they please, they are noiseless as panthers. They were discovered because, dressing her in the dark, her tippet was put on hindpart before, and she was supposed to have walked out and hung herself in a pair of brand-new shoes whose soles obviously had never touched the ground.

We ought to be grateful that anyone of us is alive, but nobody is afraid of their own Negroes. I find everyone, like myself, ready to trust their own yard. I would go down on the plantation tomorrow and stay there even if there were no white person in twenty miles. My Molly and all the rest I believe would keep me as safe as I should be in the Tower of London. . . .

CAMDEN, SOUTH CAROLINA

October 13th [1861]—Mulberry. We went in the afternoon to the Negro church on the plantation. Manning Brown, a Methodist minister, preached to a very large black congregation. Though glossy black, they were well dressed and were very stylishly gotten up. They were stout, comfortable-looking Christians. The house women, in white aprons and white turbans, were the nicest looking. How snow white the turbans on their heads appeared! But the youthful sisters flaunted in pink and sky blue bonnets which tried their complexions. For the family, they had a cushioned seat near the pulpit, neatly covered with calico. Manning Brown preached Hell fire so hot, I felt singed, if not parboiled. I could not remember any of my many sins that were worthy of an eternity in torment; but, if all the world's misery, sin, and suffering came from so small a sin as eating that apple, what mighty proportions mine take!

Jim Nelson, the driver, the stateliest darky I ever saw, tall and straight as a pine tree, with a fine face, and not so very black but a full-blooded African, was asked to lead in prayer. He became wildly excited, on his knees, facing us with his eyes shut. He clapped his hands at the end of every sentence, and his voice rose to the pitch of a shrill shriek, yet was strangely clear and musical, occasionally in a plaintive minor key that went to your heart. Sometimes it rang out like a trumpet. I wept bitterly. It was all sound, however, and emotional pathos. There was literally nothing in what he said. The words had no meaning at all. It was the devotional passion of voice and manner which was so magnetic. The Negroes sobbed and shouted and swayed backward and forward, some with aprons to their eyes, most of them clapping their hands and responding in shrill tones: "Yes, God!" "Jesus!" "Savior!" "Bless de Lord, amen," etc. It was a little too exciting for me. I would very much have liked to shout, too. Jim Nelson when he rose from his knees trembled and shook as one in a palsy, and from his eyes you could see the ecstasy had not left him yet. He could not stand at all, and sank back on his bench.

Now all this leaves not a trace behind. Jim Nelson is a good man, honest and true; but those who stole before, steal on, in spite of sobs and shouts on Sunday. Those who drink, continue to drink when they can get it. Except that for any open, detected sin they are turned out of church. A Methodist parson is no mealymouthed creature. He requires them to keep the Commandments. If they are not married—and show they ought to be—out of the church they go. If the married members are not true to their vows and it is made plain to him by their conduct, he has them up before the church. They are devoted to their church membership and it is a keen police court.

Suddenly, as I sat wondering what next, they broke out into one of those soul-stirring Negro camp-meeting hymns. To me this is the saddest of all earthly music, weird and depressing beyond my powers to describe. . . .

CAMDEN, SOUTH CAROLINA

NOVEMBER 25TH.—1861

. . . There will never be an interesting book with a Negro heroine down here. We know them too well. They are not picturesque. Only in fiction do they shine. Those beastly Negress beauties are only animals. There is not much difference, after all, between the hut where all ages, sizes and sexes sleep promiscuously, and our Negro cabins.

Now for a story taken down from Maria's lips; she who is left forlorn for the sad and involuntary crime of twins. For "Jeems" Whitaker is still unapproachable in his ire.

Martha Adamson is a beautiful mulattress, as good-looking as they ever are to me. I have never seen a mule as handsome as a horse, and I know I never will; no matter how I lament and sympathize with its undeserved mule condition. She is a trained sempstress, and "hired" her own time, as they call it; that is, the owner pays doctor's bills, finds food and clothing, and the slave pays his master five dollars a month, more or less, and makes a dollar a day if he pleases. Martha, to the amazement of everybody, married a coalblack Negro, the son of Dick the Barber, who was set free fifty years ago for faithful services rendered Mr. Chesnut's grandfather. She was asked: How could she? She is so nearly white. How could she marry that horrid Negro? It is positively shocking! She answered that she inherits the taste of her white father, that her mother was black.

The son of this marriage—a bright boy called John—is grown, reads and writes. The aforesaid Martha is now a widow. Last night there was a row. John beat a white man, who was at his mother's. Poor Martha drinks. John had forbidden Mr. T——to bring whiskey to the house, and he found him seated at table with his mother, both drunk. So he beat him all the way home to his own house. The verdict of the community: "Served him right!" Maria's word: "White people say, 'Well done, John! Give it to him!' "

HARRIET JACOBS (LINDA BRENT)

(1813–97)

Confederate diarist Mary Boykin Chesnut undoubtedly would have labeled Harriet Jacobs a "concubine" and dismissed her 1861 narrative *Incidents in the Life of a Slave Girl . . .* Jacobs expressed a "desire to arouse the women of the North," but the publication of her book in Boston at the beginning of the Civil War aroused few readers. However, by the late twentieth century, many American feminist academics—black and white—had canonized the Jacobs text as the first antebellum autobiography written by a woman of color.[1]

Jacobs was of middle age when she narrated her life as a young fugitive slave and adopted the pseudonym Linda Brent. She concealed names of other people and places, but insisted in her preface that "this narrative is not fiction." Despite the subtitle *Written by Herself,* her first and only book was considered for decades by most black scholars to be fiction by the white abolitionist author, Lydia Maria Child.[2] Although Child helped to negotiate the publishing contract, and was cited as editor on the book's title page, and admittedly made editorial changes, the "incidents" in the manuscript were the experiences of Harriet Jacobs alias Linda Brent.

Jacobs was born a slave in the town of Edenton, North Carolina, in 1813 and orphaned as a child. At age eleven she was bequeathed to a three-year-old female neighbor, whose father—fictitiously named "Dr. Flint"—increased his sexual advances as Harriet grew to puberty. To escape him, she began what her narrative termed a "deliberate calculation": a sexual liaison with a white bachelor neighbor—a lawyer, disguised as "Mr. Sands"—by whom she had a daughter and son. Threatened with retaliation by Flint, she was sent to work on a

---

[1] In 1981 Jean Fagin Yellin was the first academic scholar to publish archival evidence establishing Jacobs's authorship; through additional research on primary sources, Yellin also authenticated the names and backgrounds of the book's pseudonymous characters. See Yellin's piece, "Written by Herself: Harriet Jacobs' Slave Narrative," *American Literature* 53 (November 1981), and her introduction and notes to the reprint edition of *Incidents in the Life of A Slave Girl* published by Harvard University Press, 1987.

[2] See entry on Lydia Child in this volume. Relatedly, one black female scholar, Marion Starling, in a 1946 doctoral dissertation, "The Slave Narrative: Its Place in American History," argued for the authorship of Jacobs, but her claim was refuted by established black male critics at the time.

nearby plantation but escaped and hid for seven years in her grandmother's attic—less than a block from Flint's home. In 1842, leaving her son with her grandmother, Jacobs fled to New York City to be reunited with her daughter, whose white father sent her to Brooklyn to be a servant to his relatives.

Jacobs herself became a nursemaid in the New York household of Nathaniel P. Willis, a prominent literary journalist and editor, whose first wife died in 1844, and whose second wife arranged to purchase Harriet's freedom from Flint's heirs after the Fugitive Slave Act of 1850. Jacobs in 1849 had a chance (that she did not take) to relinquish domestic work and seek other employment in Rochester, New York, where her brother was an antislavery lecturer, and where she met white women's rights reformers such as Amy Post, who encouraged her to write an autobiography.

She began composing *Incidents* after returning to work for the Willises (fictitiously called "Mr. and Mrs. Bruce"), but kept her writing a secret from Nathaniel Willis, who was no abolitionist. His magazine pieces, however, showed him no more proslavery than *New York Tribune* editor Horace Greeley, who was lukewarm to emancipation, but who printed two of Jacobs's unsigned 1853 letters on cruelty to fugitive slaves.

She tried for several years to find a publisher in the U.S. or in England, before her book manuscript was accepted. Some of its implausible scenarios, circumlocutions, and omissions were among probable causes the work created little literary sensation. Only five pages are devoted to Jacobs's family background but five chapters describe her sexual exploitation as a slave. Inevitably, she created doubt about details of her seven-year self-confinement in a cubbyhole—three feet high, nine feet long, seven feet wide—and her remorse for having been unchaste with a white man, who broke his promise to manumit her children; such personal lament was lost on a public then occupied with a widening civil war.

Jacobs worked with Quakers to aid freed slaves during Reconstruction, but for the last three decades of her life she was not affiliated with any organization created by black women for empowerment and uplift. For her Afro-American female peers who wished to end the concubine stereotypes that had existed since slavery, the "Linda Brent" story was not heroic. Nor was her rationale that, "slave women ought not to be judged by the same standards as others." Most of the strong endorsements for her, then and later, were from white feminists, who identified her gender politics with their own.

The following is her chapter 5, "The Trials of Girlhood."

From *Incidents in the Life of a Slave Girl* . . . (1861)

During the first years of my service in Dr. Flint's family, I was accustomed to share some indulgences with the children of my mistress. Though this seemed to me no more than right, I was grateful for it, and tried to merit the kindness by the faithful discharge of my duties. But I now entered on my fifteenth year—a sad epoch in the life of a slave girl. My master began to whisper foul words in my ear. Young as I was, I could not remain ignorant of their import. I tried to treat them with indifference or contempt. The master's age, my extreme youth, and the fear that his conduct would be reported to my grandmother, made him bear this treatment for many months. He was a crafty man, and resorted to many means to accomplish his purposes. Sometimes he had stormy, terrific ways, that made his victims tremble; sometimes he assumed a gentleness that he thought must surely subdue. Of the two, I preferred his stormy moods, although they left me trembling. He tried his utmost to corrupt the pure principles my grandmother had instilled. He peopled my young mind with unclean images, such as only a vile monster could think of. I turned from him with disgust and hatred. But he was my master. I was compelled to live under the same roof with him—where I saw a man forty years my senior daily violating the most sacred commandments of nature. He told me I was his property; that I must be subject to his will in all things. My soul revolted against the mean tyranny. But where could I turn for protection? No matter whether the slave girl be as black as ebony or as fair as her mistress. In either case, there is no shadow of law to protect her from insult, from violence, or even from death; all these are inflicted by fiends who bear the shape of men. The mistress, who ought to protect the helpless victim, has no other feelings towards her but those of jealousy and rage. The degradation, the wrongs, the vices, that grow out of slavery, are more than I can describe. They are greater than you would willingly believe. Surely, if you credited one-half the truths that are told you concerning the helpless millions suffering in this cruel bondage, you at the North would not help to tighten the yoke. You surely would refuse to do for the master, on your own soil, the mean and cruel work which trained bloodhounds and the lowest class of whites do for him at the South.

Everywhere the years bring to all enough of sin and sorrow; but in slavery the very dawn of life is darkened by these shadows. Even the little child, who is accustomed to wait on her mistress and her children, will learn, before she is twelve years old, why it is that her mistress hates such and such a one among the slaves. Perhaps the child's own mother is among those hated ones. She listens to violent outbreaks of jealous passion, and cannot help understanding what is the cause. She will become prematurely knowing in evil things. Soon she will learn to tremble when she hears her master's footfall. She will be compelled to realize that she is no longer a child. If God has bestowed beauty upon her, it will prove her greatest curse. That which commands admiration in the white woman only hastens the degradation of the female slave. I know that some are too much brutalized by slavery to feel the humiliation of their position; but many slaves feel it most acutely, and shrink from the memory of it. I cannot tell how much I suffered in the presence of these wrongs, nor how I am still pained by the retrospect. My master met me at every turn, reminding me that I belonged to him, and swearing by heaven and earth that he would compel me to submit to him. If I went out for a breath of fresh air, after a day of unwearied toil, his footsteps dogged me. If I knelt by my mother's grave, his dark shadow fell on me even there. The light heart which nature had given me became heavy with sad forebodings. The other slaves in my master's house noticed the change. Many of them pitied me; but none dared to ask the cause. They had no need to inquire. They knew too well the guilty practices under that roof; and they were aware that to speak of them was an offense that never went unpunished.

I longed for someone to confide in. I would have given the world to have laid my head on my grandmother's faithful bosom, and told her all my troubles. But Dr. Flint swore he would kill me, if I was not as silent as the grave. Then, although my grandmother was all in all to me, I feared her as well as loved her. I had been accustomed to look up to her with a respect bordering upon awe. I was very young, and felt shamefaced about telling her such impure things, especially as I knew her to be very strict on such subjects. Moreover, she was a woman of a high spirit. She was usually very quiet in her demeanor; but if her indignation was once roused, it was not very easily quelled. I had been told that she once chased a white gentleman with a loaded pistol, because he insulted one of her daughters. I dreaded the consequences of a violent outbreak; and both pride and fear kept me silent. But though I did not confide in my grandmother, and even evaded her vigilant watchfulness and inquiry, her presence in the neighborhood was some protection to me. Though she had been a slave, Dr. Flint was afraid of her. He dreaded her scorching rebukes. Moreover, she was known and patronized by many people; and he did not wish to have his villainy made public. It was lucky for me that I did not live on a distant plantation, but in a town not so large that the inhabitants were ignorant of each other's affairs. Bad as are the laws and customs in a slaveholding community, the doctor, as a professional man, deemed it prudent to keep up some outward show of decency.

O, what days and nights of fear and sorrow that man caused me! Reader, it is not to awaken sympathy for myself that I am telling you truthfully what I suffered in slavery. I do it to kindle a flame of compassion in your hearts for my sisters who are still in bondage, suffering as I once suffered.

I once saw two beautiful children playing together. One was a fair white child; the other was her slave, and also her sister. When I saw them embracing each other, and heard their joyous laughter, I turned sadly away from the lovely sight. I foresaw the inevitable blight that would fall on the little slave's heart. I knew how soon her laughter would be changed to sighs. The fair child grew up to be a still fairer woman. From childhood to womanhood her pathway was blooming with flowers, and overarched by a sunny sky. Scarcely one day of her life had been clouded when the sun rose on her happy bridal morning.

How had those years dealt with her slave sister, the little playmate of her childhood? She, also, was very beautiful; but the flowers and sunshine of love were not for her. She drank the cup of sin, and shame, and misery, whereof her persecuted race are compelled to drink.

In view of these things, why are ye silent, ye free men and women of the north? Why do your tongues falter in maintenance of the right? Would that I had more ability! But my heart is so full, and my pen is so weak! There are noble men and women who plead for us, striving to help those who cannot help themselves. God bless them! God give them strength and courage to go on! God bless those, everywhere, who are laboring to advance the cause of humanity!

NATHANIEL HAWTHORNE

(1804–64)

No New England writer of his generation was as ambivalent about the Civil War as Nathaniel Hawthorne. The fratricidal warfare was a defining moment in his own psyche. Henry James's 1879 biography, *Hawthorne*, noted what "four long years of bloodshed and misery" did to the nation and to the man: "When this event occurred, he was, therefore, proportionately horrified and depressed by it; it cut from beneath his feet the familiar ground which had long felt so firm, substituting a heaving and quaking medium in which his spirit found no rest."

In 1863, the year before Hawthorne's sudden death—which some friends attributed to the war—he expressed in a few letters a wish that "New England might be a nation by itself." His preference for solitude was heightened by malaise over national events, but the tendency to insulate himself is evident in his first novel, *Fanshawe*, published anonymously at his expense in 1828, three years after he graduated from Bowdoin College. In that apprentice work, his inward-bound protagonist "deemed himself unconnected with the world, unconcerned in its feelings, and uninfluenced by it in any of his pursuits." In alienation, Hawthorne mirrored Fanshawe as much as he did a later hero of his unfinished, posthumous novel, *Septimius Felton*, who "felt himself strangely ajar with the human race, and would have given much either to be in full accord with it, or to be separated from it forever." Until Hawthorne's late but happy marriage to Sophia Peabody in July 1842—when he turned thirty-eight—he had chosen the reclusive life, single-mindedly dedicated to a literary career.

He was born on Independence Day, July 4, 1804, in Salem, Massachusetts, and reared there with two siblings in the home of his widowed mother's family. His father, a sea captain, died of fever in Surinam when Nathaniel was four; his mother withdrew in mourning for the rest of her life. A descendant of Puritan immigrants whose ghosts haunt his allegorical fiction, Hawthorne set some of his most accomplished stories in Puritan New England, including pieces in *Twice-Told Tales* (1837, 1842), *Mosses from an Old Manse* (1846), and the *Snow Image* (1851). He was aware that one of his prominent ancestors was a prosecuting judge in the Massachusetts colony witchcraft trials of 1691 and 1692; some of his fiction alludes to actual historical figures, but none to the legendary Salem figure, Tituba, a Caribbean slave accused in 1692 of serving the devil; she was ultimately spared the gallows in the mass hysteria that swept the village. Hawthorne's classic novels, *The Scarlet Letter* (1850), *The House of Seven Gables* (1851), and *The Blithedale Romance* (1852) are steeped in New England history and culture, but his artistic imagination allowed only characters of European descent, with slavery absent, and Indians barely visible.

He privately criticized abolitionists, including his sister-in-law—educator and reformer Elizabeth Peabody—but he never openly opposed his longtime friend and former Bowdoin College classmate, Franklin Pierce, for politically supporting slavery. During the Presidential campaign of 1852, Hawthorne published a biography of Pierce. The book and Pierce's career as U.S. Congressman and Senator from New Hampshire, ex-brigadier general in the Mexican War, and a defender of slaveowner's rights, all helped elect him fourteenth U.S. President. He appointed Hawthorne American consul to Liverpool, where the author and his family lived from 1853 until 1857. When the consul position ended, Hawthorne, his wife, and daughter spent two years in Italy, the setting of his last completed novel, *The Marble Faun* (1864).

Some seven years abroad had affected the exiled author who returned in 1860 to his home in Concord, believing—as he wrote in one letter—that, "the United States are fit for many excellent purposes, but they are certainly not fit to live in." That mood deepened after Lincoln's 1860 election, which Hawthorne opposed, and the Secession that soon ensued; he met Lincoln in March 1862, while part of a Massachusetts delegation to Washington, DC, to discuss the war; the result was "Chiefly about War Matters," in the July 1862 *Atlantic Monthly*—with his derisive comments about Lincoln deleted by the editor. An excerpt follows here, in Hawthorne's detached tone, on his impressions of seeing black contraband soldiers, and his predictions of their future after the end of the war.

In May 1864, thirteen months before the Union victory, he died alone in his sleep in a New Hampshire inn, while vacationing with Franklin Pierce. The year before, he had publicly dedicated to Pierce one of his last published books: a volume of sketches from travel journals in England, *Our Old Home*. He went to his grave loyal to the increasingly unpopular ex-President Pierce, who steadfastly sided with Southern slaveowners over Northern abolitionists and denounced the Emancipation Proclamation as unconstitutional.

From Chiefly about War Matters (1862)

. . . One very pregnant token of a social system thoroughly disturbed was presented by a party of contrabands, escaping out of the mysterious depths of Secessia; and its strangeness consisted in the leisurely delay with which they trudged forward, as dreading no pursuer, and encountering nobody to turn them back. They were unlike the specimens of their race whom we are accustomed to see at the North, and, in my judgment, were far more agreeable. So rudely were they attired,—as if their garb had grown upon them spontaneously,—so picturesquely natural in manners, and wearing such a crust of primeval simplicity (which is quite polished away from the northern black man), that they seemed a kind of creature by themselves, not altogether human, but perhaps quite as good, and akin to the fauns and rustic deities of olden times. I wonder whether I shall excite anybody's wrath by saying this. It is no great matter. At all events, I felt most kindly towards these poor fugitives, but knew not precisely what to wish in their behalf, nor in the least how to help them. For the sake of the manhood which is latent in them, I would not have turned them back; but I should have felt almost as reluctant, on their own account, to hasten them forward to the stranger's land; and I think my prevalent idea was, that, whoever may be benefited by the results of this war, it will not be the present generation of negroes, the childhood of whose race is now gone forever, and who must henceforth fight a hard battle with the world, on very unequal terms. On behalf of my own race, I am glad and can only hope that an inscrutable Providence means good to both parties.

There is an historical circumstance, known to few, that connects the children of the Puritans with these Africans of Virginia in a very singular way. They are our brethren, as being lineal descendants from the *Mayflower*, the fated womb of which, in her first voyage, sent forth a brood of Pilgrims on Plymouth Rock, and, in a subsequent one, spawned slaves upon the Southern soil,—a monstrous birth, but with which we have an instinctive sense of kindred, and so are stirred by an irresistible impulse to attempt their rescue, even at the cost of blood and ruin. The character of our sacred ship, I fear, may suffer a little by this revelation; but we must let her white progeny offset her dark one—and two such portents never sprang from an identical source before. . . .

ABRAHAM LINCOLN

(1809–65)

Assassinated on Good Friday, Abraham Lincoln was to many Americans the martyred Christian soldier, soon resurrected as a national icon. His fatal wound on April 14, 1865, a somber finale to the Civil War, came five days after Confederates signed papers of surrender at Virginia's Appomatox Courthouse. In the defeated South, decimated after four years of bitter battles, Lincoln's death was no cause for mourning, but throughout much of the nation, his apotheosis had already begun. The saga of Honest Abe, Man of the People, Great Debater, and Great Emancipator would proliferate in books and articles, along with the varied portraits and monuments of his image.

Until the midtwentieth century, few Afro-American intellectuals openly challenged Lincoln's deification as the Great Emancipator.[1] Although Frederick Douglass's fealty to him wavered before, during, and after the Civil War, Douglass perhaps surprised many Afro-Americans in Washington at a Freedman's Monument dedicated to the late President in April 1876, by declaring what few said aloud:

> Abraham Lincoln was not, in the fullest sense of the word, either our man or our model. In his interests, in his habits, of thought, and in his prejudices, he was a white man. . . . He was ready and willing at any time during the first years of his administration to deny, postpone, and sacrifice the rights of humanity in the colored people to promote the welfare of the white people of this country.

To some biographers and historians, Lincoln remains an enigma, his definitive image as debatable as his attitude toward race, slavery, and emancipation. Yet, on those three controversial topics, his own words are unequivocal and well-documented. When sworn in as the sixteenth President, on March 4, 1861, his inaugural address in part appeased Southern states that had recently

---

[1] Notable Afro-American critics of Lincoln in the late nineteenth century included clergyman and historian George Washington Williams, and in the early twentieth century author-editor W. E. B. Du Bois and lawyer Archibald Grimké.

seceded to form the Confederate States of America: "I have no purpose, directly or indirectly, to interfere with the institution of slavery in the states where it exists," he said, while simultaneously warning he could not sanction Southern secession: "No state upon its own mere motion can lawfully get out of the Union. . . . Acts of violence within any State or States against the authority of the United States are insurrectionary."

Three years earlier, in four debates with Stephen A. Douglas in the 1858 campaign for U.S. Senate, Douglas had won the election, but Lincoln gained the nation's attention. His stand on slavery often echoed rather than countered the antiabolitionist rhetoric of Stephen A. Douglas, who credited himself for being the voice of popular sovereignty. Lincoln, never an abolitionist, refused to urge repeal of the 1850 Fugitive Slave Law, but he opposed expansion of slavery in the territories; he argued slaveholding was unjust policy but the Federal government had no right to interfere in states where slavery existed. His was the voice of paradox.

When, as President, he announced on September 22, 1862, that his Emancipation Proclamation would take effect on January 1, 1863, his decree was one of military expediency. The Proclamation freed slaves only in rebel states, where it actually had no legal effect; it left slavery intact in border states and provided no Federal economic measures for the persons emancipated. He left unstated his preference for Negro deportation and colonization. His colonization idea, unwieldly to his image as national protector, was ultimately dropped after his Proclamation and nearly expunged in most American history books—except by populist Southerners.

On race and slavery Lincoln shared some of the same opinions and fears of Thomas Jefferson—a position he acknowledged to a Cooper Union audience in New York, during his Presidential campaign in February 1860:

"In the language of Mr. Jefferson, uttered many years ago, 'It is in our power to direct the process of emancipation, and deportation, peaceably, and in such slow degrees, as that the evil will wear off insensibly; and in their places, be *pari passu*,[2] filled up by free white laborers.' "

In that same speech, Lincoln revealed why he would later exclude border states and territories from his Emancipation Proclamation: "The Federal government," he said, "has the power of restraining the extension of the institution—the power to insure that a slave insurrection shall never occur on any American soil which is now free from slavery."

By birth and parentage Lincoln was a Southerner. But his identification as the self-made man of the frontier, the President who made it from a log cabin

---

[2] *Pari passu:* Latin, meaning "at equal pace or progress."

to the White House, is not usually associated with the South. Born in Hardin County, Kentucky, near Hodgenville, in 1809, he was age eight when his family resettled in Indiana, where he spent the rest of his youth. "I was raised to farm work, which I continued until I was twenty-two," he later wrote. His early formal schooling equaled only about one year, but his eagerness for books led him often to the Bible—which he believed "the best book God has given to men"—and to Aesop's Fables, Shakespeare, and other works that later influenced his use of parables and biblical quotes in public speeches admired for their literary style.

A man of the farm and the village, he never saw a large city before he was nineteen, when he glimpsed New Orleans while working on a flatboat on the Mississippi River. He was twenty-one when he settled in Illinois, first in the township of New Salem, then in Sangamon County, where he held jobs as a store clerk, and a wrestler, before entering legislative politics in the early 1830s. Elected to the state legislature in 1834, he served there eight years and during that time studied law, receiving his license to practice in 1836. Following his marriage to Mary Todd Lincoln in 1842, he devoted more time to law than politics, except for his one term as U.S. Congressman from Illinois (1847–49). Politically then a Whig, he dropped out of politics until 1854, when the Republican Party was founded; he was the Party's unsuccessful candidate for a vice-presidential nomination in 1856, its Presidential victor four years later.

During a Civil War he did not want, for a Union he was determined to save, his years as Chief Executive paralleled an era of internecine strife. It was the nation that he urged all citizens to restore in his second inaugural address, only six weeks before his assassination. But in private talks, as in the following "Address on Colonization"—before a five-man Negro delegation at the White House in August 1862—he spoke of a nation where blacks were unwelcome.

In his last public speech at the White House, the evening of April 11, 1865, his plea was to Southern rebels to rejoin and restore the Union. Had he lived to preside over Reconstruction, it is uncertain what policies Lincoln would have pursued—or if a majority of the black populace, then and later, would have continued to hail him North and South, in legend and history, as the Great Emancipator.

The following two pieces, which represent his painful dilemma during the Civil War, are from *The Complete Works of Abraham Lincoln*, volume 3 of the 1894 edition, compiled by John G. Nicolay and John Hay, both Lincoln's secretaries during the War, and the first biographers chosen by Lincoln's only surviving son, Robert Todd Lincoln.

Address on Colonization to a
Deputation of Colored Men (1862)

EXECUTIVE MANSION,
WASHINGTON, Thursday, August 14, 1862

This afternoon the President of the United States gave an audience to a committee of colored men at the White House. The were introduced by Rev. J. Mitchell, Commissioner of Emigration. E. M. Thomas, the chairman, remarked that they were there by invitation to hear what the Executive had to say to them.

Having all been seated, the President, after a few preliminary observations, informed them that the sum of money had been appropriated by Congress, and placed at his disposition, for the purpose of aiding the colonization in some country of the people, or a portion of them, of African descent, thereby making it his duty, as it had for a long time been his inclination, to favor that cause. And why, he asked, should the people of your race be colonized, and where? Why should they leave this country? This is, perhaps, the first question for proper consideration. You and we are different races. We have between us a broader difference than exists between almost any other two races. Whether it is right or wrong I need not discuss; but this physical difference is a great disadvantage to us both, as I think. Your race suffer very greatly, many of them, by living among us, while ours suffer from your presence. In a word, we suffer on each side. If this is admitted, it affords a reason, at least, why we should be separated. You here are freemen, I suppose?

A voice: Yes, sir.

The President: Perhaps you have long been free, or all your lives. Your race is suffering, in my judgment, the greatest wrong inflicted on any people. But even when you cease to be slaves, you are yet far removed from being placed on an equality with the white race. You are cut off from many of the advantages which the other race enjoys. The aspiration of men is to enjoy equality with the best when free, but on this broad continent not a single man of your race is made the equal of a single man of ours. Go where you are treated the best, and the ban is still upon you. I do not propose to discuss this, but to present it as a fact with which we have to deal. I cannot alter it if I would. It is a fact about which we all think and feel alike, I and you. We look to our condition.

Owing to the existence of the two races on this contiment, I need not recount to you the effects upon white men, growing out of the institution of slavery.

I believe in its general evil effects on the white race. See our present condition—the country engaged in war—our white men cutting one another's throats—none knowing how far it will extend—and then consider what we know to be the truth. But for your race among us there could not be war, although many men engaged on either side do not care for you one way or the other. Nevertheless, I repeat, without the institution of slavery, and the colored race as a basis, the war could not have an existence. It is better for us both, therefore, to be separated. I know that there are freemen among you who, even if they could better their condition, are not as much inclined to go out of the country as those who, being slaves, could obtain their freedom on this condition. I suppose one of the principal difficulties in the way of colonization is that the free colored man cannot see that his comfort would be advanced by it. You may believe that you can live in Washington, or elsewhere in the United States, the remainder of your life as easily, perhaps more so, than you can in any foreign country; and hence you may come to the conclusion that you have nothing to do with the idea of going to a foreign country.

This is (I speak in no unkind sense) an extremely selfish view of the case. You ought to do something to help those who are not so fortunate as yourselves. There is an unwillingness on the part of our people, harsh as it may be, for you free colored people to remain with us. Now, if you could give a start to the white people, you would open a wide door for many to be made free. If we deal with those who are not free at the beginning, and whose intellects are clouded by slavery, we have very poor material to start with. If intelligent colored men, such as are before me, would move in this matter, much might be accomplished. It is exceedingly important that we have men at the beginning capable of thinking as white men, and not those who have been systematically oppressed. There is much to encourage you. For the sake of your race you should sacrifice something of your present comfort for the purpose of being as grand in that respect as the white people. It is a cheering thought throughout life, that something can be done to ameliorate the condition of those who have been subject to the hard usages of the world. It is difficult to make a man miserable while he feels he is worthy of himself and claims kindred to the great God who made him. In the American Revolutionary War sacrifices were made by men engaged in it, but they were cheered by the future. General Washington himself endured greater physical hardships than if he had remained a British subject, yet he was a happy man because he was engaged in benefiting his race, in doing something for the children of his neighbors, having none of his own.

The colony of Liberia has been in existence a long time.[3] In a certain sense it is a success. The old President of Liberia, Roberts,[4] has just been with me—the first time I ever saw him. He says they have within the bounds of that colony between three and four hundred thousand people, or more than in some of our old States, such as Rhode Island or Delaware, or in some of our newer States, and less than in some of our larger ones. They are not all American colonists or their descendants. Something less than twelve thousand have been sent thither from this country. Many of the original settlers have died; yet, like people elsewhere, their offspring outnumber those deceased. The question is, if the colored people are persuaded to go anywhere, why not there?

One reason for unwillingness to do so is that some of you would rather remain within reach of the country of your nativity. I do not know how much attachment you may have toward our race. It does not strike me that you have the greatest reason to love them. But still you are attached to them, at all events.

The place I am thinking about for a colony is in Central America. It is nearer to us than Liberia—not much more than one-fourth as far as Liberia, and within seven days' run by steamers. Unlike Liberia, it is a great line of travel—it is a highway. The country is a very excellent one for any people, and with great natural resources and advantages, and especially because of the similarity of climate with your native soil, thus being suited to your physical condition. The particular place I have in view is to be a great highway from the Atlantic or Caribbean Sea to the Pacific Ocean, and this particular place has all the advantages for a colony. On both sides there are harbors—among the finest in the world. Again, there is evidence of very rich coal mines. A certain amount of coal is valuable in any country. Why I attach so much importance to coal is, it will afford an opportunity to the inhabitants for immediate employment till they get ready to settle permanently in their homes. If you take colonists where there is no good landing, there is a bad show; and so where there is nothing to cultivate and of which to make a farm. But if something is started so that you can get your daily bread as soon as you reach there, it is a great advantage. Coal land is the best thing I know of with which to commence an enterprise.

To return—you have been talked to upon this subject, and told that a speculation is intended by gentlemen who have an interest in the country, including

[3] Liberia, then in existence since 1822, was formed through the American Colonization Society to resettle freed slaves in West Africa; the nation was proclaimed a sovereign republic in 1847, after twenty-five years of negotiated treaties and land purchases from tribal chiefs.

[4] Joseph Jenkins Roberts (1809–76) was elected the Liberian republic's first president (1847–53). A freeborn mulatto from Petersburg, Virginia, he migrated to Liberia in 1829 and served successfully as first lieutenant governor and governor of the colony, before becoming president. (After several international posts, he was reelected in 1871 and served until his death.)

the coal mines. We have been mistaken all our lives if we do not know whites, as well as blacks, look to their self-interest. Unless among those deficient of intellect, everybody you trade with makes something. You meet with these things here and everywhere. If such persons have what will be an advantage to them, the question is, whether it cannot be made of advantage to you? You are intelligent, and know that success does not so much depend on external help as on self-reliance. Much, therefore, depends upon yourselves. As to the coal mines, I think I see the means available for your self-reliance. I shall, if I get a sufficient number of you engaged, have provision made that you shall not be wronged. If you will engage in the enterprise, I will spend some of the money intrusted to me. I am not sure you will succeed. The government may lose the money; but we cannot succeed unless we try; and we think, with care, we can succeed. The political affairs in Central America are not in quite as satisfactory a condition as I wish. There are contending factions in that quarter; but, it is true, all the factions are agreed[5] alike on the subject of colonization, and want it, and are more generous than we are here.

To your colored race they have no objection. I would endeavor to have you made the equals, and have the best assurance that you should be, the equals of the best.

The practical thing I want to ascertain is, whether I can get a number of able-bodied men, with their wives and children, who are willing to go when I present evidence of encouragement and protection. Could I get a hundred tolerably intelligent men, with their wives and children, and able to "cut their own fodder," so to speak? Can I have fifty? If I could find twenty-five able-bodied men, with a mixture of women and children,—good things in the family relation, I think,—I could make a successful commencement. I want you to let me know whether this can be done or not. This is the practical part of my wish to see you. These are subjects of very great importance—worthy of a month's study, instead of a speech delivered in an hour. I ask you, then, to consider seriously, not pertaining to yourselves merely, nor for your race and ours for the present time, but as one of the things, if successfully managed, for the good of mankind—not confined to the present generation, but as

---

[5] The "contending factions"—namely, Honduras, Nicaragua, Costa Rica, and to a lesser extent Panama—were not "agreed alike" on the Lincoln Cabinet's Chiriqui Project (named for the Isthmus of Chiriqui in Central America as a proposed colonization site) under study since October 1861. Lincoln's plans were already under way by August 1862 to send—through his agent, Senator Samuel Pomeroy—"five hundred able-bodied Negroes to the first colony," according to a letter later written September 10, 1862, for his signature; he did not sign it and the project was abandoned— either due to opposition by the above "contending factions" or protests by free Negroes in the United States, or the turn of events in the Civil War.

> From age to age descends the lay
>   To millions yet to be,
> Till far it echoes roll away
>   Into eternity.

The above is merely given as the substance of the President's remarks.

The chairman of the delegation briefly replied that they would hold a consultation, and in a short time give an answer.[6]

The President said: Take your full time—no hurry at all.

The delegation then withdrew.

Meditation on the Divine Will (1862)

September [30?], 1862

The will of God prevails. In great contests each party claims to act in accordance with the will of God. Both may be, and one must be, wrong. God cannot be for and against the same thing at the same time. In the present civil war it is quite possible that God's purpose is something different from the purpose of either party; and yet the human instrumentalities, working just as they do, are of the best adaptation to effect his purpose. I am almost ready to say that this is probably true; that God wills this contest, and wills that it shall not end yet. By mere great power on the minds of the new contestants, he could have either saved or destroyed the Union without a human contest. Yet the contest began. And, having begun, he could give the final victory to either side any day. Yet the contest proceeds.

---

[6] In a letter dated August 16, 1862, Edward Thomas, head of the delegation, acknowledged the meeting with Lincoln, stating further that "we would respectfully suggest that it is necessary that we should confer with leading colored men in Philadelphia, New York, and Boston." The response from persons in those cities was less than favorable to the emigration plan, which was deplored in several letters to Lincoln and in a public "Appeal from the Colored Men of Philadelphia to the President of the United States."

ISABELLA VAN WAGENEN

(SOJOURNER TRUTH)

(1797–1883)

At the White House in October 1864, Abraham Lincoln met an uninvited visitor named Sojourner Truth, who came to thank him for being an "instrument" of freedom. They were introduced by a white female abolitionist companion, who later wrote that he addressed the tall, dark figure, then in her sixties, as Aunty—"as he would his washerwoman."[1] Truth, perhaps aware that "Aunty" over "Mrs." was nomenclature by some whites for older blacks—had lived three decades a slave: from birth as Isabella Bomefree in Ulster County, New York, at the end of the eighteenth century until her freedom with the state's Emancipation Act of 1827.

Her reputation as an antislavery and women's-rights speaker predated her meeting with Lincoln, though she still spoke a dialect accented with Dutch and African words learned in childhood. Free nearly four decades in 1864, she would spend her remaining years unable to read or write. She relied on her young grandson Sammy to read newspapers aloud and white female associates to write her letters and speeches and a *Narrative of Her Life*.[2]

Her choice to remain illiterate during fifty-six years of freedom has been unchallenged by most black and white scholars who romanticize her role in American history. Nevertheless, during her itinerant years in New York and New England and Ohio and Indiana and Michigan, offers were numerous from abolitionists and feminists to instruct her to read and write. Strong-willed, yet naive to the sexual and racial politics of her day—even if acutely aware of the fetishistic curiosity of some whites toward ex-slaves—she remained unlettered, while many fugitives fled the South for school in the North. Harriet Beecher

---

[1] Lucy N. Colman, *Reminiscences*. 1891. (Lucy Colman is referred to as "Mrs. C." in the text of Truth's letter reprinted here about their visit to the White House.)

[2] See Sojourner Truth with Olive Gilbert. *Narrative of Sojourner Truth, a Northern Slave Emancipated from Bodily Servitude by the State of New York in 1828* (Boston: 1850). A later version, coauthored by Olive Gilbert and Frances Titus, appeared in 1878: *Narrative of Sojourner Truth: A Bondswoman of Olden Time, Emancipated by the New York Legislature in the Early Part of the Present Century with a History of her Labors and Correspondence Drawn from Her "Book of Life."*

Stowe reminisced that an educated Sojourner "might have spoken words as eloquent and undying as those of the African Saint Augustine or Tertullian." But in *The Atlantic Monthly*, Stowe wrote of her first encounter with a Sojourner who spoke only a folksy dialect at the author's Andover, Massachusetts, home, when she appeared unexpectedly and unannounced in 1853 for an interview: "Well, honey, I jes thought I'd like to come an' have a look at ye. You's heerd o' me, I reckon?"[3]

No advocate of abolitionism or women's rights had not then heard of Sojourner Truth—or her "Ain't I a Woman" speech in 1851 at the Akron Women's Rights Convention. There, in the border state of Ohio, she had met resistance from some white women a year after passage of the fugitive slave law; the convention president, Frances Dana Gage, later wrote how they pleaded, "Don't let her speak, . . . it will ruin us. Every newspaper in the land will have our cause mixed up with abolition and niggers, and we shall be utterly denounced."[4] Being denounced then and later was inconsequential to Sojourner. When white men heckled her at an Indiana church meeting in 1858, she exposed her breasts, lamenting how she had suckled white babies instead of her own.

Her "Ain't I a Woman" speech confessed "I have borned thirteen children and seen 'em most all sold off to slavery," but her *Narrative* concealed the fact that some were fathered by one of her four different white slavemasters, John Dumont. On his New Paltz, New York, farm she labored nearly eighteen years and also bore four or five children by an older slave named Thomas, who later died in poverty; she took only an infant daughter, Sophia, when she fled Dumont's in 1827, after his broken promise to free her by July 4, 1826. A local Quaker family, the Van Wagenens,[5] purchased Sophia from Dumont and gave Isabella the family surname and legal aid to rescue a young son who had been sold in the South.

It was as Isabella Van Wagenen that she began an odyssey in 1829 in New York City, working as a domestic for fourteen years, with little contact in the black community. She visited Manhattan's growing African Methodist Episcopal Zion church, but her discipleship was to a millenial religious cult led by a wealthy white social reformer, Robert Pierson, whose mysterious death implicated her with his accused murderer, Robert Matthews, alias "Matthias." She

---

[3] See Harriet Beecher Stowe. "Sojourner Truth, The Libyan Sibyl." *The Atlantic Monthly*. 11 (April 1863), pp. 473–81.

[4] F. D. Gage (1808–80), *National Anti-Slavery Standard*, May 2, 1863; text reprinted in various sources, including *The History of Women's Suffrage* (vol. 1) eds. Elizabeth C. Stanton, Susan B. Anthony, and Matilda F. Gage, 1881.

[5] Van Wagenen was spelled "Van Wagener" in Truth's *Narrative*.

believed the latter to be a prophet and blindly followed him until both were acquitted. In 1843 she claimed God renamed her Sojourner Truth and directed her to depart and preach.

Abolitionism through evangelism was her mission from 1843–46, after she hiked to Northampton, Massachusetts, and met social reformers in the experimental Northampton Association; they included William Lloyd Garrison, Wendell Phillips, and Frederick Douglass, whom she had seen briefly in New York. Through such contacts, she joined forces by 1850 with Lucretia Mott and other white feminists on the platform of the Wooster Women's Rights Convention. Within a month, she was addressing antislavery societies in New England, allied in the Garrisonian network of men and women who led her the following year to Akron and beyond. She continued lecturing from a base in Battle Creek, Michigan, her residence from the late 1850s until her death.

Hailed by some historians as the only black woman of her socioeconomic status in the nineteenth century women's reform effort, she told followers of Susan B. Anthony and Elizabeth Cady Stanton at the First Annual Meeting of the American Equal Rights Association in 1867 in New York that "I suppose I am about the only colored woman that goes about to speak for colored women." She was never the only one—though it says much about the ambiguity of her role and the paradox of her promoters that she did not ally with articulate black antislavery feminist writers, who were her contemporaries: Maria Stewart, Sarah Mapps Douglass, Sarah Forten, and Nancy Gardener Prince. Rather, her message to her New York audience in 1867 was, "White women are a great deal smarter and know more than colored women, while colored women do not know scarcely anything." Such comments contributed to her popularity and publicity—and ultimately to her canonization.

Her following letter, dictated to a Quaker friend, Rowland Johnson of New Jersey, appeared first in the *Anti-Slavery Standard*, December 17, 1864. She was assisting the National Freedmen's Relief Association as a Civil War volunteer at Freedmen's Village in rural Virginia, when she traveled across the Potomac to meet Lincoln. Her brief visit to the White House was later portrayed in a large painting—for which neither she nor the President ever posed.

Letter after a Visit
to President Lincoln[6] (1864)

Freedman's Village, Va.,
Nov. 17, 1864

Dear Friend,—I am at Freedman's village. After my visit to the President, I went to Mrs. Swisshelm's,[7] and remained there three weeks, and held two meetings in Washington, in Mr. Garnet's[8] Presbyterian church, for the benefit of the *Coloured Soldier's Aid Society*, both of which were largely attended. I then spent a week on Mason's Island with the freedmen there; held several meetings, and was present at the celebration of the emancipation of the slaves in Maryland, and spoke upon that occasion.

It was about eight o'clock in the morning when I called upon the President, in company with Mrs. C.[9] On entering his reception room, we found about a dozen persons waiting to see him; amongst them were two coloured women, some white women also. One of the gentlemen present knew me, and I was introduced to several others, and had a pleasant time while waiting, and enjoyed the conversation between the President and his auditors very much. He showed as much respect and kindness to the coloured persons present as to the whites. One case was a coloured woman who was sick, and likely to be turned out of her house, on account of her inability to pay her rent. The President listened to her with much attention, and replied with kindness and tenderness that he had given so much, he could give no more, but told her where she could get the needed aid, and asked Mrs. C. to direct and assist her, which she did.

He was seated at his desk. Mrs. C. and myself walked up to him, Mrs. C. said to him. "This is Sojourner Truth, who has come all the way from Michigan to see you." He then arose, gave me his hand, and said, "I am glad to see you." I said to him. "Mr. President, when you first took your seat, I feared you would be torn to pieces; for I likened you unto Daniel, who was thrown into the lion's den; for if the lions did not tear you to pieces, I knew it would be God that had saved you; and I said if He spared me, I would see you before the four years

---

[6] Title supplied by the editor.

[7] Jane Swisshelm, an abolitionist and feminist.

[8] Henry Highland Garnet, black abolitionist and Presbyterian clergyman; see pages 146–48, above.

[9] Mrs. Lucy Colman. See entry on Garnet in this volume, pages 146–54, above.

had expired. And He has done so, and I am now here to see you for myself."
He congratulated me on my having been spared. I then said, "I appreciate you,
for you are the best President who has ever taken seat." He replied thus: "I
expect you have reference to my having emancipated the slaves in my Proclamation; but," said he, mentioning the names of several of his predecessors, and
particularly Washington, "they were just as good, and would have done just as
I have, if the time had come. And if the people over the river," pointing across
the Potomac, "had behaved themselves, I could not have done what I have." I
replied, "I thank God you were the instrument selected by Him and the people
to do these things." I presented him with one of my shadows and songs, for
which he thanked me, and said he would keep them as a remembrance. He
then showed me the splendid Bible presented to him by the coloured people
of Baltimore. You doubtless have seen a description of it. I have seen it for
myself, and can say it is beautiful beyond description. After I looked it over, I
said to him, "This is beautiful; and to think that the coloured people have
given this to the head of the Government, and to think that Government ones
[once] sanctioned laws that would not permit its people to learn enough to be
able to read that book." And for what? Let them answer who can. I am proud
to say that I never was treated with more kindness and cordiality than I was by
the great and good man Abraham Lincoln, by the grace of God President of
the United States for four years more. He took my little book, and with the
same hand that signed the death warrant of Slavery, he wrote in my autograph
book as follows:

> For Auntie Sojourner Truth.
> October 29, 1864.   A. Lincoln.

I then took my leave of him, and thanked God from the bottom of my heart
that I always have advocated this cause, and done it openly and boldly; and
now I shall feel more in duty bound to do so. May God assist me! I have
obtained a little house here, through the kindness of the Captain of the Guard,
and think I will remain, and do all I can in the way of instructing the people in
habits of industry and economy. Many of them are entirely ignorant of house-
keeping. Any favors in the way of nourishment, and some sheets and pillows,
will be very acceptable, and may be forwarded to Washington, addressed to
me, care of Captain George B. Carse, Freedman's Village, V. Give my love to
all who inquire after me.

Sammy and I are both well and happy, and feel that we are in good employment, and find plenty of friends.

> Your Friend,
> Sojourner Truth.

CHARLOTTE L. FORTEN GRIMKÉ

(1837–1914)

In nineteenth-century Afro-American womanhood, a striking contrast existed between Sojourner Truth and Charlotte Forten. In appearance, background, education, expression, and temperament, they were opposites and of different generations. Charlotte was born August 17, 1837, to the prominent Forten family of Philadelphia, a lineage free and prosperous for two previous generations. Her father, Robert Bridges Forten, learned his trade as sailmaker from his affluent father, James Forten, Sr., businessman, reformer, and abolitionist, who died five years after Charlotte's birth. Although the financial position of the Afro-American élite was precarious and the Forten dynasty would decline in Charlotte's generation, her family heritage of civic service, economic independence, race advancement, cultural gentility, educational purpose, and women's rights surrounded her from the cradle. Coincidentally in the same year as her birth, an aunt, feminist-abolitionist Sarah Forten—whose poetry appeared often under the pen name "Ada" in *The Liberator*—had a poem "An Appeal to Woman" excerpted in Angelina Grimké's pamphlet for the first Anti-Slavery Convention of American Women; that same year, an uncle, James Forten, Jr., delivered an enlightened argument against male hegemony at a first annual meeting of the American Reform Society in Philadelphia. Charlotte's coming of age paralleled the rising momentum of American antislavery and reform movements in the nineteenth century—movements in which her family was accentuated.

The early death of her mother, Mary Virginia Wood Forten, and maternal grandfather left a void in the family's spacious home on Philadelphia's Lombard Street, but her father, his mother—for whom Charlotte was named—and his three sisters, Margaretta, Harriet, and Sarah, all were her tutors and role models. Harriet, married in 1831 to wealthy abolitionist Robert Purvis,[1] welcomed her niece to "Byberry," the Purvis country residence, where Charlotte saw fugitive slaves and learned about the underground railroad and the antislavery societies that her relatives had helped to organize.

The Purvis children and Charlotte were refused entry to schools near Byberry, causing Robert Forten in 1854 to send his only daughter to Massachu-

---

[1] See entry on Robert Purvis, pages 227–31, above.

setts to complete high school away from Philadelphia's segregated classrooms. He remarried and moved temporarily to Canada, while Charlotte resided in the Salem family of abolitionist Charles Lenox Remond, whose sister Sarah was briefly a mentor.[2] A year at Salem's Higginson Grammar School, led to selection as class poet and her "A Parting Hymn" at commencement in February 1855, and graduation with honors from State Normal School in July 1856, then to immediate employment at Salem's Epes Grammar School. Introspective, keen to nature and landscapes and English Romantic poets, she joined the local antislavery society but was otherwise in spiritual limbo: a member of a proscribed race teaching white pupils in an atmosphere of prejudice and mounting agitation over slavery. She left in ill health the spring of 1857 and returned to recuperate in Philadelphia.

Constrained then and later by respiratory ailments, she tried hydrotherapy cures for several summers in a clinic in Worcester, Massachusetts, but taught intermittently in her Aunt Margaretta's Philadelphia private academy until 1862, when she left to join the "Port Royal Experiment." Responding to federal recruitment of Northern instructors to teach ex-slaves in the South Carolina Sea Islands—after Union troops captured Port Royal Harbor in 1861—Charlotte Forten applied but was rejected; intervention came from a trusted friend of Forten family: poet and abolitionist John Greenleaf Whittier. In succeeding months, she shared with him her essay, "Life on the Sea Islands," which he forwarded to *The Atlantic Monthly*, where it appeared in two segments in May and June 1864; her "New Year's Day on the Islands of South Carolina" appeared a year later in *The Freedmen's Book*, edited by Lydia Maria Child.

During eighteen months in South Carolina, Forten also wrote in a diary dated October 1862 to May 1864—entries published later as part of *The Journal of Charlotte L. Forten*. She had begun writing at age sixteen in the diary in Salem but never intended her entries for the public; penciled in 1858 was a caveat: "To be burned in case of my death." In the posthumously published diaries were four sections: the first dated May 1854 to December 1856; a second January 1857 to January 1858; a third from February 1858 to February 1863, and a fourth, ended in May 1864, when she left Port Royal following her father's death that April. (His sudden death of typhoid fever, while recruiting black troops for the Union Army, is unrecorded in the diary, perhaps for reasons too traumatic and personal.) However, in many journal pages her impressions of the human drama of antebellum life, events, lectures, books, and landscapes were forged into her highest literary achievement. Although her earliest poems and letters were published in the late 1850s and early 1860s, by her idol Wil-

---

[2] See entry on Sarah Parker Remond, pages 223–26, above.

liam Lloyd Garrison in his *Liberator*, and three pieces were in the *National Antislavery Standard*, and two others anthologized by William Wells Brown in 1863, few of those works revealed the inner, very private young woman.

Not until November 1885 did she begin section five of her journal—fourteen years after arriving in Washington, DC, where she taught school, worked in the U.S. Treasury Department, and married. Her husband, a Presbyterian clergyman, Francis J. Grimké,[3] was thirteen years her junior, a devoted companion for thirty-six years—from their marriage in 1878 until her death in 1914. The journal ended in 1892. Her family manuscripts were entrusted to close friend Anna Julia Cooper,[4] who deposited them at Howard University Library.

The following excerpts, set in South Carolina during the Civil War, are taken from section four of her diary, edited by Ray Allen Billington in 1953 as *A Free Negro in the Slave Era: The Journal of Charlotte L. Forten*, and enlarged by Brenda Stevenson in 1988 as *The Journals of Charlotte Forten Grimké*.

From *The Journal of Charlotte L. Forten* (1863)

Monday, July 6, [1863]

. . . Drove hours, changed horses, and drove to school. After school, though very tired, did not neglect my invitation to tea with the officers of the 54th.[5] Drove down to Land's End with J.[ack], Mrs. H.[itchcock] and L.[izzie]. Met Col. [Quincy] G.[illmore] who went with us. Were just in time to see the Dress parade. 'Tis a splendid-looking regt [regiment]. An honor to the race. Then we went with Col. Shaw[6] to tea. Afterward sat outside the tent and listened to some very fine singing from some of the privates. Their voices blended beautifully. "Jubilo" is one of the best things I've heard lately. I am more than ever charmed with the noble little Col. [Shaw]. What purity[,] what nobleness of soul, what exquisite gentleness in that beautiful face! As I look at it I think "The bravest are the tenderest." I can imagine what he must be to his mother.

---

[3] Francis J. Grimké (1850–1937) clergyman and author, was a nephew of South Carolina abolitionists Angelina and Sarah Grimké; he was son of their brother Henry Grimké and a slave mistress, Nancy Weston; Francis and brother Archibald Grimké (1849–1930) were acknowledged and aided in their college education by Angelina and her husband Theodore D. Weld. See entries on Angelina Grimké and Theodore Weld in this book.

[4] See also entry on Anna Julia Cooper, pages 342–45, below.

[5] Reference is to the 54th Massachusetts Regiment, the first Union volunteer regiment of men of African descent to serve in the Civil War. See Luis F. Emilio, *History of the Fifty-fourth Regiment of Massachusetts Volunteer Infantry, 1863–1865* (Boston, 1891, revised edition 1894; rpt. 1968).

[6] Colonel Robert Gould Shaw (1837–63). Boston abolitionist and first commanding officer of the 54th Massachusetts. See Peter Burchard, *One Gallant Rush: Robert Gould Shaw and His Brave Black Regiment* (New York, 1965).

May his life be spared to her! Yesterday at the celebration he stood, leaning against our carriage and speaking of mother, so lovingly, so tenderly. He said he wished she c'ld [could] be there. If the regt. [regiment] were going to be stationed there for some time he sh'ld [should] send for her. "But you know," he said "we might be suddenly ordered away, and then she w'ld [would] have nobody to take care of her." I do think he is a wonderfully lovable person. Tonight, he helped me on my horse, and after carefully arranging the folds of my riding skirt, said, so kindly, "Good-bye. If I don't see you again down here I hope to see you at our house." But I hope I shall have the pleasure of seeing him many times even down here. He and his men are eager to be called into active service. Major H.[allowell] rode with L.[izzie Hunn] and me to Col. [Quincy] G.[illmore]'s tent where Lieut. and Mrs. H.[unn] were. The rest of the party played whist till a very late hour but I was thoroughly exhausted. Lay down part of the time. And part of the time sat close to the water's edge, and watched the boats, and the gleaming lights over the water, and the rising moon. A deep peace was over everything—not a sound to be heard but the low, musical murmur of the waves as they kissed the shore.

Wednesday, July 8, [1863]

Mr. T.[horpe] came over and drove down to Land's End for Lieut. W.[alton] who is still quite ill. The regiment has gone. Left this morning. My heartfelt prayers go with them—for the men and for their noble, noble young Colonel [Shaw]. God bless him! God keep him in His care, and grant that his men may do nobly and prove themselves worthy of him!

Monday, July 20, [1863]

For nearly two weeks we have waited, oh how anxiously for news of our regt. [regiment] which went, we know[,] to Morris Is.[land] to take part in the attack on Charleston. Tonight comes news oh, so sad, so heart sickening. It is too terrible, too terrible to write. We can only hope it may not all be true. That our noble, beautiful young Colonel [Shaw] is killed, and the regt. [regiment] cut to pieces! I cannot, cannot believe it. And yet I know it may be so. But oh, I am stunned, sick at heart. I can scarcely write. There was an attack on Fort Wagner. The Fifty-fourth put in advance; fought bravely, desperately, but was finally overpowered and driven back after getting into the Fort. Thank Heaven! they fought bravely! And oh, I still must hope that our colonel, *ours* especially he seems to me, is not killed.[7] But I can write no more tonight. . . .

---

[7] Colonel Shaw and many in his regiment were killed on July 18 when they led an attack on Fort Wagner, a Confederate tactical artillery base on Morris Island guarding Charleston Harbor. The battle was dramatized in the film, *Glory* (1989).

THOMAS WENTWORTH HIGGINSON

(1823–1911)

On the Civil War in the South Carolina Sea Islands, New England author Thomas Wentworth Higginson wrote a chronicle no formal historian could equal: *Army Life in a Black Regiment*—based on his experience as commander of the first Union battalion of freed slaves, known as First South Carolina Volunteers. In 1862, the War Department authorized Brigadier General Rufus Saxton—Military Governor of the Department of the South—to form a black contingent of slaves recently abandoned by fleeing Confederates on the Sea Islands captured by Union forces; he chose Higginson as colonel for the mission. A West Point–trained officer, Saxton was an abolitionist, who knew the reputation and commitment of the man he selected. Higginson, a Union volunteer recruiter in Massachusetts since early 1861, was thirty-eight years old, a graduate of Harvard College and Harvard Divinity School, an opponent of U.S. expansionism in the Mexican War of 1846–48, a foe of the Fugitive Slave Law of 1850, one of the "Secret Six" supporters of John Brown in 1859, an ordained Unitarian minister turned professional writer for the newly launched *Atlantic Monthly* magazine, which had recently published his "Travellers and Outlaws" series on slave rebellions.

A rebel with unconventional ideas, and a radical critic of society on issues ranging from slavery to physical fitness, he wrote in January 1861 to his mother: "The only way for anti-slavery men to share in the control is to share in the sacrifices. . . . All I ask now is an opportunity to fight, *under orders*." After Saxton's offer by letter, Higginson resigned as captain of the all-white Fifty-First Massachusetts Volunteers to command the South Carolina black volunteer regiment. Somewhat romantically, he wrote later: "I had always wished for an arming of the blacks, and had always felt a wish to be associated with them." He arrived in November 1862 at Port Royal Harbor, gateway to the Sea Islands between Charleston and Savannah and the nearby army camp at Beaufort, where he mobilized ex-slaves from surrounding rice plantations. In May 1863, he invited Charlotte Forten from Port Royal to teach literacy skills to his soldiers, a project that never got beyond the planning stage before the War Department banned ladies at the camp.

During his two-year command, his regiment engaged in skirmishes without the major fatalities of the Massachusetts 54th Regiment under Colonel Robert Shaw, but by July 1864 Higginson suffered a concussion and was on medical leave. Wounded also in spirit at being powerless to provide his men the same pay white soldiers received in other military units, he began a letter-writing campaign for pay equity, which he continued during his long convalescence in Rhode Island, with letters to editors and petitions to Congress—(reprinted as appendixes in his book). After he left South Carolina, his regiment fought more often in Georgia and Florida, its name changed to the Thirty-Third United States Colored Troops, its pay reduced to one dollar per month. His book documented the soldiers' valor and sacrifice in holding the Sea Islands, without which General Sherman's victorious "March to the Sea" via coastal Savannah would not have been possible.

To readers of the June 1867 *Atlantic Monthly*, Higginson introduced "Negro Spirituals"—derived from the slave songs he heard his regiment sing at campfires. His other writings of the war included *Harvard Memorial Biographies*, in tribute to fallen young men from his alma mater but *Army Life in a Black Regiment* was testament to freedmen who fought with him. From the Civil War's end until his death three years before World War I, he was preeminently a man of letters, except for two years in the Massachusetts legislature, 1880 to 1882.

His voluminous writings in every literary genre have been overshadowed by his more famous protégée: Emily Dickinson, who initiated correspondence with him in April 1862, and whose poems he encouraged and posthumously coedited with Mabel Loomis Todd for publication in 1890. However, the reclusive Dickinson is absent in his 1898 autobiographical memoir of the literati, *Cheerful Yesterdays*, due to unsettled disagreements with her family about an edition of her poems. A champion of women's advancement in literature, education, and public life, he was an egalitarian humanist, literary critic, social reformer, and pioneering environmentalist, who often went against the grain. He promoted the undiscovered Dickinson and the deceased Thoreau when his contemporaries shrugged; both are now in every college anthology of American Literature, while Higginson is not—though he deserves to be.

Though he was a legend in his own time, his fame did not long survive his death at age eighty-seven. However, at his funeral at the Cambridge First Parish Church, a black honor guard, in solemn remembrance of his service and his regiment, carried him to final rest in Cambridge, where he was born and reared.

The following excerpt of *Army Life in a Black Regiment* is taken from chapter 12, "The Negro as Soldier."

From *Army Life in a Black Regiment* (1870)

. . . I was constantly expecting to find male Topsies,[1] with no notions of good and plenty of evil. But I never found one. Among the most ignorant there was very often a childlike absence of vices, which was rather to be classed as inexperience than as innocence, but which had some of the advantages of both.

Apart from this, they were very much like other men. General Saxton,[2] examining with some impatience a long list of questions from some philanthropic Commission at the North, respecting the traits and habits of the freedmen, bade some staff officer answer them all in two words,—"Intensely human." We all admitted that it was a striking and comprehensive description.

For instance, as to courage. So far as I have seen, the mass of men are naturally courageous up to a certain point. A man seldom runs away from danger which he ought to face, unless others run; and each is apt to keep with the mass, and colored soldiers have more than usual of this gregariousness. In almost every regiment, black or white, there are a score or two of men who are naturally daring, who really hunger after dangerous adventures, and are happiest when allowed to seek them. Every commander gradually finds out who these men are, and habitually uses them; certainly I had such, and I remember with delight their bearing, their coolness, and their dash. Some of them were negroes, some mulattoes. One of them would have passed for white, with brown hair and blue eyes, while others were so black you could hardly see their features. These picked men varied in other respects too; some were neat and well-drilled soldiers, while others were slovenly, heedless fellows,—the despair of their officers at inspection, their pride on a raid. They were the natural scouts and rangers of the regiment; they had the two-o'clock-in-the-morning courage, which Napoleon thought so rare. The mass of the regiment rose to the same level under excitement, and were more excitable, I think, than whites, but neither more nor less courageous.

---

[1] "Topsies" alludes to the fictional character Topsy, an unpredictable, diabolical female child in *Uncle Tom's Cabin* by Harriet Beecher Stowe, who noted in her *Key* to the novel that, "Topsy stands a representative of a large class of the children who are growing up under the institution of slavery,—quick, active, subtle and ingenious, apparently utterly devoid of principle and conscience, keenly penetrating, by an instinct which exists in the childish mind, the degradation of their condition, and the utter hopelessness of rising above it."

[2] General Rufus Saxton, Union war general chosen by the War Department in 1862 under Lincoln to organize the first South Carolina Volunteers, the first official Union regiment of former slaves commanded by Higginson.

Perhaps the best proof of a good average of courage among them was in the readiness they always showed for any special enterprise. I do not remember ever to have had the slightest difficulty in obtaining volunteers, but rather in keeping down the number. The previous pages include many illustrations of this, as well as of their endurance of pain and discomfort. For instance, one of my lieutenants, a very daring Irishman, who had served for eight years as a sergeant of regular artillery in Texas, Utah, and South Carolina, said he had never been engaged in anything so risky as our raid up the St. Mary's. But in truth it seems to me a mere absurdity to deliberately argue the question of courage, as applied to men among whom I waked and slept, day and night, for so many months together. As well might he who has been wandering for years upon the desert, with a Bedouin escort, discuss the courage of the men whose tents have been his shelter and whose spears his guard. We, their officers, did not go there to teach lessons, but to receive them. There were more than a hundred men in the ranks who had voluntarily met more dangers in their escape from slavery than any of my young captains had incurred in all their lives.

There was a family named Wilson, I remember, of which we had several representatives. Three or four brothers had planned an escape from the interior to our lines; they finally decided that the youngest should stay and take care of the old mother; the rest, with their sister and her children, came in a "dugout" down one of the rivers. They were fired upon, again and again, by the pickets along the banks, until finally every man on board was wounded; and still they got safely through. When the bullets began to fly about them, the woman shed tears, and her little girl of nine said to her, "Don't cry, mother, Jesus will help you," and then the child began praying as the wounded men still urged the boat along. This the mother told me, but I had previously heard it from an officer who was on the gunboat that picked them up,—a big, rough man, whose voice fairly broke as he described their appearance. He said that the mother and child had been hid for nine months in the woods before attempting their escape, and the child would speak to no one,—indeed, she hardly would when she came to our camp. She was almost white, and this officer wished to adopt her, but the mother said, "I would do anything but that for *oonah*,"—this being a sort of Indian formation of the second-person plural, such as they sometimes use. This same officer afterwards saw a reward offered for this family in a Savannah paper.

I used to think that I should not care to read "Uncle Tom's Cabin" in our camp; it would have seemed tame. Any group of men in a tent would have had more exciting tales to tell. I needed no fiction when I had Fanny Wright, for instance, daily passing to and fro before my tent, with her shy little girl clinging to her skirts. Fanny was a modest little mulatto woman, a soldier's wife, and a company laundress. She had escaped from the mainland in a boat, with that child and another. Her baby was shot dead in her arms, and she reached our lines with one child safe on earth and the other in heaven. I never found it needful to give any elementary instructions in courage to Fanny's husband, you may be sure.

There was another family of brothers in the regiment named Miller. Their grandmother, a fine-looking old woman, nearly seventy, I should think, but erect as a pine tree, used sometimes to come and visit them. She and her husband had once tried to escape from a plantation near Savannah. They had failed, and had been brought back; the husband had received five hundred lashes, and while the white men on the plantation were viewing the punishment, she was collecting her children and grandchildren, to the number of twenty-two, in a neighboring marsh, preparatory to another attempt that night. They found a flatboat which had been rejected as unseaworthy, got on board,— still under the old woman's orders,—and drifted forty miles down the river to our lines. Trowbridge happened to be on board the gunboat which picked them up, and he said that when the "flat" touched the side of the vessel, the grandmother rose to her full height, with her youngest grandchild in her arms, and said only, "My God! are we free?" By one of those coincidences of which life is full, her husband escaped also, after his punishment, and was taken up by the same gunboat.

I hardly need point out that my young lieutenants did not have to teach the principles of courage to this woman's grandchildren.

I often asked myself why it was that, with this capacity of daring and endurance, they had not kept the land in a perpetual flame of insurrection; why, especially since the opening of the war, they had kept so still. The answer was to be found in the peculiar temperament of the races, in their religious faith, and in the habit of patience that centuries had fortified. The shrewder men all said substantially the same thing. What was the use of insurrection, where everything was against them? They had no knowledge, no money, no arms, no drill, no organization,—above all, no mutual confidence. It was the tradition among them that all insurrections were always betrayed by somebody. They had no mountain passes to defend like the Maroons of Jamaica,—no impenetrable swamps, like the Maroons of Surinam. Where they had these, even on a small scale, they had used them,—as in certain swamps round Savannah and in the everglades of Florida, where they united with the Indians, and would stand fire—so I was told by General Saxton, who had fought them there—when the Indians would retreat.

It always seemed to me that, had I been a slave, my life would have been one long scheme of insurrection. But I learned to respect the patient self-control of those who had waited till the course of events should open a better way. When it came they accepted it. Insurrection on their part would at once have divided the Northern sentiment; and a large part of our army would have joined with the Southern army to hunt them down. By their waiting till we needed them, their freedom was secured.

Two things chiefly surprised me in their feeling toward their former masters,—the absence of affection and the absence of revenge. I expected to find a good deal of the patriarchal feeling. It always seemed to me a very ill-applied emotion, as connected with the facts and laws of American slavery,—still I expected to find it. I suppose that my men and their families and visitors may have had as much of it as the mass of freed slaves; but certainly they had not a particle. I never could cajole one of them, in his most discontented moment, into regretting "ole mas'r time" for a single instant. I never heard one speak of the masters except as natural enemies. Yet they were perfectly discriminating as to individuals; many of them claimed to have had kind owners, and some expressed great gratitude to them for particular favors received. It was not the individuals, but the ownership, of which they complained. That they saw to be a wrong which no special kindnesses could right. On this, as on all points connected with slavery, they understood the matter as clearly as Garrison or Phillips; the wisest philosophy could teach them nothing as to that, nor could any false philosophy befog them. After all, personal experience is the best logician.

Certainly this indifference did not proceed from any want of personal affection, for they were the most affectionate people among whom I had ever lived. They attached themselves to every officer who deserved love, and to some who did not; and if they failed to show it to their masters, it proved the wrongfulness of the mastery. On the other hand, they rarely showed one gleam of revenge, and I shall never forget the self-control with which one of our best sergeants pointed out to me, at Jacksonville, the very place where one of his brothers had been hanged by the whites for leading a party of fugitive slaves. He spoke of it as a historic matter, without any bearing on the present issue.

But side by side with this faculty of patience, there was a certain tropical element in the men, a sort of fiery ecstasy when aroused, which seemed to link them by blood with the French Turcos, and made them really resemble their natural enemies, the Celts, far more than the Anglo-Saxon temperament. To balance this there were great individual resources when alone,—a sort of Indian wiliness and subtlety of resource. Their gregariousness and love of drill made them more easy to keep in hand than white American troops, who rather like to straggle or go in little squads, looking out for themselves, without being bothered with officers. The blacks prefer organization.

The point of inferiority that I always feared, though I never had occasion to prove it, was that they might show less fiber, less tough and dogged resistance, than whites, during a prolonged trial,—a long, disastrous march, for instance, or the hopeless defense of a besieged town. I should not be afraid of their mutinying or running away, but of their drooping and dying. It might not turn out so; but I mention it for the sake of fairness, and to avoid overstating the merits of these troops. As to the simple general fact of courage and reliability I think no officer in our camp ever thought of there being any difference between black and white. And certainly the opinions of these officers, who for years risked their lives every moment on the fidelity of their men, were worth more than those of all the world beside.

No doubt there were reasons why this particular war was an especially favorable test of the colored soldiers. They had more to fight for than the whites. Besides the flag and the Union, they had home and wife and child. They fought with ropes round their necks, and when orders were issued that the officers of colored troops should be put to death on capture, they took a grim satisfaction. It helped their *esprit de corps* immensely. With us, at least, there was to be no play-soldier. Though they had begun with a slight feeling of inferiority to the white troops, this compliment substituted a peculiar sense of self-respect. And even when the new colored regiments began to arrive from the North my men still pointed out this difference,—that in case of ultimate defeat, the Northern troops, black or white, would go home, while the First South Carolina must fight it out or be re-enslaved. This was one thing that made the St. John's River so attractive to them and even to me;—it was so much nearer the everglades. I used seriously to ponder, during the darker periods of the war, whether I might not end my days as an outlaw,—a leader of Maroons. . . .

PART 2

From Radical Reconstruction to the Dawn of the Harlem Renaissance

FRANCES ELLEN WATKINS HARPER

(1825–1911)

Few women of any race or nationality in her generation traveled or lectured as widely, or published as much, or for as long a time as Frances Ellen Watkins Harper. Her work, written and oral, spans the antebellum to postbellum era like a solid bridge, linking race and gender issues in poetry and prose.

Born free in Baltimore in September 1825,[1] orphaned at age three when her mother died, she was reared by a devout aunt and abolitionist uncle, William Watkins, whose Academy for Negro Youth she attended until 1839, acquiring the values and skills that shaped her career. There she learned the art of elocution and rhetoric that prepared her as an eloquent public speaker, at a time few women mounted a podium. She was trained by her aunt to be an accomplished seamstress, which led to her first paid employment—in the home of a local bookstore owner who encouraged her interest in reading and writing poetry. Her earliest verse collection was *Forest Leaves*, privately printed in 1845 but now lost.

Her second booklet, *Poems on Miscellaneous Subjects*, was published in Boston in October 1854, one month after she began lecturing for the Maine Anti-Slavery Society. The book focused on slavery and complemented her antebellum lectures with popular poems such as "The Slave Mother," "The Slave Auction," and "The Fugitive's Wife," plus other "miscellaneous subjects" on temperance, death, and faith. Then twenty-nine years old and on a path few women had tried, she would go the distance, traveling the next six years in the North, the Midwest, and Canada, as an abolitionist lecturer.

Already familiar with gender discrimination that prompted some of her verse, she had been openly opposed in 1850 as the first female teacher hired at Union Seminary operated by the African Methodist Episcopal (A.M.E.) church in Wilberforce, Ohio. She departed there after two years to teach children of fugitive slaves in a Pennsylvania village, and by early 1854 developed an acquaintance with a male contemporary who welcomed her into the Philadel-

---

[1] A death certificate and gravestone revealed 1824 as her birth date, but 1825 appeared on various personal records.

phia abolitionist network and encouraged her writings. He was William Still, employed by the Pennsylvania Society for Promoting the Abolition of Slavery, and later a coordinator of the Philadelphia Vigilance Committee to aid fugitives, and author of *The Underground Railroad* (1872), a book that included Harper's travel letters and her first biographical profile.

Her correspondence to Still reflects her commitment to end slavery and her desire for equal rights for black men and women—in a prose style both lyrical and original, without the sentimentalism and derivativeness of some of her poetry. William Still was among the first to review her *Poems on Miscellaneous Subjects* in 1854, and to point out aptly that, "Miss Watkins has been constantly engaged as a schoolteacher and seamstress during the time of writing this book, and consequently has only had . . . such leisure hours as fall the lot of those in her calling."

Called by admirers "The Bronze Muse," her poetry and prose appeared through the 1850s in black and white abolitionist journals, including the *Liberator*, the *National Antislavery Standard, Anti-Slavery Bugle, Frederick Douglass' Paper*, and *Weekly Anglo-African Magazine*; the latter printed in a September-October 1859 issue her "Two Offers"—a cautionary tale in which two female cousins approach life and marriage differently; though structurally a work of apprentice fiction, it is now considered the first published short story by an Afro-American woman. She quietly made literary history again that year, in a November 1859 letter expressing support to John Brown after Harper's Ferry, and another letter to his wife, by whose side she stayed to await the execution, while many others distanced themselves.

One year later, in November 1860, Frances Watkins became Frances Harper, when she married and moved to Ohio, briefly suspending her speaking career, shortly before the Civil War. Her short marriage to Fenton Harper, a widower and Ohio farmer, produced a daughter Mary, born in 1862, but his death in May 1864 soon left them homeless, when their modest farm near Columbus was seized by a court to pay his debts. With Mary she returned East until the war ended, then lived between North and South, from 1867 to 1871, speaking in schools and churches of newly freed people in a dozen states—and writing vivid impressions about Reconstruction to William Still.

By 1872, she and her young daughter settled permanently in Philadelphia, where both were devoted companions in the same social causes until Mary predeceased her mother in 1909. From the late 1860s, Harper's literary reputation soared with poetry collections such as *Moses: A Story of the Nile* (1869), *Poems*, (1871), *Sketches of Southern Life* (1887), and *Idylls of the Bible* (1901). Her religious denomination was Unitarian, but some of her writings appeared in black church journals, such as the A.M.E. *Christian Recorder*, which serialized three of her short novels: *Minnie's Sacrifice* (1869), *Sowing and Reaping* (1876), and *Trial and Triumph* (1888–89). She was more widely recognized as a novelist in 1892, with book publication of *Iola Leroy; or, Shadows Uplifted*—a historical novel on Reconstruction intended to be "of lasting service to the race." A year later, at age sixty-eight, she spoke on "Woman's Political Future" at the World Congress of Representative Women, for the 1893 World Columbian Exposition in Chicago—"the Chicago World's Fair."

The following piece is excerpted from her speech to the Eleventh National Women's Rights Convention in May 1866, in New York City. Her remarks there foreshadowed her position on the issue of the ballot for women, when the same Convention three years later split over the Fourteenth and Fifteenth Amendments. The heated issue weakened Harper's once cordial alliance with white reformers Susan B. Anthony and Elizabeth Cady Stanton, who had lobbied to end slavery, but argued against black American male suffrage if women were excluded. In Harper's remarks and letters on suffrage, she tactically deferred to race over gender in 1866, though she would later declare in her 1893 speech in Chicago: "I do not believe in unrestricted and universal suffrage for either men or women. I believe in moral and educational tests."

She participated in the following 1866 women's convention based on its 1850 organizing principle "Equal Rights to All."

From Speech to Eleventh National Women's Rights Convention (1866)

I am feeling something of a novice upon this platform. Born of a race whose inheritance has been outrage and wrong, most of my life had been spent in battling against those wrongs. But I did not feel as keenly as others, that I had these rights, in common with other women, which are now demanded. About two years ago, I stood within the shadows of my home. A great sorrow had fallen upon my life. My husband had died suddenly, leaving me a widow, with four children, one my own, and the others stepchildren. I tried to keep my children together. But my husband died in debt; and before he had been in his grave three months, the administrator had swept the very milk-crocks and washtubs from my hands. I was a farmer's wife and made butter for the Columbus market; but what could I do, when they had swept all away? They left me one thing—and that was a looking-glass! Had I died instead of my husband, how different would have been the result! By this time he would have had another wife, it is likely; and no administrator would have gone into his house, broken up his home, and sold his bed, and taken away his means of support.

I took my children in my arms, and went out to seek my living. While I was gone, a neighbor to whom I had once lent five dollars, went before a magistrate and swore that he believed I was a non-resident, and laid an attachment on my very bed. And I went back to Ohio with my orphan children in my arms, without a single feather bed in this wide world, that was not in the custody of the law. I say, then, that justice is not fulfilled so long as woman is unequal before the law.

We are all bound up together in one great bundle of humanity, and society cannot trample on the weakest and feeblest of its members without receiving the curse in its own soul. You tried that in the case of the negro. You pressed him down for two centuries; and in so doing you crippled the moral strength and paralyzed the spiritual energies of the white men of the country. When the hands of the black were fettered, white men were deprived of the liberty of speech and the freedom of the press. Society cannot afford to neglect the enlightenment of any class of its members. At the South, the legislation of the country was in behalf of the rich slaveholders, while the poor white man was neglected. What is the consequence to-day? From that very class of neglected poor white men, comes the man who stands to-day with his hand upon the helm of the nation. He fails to catch the watchword of the hour, and throws himself, the incarnation of meanness, across the pathway of the nation. My objection to Andrew Johnson is not that he has been a poor white man; my objection is that he keeps "poor whits" all the way through. That is the trouble with him.

This grand and glorious revolution which has commenced, will fail to reach its climax of success, until throughout the length and brea[d]th of the American Republic, the nation shall be so color-blind, as to know no man by the color of his skin or the curl of his hair. It will then have no privileged class, trampling upon and outraging the unprivileged classes, but will be then one great privileged nation, whose privilege will be to produce the loftiest manhood and womanhood that humanity can attain.

I do not believe that giving the woman the ballot is immediately going to cure all the ills of life. I do not believe that white women are dewdrops just exhaled from the skies. I think that like men they may be divided into three classes, the good, the bad, and the indifferent. The good would vote according to their convictions and principles; the bad, as dictated by preju[d]ice or malice; and the indifferent will vote on the strongest side of the question, with the winning party.

You white women speak here of rights. I speak of wrongs. I, as a colored woman, have had in this country an education which has made me feel as if I were in the situation of Ishmael, my hand against every man, and every man's hand against me. Let me go to-morrow morning and take my seat in one of your street cars—I do not know that they will do it in New York, but they will in Philadelphia—and the conductor will put up his hand and stop the car rather than let me ride.

Going from Washington to Baltimore this Spring, they put me in the smoking car. Aye, in the capital of the nation, where the black man consecrated himself to the nation's defence, faithful when the white man was faithless, they put me in the smoking car! They did it once; but the next time they tried it, they failed; for I would not go in. I felt the fight in me; but I don't want to have to fight all the time. To-day I am puzzled where to make my home. I would like to make it in Philadelphia, near my own friends and relations. But if I want to ride in the streets of Philadelphia, they send me to ride on the platform with the driver. Have women nothing to do with this? Not long since, a colored woman took her seat in an Eleventh Street car in Philadelphia, and the conductor stopped the car, and told the rest of the passengers to get out, and left the car with her in it alone, when they took it back to the station. One day I took my seat in a car, and the conductor came to me and told me to take another seat. I just screamed "murder." The man said if I was black I ought to behave myself. I knew that if he was white he was not behaving himself. Are there not wrongs to be righted? . . .

JOEL CHANDLER HARRIS

(1848–1908)

Southern journalist, humorist, short story writer, novelist, and critic, Joel Chandler Harris in his life and work was a contradictory persona: segregationist but not Negrophobe, a New South advocate yet an Old South apologist. His name became synonymous with his Uncle Remus folklore, but less known for other indigenous black and white characters he created in fiction during a forty-six-year literary career.

Unlike his Southern contemporary, Thomas Nelson Page,[1] Harris was neither a romanticist for the Confederacy or Southern chivalry or sectional politics, nor a proponent of "racial purity" propaganda advanced by a junior Southerner then writing fiction—Thomas Dixon, Jr.[2] Harris was the South's goodwill defender, but also a mythmaker as cunning in his intentions as his allegorical B'rer Rabbit, the heroic survivor in many Uncle Remus tales. Some of the Harris myths were intended to boost North–South reconciliation and to heal old animosities after the war; others were to advance his own political ideas on race and race relations.

A prolific storyteller who refused to read publicly because of a stammering speech defect, he made some of his fictional black characters mouthpieces for his rhetorical strategies, often to advance his unyielding belief that whites were superior to blacks and should always be socially separate.

His dialect depiction of blacks in tales of slavery and Reconstruction derived in part from his post–Reconstruction nostalgia, which was apparent in many nonfiction pieces he wrote for periodicals. In a 1904 article, "The Negro as the South Sees Him," for the *Saturday Evening Post*, he noted:

---

[1] Thomas Nelson Page (1853–1922), Virginia-born lawyer and author, who glorified the antebellum South and Confederates, in dialect stories such as "Marse Chan" (1884), in novels of postbellum Southern revolt, such as *Red Rock, Chronicle of Reconstruction* (1898), and in nonfiction books that included *The Negro: The Southerner's Problem* (1904), *The Old Dominion: Her Making and Her Manners* (1908), and two historical studies of Robert E. Lee, among his other works on the South, before Woodrow Wilson appointed him ambassador to Italy in 1913.

[2] Thomas Dixon, Jr. (1864–1946), North Carolina Baptist preacher and author, who celebrated postbellum segregation in novels such as *The Leopard's Spots* (1902), and *The Clansman* (1905), which led to D. W. Griffith's *The Birth of a Nation* (1915).

It is a common saying in the South that we have very few of the old-time negroes left with us; that the places that once knew them will soon know them no more forever; and we shake our heads sadly and lament the conditions that are soon to deprive us of some our most cherished and picturesque relics.

The author who devoted much of his dialect fiction to re-creating "old-time negroes" was born in the small town of Eatonton, Georgia, the county seat of Putnam, in the corn and cotton belt of the state. He was an out-of-wedlock child of Mary Harris, a thirty-one-year old seamstress and her lover, an Irish laborer, who deserted her before their son was born. At age thirteen, the boy "Joe Harris" became an apprentice compositer in a print shop at Turnwold, the plantation of Joseph Addison Turner, a slaveowner and lawyer who published a weekly newspaper, *The Countryman*. There the young apprentice tried his earliest poems and sketches and frequented the Turnwold slave quarters, the fictional setting of his adult imagination, its inhabitants the prototypes of his novels and stories extolling the Plantation Tradition. Turner, his idol and mentor, was not a secessionist, but his proslavery editorials promised a Confederate victory that ill-prepared the impressionable youth for an end to a pastoral interlude at Turnwold. Harris's four years there, from March 1862 to May 1866, closed after the Confederacy fell and *The Countryman* folded. He returned to Eatonton and later described what seemed to him the final act of a tragic drama: "When the curtain suddenly went down and the lights went out, no language can describe the grief, the despair, and the feelings of abject humiliation that fell upon the white population in the small towns and village communities." He spent most of his life writing variations on that theme.

Following a decade of editorial positions at three different small newspapers in Georgia, he became associate editor at the *Atlanta Constitution* in the autumn of 1876 and worked there until September 1900. The first of his several hundred Uncle Remus sketches appeared in the newspaper on November 28, 1876—almost as a fluke, to replace dialect sketches by another staff writer on another elderly black Atlanta man. The popular new urban (and later rural) folk hero created by Harris was his springboard to books that made him internationally famous: *Uncle Remus: His Songs and Sayings* (1880; revised edition 1895), *Nights with Uncle Remus: Myths and Legends of the Old Plantation* (1883), *Uncle Remus and His Friends* (1892), *The Tar-Baby and Other Rhymes of Uncle Remus* (1904), *Told by Uncle Remus: New Stories of the Old Plantation* (1905), *Uncle Remus and B'rer Rabbit* (1907), plus editorship of *Uncle Remus Magazine* for a year before his death, and publication of two posthumous titles: *Uncle Remus and the Little Boy* (1910), and *Uncle Remus Returns* (1918).

His other abundant fiction set on the plantation or during Reconstruction includes, *Mingo and Other Sketches in Black and White* (1884), *Free Joe and*

Other Georgian Sketches (1887), *Daddy Jake the Runaway and Short Stories Told after Dark* (1889), *Balaam and His Master and Other Sketches and Stories* (1891); *On the Plantation: The Story of a Georgia Boy's Adventures During the War* (1892), *Stories of Georgia* (1896), *The Chronicles of Aunt Minervy Ann* (1899), and *Gabriel Tolliver: A Story of Reconstruction* (1902). He abandoned seven chapters of a novel about an actual African prince—known as "Qua" to Harris's great-grandmother in colonial Middle Georgia—brother of his fictional Minervy Ann.

Credited by admirers as the first Southern author to show Negroes and poor whites as major characters in fiction, he has been criticized equally by some Afro-American scholars for stamping black stereotypes, exalting the plantation and slavery, distorting facts, misappropriating African folklore, rejecting black political enfranchisement, mocking freedmen, boosting Booker T. Washington, and fostering white paternalism.

The following piece, from the *Atlanta Constitution*, appeared on his twenty-ninth birthday, December 9, 1877, and was later included by his daughter-in-law, Julia Collier Harris, (wife of his eldest son, Julian) in her edited collection, *Joel Chandler Harris: Editor and Essayist: Miscellaneous Literary, Political, and Social Writings* (1931).

The Old Plantation (1877)

The scourge that swept slavery into the deep sea of the past gave the deathblow to one of the peculiar outgrowths of that institution. The results that made slavery impossible blotted from the Southern social system the patriarchal—I had almost written feudal—establishment known as the old plantation. Nourished into life by slavery, it soon became one of the features of Southern civilization—a peculiar feature indeed, and one which for many years exerted a powerful influence throughout the world. The genius of such men as Washington, Jefferson, Patrick Henry, Taney, Marshall, Calhoun, Stephens, Toombs and all the greatest leaders of political thought and opinion from the days of the Revolution to the beginning of the Civil War, was the result and outgrowth of the civilization made possible by the old plantation.[3] It was a cherished feature

---

[3] All of the men cited in the sentence were Southern slaveholders who held high office:
• *George Washington* (1732–99) Continental Army commander and first U.S. President (1789–97).

of Southern society, and it is not to be doubted that its demolition has been more deeply deplored by our people than all the other results of the war put together. The brave men and noble women, who at the end found themselves confronting the dire confusion and desolation of an unsuccessful struggle, have been compelled to set their faces toward the new future that is always ahead of the hopeful and truehearted; but how many times have they turned and sighed, endeavoring to get a glimpse of the ruins of the old plantation! Now that the problem of slavery, which even before the desperate cast of the die in 1861 had begun to perplex the more thoughtful of the Southern people, is successfully (but O, how cruelly!) solved, even the bare suggestion of its re-establishment is unsavory; but the memory of the old plantation will remain green and gracious forever.

What days they were, those days on the old plantation! How vividly you remember the slighest incident! How picturesque the panorama which passes before your mind's eye! There was the foxhunt planned for the especial benefit of Miss Carrie de Compton, the belle of Rockville.

It is all indelibly impressed upon your memory—the ride to Sir Reynard's range, the casting about of the hounds; the sudden burst of canine melody as the fox gets right up in the midst of the park; the hard ride at the heels of the hounds for a few minutes; and then the sudden inspiration on your part that it would be well to guide the fair de Compton to a point near which the fox (an old customer of yours) would surely pass. You remember how you vainly endeavored to convince your skeptical charge that the slight, dark shadow steal-ing across the hillside not a quarter of a mile away was the veritable fox the dogs were after; how your whole frame tingled with delight when the soul-stirring music of the hounds was borne to your ears on the crisp breeze of morning, and what a thrill came over you as the pack burst into view, running with heads up and tails down, your Flora far to the front and flying like a meteor.

What nights were the nights on the old plantation! The mellow light of the harvest moon crept through the rustling leaves of the tall oaks, fell softly upon the open space beyond, and bathed the brown old barn in a flood of golden

---

- *Thomas Jefferson* (see entry in this volume, pages 35–44.)
- *Patrick Henry* (1736–99) Virginia lawyer, governor, orator, critic of England.
- *Roger Brook Taney* (see entry in this volume, pages 190–99).
- *John Marshall* (1755–1835) Virginia Federalist; Chief Justice of Supreme Court (1801–35).
- *John C. Calhoun* (1782–1850) South Carolina representative to U.S. Congress (1811–17), Secretary of War (1817–25) U.S. Vice President (1825—resigned 1832 over Southern states' rights; U.S. Senator (1832–43, 1845–50); Secretary of State (1844–45).
- *Alexander H. Stephens* (1812–83) Georgia representative to U.S. Congress (1843–59); seces-sionist and vice president of the Confederacy (1861–65); returned to Congress (1873–82).
- *Robert Toombs* (1810–85) U.S. senator from Georgia (1853–60); secessionist (1861–65).

glory, while the songs of the negroes at the corn-pile, lusty chorus and plaintive refrain, shook the silence until it broke upon the air in far-reaching waves of melody. But alas! all these are gone. The moon pursues her pathway as serenely as of old, but she no longer looks down upon the scenes that were familiar to your youth. The old homestead and the barn are given up to decay, and the songs of the negroes have been hushed into silence by the necessities of a new dispensation. The old plantation, itself, is gone. It has passed away, but the hand of time, inexorable, yet tender, has woven about it the sweet suggestions of poetry and romance, memorials that neither death nor decay can destroy.

ALEXANDER CRUMMELL

(1819–98)

At the same time Joel Chandler Harris's unlettered hero Uncle Remus became a household name, the first black American scholar with a degree from Cambridge University was virtually unknown in the United States. He was Alexander Crummell, eulogized by W. E. B. Du Bois in *The Souls of Black Folk* (1903) as a man whose "name today, in this broad land, means little, and comes to fifty million ears laden with no incense of memory or emulation." The young Dr. Du Bois then revered but barely knew the older man; decades later, for ideological reasons, he would not remember him in his autobiography.

Crummell was the only Afro-American to graduate from Cambridge before the Civil War. (However, he believed the best trained Afro-American of his generation was James McCune Smith,[1] a British-educated physician whom he first met at New York's African Free School.) Before Cambridge, Crummell had completed his studies at Oneida Institute and been an ordained Episcopal priest for six years. Rejected at a New York diocese seminary for racial reasons, he had remained a steadfast Episcopalian apostle; while other religious denominations appointed blacks to leadership positions, the American Episcopal hierarchy then condoned white-only bishops and segregated churches, which Crummell fought in his own way.

Influenced as a youth by a black Episcopalian rector and mentor, Peter Williams, Jr., of St. Philip's Church in New York City, Crummell undertook the rigorous classical education that Williams had been denied. He believed that blacks could prove themselves the intellectual equal of whites and thereby contribute to the progress of nineteenth-century civilization; for him history was a continuum of progress in which race and nationality were subordinate to divine precepts. Both his idealism and his determination had fortified him against hardships as a young priest in Providence, Philadelphia, New Haven, Boston, and New York.

In England, his stated purpose was fund-raising for his New York parish, as well as studying at Cambridge, where he and his Afro-American wife and grow-

---

[1] James McCune Smith, M.D. (1813–65), freeborn in N.Y.C., earned three degrees from the University of Glasgow, interned abroad, and returned to New York in 1837 to practice medicine.

ing family spent five years. Aware that notable black abolitionists had preceded him in Britain in the 1830s and 1840s, he accepted invitations to speak at antislavery meetings, as he had done at conventions in the United States, but he was no spokesman in the jeremiad style of Frederick Douglass. He preferred being the reflective Victorian Afro-Anglophile, whose philosophical tracts treated moral and theological dogmas rather than political issues. His most representative literary work prior to his English sojourn was a theoretical tract in 1846, *Eulogium on the Life and Character of Thomas Clarkson.* Not until much later would he publish three collections of his political sermons and numerous articles. Meanwhile, Britain during his domicile was more racially hospitable than antebellum America, although its cultural atmosphere included Thomas Carlyle's *Discourse on the Nigger Question* (1849), and a fad for black dolls named after Topsy in Stowe's 1852 novel, *Uncle Tom's Cabin.* After completing his Cambridge study program at Queen's College in 1853, Crummell took his ideas of moral progress to Liberia, where he was a missionary-educator for seventeen years.

By some scholars he is hailed as an early Pan-Africanist, but his Pan-Africanism inevitably had its contradictions. He voiced nationalist sympathies about universal black solidarity, the "destined superiority of the Negro," claimed paternal descent from an African prince, and until the Civil War espoused the principle of emigrationism to Africa, but his credo included no protest against European imperialism encroaching on Africa by the late nineteenth century. To him the non-Western traditions and customs of Africans were "primitive" and "heathen" and could only become "civilized" through contact with Anglo-Saxon values and Christianity. In Liberia, he rejected Islamic thought as viable, doubted the Americo-Liberians' ability to elevate themselves or to end color-caste strife, or to try to improve skills of the indigenous population. His stance led ultimately to his departure in 1872 for Washington, DC, where he spent the last twenty-five years of his life.

Settling in the nation's capital during Reconstruction, he adapted his religious duties and public discourse to American concerns, while holding onto many of his earlier theories. He served two years as pastor of an integrated St. Mary's Episcopal Chapel, before founding a larger church: St. Luke's, where he remained active—often in contention with the predominantly Afro-American congregation—until his retirement in 1894. He played the role of teacher and preacher in defining his vision for race leadership and progress, stressing that the best trained must help elevate the masses (a principle embraced with some modifications by Du Bois in his 1903 essay, "The Talented Tenth"). Crummell valued a liberal arts education for the elite of the race but lobbied as forcefully for trade skills for the masses, predating, in his own way, the Du Bois–Booker T. Washington controversy on classical versus industrial training.

In 1897, the year before his death—and a year after the *Plessy v. Ferguson* Supreme Court decision—Crummell became the first president of the American Negro Academy (ANA), to promote scholarly work for "dissemination of the truth and vindication of the Negro race from vicious assaults." The group's constitution defined it as an "organization of authors, scholars, artists, and those distinguished in other walks of life, men of African descent, for the promotion of Letters, Science, and Art." Organizing and presiding over an organization that excluded educated women of African descent was a paradox of Crummell's late career, considering his earlier advocacy for the progress of uneducated black women—notably those in the South, as shown in the following excerpt of a piece he presented to the Freedman's Aid Society of the Methodist Episcopal Church, in Ocean Grove, New Jersey, August 15, 1883, and later reprinted in his book, *Africa and America: Addresses and Discourses* (1891).

From The Black Woman of the South: Her Neglects and Her Needs (1883)

. . . Ladies and gentlemen, since the day of emancipation millions of dollars have been given by the generous Christian people of the North for the intellectual training of the black race in this land. Colleges and universities have been built in the South, and hundreds of youth have been gathered within their walls. The work of your own Church in this regard has been magnificent and unrivaled, and the results which have been attained have been grand and elevating to the entire Negro race in America. The complement to all this generous and ennobling effort is the elevation of the black woman. Up to this day and time your noble philanthropy has touched, for the most part, the male population of the South, given them superiority, and stimulated them to higher aspirations. But a true civilization can only then be attained when the life of woman is reached, her whole being permeated by noble ideas, her fine taste enriched by culture, her tendencies to the beautiful gratified and developed, her singular and delicate nature lifted up to its full capacity; and then, when all these qualities are fully matured, cultivated and sanctified, all their sacred infuences shall circle around then thousand firesides, and the cabins of the humblest freedmen shall become the homes of Christian refinement and of domestic elegance through the influence and the charm of the uplifted and cultivated black woman of the South! . . .

T. THOMAS FORTUNE

(1856–1928)

One articulate adversary fo Alexander Crummell was young enough to be his son: T. Thomas Fortune, the most militant Afro-American newspaper editor of the post–Reconstruction era. At a transitional time in Southern history, his editorials probed the changing South after slavery and the complexities of black–white race relations. Born a slave named Timothy Thomas to mixed-blood parents in Marianna, Florida, five years before the Civil War, he was of Seminole, African, and European descent. As a journalist, he insisted upon the racial nomenclature *Afro-American*, to the chagrin of elders such as Crummell who preferred *Negro*, and barred Fortune from membership in The American Negro Academy. Ahead of his time, Fortune argued against using the term "*Negro, colored, or mulatto*, declaring "We are not all black and colored and yellow, but we are all Afro-American."

His surname, Fortune, adopted by his father Emanuel Fortune after Emancipation, was that of his Scottish paternal grandfather. Emanuel Fortune was one of two Afro-Americans in Florida elected to the state legislature in 1868, before a new and menacing Ku Klux Klan forced him from the capital. Young Timothy's early formal education began in Freedmen's Bureau schools after the Civil War but lasted only three academic terms between family moves. The sudden death of his mother and his father's loss of employment forged the self-reliance and resilience that characterized his own career. From printing-press jobs in Florida and Delaware, he became an expert type-setter, and at eighteen he had saved enough to enter the Howard University Preparatory Department in Washington, DC, where he completed basic courses in 1876 and considered studying law. Howard—founded for Negroes in 1867 and named for a Union general[1]—then had a small Law Department and two illustrious black lawyers: John Mercer Langston[2] and Richard T.

---

[1] Otis Oliver Howard (1830–1909), Union general in the Civil War; chief commissioner of Freedmen's Bureau (1865–72); a founder and first president of Howard University (1869–73)

[2] John Mercer Langston (1829–97) lawyer, educator, politician; educated at Oberlin College; first black-elected official in the U.S. (1855, as clerk of Brownhelm Township in Ohio); abolitionist; Union troop recruiter; inspector general, Freedmen's Bureau (1868–69) dean, Howard Law Department (1870–73) and University vice-president (1873–75); diplomatic consul, Haiti and Dominican

Greener,[3] whose credentials and comportment made an unforgettable impact on Fortune. But lacking funds to enroll in the Law Department before it suspended operations in 1880 for budgetary reasons, he began a journalistic stint in Washington. One Howard law graduate, John Wesley Cromwell, had launched a black weekly, the *People's Advocate,* where Fortune ran the printshop and began writing articles under an alias, Gustafus Bert.

After a temporary return to Florida, where he married and worked briefly at his former job on the printing press of the *Jacksonville Daily Union,* Fortune and his bride moved to New York City in early 1881. By that summer, his editorial byline, T. Thomas Fortune, became a feature of the *Globe,* a weekly paper that he quickly transformed from a black tabloid, the *Rumor,* as managing editor. The *Globe*'s objective was a "National Journal for the colored people of the United States" through an established network of correspondents and an articulate editorial page. Fortune's editorials soon proved him a radical Southern voice in the North, commenting on the growing disenfranchisement of rural blacks in America's Gilded Age of growing economic and social inequity. His columns denounced capitalistic monopolies and protective tariffs, and attacked the Republican Party for betraying his people; but he alienated some black leaders such as Frederick Douglass and John Mercer Langston who relied on Republican patronage.

In 1884, following publication of his book *Black and White: Life, Labor, and Politics in the South,* the *Globe* abruptly ceased publication due to fiscal reasons as well as Republican pressures against Fortune's unequivocal positions on civil rights, women's rights, and interracial marriage. Within months he had bounced back as sole owner of a new weekly, the *Freeman,* with columns attacking efforts to repeal the Fifteenth Amendment to overturn black voting power. He amplified his views in his 1886 pamphlet "The Negro in Politics." By 1887, to meet his debts, he renamed the *Freeman* weekly the *New York Age* and began a copartnership with a black editor–treasurer named Jerome Peterson. The *New York Age* became more editorially Republican, and Fortune published some of his more radical editorials in white newspapers such as the *New York Sun* and *Boston Transcript.* He was often broke, but his crusades persisted against race

---

Republic (1877–85); president, Virginia Normal & Collegiate Institute [Virginia State College, Petersburg] (1885–87); Congressman-elect from Virginia's Fourth District, 1888, but unseated until 1890 in a contested election; defeated for reelection. See also Charles H. Langston entry, pages 212–16, above.

[3] Richard T. Greener (1844–1922), lawyer, educator, foreign-service officer. First Afro-American undergraduate of Harvard in 1870; professor of metaphysics and logic at the University of South Carolina, where he earned a law degree in 1876; admitted to bar in District of Columbia in 1877 and as law instructor at Howard, where he was also dean, 1879–80; appointed U.S. consul in Vladivostok, Russia, 1898–1905; retired as lawyer in Chicago.

discrimination and lynching, and during the early 1890s he reached the zenith of his influence, prior to a paradoxical alliance with his contemporary Booker T. Washington. However, he already had begun foreshadowing Washington in articles and speeches on race uplift, vocational training, and industrial education, a decade before the Tuskegee educator's Atlanta Compromise speech in 1895. He hailed Washington as a "wizard" and became his ghostwriter and defender, despite their ideological differences and strong opponents. Whereas Washington rewarded him financially and often with duplicity, Fortune's autonomy decreased and his drinking increased.

In 1890 he founded the National Afro-American League, a forerunner of major twentieth-century civil rights organizations, but the League fizzled by 1893, and he tried unsuccessfully again in 1898 with a similar organization, the National Afro-American Council, which also was shortlived. He later accused some of his detractors of preempting his Council with the Niagara Movement in 1905.[4] Visionary to some and myopic to others, his severest misfortunes began in 1903 and he never completely recovered. Using Booker T. Washington's influence at the White House, Fortune accepted a political appointment in 1903 from the U.S. Treasury Department to study trade conditions in the Philippines. Returning home with malaria several months later, he was further impaired by alcoholism and impoverished by debts. In 1907 he sold his shares of the *New York Age* to a Booker T. Washington cohort. His own public prestige receded, despite a Harlem public testimonial honoring him in 1911, and praise for his occasional editorials in the *Age* until late 1914. Booker T. Washington, who abandoned him, died in November 1915, and Fortune finally exposed disillusion with his policies in an April 1916 article, "The Quick and the Dead."

That same year, he had regained his health enough to freelance for various black periodicals, and in 1923 he began editing the *Negro World*, the journal of Marcus Garvey's Universal Negro Improvement Association. The latter role stunned those who saw it as contradictory for the once-independent Fortune, an integrationist who had resisted race separatism and emigration moves like Garvey's Back to Africa, and had shunned the term *Negro* as "crude." If his final years were a sad fall from balancing on a tightrope, at his death he was eulogized in the black press for his indomitable spirit and undeniable contribution to American journalism, and for being a survivor in an era when few black weeklies survived very long. The *New York Age*, which nearly broke him, outlived him, lasting until 1960 in a different form.

The following excerpt is from Chapter 14, "Classes in the South," from his 1884 book *Black and White*. . . .

---

[4] See entry on the Niagara Movement "Declaration of Principles," pages 427–29, below.

From *Black and White: Land, Labor, and Politics in the South* (1884)

. . . The operations of the vast landed estates of the South produced all the industrial disjointments which have afflicted the South since the war. The white man was taught to look upon labor as the natural portion of the black slave; and nothing could induce a white man to put his hand to the plow, but the gaunt visage of starvation at his door. He even preferred ignominious starvation to honest work; and, in his desperate struggle to avoid the horror of the one and the disgrace of the other, he would sink himself lower in the scale of moral infamy than the black slave he despised. He would make of himself a monster of cruelty of abject servility to avoid starvation or honest work. It was from this class of vermin that the planters secured their "Nigger drivers" or overseers, and a more pliable, servile, cruel, heartless set of men never existed. They were commonly known as *"poor white trash,"* or "crackers." They were most heartily and righteously detested by the slave population. As the poor whites of the South were fifty years ago, so they are today—a careless, ignorant, lazy, but withal, arrogant set, who add nothing to the productive wealth of the community because they are too lazy to work, and who take nothing from that wealth because they are too poor to purchase. They have graded human wants to a point below which man could not go without starving. They live upon the poorest land in the South, the "piney woods," and raise a few potatoes and corn, and a few pigs, which never grow to be hogs, so sterile is the land upon which they are turned to "root, or die." These characteristic pigs are derisively called "shotes" by those who have seen their lean, lank and hungry development. They are awful counterparts of their pauper owners. It may be taken as an index of the quality of the soil and the condition of the people, to observe the condition of their livestock. Strange as it may appear, the faithful dog is the only animal which appears to thrive on "piney woods" land. The "piney woods" gopher, which may be not inappropriately termed a *highland turtle,* is a great desideratum in the food supply of the pauper denizens of these portions of the South. There is nothing enticing about the appearance of the gopher. But his flesh, properly cooked, is passably palatable.

The poor white population of the South who live in the piney woods are sunk in the lowest ignorance, and practice vices too heinous to be breathed. They have no schools, and their mental condition hardly warrants the charitable inference that they would profit much if they were supplied with them. Still, I would like to see the experiment tried. Their horrible poverty, their appalling illiteracy, their deplorable moral enervation, deserve the pity of mankind and the assistance of philanthropic men and a thoughtful government. Though sunk to the lowest moral scale, *they are men*, and nothing should be omitted to improve their condition and make them more useful members of the communities in which they are now more than an incubus.

It may not be out of place here to state that the Ku Klux Klan, the White Liners League, the Knights of the White Camelia, and other lawless gangs which have in the past fifteen years made Southern chivalry a byword and reproach among the nations of the earth, were largely recruited from this idle, vicious, ignorant class of Southerners. They needed no preparation for the bloody work perpetrated by those lawless organizations, those more cruel than Italian brigands. They instinctively hate the black man; because the condition of the black, his superior capacity for labor and receptivity of useful knowledge, place him a few pegs higher than themselves in the social scale. So these degraded white men, the very substratum of Southern population, were ready tools in the hands of the organized chivalrous brigands (as they had been of the slave oligarch), whose superior intelligence made them blush at the lawlessness they inspired, and who, therefore, gladly transferred to other hands the execution of those deeds of blood and death which make men shudder even now to think of them. It was long a common saying among the black population of the South that "I'd rudder be a niggah den a po' w'ite man!" and they were wise in their preference.

It is safe to say, that the peasantry of no country claiming to be civilized stands more in need of the labors of the schoolmaster and the preacher, than do the so-called "poor white trash" of the South. On their account, if no other, I am an advocate of a compulsory system of education, a National Board of Education, and a very large national appropriation for common school and industrial education.

I name this class first because it is the very lowest.

Next to this class is the great labor force of the South, the class upon whose ample shoulders have fallen the weight of Southern labor and inhumanity for lo! two hundred years—*the black man*. Time was, yesterday, it appears to me, when this great class were all of *one* condition, driven from the rising to the setting of the sun to enrich men who were created out of the same sod, and in the construction of whose mysterious mechanism, mental and physical, the great God expended no more time or ingenuity. Up to the close of the Rebellion, of that gigantic conflict which shook the pillars of republican government to their center, the great black population were truly the "mudsills" of Southern society, upon which rested all the industrial burdens of that section; truly, "the hewers of wood and the drawers of water"; a people who, in the mysterious providence of God, were torn root and branch from their savage homes in that land which has now become to them a dream "more insubstantial than a pageant faded," to "dwell in a strange land, among strangers," to endure, like the children of Israel, a season of cruel probation, and then to begin life in earnest; to put their shoulders to the wheel and assist in making this vast continent, this asylum of the oppressed of the world, the grandest abode of mingled happiness and woe, and wealth and pauperization ever reared by the genius and governed by the selfishness and cupidity of man. And today, as in the dark days of the past, this people are the bone and sinew of the South, the great producers and partial consumers of her wealth; the despised, yet indispensable, "mudsills" of her industrial interests.

A Senator of the United States from the South, whose hands have been dyed in the blood of his fellow citizens, and who holds his high office by fraud and usurpation, not long since declared that his State could very well dispense with her black population. That population outnumbers the white three to one; and by the toil by which that State has been enriched, by the blood and the sweat of two hundred years which the soil of that State has absorbed, by the present production and consumption of wealth by that black population, we are amazed at the ignorance of the great man who has been placed in a "little brief authority." That black population cannot and will not be dispensed with; because it is so deeply rooted in the soil that it is a part of it—the most valuable part. And the time will come when it will hold its title to the land, by right of purchase, for a laborer is worthy of his hire, and is now free to invest that hire as it pleases him best. Already some of the very best soil of that State is held by the people this great magus in the Nation's councils would supersede in their divine rights.

When the war closed, as I said, the great black population of the South was distinctively a laboring class. It owned no lands, houses, banks, stores, or livestock, or other wealth. Not only was it the distinctively laboring class but the distinctively pauper class. It had neither money, intelligence nor morals with which to begin the hard struggle of life. It was absolutely at the bottom of the social ladder. It possessed nothing but health and muscle.

I have frequently contemplated with profound amazement the momentous mass of subjected human force, a force which had been educated by the lash and the bloodhound to despise labor, which was thrown upon itself by the wording of the Emancipation Proclamation and the surrender of Robert E. Lee. Nothing in the history of mankind is at all comparable, an exact counterpart, in all particulars, to that great event. A slavery of two hundred years had dwarfed the intelligence and morality of this people, and made them to look upon labor as the most baneful of all the curses a just God can inflict upon humankind; and they were turned loose upon the land, without a dollar in their hands, and, like the great Christ and the fowls of the air, without a place to lay their head.

And yet today, this people, who, only a few years ago, were bankrupts in morality, in intelligence, and in wealth, have leaped forward in the battle of progress like *veterans*; have built magnificent churches, with a membership of over two million souls; have preachers, learned and eloquent; have professors in colleges by the hundreds and schoolmasters by the thousands; have accumulated large landed interests in country, town and city; have established banking houses and railroads; manage large coal, grocery and merchant tailoring businesses; conduct with ability and success large and influential newspaper enterprises; in short, have come, and that very rapidly, into sharp competition with white men (who have the prestige of a thousand years of civilization and opportunity) in all the industrial interests which make a people great, respected and feared. The metamorphosis has been rapid, marvelous, astounding. Their home life has been largely transformed into the quality of purity and refinement which should characterize the home; they have now successful farmers, merchants, ministers, lawyers, editors, educators, physicians, legislators—in short, they have entered every avenue of industry and thought. Their efforts are yet crude and their grasp uncertain, but they are in the field of competition, and will remain there and acquit themselves manfully.

Of course I speak in general terms of the progress the colored people have made. Individual effort and success are the indicators of the vitality and genius of a people. When individuals rise out of the indistinguishable mass and make their mark, we may rest assured that the mass is rich and capable of unlimited production. The great mass of every government, of every people, while adding to and creating greatness, go down in history unmentioned. But their glory, their genius, success and happiness, are expended and survive in the few great spirits their fortunate condition produced. The governments of antiquity were great and glorious, because their proletarians were intelligent, thrifty and brave, but the proletarians fade into vagueness, and are great only in the few great names which have been handed down to us. It has been said that a nation expends a hundred years of its vitality in the production of a great man of genius like Socrates, or Bacon, or Toussaint l'Overture, or Fulton. And this may be true. There can now be no question that the African race in the United States possess every element of vitality and genius possessed by their fellow citizens of other races, and any calculation of race possibilities in this country which assumes that they will remain indefinitely the "mudsills" only of society will prove more brittle than ropes of sand.

At this time the colored people of the South are largely the industrial class; that is, they are the producing class. They are principally the agriculturists of the South; consequently, being wedded to the soil by lifelong association and interest, and being principally the laboring class, they will naturally invest their surplus earnings in the purchase of the soil. Herein lies the great hope of the future. For the man who owns the soil largely owns and dictates to the men who are compelled to live upon it and derive their subsistence from it. The colored people of the South recognize this fact. And if there is any one idiosyncrasy more marked than another among them, it is their mania for buying land. They all live and labor in the cheerful anticipation of some day owning a home, a farm of their own. As the race grows in intelligence this mania for land owning becomes more and more pronounced. At first their impecuniosity will compel them to purchase poor hill-lands, but they will eventually get their grip upon the rich alluvial lands.

The class next to the great black class is the *small white farmers*. This class is composed of some of the "best families" of the South who were thrown upon their resources of brain and muscle by the results of the war, and of some of the worst families drawn from the more thrifty poor white class. Southern political economists labor hard to make it appear that the vastly increased production of wealth in the South since the war is to be traced largely to the phenomenally increased per centum of small white farmers, but the assumption is too transparent to impose upon any save those most ignorant of the industrial conditions of the South, and the marvelous adaptibility to the new conditions shown by colored men. I grant that these small white farmers, who were almost too inconsiderable in numbers to be taken into account before the war, have added largely to the development of the country and the production of wealth; but that the tremendous gains of free labor as against slave labor are to be placed principally to their intelligence and industry is too absurd to be seriously debated. The Charleston (S. C.) *News and Courier*, a pronounced anti-negro newspaper, recently made such a charge in all seriousness. The struggle for supremacy will largely come between the small white and black farmer; because each recurring year will augment the number of each class of small holders. A condition of freedom and open competition makes the fight equal, in many respects. Which will prove the more successful small holder, the black or the white? . . .

ALBION W. TOURGÉE

(1838–1905)

What journalist T. Thomas Fortune called the South's "poor white trash" also interested author Albion Tourgée, a Northerner whom many Southerners tagged a "carpetbagger" for migrating to North Carolina after the Civil War. Tourgée, a former Union soldier who settled in Greensboro in July 1865, soon became known for his fiction and nonfiction showing a Southern Reconstruction era doomed to failure and violence.

His popular novels included the best-seller A *Fool's Errand* (1879), which sold over two-hundred-thousand copies. It portrayed the rise of the Ku Klux Klan as mob vigilantes reacting to federal policies to empower blacks. It was a companion book to Tourgée's factual report of the origins of the KKK, *The Invisible Empire*, which he included as a supplement to later editions of his controversial novel. Twentieth-century literary critic Edmund Wilson, in his 1963 study of Civil War and Reconstruction literature, *Patriotic Gore*, wrote that "A *Fool's Errand* was received as a sensation in its day and it ought to be an historical classic in ours." Tourgée's renown in his day was fleeting, and history has since forgotten him, not only as a novelist but as a lawyer and social reformer whose books and legal cases exposed painful antagonisms between blacks and whites.

He was born Albion Winegar Tourgée in 1838 in rural Ohio, to a father of French Huguenot descent and a New England–bred mother who died when he was four. He left home at age fourteen to escape an uncongenial stepmother and lived with maternal relatives in Massachusetts. In 1859, he enrolled at the University of Rochester, where exposure to abolitionism led him to enlist as a Union soldier in the New York Volunteers when the Civil War erupted in April 1861. He was later commissioned in the Ohio Volunteers but resigned in December 1863 after complications from a spinal injury.

He studied law for a year and passed the Ohio bar before moving South to begin his legal practice after the war ended. Convinced that Northern initiative could help transform a decimated South into a new casteless society, he was soon disabused of that conviction in Dixie, where one professional setback followed another. He disagreed with partners in his law firm, which soon dissolved; he edited a local newspaper that failed; and he lost money in several small businesses before being appointed judge of the North Carolina Superior Court in 1868. His judicial appointment lasted eight years, amid increasing white hostility to his legal rulings favoring blacks victimized by mob violence. In 1876, President Ulysses S. Grant appointed him U.S. Pension Agent in Raleigh, the state capital, where he was in residence three years, until ideological adversaries threatened his life and family. In 1879, after fourteen chaotic years in North Carolina, he left and resettled in upstate New York.

Before he relocated, Tourgée had already begun fictionalizing his Southern observations under a pseudonym. His first novel, *Toinette* (1874), a miscegenation-theme tragedy, portrayed the plight of a mulatto mother and daughter, both former mistresses of white slave masters. The book appeared in 1874, before being revised and reprinted in 1880 as A *Royal Gentleman*, a year after Tourgée became nationally famous with A *Fool's Errand*. The commercial success of the latter novel in 1879 led to a sequel, *Bricks without Straw*, in 1880, and to three more melodramatic novels in quick succession: *John Eax* and *Mamelon*, both in 1882, and *Hot Ploughshares* in 1883, all socially relevant but without literary distinction.

Tourgée's popularity as a novelist declined by the late 1880s, when many white readers showed signs of collective amnesia about the Reconstruction period. To them, an uneasy truce with the postbellum New South seemed less troublesome than painful memories of the antebellum Old South. Tourgée's 1884 nonfiction tract, "An Appeal to Caesar," argued that the South's only salvation was a massive federal program of education for semifeudal communities of former slaves and dispossessed poor whites. He insisted that the way to end disharmony and hostility between them was to change old attitudes and habits.

He proposed a national-education plan to his former classmate from Ohio, James Garfield, while campaigning for him in 1880. Persuaded of the efficacy of Tourgée's educational strategy, Garfield as President-elect urged him to write a book on the subject. In March 1881, Garfield's Inaugural Address included education-reform proposals that sounded as if Tourgée wrote them. They were later excerpted prominently in "An Appeal to Caesar":

... The Census has already sounded the alarm in the appalling figures which mark how dangerously high the tide of illiteracy has risen among our voters and their children.

To the South this question is of supreme importance: but the responsibility for the existence of slavery did not rest upon the South alone. The Nation itself is responsible for the extension of the suffrage,

and is under special obligations to aid in removing the illiteracy which
it has added to the voting population. For the North and South alike
there is but one remedy.

Garfield did not live to see that remedy. He served only two hundred days
as President in 1881, before his death from an assassin's bullet—the second
Chief Executive to be slain in office (Lincoln was the first). Tourgée's "An
Appeal to Caesar"—intended as an appeal to the Executive branch—went un-
published until the autumn of 1884. It received no visible attention from Gar-
field's Vice President and successor, Chester A. Arthur (1881–85), or Grover
Cleveland (1885–89; 1893–97), the first Democrat elected President after the
Civil War.

However, in his lifetime, Tourgée's ideas on education, politics, civil rights,
and American jurisprudence evoked as much public debate as his novels. Appointed honorary professor of Legal Ethics at Buffalo Law School in 1887, he
became a major organizer of the National Citizens Rights Association, which
increased awareness of the proliferation of segregation laws and black peonage
in the South. A citizen's committee in New Orleans soon chose him one of the
lawyers for Homer Adolph Plessy, in the celebrated *Plessy v. Ferguson* case argued before the Supreme Court in 1896. In that legal case Tourgée challenged
a Louisiana segregation statute as a violation of the Thirteenth Amendment,
and argued that discriminatory "separate but equal" doctrine in intrastate rail
travel was illegal. (His plantiff–client, Homer Plessy, a Louisiana citizen of
mixed race fair enough to appear white, was arrested in 1892 on the East Louisiana Railroad, after refusing to leave a coach for white passengers and move
to one reserved for "colored.") The U.S. Supreme Court, in a majority decision,
with only Justice John M. Harlan dissenting, dismissed Tourgée's argument and
upheld Plessy's conviction. Not until fifty-eight years later, in *Brown v. Board
of Education* (1954), did the Court overturn its "separate but equal" ruling.

Tourgée was ignored by most twentieth-century American legal scholars and
literary critics. He died in relative obscurity in 1905, while serving as U.S. Consul in Bordeaux, France, in the Administration of Theodore Roosevelt. He merits remembrance for the independence of mind and egalitarianism expressed in
his writings, qualities that were absent in works by some of the more celebrated
Americans of his generation—North and South.

His "An Appeal to Caesar" has been almost perenially out of print, though
it echoes in nonfiction what his acclaimed novel *A Fool's Errand* expressed in
fiction: his conviction that Radical Reconstruction failed from a lack of commitment to prepare black freedmen for immediate citizenship and suffrage—
despite the Fourteenth and Fifteenth Amendments. Tourgée argued that the

vanquished South should have been under federal control indefinitely as a conquered territory, with a long-term Freedman's Bureau to aid former slaves in
educational and economic reforms, rather than imposing black elected officials
on a defeated and hostile white populace. Such bold ideas ultimately led to
Albion Tourgée's disappearance from the American imagination.

The following excerpt of "An Appeal to Caesar" is from his chapter titled
"Is Education a Specific?"

From An Appeal to Caesar (1884)

Is Education a Specific?

It may be admitted that the intelligence of the masses is an essential of good
government in a republic, and yet it be honestly doubted whether education is
a remedy for the evils we have depicted. We do not feel like saying with the
certainty of assured conviction that it is a specific for all the woes likely to arise
from the causes that have been noted. We can only say that we do not believe
there is any other reasonable or practicable means of sensibly alleviating, modifying, or, it may be, entirely averting these evils.

We speak with something of hesitation in regard to the efficacy of this remedy only because the elements of the problem are so intricate and terrible. If
there were no factor of race antagonism, none of the terrible prejudice that
centuries of servitude engendered; if on the part of the one race there were not
the feeling that it alone had the right to rule, and on the part of the other the
dull, unspoken conviction that the colored man has never received justice at
the hands of the whites, and perhaps never will; if there were only one race, no
matter how far apart classes or individuals might stand in the social scale; if
only the impassable barrier of color did not come between the discordant elements; if love and marriage might ever soften the asperities that prevail; if by
any means or during any conceivable period of time the two races might become one—in that case, no matter how great the discrepancy of thought or
feeling, how wide the gulf of rank or caste, how bitter the hostility that may
now exist, we should say without a moment's hesitation that education, general
intelligence, universal enlightenment, was *not only the sole remedy but would
prove almost an instant specific for the evils which now impend.* Under such
circumstances it would only be necessary to make the spelling-book the scepter

of national power until all classes clearly and distinctly appreciated the fact that the individual interest of each lay in the prosperity of all, to assure the continuance of peace and the mutual recognition of the rights of all. But alas! those elements which constitute the chief difficulties of the problem are of such a subtle and difficult character that the most exhaustive knowledge and most painstaking analysis of the existing forces of the society with which we are dealing cannot justify any positive forecast of the resultant effect of any added element or specific influence. There are some hypotheses the consideration of which may enable us to arrive at more satisfactory conclusions in regard to the probable effect of a thorough enlightenment of the ignorant masses of these States than we would be likely otherwise to reach. The first of these is a proposition which probably no man will deny, to wit:

I. *Intelligence is the chiefest foe of prejudice.*

The intelligent man is much less likely to be influenced by an insufficient motive than the ignorant one. He is more likely to act upon what he knows than upon a mere unfounded belief which he has perhaps caught from a neighbor who has no better reason for entertaining it than himself. The intelligent man is more apt to require a solid and substantial reason for his action than an ignorant one, and also more likely to be restrained in its manifestation by a knowledge of ultimate results.

II. *This being the case, we may safely conclude that if the percentage of illiterates among the native white people of the South had been for the past hundred years what it is among the whites of the North, instead of being more than five times as great, there would be very much less reason for apprehension on account of the prejudice of race than there now is.*

Although this sentiment may be as strong or even stronger among the more intelligent of the white people of that section, it cannot be doubted that if the same general intelligence had prevailed among the masses of the South as at the North, Slavery would have been peacefully eradicated and the lesson of tolerant coexistence taught to both races long before now.

III. *If ninety-five per cent of the freedmen at the date of their emancipation had been able to read and write with the facility and accuracy possessed by the like proportion of natives of Northern States, the history of the South since the close of the war would not have been one continued story of violence, humiliation, and shame.*

It is only by such a violent hypothesis as this that we are able to realize what a wonderful change in the situation of affairs might be accomplished by the general enlightenment of the masses of the South. There is no doubt that all the failure, shame, and humiliation of the past twenty years of reconstructionary growth has been, in the main, the fruit of ignorance. Had the same ratio of intelligence which prevails at the North extended also to the people of the South; had the colored man been able to master his political duty, to understand and perform the functions of citizenship, to detect fraud, and intelligently and wisely to combine in his own defense, such terms as "Ku-Klux," "Bull-Dozer," "Rifle-Clubs," "Shotgun Policy," and "Tissue Ballots" would never have disgraced the American vocabulary. Had the vast body of ignorant whites been so enlightened as to be able to comprehend the circumstances in which they were placed, the new relations which they must assume toward the freedmen, the responsibilities for the peaceful future that rested upon them— had they been accessible to reason and information upon these subjects, one of the chief impulses to violence, and perhaps the most potent evil force which threatens the future of that region, would have been obliterated. It was of course an impossibility that such a state of affairs should have existed. Slavery would long ago have been blotted from our soil if the slave had been made intelligent or the non-slave-holding whites of the South had been brought to the same average of intelligence as like classes at the North. The one great essential for the perpetuation of slavery was ignorance. Intelligence and servitude cannot co-exist: light and darkness are not less antagonistic. . . .

GEORGE WASHINGTON CABLE

(1844–1925)

George Washington Cable, the first white Southerner to emerge as a major novelist after the Civil War, shared with T. Thomas Fortune mutual antagonism for the *Atlanta Constitution*'s editor, Henry W. Grady, who promoted white supremacy for the New South. In 1885, Grady and Cable verbally jousted as Southern opponents in a Northern forum, the *Century* magazine.[1] Cable had then recently addressed the American Social Science Association in a speech he revised for *Century* as "The Freedman's Case in Equity." With that essay drawing upon history, he began a controversy on race and caste that consumed him as a writer and Christian reformer for ten years without fundamentally altering race relations in America. But his views infuriated Dixie loyalists who dubbed him a "negrophile." Due partly to that reaction, he left the South in 1885, after living in New Orleans for forty years. He resettled with his family in Northampton, Massachusetts, and resided there the next four decades, except during travels through the United States and abroad.

Some critics claimed Cable never was a true Southerner, in heart, mind, or soul, but none could dispute that he was born and reared in New Orleans and served the Confederacy in Mississippi and Alabama. The first son of a Virginia–bred father and a mother of New England lineage, his parents migrated from Indiana to Louisiana seven years before his birth. He grew up in a household that owned slaves, though the family's prosperity was short-lived after the death of his father in 1859. George, Jr., was then fourteen and obliged to quit school to help support his mother and two older sisters, and younger

---

[1] After angry letters to *Century* magazine over Cable's January 1885 article, "The Freedman's Case in Equity," the editors printed Grady's rebuttal "In Plain Black and White: A Reply to Mr. Cable" in April 1885. Cable's rejoinder appeared in the September 1885 issue as "The Silent South," and two months later in his book of the same title, along with his "The Freedman's Case in Equity" and "The Convict Lease System in the Southern States." An expanded edition of *The Silent South* appeared in 1889; eighty years later, in 1969, his biographer Arlin Turner edited an enlarged volume of *The Silent South* with eight uncollected pieces on penal and asylum reform.

Grady, who became editor of the *Atlanta Constitution* in 1881 and died by the end of that decade, was challenged in speeches and articles by T. Thomas Fortune, notably in "Civil Rights and Social Privileges" in the January 1886 issue of *A.M.E. Church Review*, as a response to Grady's *Century* article.

brother. In October 1863, he enlisted in the Confederate Army in Mississippi after the Cables were registered as Union enemies and their property confiscated, for refusing to sign an oath of allegiance when New Orleans was captured by federal troops. Paroled as a prisoner of war, he returned to begin anew in New Orleans in May 1865.

Then age twenty-one, penniless, and with limited education, he studied on his own and held jobs as errand boy, clerk, and railroad surveyor, before becoming an accountant in the cotton business. In late 1869, shortly before his marriage, his unsolicited literary contribution to the *New Orleans Picayune* brought him a part-time newspaper apprenticeship as a weekly columnist on local affairs. The position led to his study of archives on Louisiana history and duties as a *Picayune* reporter and Sunday book reviewer, and to his "Local Color" Realism short stories in the 1870s.

His first published story, "Sieur George," in *Scribner's Monthly* in October 1873, was later collected with six other Louisiana stories in his first volume, *Old Creole Days* (1879). He followed in 1880 with a first novel, *Les Grandissimes: A Story of Creole Life,* set in New Orleans at the turn of the nineteenth century. Later considered by most critics his crowning achievement, the work was nevertheless condemned by Louisiana's white Creoles,[2] who saw themselves ridiculed for their proud French and Spanish heritage, patois dialect, insulated social life, and Cable's depiction of free quadroons as victims of Creole color caste. His early fiction—including his rejected stories—proved his social vision in the 1870s and 1880s unorthodox to the white postbellum South, on the war, slavery, race, and caste. Labeled a traitor to Southern culture, and pressured by some Northern editors to delete his ideas on civil rights, Cable's autobiographical account of his political odyssey, "My Politics," written in 1889, was unpublished in his lifetime.

Cable nevertheless resigned his longstanding job in the cotton business to be a full-time man of letters by 1881. That year brought magazine serialization and book publication of his novella with a racial theme, *Madame Delphine,* in which a New Orleans quadroon mother denies parentage of a beautiful daughter to allow the girl to wed a wealthy white Creole suitor legally. Praised by critics for its artistry, the book received none of the Southern rebuke that his nonfiction on civil rights and prison reform met during the next five years. However, he made prison reform in New Orleans a major theme of his social novel, *Dr. Sevier* (1884), which was his first fiction without Creoles or quadroons as central char-

---

[2] "Creole" as used by Cable referred to white Louisiana residents who claimed ancestry from French and Spanish explorers and settlers and preferred to disassociate with Anglo-Americans after the Louisiana Purchase in 1803. The term is also used by a closed society of New Orleans natives of European, African, and Native Indian descent, who historically identify as "Creole," not "Negro" or "mulatto."

acters. A decade later, Cable used his realistic novel *Johnny March, Southerner* (1894) as a vehicle to expose social and political conditions and human frailties among blacks and whites during Reconstruction and post–Reconstruction. His 1885 appeals to public conscience and debate articulated in *The Silent South* did not generate the positive response he hoped at the time, and after *Johnny March, Southerner*, most critics saw a decline in his literary craftsmanship and in his political writing. He conceded defeat in his campaign for freedmen, and changes in tone and attitude toward race appear in his writing after his move to North-ampton. But in 1890, his book *The Negro Question* was published with six of his essays reprinted from various journals. By then, he had ended all allegiance to the South and tried in his own way to become a "Citizen of the Union," as literary critic Edmund Wilson later referred to him.

Although Cable witnessed a steady erosion of Reconstruction gains for Southern blacks, he never withdrew his advocacy for their voting rights and equal opportunities in education, the courts, and public accommodations. He firmly denied being a voice for race amalgamation and social equality. "We may reach the moon someday, not social equality," he wrote in *The Negro Question*. Some of his comments on race and ethnicity are by today's standards judged ethnocentric and racist, but in his day his civil rights positions towered publicly above those of his fellow authors of equal prominence, like Mark Twain, who occasionally joined him on the lecture podium in 1884.

Cable's canon was diverse and never devoted solely to racial concerns, al-though he returned indirectly to race and class conflicts in his late novels, *Gideon's Band* (1914), *The Flower of the Chapdelaines* (1918), and *Lovers of Louisiana [Today]* (1918), after revisiting New Orleans. A versatile writer for whom milieu was central to art, Cable had captured earlier in his career not only the ethos of Lousiana Creoles but of bayou Acadians—the rustic, French-speaking refugees from Nova Scotia—represented in his fictional *Bonaventure: A Prose Pastoral of Acadian Louisiana* (1888). Such works were equaled in in-sight only by the fiction of his contemporary Kate Chopin on Acadians and Creoles. Although none of his later creative works earned the reputation of his early ones, he produced eleven novels, five volumes of short stories, four books of social essays, a history *(The Creoles of Louisiana)*, and many miscellaneous pieces over nearly half a century.

The following is from "The Freedman's Case in Equity."

From The Freedman's Case in Equity (1885)

The greatest social problem before the American people today is, as it has been for a hundred years, the presence among us of the negro.

No comparable entanglement was ever drawn round itself by any other modern nation with so serene a disregard of its ultimate issue, or with a more distinct national responsibility. The African slave was brought here by cruel force, and with everybody's consent except his own. Everywhere the practice was favored as a measure of common aggrandizement. When a few men and women protested, they were mobbed in the public interest, with the public consent. There rests, therefore, a moral responsibility on the whole nation never to lose sight of the results of African-American slavery until they cease to work mischief and injustice.

It is true these responsibilities may not fall everywhere with the same weight; but they are nowhere entirely removed. The original seed of trouble was sown with the full knowledge and consent of the nation. The nation was to blame; and so long as evils spring from it, their correction must be the nation's duty.

The late Southern slave has within two decades risen from slavery to freedom, from freedom to citizenship, passed on into political ascendancy, and fallen again from that eminence. The amended Constitution holds him up in his new political rights as well as a mere constitution can. On the other hand, certain enactments of Congress, trying to reach further, have lately been made void by the highest court of the nation. And another thing has happened. The popular mind in the old free States, weary of strife at arm's length, bewildered by its complications, vexed by many a blunder, eager to turn to the cure of other evils, and even tinctured by that race feeling whose grosser excesses it would so gladly see suppressed, has retreated from its uncomfortable dictational attitude and thrown the whole matter over to the States of the South. Here it rests, no longer a main party issue, but a group of questions which are to be settled by each of these States separately in the light of simple equity and morals, and which the genius of American government does not admit of being forced upon them from beyond their borders. Thus the whole question, become secondary in party contest, has yet reached a period of supreme importance.

Before slavery ever became a grave question in the nation's politics—when it seemed each State's private affair, developing unmolested,—it had two different fates in two different parts of the country. In one, treated as a question of public equity, it withered away. In the other, overlooked in that aspect, it petrified and became the cornerstone of the whole social structure; and when men sought its overthrow as a national evil, it first brought war upon the land, and then grafted into the citizenship of one of the most intelligent nations in the world six millions of people from one of the most debased races on the globe.

And now this painful and wearisome question, sown in the African slave trade, reaped in our civil war, and garnered in the national adoption of millions of an inferior race, is drawing near a second seedtime. For this is what the impatient proposal to make it a dead and buried issue really means. It means to recommit it to the silence and concealment of the covered furrow. Beyond that incubative retirement no suppressed moral question can be pushed; but all such questions, ignored in the domain of private morals, spring up and expand once more into questions of public equity; neglected as matters of public equity, they blossom into questions of national interest; and, despised in that guise, presently yield the red fruits of revolution.

This question must never again bear that fruit. There must arise, nay, there has arisen, in the South itself, a desire to see established the equities of the issue; to make it no longer a question of endurance between one group of States and another, but between the moral debris of an exploded evil and the duty, necessity, and value of planting society firmly upon universal justice and equity. This, and this only, can give the matter final burial. True, it is still a question between States; but only secondarily, as something formerly participated in, or as it concerns every householder to know that what is being built against his house is built by level and plummet. It is the interest of the Southern States first, and *consequently* of the whole land, to discover clearly these equities and the errors that are being committed against them.

If we take up this task, the difficulties of the situation are plain. We have, first, a revision of Southern State laws which has forced into them the recognition of certain human rights discordant with the sentiments of those who have always called themselves the community; second, the removal of the entire political machinery by which this forcing process was effected; and, third, these revisions left to be interpreted and applied under the domination of these antagonistic sentiments. These being the three terms of the problem, one of three things must result. There will arise a system of vicious evasions eventually ruinous to public and private morals and liberty, or there will be a candid reconsideration of the sentiments hostile to these enactments, or else there will be a division, some taking one course and some the other.

This is what we should look for from our knowledge of men and history; and this is what we find. The revised laws, only where they could not be evaded, have met that reluctant or simulated acceptance of their narrowest letter which might have been expected—a virtual suffocation of those principles of human equity which the unwelcome decrees do little more than shadow forth. But in different regions this attitude has been made in very different degrees of emphasis. In some the new principles have grown, or are growing, into the popular conviction, and the opposing sentiments are correspondingly dying out. There are even some districts where they have received much practical acceptance. While, again, other limited sections lean almost wholly toward the old sentiments; an easy choice, since it is the conservative, the unyielding attitude, whose strength is in the absence of intellectual and moral debate.

Now, what are the gains, what the losses of these diverse attitudes? Surely these are urgent questions to any one in our country who believes it is always a losing business to be in the wrong. Particularly in the South, where each step in this affair is an unprecedented experience, it will be folly if each region, small or large, does not study the experiences of all the rest. And yet this, alone, would be superficial; we would still need to do more. We need to go back to the roots of things and study closely, analytically, the origin, the present foundation, the rationality, the rightness, of those sentiments surviving in us which prompt an attitude qualifying in any way peculiarly the black man's liberty among us. Such a treatment will be less abundant in incident, less picturesque; but it will be more thorough.

First, then, what are these sentiments? Foremost among them stands the idea that he is of necessity an alien. He was brought to our shores a naked, brutish, unclean, captive, pagan savage, to be and remain a kind of connecting link between man and the beasts of burden. The great changes to result from his contact with a superb race of masters were not taken into account. As a social factor he was intended to be as purely zero as the brute at the other end of his plow-line. The occasional mingling of his blood with that of the white man worked no change in the sentiment; one, two, four, eight, multiplied upon or divided into zero, still gave zero for the result. Generations of American nativity made no difference; his children and children's children were born in sight of our door, yet the old notion held fast. He increased to vast numbers, but it never wavered. He accepted our dress, language, religion, all the fundamentals of our civilization, and became forever expatriated from his own land; still he remained, to us, an alien. Our sentiment went blind. It did not see that gradually, here by force and there by choice, he was fulfilling a host of conditions that earned at least a solemn moral right to that naturalization which no one at first had dreamed of giving him. Frequently he even bought back the freedom of which he had been robbed, became a taxpayer, and at times an educator of his children at his own expense; but the old idea of alienism passed laws to banish him, his wife, and children by thousands from the State, and threw him into loathsome jails as a common felon for returning to his native land.

It will be wise to remember that these were the acts of an enlightened, God-fearing people, the great mass of whom have passed beyond all earthly accountability. They were our fathers. I am the son and grandson of slaveholders. These were their faults; posterity will discover ours; but these things must be frankly, fearlessly taken into account if we are ever to understand the true interests of our peculiar state of society.

Why, then, did this notion, that the man of color must always remain an alien, stand so unshaken? We may readily recall how, under ancient systems, he rose not only to high privileges, but often to public station and power. Singularly, with us the trouble lay in a modern principle of liberty. The whole idea of American government rested on all men's equal, inalienable right to secure their life, liberty, and the pursuit of happiness by governments founded in their own consent. Hence, our Southern forefathers, shedding their blood, or ready to shed it, for this principle, yet proposing in equal good conscience to continue holding the American black man and mulatto and quadroon in slavery, had to anchor that conscience, their conduct, and their laws in the conviction that the man of African tincture was, not by his master's arbitrary assertion merely, but by nature and unalterably, an alien. If that hold should break, one single wave of irrestistible inference would lift our whole Southern social fabric and dash it upon the rocks of negro emancipation and enfranchisement. How was it made secure? Not by books, though they were written among us from every possible point of view, but, with the mass of our slaveowners, by the calm hypothesis of a positive, intuitive knowledge. To them the statement was an axiom. They abandoned the methods of moral and intellectual reasoning, and fell back upon this assumption of a God-given instinct, nobler than reason, and which it was an insult to a freeman to ask him to prove on logical grounds.

Yet it was found not enough. The slave multiplied. Slavery was a dangerous institution. Few in the South today have any just idea how often the slave plotted for his freedom. Our Southern ancestors were a noble, manly people, springing from some of the most highly intelligent, aspiring, upright, and refined nations of the modern world; from the Huguenot, the French Chevalier, the Old Englander, the New Englander. Their acts were not always right; whose are? But for their peace of mind they had to believe them so. They therefore spoke much of the negro's contentment with that servile condition for which nature had designed him. Yet there was no escaping the knowledge that we dared not trust the slave caste with any power that could be withheld from them. So the perpetual alien was made also a perpetual menial, and the belief became fixed that this, too, was nature's decree, not ours.

Thus we stood at the close of the Civil War. There were always a few Southerners who did not justify slavery, and many who cared nothing whether it was just or not. But what we have described was the general sentiment of good Southern people. There was one modifying sentiment. It related to the slave's spiritual interests. Thousands of pious masters and mistresses flatly broke the shameful laws that stood between their slaves and the Bible. Slavery was right; but religion, they held, was for the alien and menial as well as for the citizen and master. They could be alien and citizen, menial and master, in church as well as out; and they were.

Yet over against this lay another root of today's difficulties. This perpetuation of the alien, menial relation tended to perpetuate the vices that naturally cling to servility, dense ignorance and a hopeless separation from true liberty; and as we could not find it in our minds to blame slavery with this perpetuation, we could only assume as a further axiom that there was, by nature, a disqualifying moral taint in every drop of negro blood. The testimony of an Irish, German, Italian, French, or Spanish beggar in a court of justice was taken on its merits; but the colored man's was excluded by law wherever it weighed against a white man. The colored man was a prejudged culprit. The discipline of the plantation required that the difference between master and slave be never lost sight of by either. It made our master caste a solid mass, and fixed a common masterhood and subserviency between the ruling and the serving race.[3] Every one of us grew up in the idea that he had, by birth and race, certain broad powers of police over any and every person of color.

All at once the tempest of war snapped off at the ground every one of these arbitrary relations, without removing a single one of the sentiments in which they stood rooted. . . .

---

[3] The old Louisiana Black Code says, "That free people of color ought never to . . . presume to conceive themselves equal to the white; but, on the contrary, that they ought to yield to them in every occasion, and never speak or answer to them but with respect, under the penalty of imprisonment according to the nature of the offense." (Section 21, p. 164.) [Author's note]

BOOKER T. WASHINGTON

(1856–1915)

Booker T. Washington's rising career as Southern educator coincided with George Washington Cable's lonely crusade for freedmen's equity. During the years 1885 to 1892, while Cable tried exposing Southern perfidies and black disenfranchisement in his lectures and essays, Washington was becoming known to admirers as the "Wizard of Tuskegee," the man who brought to Alabama's Black Belt a symbol of race uplift at the Tuskegee Normal and Industrial Institute, which he founded in 1881. The two men were acquainted but never allies, for reasons beyond their racial divisions as ex-slave and ex–Confederate. Cable was uncompromising toward Southern injustice at a time Washington's speeches boosted the South as a promised land for his race—a theme he later promoted in his book, *The Future of the Negro*; Washington advised his people to avoid politics and defer civil rights in pursuit of economic goals, accommodationist policies that Cable did not accept.

Privately, Washington praised some of Cable's ideas; publicly, he avoided him. When Cable wrote to him in 1889 seeking data on the casual relationship of the sharecropper system to black migration within the South, Washington politely provided a few examples but requested anonymity. Behind-the-scenes secrecy, then and later, was the modus operandi of Booker T. Washington's career. To sustain support from white Northern philanthropists and Southern politicians, who buttressed his segregated school and his growing influence, he survived by duplicity and equivocation.

Washington was born a slave in 1856 and spent his first nine years on a farm near Hale's Ford, Virginia, the son of a house servant and an unidentified white man he never met. According to his autobiography, *Up from Slavery*, he adopted the surname Washington from the first name of his black stepfather, Washington Ferguson—but hardly out of affection. After Emancipation, Ferguson put him to work in the salt mines near Malden, West Virginia, where the boy worked day shifts determined to learn to read and write. He believed education the way "up from slavery" and out of the poverty and illiteracy in which his family and most unskilled freedmen lived. He attended night classes, then day school while employed part-time in local coal mines; he left home and lived as a houseboy for a strict New England white matron who instilled in him habits that he later inculcated in Tuskegee students, and acknowledged in his autobiography: "everything kept clean," "things done promptly," and "absolute honesty." After completing rudimentary schooling at age sixteen, he entered Hampton Normal and Industrial Institute in Virginia, and for three years was a disciple of its director–founder, Samuel Chapman Armstrong, a former major general in the Union army, who had opened the school for freemen in 1868 under auspices of the American Missionary Association. Armstrong's emphasis on agricultural and industrial training for black students would become the paradigm for his protégée's educational program at Tuskegee. With savings from a janitorial job and financial aid from his brother, John, who worked in West Virginia coal mines to help him finish Hampton, Washington graduated with honors and a teacher's certificate in 1875; he tried stump speaking and spent an academic year at a seminary in Washington, DC, before returning to teach at Hampton in 1879. In 1881, Armstrong recommended him as organizer and principal of a projected school authorized by the Alabama legislature to train Negro teachers. The opportunity represented the trajectory of Washington's career and what some later termed his "Tuskegee Plantation," where he was overseer and fund-raiser for thirty-four years, and the master was an all-white board of trustees. However, Washington hired some of the nation's best-trained black teachers—including renowned plant chemist Dr. George Washington Carver—who headed the institute's Agricultural Department and its laboratory experiments.

Washington's national prominence ascended in September 1895, through a singular speech later known as the "Atlanta Compromise"—directed to a predominantly white audience at the Cotton States and International Exposition. The speech confirmed his acceptance of segregation in a "new era of industrial progress," declared that the Negro masses "shall prosper in the proportion as we learn to dignify and glorify common labor," and promised that "in all things that are purely social we can be as separate as the fingers, yet one as the hand in all things essential to mutual progress." Hailed in the white press as new national negro leader and successor to Frederick Douglass, who had died eight months before, Washington was flooded with lecture invitations and awarded an honorary degree by Harvard University in 1896.

Yet his personal rise was concurrent with legal reversals for his race, and he made no public outcry at the 1896 *Plessy v. Ferguson*—"separate but equal"—Supreme Court decision, or the increased lynchings of blacks in the South. Only the irony of being a bloody target himself of white assault in 1911 in New York City—for allegedly accosting a white woman in an unsavory neighborhood, in a contradictory incident sensationalized in the press as the "Ulrich

Case"—gave Washington self-recognition that he was not immune from racial violence or bias. However, he had occasionally incited white Southerners by personally trespassing on the social equality promise of his "Atlanta Compromise," especially by dining at the White House in 1901 as guest of Theodore Roosevelt (who never invited him to dinner again.)

Yet by 1903, Washington's most vocal opponents were influential blacks who rejected his policies and conciliation with the white South, his resistance to intellectual over vocational preparation, his manipulation of the black press, his use of espionage through a network of spies to stifle black dissent, his subterfuge in awarding patronage as White House adviser, and his hubris behind a mask of humility. His militant critics included writers who had once supported him: W. E. B. Du Bois and Ida B. Wells-Barnett, and others like Monroe Trotter, who never trusted him.[1] However, with challenges from an interracial coalition of leaders who organized the NAACP in 1909, Washington represented the past rather than the future at his death in November 1915—one of the last black spokesmen of his era born into slavery in the Old South.

Besides his Tuskegee legacy, he founded the National Negro Business League in 1901 and controlled it ideologically as president until he died. He left numerous articles, speeches, and correspondence. His books include: *The Future of the American Negro* (1899), *The Story of My Life and Work* (1900), *Up from Slavery* (1901), *Life of Frederick Douglass* (1907), *The Story of the Negro* (2 vols.) (1909), and *My Larger Education, Being Chapters from My Experience* (1911). Whereas his writings represent his personal outlook and experience, credit for most of Washington's published work is due his unheralded ghost writers, some of whom were white authors, such as Max B. Thrasher and Robert E. Park; and others black: notably journalist–editor T. Thomas Fortune and Emmett J. Scott, Washington's personal secretary, from 1897 to 1915.

The following extract, which expresses his own attitude toward the South, is from a speech presented early in his career, April 26, 1888, at a Philosophian Lyceum of Lincoln University, a historically black college in Pennsylvania. The full text was reprinted in *The Booker T. Washington Papers*, vol. 2: (1860–89), edited by Louis R. Harlan, et al., 1972.

---

[1] See Trotter and Wells-Barnett, and entries in this volume, pages 418–29 and 443–50, respectively.

The South as an Opening for a Career (1888)

Gentlemen of the Philosophian Lyceum and Friends:

What good can I do was the question I considered more than once before deciding to accept your kind invitation to address you on this occasion; indeed it is with this question before me that I try to decide on every important action of my life. After consideration I decided that perhaps I might say something to you on the subject, "The South as an Opening for a Career," that would excite your interest and cause you to think over the possibilities of achievement in that interesting and extensive part of our country.

To be permitted to address an organization that has numbered among its members men who today are counted among America's most worthy citizens,—men who in more than one walk of life are teachers and moulders of public sentiment, in the best and highest sense—brings an honor as well as a serious sense of responsibility.

Out from the classic walls of this venerable institution have gone men who were among the first to prove that God sets no limit on the development of the human intellect, no matter under what color skin it hides itself.

Gentlemen, I am perfectly aware that in your search after knowledge in science, art, and in literature, I can be of no service to you. But it has occurred to me that a few minutes spent in considering the resources of that rich and beautiful country—the South—"Where every prospect pleases, and only man is vile," would not be spent in vain. I come to speak to you of a section of country that has been purchased and paid for ten times over by the sweat and blood of our forefathers. Their 250 years of forced and unrequited toil, secured for us an inheritance which at no late day we are going to occupy and enjoy as independent and intelligent citizens.

Perhaps the most important considerations for a successful career are land, men and climate. I would put as the condition of all conditions for success in life, whether it relate to the individual or the race, ownership in the soil—cleavage to mother Earth.

Embracing what was commonly known as the Southern States, we have 877,000 square miles of land that is as well adapted to the sustenance of man as the same section found anywhere on the globe. An eminent economist has said that thirty counties in Mississippi properly cultivated could be made to produce last year's cotton crop of 1,200,000 bales. The statement will apply with equal force to other Southern States and to other products.

Can land be secured? Never, I believe, in the history of any state could such valuable property be purchased for so little money as at present in Alabama and other Southern States.

Landed estates which in Antebellum days could not be purchased for twenty-five dollars per acre can now be had for four dollars.

Landowners who twenty years ago would not part with their land to the Negro partly because of prejudice and partly because the owners thought that their information salvation lay in holding on to their lands, are now ready and anxious to sell to black or white, and often it is the old family homestead that has been sacred, where generations of slaveholders have been born and reared that is offered for sale. I do not rejoice at the misfortune of the Southern white man, for he is my brother, but I do feel it a duty to urge that his extremity is our opportunity to buy the foundation for a high civilization that is frought with the most favorable conditions.

If the sins of the fathers are visited upon the children to the third and fourth generations, who knows, but what God in His divine goodness means through the enslavers improvidence to repay the enslaved that of which he has been robbed.

The South possesses a soil as rich and productive as that of any country on the globe—a soil that is capable of producing almost every kind of vegetation and of making that section "blossom as the rose" and to become a land of plenty. But one element is wanting and that is brains—ever acre of her lowlands and hills and valleys needs to be presided over by and impregnated with brains. One Macedonian cry is for brains—brains controlled and directed by religion and conscience. The South is not crowded. Thirty-two inhabitants to every square mile is perhaps the present average population. An increase of fifty million of people in the Southern States could be accommodated and still the population would not be as dense as that of Pennsylvania.

In view of all these facts do you wonder, gentlemen, that even at the risk of disappointing you in my selection I have decided to occupy you in the discussion of a subject so utilitarian?

The time is not far distant when a larger proportion of the educated among us will seek callings outside of the schoolroom and other professional pursuits and will enter upon careers that will have material gain more directly for their object, and so might it be. It is this aspect of my subject that I shall discuss first.

To the budding capitalists, the lumber resources of the South present a field for financial gain that are presented to but few on the threshold of life in any country. There are in the Southern States perhaps 500,000 square miles of forests as valuable as any and more accessible than in other parts of the country, and these forests can be had for the pittance of two dollars per acre. At no distant day the South is to be the lumber mart of the United States. No argument is needed to prove to you that "the products of the soil are the foundations of the wealth of any nation."

If the Vanderbilts, Girards, Peabodys, Peter Coopers started out poverty-stricken with untrained minds and in competition with the shrewd and energetic Yankee amassed fortunes what superior opportunities open up before our young men who begin life with a college-trained mind and in a locality where competition is at its minimum?

To the rank and file of our aspiring youth seeking an opening in life, to me but two alternatives present themselves as matters now stand—to live a menial in the North or a semifreeman in the South.

This brings us face-to-face with Northern competition and Southern prejudice and between them I have no hesitancy in saying that the Negro can find his way to the front sooner through Southern prejudice than through Northern competition. The one decreases, the other increases.

To the really brave, earnest, energetic, ambitious, Christian young man the obstacles presented, it seems to me, by prejudice form an apology for not entering this field so weak, so unreasonable as not to *merit* serious consideration, yet prejudice does keep so large and valuable a class of those who are mentally and morally strong from that field that the question must be considered.

The most effective ammunition with which to fight prejudice is men—men such as are before me—men who in every act, word and thought give the lie to the assertion of his enemies North and South that the Negro is the inferior of the white man.

In advocating the South as a field for a career, I have no sympathy with those who would stoop to sacrifice manhood to satisfy unreasonable whims of the South, but would advise you to be there as here a man—every inch a man, and demand with reasonable patience, with proper judgment and in lawful manner every right that God and the constitution have vouchsafed to us as American citizens. I come to you from a seven years' residence in the "Black Belt" of Alabama—the heart of the South—and I speak as one who has given his strength without reserve to the amelioration of the condition of his race and to a consideration on all sides and under all circumstances of the problems that have grown out of his newly acquired citizenship. I do not wish to create the impression that all these problems have been solved yet, and that everything is just right in the South, but out of my own honest opinion that the rate at which prejudice is dying out is so rapid as to justify the conclusion that the Negro will in a quarter of a century enjoy in Alabama every right that he now does in Pennsylvania, a rate such as to furnish occasion for universal gratitude and thanksgiving to Him who controls the destinies of races. As compared with the great question of the race's acquiring education, character and property the question of prejudice, it seems to me, dwindles into insignificance.

Besides, can you afford to put along side the advantage and stimulus that the race will derive from your examples as leaders in the field of letters, professional life, and as financiers such considerations as personal inconveniences and the curtailment of political privileges—considerations which exist but for a day while the good influence that a single one of you may exert in some department of life at this auspicious time may incite the youths of far-off ages to new life and hope by rekindling their faith and aspirations.

One has said, "It may be but one colored man in a state has achieved financial independence in a decade, yet that one man is constantly an example to all others, stimulating them to renewed exertion. It may be that in a whole state but two colored men have won their way into the mystic arena of the bar, and even there may be far from encouraging examples of forensic ability, yet never one of them opens his lips in court that his example does not inspire some colored boy that listens to do as he has done."

> The smallest wave of influence
>   set in motion
> Extends and widens to the
>   eternal shore.

Just so sure as the rays of the sun dispel the frost of winter, so sure will Brains and Property and Character conquer prejudice; just so sure as right in all ages and among all races has conquered wrong, so sure will the time come and at no distant day, when the Negro South shall be triumphant over the last lingering vestige of prejudice. To believe otherwise is to deny the existence of Him who rewards virtue and condemns vice.

It is encouraging to note that there is already an entire absence of hostile feeling against business enterprises of blacks, South. A Negro merchant having a quality of goods that is in demand receives the patronage of both races. This applies in almost all branches of business.

A young man with energy, ambition and foresight can get successfully launched into business there on a capital that would not enable him to pay the first month's rent in a Northern city.

In any business enterprise requiring push, snap, tact, and continual and close attention, the wide-awake Negro has an immense advantage, for the Southern white man evades as a rule any occupation that requires early rising or late retiring that removes him very far from a shade tree or the sunless side of a house.

For three hundred years the North has been adding value to value, accumulating wealth and experience in every direction and when we, the freemen of a day, enter into competition with this it is not hard to say who will win and who will lose.

In entering the South for a career, you have the advantage of having a large number of our own kith and kin for whom to work, on whom to depend for support and with whom to cooperate. This is an advantage that perhaps outweighs all others. Notwithstanding many assertions to the contrary, I glean from my experience that the Negro is as loyal to faithful and intelligent leadership, is as ready to cooperate, to stand shoulder to shoulder for the common good as any race with no more experience in self-government, whose history we know. Show me a man among us in any walk in life who manifests to those with whom he comes in contact that he is trying to succeed for the welfare of the race as well as for his own good and I will show you a man that is supported, patronized and encouraged by the rank and file. . . .

JAMES WELDON JOHNSON

(1871–1938)

One of the talented black men of the younger generation that Booker T. Washington rewarded with political patronage was James Weldon Johnson, who later omitted the connection in his 1933 autobiography *Along This Way*. But along the way in 1904, he answered Washington's call to join the National Negro Business League, and a year later, at the League's annual convention, in tribute to Washington as founder–president, Johnson dedicated the song "Lift Every Voice and Sing"—later known as "the Negro National Anthem." He had written the lyrics to the musical score by his younger brother, Rosamond, on their front porch in Jacksonville, Florida, in 1900, for a black-school celebration of Abe Lincoln Day. Two years earlier, at a New Year's Day anniversary observance of the Emancipation Proclamation, Johnson had introduced Booker Washington to Jacksonville as "the inspiration of his race."

But in 1904, Johnson was of interest as spokesman not only to the National Business League but the New York Colored Republican Club and its political leader, Charles Anderson, who urged Johnson to campaign for Theodore Roosevelt. His enthusiastic songs and work in the Presidential election brought a nod from Washington via Anderson to Roosevelt, who appointed him to a consular post in Venezuela in 1906. He accepted but had already been initiated a political diplomat.

The son of mixed-race parents who were born free, Johnson himself was born in Jacksonville, Florida, in 1871, during the transitional era of Reconstruction. His mother, from the Bahamas, taught at Jacksonville's Stanton School, the main "colored" grammar school, where her two children attended, and where son James eventually became principal after graduation from Atlanta University in 1894. Johnson's father, headwaiter in a luxury hotel, moonlighted as a lay Baptist preacher, although the family worshiped in the local Methodist Episcopal Church, and neither denomination changed the son's ambivalence then or later for organized religion. But in 1927, he published vivid memories of black sermons in his book of sermonic poems *God's Trombones*.

The rural black masses were unknown to the future poet reared in a city then nearly fifty-percent Negro, with more job opportunities than most New South towns, and the Johnsons' proper home was unlike those he discovered in 1891 while researching the Georgia backwoods as a college freshman. An autobiography later described that discovery as an epiphany: "In all of my experience there has been no period so brief that has meant so much in my education for life as the three months I spent in the backwoods of Georgia. . . . It was this period that marked my psychological change from boyhood to manhood. It was this period which marked also the beginning of my knowledge of my own people as a 'race.' " Awareness that his race was judged as a group, not on the merit of individuals, reinforced his belief that "the whole race must be elevated" to end discrimination—a theme he began articulating in a college-prize oration in 1892: "The Best Methods of Removing the Disabilities of Caste from the Negro."

His academic preparation and communications skills acquired at Atlanta University served him as principal of the Stanton School, which he transformed from grammar level to the first black high school in the state. For nearly a year he edited his own newspaper, the *Daily American,* directed to interracial readers on local and national issues. But unlike earlier outspoken black Floridian editor T. Thomas Fortune, Johnson's editorials had the moderate-political tone he only slightly and further modified later as columnist for ten years at the *New York Age* following Fortune's selling of his interest in that newspaper. In Jacksonville, Johnson studied law with a local attorney, passed the bar in 1898, and opened an office with a partner he had known since boyhood: William Wetmore, who had attended the University of Michigan Law School, while passing as white. Wetmore would become the emotional prototype, but not the actual protagonist, in Johnson's only novel, *The Autobiography of An Ex-Colored Man,*[1] in 1912.

In 1902, realizing that his law practice interested him less than creative pursuits or a school principalship, and that preparation for a Florida teaching certificate could not change a new state law against racially integrated schools (or help him attain a higher administrative post), he resigned his official duties and left Jacksonville for New York City. In Manhattan, where he had collaborated on song lyrics with his brother for several previous summers, the Johnson duo entered a partnership trio with Bob Cole—a black composer, dancer, singer, actor—to create musical productions, at a time when vaudeville, ragtime, "coon songs" and the cakewalk were American fads. The trio lasted four years, producing nearly two hundred songs for various Broadway musical comedies—none worthy enough for citation in Johnson's autobiography. Few of the Johnson–Cole songs broke with racial stereotypes, and some, written in crude

---

[1] In the first edition, the author's name was anonymous; in the second edition, reprinted in 1927 (at the apex of the Harlem Renaissance, which will be covered in a planned sequel to the present book), Johnson's name as author was added and the spelling of "*Colored*" changed to "*Coloured.*"

stereotypical dialect, pandered to white theatergoers and showed the influence of the popular dialect librettos of their friend, Paul Laurence Dunbar. The trio gained fame from Broadway, road tours, and a six-week engagement at London's Palace Theatre, but their Tin Pan Alley music publishers profited more financially from their "coon songs," which were hardly commensurate with Rosamond's training at the New York Conservatory, or of his brother's graduate courses in drama at Columbia University. Bob Cole, whom they considered a genius, suffered a nervous breakdown and committed suicide.

James Weldon Johnson—whose middle name he changed from William in 1913—was too proud to consider himself emblematic of the paradoxes and dilemmas of a black man trapped between the late 1870s and 1901, an era that one historian later termed the "nadir" of Negro progress.[2] Johnson's rite of passage coincided with that "nadir" and perhaps influenced him to stay nearly seven years in Latin America, accepted by indigenous peoples as a social equal, while serving two Republican Presidents at low wages. After three years at minor rank in Puerto Cabello, Venezuela, and four as Consul in Corinto, Nicaragua, he resigned in 1913 when Democrat Woodrow Wilson was inaugurated President.

But in his unusual life, the end of one career often led to another, and by 1914 he was a contributing editor for the *New York Age*, and soon collaborating with his brother on librettos for classical works. With Booker T. Washington dead, Johnson joined the late leader's foes in the newly organized NAACP; he began his official duties as NAACP field secretary in late 1916, after attending an interracial "Amenia Conference" sponsored by NAACP board president Joel Spingarn. Within four years, he substantially increased national membership, prepared the first statistical data on lynching, and supported United States entry into World War I. He was appointed the first Afro-American NAACP executive secretary in 1920 and served until December 1930, when he resigned to concentrate on his writing and teach literature at New York University, and Fisk University in Nashville. His energy during the Harlem Renaissance added to his literary canon: articles, pamphlets, poems, two edited anthologies of Negro poetry, and two collections of Negro spirituals compiled with his brother. His cultural history, *Black Manhattan* (1930), followed by *Along This Way*, were his final major works before his sudden death in an automobile accident in Maine.

The following extract of his oratorical prize speech first appeared in the *Atlanta University Bulletin*, May 1892.

---

[2] Rayford W. Logan, *The Betrayal of the Negro: From Rutherford B. Hayes to Woodrow Wilson* (1965); originally *The Negro in American Life and Thought: The Nadir, 1877–1901*.

Best Methods of Removing the Disabilities
of Caste from the Negro (1892)

Before we can intelligently discuss this question we must first consider what is caste and what are the disabilities of caste under which the Negro labors. Caste in America is not what it is in most countries. In India it is the distinction made between people of different trades, professions, or religious sects. In most European countries it is the distinction made by society between people of different rank, wealth and position. In America it is neither. In this country the work in which a man is engaged, if it is honest, does not bring upon him odium or contempt; neither does his religious beliefs separate him from his fellowman nor need he, however lowly born, despair of rising to the highest positions of wealth and honor. That is provided he is a white man. But caste in America is the distinction between two great races, the white and the black. The whites make this distinction. It is not mutual. And this vast superiority, in regard to numbers, wealth, and power, enable them to enforce it.

The disabilities of caste under which the Negro labors are many, especially in the South. He is not allowed in hotels, restaurants, or any other such public place, however wealthy he may be. He is compelled to ride in a dirty, smoky railroad car, however refined and cultured. He does not get justice in the courts; and for every slight offense the fullest extent of the law is meted out to him. He is debarred from many of the trades and professions on account of his race. In fact he is subjected to every form of humiliation and oppression which humanity and a republican form of government will allow.

Now before we suggest any remedies let us look at the causes for this state of affairs. Was this caste born in America? No, for we can see traces of it all through history. Hannibal is said to have had in his army one officer who was a Negro and to whom much of his success was due; but the other officers would not associate with him because he was a Negro. Undoubtedly the primary cause of caste, with respect to the Negro, was his color and features; but this is not a cause in America; for a man may be as fair and his features as regular as the purest Caucasian, but if in his veins there is one single drop of African blood, it is sufficient to cause him to be subjected to the same indignities to which a pure Negro would be subjected. Not long ago a physician, a recognized authority on certain subjects, applied for membership in the District Medical Association of Washington. Upon the eve of his election a card was sent to certain members conveying a hint of the taint in his blood. The result was a blackball. Moreover, there are other races as dark or darker than many colored people, who are not disabled in the least by any caste regulations.

Neither is this caste merely on account of ignorance; for there are many educated, refined and cultured Negroes against whom prejudice is just as bitter as against the most ignorant of that race. Nor is it wholly on account of poverty, since there are among the colored people many men of wealth, who own beautiful homes and drive their own horses; but whose money would not be taken in exchange for many of the common pleasures of life. How many times have colored men who have the money to pay whatever is charged driven away from hotels and other places of public resort? Several years ago the Hon. Frederick Douglass, a man of considerable wealth and of high position, while lecturing in a certain Southern city was unable to secure accommodations at any one of the hotels.

Now if this line of caste, which is drawn so tightly against the Negro is not due primarily to color, ignorance, or poverty, what then can be the true cause? When I take into consideration the blind and bitter prejudice in which the white race, particularly in the South, judges the colored people, unjustly classing them altogether as ignorant and depraved, no matter what might be the progress and advancement of some, refusing to recognize in them ability, no matter to what some may have attained, before God as I stand here, I believe that the white man feels in his innermost soul that any man whose blood is tinged much or little with African blood is an inferior being, not worthy to be thought of as a man, but a fit object only for his bitterest hatred or greatest contempt. The Negro is hated simply because he is a Negro, no matter what might be his attainments. The most ignorant and depraved white man in this country has rights and privileges for which educated and respectable colored men dare not even ask. A Negro is hated because he belongs to a race which is despised because it is believed to be an inferior one.

If this be so then it will take not only courage, determination, a perseverance on the part of the Negro, but it will take time. It is a feeling which cannot be dispelled in a day, whatever may be the methods employed for removing it.

Perhaps there may be some ground for this feeling. In the first place, never before has the Negro stood before the world civilized as a race. Then again, his long slavery no doubt makes it hard for those who once owned him as a mere chattel to recognize in him an equal being, endowed with the same faculties and desires of mankind in common. But whatever may be the causes or grounds for this feeling of Negro inferiority it nevertheless does exist, and is the fountain spring from which flows all prejudice against the black man.

Now since the cause of caste is not merely due to color, poverty nor ignorance, but to the fact that the Negro is regarded by his white brother as an
inferior being, the only method for removing the disabilities of caste will be to
remove the idea of Negro inferiority. The Negro must prove that as a race he is
the equal mentally, morally and physically of any other race of man ever created
by God. He must remove the odium which the very name Negro bears; and the
race as a whole must be so elevated that the fact that a man has Negro blood
in his veins will not be considered as a disgrace. The race as a whole must
command the respect of men as much as any other race. Then and not until
then will the Negro have an equal chance with the other races in the struggle
for supremacy. Then and not until then, when every man is gauged by ability
and weighed only in the scale of true worth will it ever become possible to
remove the disabilities.

But, how shall this be done? I do not wish to appear pessimistic, but at times
the outlook is very dark. It seems that here in the South prejudice against the
Negro is growing more bitter; that he is tolerated so long as he remains in a
subservient and mental position, but as soon as he attempts to rise, the heel of
oppression is put down upon him with greater weight. But if the Negro was
only given fair unprejudiced judgment the question of caste would very soon
take care of itself.

As I have said, the whole race must be so elevated that it will cast no reflection on a man from the fact that he is a Negro. But this will take time; for it
cannot be expected that the Negro, after having been held in slavery for more
than two hundred years, a slavery which tended not only to crush out of him
every semblance of manhood, intelligence and virtue, but also to inscribe in his
very nature every form of vice, superstition and immorality, can be raised in a
single day to the level of a race which has an ancestry of thousands of years.
But one of the best and quickest means of hastening it on will be through
education of the masses. As long as the masses are ignorant, intelligent Negroes, still being classed with the race, will be thought of as ignorant.

Now education will prove a method for removing the disabilities of caste
only in as much as it removes from the whites the idea of Negro inferiority.
Will it do this let us see. Education of the masses will raise the moral standard
of the race, so that it will take a higher and nobler view of life and be able to
see more in it than the mere gratification of animal passion and provision of
physical wants. The Negro as a race is very religious—all ignorant races are—
but is sometimes sadly immoral: education is the only means of elevating the
morals of any people. It has raised nations from the level of beasts to the
heights of civilization: the Negro will prove no exception. Let the Negro first
become educated, then wealth, power and all of the other attitudes of a civi-

lized and powerful people will follow as a natural sequence. Wealth and power may be given the Negro, but if he is still ignorant he will waste the one and misuse the other.

Again, education will better the home life of the masses. It will make the Negro a better citizen. Through education the Negro can prove that mentally and morally he is the equal of any other man. He can do it in no other way. As a result of education of the masses the whole race will be inspired with a self-respect, which in time will command and receive respect of others.

The Negro must accumulate wealth. He must become independent. As long as he is, as a race, dependent upon the white man for his bread, he will be treated as dependents always are. The Negro must become able not only to employ and pay men of his own color, but white men also. For as it is now, in the South, if any colored man is respected more than another, it is the one who has some share of this world's goods laid by.

The Negro must also prove his physical equality. Now I do not advocate any shotgun or torch policy, but the Negro should defend his rights; and here in the South it often becomes necessary for him to defend his life and his home. If the Negro asserted himself more, he would not have to suffer one-half of what he does now. Has history ever recorded any people, who have fought and died for their rights and liberty, whom we have not admired and respected even though they are heathen and barbarous? Or on the other hand, has any people been recorded, who have humbly submitted to every wrong and injury inflicted upon them without ever themselves attempting to throw off the yoke of oppression, whom we have not despised no matter what may have been their other virtues? It is human nature to admire and respect physical courage. Here in the South scores of colored men are lynched, and even burned alive every year, the newspapers encourage it, the authorities wink at it. What will stop it? Nothing but the physical resistance of the Negro himself; and when he has done this he will have done a great part toward removing the disabilities of caste.

But the Negro cannot do it all. The white people must do their part. They must be willing to fairly give to the Negro what he deserves, and be as ready to recognize ability in him as in any other man; for the Negro might rise to rival the Greeks in learning and the Carthaginians in wealth and all the saints in morality, but until his white brother is ready to judge him fairly, the disabilities of caste will never be removed. But when he is ready to do this, and the Negro proves that as a race he is inferior to none, then shall caste and all of its disabilities be forever removed from the Negro, and this youngest child of civilization shall stand before the world clad in all the rights and privileges of full manhood, an unprecedented example of progress and advancement.

WILLIAM DEAN HOWELLS

(1837–1920)

From his "Editor's Study" column in *Harper's*, and "Easy Chair" essays published in other journals, William Dean Howells was the foremost American literary critic from 1886 until the early twentieth century. His position as dean of American letters was coincidental to disenfranchisement of Afro-Americans, of whose lives and literature he knew little. He was a greenhorn to distinctions between Frederick Douglass and Booker T. Washington, whose autobiographies he reviewed; paternalistic to the dialect poetry of Paul Laurence Dunbar, whom he promoted; and inconsistent on the fiction of Charles Chesnutt,[1] if it did not conform to his own race prejudices.

Like many of his white American readers at the time, Howells lumped together people of African descent into a stereotyped box of fixed notions. He never understood the diversity that the race represented, before or after he signed an interracial petition to found the NAACP in 1909. In the postbellum North, where most blacks were yet unassimilated, Howells's closest exposure to them was his cook, whom he depicted fictionally as emotionally disparate from whites in his short story "Mrs. Johnson" (*Atlantic Monthly*, January 1868); in his 1892 novel, *An Imperative Duty*, his own social attitude perhaps matched the quip of his white hero, Dr. Olney, "that one would be quite as likely to meet a cow or a horse in an American drawing room as a person of color."

Howells was born of humble origins in antebellum Ohio, and self-transplanted to New England and New York City after extended periods abroad. In Ohio, called "the West" in 1837 when he was born (a year before Albion W. Tourgée, also in Ohio) in rural Martin's Ferry, he had little formal schooling. But early literary inclinations and journalistic training came from his father, an itinerant newspaper editor and printer of Quaker background and antislavery sentiments. Those same sentiments were shared by Howells's mother, who imparted them to her eight children, as the struggling family moved between towns and villages in their horse-drawn wagon, occasionally to escape pro-slav-

---

[1] See entries on Dunbar and Chesnutt in this volume, pages 370–78 and 393–411, respectively.

ery communities in the nonslave state. In Hamilton, Howells's father was chased out for his abolitionism, leaving his son with a feeling of an "impassable gulf" between the races.

In his memoirs, written late in life about his Ohio boyhood, no black companions appear in *A Boy's Town* (1890), or *My Year in a Log Cabin* (1893), or *Years of My Youth* (1916). Howells, as child and adult, identified with white martyrs like his family rather than proscribed blacks, who most of his life he saw as inferior, even if their formal education was superior to his own. He never finished grammar school in the towns in which his family lived before he was twelve, but he learned to set type for his father's rural newspapers. At age nineteen, he began his own journalistic career—first in Cincinnati, then in the capital, Columbus, as editor of the *Ohio State Journal*, while writing poems and devouring the books described in *My Literary Passions* (1895).

In 1860, at age twenty-three, his first poetry volume—*Poems of Two Friends*, co-authored by fellow journalist, John J. Piatt—appeared, as did a short biography Howells wrote on Abraham Lincoln for the presidential campaign. Inspired by young Abe, who like himself had lived in a log cabin, and come from nowhere to go somewhere, Howells took his book on a short trip to New England, where he met literary high priests he had worshiped from afar: Emerson, Hawthorne, Oliver Wendell Holmes, Sr., and James Russell Lowell.

A year later, with Lincoln in the White House, the twenty-four-year-old Howells was appointed U.S. consul to Venice, where he lived on the Grand Canal, detached from the Civil War, from late 1861 to 1865. His consular experience yielded less understanding of American politics than of Italian literature, but in 1866 he produced a travel book called *Venetian Life*, plus two later books of travel reminiscences, essays on Italian poets, as well as four novels set in Italy. From Venice, he wrote his father that he would not resettle in Ohio: "I must seek my fortune at the great literary centres." After a stint at *The Nation* in New York, in 1866 Howells settled in Cambridge, near intellectual Harvard and literati such as Lowell, Whittier, and Longfellow, and the city of Boston, where in 1871 he became editor of the eminent *Atlantic Monthly*, whose first editor had been Lowell in 1857.

During his ten years at the *Atlantic*, Howells wrote six novels in the fictional style of American literary Realism, a style he fostered for the next two decades in criticism. He urged fiction that rejected romanticized plots and concentrated on close attention to "the motives, the impulses, the principles that shape the life of actual men and women." His theories were evident in his first two novels in 1872: the quasiautobiographical *Their Wedding Journey* and *A Chance Acquaintance*. He also soon influenced two literary friends who were complete opposites in their own fictional techniques of Realism: Henry James and Mark Twain.

In 1881, Howells resigned his *Atlantic* editorship to write full-time and travel abroad. He revisited Europe in 1882, while Americans debated his first daring Realistic novel, A *Modern Instance*; it was his best-known fiction before his classic, *The Rise of Silas Lapham* (1885). He nearly suffered nervous break-downs while writing both books. He began his "Easy Chair" columns in *Harper's* magazine in 1886 and continued them until 1892, many collected in 1891 as *Criticism and Fiction*. During those same years, his novels began to show the influence of theoretical socialism, from reading and reviewing Russian novelist Lev Tolstoy and English poet–social reformer William Morris. Howells now emphasized *critical* social Realism, to expose the ills of society and arouse Americans to action. He jumped into the fray himself and marched for women's suffrage. He defended the 1886 Chicago Haymarket Square labor strikers and used his fiction to contrast the lives of rich and poor.

By 1889 Howells moved to New York City, which had replaced Boston as a literary mecca. To him, New York symbolized the new democratic center of the nation. His writings of the 1890s and into the next decade brought new fiction and criticism, with some novels that raised his reputation and America's consciousness—among them, *The Hazard of New Fortunes* (1890), A *Traveler from Altruria* (1894), and *The Landlord at Lion's Head* (1897). An *Imperative Duty* (1892), a novelette that was Howells's longest fiction on a racial theme, did not add to his reputation for creating verisimilitude. His contrived tale, set in Boston, portrays a white suitor, Dr. Edward Olney, who first "recoils" at discovering that his beautiful, intended bride, Rhoda Aldgate, is of "Negro descent"; Rhoda, reared as white, and anguished to learn her racial origins, threatens to end their engagement and do her "imperative duty" to serve her people, but is dissuaded by Olney. The pair decide to marry and resettle in Italy to conceal her "secret."

The book was dismissed by the few American critics who reviewed it, rejected by British critics and readers, and was out of print between 1903 and 1962. In the late twentieth century, a few scholars praised Howells for being a forerunner to Chesnutt on the miscegenation theme and a satirist on the issue of racial "passing." The novel is neither satirical nor groundbreaking. Before Chesnutt, the most honest and authentic treatment of miscegenation or passing was not by Howells but his contemporary, George Washington Cable, who knew his own milieu, characters, and social history in depth.

In Howells's early notes, he intended his book title to be "The Letters of Olney," but the title changed, as did the final text, after it was serialized in *Harper's Monthly* in four installments as An *Imperative Duty*, in 1891.

The following excerpt, from chapter 8 of the book, reprinted in 1970,[2] reveals Howells's own racial attitudes through Rhoda, who after learning her racial identity, takes a frenetic walk through a black neighborhood in Boston.

From *An Imperative Duty* (1892)

8

In the street where Rhoda found herself the gas was already palely burning in the shops, and the moony glare of an electric globe was invading the flush of the sunset whose afterglow still filled the summer air in the western perspective. She did not know where she was going, but she went that way, down the slope of the slightly curving thoroughfare. She had the letter which she meant to post in her hand, but she passed the boxes on the lampposts without putting it in. She no longer knew what she meant to do, in any sort, or what she desired; but out of the turmoil of horror, which she whirled round and round in, some purpose that seemed at first exterior to herself began to evolve. The street was one where she would hardly have met ladies of the sort she had always supposed herself of; gentility fled it long ago, and the houses that had once been middle-class houses had fallen in the social scale to the grade of mechanics' lodgings, and the shops, which had never been fashionable, were adapted strictly to the needs of a neighborhood of poor and humble people. They were largely provision stores, full of fruit, especially watermelons; there were some groceries, and some pharmacies of that professional neatness which pharmacies are of everywhere. The roadway was at this hour pretty well deserted by the express wagons and butcher carts that bang through it in the earlier day; and the horsecars, coming and going on its incline and its final westward level, were in the unrestricted enjoyment of the company's monopoly of the best part of its space.

At the first corner Rhoda had to find her way through groups of intense-faced suburbans who were waiting for their respective cars, and who heaped themselves on board as these arrived, and hurried to find places, more from force of habit than from necessity, for the pressure of the evening travel was already over. When she had passed these groups she began to meet the proper

[2] William Dean Howells, *The Shadow of a Dream* and *An Imperative Duty*, eds. Martha Banta, Ronald Gottesman, and David Nordloh. (Bloomington: Indiana University Press, 1970).

life of the street—the women who had come out to cheapen the next day's provisions at the markets, the men, in the brief leisure that their day's work had left them before bedtime, lounging at the lattice doors of the drinking shops, or standing listlessly about on the curbstones smoking. Numbers of young fellows, of the sort whose leisure is daylong, exchanged the comfort of a mutual support with the house walls, and stared at her as she hurried by; and then she began to encounter in greater and greater number the colored people who descended to this popular promenade from the uphill streets opening upon it. They politely made way for her, and at the first meeting that new agony of interest in them possessed her.

This was intensified by the deference they paid her as a young white lady, and the instant sense that she had no right to it in that quality. She could have borne better to have them rude and even insolent; there was something in the way they turned their black eyes in their large disks of white upon her, like dogs, with a mute animal appeal in them, that seemed to claim her and own her one of them, and to creep nearer and nearer and possess her in that late-found solidarity of race. She never knew before how hideous they were, with their flat wide-nostriled noses, their out-rolled thick lips, their mobile, bulging eyes set near together, their retreating chins and foreheads, and their smooth, shining skin: they seemed burlesques of humanity, worse than apes, because they were more like. But the men were not half so bad as the women, from the shrill-piped young girls, with their grotesque attempts at fashion, to the old grandmothers, wrinkled or obese, who came down the sloping sidewalks in their bare heads, out of the courts and alleys where they lived, to get the evening air. Impish black children swarmed on these uphill sidewalks, and played their games, with shrill cries racing back and forth, catching and escaping one another.

These colored folk were of all tints and types, from the comedy of the pure black to the closest tragical approach to white. She saw one girl, walking with a cloud of sable companions, who was as white as herself, and she wondered if she were of the same dilution of negro blood; she was laughing and chattering with the rest, and seemed to feel no difference, but to be pleased and flattered with the court paid her by the inky dandy who sauntered beside her.

"She has always known it; she has never felt it!" she thought, bitterly. "It is nothing; it is natural to her; I might have been like her."

She began to calculate how many generations would carry her back, or that girl back, in hue to the blackest of those loathsome old women. She knew what an octoroon was, and she thought, "I am like her, and my mother was darker, and my grandmother darker, and my great-grander like a mulatto, and then it was a horrible old negress, a savage stolen from Africa, where she had been a cannibal."

A vision of palm-tree roofs and grass huts, as she had seen them in pictures, with skulls grinning from the eaves, floated before her eyes; then a desert, with a long coffle of captives passing by, and one black naked woman, fallen out from weakness, kneeling, with manacled hands, and her head pulled back, and the Arab slaver's knife at her throat. She walked in a nightmare of these sights; all the horror of the wrong by which she came to be, poured itself round and over her.

She emerged from it at moments with a refusal to accept the loss of her former self: like that of the mutilated man who looks where his arm was, and cannot believe it gone. Like him, she had the full sense of what was lost, the unbroken consciousness of what was lopped away. At these moments, all her pride reasserted itself; she wished to punish her aunt for what she had made her suffer, to make her pay pang for pang. Then the tide of reality overwhelmed her again, and she groveled in self-loathing and despair. From that she rose in a frenzy of longing to rid herself of this shame that was not hers; to tear out the stain; to spill it with the last drop of her blood upon the ground. By flamy impulses she thrilled towards the mastery of her misery through its open acknowledgment. She seemed to see herself and hear herself stopping some of these revolting creatures, the dreadfulest of them, and saying, "I am black, too. Take me home with you, and let me live with you, and be like you every way." She thought, "Perhaps I have relations among them. Yes, it must be. I will send to the hotel for my things, and I will live here in some dirty little back court, and try to find them out."

The emotions, densely pressing upon each other, the dramatizations that took place as simultaneously and unsuccessively as the events of a dream, gave her a new measure of time; she compassed the experience of years in the seconds these sensations outnumbered.

All the while she seemed to be walking swiftly, flying forward; but the ground was uneven: it rose before her, and then suddenly fell. She felt her heart beat in the middle of her throat. Her head felt light, like the blowball of a dandelion. She wished to laugh. There seemed two selves of her, one that had lived before that awful knowledge, and one that had lived as long since, and again a third that knew and pitied them both. She wondered at the same time if this were what people meant by saying one's brain was turned; and she recalled the longing with which her aunt said, "If I were *only* crazy!" But she knew that her own exaltation was not madness, and she did not wish for escape that way. "There must be some other," she said to herself; "if I can find the courage for it, I can find the way. It's like a ghost: if I keep going towards it, it won't hurt me; I mustn't be afraid of it. Now, let me see! What *ought* I to do? Yes, that is the key: *Duty*." Then her thought flew passionately off. "If *she* had done her duty all this might have been helped. But it was her cowardice that made her murder me. Yes, she has killed me!"

The tears gushed into her eyes, and all the bitterness of her trial returned upon her, with a pressure of lead on her brain.

In the double consciousness of trouble she was as fully aware of everything about her as she was of the world of misery within her; and she knew that this had so far shown itself without that some of the passers were noticing her. She stopped, fearful of their notice, at the corner of a street she had come to, and turned about to confront an old colored woman, yellow like saffron, with the mind, sad face we often see in mulattoes of that type, and something peculiarly pitiful in the straight underlip of her appealing mouth, and the cast of her gentle eyes. The expression might have been merely physical, or it might have been a hereditary look, and no part of her own personality, but Rhoda felt safe in it.

"What street is this?" she asked, thinking, suddenly, "She is the color of my grandmother; that is the way she looked," but though she thought this she did not realize it, and she kept an imperious attitude towards the old woman.

"Charles Street, lady."

"Oh, yes; Charles. Where are all the people going?"

"The colored folks, lady?"

"Yes."

"Well, lady, they's a kyind of an evenin' meetin' at ouah choach tonight. Some of 'em's goin' there, I reckon; some of 'em's just out fo' a walk."

"Will you let me go with you?" Rhoda asked.

"Why, certainly, lady," said the old woman. She glanced up at Rhoda's face as the girl turned again to accompany her. "But *I'm* a-goin' to choach."

"Yes, yes. That's what I mean. I want to go to your church with you. Are you from the South—Louisiana? She would be the color," she thought. "It might be my mother's own mother."

"No, lady: from Voginny. I was bawn a slave; and I lived there till after the wa'. Then I come Nawth."

"Oh," said Rhoda, disappointed, for she had nerved herself to find this old woman her grandmother.

They walked on in silence for a while; then the old woman said, "I thought you wasn't very well, when I noticed you at the cawnah."

"I am well," Rhoda answered, feeling the tears start to her eyes again at the note of motherly kindness in the old woman's voice. "But I am in trouble; I am in trouble."

"Then you're gwine to the right place, lady," said the old woman, and she repeated solemnly these words of hope and promise which so many fainting hearts have stayed themselves upon: " 'Come unto me, all ye that labor and are heavy laden, and I will give you rest unto your souls.' Them's the words, lady; the Lawd's own words. Glory be to God; glory be to God!" she added in a whisper.

"Yes, yes," said Rhoda, impatiently. "They are good words. But they are not for me. He can't make *my* burden light; He can't give *me* rest. If it were sin, He could; but it isn't sin; it's something worse than sin; more hopeless. If I were only a sinner, the vilest, the wickedest, how glad I should be!" Her heart uttered itself to this simple nature as freely as a child's to its mother.

"Why, sholy, lady," said the old woman, with a little shrinking from her as if she had blasphemed, "sholy you's a sinnah?"

"No, I am not!" said the girl, with nervous sharpness. "If I were a sinner, my sin could be forgiven me, and I could go free of my burden. But nothing can ever lift it from me."

"The Lawd kin do anything, the Bible says. He kin make the dead come to life. He done it once, too."

The girl turned abruptly on her. "Can He change your skin? Can He make black white?"

The old woman seemed daunted; she faltered. "I don't know as He ever tried, lady; the Bible don't tell." She added, more hopefully, "But I reckon He could do it if He wanted to."

"Then why doesn't He do it?" demanded the girl. "What does He leave you black for, when He could make you white?"

"I reckon He don't think it's worthwhile, if He can make me *willing to be black* so easy. Somebody's got to be black, and it might as well be me," said the old woman with a meek sigh.

"No, no one need be black!" said Rhoda, with a vehemence that this submissive sigh awakened in her. "If He cared for us, no one would be!"

" 'Sh!" said the old woman, gently.

They had reached the church porch, and Rhoda found herself in the tide of black worshipers who were drifting in. The faces of some were supernaturally solemn, and these rolled their large-whited eyes rebukingly on the young girls showing all their teeth in the smiles that gashed them from ear to ear, and carrying on subdued flirtations with the polite young fellows escorting them. It was no doubt the best colored society, and it was bearing itself with propriety and self-respect in the court of the temple. If their natural gayety and lightness of heart moved their youth to the betrayal of their pleasure in each other in the presence of their Maker, He was perhaps propitiated by the gloom of their elders.

" 'Tain't a regular evenin' meetin'," Rhoda's companion explained to her. "It's a kind o' lecture." She exchanged some stately courtesies of greeting with the old men and women as they pushed into the church; they called her sister, and they looked with at least as little surprise and offense at the beautiful young white lady with her as white Christians would have shown a colored girl come to worship with them. "De preacher's one o' the Southern students; I 'ain't hud him speak; but I reckon the Lawd's sent him, anyway."

Rhoda had no motive in being where she was except to confront herself as fully and closely with the trouble in her soul as she could. She thought, so far as such willing may be called thinking, that she could strengthen herself for what she had henceforth to bear, if she could concentrate and intensify the fact to her outward perception; she wished densely to surround herself with the blackness from which she had sprung, and to reconcile herself to it, by realizing and owning it with every sense.

She did not know what the speaker was talking about at first, but phrases and words now and then caught in her consciousness. He was entirely black, and he was dressed in black from head to foot, so that he stood behind the pulpit light like a thick, soft shadow cast upon the wall by an electric. His absolute sable was relieved only by the white points of his shirt collar, and the glare of his spectacles, which, when the light struck them, heightened the goblin effect of his presence. He had no discernible features, and when he turned his profile in addressing those who sat at the sides, it was only a wavering blur against the wall. His voice was rich and tender, with those caressing notes in it which are the peculiar gift of his race.

The lecture opened with prayer and singing, and the lecturer took part in the singing; then he began to speak, and Rhonda's mind to wander, with her eyes, to the congregation. The prevailing blackness gave back the light here and there in the glint of a bald head or from a patch of white wool, or the cast of a rolling eye. Inside of the bonnets of the elder women, and under the gay hats of the young girls, it was mostly lost in a characterless dark; but nearer by, Rhoda distinguished faces, sad repulsive visages of a froglike ugliness added to the repulsive black in all its shades, from the unalloyed brilliancy of the pure negro type to the pallid yellow of the quadroon. These mixed bloods were more odious to her than the others, because she felt herself more akin to them; but they were all abhorrent. Some of the elder people made fervent responses to thoughts and sentiments in the lecture as if it had been a sermon. "That is so!" they said. "Bless the Lord, that's the truth!" and "Glory to God!" One old woman who sat in the same line of pews with Rhoda opened her mouth like a catfish to emit these pious ejaculations.

The night was warm, and as the church filled, the musky exhalations of their bodies thickened the air, and made the girl faint; it seemed to her that she began to taste the odor; and these poor people, whom their Creator has made so hideous by the standards of all his other creatures, roused a cruel loathing in her, which expressed itself in a frantic refusal of their claim upon her. In her heart she cast them off with vindictive hate. "Yes," she thought, "I should have whipped them, too. They are animals; they are only fit to be slaves." But when she shut her eyes, and heard their wild, soft voices, her other senses were holden, and she was rapt by the music from her frenzy of abhorrence. In one of these suspenses, while she sat listening to the sound of the lecturer's voice, which now and then struck a plangent note, like some rich, melancholy bell, a meaning began to steal out of it to her whirling thoughts.

"Yes, my friends," it went on saying, "you got to commence doing a person good if you expect to love them as Jesus loved us when he died for us. And oh, if our white brethren could only understand—and they're gettin' to understand it—that if they would help us a little more, they needn't hate us so much, what a great thing," the lecturer lamely concluded—"what a great thing it would be all round!"

"Amen! Love's the thing," said the voice of the old woman with the catfish mouth; and Rhoda, who did not see her, did not shudder. Her response inspired the lecturer to go on. "I believe it's the one way out of all the trouble in this world. You can't fight your way out, and you can't steal your way out, and you can't lie your way out. But you can *love* your way out. And how can you love your way out? By helpin' somebody else! Yes, that's it. Somebody that needs your help. And now if there's any one here that's in trouble, and wants to get out of trouble, all he's got to do is to help somebody else out. Remember that when the collection is taken up durin' the singin' of the hymn. Our college needs help, and every person that helps our college helps himself. Let us pray!"

The application was apt enough, and Rhoda did not feel anything grotesque in it. She put into the plate which the old woman passed to her from the collector all the money she had in her purse, notes and silver, and two or three gold pieces that had remained over to her from her European travel. Her companion saw them, and interrupted herself in her singing to say, "The Lawd 'll bless it to you; He'll help them that helps others that can't help themselves."

"Yes, that is the clew," the girl said to herself. "That is the way out; the only way. I can endure them if I can love them, and I shall love them if I try to help them. This money will help them."

But she did not venture to look round at the objects of her beneficence; she was afraid that the sight of their faces would harden her heart against them in spite of her giving, and she kept her eyes shut, listening to their pathetic voices. She stood forgetful after the lecturer had pronounced the benediction—he was a divinity student, and he could not forego it—and her companion had to touch her arm. Then she started with a shiver, as if from a hypnotic trance.

Once out on the street she was afraid, and begged the old woman to go back to her hotel with her.

"Why, sholy, lady," she consented.

But Rhoda did not hear. Her mind had begun suddenly to fasten itself upon a single thought, a sole purpose, and "Yes," she pondered, "that is the first thing of all: to forgive her; to tell her that I forgive her, and that I understand and pity her. But how—how shall I begin? I shall have to do her some good to begin with, and how can I do that when I hate her so? I do hate her; I do hate her! It is her fault!"

As she hurried along, almost running, and heedless of the old woman at her side, trying to keep up with her, it seemed to her that if her aunt had told her long ago, when a child, what she was, she would somehow not have been it now.

It was not with love, not with pardon, but with frantic hate and accusal in her heart, that she burst into the room, and rushed to Mrs. Meredith's sofa, where she lay still.

"Aunt Caroline, wake up! Can you sleep when you see me going perfectly crazy? It is no time for sleeping! Wake!"

The moony pallor of an electric light suspended over the street shone in through the naked window, and fell upon Mrs. Meredith's face. It was white, and as the girl started back her foot struck the empty bottle from which the woman had drained the sleeping medicine, and let lie where she had let it fall upon the floor. Rhoda caught it up, and flew with it to the light. . . .

ANNA JULIA COOPER

(1858–1964)

The social consequences of fiction in Howells's *An Imperative Duty* were argued by Afro-American feminist and educator Anna Julia Cooper in her 1892 book of essays *A Voice from the South*. "Mr. Howells's point of view is precisely that of a white man who sees colored people at long range or only in certain capacities," she wrote. She chose white Southern author Albion W. Tourgée[1] as "foremost among the champions of the black man's cause through the medium of fiction," and George Washington Cable[2] as "brave and just," but lambasted Howells's literary "misrepresentations." Her book of eight social essays on race and gender was reviewed by a few Northern newspapers, but not by the prestigious magazines where Howells's pieces often appeared: the *Atlantic Monthly, Century, Harper's,* and *North American Review,* all of which in the early 1890s were still determined to let Northern and Southern whites speak for blacks, to advance post–Civil War sectional "reconciliation."

Cooper was a black female voice from the South, one heard mainly by intellectuals of her race, whose numbers were then too few to influence national policy or white publishers. Knowing her essays defied race stereotypes and gender roles, she paid an Ohio printer for publication of her book. She did not write a confession or autobiographical narrative, à la Frederick Douglass or Booker T. Washington. Hers was the voice of an interpreter, offering "the open-eyed but hitherto voiceless Black Woman of America." Her title page, minus her name, cited her book *By a Black Woman of the South*.

She was born Annie Haywood in Raleigh, North Carolina, the daughter of a slave woman, Hannah Stanley Haywood, and a white master, Dr. Fabius J. Haywood, whose name her mother "was always too modest and shamefaced

---

[1] Albion W. Tourgée (1838–1905), Ohio-born writer; served in Union Army, became resident of Greensboro, North Carolina, during Reconstruction and later wrote a series of historical novels documenting black-white relations he observed during fourteen years there as lawyer, businessman, and court judge; his novels include: *A Fool's Errand* (1879), *Figs and Thistles* (1879), *A Royal Gentleman* (1880, published as *Toinette* in 1874); *Bricks without Straw* (1880); plus his factual studies, *The Invisible Empire* (1880), and *An Appeal to Caesar* (1884), which is excerpted in this volume. See also the biographical entry on Tourgée, above, pages 302–5.

[2] See Cable biography and nonfiction excerpt in this volume, above, pages 308–15.

ever to mention." If her paternity gave her no identity, her formal education did; during Reconstruction she enrolled at Augustine's Normal School and Collegiate Institute—established by the Episcopal Church Board to train freed persons to become teachers. She completed a prescribed curriculum there before marrying Reverend George Cooper, an Episcopal clergyman and professor of Greek. Widowed after two years, she entered Oberlin College in 1881, earned an A.B. in 1884, and taught at Ohio's black Wilberforce University, before receiving her M.A. in mathematics at Oberlin in 1887.

Cooper's qualifications led to a teaching job in DC, at the only secondary school then open to her race: Washington Colored High School—commonly called the "M Street School," later renamed DunBar after 1916. She remained nearly forty years, as a teacher of mathematics, Latin, and modern languages (1887 through 1901), as principal (January 1902–6), and again as teacher (1910–30), after four years at Lincoln University in Missouri. She left Washington temporarily in 1906 after dismissal by the DC Board of Education, over alleged "insubordination" "inefficiency," and rumors of a romance with her foster son, John Love, Jr., a teacher of English at the DC high school.

The 1905–6 allegations against Cooper as school principal were a cause célèbre, but her supporters charged white administrators with persecution, especially for her insistence on college-preparatory courses that sent some of her best students to Ivy League colleges at a time when Booker T. Washington urged blacks to keep their hands on the plow. Her 1892 book revealed that she endorsed both academic and industrial education, a decade before the Booker T. Washington–W. E. B. Du Bois feud about classical-versus-manual training. But she was never beholden to the Tuskegee leader or desirous of the patronage he rewarded his supporters in the capital, such as Robert J. Terrell, who preceded Cooper as principal of the M Street School before he was appointed a justice of the peace.

Cooper believed higher education essential to race progress and to the status of women, emphasizing that "intellectual development, with the self-reliance and capacity for earning a livelihood which it gives, renders woman less dependent on the marriage relation." She resented an arcane law in DC and some states forbidding married women to teach; she never remarried but in 1915 adopted five young children of a widowed relative and reared them as hers. Her feminist viewpoint in the opening essay of her book, "Womanhood: A Vital Element in the Regeneration and Progress of a Race," was first presented in 1886 in Washington, DC—to the Colored Clergy of the Protestant Episcopal Church—where Alexander Crummell was present, and where she mentioned his 1883 pamphlet "The Black Woman of the South." Yet she eschewed the notions of color and caste that Crummell developed while in exile in Liberia—

which led him to say, after his return to America: "In speaking of the 'black woman,' I must make a very clear distinction. The African race in this country is divided into two classes . . . the colored people and the . . . black or negro population." Cooper suggested he add a "plea for the *Colored Girls of the South*," and she stressed that "the whole Negro race enters with me."

She lived to age 105 and saw racial nomenclature change with the times, but she proudly used the word *black* interchangeably with *colored* and *Negro*, when the latter two terms were more popular. With publication of only one full-length book in her early career, and a few monographs and articles later, her reputation was as an educator, not as a writer; one of a few black women to address the World Congress of Representative Women at the Columbian Exposition (Chicago World's Fair) of 1893, and the First Pan–African Conference in London in 1900. In 1925, in her sixties, she earned a doctorate at the Sorbonne, with a thesis published that year in Paris: "L'Attitude de la France à l'égard de l'esclavage pendant la revolution" ("France's attitude toward slavery during the revolution"). She spent the final decades of her professional life as President and Registrar of the Frelinghuysen University/Group of Schools for Colored Working People, an experiment that she helped initiate to provide evening classes to adults. The concept ended for lack of endowment.

The following excerpt, from *A Voice from the South*, is part of her commentary on William Dean Howells, from the essay "The Negro as Presented in American Literature."

From *A Voice from the South* (1892)

. . . Among our artists for art's sweet sake, Mr. Howells has recently tried his hand also at painting the Negro, attempting merely a sidelight in halftones, on his life and manners; and I think the unanimous verdict of the subject is that, in this single department at least, Mr. Howells does not know what he is talking about. And yet I do not think we should quarrel with *An Imperative Duty* because it lacks the earnestness and bias of a special pleader. Mr. Howells merely meant to press the button and give one picture from American life involving racial complications. The Kodak does no more; it cannot preach sermons or solve problems.

Besides, the portrayal of Negro characteristics was by no means the main object of the story, which was rather meant, I judge, to be a thumbnail sketch containing a psychological study of a morbidly sensitive conscience hectoring over a weak and vacillating will and fevered into increased despotism by reading into its own life and consciousness the analyses and terrible retributions of fiction,—a product of the Puritan's uncompromising sense of *"right though the heavens fall,"* irritated and kept sore by being unequally yoked with indecision and cowardice. Of such strokes Mr. Howells is undoubtedly master. It is true there is little point and no force of character about the beautiful and irresponsible young heroine; but as that is an attainment of so many of Mr. Howells's models, it is perhaps not to be considered as illustrating any racial characteristics. I cannot help sharing, however, the indignation of those who resent the picture in the colored church,—"evidently," Mr. Howells assures us, "representing *the best colored society"*; where the horrified young prig, Rhoda Aldgate, meets nothing but the froglike countenances and catfish mouths, the musky exhalations and the "bress de Lawd, Honey," of an uncultivated people. It is just here that Mr. Howells fails—and fails because he gives only a half-truth, and that a partisan half-truth. One feels that he had no business to attempt a subject of which he knew so little, or for which he cared so little. There is one thing I would like to say to my white fellow countrymen, and especially to those who dabble in ink and affect to discuss the Negro; and yet I hesitate because I feel it is a fact which persons of the finer sensibilities and more delicate perceptions must know instinctively: namely, that it is an insult to humanity and a sin against God to publish any such sweeping generalizations of a race on such meager and superficial information. We meet it at every turn—this obtrusive and offensive vulgarity, this gratuitous sizing up of the Negro and conclusively writing down his equation, sometimes even among his ardent friends and bravest defenders. Were I not afraid of falling myself into the same error that I am condemning, I would say it seems an *Anglo-Saxon characteristic* to have such overweening confidence in his own power of induction that there is no equation which he would acknowledge to be indeterminate, however many unknown quantities it may possess. . . .

FANNIE BARRIER WILLIAMS

(1855–1944)

A contemporary of Anna Julia Cooper was the outspoken Fannie Barrier Williams, who joined Cooper and four other Afro-American women on a rostrum at the World Congress of Representative Women in Chicago in May 1893.[1] Featured as part of the international Columbian Exposition—as noted, also called the Chicago World Fair—the six black speakers addressed a predominantly white audience at the *Women's Building*, in a forum titled "The Solidarity of Human Interests." Williams, then unknown, and the only one of the six a resident of Chicago, had prodded the Exposition's "Board of Control" for "colored" representation, and the session opened with her speech, "The Intellectual Progress of the Colored Women of the United States since the Emancipation Proclamation."

The event was little noticed in the opening month of a colossal exposition intended to showcase America's technology and wealth. But present was septuagenarian Frederick Douglass, who had collaborated with Ida B. Wells[2] to write and distribute a querulous pamphlet, "The Reason Why the Colored American Is Not in the Columbian Exposition." He rose to praise the women's presentations but displayed limited exposure to females of his race, when he said, "I have heard tonight what I hardly expected ever to live to hear. I have heard refined, educated colored ladies addressing—and addressing successfully—one of the most intelligent white audiences that I have ever looked upon."

Williams knew better than Douglass that "refined, educated colored ladies" were numerous but invisible to most white Americans. As she later wrote, "progress included a great deal more than what is generally meant by the terms culture, education, and contact." A frequent theme of her articles and speeches for the next decade was that educated colored women were perceived by whites not by class, but by race, not distinctive as individuals but indistinguishable from the underprivileged, uneducated masses. She tried to resolve that binary image as lecturer, community activist, journalist, and leader in the national

---

[1] The six women were Hallie Quinn Brown, Anna Julia Cooper, Fannie Jackson Coppin, Frances E. W. Harper, Sarah J. W. Early, and Fannie Barrier Williams.

[2] See in this volume Ida B. Wells-Barnett (who took a married name in 1895), pages 443–50.

black women's civic club movement. Her personal background prepared her to be genteel; social conditions made her a militant, and she tried being both—often in conflict.

A mulatto born to free and self-employed parents in Brockport, New York, reared among white neighbors and classmates without prejudice, she graduated from the State Normal School of Brockport in 1870, studied at the New England Conservatory of Music in Boston, and the School of Fine Arts in Washington, DC. But such training then offered few options open to her race to succeed professionally, and she taught in the South before her marriage in 1887 to S. Laing Williams, a graduate of the University of Michigan and Columbian Law School (later George Washington Law School). They settled in Chicago and joined a striving upper class in a black population then numbering fewer than 15,000, where her husband began his law practice and Fannie her volunteer service in the community. She helped to organize Provident Hospital, which opened in 1891 with the first integrated staff of nurses and doctors, headed by noted Negro surgeon Dr. Daniel Hale Williams. She lectured and wrote increasingly after her speech at the 1893 Columbian Exposition, and in 1895 was elected the first "colored member" of the prestigious Chicago Woman's Club. Simultaneously, she helped to galvanize the Illinois branch of the National League of Colored Women, and its 1896 successor, the National Association of Colored Women (NACW), headed by Mary Church Terrell[3] in Washington, DC. The NACW's motto, "Lifting as We Climb," fit the group's mission of race uplift through services to the indigent, orphaned, and aged, as well as programs to combat Jim Crow segregation. The civic-club movement mushroomed in the late nineteenth century, and had its counterpart in the all-white General Federation of Women's Clubs, founded in 1890—with no welcome sign to black women's clubs to affiliate as members.

Williams recorded her observations in articles such as "The Club Movement among Colored Women in America," and "The Clubs and Their Location in All the States of the National Association of Colored Women and Their Mission," which both appeared in 1900 in a volume of essays, *New Negro for a New Century*, which was privately printed in Chicago, and later credited by some to Booker T. Washington as editor, though he was a only contributor. Two major hands behind the book were Fannie and S. Laing Williams, who by 1900 were both in the grip of the "Tuskegee Wizard." That year, the couple helped to

---

[3] Mary Church Terrell (1863–1954), teacher, women's rights and civil rights leader, author; Memphis-born, Oberlin-educated; married educator–lawyer Robert Terrell in 1891; formed the National League of Colored Women in 1895 and united it in 1896 with the National Federation of Afro-American Women; the merged organization became the National Association of Colored Women (NACW) and Terrell its first President.

organize a Chicago reception of 2,500 at Armory Hall to honor him and his new National Negro Business League. One of its Chicago officers was Attorney Williams, whose photograph appeared a year later in the second edition of Washington's *The Story of My Life and Work*; for the next decade he served as the Wizard's Chicago line of defense, controlling his Tuskegee image in the black press, ghostwriting a book on Frederick Douglass (with help from Fannie and T. Thomas Fortune), and receiving a political reward from Theodore Roosevelt in 1908 to become federal assistant district attorney in Chicago. Meanwhile, Fannie worked in the women's-club movement with Margaret Murray Washington, who in 1893 became the third wife of Booker T. Washington, and soon vice-president of the National Association of Colored Women from 1896 to 1901, and its president from 1912 to 1916.

In 1907, after T. Thomas Fortune's misadventure with the *New York Age*, Fannie wrote for the then-conservative newspaper, in which Washington owned a secret interest. Her columns reveal the paradoxes of class, race, and gender in which women of the black elite found themselves. "We must not despise the coming of the Negro aristocrat," she wrote in the *New York Age* in 1905. "He is very much needed and has good services to perform." After her husband's death in 1921, she shunned writing or speaking on race issues, feeling more keenly the class stratifications created in Chicago by the Great Migration and the formation of urban ghettos. Her final community service in Chicago was as the first woman and Afro-American on the city's Library Board. She spent her final years living with her sister, Ella D. Barrier, who taught for a long time with Anna Julia Cooper in Washington.

The following excerpt is from Williams's 1893 speech, reprinted after the Chicago Exposition as a pamphlet entitled "The Present Status and Intellectual Progress of Colored Women."

From The Present Status and Intellectual Progress of Colored Women (1893)

Less than thirty years ago the term *progress* as applied to colored women of African descent in the United States would have been an anomaly. The recognition of that term today as appropriate is a fact full of interesting significance. That the discussion of progressive womanhood in this great assemblage of the representative women of the world is considered incomplete without some account of the colored women's status is a most noteworthy evidence that we have not failed to impress ourselves on the higher side of American life.

Less is known of our women than of any other class of Americans.

No organization of far-reaching influence for their special advancement, no conventions of women to take note of their progress, and no special literature reciting the incidents, the events, and all things interesting and instructive concerning them are to be found among the agencies directing their career. There has been no special interest in their peculiar condition as native-born American women. Their power to affect the social life of America, either for good or for ill, has excited not even a speculative interest.

Though there is much that is sorrowful, much that is wonderfully heroic, and much that is romantic in a peculiar way in their history, none of it has as yet been told as evidence of what is possible for these women. How few of the happy, prosperous, and eager living Americans can appreciate what it all means to be suddenly changed from irresponsible bondage to the responsibility of freedom and citizenship!

The distress of it all can never be told, and the pain of it all can never be felt except by the victims, and by those saintly women of the white race who for thirty years have been consecrated to the uplifting of a whole race of women from a long-enforced degradation.

The American people have always been impatient of ignorance and poverty. They believe with Emerson that "America is another word for opportunity," and for that reason success is a virtue and poverty and ignorance are inexcusable. This may account for the fact that our women have excited no general sympathy in the struggle to emancipate themselves from the demoralization of slavery. This new life of freedom, with its far-reaching responsibilities, had to be learned by these children of darkness mostly without a guide, a teacher, or a friend. In the mean vocabulary of slavery there was no definition of any of the virtues of life. The meaning of such precious terms as marriage, wife, family, and home could not be learned in a schoolhouse. The blue-back speller, the arithmetic, and the copybook contain no magical cures for inherited inaptitudes for the moralities. Yet it must ever be counted as one of the most wonderful things in human history how promptly and eagerly these suddenly liberated women tried to lay hold upon all that there is in human excellence. There is a touching pathos in the eagerness of these millions of new homemakers to taste the blessedness of intelligent womanhood. The path of progress in the picture is enlarged so as to bring to view these trustful and zealous students of freedom and civilization striving to overtake and keep pace with women whose emancipation has been a slow and painful process for a thousand years. The longing to be something better than they were when freedom found them has been the most notable characteristic in the development of these women. This constant striving for equality has given an upward direction to all the activities of colored women.

Freedom at once widened their vision beyond the mean cabin life of their bondage. Their native gentleness, good cheer, and hopefulness made them susceptible to those teachings that make for intelligence and righteousness. Sullenness of disposition, hatefulness, and revenge against the master class because of two centuries of ill-treatment are not in the nature of our women.

But a better view of what our women are doing and what their present status is may be had by noticing some lines of progress that are easily verifiable.

First it should be noticed that separate facts and figures relative to colored women are not easily obtainable. Among the white women of the country independence, progressive intelligence, and definite interests have done so much that nearly every fact and item illustrative of their progress and status is classified and easily accessible. Our women, on the contrary, have had no advantage of interests peculiar and distinct and separable from those of men that have yet excited public attention and kindly recognition.

In their religious life, however, our women show a progressiveness parallel in every important particular to that of white women in all Christian churches. . . .

While there has been but little progress toward the growing rationalism in the Christian creeds, there has been a marked advance toward a greater refinement of conception, good taste, and the proprieties. It is our young women coming out of the schools and academies that have been insisting upon a more godly and cultivated ministry. It is the young women of a new generation and new inspirations that are making tramps of the ministers who once dominated the colored church, and whose intelligence and piety were mostly in their lungs. . . .

Another evidence of growing intelligence is a sense of religious discrimination among our women. Like the nineteenth-century woman generally, our women find congeniality in all the creeds, from the Catholic creed to the no-creed of Emerson. There is a constant increase of this interesting variety in the religious life of our women.

Closely allied to this religious development is their progress in the work of education in schools and colleges. For thirty years education has been the magic word among the colored people of this country. That their greatest need was education in its broadest sense was understood by these people more strongly than it could be taught to them. It is the unvarying testimony of every teacher in the South that the mental development of the colored women as well as men has been little less than phenomenal. In twenty-five years, and under conditions discouraging in the extreme, thousands of our women have been educated as teachers. They have adapted themselves to the work of mentally lifting a whole race of people so eagerly and readily that they afford an apt illustration of the power of self-help. Not only have these women become good teachers in less than twenty-five years, but many of them are the prize teachers in the mixed schools of nearly every Northern city.

These women have also so fired the hearts of the race for education that colleges, normal schools, industrial schools, and universities have been reared by a generous public to meet the requirements of these eager students of intelligent citizenship. As American women generally are fighting against the nineteenth-century narrowness that still keeps women out of the higher institutions of learning, so our women are eagerly demanding the best of education open to their race. They continually verify what President Rankin[+] of Howard University recently said, "Any theory of educating the Afro American that does not throw open the golden gates of the highest culture will fail on the ethical and spiritual side."

It is thus seen that our women have the same spirit and mettle that characterize the best of American women. Everywhere they are following in the tracks of those women who are swiftest in the race for higher knowledge.

Today they feel strong enough to ask for but one thing, and that is the same opportunity for the acquisition of all kinds of knowledge that may be accorded to other women. This granted, in the next generation these progressive women will be found successfully occupying every field where the highest intelligence alone is admissible. In less than another generation American literature, American art, and American music will be enriched by productions having new and peculiar features of interest and excellence.

The exceptional career of our women will yet stamp itself indelibly upon the thought of this country.

American literature needs for its greater variety and its deeper soundings that which will be written into it out of the hearts of these self-emancipating women.

The great problems of social reform that are now so engaging the highest intelligence of American women will soon need for their solution the reinforcement of that new intelligence which our women are developing. In short, our women are ambitious to be contributors to all the great moral and intellectual forces that make for the greater weal of our common country.

[+] Jeremiah E. Rankin (1828–1904), white theologian and and minister, who was then president of Howard University (1890–1903).

If this hope seems too extravagant to those of you who know these women only in their humbler capacities, I would remind you that all that we hope for and will certainly achieve in authorship and practical intelligence is more than prophesied by what has already been done, and more that can be done, by hundreds of Afro-American women whose talents are now being expended in the struggle against race resistance.

The power of organized womanhood is one of the most interesting studies of modern sociology. Formerly women knew so little of each other mentally, their common interests were so sentimental and gossipy, and their knowledge of all the larger affairs of human society was so meager that organization among them, in the modern sense, was impossible. Now their liberal intelligence, their contact in all the great interests of education, and their increasing influence for good in all the great reformatory movements of the age has created in them a greater respect for each other, and furnished the elements of organization for large and splendid purposes. The highest ascendancy of woman's development has been reached when they have become mentally strong enough to find bonds of association interwoven with sympathy, loyalty, and mutual trustfulness. Today union is the watch-word of woman's onward march.

If it be a fact that this spirit of organization among women generally is the distinguishing mark of the nineteenth-century woman, dare we ask if the colored women of the United States have made any progress in this respect? . . .

Benevolence is the essence of most of the colored women's organizations. The humane side of their natures has been cultivated to recognize the duties they owe to the sick, the indigent and ill-fortuned. No church, school, or charitable institution for the special use of colored people has been allowed to languish or fail when the associated efforts of the women could save it. . . .

The hearts of Afro-American women are too warm and too large for race hatred. Long suffering has so chastened them that they are developing a special sense of sympathy for all who suffer and fail of justice. All the associated interests of church, temperance, and social reform in which American women are winning distinction can be wonderfully advanced when our women shall be welcomed as coworkers, and estimated solely by what they are worth to the moral elevation of all the people.

I regret the necessity of speaking to the question of the moral progress of our women, because the morality of our home life has been commented upon so disparagingly and meanly that we are placed in the unfortunate position of being defenders of our name.

It is proper to state, with as much emphasis as possible, that all questions relative to the moral progress of the colored women of America are impertinent and unjustly suggestive when they relate to the thousands of colored women in the North who were free from the vicious influences of slavery. They are also meanly suggestive as regards thousands of our women in the South whose force of character enabled them to escape the slavery taints of immorality. The question of the moral progress of colored women in the United States has force and meaning in this discussion only so far as it tells the story of how the once-enslaved women have been struggling for twenty-five years to emancipate themselves from the demoralization of their enslavement.

While I duly appreciate the offensiveness of all references to American slavery, it is unavoidable to charge to that system every moral imperfection that mars the character of the colored American. The whole life and power of slavery depended upon an enforced degradation of everything human in the slaves. The slave code recognized only animal distinctions between the sexes, and ruthlessly ignored those ordinary separations that belong to the social state.

It is a great wonder that two centuries of such demoralization did not work a complete extinction of all the moral instincts. But the recuperative power of these women to regain their moral instincts and to establish a respectable relationship to American womanhood is among the earlier evidences of their moral ability to rise above their conditions. In spite of a cursed heredity that bound them to the lowest social level, in spite of everything that is unfortunate and unfavorable, these women have continually shown an increasing degree of teachableness as to the meaning of woman's relationship to man.

Out of this social purification and moral uplift have come a chivalric sentiment and regard from the young men of the race that give to the young women a new sense of protection. I do not wish to disturb the serenity of this conference by suggesting why this protection is needed and the kind of men against whom it is needed.

It is sufficient for us to know that the daughters of women who thirty years ago were not allowed to be modest, not allowed to follow the instincts of moral rectitude, who could cry for protection to no living man, have so elevated the moral tone of their social life that new and purer standards of personal worth have been created, and new ideals of womanhood, instinct with grace and delicacy, are everywhere recognized and emulated.

This moral regeneration of a whole race of women is no idle sentiment—it is a serious business; and everywhere there is witnessed a feverish anxiety to be free from the mean suspicions that have so long underestimated the character strength of our women.

These women are not satisfied with the unmistakable fact that moral progress has been made, but they are fervently impatient and stirred by a sense of outrage under the vile imputations of a diseased public opinion. . . .

It may now perhaps be fittingly asked, What mean all these evidences of mental, social, and moral progress of a class of American women of whom you know so little? Certainly you can not be indifferent to the growing needs and importance of women who are demonstrating their intelligence and capacity for the highest privileges of freedom.

The most important thing to be noted is the fact that the colored people of America have reached a distinctly new era in their career so quickly that the American mind has scarcely had time to recognize the fact, and adjust itself to the new requirements of the people in all things that pertain to citizenship. . . .

It seems to daze the understanding of the ordinary citizen that there are thousands of men and women everywhere among us who in twenty-five years have progressed as far away from the nonprogressive peasants of the "black belt" of the South as the highest social life in New England is above the lowest levels of American civilization.

This general failure of the American people to know the new generation of colored people, and to recognize this important change in them, is the cause of more injustice to our women than can well be estimated. Further progress is everywhere seriously hindered by this ignoring of their improvement.

Our exclusion from the benefits of the fair play sentiment of the country is little less than a crime against the ambitions and aspirations of a whole race of women. The American people are but repeating the common folly of history in thus attempting to repress the yearnings of progressive humanity.

In the item of employment colored women bear a distressing burden of mean and unreasonable discrimination. . . .

It is almost literally true that, except teaching in colored schools and menial work, colored women can find no employment in this free America. They are the only women in the country for whom real ability, virtue, and special talents count for nothing when they become applicants for respectable employment. Taught everywhere in ethics and social economy that merit always wins, colored women carefully prepare themselves for all kinds of occupation only to meet with stern refusal, rebuff, and disappointment. One of countless instances will show how the best as well as the meanest of American society are responsible for the special injustice to our women.

Not long ago I presented the case of a bright young woman to a well-known bank president of Chicago, who was in need of a thoroughly competent stenographer and typewriter. The president was fully satisfied with the young woman as exceptionally qualified for the position, and manifested much pleasure in commending her to the directors for appointment, and at the same time disclaimed that there could be any opposition on account of the slight tinge of African blood that identified her as a colored woman. Yet, when the matter was brought before the directors for action, these mighty men of money and business, these men whose prominence in all the great interests of the city would seem to lift them above all narrowness and foolishness, scented the African taint, and at once bravely came to the rescue of the bank and of society by dashing the hopes of this capable yet helpless young woman. . . .

Can the people of this country afford to single out the women of a whole race of people as objects of their special contempt? Do these women not belong to a race that has never faltered in its support of the country's flag in every war since Attucks fell in Boston's streets?

Are they not the daughters of men who have always been true as steel against treason to everything fundamental and splendid in the republic? In short, are these women not as thoroughly American in all the circumstances of citizenship as the best citizens of our country?

If it be so, are we not justified in a feeling of desperation against that peculiar form of Americanism that shows respect for our women as servants and contempt for them when they become women of culture? We have never been taught to understand why the unwritten law of chivalry, protection, and fair play that are everywhere the conservators of women's welfare must exclude every woman of a dark complexion.

We believe that the world always needs the influence of every good and capable woman, and this rule recognizes no exceptions based on complexion. In their complaint against hindrances to their employment colored women ask for no special favors. . . .

Another, and perhaps more serious, hindrance to our women is that nightmare known as "social equality." The term equality is the most inspiring word in the vocabulary of citizenship. It expresses the leveling quality in all the splendid possibilities of American life. It is this idea of equality that has made room in this country for all kinds and conditions of men, and made personal merit the supreme requisite for all kinds of achievement.

When the colored people became citizens, and found it written deep in the organic law of the land that they too had the right to life, liberty, and the pursuit of happiness, they were at once suspected of wishing to interpret this maxim of equality as meaning social equality.

Everywhere the public mind has been filled with constant alarm lest in some way our women shall approach the social sphere of the dominant race in this country. Men and women, wise and perfectly sane in all things else, become instantly unwise and foolish at the remotest suggestion of social contact with colored men and women. At every turn in our lives we meet this fear, and are humiliated by its aggressiveness and meanness. If we seek the sanctities of religion, the enlightenment of the university, the honors of politics, and the natural recreations of our common country, the social equality alarm is instantly given, and our aspirations are insulted. "Beware of social equality with the colored American" is thus written on all places, sacred or profane, in this blessed land of liberty. The most discouraging and demoralizing effect of this false sentiment concerning us is that it utterly ignores individual merit and discredits the sensibilities of intelligent womanhood. The sorrows and heartaches of a whole race of women seem to be matters of no concern to the people who so dread the social possibilities of these colored women.

On the other hand, our women have been wonderfully indifferent and unconcerned about the matter. The dread inspired by the growing intelligence of colored women has interested us almost to the point of amusement. It has given to colored women a new sense of importance to witness how easily their emancipation and steady advancement is disturbing all classes of American people. It may not be a discouraging circumstance that colored women can command some sort of attention, even though they be misunderstood. We believe in the law of reaction, and it is reasonably certain that the forces of intelligence and character being developed in our women will yet change mistrustfulness into confidence and contempt into sympathy and respect. It will soon appear to those who are not hopelessly monomaniacs on the subject that the colored people are in no way responsible for the social equality nonsense. We shall yet be credited with knowing better than our enemies that social equality can neither be enforced by law nor prevented by oppression. Though not philosophers, we long since learned that equality before the law, equality in the best sense of that term under our institutions, is totally different from social equality.

We know, without being exceptional students of history, that the social relationship of the two races will be adjusted equitably in spite of all fear and injustice, and that there is a social gravitation in human affairs that eventually overwhelms and crushes into nothingness all resistance based on prejudice and selfishness.

Our chief concern in this false social sentiment is that it attempt to hinder our further progress toward the higher spheres of womanhood. On account of it, young colored women of ambition and means are compelled in many instances to leave the country for training and education in the salons and studios of Europe. On many of the railroads of this country women of refinement and culture are driven like cattle into human cattle-cars lest the occupying of an individual seat paid for in a first-class car may result in social equality. This social quarantine on all means of travel in certain parts of the country is guarded and enforced more rigidly against us than the quarantine regulations against cholera.

Without further particularizing as to how this social question opposes our advancement, it may be stated that the contentions of colored women are in kind like those of other American women for greater freedom of development. Liberty to be all that we can be, without artificial hindrances, is a thing no less precious to us than to women generally.

We come before this assemblage of women feeling confident that our progress has been along high levels and rooted deeply in the essentials of intelligent humanity. We are so essentially American in speech, in instincts, in sentiments and destiny that the things that interest you equally interest us.

We believe that social evils are dangerously contagious. The fixed policy of persecution and injustice against a class of women who are weak and defenseless will be necessarily hurtful to the cause of all women. Colored women are becoming more and more a part of the social forces that must help to determine the questions that so concern women generally. In this Congress we ask to be known and recognized for what we are worth. If it be the high purpose of these deliberations to lessen the resistance to woman's progress, you cannot fail to be interested in our struggles against the many oppositions that harass us. . . .

SAMUEL L. CLEMENS [MARK TWAIN]

(1835–1910)

Concurrent with the 1893 Columbian Exposition in Chicago, the American Historical Association meeting there heard a paper on "The Significance of the Frontier in American History" by a young professor named Frederick Jackson Turner. It influenced scholarship for the next quarter century, including social historian Bernard DeVoto's seminal books on Mark Twain. The "frontier is the whole truth about the books of Mark Twain," wrote DeVoto in *Mark Twain's America* (1932).

Twain's frontier influences are enfabled in *Old Times on the Mississippi* (1875), *The Adventures of Tom Sawyer* (1876), *Adventures of Huckleberry Finn* (1885); and in his sketches of backwoods humor of the Wild West in "The Celebrated Jumping Frog of Calaveras County" (1867), and in eyewitness tales of Westward expansion in his travelogue *Roughing It* (1872). Central to novels about his youth is the specter of the Negro—about whom Twain showed ambiguity all his literary life, though after his death he was hailed as a writer without prejudice by those who chose to ignore his paradoxes.

The man who renamed himself Mark Twain in 1865 was born Samuel Langhorne Clemens in 1835 in Missouri—then a slaveholding state newly admitted to the Union—when his parents arrived to buy land on a new frontier. From his village birthplace in Florida, Missouri, near the Salt Lick River, the family moved four years later to nearby Hannibal, on the Mississippi, where Sam spent his first two decades, witness to a Southern frontier cosmos of slaves and fugitive slaves like his fictional Jim, so-called poor white trash like Huck's Pap, and the fallen yet aspiring gentry such as his parents, Jane Lampton Clemens, a Kentuckian and John Marshall Clemens, a Virginian who suffered reverses as a lawyer, landowner, and storekeeper before his death in 1847. The future author, who disliked school as much as his hero Huck Finn, went to work in a printing office at age twelve, with his refuge the river and the prairies, his classroom the frontier port of piracies, lynchings, minstrel shows, slave superstitions, and the Southwestern dialects he re-created.

His father had inherited three slaves whom he sold, but one female slave traveled to Missouri with his mother, who he later memorialized in his *Autobiography* as oblivious "that slavery was a bald, grotesque and unwarrantable usurpation":

> She had never heard it assailed in any pulpit, but had heard it defended and sanctioned in a thousand; her ears were familiar with Bible texts that approved it, but if there were any that disapproved it they had not been quoted by her pastors; as far as her experience went, the wise and the good and the holy were unanimous in the conviction that slavery was right.

Twain fought briefly for the slaveocracy as a Confederate in Marion County, Missouri, until his "Marion Rangers" regiment was demobilized the summer of 1861. Then twenty-five-years-old, he deserted to go West with his brother Orion, a Unionist, who was appointed Secretary of Nevada Territory. The Civil War was to Twain a silent memory until 1885, when he wrote "The Private History of a Campaign That Failed"—for *Century*'s Battles and Leaders series, which the magazine intended as a catharsis for North and South.

The Southerner who went West on the stagecoach route in July 1861 had rarely been far from Hannibal, except during the summer of 1853, when he wandered between St. Louis, New York, Philadelphia, Keokuk, and Cincinnati as a journeyman compositer and printer. He worked some nine years as a printer before becoming a riverboat pilot on the Mississippi in the spring of 1857—a job that the Civil War ended. Decades later, he claimed no experience had been as glorious, and that he never met a man he had not already met on steamboats.

Before his books made him a culture hero, Clemens made his name as a newspaper reporter in the Gold Rush West: from 1862 to 1864 for the *Virginia City Territorial Enterprise,* and two more years freelancing for the *San Francisco Morning Call* and other California papers, such as the *Sacramento Union,* which sent him as correspondent in 1866 to the Sandwich Islands (now Hawaii). He published a book of his Western sketches with the popular "The Celebrated Jumping Frog" after success with frontier humor as a platform lecturer; that same summer of 1867 he traveled to Europe and the Holy Land for the *San Francisco Alta California.* In late 1868, he headed to New York, and in 1869 saw publication of the satirical *Innocents Abroad,* which soon sold ten-thousand copies. He was the most widely read American writer after 1869, and he joked that, "Everything I touch turns to gold."

He did seem to strike it rich, and in 1870 his marriage to an Elmira, New York, heiress included a mansion as a wedding gift from his father-in-law. In 1871, after a lecture trip to Europe, and failure at editing a newspaper in Buffalo, the little Clemens family built a spacious home in Hartford, Connecticut. There for the next twenty years at "Nook Farm," he wrote novels of his Southern heritage, believing his frontier past insulated him from the Gilded Age he despised but in which he was complicit by his ostentatious spending. During the 1890s, he lectured widely abroad, lived mostly in Europe, but filed for bankruptcy in 1894. With his finances restored by late 1900, he returned to the United States with enhanced resilience, until his wife died in 1904, a loss compounded by the sudden death of his favorite daughter when he was in London back in 1896. The books of his final decade reflected a brooding but still feisty Twain, in the *The Man That Corrupted Hadleyburg and Other Stories and Essays* (1900), *The Mysterious Stranger*, a posthumous novel, and *What Is Man?*, a somber document published anonymously in 1906, a year in which his divided psyche and increasing despair appeared in two other books, *Eve's Diary* and *"The $30,000 Bequest" and Other Stories*.

In his last period of undiminished talent but often inconsistent social criticism, he worked on his *Autobiography* and *The Damned Human Race*, as well as *Letters from the Earth*; his published writings attacked American imperialism, indicted the commercial motives of Christian Scientist Mary Baker Eddy, and questioned the true existence of Shakespeare. But at his death he was still the most popular writer in the nation, who left behind as many unpublished as published manuscripts.

His friend of forty years, William Dean Howells, eulogized him as "the most desouthernized Southerner" and "the Lincoln of our literature." In reality, Twain was more Southerner than Connecticut Yankee, and he never psychologically emancipated the slaves in his fiction. And only once in his early career did he document slavery as tragedy, with "A True Story: Repeated Word for Word as I Heard It"—from a slave's viewpoint—in the November 1874 *Atlantic Monthly* (edited by Howells). Yet a year earlier, in his first novel *The Gilded Age* (1873), written in collaboration with Charles Dudley Warner, slaves made cameo appearances as childlike stereotypes. Over the next two decades, the few black characters in his novels were all slaves or ex-slaves speaking dialect, usually for comic relief. The author best known for his humor often made blacks a butt of it. Not until slavery had ended did he obliquely attack it in *Adventures of Huckleberry Finn*, a book set in the antebellum period, but begun in the late 1870s and published in 1885. Nine years later came *The Tragedy of Puddn'head Wilson*, his most corrosive but contradictory condemnation of slavery. Those two novels are his only ones with slave heroes, namely Jim and Roxy, who are portrayed sympathetically. He distinguished between blacks and mulattos, but he allowed neither to speak as free-and-educated members of their race in his imagination.

"The Celebrated Jumping Frog" originated as a slave tale but was uncredited as such in his refashioned sketch published in 1865 as "Jim Smiley and His Jumping Frog," and in 1867 under its more famous title. The latter version had a white storyteller, Simon Wheeler, who resurfaced a decade later in Twain's uncompleted, posthumous novel *Simon Wheeler, Detective*—with an illiterate slave, Toby, as comic buffoon. He reintroduced from *The Gilded Age* former slaves turned into shiftless freedmen in the *The American Claimant* (1892). And in 1896 in *Tom Sawyer Abroad*, Jim of Huck Finn fame reemerged as a middle-aged black servant clown. An admirer of Joel Chandler Harris's stories, Twain had his own black caricatures and white paternalism in a reactionary era.

Whereas *Adventures of Huckleberry Finn* was being read by millions—yet censored and purged from some libraries—Twain's *Pudd'nhead Wilson* had less popular appeal. The complex thematic interconnections and characters of the novel, and its arc of what Twain called "farce to tragedy," disappointed some readers discomfited also by the reality of miscegenation. The tragic plot showed a sacrificial female-slave heroine, Roxy, whom Twain described "as white as anybody," as was her son. When her owner threatens to sell his slaves "down the river," Roxy interchanges the cradle of her slavemaster's white baby with her own "black" baby. In that reversal, the transposed white heir becomes a scorned slave, while Roxy's son, Tom, evolves into a despotic slaveowner who sells *her* down the river. In final vengeance, she discloses to him he is *"bawn a nigger en a slave"* and he turns against her, himself, and whites, murdering Judge Driscoll—the brother of Roxy's master—in attempted robbery. His guilt and identity are exposed through forensic fingerprinting in a court trial by a Yankee lawyer and detective, David Wilson—known as "Puddn'head" to local citizens—who in the full circle of master–slave decides Tom's fate is to be sold into servitude. The following excerpts are from chapters 2 and 3.

From *The Tragedy of Pudd'nhead Wilson* (1894)

. . . In front of Wilson's porch stood Roxy, with a local handmade baby wagon, in which sat her two charges—one at each end and facing each other. From

Roxy's manner of speech, a stranger would have expected her to be black, but she was not. Only one-sixteenth of her was black, and that sixteenth did not show. She was of majestic form and stature, her attitudes were imposing and statuesque, and her gestures and movements distinguished by a noble and stately grace. Her complexion was very fair, with the rosy glow of vigorous health in the cheeks, her face was full of character and expression, her eyes were brown and liquid, and she had a heavy suit of fine soft hair which was also brown, but the fact was not apparent because her head was bound about with a checkered handkerchief and the hair was concealed under it. Her face was shapely, intelligent, and comely—even beautiful. She had an easy, independent carriage—when she was among her own caste—and a high and "sassy" way, withal; but of course she was meek and humble enough where white people were.

To all intents and purposes Roxy was as white as anybody, but the one-sixteenth of her which was black outvoted the other fifteen parts and made her a Negro. She was a slave, and salable as such. Her child was thirty-one parts white, and he, too, was a slave, and by a fiction of law and custom a Negro. He had blue eyes and flaxen curls like his white comrade, but even the father of the white child was able to tell the children apart—little as he had commerce with them—by their clothes: for the white babe wore ruffled soft muslin and a coral necklace, while the other wore merely a coarse tow-linen shirt which barely reached to its knees, and no jewelry.

The white child's name was Thomas à Becket Driscoll, the other's name was Valet de Chambre: no surname—slaves hadn't the privilege. Roxana had heard that phrase somewhere, the fine sound of it had pleased her ear, and as she had supposed it was a name, she loaded it on to her darling. It soon got shortened to "Chambers," of course.

Wilson knew Roxy by sight, and when the duel of wit began to play out, he stepped outside to gather in a record or two. Jasper went to work energetically, at once, perceiving that his leisure was observed. Wilson inspected the children and asked:

"How old are they, Roxy?"

"Bofe de same age, sir—five months. Bawn de fust o' Feb'uary."

"They're handsome little chaps. One's just as handsome as the other, too."

A delighted smile exposed the girl's white teeth, and she said:

"Bless yo' soul, Misto Wilson, it's pow'ful nice o' you to say dat, 'ca'se one of 'em ain't on'y a nigger. Mighty prime little nigger, *I* al'ays says, but dat's 'ca'se it's mine, o' course."

"How do you tell them apart, Roxy, when they haven't any clothes on?"

Roxy laughed a laugh proportioned to her size, and said:

"Oh, *I* kin tell 'em 'part, Misto Wilson, but I bet Marse Percy couldn't, not to save his life."

Wilson chatted along for awhile, and presently got Roxy's fingerprints for his collection—right hand and left—on a couple of his glass strips; then labeled and dated them, and took the "records" of both children, and labeled and dated them also.

Two months later, on the third of September, he took this trio of finger marks again. He liked to have a "series," two or three "takings" at intervals during the period of childhood, these to be followed by others at intervals of several years.

The next day—that is to say, on the fourth of September—something occurred which profoundly impressed Roxana. Mr. Driscoll missed another small sum of money—which is a way of saying that this was not a new thing, but had happened before. In truth, it had happened three times before. Driscoll's patience was exhausted. He was a fairly humane man toward slaves and other animals; he was an exceedingly humane man toward the erring of his own race. Theft he could not abide, and plainly there was a thief in his house. Necessarily the thief must be one of his Negroes. Sharp measures must be taken. He called his servants before him. There were three of these, besides Roxy: a man, a woman, and a boy twelve years old. They were not related. Mr. Driscoll said:

"You have all been warned before. It has done no good. This time I will teach you a lesson. I will sell the thief. Which of you is the guilty one?"

They all shuddered at the threat, for here they had a good home, and a new one was likely to be a change for the worse. The denial was general. None had stolen anything—not money, anyway—a little sugar, or cake, or honey, or something like that, that "Marse Percy wouldn't mind or miss," but not money—never a cent of money. They were eloquent in their protestations, but Mr. Driscoll was not moved by them. He answered each in turn with a stern "Name the thief!"

The truth was, all were guilty but Roxana; she suspected that the others were guilty, but she did not know them to be so. She was horrified to think how near she had come to being guilty herself; she had been saved in the nick of time by a revival in the colored Methodist Church, a fortnight before, at which time and place she "got religion." The very next day after that gracious experience, while her change of style was fresh upon her and she was vain of her purified condition, her master left a couple of dollars lying unprotected on his desk, and she happened upon that temptation when she was polishing around with a dustrag. She looked at the money awhile with a steadily rising resentment, then she burst out with:

"Dad blame dat revival, I wisht it had 'a' be'n put off till tomorrow!"

Then she covered the tempter with a book, and another member of the kitchen cabinet got it. She made this sacrifice as a matter of religious etiquette; as a thing necessary just now, but by no means to be wrested into a precedent; no, a week or two would limber up her piety, then she would be rational again, and the next two dollars that got left out in the cold would find a comforter— and she could name the comforter.

Was she bad? Was she worse than the general run of her race? No. They had an unfair show in the battle of life, and they held it no sin to take military advantage of the enemy—in a small way; in a small way, but not in a large one. They would smouch provisions from the pantry whenever they got a chance; or a brass thimble, or a cake of wax, or an emery bag, or a paper of needles, or a silver spoon, or a dollar bill, or small articles of clothing, or any other property of light value; and so far were they from considering such reprisals sinful, that they would go to church and shout and pray the loudest and sincerest with their plunder in their pockets. A farm smokehouse had to be kept heavily pad- locked, for even the colored deacon himself could not resist a ham when Provi- dence showed him in a dream, or otherwise, where such a thing hung lonesome, and longed for someone to love. But with a hundred hanging before him, the deacon would not take two—that is, on the same night. On frosty nights the humane Negro prowler would warm the end of a plank and put it up under the cold claws of chickens roosting in a tree; a drowsy hen would step on to the comfortable board, softly clucking her gratitude, and the prowler would dump her into his bag, and later into his stomach, perfectly sure that in taking this trifle from the man who daily robbed him of an inestimable treasure—his lib- erty—he was not committing any sin that God would remember against him in the Last Great Day.

"Name the thief!"

For the fourth time Mr. Driscoll had said it, and always in the same hard tone. And now he added these words of awful import:

"I give you one minute." He took out his watch. "If at the end of that time, you have not confessed, I will not only sell all four of you, *but*—I will sell you DOWN THE RIVER!"

It was equivalent to condemning them to hell! No Missouri Negro doubted this. Roxy reeled in her tracks, and the color vanished out of her face; the others dropped to their knees as if they had been shot; tears gushed from their eyes, their supplicating hands went up, and three answers came in the one instant.

"I done it!"

"I done it!"

"I done it!"—have mercy, marster—Lord have mercy on us po' niggers!"

"Very good," said the master, putting up his watch, "I will sell you *here* though you don't deserve it. You ought to be sold down the river."

The culprits flung themselves prone, in an ecstasy of gratitude, and kissed his feet, declaring that they would never forget his goodness and never cease to pray for him as long as they lived. They were sincere, for like a god he had stretched forth his mighty hand and closed the gates of hell against them. He knew, himself, that he had done a noble and gracious thing, and was privately well pleased with his magnanimity; and that night he set the incident down in his diary, so that his son might read it in after years, and be thereby moved to deeds of gentleness and humanity himself.

3

> Whoever has lived long enough to find out what life is, knows how deep a debt of gratitude we owe to Adam, the first great benefactor of our race. He brought death into the world.
> —*Pudd'nhead Wilson's Calendar*

Percy Driscoll slept well the night he saved his house minions from going down the river, but no wink of sleep visited Roxy's eyes. A profound terror had taken possession of her. Her child could grow up and be sold down the river! The thought crazed her with horror. If she dozed and lost herself for a moment, the next moment she was on her feet flying to her child's cradle to see if it was still there. Then she would gather it to her heart and pour out her love upon it in a frenzy of kisses, moaning, crying, and saying, "Dey sha'n't, oh, dey *sha'n't!*'—yo' po' mammy will kill you fust!"

Once, when she was tucking it back in its cradle again, the other child nestled in its sleep and attracted her attention. She went and stood over it a long time communing with herself.

"What has my po' baby done, dat he couldn't have yo' luck? He hain't done noth'n'. God was good to you; why warn't he good to him? Dey can't sell *you* down de river. I hates yo' pappy; he hain't got no heart—for niggers, he hain't, anyways. I hates him, en I could kill him!" She paused awhile, thinking; then she burst into wild sobbings again, and turned away, saying, "Oh, I got to kill my chile, dey ain't no yuther way—killin' *him* wouldn't save de chile fum going' down de river. Oh, I got to do it, yo' po' mammy's got to kill you to save you, honey." She gathered her baby to her bosom now, and began to smother it with caresses. "Mammy's got to kill you—how *kin* I do it! But yo' mammy ain't gwine to desert you—no, no; *dah*, don't cry—she gwine *wid* you, she gwine to kill herself too. Come along, honey, come along wid mammy; we gwine to jump in de river, den de troubles o' dis worl' is all over—dey don't sell po' niggers down the river over *yonder*."

She started toward the door, crooning to the child and hushing it; midway she stopped, suddenly. She had caught sight of her new Sunday gown—a cheap curtain-calico thing, a conflagration of gaudy colors and fantastic figures. She surveyed it wistfully, longingly.

"Hain't ever wore it yet," she said, "en it's jist lovely." Then she nodded her head in response to a pleasant idea, and added, "No, I ain't gwine to be fished out, wid everybody lookin' at me, in dis mis'able ole linsey-woolsey."

She put down the child and made the change. She looked in the glass and was astonished at her beauty. She resolved to make her death toilet perfect. She took off her handkerchief turban and dressed her glossy wealth of hair "like white folks"; she added some odds and ends of rather lurid ribbon and a spray of atrocious artificial flowers; finally she threw over her shoulders a fluffy thing called a "cloud" in that day, which was of a blazing red complexion. Then she was ready for the tomb.

She gathered up her baby once more; but when her eye fell upon its miserably short little gray tow-linen shirt and noted the contrast between its pauper shabbiness and her own volcanic eruption of infernal splendors, her mother-heart was touched, and she was ashamed.

"No, dolling, mammy ain't gwine to treat you so. De angels is gwine to 'mire you jist as much as dey does yo' mammy. Ain't gwine to have 'em putt'n dey han's up 'fo' dey eyes en sayin' to David en Goliah en dem yuther prophets, 'Dat chile is dress' too indelicate fo' dis place.' "

By this time she had stripped off the shirt. Now she clothed the naked little creature in one of Thomas à Becket's snowy, long baby gowns, with its bright blue bows and dainty flummery of ruffles.

"Dah—now you's fixed." She propped the child in a chair and stood off to inspect it. Straightway her eyes began to widen with astonishment and admiration, and she clapped her hands and cried out, "Why, it do beat all! I *never* knowed you was so lovely. Marse Tommy ain't a bit puttier—not a single bit."

She stepped over and glanced at the other infant; she flung a glance back at her own; then one more at the heir of the house. Now a strange light dawned in her eyes, and in a moment she was lost in thought. She seemed in a trance; when she came out of it, she muttered, "When I 'uz a-washin' 'em in de tub, yistiddy, his own pappy asked me which of 'em was his'n."

She began to move about like one in a dream. She undressed Thomas à Becket, stripping him of everything, and put the tow-linen shirt on him. She put his coral necklace on her own child's neck. Then she placed the children side by side, and after earnest inspection she muttered:

"Now who would b'lieve clo'es could do de like o' dat? Dog my cats if it ain't all *I* kin do to tell t' other fum which, let alone his pappy."

She put her cub in Tommy's elegant cradle and said:

"You's young Marse *Tom* fum dis out, en I got to practice and git used to 'memberin' to call you dat, honey, or I's gwine to make a mistake sometime en git us bofe into trouble. Dah—now you lay still en don't fret no mo', Marse Tom. Oh, thank de good Lord in heaven, you's saved, you's saved! Dey ain't no man kin ever sell mammy's po' little honey down de river now!"

She put the heir of the house in her own child's unpainted pine cradle, and said, contemplating its slumbering form uneasily:

"I's sorry for you, honey; I's sorry, God knows I is—but what *kin* I do, what *could* I do? Yo' pappy would sell him to somebody, sometime, en den he'd go down de river, sho', en I couldn't, couldn't, *couldn't* stan' it."

She flung herself on her bed and began to think and toss, toss and think. By and by she sat suddenly upright, for a comforting thought had flown through her worried mind.

" 'Tain't no sin—*white* folks has done it! It ain't no sin; glory to goodness, it ain't no sin! *Dey's* done it—yes, en dey was de biggest quality in de whole bilin', too—*kings!*"

She began to muse; she was trying to gather out of her memory the dim particulars of some tale she had heard sometime or other. At last she said:

"Now I's got it; now I 'member. It was dat ole nigger preacher dat tole it, de time he come over here fum Illinois en preached in de nigger church. He said dey ain't nobody kin save his own self—can't do it by faith, can't do it by works, can't do it no way at all. Free grace is de *on'y* way, en dat don't come fum nobody but jis' de Lord; en *He* kin give it to anybody He please, saint or sinner—*He* don't kyer. He do jis' as He's a mineter. He s'lect out anybody dat suit Him, en put another one in his place, en make de fust one happy forever en leave t' other one to burn wid Satan. De preacher said it was jist like dey done in Englan' one time, long time ago. De queen she lef' her baby layin' aroun' one day, en went out callin'; en one o' de niggers roun'bout de place dat was 'mos' white, she come in en see de chile layin' aroun', en tuck en put her own chile's clo'es on de queen's chile, en put de queen's chile's clo'es on her own chile, en den lef' her own chile layin' aroun', en tuck en toted de queen's chile home to de nigger quarter, en nobody ever foun' it out, en her chile was de king bimeby, en sole de queen's chile down de river one time when dey had to settle up de estate. Dah, now—de preacher said it his own self, en it ain't no sin, 'ca'se white folks done it. *Dey* done it—yes, *dey* done it; en not on'y jis' common white folks nuther, but de biggest quality dey is in de whole bilin'. Oh, I's *so* glad I 'member 'bout dat!"

She got up lighthearted and happy, and went to the cradles, and spent what was left of the night "practicing." She would give her own child a light pat and say humbly, "Lay still, Marse Tom," then give the real Tom a pat and say with severity, "Lay *still*, Chambers! Does you want me to take somep'n' *to* you?"

As she progressed with her practice, she was surprised to see how steadily and surely the awe which had kept her tongue reverent and her manner humble toward her young master was transferring itself to her speech and manner toward the usurper, and how similarly handy she was becoming in transferring her motherly curtness of speech and peremptoriness of manner to the unlucky heir of the ancient house of Driscoll.

She took occasional rests from practicing, and absorbed herself in calculating her chances.

"Dey'll sell dese niggers today fo' stealin' de money, den dey'll buy some mo' dat don't know de chillen—so *dat's* all right. When I takes de chillen out to git de air, de minute I's roun' de corner I's gwine to gaum dey mouths all roun' wid jam, den dey can't *nobody* notice dey's changed. Yes, I gwine ter do dat till I's safe, if it's a year.

"Dey ain't but one man dat I's afeard of, en dat's dat Pudd'nhead Wilson. Dey calls him a pudd'nhead, en says he's a fool. My lan', dat man ain't no mo' fool den I is! He's de smartes' man in dis town, less'n it's Jedge Driscoll or maybe Pem Howard. Blame dat man, he worries me wid dem ornery glasses o' his'n; *I* b'lieve he's a witch. But nemmine, I's gwine to happen aroun' dah one o' dese days en let on dat I reckon he wants to print de chillen's fingers ag'in; en if *he* don't notice dey's changed, I bound dey ain't nobody gwine to notice it, en den I's safe, sho'. But I reckon I'll tote along a hoss-shoe to keep off de witch work."

The new Negroes gave Roxy no trouble, of course. The master gave her none, for one of his speculations was in jeopardy, and his mind was so occupied that he hardly saw the children when he looked at them, and all Roxy had to do was to get them both into a gale of laughter when he came about; then their faces were mainly cavities exposing gums, and he was gone again before the spasm passed and the little creatures resumed a human aspect.

Within a few days the fate of the speculation became so dubious that Mr. Percy went away with his brother, the judge, to see what could be done with it. It was a land speculation as usual, and it had gotten complicated with a lawsuit. The men were gone seven weeks. Before they got back, Roxy had paid her visit to Wilson, and was satisfied. Wilson took the fingerprints, labeled them with the names and with the date—October the first—put them carefully away, and continued his chat with Roxy, who seemed very anxious that he should admire the great advance in flesh and beauty which the babies had made since he took their fingerprints a month before. He complimented their improvement to her contentment; and as they were without any disguise of jam or other stain, she trembled all the while and was miserably frightened lest at any moment he—

But he didn't. He discovered nothing; and she went home jubilant, and dropped all concern about the matter permanently out of her mind. . . .

PAUL LAURENCE DUNBAR

(1872–1906)

In the 1890s' parade of comic and sentimental Negro iconography popularized by Mark Twain, Joel Chandler Harris, Thomas Nelson Page, and others less famous, came the creations of a young black writer, Paul Laurence Dunbar, whose literary imagination reinforced some stereotypical conceptions among whites in postbellum America. For reasons kindled as much by what he produced as who promoted him, his career blazed brightly at the end of the nineteenth century and smoldered within a decade. But admirers then and later tagged him the first "Negro poet laureate." His ascendancy from 1896 until his early death in 1906 paralleled the apogee of Booker T. Washington, but both would later come under scrutiny by black and white critics who found them equally ambiguous accommodationists—despite their defenders.

Dunbar wrote over five-hundred poems, many in traditional poetic forms, some experimental, a few in noble tribute to his race, but one-third preeminently in a stylized Negro dialect; he published four volumes of short stories heavy on nostalgia and apology for Old South plantation days; and four uneven novels in which Caucasian characters are the principal figures in all but one. These works plus librettos, articles, plays, and letters reveal a complex author too young and ingenuous in his swift climb to popularity and prosperity to recognize the decreasing probity of his prolific canon, or the increasing alcoholism he believed could "cure" the tuberculosis that killed him at age thirty-three. To navigate Dunbar is to witness the contradictions in the life and work of the *first* black American creative writer popularized by hype and fanfare, one who often compromised his artistry to please a white majority audience in an age of Jim Crow.

If "Jim Crow" in the 1890s was a political synonym for segregation and lynching, its cultural meaning had existed since 1830 in the blackface minstrelsy "Jim Crow" caricatures by white entertainer T. D. Rice,[1] whose comic

---

[1] Thomas Dartmouth Rice (1808–60) is often called the "inventor of American minstrelsy." His burlesque imitations became a sensation after his solo appearances at theaters in Cincinnati, Pittsburgh, Boston, New York, and Washington, DC, between 1828 and 1832, and an 1837 tour of

impersonations of Negroes began in road shows in the Ohio Valley and were performed by burned-cork imitators when Dunbar grew up in Dayton, where he was born seven years after the Civil War. Rice created a dialect lyric popularly called "Jump Jim Crow," patterned after a song-and-dance step he saw a male slave improvise in a Kentucky stable-yard, and it was familiar in its refrain to Dunbar's boyhood generation:

> *First on de heel tap, den on de toe,*
> *Wheel about, turn about, Do jis so,*
> *An' ebery time I wheel about*
> *I jump Jim Crow*

By the late 1890s and early 1900s, when black entertainers began the slow process of their own self-created minstrel mimicry on stage—while living as social outcasts offstage—Dunbar was among those who contributed some of the lyrics.

He was a multitalented Doppelgänger, a bard of double-consciousness who could compose as well in standard English as in dialect. A son of Kentucky ex-slaves, Dunbar attended predominantly white Dayton schools and published his earliest poems on nonracial themes in the *Dayton Herald*, the summer of 1888. Two years later, at age eighteen, he launched and edited a short-lived four-page weekly newspaper for black readers, the *Dayton Tattler*, printed with the help of two white classmates, Orville and Wilbur Wright—later famous aviators. He believed then and wrote later that gifted Negro individuals could exalt his race, and his sympathies were with them more than with the masses. But he owed the encouragement of his literary ambitions to his mother, a laundress, who reared him alone from age four, after she divorced his elderly, embittered father, who had escaped slavery in Kentucky via the Underground Railroad, returned to enlist for the Union in a black regiment, then settled in Dayton as a low-wage plasterer before his death in a veteran's home in 1885. Economic hardships of freedmen in the North became a Dunbar theme and, like Booker T. Washington, he prosetylized for blacks to remain in the South.

In a July 1895 letter to a white mentor, Toledo physician Henry A. Tobey, Dunbar expressed a wish "to interpret my own people through song and story and to prove to the many that, after all, we are more human than African." Tobey helped him finance printing of *Majors and Minors* (1895), Dunbar's

---

the British Isles. He multiplied "Jim Crow" stanzas in hundreds of performances, and his success led to the rise of minstrel troupes, the most popular form of American entertainment from 1835 to 1880.

second poetry volume, which included select poems from a first book, *Oak and Ivy*, printed at the poet's own expense in 1892. He had been encouraged to collect his verses following plaudits for his public reading at the 1892 Western Association of Writers in Dayton, which also brought a note of recognition from his literary idol, the popular Hoosier poet James Whitcomb Riley. When *Oak and Ivy* appeared, Dunbar was twenty, an 1891 graduate of Central High School, where he was the only Negro in his class, president of the literary society, and editor of the student paper. But his color closed Dayton office jobs to him, except as an elevator operator at four dollars a week. Without funds for college, or success in finding a job in Chicago—where he clerked briefly at the Columbian Exposition and read his poems for "Colored American Day"—he was running elevators and errands in Dayton when William Dean Howells reviewed *Majors and Minors* in *Harper's Weekly*, June 27, 1896. The date coincidentally was the poet's twenty-fourth birthday, and the lengthy review by Howells, as we have seen the l'éminence grise of American letters, was a turning point in Dunbar's career. The Howells piece, well-intentioned at the time, is by today's standards a vestige of how insular and racially segregated American literature was in 1896, provincial in its readership, and narrow in its criticism. Howells presented Dunbar as a black curio to a white audience, describing the poet's frontispiece portrait in language reminiscent of the critic's own novel, *An Imperative Duty*: "The face which confronted me when I opened the volume was the face of a young Negro, with the race traits strangely accented: the black skin, wooly hair, the thick out-rolling lips, and the mild, soft eyes of the pure African type." Howells dismissed the "literary English" poems Dunbar intended as "majors" in the front of his book of ninety-three verses, and targeted his "Humor and Dialect" works at the end.

But Dunbar bowed to Howells, who soon answered requests of the poet's white friends in Ohio to recommend a lecture-tour agent as well as a literary agent, who in turn engaged New York publisher Dodd, Mead and Company, which gave Dunbar a $400 advance for his third poetry volume, *Lyrics of Lowly Life*, comprising earlier poems and eleven new ones. Howells wrote the introduction, amplifying his *Harper's* review of Dunbar's dialect verses, stressing how "he reveals in these a finely ironical perception of the Negro's limitations." But he put critical blinders on to "We Wear the Mask," "Ode to Ethiopia," and "Frederick Douglass"—rare expressions of Dunbar's militancy and likewise unmatched until "The Haunted Oak" in 1900, on lynching. Dunbar's extant thank-you letters to Howells are deferential, without evidence to support a claim of an early biographer, Benjamin Brawley, that the poet on an 1897 lecture tour in England complained in a letter to a friend: "I see now very clearly that Mr. Howells has done me irrevocable harm in the dictum he laid down regarding my dialect verse. I am afraid it will even influence English criticism."

Despite his private disappointment over public preference for what some whites termed his "darky dialect," Dunbar churned it out on stages; in regional newspapers; and national magazines such as *Century, Saturday Evening Post, Ladies' Home Journal,* and others that had never published a black writer. His co-option to myth and minstrelsy dismayed his beautiful and dignified wife, Alice Moore, a New Orleans–born teacher and writer, who married him in March 1898 and left in 1902. But between late 1897 and 1902—due partly to her urging for him to redeem himself, and to restore his failing health in 1899—he lived at intervals in Colorado and Washington, DC, where before marriage he worked a year as a Library of Congress clerk; he also contributed a dozen serious articles on racial issues to various newspapers, including "Our New Madness" (September 15, 1898, the *Independent*) criticizing the ardor for industrial education at Booker T. Washington's Tuskegee. But in 1902, at Washington's request, Dunbar wrote "The Tuskegee Song" for the school's commencement.

Meanwhile, he satisfied public demand for dialect with reprints and new poetry collections: *Lyrics of the Hearthside* (1899), *Poems of Cabin and Field* (1899), *Candle-Lightin' Time* (1901), *Lyrics of Love and Laughter* (1903), *When Malindy Sings* (1903), *Li'l' Gal* (1904), *"Chris'mus Is a-Comin'"* and Other Poems (1905), *Howdy, Honey Howdy* (1905), *Lyrics of Sunshine and Shadow* (1905), *A Plantation Portrait* (1905), and *Joggin' Erlong* (1906). Simultaneously came short stories, many in the Plantation Tradition, collected in *Folks from Dixie* (1898), *"The Strength of Gideon" and Other Stories* (1900), *In Old Plantation Days* (1903), and *The Heart of Happy Hollow* (1904), plus lyrics set to music by black composer Will Marion Cook as well as four novels, the first and last serialized in *Lippincott's Monthly Magazine: The Uncalled* (1898), *The Love of Landry* (1900), *The Fanatics* (1901), and *The Sport of the Gods* (1902)—the final and only one with central black characters.

The fiction that follows is from his first collection of tales primarily on plantation themes, *Folks from Dixie.*

The Intervention of Peter (1898)

No one knows just what statement it was of Harrison Randolph's that Bob Lee doubted. The annals of these two Virginia families have not told us that. But these are the facts:—

It was at the home of the Fairfaxes that a few of the sons of the Old Dominion were giving a dinner,—not to celebrate anything in particular, but the joyousness of their own souls,—and a brave dinner it was. The courses had come and gone, and over their cigars they had waxed more than merry. In those days men drank deep, and these men were young, full of the warm blood of the South and the joy of living. What wonder then that the liquor that had been mellowing in the Fairfax cellars since the boyhood of their revolutionary ancestor should have its effect upon them?

It is true that it was only a slight thing which Bob Lee affected to disbelieve, and that his tone was jocosely bantering rather than impertinent. But sometimes Virginia heads are not less hot than Virginia hearts. The two young men belonged to families that had intermarried. They rode together. They hunted together, and were friends as far as two men could be who had read the message of love in the dark eyes of the same woman. So perhaps there was some thought of the long-contested hand of Miss Sallie Ford in Harrison Randolph's mind when he chose to believe that his honor had been assailed.

His dignity was admirable. There was no scene to speak of. It was all very genteel.

"Mr. Lee," he said, "had chosen to doubt his word, which to a gentleman was the final insult. But he felt sure that Mr. Lee would not refuse to accord him a gentleman's satisfaction." And the other's face had waxed warm and red and his voice cold as he replied: "I shall be most happy to give you the satisfaction you demand."

Here friends interposed and attempted to pacify the two. But without avail. The wine of the Fairfaxes has a valiant quality in it, and these two who had drunken of it could not be peaceably reconciled.

Each of the young gentlemen nodded to a friend and rose to depart. The joyous dinner-party bade fair to end with much more serious business.

"You shall hear from me very shortly," said Randolph, as he strode to the door.

"I shall await your pleasure with impatience, sir, and give you such a reply as even you cannot disdain."

It was all rather high-flown, but youth is dramatic and plays to the gallery of its own eyes and ears. But to one pair of ears there was no ring of anything but tragedy in the grandiloquent sentences. Peter, the personal attendant of Harrison Randolph, stood at the door as his master passed out, and went on before him to hold his stirrup. The young master and his friend and cousin, Dale, started off briskly and in silence, while Pete, with wide eyes and disturbed face, followed on behind. Just as they were turning into the avenue of elms that led to their own house, Randolph wheeled his horse and came riding back to his servant.

"Pete," said he, sternly, "what do you know?"

"Nuffin', Mas' Ha'ison, nuffin' 't all. I do' know nuffin'."

"I don't believe you." The young master's eyes were shining through the dusk. "You're always slipping around spying on me."

"Now dah you goes, Mas' Randolph. I ain't done a t'ing, and you got to 'mence pickin' on me—"

"I just want you to remember that my business is mine."

"Well, I knows dat."

"And if you do know anything, it will be well for you to begin forgetting right now." They were at the door now and in the act of dismounting. "Take Bess around and see her attended to. Leave Dale's horse here, and—I won't want you any more tonight."

"Now how does you an' Mas' Dale 'spect dat you gwine to wait on yo'se'ves tonight?"

"I shall not want you again tonight, I tell you."

Pete turned away with an injured expression on his dark face. "Bess," he said to the spirited black mare as he led her toward the stables, "you jes' bettah t'ank yo' Makah dat you ain't no human-bein', 'ca'se human-bein's is cur'ous articles. Now you's a hoss, ain't you? An' dey say you ain't got no soul, but you got sense, Bess, you got sense. You got blood an' fiah an' breedin' in you too, ain't you? Co'se you has. But you knows how to answah de rein. You's a high steppah, too: but you don' go to work an' try to brek yo' naik de fus' chanst you git. Bess, I 'spect you 'ca'se you got jedgment, an' you don' have to have a black man runnin' 'roun aftah you all de time plannin' his haid off jes' to keep you out o' trouble. Some folks dat's human-bein's does. Yet an' still, Bess, you ain't nuffin' but a dumb beas', so dey says. Now, what I gwine to do? Co'se dey wants to fight. But whah an' when an' how I gwine to stop hit? Do' want me to wait on him tonight, huh! No, dey want to mek dey plans an' do' want me 'roun' to hyeah, dat's what's de mattah. Well, I lay I 'll hyeah somep'n' anyhow."

Peter hurried through his work and took himself up to the big house and straight to his master's room. He heard voices within, but though he took many liberties with his owner, eavesdropping was not one of them. It proved too dangerous. So, though "he kinder lingered on the mat, some doubtful of the sekle," it was not for long, and he unceremoniously pushed the door open and walked in. With a great show of haste, he made for his master's wardrobe and began busily searching among the articles therein. Harrison Randolph and his cousin were in the room, and their conversation, which had been animated, suddenly ceased when Peter entered.

"I thought I told you I did n't want you any more tonight."

"I's a-lookin' fu' dem striped pants o' yo'n. I want to tek 'em out an' bresh 'em: dey's p'intly a livin' sight."

"You get out o' here."

"But, Mas' Ha'ison, now—now—look—a—hyeah—"

"Get out, I tell you—"

Pete shuffled from the room, mumbling as he went: "Dah now, dah now! driv' out lak a dog! How's I gwine to fin' out anyt'ing dis away? It do 'pear lak Mas' Ha'ison do try to gi'e me all de trouble he know how. Now he plannin' an' projickin' wif dat cousin Dale, an' one jes' ez scattah-brained ez de othah. Well, I 'low I got to beat dey time somehow er ruther."

He was still lingering hopeless and worried about the house when he saw young Dale Randolph come out, mount his horse and ride away. After a while his young master also came out and walked up and down in the soft evening air. The rest of the family were seated about on the broad piazza.

"I wonder what is the matter with Harrison tonight, said the young man's father, "he seems so preoccupied."

"Thinking of Sallie Ford, I reckon," some one replied; and the remark passed with a laugh. Pete was near enough to catch this, but he did not stop to set them right in their conjectures. He slipped into the house as noiselessly as possible.

It was less than two hours after this when Dale Randolph returned and went immediately to his cousin's room, where Harrison followed him.

"Well?" said the latter, as soon as the door closed behind them.

"It's all arranged, and he's anxious to hurry it through for fear some one may interfere. Pistols, and tomorrow morning at daybreak."

"And the place?"

"The little stretch of woods that borders Ford's Creek. I say, Harrison, it isn't too late to stop this thing yet. It's a shame for you two fellows to fight. You're both too decent to be killed for a while yet."

"He insulted me."

"Without intention, every one believes."

"Then let him apologize."

"As well ask the devil to take Communion."

"We'll fight then."

"All right. If you must fight, you must. But you'd better get to bed; for you'll need a strong arm and a steady hand tomorrow."

If a momentary paleness struck into the young fellow's face, it was for a moment only, and he set his teeth hard before he spoke.

"I am going to write a couple of letters," he said, "then I shall lie down for an hour or so. Shall we go down and drink a steadier?"

"One won't hurt, of course."

"And, by the way, Dale, if I—if it happens to be me tomorrow, you take Pete—he's a good fellow."

The cousins clasped hands in silence and passed out. As the door closed behind them, a dusty form rolled out from under the bed, and the disreputable, eavesdropping, backsliding Pete stood up and rubbed a sleeve across his eyes.

"It ain't me dat's gwine to be give to nobody else. I hates to do it, but dey ain't no othah way. Mas' Ha'ison cain't be spaihed." He glided out mysteriously, some plan of salvation working in his black head.

Just before daybreak next morning, three stealthy figures crept out and made their way toward Ford's Creek. One skulked behind the other two, dogging their steps and taking advantage of the darkness to keep very near to them. At the grim trysting place they halted and were soon joined by other stealthy figures, and together they sat down to wait for the daylight. The seconds conferred for a few minutes. The ground was paced off, and a few low-pitched orders prepared the young men for business.

"I will count three, gentlemen," said Lieutenant Custis. "At three, you are to fire."

At last daylight came, gray and timid at first, and then red and bold as the sun came clearly up. The pistols were examined and the men placed face to face.

"Are you ready, gentlemen?"

But evidently Harrison Randolph was not. He was paying no attention to the seconds. His eyes were fixed on an object behind his opponent's back. His attitude relaxed and his mouth began twitching. Then he burst into a peal of laughter.

"Pete," he roared, "drop that and come out from there!" and away he went into another convulsion of mirth. The others turned just in time to see Pete cease his frantic grimaces of secrecy at his master, and sheepishly lower an ancient fowling piece which he had had leveled at Bob Lee.

"What were you going to do with that gun level at me?" asked Lee, his own face twitching.

"I was gwine to fiah jes' befo' dey said free. I wa'n't gwine to kill you, Mas' Bob. I was on'y gwine to lame you."

Another peal of laughter from the whole crowd followed this condescending statement.

"You unconscionable scoundrel, you! If I was your master, I'd give you a hundred lashes."

"Pete," said his master, "don't you know that it is dishonorable to shoot a man from behind? You see you have n't in you the making of a gentleman."

"I do' know nuffin' 'bout mekin' a gent'man, but I does know how to save one dat's already made."

The prime object of the meeting had been entirely forgotten. They gathered around Pete and examined the weapon.

"Gentlemen," said Randolph, "we have been saved by a miracle. This old gun, as well as I can remember and count, has been loaded for the past twenty-five years, and if Pete had tried to fire it, it would have torn up all of this part of the county." Then the eyes of the two combatants met. There was something irresistibly funny in the whole situation, and they found themselves roaring again. Then, with one impulse, they shook hands without a word.

And Pete led the way home, the willing butt of a volume of good-nature abuse.

SUTTON GRIGGS

(1872–1930)

A contemporary of Paul Laurence Dunbar, Sutton Griggs was a more militant and unshackled writer, who introduced the term "New Negro" in his first
novel.[1] Unknown to the white audience that celebrated Dunbar, Griggs was
identifiable as a voice of self-determination to a generation of black readers
who saw him practice what he preached. He established his own publishing
company and distributed his novels and pamphlets at his expense, and he exposed yet tried to resolve class contradictions and tensions within his race. He
emerged as an author a decade before the NAACP and Urban League arose,
and after black-political influence had waned with post–Reconstruction. To
a powerless, oppressed people in transition, he urged self-reliance, economic
independence, and an end to servility and docility inherited from slavery.

His roots were in Texas, where he was born in 1872 in Chatfield, and educated in the schools of Dallas, and at Bishop College in Marshall. Griggs was
the son of a Southern black Baptist preacher, Reverend Allen Griggs, who instilled in his son a faith in the black church to lead their race. Griggs began his
own career in the ministry after completing academic training at Richmond
Theological Seminary in Virginia, and he soon became a progenitor of the
activist black Baptist preachers to follow him later in the twentieth century.
His pastorate began in Berkey, Virginia, and continued for over thirty years in
Tennessee, before he returned to work in his native state shortly before he died.

During his years as pastor of the First Baptist Church in Nashville, Tennessee, he turned to writing novels to redress the political and social grievances
inappropriate to Sunday sermons. He produced five novels, in which almost all
the major characters are of African descent: *Imperium in Imperio, Overshadowed*
(1901), *The Unfettered* (1902), *The Hindered Hand* (1905), and *Pointing the
Way* (1908)—the last four published by his Orion Publishing Company. More

---

[1] Griggs was the first Afro-American writer to introduce the term *New Negro*, which appears in
his 1899 novel *Imperium in Imperio*. The term was subsequently used by others in other contexts in
early twentieth-century book titles, including *New Negro for a New Century* (1901) [see entry on
Fannie Barrier Williams, above, pages 346–57.]; *The New Negro* (1916), a collection of essays by
William Pickens; and *The New Negro* (1925), an anthology edited by Alain Locke.

dedicated to serving his flock than in mastering techniques of fiction, Griggs wrote unstructured novels with contrived plots and subplots, implausible time lines, clichéd descriptions, and undeveloped characters. He did not contribute to the art of the novel, but he was ahead of his time in inventing situations previously unseen in black American fiction—and unimagined again until decades later. He likewise created some of the first independent, educated Southern black characters in literature, though his older contemporary Charles Chesnutt[2] excelled him in literary craftmanship and style, with more realistic portraits of the descendants of miscegenation. But Griggs was a visionary, a purveyor of bold ideas, a writer without literary patronage, a self-made novelist, who knew that most white publishers "might hesitate to father books not in keeping with the prevailing sentiment of Southern white people." He offered that quote through his fictional Negro preacher, Ensal Elwood, in early editions of *The Hindered Hand*, but deleted it in subsequent printings (along with a lengthy polemic on racist author Thomas Dixon). His interest in ideology over aesthetics caused him to concentrate on nonfiction after 1910 to further his ideas of race progress and solidarity.

Griggs's outlook became more conciliatory during the last decade of his life, and he was criticized by some colleagues as being too willing to cooperate with whites, yet dubbed by others a Negro nationalist. Both his fiction and nonfiction demonstrate a conflict between conservatives and radicals, a dissension between mixed-bloods and full-bloods, and his own vacillation toward the goal of interracial harmony. He rejected an exodus to Africa, unlike some Afro-American clergy of his generation, such as Bishop Henry M. Turner, who argued, "Africa is our home, and is the one place that offers us manhood and freedom."[3] Despite Griggs's own chagrin with American injustice, he was ultimately the reluctant American patriot. His veiled American allegiance is seen in early and late writings, notably in an undated tract, *Building Our Own: A Plea for a Parallel Civilization*, which he printed after moving to Memphis, where by 1920 he pastored the Tabernacle Baptist Church and founded The Nehemiah Brotherhood, a black self-help organization. In *Building Our Own*, he noted:

> Let it be clearly understood that the civilization for which we plead is not to be an alien one, but American throughout, for we are Americans.

---

[2] See the entry on Chesnutt in this volume, pages 393–410, below.

[3] Henry MacNeal Turner (1834–1915) pastor, chaplain, orator, Freedom's Bureau appointee, Georgia legislator; A.M.E. bishop; president of Morris Brown College; colonization advocate; author. The above quote is from his "The Negro Has Not Sense Enough," published in *Voice of Missions* journal, July 1, 1900, following his four trips to Africa between 1891 and 1898.

Nor is it planned that our civilization shall be antagonistic to that of whites. It is to serve, rather as a supplement, rounding out the American ideal as one of equal opportunity to all.

One may compare the philosophy of *Building Our Own* with the opinions of Belmont Piedmont in *Imperium in Imperio,* and its theme of the political struggle between race separatism and assimilationism. In the novel—an excerpt of which follows—the "Imperium" is a secret black "nation within a nation," functioning as an underground paramilitary cadre: its paired protagonists are rivals since childhood, and in the checkerboard-color game of Griggs his character Bernard Belgrade is mulatto, and Belton Piedmont, black; both are college-educated but thwarted by racism in their respective lives. Bernard, the "Imperium's" revolutionary president, seeks a declaration of war and immediate seizure of Texas for a separate, autonomous state. Belton, the more moderate cohort, who introduced Bernard to the secret organization, offers a less radical proposal to "spend four years in endeavors" before emigrating to Texas. He rejects Bernard's plan as treasonous and resigns when it is accepted, knowing that his own defection, according to "Imperium" law, means execution by firing squad. After his death, one of his executioners turns traitor to inform the federal government of the existence of the "Imperium"—thereby destroying it. The extract is from Belton Piedmont's ideas and his mediation proposal, in chapter 18 of the novel.

From *Imperium in Imperio* (1899)

. . . "Now, hear my solution of the race problem. The Anglo-Saxon does not yet know that we have caught the fire of liberty. He does not yet know that we have learned what a glorious thing it is to die for a principle, and especially when that principle is liberty. He does not yet know how the genius of his institutions has taken hold of our very souls. In the days of our enslavement we did not seem to him to be much disturbed about physical freedom. During the whole period of our enslavement we made only two slight insurrections.

"When at last the war came to set us free we stayed in the field and fed the men who were reddening the soil with their blood in a deadly struggle to keep us in bondage forever. We remained at home and defended the helpless wives and children of men, who if they had been at home would have counted it no crime to have ignored all our family ties and scattered husbands and wives, mothers and children as ruthlessly as the autumn winds do the falling leaves.

"The Anglo-Saxon has seen the eyes of the Negro following the American eagle in its glorious flight. The eagle has alighted on some mountaintop and the poor Negro has been seen climbing up the rugged mountainside, eager to caress the eagle. When he has attempted to do this, the eagle has clawed at his eyes and dug his beak into his heart and has flown away in disdain; and yet, so majestic was its flight that the Negro, with tears in his eyes, and blood dripping from his heart has smiled and shouted: 'God save the eagle.'

"These things have caused us to be misunderstood. We know that our patient submission in slavery was due to our consciousness of weakness; we know that our silence and inaction during the Civil War was due to a belief that God was speaking for us and fighting our battle; we know that our devotion to the flag will not survive one moment after our hope is dead; but we must not be content with knowing these things ourselves. We must change the conception which the Anglo-Saxon has formed of our character. We should let him know that patience has a limit; that strength brings confidence; that faith in God will demand the exercise of our own right arm; that hope and despair are each equipped with swords, the latter more dreadful than the former. Before we make a forward move, let us pull the veil from before the eyes of the Anglo-Saxon that he may see the New Negro standing before him humbly, but firmly demanding every right granted him by his maker and wrested from him by man.

"If, however, the revelation of our character and the full knowledge of our determined attitude does not procure our rights, my proposition, which I am about to submit, will still offer a solution.

Resolutions

"1. Be it *Resolved:* That we no longer conceal from the Anglo-Saxon the fact that the Imperium exists, so that he may see that the love of liberty in our bosoms is strong enough to draw us together into this compact government. He will also see that each individual Negro does not stand by himself, but is a link in a great chain that must not be broken with impunity.

"2. *Resolved:* That we earnestly strive to convince the Anglo-Saxon that we are now thoroughly wedded to the doctrine of Patrick Henry: 'Give me liberty or give me death.' Let us teach the Anglo-Saxon that we have arrived at the stage of development as a people, where we prefer to die in honor rather than live in disgrace.

"3. *Resolved:* That we spend four years in endeavors to impress the Anglo-Saxon that he has a New Negro on his hands and must surrender what belongs to him. In case we fail by these means to secure our rights and privileges we shall all, at once, abandon our several homes in the various other states and emigrate in a body to the state of Texas, broad in domain, rich in soil and salubrious in climate. Having an unquestioned majority of votes we shall secure possession of the state government.

"4. *Resolved:* That when once lawfully in control of that great state we shall, every man, die in his shoes before we shall allow vicious frauds or unlawful force to pursue us there and rob us of our acknowledged right.

"5. *Resolved:* That we sojourn in the state of Texas, working out our destiny as a separate and distinct race in the United States of America.

"Such is the proposition which I present. It is primarily pacific: yet it is firm and unyielding. It courts a peaceable adjustment, yet it does not shirk war, if war is forced.

"But in concluding, let me emphasize that my aim, my hope, my labors, my fervent prayer to God is for a peaceable adjustment of all our differences upon the high plane of the equality of man. Our beloved President, in his message to this Congress, made a serious mistake when he stated that there were only two weapons to be used in accomplishing revolutions. He named the sword (and spear) and ballot. There is a weapon mightier than either of these. I speak of the pen. If denied the use of the ballot let us devote our attention to that mightier weapon, the pen.

"Other races which have obtained their freedom erect monuments over bloody spots where they slew their fellowmen. May God favor us to obtain our freedom without having to dot our land with these relics of barbaric ages.

"The Negro is the latest comer upon the scene of modern civilization. It would be the crowning glory of even this marvelous age; it would be the grandest contribution ever made to the cause of human civilization; it would be a worthy theme for the songs of the Holy Angels, if every Negro, away from the land of his nativity, can by means of the pen, force an acknowledgment of equality from the proud lips of the fierce, all-conquering Anglo-Saxon, thus eclipsing the record of all other races of men, who without exception have had to wade through blood to achieve their freedom. . . .

CAROLINE HOLLINGSWORTH PEMBERTON

(186?–1927)

Caroline H. Pemberton is perhaps the most invisible white author in American letters. Absent from every printed biographical dictionary, encyclopedia,[1] and bibliography on women in the English-speaking world, the available details of her life are few, but what is on record points to probable causes of her literary obscurity, despite an unusual career.

Born in Philadelphia to an aristocratic family, she spent part of her professional life and personal fortune to advance equal opportunities for blacks and to improve foster care for underprivileged white children—concerns to which she devoted most of her published writings. Her name is unassociated with feminism, in an era when many women concentrated their efforts on attaining female suffrage. From the mid–1890s through the early years of the twentieth century her public activities were devoted to a crusade to help the economically disadvantaged; she was briefly an unremitting voice against the second-class citizenship of blacks, North and South—apart from any national or local organized movement. A well-bred white American woman who took that step alone in a segregated society in her era risked censure from her own race. The independent role Pemberton chose differed from upper-class female social reformers like Jane Addams, who in 1889 founded Hull House for foreign immigrants in the slums of Chicago. Pemberton founded no organization, although she generously financed the Children's Aid Society of Pennsylvania of which she was volunteer superintendent and spokesperson in the mid-1890s.

But her main instrument was her pen, and she received brief attention for her first novel, *Your Little Brother James* (1896), about a white boy reared as a thief by a prostitute mother in an urban slum and saved by foster parents and religious conversion. Her belief in the importance of environment over heredity was echoed in her magazine articles and a short story, "The Putting Away of the McPhersons." Her second novel, *Stephen the Black* (1899), racial in content, went unreviewed by critics, ignored by the public, and all but forgotten

---

[1] This biographical entry on Caroline Pemberton also appears in *The Continuum Encyclopedia of American Literature*, Steven R. Serafin, general editor, Alfred Bendixen, associate editor, pages 877–78, published by Continuum International, 1999. Reprinted by permission of Faith Berry.

until 1972 when it was reprinted by Books for Library Press (with no information about her).

Stephen the Black, with its nonstereotypical black characters, was uncharacteristic of any race fiction published by a white American author in 1899. For most white readers, it was undoubtedly unrealistic, too sympathetic, and its writer too indignant. That it received no critical attention can be attributed not to its stylistic and structural defects (which were fewer than in her first novel reviewed by the *New York Times*) but because the text defied racial boundaries, exposed and satirized the hypocrisy and race paternalism of Northern white philanthropists, attacked the venal sharecropper system that replaced slavery, and assailed the murder by extremists of a black woman wed to a wealthy white man in the South. In an article in the January 1900 issue of *Arena* magazine, "The Barbarism of Civilization," Pemberton impugned lynching, scorned the illogic of illegal interracial marriage, urged literacy for the black-and-white masses, and an end to race discrimination in skilled trades. She went further in the early 1900s by becoming an active socialist. However, when she found some socialists not immune from racism, she broke ranks and dissented in print.[2]

Her progressive political views were far to the left of her Quaker background. In her old-line family of merchants and scholars prominent in Philadelphia from the days of William Penn, the most famous relative was a West Point–educated uncle who joined the Confederacy: John Clifford Pemberton, the defender of Vicksburg, until Grant forced his unconditional surrender. At Civil War's end, her uncle settled with his wife and children on a farm in Warrenton, Virginia, where a young Caroline first visited the South before the ex-general relocated to Philadelphia in 1876. Her father was John's younger brother, Henry, a Unionist, who later made his name as author of *The Path of Evolution through Ancient Thought and Modern Science* (1902), and as a member of the American Philosophical Society, the Academy of Natural Sciences, and the Historical Society of Pennsylvania. Her mother, who named her only daughter after herself, was born in London, where she died in 1883 while traveling with Caroline and an elder son, Harry. Mrs. Pemberton's last will and testament made Caroline sole heir to a fortune valued at nearly one-million dollars—in income and property throughout England and the United States. The legal will was contested for more than a year by Caroline's two older brothers, both

---

[2] Historian Philip S. Foner is the pioneer scholar of her socialist activities. See his "Caroline Hollingsworth Pemberton: Philadelphia Socialist Champion of Black Equality," *Pennsylvania History*, July 1976, pages 227–51, written as part of his *The Black Experience in American Socialism*. Other interpretations and facts in this entry are based on primary and secondary research by the editor–narrator.

physicians, who ultimately lost to her in a New Jersey court. The *New York Times* reported her legal victory with a poignant sidelight of her personal life that is still veiled in mystery, even if it reads like a sketch of a Henry James novel:

> . . . The lady who wins this great legal battle has a romantic history. While traveling with her mother in Europe, Caroline, then a miss of about 18, fell in love with a young Jewish gentleman who was a student at one of the Parisian academies. A clandestine marriage was the result. Later, it is said through the influence of the young wife's family, the husband of Caroline left for parts unknown. A child was afterward born to the young wife, but when she—the mother—regained her health the child was missing. The young mother was told that it had died immediately after birth. After the death of her mother, Caroline, who still kept her maiden name, found herself a wealthy woman. Visiting Europe, the lady with her wealth, used every effort to find her husband and child, both of whom she believed to be alive, but without success.[3]

The final decades of her career are unknown, and her private life concealed by a family reluctant to reopen it. Ahead of her time, she left various pieces in newspapers, black-church journals, and now defunct magazines like *Lend a Hand*, and other works yet to be discovered.[4] Revived here is a portion of *Stephen the Black*, featuring protagonist Stephen Wells, a Tuskegee graduate determined to help end Southern poverty and peonage by raising money to build his own school, a venture impeded by white Southern violence and Northern indifference. The excerpt is from chapter 19.

From *Stephen the Black* (1899)

. . . Although Stephen was a good penman, an accurate accountant and a clever carpenter, he was too well acquainted with the peculiar form of race prejudice in the North to waste time seeking employment in any of these lines. Through

---

[3] The *New York Times*, "Romantic Incident in the Life of Mrs. Caroline H. Pemberton," July 21, 1884: 1.

[4] It is undocumented whether she is the same Caroline Pemberton who edited *Queen Elizabeth's Englishings*, published in London in 1899, with no background data about the editor.

the efforts of a friend, he secured a position as waiter in a large summer hotel situated at a fashionable seaside resort, and as it was now open and guests were pouring in plentifully, his services began without delay.

Stephen had never "waited" before in a professional sense, but this humble waiting on individuals instead of on time and opportunity seemed to him only a more acute stage of his chronic condition.

Some of his comrades were wild young blacks who shifted from city to city in winter and from mountain to seashore in summer. The habits of these individuals were extravagant; but others were sedate young fellows intent on making hay while their brief summer sun shone. All of them, however, were good-natured, and they gave Stephen invaluable points in the science of remembering orders, serving dishes, carrying heavy trays, and bowing with exquisite grace. Some of the men were graduates of training schools established for the industrial development of the race. They had become skilled craftsmen and were striking examples of the satirical benevolence of the North which bestows the handsome accomplishment of a trade on a black, and then commands him to starve or steal rather than live by it. That these individuals had succeeded in prolonging their existence without either starving or stealing was certainly a proof of their ingenuity. We need not lose self-esteem by giving them credit for ingenuity.

The headwaiter was a graduate of Harvard and had been selected with great care, not because of his Greek and Hebrew accomplishments (of which the proprietor indeed knew nothing) but because his honesty was unquestioned, his habits beyond reproach, and his command of men, napkins and china equal to that of a great general over an army. His name was Henry Howards; he was a coal black negro of good height and heavy build; his expression was thoughtful and his smile pleasing. Stephen looked up to him as a man of profound learning and was delighted when Howards condescended to notice him, and invited him more than once to spend an evening in his room.

Stephen served at a table monopolized by a wealthy Boston family by the name of Ormsby; he understood vaguely that they were great people in the social world, and he heard them described also as philanthropists. The term made him quake in his low shoes, for he still believed that the future of his race lay in the hands of this class.

Accordingly he ran his legs off cheerfully to obtain for the Ormsbys the hottest rolls and the choicest lamb chops, and in every way presented himself to their languid perceptions as a being whose head had grown to one side in an anxious stoop to receive their indistinct commands. Such a beneficent adaptation of means to an end may possibly have required a special act of creation—of which the Ormsbys doubtless believed they were deemed not unworthy.

In the evening the waiters sat together in the kitchen and displayed their social graces in various ways. They were quite as merry notwithstanding their hard work, as the guests in the hotel parlor; in fact, I do not know that they were not merrier for they had such good stories to tell of the number of dishes ordered by the great ones of the earth, the amount they devoured, the absurdity of their complaints, and the gossip that was repeated at their tables.

As the men were excellent singers, Howards one day suggested that they should give a concert for the benefit of Stephen's school.

The day on which the performance was to be given, every waiter laid an assortment of tickets and programs on the table before the guests had assembled. During the dinner Stephen's hopes ran high for he heard enough to know that the programs were read aloud amid laughter and comment. He brought on the dessert with a beating heart and hastened after the coffee. On his return he found words to make a short plea in behalf of his school.

Mrs. Ormsby drank her coffee and addressing the coffeepot, observed that she had once been a great friend of the negro but had now come to the conclusion that a great deal of money had been thrown away on educating him above his position. The race had become shiftless and good-for-nothing. The colored people needed to be made to work. Freedom had done them no good.

Stephen fixed his grey eyes haughtily upon her. He answered in utter defiance of every precedent in his experience as a menial:

"My people have never eaten bread that they've not earned,—they've paid double the price for every mouthful that the white man has paid!"

The great lady stared, rose majestically from her seat and swept out of the room. He learned later from one of his comrades who had been summoned to the parlor on an errand, that she expressed her indignation at great length to sympathetic circles in the parlor, and declared it to be her choice henceforth to be surrounded and served by members of her own race. Howards reproved him severely for his folly.

"You might as well invite an iceberg to roll over you, and expect to melt it with your fiery heart. Keep out of the way of icebergs! All humanity flees from them—and are *you* going to block their progress?"

The upshot of it was that nearly all the guests with the exception of the nurses and children stayed away from the concert. The receipts amounted to next to nothing, and Stephen went to bed that night with his hopes crushed. To add to his depression, the evening papers told a terrible tale of massacre in one of the Southern states—the victims being as usual, accused, untried, defenseless blacks.

He hugged his pillow with angry eyes, and tossed in sorrow and despair many hours. What was to become of his school if money could not be raised for it in the North,—ay,—what was to become of his race if the whole nation turned against it with the cold scorn of Mrs. Ormsby and her friends?

At last he fell asleep and dreamed that he was clinging to the steep, rocky side of a mountain; his hands clutched rootless shrubs and saplings, his feet were planted in loose gravel. Vainly he sought a path upward. . . .

GEORGE HENRY WHITE

(1852–1918)

The end of the nineteenth century coincided with a temporary phaseout of Afro-Americans elected to the United States Congress. Of the total twenty-two black Congressmen who took office between February 1870 and March 1901,[1] the last member of the post–Reconstruction era was George White, chosen by voters of North Carolina in 1896 and 1898. He sought no third term in his district, for by early 1900 white supremacy had inundated the state press, including the influential *Raleigh News and Observer*, which editorialized without apology or temerity, "It is bad enough that North Carolina should have the only nigger Congressman."

The last former slave in the U.S. House of Representatives, White was a political beneficiary of the Thirteenth, Fourteenth, and Fifteenth Amendments passed between 1865 and 1870 by a radical Republican Congress. It also passed four Reconstruction bills and two Civil Rights Acts to offset "Black Codes" triggered by Southern state legislators of the Old Order. Conservative historians would later interpret Congressional Reconstruction as an era that yielded "Negro rule," "carpetbaggers," "scalawags," and "tragedy" for the South—an interpretation that resounded nationally in many American textbooks and classrooms until the mid-twentieth century. But to George White, born in 1852 of Native Indian, African, and Irish ancestry in rural North Carolina, radical Reconstruction offered black men legal rights on an equal basis with white citizens. But he saw those new opportunities collapse, all too soon.

White attended local public schools after emancipation and worked on his family's farm, saving enough to finance a four-year college education at Howard University. Graduating with a liberal arts degree in 1877, he returned to North Carolina and worked as a school teacher and principal in the state's former capital, New Bern. After studying law there and in Raleigh part-time under a superior-court judge for two years, he passed the bar examination and opened

---

[1] Of those twenty-two black Congressmen, all were elected from the South; two served in the U.S. Senate (both from Mississippi) and twenty in the House of Representatives: eight from South Carolina, four from North Carolina, three from Alabama, and one each from Florida, Mississippi, Louisiana, and Virginia, respectively.

a law office. His political career began with his election as a Republican to the state house of representatives in 1880, and to the state senate in 1884. A year later, he won Republican endorsement for solicitor and prosecuting attorney, serving two terms until 1894. A skillful orator and effective organizer, he was nominated from North Carolina's second district in 1896 for the U.S. House of Representatives, over opposition from his hard-working but less flamboyant brother-in-law, Henry Cheatham, a former congressman who represented the same district from late 1889 to early 1893. White won the 1896 election, and on March 15, 1897, was the lone black man seated in the Fifty-fifth Congress.

During his first term, he was a frequent absentee who introduced no substantial legislation but angered Southern whites by urging inclusion of Negro military units in the armed services, as the United States entered war with Spain after the battleship *Maine* exploded in Havana harbor in February 1898. In his second term, his retorts to Southern verbal attacks upon Negroes as "savages," "aliens," "brutes," and "inferiors" sapped his energies. In such an atmosphere it was perhaps inevitable that his most important legislation, H. R. Bill 6963—the earliest proposal to make mob lynching a federal offense—was defeated. He occasionally read into the *Congressional Record* racial insults he faced inside and outside the halls of Congress—remarks that put him on the defensive to enumerate the success stories of his race. On January 29, 1901, he spoke for nearly an hour, after floor time was yielded to him (by Representative Wadsworth of New York, who asked the Chairman that "the gentleman from North Carolina be recognized in his own right") to enter an agriculture debate. Thereupon White began his historic "farewell" to Congress:

> I want to enter a plea for the colored man, the colored woman, the
> colored boy, and the colored girl of this country. I would not thus di-
> gress from the question at issue and detain the House in a discussion of
> the interests of this particular people, at this time, but for the constant
> and the persistent efforts of certain gentlemen upon this floor to mold
> and rivet public sentiment against us as a people.

The conclusion of that speech on January 29, 1901, to the Second Session of the Fifty-sixth Congress, is excerpted here from the *Congressional Record*, volume 34, part 2. White was the last Afro-American to serve in Congress from North Carolina for the next nine decades.[2] After leaving office, he practiced

---

[2] Representative Eva M. Clayton (D), elected in 1992 from North Carolina's First District, was the first black member since George White from that state, and the first woman to represent North Carolina in Congress for a full term; she was reelected in 1994 and 1996.

law in Washington, DC, and invested with several partners in land for an all–
Negro rural community in Whitesboro, New Jersey. In 1905, he moved to Phila-
delphia, where he founded the People's Savings Bank and was active in local
civic projects, and the NAACP, until his death in 1918. During his post–
Congressional career, White chose not to resettle in his home state of North
Carolina.

From The Negroes' Temporary Farewell
to Congress[3] (1901)

. . . Now, Mr. Chairman, before concluding my remarks I want to submit a
brief recipe for the solution of the so-called American negro problem. He asks
no special favors, but simply demands that he be given the same chance for
existence, for earning a livelihood, for raising himself in the scales of manhood
and womanhood that are accorded to kindred nationalities. Treat him as a man;
go into his home and learn of his social conditions; learn of his cares, his troubles, and his hopes for the future; gain his confidence; open the doors of industry to him; let the word *negro, colored,* and *black* be stricken from all the
organizations enumerated in the federation of labor.

Help him to overcome his weaknesses, punish the crime-committing class
by the courts of the land, measure the standard of the race by its best material,
cease to mold prejudicial and unjust public sentiment against him, and my
word for it, he will learn to support, hold up the hands of, and join in with that
political party, that institution, whether secular or religious, in every community where he lives, which is destined to do the greatest good for the greatest
number. Obliterate race hatred, party prejudice, and help us to achieve nobler
ends, greater results, and become more satisfactory citizens to our brother
in white.

This, Mr. Chairman, is perhaps the negroes' temporary farewell to the American Congress; but let me say, Phoenix-like he will rise up some day and come
again. These parting words are in behalf of an outraged, heartbroken, bruised,
and bleeding, but God-fearing people, faithful, industrious, loyal people—
rising people, full of potential force. . . .

---

[3] Title supplied by the editor.

CHARLES W. CHESNUTT

(1858–1932)

In the same year that North Carolina Representative George H. White bid "farewell" to Congress and his state, author Charles Chesnutt dramatized the history of racial conflict through a fictional North Carolina in his literary masterpiece *The Marrow of Tradition*. Written in reaction to the Wilmington, North Carolina, massacre of black citizens during the election of November 1898, Chesnutt gave the town the imaginary name "Wellington" and presented it as a microcosm of racial and sociopolitical upheavals in the South. The 1901 narrative was termed "bitter" by literary critic William Dean Howells, but it was the principal Afro-American social protest novel at the turn of the century. It was Chesnutt's second and penultimate novel about post–Civil War antagonism in the state, where he grew to manhood during what he once called "one of the most eventful eras of history."

Born June 20, 1858, in Cleveland, he was the first son of Ann Maria and Andrew Jackson Chesnutt, free mulattos who met on a wagon train traveling from North Carolina to Ohio in 1856. After the Civil War, the family returned to Fayetteville, where Andrew, a former Union soldier, made peace with his aging white father, once a prosperous tobacco farmer and slaveowner, who had freed his illegitimate children by his mulatto mistress and now funded Andrew to open a grocery store. Young Charles spent his boyhood years of the late 1860s working in the store and attending Howard School, which was operated by the Freedmen's Bureau. At fourteen, he was a wage-earning pupil-teacher, helping to support five younger siblings on the family farm after the grocery closed in debt and his failing mother died from seven childbirths.

In Fayetteville, Chesnutt came of age during Reconstruction, absorbing what later came into focus in his fiction: the clash between the old regime and the new; the tensions of racial, economic, and political injustice; the frictions of social caste consciousness; and the scorn of white Southerners toward a mixed-blood population whom they considered illegitimate and inferior heirs of slaves. Chesnutt himself bore the stigma: he was indistinguishable from a white person in features and complexion. But he refused to follow some of his relatives in passing for white. In a speech, he later said, "My physical makeup was such that I knew the psychology of people of mixed blood insofar as it differed from other people, and most of my writings ran along the color line."

His "color line" stories probed the social complications of mixed ancestry and psychological dilemmas of racial passing. Such themes were then hushed in American literature but he introduced them boldly, examining intraracial as well as interracial relations. He was a counterpoint to the younger Paul Laurence Dunbar, the only Afro-American creative writer then critically and nationally recognized. Dunbar's popularity was never attained by Chesnutt, who began writing and appearing in mass-market magazines earlier, but whose fiction in book form commercial publishers rejected until 1899. In an era when white readers were eager to be entertained by Dunbar's books that satisfied the public taste for a romanticized view of blacks, Chesnutt labored behind the scenes to master his own literary craft. But he soon discovered American literature had the same barriers, biases, and prejudices of American society. He was the first Afro-American writer to distinguish himself in the art of fiction with a social purpose, the first to create characters who fit no stereotype; the first to persuade Northern white editors and publishers that truthful books on race relations were a step toward the "moral progress of the American people."

By age twenty-two, he had taught eight years in rural schoolhouses and towns in North and South Carolina, married a local school teacher, become a parent, and been chosen the principal of a new State Normal School in Fayetteville, succeeding his Afro-American mentor, Robert Harris, who died in 1880. To overcome a limited formal education, Chesnutt educated himself, reading widely in European and American literature, studying music, mathematics, and the basics of Greek, Latin, German, and French, with the aid of white tutors— some of them reluctant, he wrote later, "to teach a nigger." He hoped to educate prejudiced whites about his race, and he affirmed his goals in his journal: "to live down the prejudice . . . exalt my race . . . to be judged according to my merit . . . get employment in some literary avocation."

Desiring to support his wife and young children outside the South, he mastered stenography. In 1883 he practiced it for six months in New York City, both as a Wall Street reporter for the Dow Jones news agency and as part-time columnist for the *New York Mail and Express*. The Gilded Age of America's new fortunes of the 1880s influenced his early nonracial fiction with characters from his Wall Street experience. In late 1883 he relocated to his birthplace, Cleveland, where his family soon joined him. The city became his permanent home and the imaginary "Groveland" in some of his fiction.

While employed as an accountant and stenographer at Cleveland's Nickel Plate Railroad Company, Chesnutt studied law under the company's legal counsel and in 1887 passed the Ohio bar. While developing his law practice, he earned an annual income as a stenographic reporter in the courts, and in his spare time continued to write fiction. His first published story, "Uncle Peter's House," about a black freedman's struggle for survival after emancipation, appeared in December 1885 in the *Cleveland News and Herald*. The story was his subtle but subversive effort to counter white–Southern propagandists depicting ex-slaves as comic buffoons or brutes. His published story began his apprenticeship phase of the mid–1880s with short sketches sold to the McClure newspaper syndicate, which gave him exposure in the *Atlanta Constitution, Chicago Ledger, Puck, Tid-Bits, Family Fiction, Household Realm, the New Haven Register,* and *Overland Monthly*. Some of his apprenticeship pieces were Southern–dialect sketches of his imagination but more representative of true black folk characters than the Joel Chandler Harris folktales then in vogue. However, Chesnutt soon found himself identified with one story he never intended as his trademark, when he revived a folktale of witchcraft told to him by a black gardener in Fayetteville. He sold it to the *Atlantic Monthly*, where it appeared as "The Goophered Grapevine" in August 1887, his first in a national magazine.

To *Atlantic Monthly* readers and white literary circles, Chesnutt's racial identity was then unknown. In 1888, author George Washington Cable located him and a correspondence ensued. His advice to Chesnutt was to keep quiet on publicizing his race to assure more favorable public reception. Such was the mood of the nation in the 1880s: most white editors, to safeguard their readership, welcomed white but not black writers to write about racial issues, even in fiction. However, Chesnutt learned from his own experience that well-crafted nonracial fiction by nonwhite writers was also unwelcome. Social equality between the races was not yet acceptable. In his first published essay, "What Is a White Man?" in the *Independent*, May 30, 1889, Chesnutt left no doubt about his race in his attack on laws of various states denying legitimacy to people of mixed blood.

To support his family and continue to write, he opened a legal-stenographic reporting business in Cleveland in 1890. He did not depend on literary pursuits for financial security. Rejections, demands for revisions, and indifferent excuses from editors and publishers to some of his works did not deter him, though they might have discouraged a less dedicated writer. In September 1891, in a letter to the Houghton Mifflin publishing house, then owner of the *Atlantic Monthly*, which had published three of his stories, he introduced himself as "An American with acknowledged African descent," and inquired of interest in publishing a volume of his fiction. Eight years and many polite rejection letters later, Houghton Mifflin published two distinctly different collections of his fiction—both in 1899: *The Conjure Woman* and *"The Wife of His Youth" and Other Stories of the Color Line*. Publication of the two books might not have happened without Walter Hines Page, a liberal Southerner from North Carolina who joined the *Atlantic Monthly* as editor in 1895 and published several new Chesnutt stories that he championed as a literary adviser to the publishing house. From Page also came the sobriquet *conjure*, for the dialect stories set in a Southern locale.

Favorable public reaction to Chesnutt's two books, and his short biography of Frederick Douglass the same year, encouraged him to take a leave of absence from his business firm to write full time. A year later, in 1900, Houghton Mifflin issued his novel on miscegenation, *The House behind the Cedars*, begun a decade earlier as a short story, "Rena Walden," but revised many times and expanded, following rejections by *Century* magazine editor Richard Watson Gilder.

Chesnutt had hoped to write fiction about the American South equal to white author Albion Tourgée's best-selling 1879 novel of Reconstruction *A Fool's Errand*, which earned over $20,000. In his March 1880 journal, Chesnutt hoped to be the literary man "yet to make his appearance." As man and artist, he was praised by Tourgée himself, but none of Chesnutt's novels received the popular response his short stories did, or the critical and financial success his artistry deserved. In December 1901, he wrote to Houghton Mifflin after anemic sales of *The Marrow of Tradition*:

> I am beginning to suspect that the public as a rule does not care for books in which the principal characters are colored people, or written with a striking sympathy with that race as contrasted with the white race. . . . If a novel is generally acknowledged to be interesting, dramatic, well constructed, well written—which qualities have been pretty generally ascribed to *The Marrow of Tradition* . . . there must be something radically wrong . . . and I do not know where it is unless it be in the subject.

In 1905, guided by Page, who by then had co-founded his own publishing house, Chesnutt made a last try with a Southern exposé novel, *The Colonel's Dream*. Set in North Carolina at the turn of the century, with an idealistic white protagonist crusading for democracy in the New South, it was reviewed more favorably than *The Marrow of Tradition*, but the public did not buy it. Foundering sales signaled a return to the legal-stenography business and retreat from a writing career. Chesnutt engaged in little literary work for the next two decades, but he was active in civic and professional affairs, and he traveled abroad. In 1928, the NAACP awarded him the Spingarn Medal, for "pioneer work as a literary artist." That same year, he completed two novels, *The Quarry* and *Paul Marchant, F. M.C. (Free Man of Color)*; both were rejected. Among other unpublished works, he left three early novellas: *Mandy Oxendine* (1897), on a mulatto protagonist's attempt to pass into the North Carolina aristocracy; and two nonracial Northern romances: *A Business Career* (1898) and *The Rainbow Chasers* (1900). *Mandy Oxendine* was published for the first time in 1997, a century after Chesnutt wrote it. His last published story, "Concerning Father," appeared in the NAACP national magazine the *Crisis* in May 1930.

Of over sixty published short stories in his prolific canon of literary realism and local color writing, American college anthologies usually feature his dialect stories. Black folklore is a thread in the complex and historic tapestry he created, but he would be the first to say that his dialect fiction was not how he wished to be remembered. In 1931, in his last-commissioned essay "Post-Bellum-Pre-Harlem," published one year before his death, Chesnutt wrote: "As a matter of fact, substantially all my writings, with the exception of *The Conjure Woman*, have dealt with the problems of people of mixed blood. . . ."

The following story, "White Weeds," on the social ironies of American racial identity, was unpublished in his lifetime. It first appeared in *The Short Fiction of Charles W. Chesnutt* (1974, 1981), edited by Sylvia Lyons Render, a pioneering scholar of the author, until her death in 1986.

White Weeds (ca. 1903)

Students of Danforth University during the late nineties may remember the remarkable events following the death of Professor Carson of that institution.

At three o'clock one afternoon Professor Carson left his own apartments in Merle Hall and crossed the university campus toward the president's house. It was obvious to the few students whom he encountered during his short walk that Professor Carson was deeply absorbed in thought, because, ordinarily a model of politeness, upon this occasion he either passed them as though unaware of their presence, or responded to their respectful salutations with a very palpable perfunctoriness. There was reason enough, the students knew, for a certain degree of preoccupation on the part of Professor Carson, but hardly sufficient to account for an agitation so extreme as not only to disturb his usually grave and composed countenance but to make him forget his punctilious manners. A man might well be absentminded upon his wedding day, but he need not look as though he were under sentence of death and straining every effort to secure a reprieve. For Professor Carson, as everyone knew, was to be married at seven o'clock in the evening to Miss Marian Tracy, by common consent of the university faculty and the student body the most beautiful woman of her years in Attica.

It was a noble campus that Professor Carson crossed. Founded by a wealthy merchant of a past generation, before the days of colossal and burdensome fortunes, the university had never been regarded as a medium of self-advertisement, but as the contribution of an enlightened philanthropist to the training of youth and the advancement of a science. There was a broad quadrangular sweep of velvety turf, crossed by two intersecting avenues of noble elms. while distributed symmetrically around the square were a dozen stately stone buildings, some ivy-clad, others beginning already to show, though the institution was only fifty years old, the markings of frost and snow and sun and rain which in a strenuous Northern climate so soon simulate the mellowness of age.

Professor Carson found the president at home and was ushered into his presence. President Trumball of Danforth University was a suave and learned gentleman of fifty, in whom a fine executive mind had not overborne a zeal for scholarship, in which he had achieved deserved renown before assuming the cares of administration. A more striking contrast than that between the two men it would be difficult to imagine; physically they were almost the antitheses of each other. Professor Carson was tall and slender with fair hair, which he wore much longer than most men; the president was sturdy and his hair dark, with a very slight sprinkling of white, and ruddy of complexion. The professor's forehead was high and narrow, the president's lower but broader. The president's eye was a gray, keen and steady; the professor's blue, weak and wavering. The one was the face of a man of affairs, who welcomed responsibilities as a fit exercise for high powers; the other that of a man lacking resolution and prone, in the crises of life, to seek the support and direction of stronger minds. It was, indeed, Dr. Trumbull's well-known decision of character which had brought Professor Carson, torn by conflicting emotions, across the campus to the president's house. Both were men of striking appearance, not to say handsome men, Professor Carson's manner being marked by a certain distinction, accounted for in some measure by his consciousness that he was of an old and distinguished ancestry. He was deeply wedded to his work, and punctiliously conscientious in its performance; he was professor of mathematics, a science governed by exact rules and requiring little exercise of judgment or imagination. He had been connected with the school longer than President Trumbull and was loyal to its ideals and traditions, with the tenacity of a vine which has thrust its slender roots into the interstices of a rock.

President Trumbull was in his study, in company with his daughter Marcia, a handsome and intelligent child of twelve who sat beside a window reading, while her father wrote at his desk. At a glance from his visitor, the president, with another glance, dismissed Marcia. Professor Carson, murmuring a request for permission, closed the door of the room and sat, or rather sank into a chair near the president.

"Well, Professor Carson, what can I do for you? I see that you have something on your mind."

"Dr. Trumbull," said the other, "I am in the greatest trouble of my life."

"Bless me, Professor! What can it be? Nothing serious, I hope?"

"Serious is hardly the name for it—it is more than serious. It is a matter that concerns my whole future—almost a matter of life and death. As you know, I am—I was to be married tonight."

"Yes, and to an exceedingly beautiful and charming lady."

This statement was made in all sincerity, and not without a certain degree of regret. Dr. Trumbull was a widower of less than a year's standing. Had Professor Carson waited a while longer, he would not have been without a formidable rival.

"Exactly," said Professor Carson, extending his hand with a gesture unconsciously tragic, "and an hour ago I received this letter."

Dr. Trumbull took the letter, and as he read it an air of astonishment overspread his features.

"An extraordinary statement," he exclaimed, "most extraordinary! But surely it is not true—surely you cannot believe it?"

"I—don't—know what to believe. It is possible—most things are possible."

"But, my dear sir, this is an anonymous letter—the weapon of malice—the medium of slander."

"I know it, sir. In the ordinary affairs of life I should have tossed it into the fire. But this is a matter vital to my happiness. And there is always the possibility that someone might wish to tell another the truth, without seeming to do an unkind thing. An anonymous letter *might* be written with the best of motives."

"The method throws suspicion on the motive. Is there no clue to the writer? Have you any enemy?"

"None that I know of," replied Professor Carson promptly. "I don't know of a man in the world who should wish me other than well."

"Or a woman?"

"Or a woman," came the reply with equal promptness.

"It is more calculated to injure the lady than you," said the president reflectively. "*She* may have enemies."

"She is the soul of candor, and popular with her own sex."

"She is beautiful, and popular with the other sex—sufficient reasons why she might be the object of envy or malice."

"The letter is from another city. It is postmarked 'Drexel.' "

"Drexel is forty miles away," returned the president. "One might take the ten o'clock train from here, post the letter at Drexel, and be back here by twelve o'clock. The letter would be here for afternoon delivery."

Professor Carson examined the envelope.

"It was postmarked at Drexel at eleven o'clock. The receiving stamp shows it delivered at the post office here at 12:15. It reached me in the afternoon delivery. It is typewritten, so there is no penmanship to afford a clue."

"I have passed the point of concern about its origin," returned Professor Carson. "It is the fact itself that worries me. The mere suggestion is torture. If the statement be true, it means the ruin of my happiness. If it be false—and pray God it is—I have no time, before the hour set for the wedding, to ascertain the fact. I must decide now, with such light as I have. As my friend and superior in office, what would you advise me to do?"

"Why not ask the lady?"

"I could not do it. If it were true, I could not marry her."

"Nor, as I understand, would you wish to. And if it were false, your mind would be at ease."

"But if I should ask her, she might not marry me; and if it is false, I would not lose her for the world."

"You would trust her word?"

"Implicitly. She is too proud to lie."

"Then, my dear Professor Carson, if you feel that way. . . ."

"Then you would advise me?"

"Is it so important?" asked the president, perplexed. "The world would never know it, even if it were true."

"Someone knows it—if it be true," returned the other. "And then, I should wish to have children, and it is of them I should have to think—it would be criminal not to think of them. The time is so short that I don't know what to do nor where to turn. I thought you might advise me—you are so prompt, so resourceful. I should wish to adopt a course that would protect myself, and yet in no way reflect upon the lady, or upon the university, or impair my usefulness here."

"Such delicacy was to be expected of you, Professor Carson. If it were my own affair, I could decide it promptly, but unless I could put myself exactly in your place, as perhaps I should be unable to do, I should hesitate to advise a man upon a matter so vital. Your problem is a difficult one from your own point of view—perhaps from any man's. You are engaged to be married, within a few hours, to a most charming woman, in whose worth and worthiness you have had entire confidence. The wedding preparations are made, the guests invited. Even now, in all probability, the bride is dressing for the wedding. At this moment you receive an anonymous letter, purporting to convey information which, if true, renders the lady ineligible for marriage with you. I see but three courses open to you as a gentleman—and those who know you would expect you to consider the subject first from that point of view. You can take the letter to the lady, ask her frankly if the charge be true, and marry her or not, as she may answer. A less frank but at least forgivable step would be to postpone the marriage on account of sudden indisposition—you are looking far from well just now. If she confirmed the statement of the letter, you would have to make some such excuse, in order to spare her feelings. A third course, which a man—some men at least—who loved the lady well enough would follow, would be to throw the letter into the fire and marry her."

"But which do you think—" began Professor Carson desperately, "which do you think—"

"I think," said the president, interrupting him, "that you had better choose between the three. A gentleman of your character and antecedents can hardly fail to select a course consistent with—"

"With honor," murmured the poor professor. "Thank you, sir," he added with dignity, "I shall trouble you no further. But whatever course I decide upon, I may ask you to hold in strict confidence all that I have said, and the contents of this letter?"

"You need hardly ask it. It is not a matter to be repeated. Whether the marriage take place or no, we should have no right to compromise the lady."

At seven o'clock the same evening the marriage of Professor John Marshall Carson to Miss Marian Tracy took place at the latter's residence. Miss Tracy was alone in the world, having neither parents nor near relatives living. She had been a teacher in a ladies' seminary, and made her home with a distant connection who lived in the town. To the college world the event was a notable one. Professor Carson was, if not exactly popular, at least very highly esteemed by his colleagues. If he seemed at times to hold himself aloof from the other professors, his attitude was instinctively ascribed to a natural reserve rather than to undue self-esteem. If any new-fledged tutor or professor ever attempted to be familiar with the professor of mathematics, he was brought back to the conventional by a tact so delicate, a courtesy so refined, that no offense was taken, and respect took the place of what, at a ruder rebuff, might easily have been dislike. The wedding was attended by all the professors and their wives, as well as by many of the townspeople.

The house was decorated for the wedding with red and white roses. Festoons of smilax ran from the chandeliers in the center to the corners of the rooms. The floors were covered with white canvas. Gorman and McAlee's orchestra, screened behind palms in the back hall, played a varied program of classical and popular music, ranging from Mendelssohn to ragtime. These details are mentioned because they are important to the remainder of the story. The bride,

> Clothed in white samite,
> Mystic, wonderful,

as Dr. Trumbull murmured when the vision dawned upon him—was radiant in the well-preserved beauty of thirty years, for Miss Tracy was no longer in her first youth. When she entered the front parlor upon the arm of her cousin, to the strains of the wedding march, there was not a man present who did not think Professor Carson an extremely lucky man. It was observed, however, by those who paid the bridegroom any attention, that he did not seem as happy as the occasion demanded; that the voice with which he spoke the irrevocable vows had not the vibrant ring that might be expected from the virile man united to his mate; that the hand which he gave to those who congratulated him was limp and cold; that while from time to time during the evening his eyes sought the bride's face with a look of longing, behind this lay a haunting distrust—that he seemed to be seeking something which he did not find; that at other times his manner was *distrait* and his smile forced; and that when the last guests were departing, his expression alternated between anticipation and dread. President Trumbull, the most distinguished guest, responded at the supper table to a toast in which he wished the couple every felicity. At no time during the evening did Professor Carson allude to the interview of the afternoon, nor did the president mention it to him then or thereafter. There had been no scandal, no sensation, and Dr. Trumbull had no disposition to pry into another's secrets.

If there were any lingering curiosity on Dr. Trumbull's part concerning which of the two possible courses open to him besides postponement of the marriage Professor Carson had adopted, it was not lessened by his observation of the married couple during the succeeding months. He went to Europe for the summer, but upon his return in the autumn to his duties, he met Professor Carson daily, in the routine of the university work, and the lady from time to time in the social life of which the university was the center. Only a few meetings were necessary to convince him that neither husband nor wife was happy. Professor Carson, at the end of what should have been a restful vacation, had visibly declined in health. Always slender, he had become emaciated. His natural gravity had developed into an almost sepulchral solemnity, his innate reserve into a well-nigh morbid self-absorption. The rare smile which had at times flickered upon his features seemed to have gone out forever.

His efforts to overcome this melancholy were at times very apparent. Mrs. Carson was fond of society, and they often went out together. On such occasions their bearing toward one another was perfect, of its kind. Professor Carson was the embodiment of chivalrous courtesy—a courtesy so marked that in the bearing of any other man toward his own wife it would have provoked a smile. The lady, in her demeanor toward her husband responded in a manner so similar as to seem at times ironical. In a free and familiar society of intimates they were, when together, conspicuous. The lady when alone could unbend; but Professor Carson after his marriage never appeared in society alone.

In spite, however, of this elaborate deference toward one another, more than one observer besides Dr. Trumbull suspected that their union was not one of perfect happiness. Dr. Trumbull wondered, more than once, whether Carson had asked her, before their marriage, the question suggested by the anonymous letter, and, receiving a negative answer, had had his faith shaken after marriage, or whether he had loyally burned the letter, but had been unable to divest himself of the hateful doubt it had engendered, which was slowly sapping his vitality. That some cause was producing this unfortunate result became more and more apparent, for before the next summer vacation came around, Professor Carson took to his bed, and, after a brief illness, was enrolled among the great majority.

The number of those who were interested in the Carsons household was largely increased during the two days succeeding the professor's death. Announcement was duly made that the funeral services would take place on Saturday afternoon—Professor Carson had died on Thursday—and were to be conducted by old Dr. Burridge, rector emeritus of St. Anne's. This in itself was a novelty, for Dr. Burridge was purblind and hard of hearing, and rarely performed any priestly function except some service where sight and hearing were not prime essentials. Some surprise being expressed that Dr. McRae, the rector in charge, had not been requested to officiate, it was learned that Dr. Burridge would act by special request of the widow.

This, however, was a trivial preliminary. The real surprise began when those who entered the house shortly before the hour fixed for the service, found none of the customary trappings of woe, but on the contrary, a house decked as for a wedding ceremony. It required only a moment for those who had been present at Professor Carson's marriage a few months before to perceive with a sort of dazed wonder, that an effort had seemingly been made to reproduce, as near as the plan of the rooms would permit, the decorations upon that occasion.

Roses, white and red, were banked in the corners; long streamers of smilax ran from the chandeliers to the corners of the room, and were twined around the stair railing. Where, at the wedding ceremony a floral altar had been reared, the body of Professor Carson, in immaculate evening dress, lay upon a bier, composed of a casket the sides of which were let down so as to resemble more a couch than the last narrow house of a mortal man.

The troubled wonder of the funeral guests was still further augmented when in the rear hall, behind a screen of palms, Gormand and McAlee's orchestra began to play Wagner's "O du mein holder Abendstern." For a moment, while the gathering audience were realizing that a bank associated only with pleasure parties was playing music, which, while not exactly profane, was certainly not religious—for a few moments the audience was silent, and then the room was as murmurous with whispered comment as a wheat-field shaken by the wind.

One of the professors spoke to the undertaker, who was hovering, like a bird of prey, around the hall.

"What is the meaning," he asked, "of this extraordinary performance?"

"Don't ask me, sir. It is the widow's orders. I don't approve of it, sir, but business is business with me. It is the widow's orders, and, as the person chiefly interested, the widow's wishes are sacred."

While Dr. Burridge, in full canonicals, having taken his place before the bier, to which he was led by one of the ushers, was reading the first part of the beautiful Episcopal service for the burial of the dead, there was opportunity for those present to reach in some degree the frame of mind befitting so solemn an occasion. At that point, following the first lesson, where a hymn is sung or an anthem, the discomfort returned with even greater force when a hired quartet, which some of those present recognized as belonging to the neighboring town of Drexel, began to sing, to a soft accompaniment by the orchestra, not the conventional and the expected "Abide with Me" or "Lead, Kindly Light," but Graben Hoffman's exquisite love song, "Dere schoenste Engel." As the words were German only a few understood them, but in the bosoms of the rest there was a vague intuition that the song was of a piece with the other unusual features of the occasion.

Good old Dr. Burridge, however, to whose dull hearing all music was the same, had neither seen nor heard anything to mar the solemnity of the service. He repeated the Creed, in which he was joined by those who were sufficiently collected, and added the fitting prayers. When he had concluded the portion of the service which could be performed at the home, and the undertaker had announced that the remainder of the service would take place at the cemetery, the guests instead of rising returned to their seats as though by a common premonition that there was something more to happen. Nor were they disappointed, for almost immediately the orchestra struck up the "Wedding March" from *Lohengrin*, and Mrs. Carson, clad not in widow's weeds but in bridal array, her face set in a tragic smile, entered the back parlor and moved in time to the music down the narrow lane which had been left between the chairs, and pausing before the bier took off her wedding ring and placed it in her dead husband's hand; took off her wreath of orange blossoms and laid it among the flowers by his side. Then, turning, she left the room by the side door. A few moments later, when the casket had been closed and the body was ready for sepulture, she came downstairs dressed in an ordinary street costume of dark cloth, took her place in the mourner's carriage, and followed the remains to the grave, by the side of which she stood like any ordinary spectator until ashes had been consigned to ashes, and dust to dust, after which she immediately entered her carriage and was driven away, leaving the mystified throng morally certain that nothing but a pronounced mental aberration on the part of Mrs. Carson could account for so extraordinary, not to say shocking a funeral. To more than one the mad scene in Hamlet occurred as at least a distant parallel, though no one of them had ever dreamed that the stately Mrs. Carson had loved her middle-aged husband so deeply as, like Ophelia, to go mad for love of him.

So paralyzed with amazement had been everyone at the funeral, and brief had been Mrs. Carson's appearances, that not anyone had uttered a word of condolence or spoken to her during the afternoon. That very night she left Attica. Her house was closed and her affairs settled by her distant cousin, and it was learned that she had gone abroad for an indefinite sojourn. By the will of Professor Carson, which was presented for probate shortly after his decease, he left to his widow the whole of his estate, which amounted to some twenty thousand dollars in money and securities.

A little more than a year after Professor Carson's death, at the close of the school year, Dr. Trumbull, accompanied by his daughter Marcia—he had been a widower now for three years—left home to spend the summer in Europe. A few weeks later, upon stepping aboard the steamer at Mainz for the trip down the Rhine, he saw seated upon the deck, at a little distance, a lady whose outlines, though her face was turned away, seemed familiar. Having seen his daughter comfortably seated and their hand baggage placed, he went over to the lady, who, upon his addressing her by name, looked up with a start, and then extended both her hands.

"Why, Dr. Trumbull, what a surprise! You are the last person whom I should have expected to see!"

"And, I suppose, the one whom it gives you the least pleasure to see?"

"By no means! Indeed, I am glad to see you. One's home friends are never so welcome as when one meets them in a foreign land."

"Yes, I believe it is understood that a mere bowing acquaintance at home becomes an intimate friend abroad."

"Now, doctor, I shall not follow your very palpable lead; you must take my friendship at its face value."

"My dear Mrs. Carson, I am only too glad to do so, and am sincerely delighted, on my part, that our paths have met."

The president's daughter, finding herself deserted, and recognizing Mrs. Carson, came over at this juncture, and was duly hugged and kissed.

"How tall you are growing, dear!" said the lady. "It is only about a year since I saw you, and you look three years older."

"My dresses are longer," said Marcia ingenuously. "Oh, I'm so glad we've met you. You know, I always liked you, Mrs. Carson, even before you were married."

"You dear child! And as for you, who could help loving you? But, there, how selfish I am! In my pleasure at our meeting, I had forgotten all about Professor and Mrs. Gilman. I'm traveling with them, you know. Professor Gilman has had his 'sabbatical year,' and I've been with them ever since they came over last July. At school Mrs. Gilman was my dearest friend, and they have been very good to me."

"And you never give up your friends?"

"Never! So long as they are good to me. But excuse me a moment, and I will look them up."

She returned shortly with her friends. The two gentlemen were old acquaintances and former intimates. Professor Gilman, an authority on medieval history, had been a colleague of Dr. Trumbull's at Brown, many years before. After the exchange of cordial greetings, the ladies, accompanied by Marcia, went over to the side of the boat, leaving the gentlemen together.

They spoke of their work and their travels, and then the conversation turned on Mrs. Carson.

"She is looking well," said President Trumbull.

"A fine woman," returned Professor Gilman, "a woman of character, capable of forming a definite purpose, and of carrying it out; and yet not at all hard, and in some ways exceedingly feminine. My wife loves her dearly, and we have enjoyed having her with us."

"I never thought," said Dr. Trumbull, "that she was quite happy with Carson."

"Happy! Far from it! I suppose, after Carson's remarkable funeral, that all Attica imagined her out of her mind?"

"Her conduct was unusual, certainly, and in default of explanation, such a suspicion might really have seemed charitable."

"Did it ever occur to you that there might be a reasonable explanation, without that hypothesis?"

"Frankly, yes, though I could never have imagined what it was. I happened to know something of Carson's antecedents, and of certain events preceding his marriage, which I have thought might in some obscure way have accounted for Mrs. Carson's eccentric conduct upon that occasion. But the knowledge came to me in such a manner that I shall probably never know any more about it."

"Did it concern a letter?"

"Yes."

"An anonymous letter?"

"Yes."

"Then I know it already. Mrs. Carson is my wife's other self—even I play only second fiddle. They have no secrets from one another. I know that Mrs. Carson values your good opinion, and since you know so much, I imagine she would not be unwilling for you to know all the facts—if you could dream them, say. Indeed, you ought to know them."

It was a warm day. Their cigars were good. The ladies left them alone for half an hour. The steamer glided smoothly down the Rhine. Two gentlemen in middle life, upon their vacation, might have dozed and might have dreamed. At any rate, before the ladies rejoined them, each knew all that the other knew of Mrs. Carson's story, and what they did not know required no supernatural wisdom to divine it.

When, after the wedding, the guests had departed and the wedded pair were left alone, the bride observed that Professor Carson was ill at ease, and that his embarrassment was serious. For a while he wandered about the room. At length he sat down beside her and began to speak.

"Marian," he said, "I have a very painful duty to perform. This afternoon, only a few hours ago, I received through the mail an anonymous letter, containing a certain statement with reference to yourself."

To say that his wife was surprised is a mild statement. She was not a child, but a mature woman, and the inference seemed plain; a wedding, an anonymous letter upon the eve of it. That he had not believed the statement, whatever it had been, was apparent, for he had married her. But right upon the heels of this conviction came the first false note in her conception of Professor Carson's character—a doubt of his taste. She had considered him the flower of courtesy—had looked upon his chivalrous deference for women as a part of his Southern heritage. It was this attribute of his, which, more than anything else, had attracted her. That having loyally ignored such a letter, he should now tell her of it was hardly to have been expected of him.

"I could not believe the statement," he went on, "and therefore, as honor required of me, I threw the letter into the fire, and fulfilled my contract."

Again the lady winced. It hardly required a sensitive mind to infer, from his language, that he had married her because of their previous engagement. His choice of words was at least unfortunate.

"I am sorry," she said with spirit, "that you should have felt under any compulsion."

"There was none," he replied, "except that of my love. And I did not believe the story."

"Then why mention it?"

"Because I must know," he replied, "and yet I dared not run the risk of losing you. Had I asked you the question before our marriage, your pride, which in my eyes is one of your greatest charms, might have made you refuse to marry me."

"Quite likely," she replied, with rising anger. "But, since you ignored the letter, and disbelieve the story, why, oh, why, do you tell me now?"

"Because," he said wildly, "because I love you, and because my happiness is so bound up in you, and because this charge is of such a nature, that I can never shake off its memory until I learn from your own lips that it is false. I know it is false—I am sure it is false—it must be false; but I want your lips to give it the lie. Whatever you say, I shall believe."

She was a woman, and for a moment curiosity replaced indignation.

"And what," she asked, "is this terrible charge which I must meet, this crime I must deny?"

"It is a monstrous calumny. Could anyone, looking at your fair face, at your clear eye, your frank and noble countenance, believe that one drop of Negro blood coursed through your veins? Preposterous!"

His words were confident, but his voice scarcely rang true, and she could read the lingering dread in his eyes. This, then, that some unknown person had said of her, was the offense with which she was charged?

She was silent. He watched her anxiously.

"Suppose," she answered with a forced smile, "suppose, for the sake of the argument, it had been true—what then?"

"Ah, dearest," he replied, reassured by her smile, and drawing nearer to her, while she retreated behind a convenient chair. "I should have suffered a severe shock. For the sake of the university, and to avoid scandal, I should have lived with you, had you been willing, and to the outer world we should have been husband and wife; but to ourselves the relationship would have existed in name only."

"And you married me," she said coldly, "with such a doubt in your mind, and with such a purpose, should the doubt be wrongly resolved? It seems scarcely fair to me. I might have answered yes."

He explained his state of mind, or at least endeavored to make it clear, plainly surprised that he should find it necessary; for to his mind, the mere statement of the race was its own explanation.

His father had been a planter, with wide estates and numerous slaves. His mother had suffered deeply in her pride and her affections, because of some poor unfortunate of color. With his mother's milk he had drunk in a deadly antipathy to the thought of any personal relation between white people and black but that of master and servant. The period of his adolescence had coincided with the tense years during which the white South, beaten on the field, had sought in a fierce and unreasoning pride a refuge from the humiliation of defeat, and with equal unreason, but very humanly, had visited upon the black pawns in the game, who were near at hand, the hatred they felt for their conquerors. Most of this feeling Professor Carson had overcome, but this one thing was bred in the bone.

"It is part of me," he said. "Nothing could ever make me feel that the touch of a Negress was not pollution. Beside my mother's deathbed I swore a solemn vow that this sin should never be laid at my door."

His bride was not flattered by the suggestion. She, a Negress, to whom his vow might apply!

"How white," she asked, "must one be, to come within the protection of the code of Southern chivalry?"

"There are no degrees," he explained. "To me, and those who think like me, men and women are either white or black. Those who are not at all white are all black. Were I married in fact to a woman even seemingly as white, as you, yet not entirely white, I should feel guilty of mortal sin. I should lie awake at night, dreading lest my children should show traces of their descent from an inferior and degraded race. I should never know a moment's happiness."

"Pardon my curiosity," she said, "but this is interesting—at least. What, may I ask, was to have been—my attitude in this marriage? In this state there would have been no legal objection to our union. We are both Episcopalians, and our church looks upon divorce with disfavor. Was I to have submitted without protest to a plan which left me married, yet no wife?"

"It would have been for you to say," he replied. "I could not blame you for concealing your antecedents. For me to seek a divorce would have been to reveal your secret, which honor would scarcely have permitted, and the same reason, I imagined, might constrain you. But, let us thank heaven! I am spared the trial, and with your assurance that all is well we shall be happy all the rest of our lives."

He moved toward her to take her in his arms.

"You forget," she answered quickly, and still evading him, "that I have given you no such assurance."

Professor Carson turned white to the lips. She thought he would have fainted at her feet; he clutched the table beside him for support. She would have pitied him, had she despised him less.

"What," he faltered, "can it be possible?"

"I shall certainly not deny it," she replied.

And she never did. They lived together according to his program. He was never certain, and in his doubt he found his punishment. When he died, she yielded to a woman's weakness. She was not a widow, but a bride. She owed Professor Carson no affection and felt for him no regret. He had outraged her finest feelings, and she had stooped to a posthumous revenge, which had satisfied her mind, while it only mystified others; indeed, she had cared very little, at the time, for what others might think. That having known her, and loved her, and married her, a prejudice which reflected in no wise upon her character, her intelligence or her beauty could keep them apart, was the unpardonable sin. She must be loved for what she was.

"It is curious," said Dr. Trumbull, reflectively, "how the fixed idea dominates the mind. Perfectly reasonable and logical and fair-minded upon every other topic, upon one pet aversion a man may skirt the edge of mania. Nature has set no impassable barrier between races. A system which, assuming the Negro race to be inferior, condemns Mrs. Carson, because of some remote strain of its blood, to celibacy and social ostracism, or throws her back upon the inferior race, is scarcely complimentary to our own. The exaggerated race feeling of men like Carson is more than a healthy instinct for the preservation of a type; it is more than a prejudice. It is an obsession."

"A disease," returned Professor Gilman. "In all probability, had she given Professor Carson the answer he wanted, it would never have satisfied him. The seed had been planted in his mind; it was sure to bring forth a harvest of suspicion and distrust. He would in any event have worried himself into a premature grave. His marriage, while the doubt existed, was a refinement of Quixotry—and of unconscious selfishness; to spare the feelings of the possible white woman, and to save her for himself, he deliberately contemplated the destruction of the happiness of the possible—Negress."

Across the deck, Dr. Trumbull studied the graceful contour of Mrs. Carson's figure, the fine lines of her profile. A widow, and yet no wife! It was interesting.

It would be a brave man who would marry her—but surely she had never loved Carson.

Dr. Trumbull had always admired her, since he had known her. Had she been willing, and had she waited a little longer, she might have been spared the somewhat tragic interlude with Carson.

"I had always wondered," he said, reflectively, "which of the three courses open to Carson he adopted—to postpone the marriage—to burn the letter—or to ask her frankly whether its contents were true. It seems that he did all three—he asked whether or not the statement was true; he burned the letter and married her without mentioning it; and—he deferred the marriage—the real marriage. It was the order in which he did them that destroyed his happiness and shortened his life."

"And all," said Professor Gilman, "for nothing, absolutely nothing. What malicious mind conceived and wrote the letter, Mrs. Carson never learned, but there was not a word of truth in it! Her blood is as entirely pure as Professor Carson's could have been. My wife knew her people, and her line of descent for two hundred years is quite as clear, quite as good, as that of most old American families. But here come the ladies."

"Oh, papa," cried Marcia, "you and Professor Gilman have been so busy talking that you have missed the most beautiful scenery—the Lorelei, and Bingen, and Ehrenbreitstein, and—oh, my! If it hadn't been for Mrs. Carson, who has been telling me all the legends, I shouldn't have known anything about them."

"I saw you with her and Mrs. Gilman, dear, and I knew it was all right. Perhaps Mrs. Carson will show them to me—some other time."

PAULINE ELIZABETH HOPKINS

(1859–1930)

A contemporary of Charles Chesnutt, Pauline Hopkins explored some of the same literary themes for a different audience. A venerable Boston publisher of classic American authors opened doors to him. But her literary entrée was Boston's Colored Co-operative Publishing Company, a struggling and small enterprise that she helped to develop. At a time when few American women writers—black or white—were recognized in journalism or literature, she was self-taught and prolific in both, though her artistry in fiction never equaled Chesnutt's. Her short stories and novels were those of a forerunner, as were the biographical profiles she wrote of notable black figures then absent in American textbooks. She pioneered at the beginning of a new century, but her efforts were not duly recognized in her lifetime.[1]

Born in 1859 in Portland, Maine, and reared in Boston, she graduated from Boston Girls High School, conscious of her family's significant heritage in New England history. On her mother's side, she was descended from a free-born New Hampshire family of prominent black clergyman, who included Thomas Paul, Sr. (1773–1831), a Revolutionary War veteran who settled in Boston and organized the First African Baptist Church (later called the First Independent Baptist Church) and the African Meetinghouse, a center of abolitionism in the 1820s and 1830s (now in the National Register of Historic Places). The Boston of her youth was then home to the antebellum abolitionist and novelist William Wells Brown, who provided a literary prize of ten dollars in gold that she won at age fifteen in a school-essay contest sponsored by the Congregational Publishing Society.

---

[1] Author and archivist Ann Allen Shockley was the first to revive interest in the author legacy in a seminal piece "Pauline Hopkins: A Biographical Excursion into Obscurity," *Phylon*, 33, 1972, pages 22–26. An Associate Librarian for Special Collections at Fisk University (until her retirement in 1998), Shockley researched the Pauline Hopkins Papers left by Charles S. Johnson, the University president from 1928 to 1956. Shockley expanded her research for her 1988 anthology *Afro-American Women Writers, 1746–1933*, which acknowledges the significance of additional new biographical information presented by archivist Dorothy B. Porter in the *Dictionary of American Negro Biography*, edited by Rayford Logan and Michael R. Winston (New York, 1982). *The Magazine Novels of Pauline Hopkins* were reprinted in 1988.

Her early ambition was to write for the theater, and she achieved limited success before she was twenty with two scripts for the musical stage. Written for performance by the famed Hyers Sisters, who moved from California to Boston in 1876 to found the first black musical repertory company, Pauline's two song plays for them were the three-act *Colored Aristocracy* (1877) and the four-act *Peculiar Sam; or, The Underground Railroad* (1879).[2] In 1880, the Company featured Pauline, her mother, and stepfather with the chorus for five performances billed as "The Hopkins Colored Troubadours in the Great Musical Drama, *Escape from Slavery.*" But when the Hyers team joined the black minstrelsy circuit in the early 1880s, Pauline chose another direction.

Advised by the stage manager at the Boston Museum to try writing short stories instead of dramas, she took that path, believing that fiction was universal and a means to present the lives, manners, and social conditions of her people from generation to generation. She was forty before she saw any of her fiction in print. In the interim, like Chesnutt, she studied stenography to acquire a skill to earn a livelihood. She worked as a stenographer for local Republicans, passed the Civil Service exam, and obtained employment at the Massachusetts Bureau of Statistics.

It is uncertain if, during her apprenticeship years, she submitted stories to commercial white magazines or book publishers. The short story was a new literary genre for black authors in the 1890s. No men except Dunbar and Chesnutt then had commercial publishers for their stories, and the female exception was Dunbar's wife, Alice, whose collection *The Goodness of St. Rocque* was issued by *his* publisher in 1899. Hopkins's first published short story, "The Mystery within Us," was nonracial and she perhaps submitted it to various outlets before it appeared in May 1900 in the first issue of *Colored American* magazine[3]—an illustrated monthly "Devoted to Literature, Science, Music, Art, Religion, Facts, Fiction, and Traditions of the Negro Race"—the first such monthly magazine in the twentieth century.

The four male associates who conceived the magazine in Boston announced in the premiere issue that, "Recognizing an immediate need for a Race Journal, otherwise than our current local periodicals, we have organized a Company, to be known as the Colored Co-operative Publishing Company." Hopkins became a member of the editorial board by investing in the cooperative, which issued certificates of deposit and dividends and accepted manuscripts as cash. Later that year, in a kind of barter arrangement, they published her first full-length

---

[2] The title of *Peculiar Sam* and its script length varied in several different versions by Hopkins. For further information, see Eileen Southern's *African American Musical Theater* (1991) and *The Music of Black Americans* (1997 rpt.)

[3] This periodical had no affiliation with the *Colored American* newspaper (1827–42), founded by free blacks in New York City, and mentioned elsewhere in this volume.

novel, *Contending Forces: A Romance Illustrative of Negro Life North and South,* a saga of miscegenation and family intrigue dating from slavery to post–Reconstruction—based on incidents that, according to her preface, can be found in court records in North Carolina. She copyrighted the text in 1899 and read portions to the Women's Era Club of Boston. The magazine advertised the novel, promoted it by mail subscription at $1.50 per copy, and distributed it nationally through commissioned agents, who also arranged public readings. Her audience was the emerging middle-class of black women active in civic clubs who bought the book and also increased the magazine circulation.

Appointed literary editor in May 1903, her contributions between 1900 and early 1904 were prodigious. These include varied essays, a biographical series on Famous Women of the Negro Race and Famous Men of the Negro Race, six short stories, and three serialized novels: *Hagar's Daughter—A Story of Southern Caste Prejudice* (1901, under the pseudonym Sarah A. Allen, her mother's maiden name); *Winona: A Tale of Negro Life in the South and Southwest* (1902); and *Of One Blood; or, the Hidden Self* (1902–3).

In August 1904, the *Colored American* moved to New York "Under New Management"—and the November issue surprised readers with an announcement on the last page:

> On account of ill-health—Miss Pauline Hopkins has found it necessary to sever her relations with this Magazine and has returned to her home in Boston. Miss Hopkins was a faithful and conscientious worker, and did much toward building up the Magazine.

She gave no public explanation, but her byline that December was in a new journal, *Voice of the Negro,* launched by black intellectuals in Atlanta to counter Booker T. Washington's covert efforts to influence the Negro press. The Hopkins transition aroused speculation—yet persistent—that her exit from *Colored American* magazine was due to its new editor–publisher, Fred R. Moore, Booker T. Washington's National Business League Secretary, who hired the nephew of Washington's wife as associate editor. The revamped magazine became a public-relations organ for Washington and was defunct by 1910. Blame for the collapse was later falsely pinned to Hopkins by misinformed outsiders like sociologist Charles S. Johnson, who, eighteen years later, in "The Rise of the Negro Magazine" for the *Journal of Negro History,* singled her out: "The *Colored American,* edited in Boston by Miss Pauline Hopkins, reached a circulation of 15,000 but through poor management was sold for debt. . . ."

Whether Hopkins resigned or was removed in 1904 is unknown. Her 1900 novel, *Contending Forces,* shows her awareness of opposing factions in black leadership—especially in the Washington–Du Bois controversy—and her ambivalence toward Washington's philosophy of industrial education. Yet her lengthy article, "Booker T. Washington," in the October 1901 *Colored American*, concludes with a turgid note that she perhaps would have changed by 1904:

> View his career in whatever light we may, be we for or against his theories, his personality is striking, his life uncommon, and the magnetic influence which radiates from him in all directions, bending and swaying great minds and pointing the ultimate conclusion of colossal schemes as the wind the leaves of the trees, is stupendous. When the happenings of the Twentieth Century have become matters of history, Dr. Washington's motives will be open to as many constructions and discussions as are those of Napoleon today, or of other men of extraordinary ability, whether for good or evil, who have had like phenomenal careers.

To *Voice of the Negro*, Hopkins contributed a piece on "The New York Subway" in 1904, and a series on The Dark Races of the Twentieth Century in 1905. Their content could not have displeased the white financiers or black editors of *Voice of the Negro*, unlike her stories of interracial romance, which upset some white investors of *Colored American*. Before *Voice of the Negro* fell silent in 1907, she briefly tried her own publishing venture, P. E. Hopkins and Company, in Cambridge, where she privately printed *A Primer of Facts Pertaining to the Early Greatness of the African Race and the Possibility of Restoration by Its Descendants, with Epilogue* (1905). Her byline was not evident again until 1916, when the New Era Publishing Company of Boston introduced *New Era* magazine, "a monthly devoted to the world-wide interest of the Negro race." She contributed one work of fiction and two biographical profiles, before *New Era*'s early demise. It signaled the end of an era for her literary efforts. She could have found an audience in the NAACP's new magazine, *The Crisis*, launched in 1910, but no contributions from her appeared in its pages, then or later—undoubtedly because its mordant editor, W. E. B. Du Bois, whose editorial reign lasted the rest of her life, said publicly in 1912 that she was "not conciliatory enough" at the *Colored American*.

Hopkins's final years were spent in low profile, working as a stenographer at the Massachusetts Institute of Technology. She died in a Cambridge hospital, August 13, 1930, at age 71: severe burns suffered when her garment caught fire from an oil stove in her room. If her tragic end had an analogue in her fiction, it was in her first published short story, with a sober line from a protagonist saved from death by a mysterious force: "What is life . . . but a flame easily extinguished by the rude hand of destiny or misfortune." Her following short story excerpt is from the November 1903 issue of *Colored American*.

From As the Lord Lives, He Is One
of Our Mother's Children (1903)

It was Saturday afternoon in a large Western town, and the Rev. Septimus Stevens sat in his study writing down the headings for his Sunday sermon. It was slow work; somehow the words would not flow with their usual ease, although his brain was teeming with ideas. He had written for his heading at the top of the sheet these words for a text: "As I live, he is one of our mother's children." It was to be a great effort on the Negro question, and the reverend gentleman, with his New England training, was in full sympathy with his subject. He had jotted down a few headings under it, when he came to a full stop; his mind simply refused to work. Finally, with a sigh, he opened the compartment in his desk where his sermons were packed and began turning over those old creations in search of something suitable for the morrow.

Suddenly the whistles in all directions began to blow wildly. The Rev. Septimus hurried to the window, threw it open and leaned out, anxious to learn the cause of the wild clamor. Could it be another of the terrible "cave-ins," that were the terror of every mining district? Men were pouring out of the mines as fast as they could come up. The crowds which surged through the streets night and day were rushing to meet them. Hundreds of policemen were about; each corner was guarded by a squad commanded by a sergeant. The police and the mob were evidently working together. Tramp, tramp, on they rushed; down the serpentine boulevard for nearly two miles they went swelling like an angry torrent. In front of the open window where stood the white-faced clergyman, they paused. A man mounted the empty barrel and harangued the crowd: "I am from Dover City, gentlemen, and I have come here today to assist you in teaching the blacks a lesson. I have killed a nigger before," he yelled, "and in revenge of the wrong wrought upon you and yours I am willing to kill again. The only way you can teach these niggers a lesson is to go to the jail and lynch these men as an object lesson. String them up! That is the only thing to do. Kill them, string them up, lynch them! I will lead you. On to the prison and lynch

Jones and Wilson, the black fiends!" With a hoarse shout, in which were mingled cries like the screams of enraged hyenas and the snarls of tigers, they rushed on.

Nora, the cook burst open the study door, pale as a sheet, and dropped at the minister's feet. "Mother of God!" she cried, "and is it the end of the wurruld?"

On the maddened men rushed from north, south, east and west, armed with everything from a brick to a horse-pistol. In the melee a man was shot down. Somebody planted a long knife in the body of a little black newsboy for no apparent reason. Every now and then a Negro would be overwhelmed somewhere on the outskirts of the crowd and left beaten to a pulp. Then they reached the jail and battered in the door.

The solitary watcher at the window tried to move, but could not; terror had stricken his very soul, and his white lips moved in articulate prayer. The crowd surged back. In the midst was only one man; for some reason the other was missing. A rope was knotted about his neck—charged with murder, himself about to be murdered. The hands which drew the rope were too swift, and, half-strangled, the victim fell. The crowd halted, lifted him up, loosened the rope and let the wretch breathe.

He was a grand man—physically—black as ebony, tall, straight, deep-chested, every fiber full of that life so soon to be quenched. Lucifer, just about to be cast out of heaven, could not have thrown around a glance of more scornful pride. What might not such a man have been, if—but it was too late. "Run fair, boys," said the prisoner, calmly, "run fair! You keep up your end of the rope and I'll keep up mine."

The crowd moved a little more slowly, and the minister saw the tall form "keeping up" its end without a tremor of hesitation. As they neared the telegraph pole, with its outstretched arm, the watcher summoned up his lost strength, grasped the curtain and pulled it down to shut out the dreadful sight. Then came a moment of ominous silence. The man of God sank upon his knees to pray for the passing soul. A thousand-voiced cry of brutal triumph arose in cheers for the work that had been done, and curses and imprecations, and they who had hunted a man out of life hurried off to hunt for gold.

To and fro on the white curtain swung the black silhouette of what had been a man.

For months the minister heard in the silence of the night phantom echoes of those frightful voices, and awoke, shuddering, from some dream whose vista was closed by that black figure swinging in the air. . . .

WILLIAM MONROE TROTTER

(1872–1934)

The year 1901 brought Boston a militant new newspaper, whose founder and managing editor, twenty-nine-year-old Monroe Trotter, had as his role model William Lloyd Garrison and the *Liberator*. Trotter's new weekly was the *Guardian*, and its motto was "For Every Right with All Thy Might." For three decades he tried to abide by it, as one of the first Afro-American editors to make a life-long career with a weekly newspaper in the twentieth century.

In Boston, Trotter's family history was linked to the making of the *Guardian*. His father, James Monroe Trotter, Mississippi–born son of a slaveowner, freed and educated in Ohio, was recruited as a Union soldier for the Massachusetts 55th Regiment, and after the Civil War appointed the first Afro-American postal clerk in Boston. In 1868 he married Virginia Isaacs, whom he had met while teaching school in Ohio. She was reputed to be a great-granddaughter of Thomas Jefferson, whose liaison with his mulatto chambermaid Sally Hemings produced Eston Hemings, who married and settled for several years in Chillicothe, leaving three offspring before his death in Wisconsin in the 1850s. On April 7, 1872, on a Chillicothe farm belonging to Virginia Isaacs Trotter's parents, William Monroe Trotter was born, the first and only son among three Trotter children who were reared in Boston.

Called "Monroe" from infancy, he grew up with two younger sisters, Bessie and Maude, in a home steeped in New England ideals of family and society, inspired with principles of religions from his mother, and temperance, hard work, and other values requisite for success from his father. Growing up in the 1870s and 1880s, he was taught to transcend barriers that might be imposed by race prejudice and told about both black and white abolitionists. In a Boston the population of which then included fewer than 10,000 Afro-Americans, the Trotters found little opposition to their presence in largely white neighborhoods, schools, and churches—first in Cambridge, later in Boston's South End, and finally in suburban Hyde Park—once known as Fairmount after the Civil War—when abolitionists Angelina Grimké Weld and husband Theodore moved there and helped to organize the first public schools and library. Monroe

Trotter excelled at Hyde Park high school, where he was the only Afro-American student and the senior class president.

In 1891 he entered Harvard, was elected to Phi Beta Kappa his junior year, and graduated magna cum laude in 1895. In February 1892, while a college freshman, he lost the father whose influence on him never waned: the Civil War lieutenant who demanded equal pay for black soldiers in his Massachusetts 55th Regiment commanded by whites; the senior postal employee who resigned when white clerks were promoted over him; the erstwhile Republican who urged black men in the early 1880s to use the Fifteenth Amendment and vote for Democrats. The son was old enough to understand politics when his father won Senate confirmation in 1887 as U.S. Recorder of Deeds for the District of Columbia, appointed by Grover Cleveland, the first Democrat elected President in a quarter century. The federal job—held earlier in the decade by Republican Frederick Douglass—was over in 1889 after Cleveland lost the 1888 election. James Trotter returned to Boston and began a real-estate business profitable enough at his death to leave his family a substantial inheritance.

At Harvard, while concentrating on courses in politics and history, Monroe's goal was to enter a business career—having observed his father's acumen, and hearing about onetime Harvard student Horatio Alger's luck-and-pluck stories on the American–dream theme of success and fortune. Using his late father's contacts, after graduation Trotter apprenticed in a white-owned firm of real-estate mortgage negociants, becoming successful enough to open his own office by 1899. That year he married Geraldine Pindell, an intelligent and attractive young woman trained as a bookkeeper, who was blond and blue-eyed but "colored" according to America's divided identity "one drop" race phobia. In Boston, as in other cities North and South after the Civil War, a mixed-blood population of racially indeterminate individuals dotted the landscape, some of its members publicly known as the offspring of slave and master, like the Trotters' Hyde Park neighbor, Archibald Henry Grimké,[1] prominent Boston attorney and former editor, who was United States Consul to the Dominican Republic, 1894–98.

In 1901, the newlywed Trotters helped to organize the Boston Literary and Historical Association, for both races "to promote the intellectual life of the community." As noted, social life in Boston between the races was then rare, and upper-class society among Afro-Americans had its distinct and exclusive rival sets living in the West End and the South End of the city. Education,

---

[1] See the biographical footnote on Archibald H. Grimké in the entry on Theodore D. Weld in this volume, p. 137.

family background, and color caste counted more than wealth for entry into those ranks. The Trotters, for a time, were part of that closed elite, which was more successful and prosperous than in any turn-of-the century city except Chicago in terms of numbers of college-educated persons distinguished in the professions and politics. Many of those in Boston were not newcomers after the Civil War like the Trotters but descendants of Revolutionary War veterans and abolitionists. (Among them Edmund Garrison Walker, son of martyred abolitionist David Walker[2] but venerated on his merit as Boston lawyer and legislator, the first of his race in 1866 elected to the Massachusetts General Court. He died in January 1901, and Pauline Hopkins eulogized him in *Colored American* magazine.)

Trotter had the future as well as history in mind when, after much soul-searching and painful awareness of Jim Crow obstacles facing him in the business world, he invested from his inheritance to launch the *Guardian* on November 9, 1901—promising a new editorial voice for the "needs and aspirations of the colored American." Circulation soared to 3,000 in nine months. Co-edited the first two years with George Forbes, an Amherst graduate who earned his living at the Boston Public Library, and assisted by Geraldine Trotter as collaborator and bookkeeper, the paper was soon solvent, with steady advertisers and subscribers. The editorial content was like Trotter himself: audacious, forthright, self-righteous, unpredictable, and unrelenting—especially against the policies of Booker T. Washington, then at the apex of his power. So regularly satirized and mocked was Washington in the *Guardian's* editorials and cartoons that he secretly subsidized three new black Boston weeklies to challenge Trotter: the *Advocate*, which lasted less than a year in 1902; the *Enterprise*, which fell after six months in 1903; and the *Colored Citizen*, which held on weekly from late 1903 to 1905. Washington was also sending checks via his conduits to Bostonian Charles Alexander, a Tuskegee graduate, to edit *Alexander's* magazine, and by late 1904 in control of *Colored American*, after James Trotter's brother-in-law, William Dupree, invested as publisher in May 1903.

Washington never bought or influenced the resolute Trotter, as he succeeded in doing with the once fiercely independent journalist T. Thomas Fortune,[3] who then was firmly in Washington's camp and calling the young *Guardian* editor "a public nuisance." Trotter was arrested by a police squad the night of July 30, 1903, for confronting Washington and Fortune, and their entourage, at a program at Boston's Columbus Avenue A.M.E. Zion Church, and demanding Washington answer a list of nine questions. The heckling, hiss-

---

[2] See the biographical entry on David Walker in this volume, pages 87–88, above.

[3] See the biographical entry on T. Thomas Fortune in this volume, pages 294–96, above.

ing, pushing, and shouting that ensued on both sides was reported by Boston's white press as a "riot." Trotter was soon convicted by a judge and served thirty days in jail. He wrote his version of events for the *Guardian*, where a long article in the August 1 issued displayed three bold captions:

> BOOKER T. WASHINGTON SPEAKS UNDER A CORDON OF POLICE
> *Tuskegeean Two Hours Trying to Make Himself Heard*
> *His Hirelings Protect Him From the Consequences of*
> *Facing His Own Previous Statements—Attempt to Deny Free*
> *Speech Foiled.*

In Trotter's long and contentious career, the July 1903 episode made him both famous and infamous; it was also the genesis of a more significant event later explained in retrospect by W. E. B. Du Bois in his *Autobiography*:

> I did not know beforehand of the meeting in Boston, nor the projected plan to heckle Mr. Washington. But when Trotter went to jail, my indignation overflowed. I did not always agree with Trotter, then or later. But he was an honest, brilliant, unselfish man, and to treat as a crime that which was at worst mistaken judgment was an outrage. I sent out from Atlanta in June 1905 a call to a few selected persons "for organized determination and aggressive action on the part of men who believe in Negro freedom and growth." I proposed a conference during the summer "to oppose firmly present methods of strangling honest criticism; to organize intelligent and honest Negroes; and to support organs of news and public opinion."

The organization Du Bois proposed became the Niagara Movement. Trotter was a catalyst for it and an early participant, but he broke away in 1907. For reasons more to do with his temperament than with Niagara Movement principles, he adopted his own strategy for civil rights and race relations, with himself and his newspaper at the center. A master of protest demonstrations, mass rallies, and editorials, he galvanized crowds at several political conferences that he initiated—but they lasted as long as a Presidential campaign—and overestimated the numerical strength of the black ballot when women could not yet vote (an issue he avoided).

The pressure groups Trotter founded were said to be "organizations," but were primarily all-male conventions for Presidential campaign electoral strategy, focusing on which national political party and candidate to support. He aimed to offer an alternative to the Niagara Movement and an end to Booker T. Washington as power broker of black political patronage via the White House. Hence a call to attend his Negro–American Political League, which met in Philadelphia in 1908, and his National Independent League, which convened in Boston in 1911. His endorsement of Woodrow Wilson in the 1912 election was one the *Guardian* never lived down. Wilson's victory brought instant Jim Crow federal policies that led an embarrassed and caustic Trotter with a delegation to the White House in 1914, only to be abruptly dismissed. He miscalculated by believing he could do as his father had done and pressure Democrats and Republicans with the black vote and thereby receive civil rights gains and political plums. The last group he mobilized was the National Independent Equal Rights League, which sponsored his Midwest speaking tour in 1915, and supported his Boston demonstration against D. W. Griffith's racist film *The Birth of a Nation*, which was released the same year.

After Booker T. Washington's death in November 1915, the *Guardian*'s main target was gone; its circulation dwindled as larger black national weekly newspapers emerged in other cities. The then five-year-old NAACP, which Trotter saw as an organization led by whites with black followers, moved ahead without him, as did its new official organ, the *Crisis*. Over the years, Trotter spearheaded commemorative Boston celebrations to honor abolitionists William Lloyd Garrison, Charles Sumner, and Elijah Lovejoy, but he was unable to work harmoniously with black and white intellectuals in the NAACP.[4]

In 1919, following World War I, Trotter traveled in disguise on an ocean liner as one of the kitchen crew to attend the Paris Peace Conference, after the Wilson administration refused him a passport. By then he had lost his wife in the influenza epidemic of 1918, and the *Guardian* was losing money, but the paper continued a fight against segregation, police brutality, and deteriorating economic conditions as the black masses moved into Boston with the Great Migration.

The world of his readership had been outside a "ghetto," a word then increasingly heard as social-caste tensions increased within the race and baleful resentments mounted between the races. The Boston he had known and made the compass of his universe began to move toward more invidious ethnic tensions in changing neighborhoods with the Great Depression. In April 1934, on his sixty-second birthday, in despair after years of personal sacrifice and declining support, and with few relatives remaining, Trotter fell or jumped from the roof of his apartment building. His funeral, one of the largest in Boston's history, vindicated him as the city's foremost black voice of protest of his generation.

---

[4] See the entry of Oswald Garrison Villard in this volume, pages 451–57, below.

The following selection, from the *Guardian,* January 10, 1903, represents Trotter's disagreements with Booker T. Washington.

Has the Race the Element
of Self-Salvation in It? (1903)

Nothing tends so much to disparage a class of people in the estimation of others as the manifestation of inherent mental weakness on the part of its leaders in the discussion of everyday public questions. Other sins of both commission and omission may be pardoned, but those of deficiency in mental grasp of elementary questions of primal importance such as concern our very existence raise at once doubt in the mind of others as to the wisdom of clothing such a class of people with the same rights and equality as themselves. For if the salt of the leaders has lost its savor wherewith shall the followers be salted or saved? We have been led to these observations by the attitude which the *New York Age* and the (Philadelphia) *Christian Recorder,* two supposed leading Colored journals, take of late toward some very elementary race questions.

Some weeks ago, as will be recalled, the *Guardian* called attention to a very dangerous statement contained in the letter which Prof. Booker T. Washington sent to a Southern newspaper on Thanksgiving Day. The statement was that every revised [state] constitution had put at the South a premium on intelligence, character and thrift, etc. We thought that with the knowledge that every Colored editor must have—regarding the aim and declared purpose of the Southern constitution—nothing else was needed than to call the attention to the professor's statement. We went so far as to quote several comments from daily papers hereabout, among them this from the *Boston Herald:*

> It is very considerate of Booker T. Washington to say that every revised constitution throughout the southern states has put a premium upon intelligence, ownership of property, thrift and character. In fact, it sounds somewhat too considerate at first glance.

And also the following from the *Boston Evening Record:*

> Booker T. Washington says that the Negroes are disenfranchised, and he sees no hope of reversing the situation, except through the process

of education, which may not, result in enfranchisement. It never will, so long as the Caucasians in the south, feel as they do now. Perhaps the anti-Negro feeling will moderate with time. But Booker Washington's position settles the fact that for the present all hope of political participation in the South is denied to the Negro. And no party in Congress will take up the issue. We may, as Republicans, talk about it, and that is all. And we shall not attempt to reduce the representation of the southern states in Congress.

These two journals, here quoted, speak of this disfranchising business as it strikes white men; they have not yet learned to mix their liberty with alloy. Now how about the Colored papers above named? The *New York Age*—which was once trumpet-voiced in public affairs, but which now had died away to the almost inaudible and feeble chirp of a katydid, reasons thus as to the *Herald*'s remarks (making use even of the antiquated and forgotten term, *Mugwump*[5]):

> Other folks lacking the intellectual acumen of the Mugwump mind have felt something of the same sort, perhaps, more bluntly expressed. In fact, it has required a little reflection to see through the apparent approval of recent southern legislation enunciated by Dr. Washington—and discern beneath it a deeper meaning in the future results to be looked for from that policy. It is a question whether the utterance is more significant of the optimism or the sagacity of the author. At any rate, it demonstrates that he is both farsighted and longheaded.

Without a minute's further parley, "The *Guardian* hastens to confess itself in the class with those here thought to be 'lacking the intellectual acumen.'" No amount of reflection can bring us to the approval of "Dr. Washington's deeper meaning." The *Guardian* would a thousand times prefer the interpretation put upon "Dr. Washington's" meaning by the disinterested white press, than any amount of inane babble of a sycophantic sheet running without rhyme or reason. From such "farsightedness" we pray earnestly for eternal deliverance.

---

[5] *Mugwump*: Originally an Algonquin Indian word meaning *chief*, the term was used in nineteenth-century politics to refer to persons who acted independently, notably Republicans who opposed the party candidate James Blaine and supported Grover Cleveland in the presidential election of 1884.

THE NIAGARA MOVEMENT:

THE MEN AND IDEAS BEHIND IT

Two years elapsed between the so-called Boston Riot of July 1903 when Monroe Trotter was arrested and the corollary summons by Du Bois for a conference in June 1905. Other reasons were then tantamount when twenty-nine black men from fourteen states joined Du Bois to cross from Buffalo, New York, to the Canadian side of Niagara Falls at Fort Erie, Ontario. The three-day meeting there July 11 to 15, 1905, initiated the first black protest organization of the twentieth century—one intended to do more than the Afro-American Council begun by T. Thomas Fortune in 1898. Du Bois had circulated a statement of purpose to over fifty colleagues he thought receptive to a conference focusing on alternatives to the accommodationist policies of Booker T. Washington. During the Niagara assembly, the participants discussed how to promote social, political, and racial justice, through a signed Declaration of Principles.

"Who are the men back of these principles?" Du Bois asked readers in "The Growth of the Niagara Movement," in *Voice of the Negro,* January 1906. "We can say in all modesty," he wrote, "that no organization in the United States, white or black, represents today in membership a higher grade of character and efficiency. We have on our rolls ministers, lawyers, journalists, teachers, merchants, artisans and servants." Membership by December 1905 increased to 150 men in 30 states. The initial meeting voted to restrict maximum membership to five hundred in subsequent years. The objective was never to swell the ranks but to work in small groups in local communities. Yet, their programmatic emphasis was cosmetic at best, without one idea on economic aims to counter Booker T. Washington. Instead, Niagara's push was "freedom of speech and criticism," "an unfettered and unsubsidized press," "manhood suffrage," "the abolition of all caste distinctions based simply on race and color," "the recognition of the highest and best training as the monopoly of no class or race," and "united effort to realize these ideals under wise and courageous leadership."

The Niagara Movement was incorporated January 31, 1906, in the District of Columbia, with Du Bois as General Secretary. Although the organization was entirely Afro-American, it inaugurated tributes to honor abolitionists such as John Brown—a reason its second annual meeting was held at Harper's Ferry in August 1906. To advance the movement's ideas and goals, Du Bois edited a weekly, *Moon*, though it faded due to finances by the summer conclave of 1906. In January 1907, he began publishing a new monthly, *Horizon: A Journal of the Color Line*, which lasted through the third Niagara conference in August 1907, in Boston, and beyond the fourth one in August 1908, at Oberlin. The latter meeting was the last annual forum before the movement dissolved in 1911. Contrary to popular opinion, it did not dissolve into the biracial NAACP, which some of its members joined after 1910.

In its five-year existence, the Niagara Movement was integrally an organization *of* men, and essentially *for* men. Nothing in its Declaration of Principles acknowledges the status of women, the condition of girls, or a concern for female suffrage. Its accent is on "manhood suffrage," "manhood rights," "black men," "black boys," "black soldiers," "manly agitation," and "all men of all races." Womanhood is cited once: in the context of "protest against the 'Jim Crow' car.'" Du Bois did not invite women to the first conference in 1905, and his aforementioned 1906 article did not appear to welcome them: "The Niagara Movement has grown and will grow," he wrote. "And we welcome to it intelligent, manly men who are not afraid to stand up and be counted." Monroe Trotter consistently opposed official admission of women to the movement before he left it in 1907. By then, Du Bois was writing poems like "The Burden of Black Women" with a lament about their plight during slavery, but he then also saw a need for a few Niagara members' wives to help out in state auxiliaries, even though women were excluded from plenary sessions at annual meetings. Such chauvinism found little dissent, despite the growing number of women among the "Talented Tenth"—the educated élite of the race Du Bois defended in his 1903 essay—with its doctrinaire opening sentence: "The Negro race, like all races, is going to be saved by its exceptional men." While "exceptional men" of Niagara forged ahead, their wives gained respect in their own national organizations, working in the rear guard—seen and heard mainly among themselves. Women were likewise banned from the all-male American Negro Academy (1897–1928), which had among its distinguished intellectuals some who were also in the Niagara Movement, including Du Bois, the ANA's second president, who proposed a merger of the two with other black organizations in 1908.[1]

---

[1] For a full history of the ANA, see Alfred A. Moss, Jr., *The American Negro Academy: Voice of the Talented Tenth*, (Baton Rouge: Louisiana State University Press, 1981), which explains why the Du Bois proposal was rejected by the learned society. Founded in March 1897 as "an organization of authors, scholars, artists and those distinguished in other walks of life, men of African descent, for the promotion of Letters, Science and Art," according to Moss's book, "no efforts were made by

The following text is the mandate of guiding principles adopted by the Niagara Movement in 1905.

From *The Niagara Movement* *"Declaration of Principles"* (1905)

. . . We believe in manhood suffrage; we believe that no man is so good, intelligent or wealthy as to be entrusted wholly with the welfare of his neighbor.

We believe also in protest against the curtailment of our civil rights. All American citizens have the right to equal treatment in places of public accommodation according to their behavior and deserts. . . .

We especially complain against the denial of equal opportunities to us in economic life; in the rural districts of the South this amounts to peonage and virtual slavery; all over the South it tends to crush labor and small business enterprises; and everywhere American prejudice, helped often by iniquitous laws, is making it more difficult for Negro-Americans to earn a decent living.

Common school education should be free to all American children and compulsory. High school training should be adequately provided for all, and college training should be the monopoly of no class or race in any section of our common country. We believe that, in defense of our own institutions, the United States should aid common school education, particularly in the South, and we especially recommend concerted agitation to this end. We urge an increase in public high school facilities in the South, where Negro-Americans are almost wholly without such provisions. We favor well-equipped trade and technical schools for the training of artisans, and the need of adequate and liberal endowment for a few institutions of higher education must be patent to sincere well-wishers of the race.

We demand upright judges in courts, juries selected without discrimination on account of color and the same measure of punishment and the same efforts at reformation for black as for white offenders. We need orphanages and farm

---

any academy member . . . to recruit black women who were 'Authors, Scholars, Artists,' " despite a suggestion to do so by one founding member, George N. Grisham, who terminated his relationship with the ANA in 1908."

For other references to ANA in this volume, see entries on Alexander Crummell, T. Thomas Fortune, and Kelly Miller, pages 291–93, 294–301, and 430–42, respectively.

schools for dependent children, juvenile reformatories for delinquents, and the abolition of the dehumanizing convict-lease system.

We note with alarm the evident retrogression in this land of sound public opinion on the subject of manhood rights, republican government and human brotherhood, and we pray God that this nation will not degenerate into a mob of boasters and oppressors, but rather will return to the faith of the fathers, that all men were created free and equal, with certain unalienable rights.

We plead for health—for an opportunity to live in decent houses and localities, for a chance to rear our children in physical and moral cleanliness.

We hold up for public execration the conduct of two opposite classes of men: The practice among employers of importing ignorant Negro-American laborers in emergencies, and then affording them neither protection nor permanent employment; and the practice of labor unions in proscribing and boycotting and oppressing thousands of their fellow toilers, simply because they are black. These methods have accentuated and will accentuate the war of labor and capital, and they are disgraceful to both sides.

We refuse to allow the impression to remain that the Negro-American assents to inferiority, is submissive under oppression and apologetic before insults. Through helplessness we may submit, but the voice of protest of ten million Americans must never cease to assail the ears of their fellows, so long as America is unjust.

Any discrimination based simply on race or color is barbarous, we care not how hallowed it be by custom, expediency, or prejudice. Differences made on account of ignorance, immorality, or disease are legitimate methods of fighting evil, and against them we have no word of protest; but discrimination based simply and solely on physical peculiarities, place of birth, color of skin, are relics of that unreasoning human savagery of which the world is and ought to be thoroughly ashamed.

We protest against the "Jim Crow" car, since its effect is and must be, to make us pay first-class fare for third-class accommodations, render us open to insults and discomfort and to crucify wantonly our manhood, womanhood and self-respect.

We regret that this nation has never seen fit adequately to reward the black soldiers who, in its five wars, have defended their country with their blood, and yet have been systematically denied the promotions which their abilities deserve. And we regard as unjust, the exclusion of black boys from the military and navy training schools.

We urge upon Congress the enactment of appropriate legislation for securing the proper enforcement of those articles of freedom, the thirteenth, fourteenth and fifteenth amendments of the Constitution of the United States.

We repudiate the monstrous doctrine that the oppressor should be the sole authority as to the rights of the oppressed.

The Negro race in America, stolen, ravished and degraded, struggling up through difficulties and oppression, needs sympathy and receives criticism; needs help and is given hindrance, needs protection and is given mob violence, needs justice and is given charity, needs leadership and is given cowardice and apology, needs bread and is given a stone. This nation will never stand justified before God until these things are changed.

Especially are we surprised and astonished at the recent attitude of the church of Christ—on the increase of a desire to bow to racial prejudice, to narrow the bounds of human brotherhood, and to segregate black men in some outer sanctuary. This is wrong, unchristian and disgraceful to the twentieth-century civilization.

Of the above grievances we do not hesitate to complain, and to complain loudly and insistently. To ignore, overlook, or apologize for these wrongs is to prove ourselves unworthy of freedom. Persistent manly agitation is the way to liberty, and toward this goal the Niagara Movement has started and asks the cooperation of all men of all races.

At the same time we want to acknowledge with deep thankfulness the help of our fellowmen from the abolitionist down to those who today still stand for equal opportunity and who have given and still give of their wealth and of their poverty for our advancement.

And while we are demanding, and ought to demand, and will continue to demand the rights enumerated above, God forbid that we should ever forget to urge corresponding duties upon our people:

The duty to vote.
The duty to respect the rights of others.
The duty to work.
The duty to obey the laws.
The duty to be clean and orderly.
The duty to send our children to school.
The duty to respect ourselves, even as we respect others. . . .

KELLY MILLER

(1863–1939)

While the Niagara Movement struggled to gain equal rights and the American Negro Academy due respect for a beleaguered people in the first decade of the new century, a fictional trilogy with a bitter racial view from a white Southerner drew wider national attention. The extremist author was Thomas Dixon, Jr., a North Carolina Baptist preacher of "racial purity" and antiblack propaganda in three "historical novels" about Reconstruction: *The Leopard's Spots: A Romance of the White Man's Burden—1865–1900* (1902); *The Clansman: An Historical Romance of the Ku Klux Klan* (1905); and *The Traitor: A Story of the Fall of the Invisible Empire* (1907). After *The Leopard's Spots* hit best-sellerdom and Broadway in 1903, Dixon was challenged in an open letter by a then obscure scholar named Kelly Miller. His reasoned argument did not stop Dixon's two successive novels (or D. W. Griffith's million-dollar movie, *The Birth of a Nation,* based on *The Clansman*), but the letter offered a fervent reply from a black Southerner unlike any in Dixon's fiction.

Of the civil rights figures born and reared in the South during Reconstruction, Miller was undoubtedly the only one whose namesake father, a black freeman, chose to fight in the Confederate Army. Born in 1863 in rural Winnsboro, South Carolina, to a slave mother during the Civil War, Kelly, Jr., was the sixth of ten children. His schooling during Reconstruction was in the town's first classroom, where Presbyterian missionaries recognized his genius for mathematics and enrolled him at the local Fairfield Institute. In the early 1880s, he won a scholarship to the Howard University Preparatory Department and completed a three-year liberal arts program in two years, while working part-time as a clerk in the U.S. Pension Office. Graduate work followed at Johns Hopkins University, where he studied mathematics and physics from 1887 to 1889, the first Afro-American admitted to that institution. In 1890, he was appointed professor of mathematics at Howard, his alma mater.

His own "up from slavery" success in higher education made him first an opponent of Booker T. Washington's industrial-training doctrine, but then an advocate of both manual and classical education as necessary for progress. He rejected Washington's "Atlanta Compromise" speech of 1895, and that same year successfully lobbied Howard's board of trustees to add the new discipline of sociology to the curriculum, as a way to explore and discuss race relations. Between 1895 and 1907, he taught both sociology and mathematics and began publishing articles—some of which inevitably swept him into the controversies surrounding Booker T. Washington. In those disputes, from 1903 to 1907, Miller's position varied between neutrality to open criticism, to identification with both Du Bois and Washington. The three men were briefly part of the improbable Committee of Twelve for the Advancement of Interests of the Negro Race, set in motion by Washington in January 1904 and funded by wealthy industrialist Andrew Carnegie. Du Bois tipped his hat good-bye after seven months on that Committee, but Miller remained until 1908. Earlier, he had disclaimed the so-called Boston Riot as "regrettable," in an anonymous article, "Washington's Policy," for the *Boston Transcript* in September 1903, reprinted two months later under the pseudonym "Fair Play" in *Colored American* magazine. In 1908, he amended that essay into a more uncompromisingly critical view of both Trotter and Du Bois in his book *Race Adjustment*—for by then the two militants had excluded him from the Niagara Movement.

To some of his critics, Miller was the middle-of-the-road straddler, an equivocal voice of expediency, though others respected him as an objective analyst, a quiet conciliator, who wrote about race problems with a recognition of white paternalism, which he had learned to accept as a student in the South, and as an academic under Howard's white presidents. He was appointed acting dean of Howard's College of Arts and Sciences in 1907 (a position his critics claimed was due to Booker T. Washington's election as a trustee that same year). In 1908, he became "Dean Miller," a position he held until a 1919 demotion by the University's last white president. From 1915 to 1925, he remained professor and chair of the Department of Sociology, where he taught until he retired in 1934.

His efforts to make Howard a research center on "Negro–Americana" are now enshrined at the University's Moorland–Spingarn Research Center, whose "Visitor's Guide" notes:

> . . . The increasing interest in Negro history at the turn of the century was reflected most forcibly at Howard University by Professor Kelly Miller. . . . He succeeded in persuading Dr. Jesse E. Moorland (1863–1940), an alumnus and trustee who was a secretary of the YMCA, that he should donate to Howard his sizable private library on black people in Africa and in America, so that the University might develop a Negro–American Museum and Library that could be a center for research and instruction.

Miller's own articles as educator and sociologist on issues about "the race problem" began in the early 1900s in scholarly periodicals such as *Journal of Social Science, Educational Review, Scientific Monthly, Dial,* and *Forum,* though he was better known for controversial "open letter" pamphlets and his essays compiled as books, including *Out of the House of Bondage* (1914) and *The Everlasting Stain* (1924). His weekly columns in several black weekly newspapers in the 1920s and 1930s increased his impact as one of the most influential educators of the day. But in the early 1930s, he was in contention with historian and former Howard colleague Carter G. Woodson[1] on black progress in higher education, and at odds with the radical Du Bois, who insisted, as Miller did not, that segregation and discrimination existed in the North.

A week after Miller's death on December 29, 1939, Du Bois had the last word in an unsentimental obituary note that was no encomium but a reflection of their growing differences over the decades. Du Bois, then nearly seventy-two, solemnly concluded: "Miller had gained a widespread reputation for instability of judgment and disloyalty to most causes."

Following is the text of "As to the Leopard's Spots: An Open Letter to Thomas Dixon," Miller's first major pamphlet, published in September 1905. Dixon's allusion to "Leopard's Spots" is from the Biblical Jeremiah 13:23— "Can the Ethiopian change his skin, or the leopard his spots?"

An Open Letter to Thomas Dixon, Jr. (1905)

September, 1905.

Dear Sir:—

I am writing you this letter to express the attitude and feeling of ten millions of your fellow citizens toward the evil propagandism of race animosity to which you have lent your great literary powers. Through the widespread influence of your writings you have become the chief priest of those who worship at the shrine of race hatred and wrath. This one spirit runs through all your books and published utterances, like the recurrent theme of an opera. As the general trend of your doctrine is clearly epitomized and put forth in your contribution to the *Saturday Evening Post* of August 19, I beg to consider chiefly the issues

---

[1] See the entry on Carter G. Woodson in this volume, pages 465-72, below.

therein raised. You are a white man born in the midst of the Civil War, I am a Negro born during the same stirring epoch. You were born with a silver spoon in your mouth, I was born with an iron hoe in my hand. Your race has inflicted accumulated injury and wrong upon mine, mine has borne yours only service and goodwill. You express your views with the most scathing frankness; I am sure, you will welcome an equally candid expression from me.

Permit me to acknowledge the personal consideration which you have shown me. You will doubtless recall that when I addressed the Congregational Ministers, of New York City, some year or more ago, you asked permission to be present and listened attentively to what I had to say, although as might have been expected, you beat a precipitous retreat when luncheon was announced. In your article in the *Post* you make several references to me and to other colored men with entire personal courtesy. So far as I know you have never varied from this rule in your personal dealings with members of my race. You are merciless, however, in excoriating the race as a whole, thus keenly wounding the sensibilities of every individual of that blood. I assure you that this courtesy of personal treatment will be reciprocated in this letter, however sharply I may be compelled to take issue with the views you set forth and to deplore your attitude. I shall endeavor to indulge in no bitter word against your race nor against the South, whose exponent and special pleader you assume to be.

I fear that you have mistaken personal manners, the inevitable varnish of any gentleman of your antecedents and rearing, for friendship to a race which you hold in despite. You tell us that you are kind and considerate to your personal servants. It is somewhat strange that you should deem such assurance necessary, any more than it is necessary for you to assure us that you are kind to and fond of your horse or your dog. But when you write yourself down as "one of their best friends," you need not be surprised if we retort the refrain of the ritual: "From all such proffers of friendship, good Lord deliver us."

Your fundamental thesis is that "no amount of education of any kind, industrial, classical, or religious, can make a Negro a white man or bridge the chasm of the centuries which separates him from the white man in the evolution of human history." This doctrine is as old as human oppression. Calhoun made it the arch stone in the defense of Negro slavery—and lost.

This is but a recrudescence of the doctrine which was exploited and exploded during the antislavery struggle. Do you recall the school of proslavery scientists who demonstrated beyond doubt that the Negro's skull was too thick to comprehend the substance of Aryan knowledge? Have you not read in the discredited scientific books of that period, with what triumphant acclaim it was shown that the Negro's shape and size of skull, facial angle, and cephalic configuration rendered him forever impervious to the white man's civilization? But all enlightened minds are now as ashamed of that doctrine as they are of the onetime dogma that the Negro had no soul. We become aware of mind through its manifestations. Within forty years of only partial opportunity, while playing as it were in the backyard of civilization, the American Negro has cut down his illiteracy by over fifty percent; has produced a professional class, some fifty thousand strong, including ministers, teachers, doctors, lawyers, editors, authors, architects, engineers and all higher lines of listed pursuits in which white men are engaged; some three thousand Negroes have taken collegiate degrees, over three hundred being from the best institutions in the North and West established for the most favored white youth; there is scarcely a first-class institution in America, excepting some three or four in the South, that is without colored students who pursue their studies generally with success, and sometimes with distinction; Negro inventors have taken out four hundred patents as a contribution to the mechanical genius of America; there are scores of Negroes who, for conceded ability and achievements, take respectable rank in the company of distinguished Americans.

It devolves upon you, Mr. Dixon, to point out some standard, either of intelligence, character, or conduct to which the Negro can not conform. Will you please tell a waiting world just what is the psychological difference between the races? No reputable authority, either of the old or the new school of psychology, has yet pointed out any sharp psychic discriminant. There is not a single intellectual, moral, or spiritual excellence attained by the white race to which the Negro does not yield an appreciative response. If you could show that the Negro was incapable of mastering the intricacies of Aryan speech, that he could not comprehend the intellectual basis of European culture, or apply the apparatus of practical knowledge, that he could not be made amenable to the white man's ethical code or appreciate his spiritual motive, then your case would be proved. But in default of such demonstration, we must relegate your eloquent pronouncement to the realm of generalization and prophecy, an easy and agreeable exercise of the mind in which the romancer is ever prone to indulge.

The inherent, essential, and unchangeable inferiority of the Negro to the white man lies at the basis of your social philosophy. You disdain to examine the validity of your fondly cherished hope. You follow closely in the wake of Tom Watson, in the June number of his homonymous magazine. You both hurl your thesis of innate racial inferiority at the head of Booker T. Washington. You use the same illustrations, the same arguments, set forth in the same order of recital, and for the most part in identical language. This seems to be an instance of great minds, or at least of minds of the same grade, running in the same channel.

These are your words: "What contribution to human progress have the millions of Africa who inhabit this planet made during the past four thousand years? Absolutely nothing." These are the words of Thomas Watson spoken some two months previous: "What does civilization owe to the Negro race? Nothing! Nothing!! Nothing!!!" You answer the query with the most emphatic negative noun and the strongest qualifying adjective in the language. Mr. Watson, of a more ecstatic temperament, replies with the same noun and six exclamation points. One rarely meets, outside of yellow journalism, with such lavishness of language, wasted upon a hoary dogma. A discredited dictum that has been bandied about the world from the time of Canaan to Calhoun, is revamped and set forth with as much ardor and fervency of feeling as if discovered for the first time and proclaimed for the illumination of a waiting world.

But neither boastful asseveration on your part nor indignant denial on mine will affect the facts of the case. That Negroes in the average are not equal in developed capacity to the white race, is a proposition which it would be as simple to affirm as it is silly to deny. The Negro represents a backward race which has not yet taken a commanding part in the progressive movement of the world. In the great cosmic scheme of things, some races reach the limelight of civilization ahead of others. But that temporary forwardness does not argue inherent superiority is as evident as any fact of history. An unfriendly environment may hinder and impede the one, while fortunate circumstances may quicken and spur the other. Relative superiority is only a transient phase of human development. You tell us that "The Jew had achieved a civilization—had his poets, prophets, priests, and kings, when our Germanic ancestors were still in the woods cracking cocoanuts and hickory-nuts with the monkeys." Fancy some learned Jew at that day citing your query about the contribution of the Germanic races to the culture of the human spirit, during the thousands of years of their existence! Does the progress of history not prove that races may lie dormant and fallow for ages and then break suddenly into prestige and power? Fifty years ago you doubtless would have ranked Japan among the benighted nations and hurled at their heathen heads some derogatory query as to their contribution to civilization. But since the happenings at Mukden and Port Arthur, and Portsmouth, I suppose that you are ready to change your mind. Or maybe since the Jap has proved himself "a first-class fighting man," able to cope on equal terms with the best breeds in Europe, you will claim him as belonging to the white race, notwithstanding his pig eye and yellow pigment.

The Negro enters into the inheritance of all the ages on equal terms with the rest, and who can say that he will not contribute his quota of genius to enrich the blood of the world?

The line of argument of every writer who undertakes to belittle the Negro is a well-beaten path. Liberia and Haiti are bound to come in for their share of ridicule and contemptuous handling. Mr. Watson calls these experiments freshly to mind, lest we forget. We are told all about the incapacity of the black race for self-government, the relapse into barbarism and much more of which we have heard before; and yet when we take all the circumstances into account, Haiti presents to the world one of the most remarkable achievements in the annals of human history. The panegyric of Wendell Phillips on Toussaint L'Ouverture is more than an outburst of rhetorical fancy; it is a just measure of his achievements in terms of his humble environment and the limited instrumentalities at his command. Where else in the course of history has a slave, with the aid of slaves, expelled a powerfully intrenched master class, and set up a government patterned after civilized models and which without external assistance or reinforcement from a parent civilization, has endured for a hundred years in face of a frowning world? When we consider the difficulties that confront a weak government, without military or naval means to cope with its more powerful rivals, and where commercial adventurers are ever and anon stirring up internal strife, thus provoking the intervention of stronger governments, the marvel is that the republic of Haiti still endures, the only self-governing state of the Antilles. To expect as effective and proficient government to prevail in Haiti as at Washington would be expecting more of the black men in Haiti than we find in the white men of South America. And yet, I suspect that the million Negroes in Haiti are as well governed as the corresponding number of blacks in Georgia, where only yesterday eight men were taken from the custody of the law and lynched without judge or jury. It is often charged that these people have not maintained the pace set by the old master class, that the plantations are in ruin and that the whole island wears the aspect of dilapidation. Wherever a lower people overrun the civilization of a higher, there is an inevitable lapse toward the level of the lower. When barbarians and semicivilized hordes of northern Europe overran the southern peninsulas, the civilization of the world was wrapped in a thousand years of darkness. Relapse inevitably precedes the rebound. Is there anything in the history of Haiti contrary to the law of human development?

You ask: "Can you change the color of the Negro's skin, the kink of his hair, the bulge of his lip, or the beat of his heart, with a spelling book or a machine?" This rhetorical outburst does great credit to your literary skill, and is calculated to delight the simple; but analysis fails to reveal in it any pregnant meaning. Since civilization is not an attribute of the color of skin, or curl of hair, or curve of lip, there is no necessity for changing such physical peculiarities, and if there was, the spelling book and the machine would be very unlikely instruments for its accomplishment. But why, may I ask, would you desire to change the Negro's heartthrob, which already beats at a normal human pace? You need not be so frantic about the superiority of your race. Whatever superiority it may possess, inherent or acquired, will take care of itself without such rabid support. Has it ever occurred to you that the people of New England blood, who have done and are doing most to make the white race great and glorious in this land, are the most reticent about extravagant claims to everlasting superiority? You protest too much. Your loud pretensions, backed up by such exclamatory outbursts of passion, make upon the reflecting mind the impression that you entertain a sneaking suspicion of their validity.

Your position as to the work and worth of Booker T. Washington is pitiably anomalous. You recite the story of his upward struggle with uncontrolled admiration: "The story of this little ragged, barefooted pickaninny, who lifted his eyes from a cabin in the hills of Virginia, saw a vision and followed it, until at last he presides over the richest and most powerful institution in the South, and sits down with crowned heads and presidents, has no parallel even in the Tales of the Arabian Nights." You say that his story appeals to the universal heart of humanity. And yet in a recent letter to the *Columbia States*, you regard it as an unspeakable outrage that Mr. Robert C. Ogden[2] should walk arm in arm with this wonderful man who "appeals to the heart of universal humanity," and introduce him to the lady clerks in a dry goods store. Your passionate devotion to a narrow dogma has seriously impaired your sense of humor. The subject of your next great novel has been announced as "The Fall of Tuskegee." In one breath you commend the work of this great institution, while in another you condemn it because it does not fit into your preconceived scheme in the solution of the race problem. The Tuskegee ideal: "to make Negroes producers, lovers of labor, independent, honest, and good" is one which you say that only a fool or a knave can find fault with, because, in your own words, "it rests squarely upon the eternal verities." Over against this you add with all the condemnatory emphasis of italics and exclamation point: *"Tuskegee is not a servant training school!"* And further: "Mr. Washington is not training Negroes to take their places in the industries of the South in which white men direct and control them. He is not training students to be servants and come at the beck and call of any man. He is training them to be masters of men, to be independent, to own and operate their own industries, plant their own field, buy and sell their own goods." All of which you condemn by imperative inference ten times stronger than your faint and forced verbal approval. It is a heedless man

---

[2] Wealthy white philanthropist, trustee of Booker T. Washington's Tuskegee Institute, and president of the Southern Education Board.

who willfully flaunts his little philosophy in the face of "the eternal verities." When the wise man finds that his prejudices are running against fixed principles in God's cosmic plan, he speedily readjusts them in harmony therewith. Has it never occurred to you to reexamine the foundation of the faith, as well as the feeling, that is in you, since you admit that it runs afoul of the "eternal verities?"

Mr. Washington's motto, in his words, is that "the Negro has been worked; but now he must learn to work." The man who works for himself is of more service to any community than the man whose labor is exploited by others. You bring forward the traditional bias of the slave regime to modern conditions, viz.: that the Negro did not exist in his own right and for his own sake, but for the benefit of the white man. This principle is as false in nature as it is in morals. The naturalists tell us that throughout all the range of animal creation, there is found no creature which exists for the sake of any other, but each is striving after its own best welfare. Do you fear that the Negro's welfare is incompatible with that of the white man? I commend to you a careful perusal of the words of Mr. E. Gardner Murphy who, like yourself, is a devoted Southerner, and is equally zealous to promote the highest interest of that section: "Have prosperity, peace and happiness ever been successfully or permanently based upon indolence, inefficiency, and hopelessness? Since time began, has any human thing that God has made taken damage to itself or brought damage to the world through knowledge, truth, hope, and honest toil?" Read these words of your fellow Southerner, Mr. Dixon, meditate upon them; they will do you good as the truth doeth the upright heart.

You quote me as being in favor of the amalgamation of the races. A more careful reading of the article referred to would have convinced you that I was arguing against it as a probable solution of the race problem. I merely stated the intellectual conviction that two races cannot live indefinitely side by side, under the same general regime without ultimately fusing. This was merely the expression of a belief, and not the utterance of a preference nor the formulation of a policy. I know of no colored man who advocates amalgamation as a feasible policy of solution. You are mistaken. The Negro does not "hope and dream of amalgamation." This would be self-stultification with a vengeance. If such a policy were allowed to dominate the imagination of the race, its women would give themselves over to the unrestrained passion of white men, in quest of tawny offspring, which would give rise to a state of indescribable moral debauchery. At the same time you would hardly expect the Negro, in derogation of his common human qualities, to proclaim that he is so diverse from God's other human creatures as to make the blending of the races contrary to the law of nature. The Negro refuses to become excited or share in your frenzy on this subject. The amalgamation of the races is an ultimate possibility, though not an immediate probability. But what have you and I to do with ultimate questions, anyway? Our concern is with duty, not destiny.

But do you know, Mr. Dixon, that you are probably the foremost promoter of amalgamation between the two races? Wherever you narrow the scope of the Negro by preaching the doctrine of hate, you drive thousands of persons of lighter hue over to the white race carrying more or less Negro blood in their train. The blending of the races is less likely to take place if the self-respect and manly opportunity of the Negro are respected and encouraged, than if he is to be forever crushed beneath the level of his faculties for dread of the fancied result. Hundreds of the composite progeny are daily crossing the color line and carrying as much of the despised blood as an albicant skin can conceal without betrayal. I believe that it was Congressman Tillman, brother of the more famous Senator of that name, who stated on the floor of the constitutional convention of South Carolina, that he knew of four hundred white families in that State who had a taint of Negro blood in their veins. I personally know, or know of, fifty cases of transition in the city of Washington. It is a momentous thing for one to change his caste. The man or woman who affects to deny, ignore, or scorn the class with whom he previously associated is usually deemed deficient in the nobler qualities of human nature. It is not conceivable that persons of this class would undergo the self-degradation and humiliation of soul necessary to cross the great "social divide" unless it be to escape for themselves and their descendants an odious and despised status. Your oft-expressed and passionately avowed belief that the progressive development of the Negro would hasten amalgamation is not borne out by the facts of observation. The refined and cultivated class among colored people are as much disinclined to such unions as the whites themselves. I am sorry that you saw fit to characterize Frederick Douglass as "a bombastic vituperator." You thereby gave poignant offense to ten millions of his race who regard him as the best embodiment of their possibilities. Besides millions of your race rate him among the foremost and best beloved of Americans. How would you feel if some one should stigmatize Jefferson Davis or Robert E. Lee in such language, these beau ideals of your Southern heart? But I will not undertake to defend Frederick Douglass against your calumniations. I am frank to confess that I do not feel that he needs it. The point I have in mind to make about Mr. Douglass is that he has a hold upon the affection of his race, not on account of his second marriage, but in spite of it. He seriously affected his standing with his people by that marriage.

It seems to me, Mr. Dixon, that this frantic abhorrence of amalgamation is a little late in its appearance. Whence comes this stream of white blood, which flows with more or less spissitude, in the veins of some six out of ten million Negroes? The Afro-American is hardly a Negro at all, except constructively; but a new creature. Who brought about this present approachment between the races? Do you not appreciate the inconsistency in the attitude and the action on the part of many of the loudmouthed advocates of race purity? It is said that old Father Cronos[3] devoured his offspring in order to forestall future complications. But we do not learn that he put a bridle upon his passion as the surest means of security. The most effective service you can render to check the evil of amalgamation is to do missionary work among the males of your own race. This strenuous advocacy of race purity in face of proved proneness for miscegenation affords a striking reminder of the lines of *Hudibras*:[4]

> *The selfsame thing they will abhor,*
> *One way, and long another for.*

Again, you say that "we have spent about $800,000,000 on Negro education since the war." This statement is so very wide of the mark, that I was disposed to regard it as a misprint, if you had not reinforced it with an application implying a like amount. In the report of the Bureau of Education for 1901, the estimated expenditure for Negro education in all the former slave States since the Civil War was put down at $121,184,568. The amount contributed by Northern philanthropy during that interval is variously estimated from fifty to seventy-five millions. Your estimate is four times too large. It would be interesting and informing to the world if you would reveal the source of your information. These misstatements of fact are not of so much importance in themselves, as that they serve to warn the reader against the accuracy and value of your general judgments. It would seem that you derive your figures of arithmetic from the same source from which you fashion your figures of speech. You will not blame the reader for not paying much heed to your sweeping generalizations, when you are at such little pains as to the accuracy of easily ascertainable data.

Your proposed solution of the race problem by colonizing the Negroes in Liberia reaches the climax of absurdity. It is difficult to see how such a proposition could emanate from a man of your reputation. Did you consult Cram's Atlas about Liberia? Please do so. You will find that it has an area of forty-eight

---

[3] Reference is to the *Theogony* of eighth century B.C.E. poet Hesiod, whose mythological/genealogical origin of gods and creation includes the lines: "Great Cronus [Cronos] swallowed his children." In Hesiod's account of the myth, Cronus devours all his children except Zeus.

[4] *Hudibras*: the title of a three-part poem (1603, 1664, 1678) by English poet Samuel Butler attacking hypocrisy of Puritans.

thousand square miles and a population of 1,500,000, natives and immigrants. The area and population are about the same as those of North Carolina, which, I believe, is your native State. When you tell us that this restricted area, without commerce, without manufacture, without any system of organized industry, can support every Negro in America, in addition to its present population, I beg mildly to suggest that you recall your plan for revision before submitting it to the judgment of a critical world. Your absolute indifference to and heedlessness of the facts, circumstances, and conditions involved in the scheme of colonization well befit the absurdity of the general proposition.

The solution of the race problem in America is indeed a grave and serious matter. It is one that calls for statesmanlike breadth of view, philanthropic tolerance of spirit, and exact social knowledge. The whole spirit of your propaganda is to add to its intensity and aggravation. You stir the slumbering fires of race wrath into an uncontrollable flame. I have read somewhere that Max Nordau, on reading *The Leopard's Spots*, wrote to you suggesting the awful responsibility you had assumed in stirring up enmity between race and race. Your teachings subvert the foundations of law and established order. You are the high priest of lawlessness, the prophet of anarchy. Rudyard Kipling places this sentiment in the mouth of the reckless stealer of seals in the Northern Sea: "There's never a law of God nor man runs north of fifty-three." This description exactly fits the brand of literature with which you are flooding the public. You openly urge your fellow citizens to override all law, human and divine. Are you aware of the force and effect of these words? "Could fatuity reach a sublimer height than the idea that the white man will stand idly by and see the performance? What will he do when put to the test? He will do exactly what his white neighbor in the North does when the Negro threatens his bread—kill him!" These words breathe out hatred and slaughter and suggest the murder of innocent men whose only crime is quest for the God-given right to work. You poison the mind and pollute the imagination through the subtle influence of letters. Are you aware of the force and effect of evil suggestion when the passions of men are in a state of unstable equilibrium? A heterogeneous population, where the elements are, on any account, easily distinguishable, is an easy prey for the promotor of wrath. The fuse is already prepared for the spark. The soul of the mob is stirred by suggestion of hatred and slaughter, as a famished beast at the smell of blood. The rabble responds so much more readily to an appeal to passion than to reason. To wantonly stir up the fires of race antipathy is as execrable a deed as flaunting a red rag in the face of a bull at a summer's picnic, or raising a false cry of "fire" in a crowded house. Human society could not exist one hour except on the basis of law, which holds the baser passions of men in restraint.

In our complex situation it is only the rigid observance of law reenforced by higher moral restraint that can keep these passions in bound. You speak about giving the Negro a "square deal." Even among gamblers, a "square deal" means to play according to the rules of the game. The rules which all civilized States have set for themselves are found in the Ten Commandments, the Golden Rule, the Sermon on the Mount, and the organic law of the land. You acknowledge no such restraints when the Negro is involved, but waive them all aside with frenzied defiance. You preside at every crossroad lynching of a helpless victim; wherever the midnight murderer rides with rope and torch, in quest of the blood of his black brother, you ride by his side; wherever the cries of the crucified victim go up to God from the crackling flame, behold you are there; when women and children, drunk with ghoulish glee, dance around the funeral pyre and mock the death groans of their fellowman and fight for ghastly souvenirs, you have your part in the inspiration of it all. When guilefully guided workmen in mine and shop and factory, goaded by a real or imaginary sense of wrong, begin the plunder and pillage of property and murder of rival men, your suggestion is justifier of the dastardly doings. Lawlessness is gnawing at the very vitals of our institutions. It is the supreme duty of every enlightened mind to allay rather than spur on this spirit. You are hastening the time when there is to be a positive and emphatic show of hands—not of white hands against black hands, God forbid; not of Northern hands against Southern hands, heaven forfend; but a determined show of those who believe in law and God and constituted order, against those who would undermine and destroy the organic basis of society, involving all in a common ruin. No wonder Max Nordau exclaimed: "God, man, are you aware of your responsibility!"

But do not think, Mr. Dixon, that when you evoke the evil spirit, you can exorcise him at will. The Negro in the end will be the least of his victims. Those who become inoculated with the virus of race hatred are more unfortunate than the victims of it. Voltaire tells us that it is more difficult and more meritorious to wean men of their prejudices than it is to civilize the barbarian. Race hatred is the most malignant poison that can afflict the mind. It freezes up the fount of inspiration and chills the higher faculties of the soul. You are a greater enemy to your own race than you are to mine.

I have written you thus fully in order that you may clearly understand how the case lies in the Negro's mind. If any show of feeling or bitterness of spirit crops out in the treatment or between the lines, it is wholly without vindictive intent; but is the inevitable outcome of dealing with issues that verge upon the deepest human passion.

Yours truly,
Kelly Miller

IDA B. WELLS-BARNETT

(1862–1931)

To many she was still "Ida B. Wells" when she added her married surname, Barnett, in 1895. When the septuagenarian-suffrage leader Susan B. Anthony bristled at calling her "Mrs. Barnett," she asked, "Miss Anthony, don't you believe in women getting married?" "Oh yes," she answered, "but not women like you who had a special call for special work." That special work was the antilynching crusade—which Wells pioneered in the press and on lecture podiums in the United States and Britain. A school teacher turned journalist, civil rights activist, social reformer, community organizer, errant feminist, and political candidate, she became for many people an icon—from her first article on lynching in 1892 until long after her death.

The Joan of Arc for justice, as some called her, was of humble beginnings in Holly Springs, Mississippi, born in 1862 to slave parents who wed after emancipation. The eldest of eight children, she grew up in a devout and close family, in a house built by her father, Jim Wells, a skilled carpenter, who apprenticed as the son of his master. In their small hillside town, she learned to read and write at the local Shaw University (later Rust College) opened in 1866 by the Methodist Freedmen's Aid Society, whose teachers she credited many years later in her memoirs:

> All my teachers had been the consecrated white men and women from
> the North who came into the South to teach immediately after the end
> of the war. It was they who brought us the light of knowledge and their
> splendid example of Christian courage.

Her remembrance of Southern whites was a different story. After the Reconstruction Act of 1867 provided black males the franchise in the state, they became a Republican majority, causing angry white citizens to wave the flag of "Negro Domination." Ida's father was "locked out" by a contractor who had hired him as carpenter but fired him for refusing to vote for a ticket of white Democrats. She was eight-years old in 1870 when Mississippi, former bastion of the Confederacy, was readmitted to the Union, after finally ratifying the

Fourteenth Amendment (making "all persons born or naturalized in the United States . . . citizens of the United States and the state wherein they reside.") Also in that year, Mississippi elected the first Afro-American to the United States Senate: Hiram Revels, whose brief term in office followed a bitter debate to seat him. Ferment increased in Mississippi, where by 1875 white political rule was restored.

In 1878, a yellow-fever epidemic struck Holly Springs, killing Ida's parents and a nine-month old brother. At age sixteen, she found herself head of a family, the nurturer, protector, matriarch role that she later accentuated throughout her career. With $300 left by her father, supplemented by her earnings as a teacher in rural schools, she kept five surviving siblings together at home until 1883, when two brothers were old enough to work, and she moved to Memphis to study and qualify for teacher certification.

In May 1884, her civil-rights activism began when she sued the Chesapeake, Ohio and Southwestern Railroad, after a conductor and baggage man dragged her from a seat in the "Ladies' Car" and put her off the train in Shelby County, Tennessee, for refusing to sit in a "first class" segregated smoking car. In December 1884, a judge, who was a Union Army veteran, awarded her a $500 settlement. The railway company appealed it, and the Tennessee Supreme Court reversed the lower court decision in April 1887. In her litigation, she ignored the U.S. Supreme Court ruling of 1883 revoking the 1875 Civil Rights Law passed by Congress to prohibit discrimination in public accommodations. Her family and friends had yawned at the developments. "None of my people had ever seemed to feel that it was a race matter and they should help me with the fight," she wrote later. By 1896, interstate-rail transportation in the South was a "race matter," after the Supreme Court legally sanctioned "separate but equal" accommodations in the *Plessy v. Ferguson* decision.

Wells's lawsuit led to her first published articles—under a pen name "Iola"—in a Baptist weekly newspaper, the *Living Way*, in 1884. For the next three years, she wrote part-time for American Baptist periodicals and attended the Negro Press Association convention in Louisville in 1888, and in 1889 in Washington, DC, where she met Frederick Douglass and T. Thomas Fortune. That 1889, she invested her savings in a small, black weekly newspaper in Memphis, *Free Speech and Headlight*, becoming its co-editor, co-owner, and reporter. Her articles critical of the Memphis Board of Education led to her dismissal as a teacher in 1891, but was her beginning as a full-time journalist. She changed the name of the paper to *Free Speech*, and on May 21, 1892, wrote an outspoken editorial on eight lynchings in Southern states—ending it with a threatening taunt to white men. In retaliation, a lawless mob destroyed the *Free Speech* office equipment, and threatened "the wretch who uttered these calumnies to a stake." She was safely in Philadelphia at an A.M.E. Church convention, but the editorial risked the life of her male business partner who, had he not been forewarned by a sympathetic Memphis citizen, might have become a statistic. Many years later, she wrote, "He blamed me very bitterly for that editorial, and perhaps he was justified in doing so."

Wells would not see Memphis again for the next thirty years. Few could build bridges better or burn them faster than Ida B. Wells, who later admitted that her temper was her greatest flaw. She retreated to New York City, where on June 25, 1892, in an article in T. Thomas Fortune's *New York Age*, she told her story and urged the black population of Memphis to pack up and move West. Fresh in her memory was the tragic murder three months earlier of three black Memphis friends who owned the People's Grocery Company, raided when they were gunned down by hostile white merchant competitors. Herself with a bounty on her head, in exile and uncertain of her future, she was soon a national figure and public speaker.

She addressed her first audience at a testimonial dinner in her honor, October 5, 1892, sponsored by over two-hundred Afro-American women at Lyric Hall, in New York City. From a $500 donation presented there, she published her first pamphlet, "Southern Horrors: Lynch Law in All Its Phases" (1892), introduced with a letter from Frederick Douglass. Years later, her memoirs noted that the testimonial also brought "the real beginning of the club movement among the colored women in this country." The goals of that developing club movement were diverse, however, and her focus was less in consensus building than in her own program, which later brought criticism from allies who had other national concerns. She spent most of April and May 1893 lecturing in England, Scotland, and Wales, where her pamphlet appeared in a British edition, "United States Atrocities: Lynch Law."

Returning to the United States, she moved to Chicago to collaborate on an eighty-page pamphlet: "The Reason Why the Colored American Is Not in the World's Columbian Exposition," which she co-wrote with Frederick Douglass, journalist I. Garland Penn, and future husband, Chicago newspaper editor and lawyer Ferdinand Barnett. Their exposé on what Douglass blasted as "the white American's World Fair" at Chicago's Jackson Park that 1893, has been projected by some modern feminists as the putative work of Wells, whom Douglass gave his office at the Exposition's Haitian Pavillion, and who supposedly circulated the pamphlet outside the World Congress of Representative Women, where six Afro-American doyennes were guest speakers on May 20, 1893. On that date she was still abroad. However, as a busy-bee newcomer to Chicago, she soon alienated a queen bee of the city, Fannie Barrier Williams,[1]

---

[1] See the entry on Fannie Barrier Williams in this volume, pages 346–57, above.

a World Congress of Representative Women speaker, who kept a distance from her in social, civic, and political circles, where the two (and eventually their husbands) were also at odds over Booker T. Washington. In Wells's memoirs, Fannie Barrier Williams is invisible in spite of her wide influence.

After completing a second lecture tour of Britain in 1894, as correspondent for Chicago's liberal white *Inter Ocean* newspaper with her series of articles, Ida Wells Abroad, she released her second pamphlet on lynching, "A Red Record: Tabulated Statistics and Alleged Causes of Lynchings in the United States, 1892–1893–1894." Before and after her marriage to Ferdinand Barnett on June 17, 1895, she contributed to his *Chicago Conservator*, the city's first black newspaper, which she bought but sold after the birth of their second son in 1897. She had four children within eight years but continued to combine careers as wife, mother, public speaker, and activist, often taking her babies to the Ida B. Wells Club, and attending community meetings, despite many public avowals of "retirement." The birth of her first son in 1896 prevented her being in Boston at the historic founding convention of the National Association of Colored Women, but she was at its second meeting the following year in Washington, DC, with her second son, then four-months old.

Her research on lynching statistics continued, resulting in her third and last pamphlet, "Mob Rule in New Orleans," in 1900. The varied organizations in which she was active in the next decades included two which she founded in Chicago: in 1910, the Negro Fellowship League, a community settlement house for Southern black migrants, modeled after Chicago's Hull House begun by her friend and role model, Jane Addams; and in 1913, the Alpha Suffrage Club, the first black female suffrage organization in Illinois. In 1930, ten years after American women gained the right to vote, and one year before Wells-Barnett died, she ran unsuccessfully as an independent candidate for Illinois state Senator. She attributed her electoral defeat to women who did not vote.

Her career spanned what American cultural historians call the "Progressive Era" 1890 to 1920—when muckraking journalists were part of a societal effort at major reform. She belongs in the muckraking pantheon but has been viewed outside it. Most so-called Progressives ignored the status of black Americans. Wells exposed lynching and presented readers with proposals for economic pressure and legislation against the South. Her facts and statistics were partly responsible for the Dyer Antilynching Bill, introduced in the House of Representatives by Missouri Congressman Leonidas Dyer in 1918, but that bill and similar ones never passed, despite efforts by the NAACP to make lynching a federal crime.

She likewise left a compelling but panegyrical story in her unfinished *Crusade for Justice: The Autobiography of Ida B. Wells*, published posthumously in 1970, through the diligent efforts of her youngest daughter, Alfreda M. Duster.

The following piece, "Brutal Burnt Offerings"—a title supplied by the editor—was untitled by Wells-Barnett when presented at Proceedings of the National Negro Committee Conference in 1909, in New York City. That Committee at its second conference in 1910 took the historic new name, National Association for the Advancement of Colored People: NAACP.

"Brutal Burnt Offerings"[2] (1909)

The lynching record for a quarter of a century merits the thoughtful study of the American people. It presents three salient facts:

First: Lynching is color line murder.

Second: Crimes against white women is the excuse, not the cause.

Third: It is a national crime and requires a national remedy.

Proof that lynching follows the color line is to be found in the statistics which have been kept for the past twenty-five years. During the few years preceding this period and while frontier lynch law existed, the executions showed a majority of white victims. Later, however, as law courts and authorized judiciary extended into the far West, lynch law rapidly abated and its white victims became few and far between.

Just as the lynch law regime came to a close in the West, a new mob movement started in the South. This was wholly political, its purpose being to suppress the colored vote by intimidation and murder. Thousands of assassins banded together under the name of Ku Klux Klans, "Midnight Raiders," "Knights of the Golden Circle," etc., spread a reign of terror, by beating, shooting and killing colored people by the thousands. In a few years, the purpose was accomplished and the black vote was suppressed. But mob murder continued.

From 1882, in which year 52 were lynched, down to the present, lynching has been along the color line. Mob murder increased yearly until in 1892 more than 200 victims were lynched and statistics show that 3,284 men, women and children have been put to death in this quarter of a century. During the last ten years from 1899 to 1908 inclusive the number lynched was 959. Of this number 102 were white while the colored victims numbered 857. No other nation, civilized or savage, burns its criminals; only under the stars and stripes is the human holocaust possible. Twenty-eight human beings burned at the

---

[2] Title supplied by the editor.

stake, one of them a woman and two of them children, is the awful indictment against American civilization—the gruesome tribute which the nation pays to the color line.

Why is the mob murder permitted by a Christian nation? What is the cause of this awful slaughter? This question is answered almost daily—always the same shameless falsehood that "Negroes are lynched to protect womanhood." Standing before a Chautauqua assemblage, John Temple Graves, at once champion of lynching and apologist for lynchers, said: "The mob stands today as the most potential bulwark between the women of the South and such a carnival of crime as would infuriate the world and precipitate the annihilation of the Negro race." This is the never-varying answer of lynchers and their apologists. All know that it is untrue. The cowardly lyncher revels in murder, then seeks to shield himself from public execration by claiming devotion to woman. But truth is mighty and the lynching record discloses the hypocrisy of the lyncher as well as his crime.

The Springfield, Illinois, mob rioted for two days, the militia of the entire state was called out, two men were lynched, hundreds of people were driven from their homes, all because a white woman said a Negro had assaulted her. A mad mob went to the jail, tried to lynch the victim of her charge and, not being able to find him, proceeded to pillage and burn the town and to lynch two innocent men. Later, after the police had found that the woman's charge was false, she published a retraction, the indictment was dismissed and the intended victim discharged. But the lynch victims were dead. Hundreds were homeless and Illinois was disgraced.

As a final and complete refutation of the charge that lynching is occasioned by crimes against women, a partial record of lynchings is cited; 285 persons were lynched for causes as follows:

Unknown cause, 92; no cause, 10; race prejudice, 49; miscegenation, 7; informing, 12; making threats, 11; keeping saloon, 3; practicing fraud, 5; practicing voodooism, 2; bad reputation, 8; unpopularity, 3; mistaken identity, 5; using improper language, 3; violation of contract, 1; poisoning well, 2; by white caps, 9; vigilantes, 14; Indians, 1; moonshining, 1; refusing evidence, 2; political causes, 5; disputing, 1; disobeying quarantine regulations, 2; slapping a child, 1; turning state's evidence, 3; protecting a Negro, 1; to prevent giving evidence, 1; knowledge of larceny, 1; writing letter to white woman, 1; asking white woman to marry, 1; jilting girl, 1; having smallpox, 1; concealing criminal, 2; threatening political exposure, 1; self-defense, 6; cruelty, 1; insulting language to woman, 5; quarreling with white man, 2; colonizing Negroes, 1; throwing stones, 1; quarreling, 1; gambling, 1.

Is there a remedy, or will the nation confess that it cannot protect its protectors at home as well as abroad? Various remedies have been suggested to abolish the lynching infamy, but year after year, the butchery of men, women and children continues in spite of plea and protest. Education is suggested as a preventive, but it is as grave a crime to murder an ignorant man as it is a scholar. True, few educated men have been lynched, but the hue and cry once started stops at no bounds, as was clearly shown by the lynchings in Atlanta, and in Springfield, Illinois.

Agitation, though helpful, will not alone stop the crime. Year after year statistics are published, meetings are held, resolutions are adopted and yet lynchings go on. Public sentiment does measurably decrease the sway of mob law, but the irresponsible bloodthirsty criminals who swept through the streets of Springfield, beating an inoffensive law-abiding citizen to death in one part of the town, and in another torturing and shooting to death a man who, for three-score years, had made a reputation for honesty, integrity and sobriety, had raised a family and had accumulated property, was not deterred from its heinous crimes by either education or agitation.

The only certain remedy is an appeal to law. Lawbreakers must be made to know that human life is sacred and that every citizen of this country is first a citizen of the United States and secondly a citizen of the state in which he belongs. This nation must assert itself and defend its federal citizenship at home as well as abroad. The strong arm of the government must reach across state lines whenever unbridled lawlessness defies state laws and must give to the individual citizen under the Stars and Stripes the same measure of protection which it gives to him when he travels in foreign lands.

Federal protection of American citizenship is the remedy for lynching. Foreigners are rarely lynched in America. If, by mistake, one is lynched, the national government quickly pays the damages. The recent agitation in California against the Japanese compelled this nation to recognize that federal power must yet assert itself to protect the nation from the treason of sovereign states. Thousands of American citizens have been put to death and no President has yet raised his hand in effective protest, but a simple insult to a native of Japan was quite sufficient to stir the government at Washington to prevent the threatened wrong. If the government has power to protect a foreigner from insult, certainly it has the power to save a citizen's life.

The practical remedy has been more than once suggested in Congress. Senator Gallinger of New Hampshire in a resolution introduced in Congress called for an investigation "with a view of ascertaining whether there is a remedy for lynching which Congress may apply." The Senate Committee has under consideration a bill drawn by A. E. Pillsbury, formerly Attorney General of

Massachusetts, providing for federal prosecution of lynchers in cases where the state fails to protect citizens or foreigners. Both of these resolutions indicate that the attention of the nation has been called to this phase of the lynching question.

As a final word, it would be a beginning in the right direction if this conference can see its way clear to establish a bureau for the investigation and publication of the details of every lynching, so that the public could know that an influential body of citizens has made it a duty to give the widest publicity to the facts in each case; that it will make an effort to secure expressions of opinion all over the country against lynching for the sake of the country's fair name; and lastly, but by no means least, to try to influence the daily papers of the country to refuse to become accessory to mobs either before or after the fact. Several of the greatest riots and most brutal burnt offerings of the mobs have been suggested and incited by the daily papers of the offending community. If the newspaper which suggests lynching in its accounts of an alleged crime, could be held legally as well as morally responsible for reporting that "threats of lynching were heard"; or, "It is feared that if the guilty one is caught, he will be lynched"; or "There were cries of 'lynch him,' and the only reason the threat was not carried out was because no leader appeared," a long step toward a remedy will have been taken.

In a multitude of counsel there is wisdom. Upon the grave question presented by the slaughter of innocent men, women and children there should be an honest courageous conference of patriotic, law-abiding citizens anxious to punish crime promptly, impartially and by due process of law, also to make life, liberty, and property secure against mob rule.

Time was when lynching appeared to be sectional, but now it is national—a blight upon our nation, mocking our laws and disgracing our Christianity. "With malice toward none but with charity for all" let us undertake the work of making the "law of the land," effective and supreme upon every foot of American soil—a shield to the innocent and to the guilty punishment swift and sure.

OSWALD GARRISON VILLARD

(1872–1949)

Ida Wells-Barnett's testimony to the National Negro Committee in 1909 was part of "a national conference to discuss the plight of the Negro"—as Oswald Garrison Villard put it three decades later in *Fighting Years: Memoirs of a Liberal Editor.* The "conference was instigated by Mary White Ovington, William English Walling, Henry Moskowitz and myself," so he said. Actually, he was enlisted by the other three for a "Call" to the conference which, a year later, as noted (p. 447), became the National Association for the Advancement of Colored People, better known as the NAACP.

Of the three "instigators," Ovington, forty-three, a Brooklyn–born, Radcliffe–educated social worker and settlement-house organizer, was an occasional reporter for Villard's *New York Evening Post.* Walling, thirty-two, a wealthy Southerner turned New York labor reformer, was a socialist writer, whose article, "The Race War in the North" in the September 3, 1908, *Independent,* protested that summer's Springfield, Illinois race riot, and urged an interracial conference. Their associate, Dr. Henry Moskowitz, a Rumanian–born social worker reared on New York's Lower East Side, was working among Jewish immigrants, after graduate study in Berlin. The three in early January 1909 showed Villard their idea for a "Call" to be printed on February 9, Lincoln's birthday centennial, seeking like-minded individuals for a conference on race relations. Villard's life was full of social-reform causes, but when asked to write *The Call,* he said later, "no greater compliment has ever been paid me."

"Oswald Garrison Villard, we agreed, was the man to write *The Call,*" Ovington wrote in her 1947 memoir *The Walls Came Tumbling Down.* Villard, at thirty-seven, was viewed differently by different people in 1909, but he was not yet the controversial pacifist he would become by World War I. Like a prism, he refracted different kinds of light. To Ovington, he was the liberal editor of the *New York Evening Post,* and its weekly supplement, *The Nation,* which he had inherited and owned since 1897 when he was twenty-five. To the Socialist William English Walling, who like Villard had gone to Harvard, but unlike him worked in a factory and spent a few months in Russia, Villard was just a good capitalist. His first book was *The History of Wall Streeet* (1897), but his work then in progress was *John Brown: A Biography of Fifty Years* (1910). The mater-

nal grandson of abolitionist William Lloyd Garrison, he was the son of a mil-
lionaire owner of railways, banks, and newspapers. A member of half a dozen
wealthy men's private clubs, he was an experienced yachtsman who founded
Yachting magazine in 1907. A man of divided interests, and with a public and
private soul; he was also a philanthropist who in 1903 became President of the
Board of Directors of the Manassas, Virginia, Industrial School for Negroes. In
the same year he married a Southerner loyal to her Confederate background
and disinterested in anything interracial.

Villard could draw both the liberal reformers and the monied philanthropists, as Ovington knew when she suggested he make *The Call*. In a "Reminiscence" two decades later in the *Baltimore Afro-American* newspaper, she noted
that, "It was most important, for the sake of publicity, to have this *Call* signed
by people of national reputation." Villard later acknowledged "securing the
cooperation of able and representative men and women." However, it was
Ovington, the conceptualizer and principal organizer of the conference, who
suggested many of the people to invite: social scientists, clergymen, educators,
editors, and socialist friends of Walling and herself, such as Charles Edward
Russell and J. G. Phelps Stokes. Ironically omitted was the constitutional lawyer, Moorfield Storey of Boston, who became the first national president of the
NAACP in 1910. Villard's abolitionist uncles in Boston helped him recruit Storey for the conference, and he participated as a sponsor.

Of the sixty persons whose names joined Villard's in *The Call*, seven were
black; five of them men: educators like W. E. B. Du Bois, and clergymen like
Francis J. Grimké (brother of lawyer Archibald Henry Grimké, who though not
a signer was a member of the Committee of Forty selected at the conference.)
One-third of the names were female; two of them Afro-American: Ida Wells-
Barnett and Mary Church Terrell, the Oberlin–educated founder and president
of the thirteen-year-old National Association of Colored Women. Among the
white women who signed *The Call*, were some of Ovington's associates in professional social work—Jane Addams, Florence Kelley, and Lillian Wald, who
often had investigated conditions among women and children but not among
black-urban dwellers, as had Ovington, whose findings would appear in her first
book, *Half a Man: The Status of the Negro in New York* (1911). It included a
chapter "The Colored Woman as Bread Winner."

Those who attended the two-day event in New York City May 30 to June 1,
1909, heard speakers by day in the Charity Organization Building, and at night
in larger public sessions at Cooper Union. Nearly one thousand invitations to
the "Conference on the Status of the Negro" had been sent mostly to white
people, but among the black invitees was *Guardian* editor Monroe Trotter, who
argued at public meetings for stronger amendments against lynching and Jim
Crow segregation. Ovington later remarked in *The Walls Came Tumbling*

Down: "I remember Monroe Trotter of Boston and Ida Wells Barnett. . . . They were powerful personalities who had gone their own ways fitted for courageous work, but perhaps not fitted to accept the restraint of organization." Trotter could not accept Ovington's assumption that a predominantly white group could name itself a National Negro Committee and make all the major decisions for Negroes. Ovington wrote later, "We were a group primarily of white people who felt that while the Negro would aid in the Committee's work . . . the whites, who were largely responsible for conditions and who controlled the bulk of the nation's wealth, ought to finance the movement." Such was the maternalistic/paternalistic mood of the time, but a one-sided "movement" was a comedy of errors and contrary to the "equality of the races" concept the group espoused. It was also the beginning of an economic and political dependence of civil rights organizations on white philanthropy—a situation that persisted into the twentieth century, by those who accepted and perpetuated it.

Most of *The Call* signatories did not know each other. Some who signed did not attend. Many others who did had positive reactions. The few writers whose names were on the roster with Villard's—such as critic novelist William Dean Howells and journalist Ray Stannard Baker—had written little to improve race relations; Baker, who in 1908 had published *Following the Color Line: American Negro Citizenship in the Progressive Era*, was still following the line of Booker T. Washington. Villard himself leaned in that direction at the time of the 1909 conference, but he visibly changed with an April 1, 1910, editorial, "Mr. Washington in Politics" in his *Evening Post*, delineating differences between the philosophy of Du Bois and Washington, and rejecting the latter as the "political boss of his race." Villard had informed Tuskegee that the National Negro Committee would not take sides between Du Bois and Washington. Du Bois believed it should be otherwise, since "I myself and most of the Niagara Movement were willing to join," he wrote.

Villard and Du Bois had ideological and personal differences then and later. They glared and grimaced at each other when they served on the NAACP Board of Directors. Villard balked that Du Bois, as a salaried Director of Publicity and Research, and editor of *The Crisis* journal, often acted as if he had his own fiefdom separate from the NAACP. His memoirs dismiss "Doctor W. E. B. Du Bois" in less than two polite sentences, but the Du Bois *Autobiography* takes vengeful aim at the man who was four years his junior but his "boss" as NAACP Chairman of the Executive Committee, and then Chairman of the Board. "To a white philanthropist like Villard," he wrote, "a Negro was quite naturally expected to be humble and thankful or certainly not assertive and aggressive; this Villard resented."

Villard occasionally disagreed with Ovington, who often sided with Du Bois, but he praised her in retrospect in *Fighting Years* as "having been fired with a desire to aid the Negro; she was at that moment living in a Negro tenement on a Negro street in New York and had been for four years studying the terrible conditions under which Negroes were then living. . . . To the Negroes she has given the greater part of her life with an unselfishness, a patience, a sweetness of spirit, and a kindliness hard to describe adequately."

Ovington's humanitarian search had taken her from Unitarianism to Socialism and tours of London's East End slums to the rural and urban American South, to her discovery in 1904 of what she termed later "a thrilling subject, the American Negro." Having read Du Bois's *Souls of Black Folk* in 1903, initiated correspondence with him in 1904, met him in Atlanta in 1908, covered his Niagara Movement at Harper's Ferry in 1906 for the *New York Evening Post*, and become disenchanted after reporting on Booker T. Washington's Negro Business League and Tuskegee Institute, she had slowly pledged allegiance to Du Bois—recruiting him for *The Call*, the conference, and soon after the NAACP. Ovington and Villard worried they could not raise money from Andrew Carnegie without Washington on their side; finally, the Tuskegee Wizard was not invited at all, but a compromise was reached to have a committee of contrasting opinions.

From the large public meeting on the final evening of the 1909 Conference, resolutions emerged to demand enforcement of the Fourteenth and Fifteenth Amendments as well as equal education. A Committee of Forty was elected to continue the group's work; included were sixteen Afro-Americans (three women and thirteen men), but Ida B. Wells-Barnett's name was deleted by Du Bois—the only black member on the nominating committee—to substitute a Niagara Movement colleague, Dr. Charles Bentley. When Wells-Barnett remonstrated and Du Bois agreed to reinstate her, she demurred: "I told him that as he had done this purposely, I was opposed to making any change," she wrote later. Ovington penned another version in her own "Reminiscence"[1]—in the *Afro-American* newspaper a year after Barnett's death:

> Ida Wells-Barnett's name was omitted in the committee's list brought before the conference. But she got it put on in the next few days. And there it stands, where it ought to be. She was a great fighter, but we

---

[1] Mary White Ovington (1865–1951) published her "Reminiscences" serially September 17, 1932 to February 25, 1933, in the weekly *Baltimore Afro-American* newspaper, at the invitation of the editor, Carl Murphy. The newspaper reprinted the pieces in 1951–52, following Ovington's death. They were collected in book form as *Black and White Sat down Together: The Reminiscences of an NAACP Founder.* Edited by Ralph E. Lukor (New York: The Feminist Press, 1995).

knew that she had to play a lone hand. And if you have too many players of lone hands in your organization, you soon have no game.

In *Crusade for Justice*, Barnett complained that Ovington "basked in the sunlight of the adoration of the few college-bred Negroes who have surrounded her, but has made little effort to know the soul of the black woman." Those comments appeared after both women died. Hence, Ovington never read them, but she knew that Wells-Barnett, with no major role in the NAACP, soon lost interest in it (as did Monroe Trotter).[2]

Of more than fifty names included in the 1909 *Call*, and of several hundred who attended the first National Negro Committee Conference and the second conference the following year—under the new acronym NAACP—many were later called "founders," but only five were actually incorporators when the new NAACP became an official organization under laws of the state of New York. The five were: Du Bois, Ovington, Villard, Reverend John Haynes Holmes, and Walter Sachs, the treasurer (the only one not among signers of *The Call*.) Ovington served the longest uninterrupted term of any executive in the first forty years of the organization, as Acting Executive Secretary for one year, chairman of the Board of Directors for thirteen years, and treasurer for fifteen. She resigned three years before her death in 1951. Villard predeceased her in 1949. Du Bois would survive them both.

The following text of *The Call*—with names of signers—is from the Oswald Garrison Villard Papers (Houghton Library, Harvard University), and the NAACP Papers, Library of Congress.

"A Call to Action"—
The Advent of the NAACP[3] (1909)

The celebration of the centennial of the birth of Abraham Lincoln widespread and grateful as it may be, will fail to justify itself if it takes no note and makes no recognition of the colored men and women to whom the great emancipator

---

[2] Wells-Barnett was on the NAACP Executive Committee and Trotter on the General Committee in 1910. Neither was elected to the board of directors after the organization was legally incorporated in 1911.

[3] Title supplied by the editor. In the Oswald Garrison Villard Papers, the text is titled "The Call" and subtitled "To Discuss Means for Securing Political and Civil Equality for the Negro."

labored to assure freedom. Besides a day of rejoicing, Lincoln's birthday in 1909 should be one of taking stock of the nation's progress since 1865. How far has it lived up to the obligations imposed upon it by the Emancipation Proclamation? How far has it gone in assuring to each and every citizen, irrespective of color, the equality of opportunity and equality before the law, which underlie our American institutions and are guaranteed by the Constitution?

If Mr. Lincoln could revisit this country he would be disheartened by the nation's failure in this respect. He would learn that on January 1st, 1909, Georgia had rounded out a new oligarchy by disfranchising the negro after the manner of all the other Southern states. He would learn that the Supreme Court of the United States, designed to be a bulwark of American liberties, had failed to meet several opportunities to pass squarely upon this disfranchisement of millions by laws avowedly discriminatory and openly enforced in such a manner that white men may vote and black men be without a vote in their government; he would discover, there, that taxation without representation is the lot of millions of wealth-producing American citizens, in whose hands rests the economic progress and welfare of an entire section of the country. He would learn that the Supreme Court, according to the official statement of one of its own judges in the Berea College case, has laid down the principle that if an individual State chooses it may "make it a crime for white and colored persons to frequent the same marketplace at the same time, or appear in an assemblage of citizens convened to consider questions of a public or political nature in which all citizens, without regard to race, are equally interested." In many States Lincoln would find justice enforced, if at all, by judges elected by one element in a community to pass upon the liberties and lives of another. He would see the black men and women, for whose freedom a hundred thousand of soldiers gave their lives, set apart in trains, in which they pay first-class fares for third-class service, in railway stations and in places of entertainment, while State after State declines to do its elementary duty in preparing the negro through education for the best exercise of citizenship.

Added to this, the spread of lawless attacks upon the negro, North, South and West—even in the Springfield made famous by Lincoln—often accompanied by revolting brutalities, sparing neither sex, nor age nor youth, could not but shock the author of the sentiment that "government of the people, by the people, for the people shall not perish from the earth."

Silence under these conditions means tacit approval. The indifference of the North is already responsible for more than one assault upon democracy, and every such attack reacts as unfavorably upon whites as upon blacks. Discrimination once permitted cannot be bridled; recent history in the South shows that in forging chains for the negroes, the white voters are forging chains for themselves. "A house divided against itself cannot stand"; this government cannot exist half-slave and half-free any better today than it could in 1861. Hence we call upon all the believers in democracy to join in a national conference for the discussion of present evils, the voicing of protests, and the renewal of the struggle for civil and political liberty.

Miss Jane Addams, Chicago
Ray Stannard Baker, New York
Mrs. Ida Wells-Barnett, Chicago
Mrs. Harriet Stanton Blatch, New York
Mr. Samuel Bowles, (*Springfield Republican*)
Prof. W. L. Bulkley, New York
Miss Kate Claghorn, New York
E. H. Clement, Boston
Prof. John Dewey, New York
Miss Mary E. Dreier, Brooklyn
Rev. Walter Laidlaw, New York
Rev. Frederick Lynch, New York
Miss Helen Marot, New York
Miss Mary E. McDowell, Chicago
Prof. J. G. Merrill, Connecticut
Mr. John E. Milholland, New York
Dr. Henry Moskowitz, New York
Miss Leonora O'Reilly, New York
Miss Mary W. Ovington, New York
Rev. Charles H. Parkhurst, New York
Rev. John P. Peters, New York
J. G. Phelps-Stokes, New York
Louis F. Post, Chicago
Dr. Jane Robbins, New York
Charles Edward Russell, New York
William M. Salter, Chicago
Joseph Smith, Boston
Mrs. Anna Garlin Spencer, New York
Judge Wendell S. Stafford, Washington, D.C.
Lincoln Steffens, Boston
Miss Helen Stokes, New York

Prof. W. E. B. DuBois, Atlanta
Dr. John L. Elliott, New York
Mr. William Lloyd Garrison, Boston
Rev. Francis J. Grimke, Washington, D.C.
Prof. Thomas C. Hall, New York
Rabbi Emil G. Hirsch, Chicago
Rev. John Haynes Holmes, New York
Hamilton Holt, New York
William Dean Howells, New York
Rev. Jenkin Lloyd Jones, Chicago
Mrs. Florence Kelley, New York
Mrs. Mary Church Terrell, Washington, D.C.
Prof. W. I. Thomas, Chicago
President Charles F. Thwing, Western Reserve University
Oswald Garrison Villard, New York
Mrs. Henry Villard, New York
Miss Lillian D. Wald, New York
Dr. J. Milton Waldron, Washington, D.C.
William English Walling, New York
Bishop Alexander Walters, New York
Dr. William H. Ward, New York
Mrs. Rodman Wharton, Philadelphia
Miss Susan P. Wharton, Philadelphia
Horace White, New York
Mayor Brand Whitlock, Toledo
Rabbi Stephen S. Wise, New York
President Mary E. Wooley, Mt. Holyoke College
Rev. M. St. Croix Wright, New York
Prof. Charles Zueblin, Boston

WILLIAM PICKENS

(1881–1954)

Educator, orator, writer, and first director of the national branches of the NAACP, William Pickens for two decades was one of the few black men on the national staff in the early years of the organization. His name, however, slipped into public oblivion, buried at sea like Pickens himself, following his sudden death aboard a ship in the West Indies, twelve years after he left NAACP.

He began his full-time work for civil rights in early 1920, nearly five years after the death of Booker T. Washington, whose up-from-the-boot-straps philosophy influenced Pickens's life and thought. A South Carolina–born heir of slaves, he took different routes to distance himself from Washington's myth and image, and to develop personal intellectual and political independence. But that distance was never wide enough in the minds of some. Yet, if any black man younger than Washington knew the mind of the South or tried harder to work his way up from the bottom, it was William Pickens.

Born in 1881, the sixth of ten children to sharecroppers illiterate but determined to educate their offspring, Pickens was reared in the rural Black Belt: in South Carolina, then in Arkansas, where his parents moved when he was seven, and where a decade later he graduated first in his class from a black high school in Little Rock; then in Alabama, where he finished Talladega College in 1902 and was encouraged by its American Missionary Association to satisfy his desire to go to Yale, where he graduated summa cum laude in 1904.

He financed his college expenses with summer jobs as a ferryman, window washer, shop clerk, and ironworks employee, driven by the "endurance and struggle" challenge of Booker T. Washington's then-popular memoir *Up from Slavery*. Pickens opted for no industrial training but for a curriculum in the classics. In 1911, his slim autobiographical text, *Heir of Slaves*—reprinted in 1923 as *Bursting Bonds*[1]—ended with his Yale accolades: "honors in all studies," and a Phi Beta Kappa key (which some in the honorary society opposed).

Heir of Slaves included a chapter on his 1903 award in Yale's Henry James Ten Eyck Oratorical Contest, which he won for an oration on Haiti, (then

---

[1] *Bursting Bonds* was expanded to fourteen chapters that included the original nine chapters in *Heir of Slaves*.

spelled "Hayti"). The account is revealing of Pickens and the era, and how he "decided to win first prize" when "Negro students were less than one-half of one percent of the three thousand men at Yale." But it is silent on the content of his oration, or an attack on it by Monroe Trotter, the first black student elected to Phi Beta Kappa at Harvard. In his Boston newspaper, the *Guardian*, on April 11, 1903, Trotter printed the first of several onslaughts against Pickens's 1903 speech, for claiming "Hayti needed the advantages of a civilizing influence." The *Guardian* concluded:

> Like . . . several other young colored men in New England colleges, Pickens seems to have been unable to write except in a destructive way, about his own race, and like them seems to have been well rewarded for his pains. Such a tendency is to be deplored.

A month later, the *Guardian* deplored that "the little black freak student" was invited by Citizens Trade Association of Cambridge, Massachusetts, to speak on "Misery in Haiti."

After Yale, Pickens returned to Alabama to teach languages at his other alma mater, Talladega. His articles on various subjects began appearing in the Atlanta–based *Voice of the Negro*, edited by Southern friend Jesse Max Barber, whose contributors included Du Bois and others in the Niagara Movement, which Pickens quietly joined without publicizing it in order not to risk alienating Booker T. Washington. In the June 1906 issue of *Voice of the Negro*, he contributed an essay titled "Choose!," laying out the differences in the positions of Washington and Du Bois. But he chose not to take a stand or to name either man, alluding instead to Roman generals, Latin phrases, and Biblical parables. As he later admitted in *Bursting Bonds*:

> In my last two years in Alabama, I was president of the Alabama State Teachers' Association, of colored educators, and had many a cordial day with Booker T. Washington. Since I was nineteen years old, we had repeatedly found ourselves together as speakers on many large occasions, North and South. I introduced him in his last important address in Birmingham and Montgomery, Alabama, and presided at the banquet closing the last of his "state tours" in Shreveport. . . .

Meanwhile, in 1910 Pickens attended the NAACP founding conference and was selected for its "Committee of One Hundred," which pledged to increase membership and raise $100. He participated in the NAACP's annual summer conventions and its programs in churches to recruit and mobilize members in the South. Between 1910 and 1916, when the NAACP's top-level leadership—except for Du Bois—consisted of unsalaried white volunteers in administrative positions, and half a dozen "colored people" on the thirty-member board of directors, Pickens was a visible volunteer black recruiter. He traveled to Southern locations with Joel Spingarn,[2] the Jewish chairman of the board chosen by the NAACP in 1914. With the outbreak of World War I in Europe, Pickens joined Spingarn in the NAACP's efforts to urge the Secretary of War to create training camps for prospective black officers of black troops in the United States fighting force in Europe. Pickens had spent his summer vacation of 1913 on his first European tour, with no apprehension that World War I was imminent.

In late 1916, after publication of his volume of essays *The New Negro: His Political, Civil and Mental Status*, a few in the NAACP hierarchy preferred Pickens to James Weldon Johnson[3] for the first Afro-American National Secretary. However, unbeknownst to Pickens, Spingarn with a nod from Du Bois solicited John Hope, then President of Morehouse College. When Hope declined, Spingarn offered the position to Johnson, who accepted, with no previous involvement in the NAACP. Pickens, ten years Johnson's junior, was chosen as his field assistant in late 1919. With Johnson, Pickens, and Du Bois, the NAACP had a trio that once believed, in different ways, in Booker T. Washington, but only Pickens and Du Bois were honest enough to admit it in their respective memoirs. Johnson's 1933 autobiography, *Along This Way*, neither acknowledged his friendship with Washington nor his refusal to join the Niagara Movement.

When Pickens moved to New York to accept a full-time position at the NAACP, he had spent some sixteen years teaching in black colleges: Talladega (1904–14), Wiley College, in Marshall, Texas (1914–15), and Morgan College (later Morgan State University) in Baltimore (1915–20). At Morgan, he was dean when he resigned. His self-portrait, *Bursting Bonds*, ends with a chapter "Morgan College and After," with only one sentence about his entry into the NAACP: "Finally, on February 1, 1920, I accepted a position in the organization."

He did not write a sequel about his twenty-two years with the NAACP, perhaps because they were not the years of his greatest triumph, though he

---

[2] Joel E. Spingarn (1875–1939), President of the NAACP board of directors 1914–19; established in 1915 the Spingarn Medal award annually "for the highest and noblest achievement of an American Negro." He remained active in the organization until his death. By profession he was a literary critic and author of *New Criticism* (1911) and *Creative Criticsim* (1917); he was an academician on the faculty at Columbia University, 1899–1911.

[3] See the entry on James Weldon Johnson in this volume, pages 324–30, above.

worked diligently and was quickly promoted from assistant to associate field director, then to director of national branches. Responsibilities in the New York office were those of Johnson and his assistant national director, Walter White, who had arrived in 1918, twenty-four years old, "self-centered and egotistical" as Du Bois later described him. For Pickens, White was more domineering when he succeeded Johnson, who resigned in late 1930. Searching to find his own political voice, Pickens took some stands independent of Johnson and White; he flirted with Garveyism in the early 1920s; he traveled to Russia the summer of 1927; and after his return urged the NAACP board to take up the cause of labor and the working class, which the more conservative Johnson refused to do. In 1931, after the Scottsboro case became an international cause celèbre, Pickens wrote to the communist *Daily Worker* commending the communist–led International Labor Defense (ILD) for being ahead of the NAACP in legal defense of the Scottsboro Boys, but he later joined NAACP critics of ILD in the case. He sided with the NAACP board's resolution against the pro-segregation editorials that led to a resignation of Du Bois from the *The Crisis* and the NAACP in June 1934.

In 1942, Pickens himself was dismissed from the organization. While on a leave of absence as director of the Interracial Section of the Treasury Department's War Savings Bonds Division, he made public his dissent for Walter White's policy of opposing segregation in the armed forces while simultaneously supporting the war effort. Pickens believed such opposition should wait until the war ended. Despite his patriotism and support of the war (even before Japan bombed Pearl Harbor), in 1943 the House Committee on Un-American Activities accused him of being a Communist, and tried to oust him from the Treasury Department; he succeeded in holding onto the job until he retired in 1950.

Concerned throughout his career that the handicap of prejudice was due to "the ignorance of the better class of white people concerning the better class of colored people," he made that a recurring theme of his 1916 volume of essays, *The New Negro*. The following excerpt of his homonymous essay is from that book. The fourteen essays in the volume focus on problems and achievements since slavery—predating with a different emphasis the term *New Negro* used in an artistic and cultural context in the Harlem Renaissance of the 1920s.[4] Pickens lived in Harlem during that decade but was not identified with its artistic and literary circles. He published one collection of fiction, *"The*

[4] See also the biographical entry on Fannie Barrier Williams, above, pages 346–48, regarding the 1900 title *A New New Negro for a New Century.* That book, and an article by Williams's husband, S. Laing Williams, "The New Negro" in *Alexander's Magazine* (8 November 1908), 17–22, are believed to be the first publications using the term "New Negro" in the twentieth century.

Vengeance of the Gods" and Three Other Stories of the Real American Color
Line (1922), without success.

From *The New Negro* (1916)

The average white man of the present generation who sees the Negro daily,
perhaps knows less of the Negro than did the similarly situated white man of
any previous generation since the black race came to America. This lack of
knowledge has a fearful influence on the judgment: it is both history and psychology that where knowledge is wanting, imagination steps in. What naive
explanations men once gave of natural phenomena, what odd shapes they ascribed to the earth, and what erroneous proportions and fanciful relations they
imagined among the heavenly bodies. The most serious handicap to the creation of a wholesome public opinion on matters affecting the Negro, is the
ignorance of the better class of white people concerning the better class of
colored people who live in their community. They often know the other classes:
the servants through their kitchens and the criminals through the newspapers.
In a large Southern city lived the most experienced Negro banker in the United
States, with his bank, for twenty-five or thirty years; but, excepting the few
bankers and others with whom, he came into business contact, practically the
whole group of intelligent white people in that city were ignorant of the fact
that this Negro existed. In another Southern town of seven thousand people,
half-white and half-colored, an elderly, cultured, Christian white woman, who
had lived there all her life, did not know that the Negroes were not given a
public school building by her municipality, and had supposed that a primary
school for Negroes which had been maintained by a missionary society for thirty
or forty years, was the Negro public school. From an old Maryland community
a young Negro went out, got an education in some of the best schools, took a
course in theology at Yale, and then returned to that community to pastor a
church. He worked with great energy, aroused his people to build a fine new
church, and awakened so much enthusiasm in the colored masses that finally
some inklings of his success trickled in behind the ivied walls of an old mansion
where lived two wealthy white ladies of the "good old days," when the Negro
was so much better than he is now, as they could well testify from the superb
character of the "black mammy," now dead and gone, but who had been for

many years an indispensable part of their household conveniences. Hearing of the fine new building, for the first time in their lives they decided to attend the dedication of a Negro church. On learning the name and antecedents of the young pastor they found him to be the son of their bemoaned "black mammy,"—him whom they supposed had long since gone to the dogs, whither their daily newspapers were saying all the young and aspiring Negroes were bound. The mother had been a "member" of their family, but the son had struggled against poverty and prejudice, had got his education and done his work without any encouragement from them, without even so much as their confidence or their knowledge. How can a people so hedged about by tradition and handicapped by prejudice "know the Negro" as he now is, even though they be good people and knew him as he once was?

Not only does this ignorance of the Negro prevent many white people from sympathizing with his condition and struggles, but it does a mischief more positive than that: it prepares them to believe any charge of crime or viciousness or depravity which may be brought against the race. They will not analyze the evidence. If it is said that in proportion to their population there are four or five times as many blacks as whites in a Southern penitentiary, men will conclude at once, without thought or investigation, that such is the ratio of the criminality of the Negro and the white man. They overlook the multitude of other differences which may account for this difference in criminal statistics: the poverty, the ignorance, the homelessness and helplessness, and the very sort of prejudice which they themselves are substituting for thought. The ease with which a Negro can be lynched in the South should make them know how much more easily he can get into the penitentiary. Another thing that largely accounts for the Negro's superior numbers among the prisoners: most Southern states allow the discretion of the court a very wide latitude as to the number of years for which the condemned is to be sentenced. The law is often like this: a fine of so many dollars, or ten years in prison, or both. The Negro usually gets the limit, perhaps "both." To make an extreme but simplifying case, suppose one Negro and one white man commit a certain crime every year; if the white criminal is either fined or given only one year in prison, while the colored criminal is given ten years, in the tenth year when the visitor goes to that prison he will find nine or ten Negroes there for a certain crime, but only one white man. The easygoing investigator might conclude that the Negro is ten times as criminal in that respect as is the white man, while as a matter of fact both races would have committed exactly the same number of crimes. The long-term sentences of Negroes cause them to *accumulate* in prison. There are much more scientific ways of explaining the Negro's situation in this country than by reference to an unprovable something like innate depravity.

One of the greatest handicaps under which the new Negro lives is the handicap of the lack of acquaintanceship between him and his white neighbor. Under the former order, when practically all Negroes were either slaves or servants, every Negro had the acquaintance of some white man; as a race he was better known, better understood, and was therefore the object of less suspicion on the part of the white community. But under the present order there are many Negroes who are independent, in occupation or in fortune, doing business for themselves, rendering professional service to their own race or living independently at home. These Negroes, unknown to the white mass, are the objects of its special suspicions and distrust, for they are "something new under the sun." When riots break out, this unknown Negro, well-to-do and equally well behaved, the one who ought to be safest, is the one most liable to attack by the mob. This is because ignorance and prejudice have made the very things which pass for virtues in white men, seem like vices in the Negro; pride, ambition, self-respect, unsatisfaction with the lower positions of life, and the desire to live in a beautiful house and to keep his wife and children at home and out of "service." There can be no sympathy where there is no knowledge, and the Negro of this class, being rather a stranger to his white neighbors, is regarded as a bad example to those humbler and more helpless Negroes who are servants. This is not so in every case, but this is the rule, and the rule is the thing. And we are not talking hearsay but speaking out of the experiences of our lifetime.

If prejudice could only reason, it would dispel itself. If it could think, its thoughts might run like this: If it be true that the Negro is innately low and criminal in his instincts, then the Negro must be the same in all places—but the Negroes of other countries do not bear this reputation; those of Brazil and the rest of South America, of Central America, of the West Indies and of Mexico, are no distinguished as criminals. There are great numbers of Negroes in parts of these countries, and being in many of them unrestricted as to the position to which they may aspire in society and state, they would have a better chance to demonstrate any essential inferiority in those lands than in the United States. . . .

CARTER G. WOODSON

(1875–1950)

Four years after incorporation of the NAACP came another new organization, the Association for the Study of Negro Life and History, founded September 9, 1915. It was the idea of Carter G. Woodson—later known as the "Father of Negro History," whose numerous outreach programs included Negro History Week, an annual observance that began in 1926; it developed by 1976 into Black History Month, still celebrated annually each February in the United States.

Once a sharecropper, coal miner, and teacher, Woodson, the Virginia–born son of ex-slaves, graduated from Berea College in 1903; taught in the Philippines for three years (1903–6); traveled six months in Asia, North Africa, the Middle East, and Europe; and returned to the United States to earn a B.A. and M.A. in 1908 at the University of Chicago, and a Ph.D. from Harvard University in 1912. He incorporated the Association for the Study of Negro Life and History (ASNLH) in Washington, DC, in October 1915, established an executive council, and three months later launched the first issue of the quarterly *Journal of Negro History*, borrowing against his life-insurance policy to pay the printing costs. Edited by Woodson from January 1916 until his death in April 1950, the *Journal* promoted research and articles by black and white scholars on black history and achievements; it aimed at correcting omissions and distortions in American textbooks and culture—especially *The Birth of Nation*, as noted released in 1915 to a curious public in packed movie houses that were also picketed by many NAACP branches.

In the first few years of the Association, Woodson struggled almost single-handedly, soliciting articles, lecturing, fund raising with letter campaigns to newspaper editors, libraries, scholars, and philanthropists, seeking subscribers and membership donations. His venture would have failed without early support from wealthy whites, but the stern and spartan-living bachelor Woodson refused to become dependent on those sources, or discouraged when prestigious white foundations turned him down. His early black contributors were colleagues at the Armstrong Manual Training School, where he was principal from 1918 to 1919, and at Howard University, where he was Dean of the College of Liberal Arts from 1919 to 1920. Dismissed from Howard due to a conflicted relationship with University president J. Stanley Durkee—who hired him after demoting Dean Kelly Miller[1]—Woodson accepted a deanship at West Virginia Collegiate Institute (later West Virginia State College).

From West Virginia, he continued to handle duties of the Association and fund-raising efforts for a new publishing division, Associated Publishers, intended for publication of monographs and books by black scholars unwelcomed by white publishers. The July 1921 issue of his *Journal* announced the formation of the new publishing wing, with stock options open to future investors. After fulfilling administrative obligations of his two-year contract in West Virginia, Woodson returned to Washington during the summer of 1922 to devote full time to research, writing, and directorship of the ASNLH. With a loan, he purchased a modest three-story row house for his home and office, relocating the Association and Associated Publishers to 1538 Ninth Street—a permanent headquarters for the rest of his life.

Woodson's first book, *The Education of the Negro Prior to 1861*, published by the New York house of G. P. Putnam Sons, in early 1915, was his first and last title released by a commercial white publisher. His second book, *A Century of Negro Migration* (1918), and all his titles between 1921 and 1942 had the imprint of the Association for the Study of Negro Life and History, or Associated Publishers. His own texts covered a range of topics, some for a scholarly audience, most for the black masses and black schools on previously neglected aspects of history, including *The History of the Negro Church* (1921); *The Negro in Our History* (1922); *Free Negro Owners of Slaves in the United States in 1830* . . . (1924); *Negro Orators and Their Orations* (1926); *The Mind of the Negro as Reflected in Letters Written during the Crisis, 1800–1860* (1926); *The Negro as Businessman* (co-written with John H. Harmon, 1929); *The Negro Wage Earner* (with Lorenzo Greene, 1930); *The Rural Negro* (1930); *The Mis-Education of the Negro* (1933), *The Negro Professional Man and the Community; The Story of the Negro Retold* (1935); *The African Background Outlined* (1936); *African Heroes and Heroines* (1939); and *The Works of Francis J. Grimké* (1942).

Publishing his own manuscripts under his own editorial and administrative control, often in haste, and with limited resources and staff, accounts for the reason that they drew criticism from some black and white scholars who judged them deficient in style, structure, and documentation. Woodson was duly credited, however, for pioneering in the use of hitherto-ignored primary sources: letters, speeches, sermons, diaries, oral histories, interviews, and public records. The Woodson method was to popularize black history for the lay reader rather

---

[1] See the entry on Kelly Miller in this volume, pages 430–42, above.

than to write for recognition by professional historians. The content of his *Journal* was for a scholarly audience, but his illustrated *Negro History Bulletin*, started in 1937, was for the general public of all ages, with monthly features, events, and significant dates and figures in history.

The outspoken and no-nonsense Woodson was not only a historian but an activist "people's scholar" whose major concerns were education through outreach such as forums, source materials, and meetings sponsored by the Association. He was often critical of the consumer-oriented values of both the black middle class and the black masses. His ideas for solutions to socioeconomic change varied over the decades and often seemed contradictory. But he was steadfast in his strategies for uplift through self-knowledge and economic self-help. During the Great Depression years of the 1930s, he appealed through black newspapers to readers in regular weekly columns.

Following World War I, Woodson wrote increasingly of the results of the Northward migration of Southern blacks, offering solutions to class and race tensions, stressing education as the crucial link to progress. The following excerpt from A *Century of Negro Migration* is from chapter 9, "The Exodus during the World War." It closes this collection, taking readers to the dawn of The Harlem Renaissance and the beginnings of our own times.

From *A Century of Negro Migration* (1918)

. . . Within the last two years there has been a steady stream of Negroes into the North in such large numbers as to overshadow in its results all other movements of the kind in the United States. These Negroes have come largely from Alabama, Tennessee, Florida, Georgia, Virginia, North Carolina, Kentucky, South Carolina, Arkansas and Mississippi. The given causes of this migration are numerous and complicated. Some untruths centering around this exodus have not been unlike those of other migrations. Again we hear that the Negroes are being brought North to fight organized labor,[2] and to carry doubtful States for the Republicans.[3] These numerous explanations themselves, however, give rise to doubt as to the fundamental cause.

Why then should the Negroes leave the South? It has often been spoken of as the best place for them. There, it is said, they have made unusual strides

---

[2] *New York Times*, September 5, 9, 28, 1916.
[3] Ibid., October 18, 28; November 5, 7, 12, 15; December 4, 9, 1916.

forward. The progress of the Negroes in the South, however, has in no sense been general, although the land owned by Negroes in the country and the property of thrifty persons of their race in urban communities may be extensive. In most parts of the South the Negroes are still unable to become land-owners or successful businessmen. Conditions and customs have reserved these spheres for the whites. Generally speaking, the Negroes are still dependent on the white people for food and shelter. Although not exactly slaves, they are yet attached to the white people as tenants, servants or dependents. Accepting this as their lot, they have been content to wear their lord's cast-off clothing, and live in his ramshackled barn or cellar. In this unhappy state so many have settled down, losing all ambition to attain a higher station. The world has gone on but in their sequestered sphere progress has passed them by.

What then is the cause? There have been *bulldozing*, terrorism, maltreatment and what not of persecution; but the Negroes have not in large numbers wandered away from the land of their birth. What the migrants themselves think about it, goes to the very heart of the trouble. Some say that they left the South on account of injustice in the courts, unrest, lack of privileges, denial of the right to vote, bad treatment, oppression, segregation or lynching. Others say that they left to find employment to secure better wages, better school facilities, and better opportunities to toil upward. Southern white newspapers unaccustomed to give the Negroes any mention but that of criminals have said that the Negroes are going North because they have not had a fair chance in the South and that if they are to be retained there, the attitude of the whites toward them must be changed. Professor William O. Scroggs, of Louisiana State University, considers as causes of this exodus "the relatively low wages paid farm labor, an unsatisfactory tenant or crop-sharing system, the boll weevil, the crop failure of 1916, lynching, disfranchisement, segregation, poor schools, and the monotony, isolation and drudgery of farm life." Professor Scroggs, however, is wrong in thinking that the persecution of the blacks has little to do with the migration for the reason that during these years when the treatment of the Negroes is decidedly better they are leaving the South. This does not mean that they would not have left before, if they had had economic opportunities in the North. It is highly probable that the Negroes would not be leaving the South today, if they were treated as men, although there might be numerous opportunities for economic improvement in the North.

The immediate cause of this movement was the suffering due to the floods aggravated by the depredations of the boll weevil . . . The boll weevil is an insect about one-fourth of an inch in length, varying from one-eighth to one-third of an inch with a breadth of about one-third of the length. When it first emerges it is yellowish, then becomes grayish brown and finally assumes a black shade. It breeds on no other plant than cotton and feeds on the boll. This little animal, at first attacked the cotton crop in Texas. It was not thought that it would extend its work into the heart of the South so as to become of national consequence, but it has, at the rate of 40 to 160 miles annually, invaded all of the cotton district except that of the Carolinas and Virginia. The damage it does, varies according to the rainfall and the harshness of the winter, increasing with the former and decreasing with the latter. At times the damage has been to the extent of a loss of 50 percent of the crop, estimated at 400,000 bales of cotton annually, about 4,500,000 bales since the invasion or $250,000,000 worth of cotton. The output of the South being thus cut off, the planter has less income to provide supplies for his black tenants and, the prospects for future production being dark, merchants accustomed to give them credit have to refuse. This, of course, means financial depression, for the South is a borrowing section and any limitation to credit there blocks the wheels of industry. It was fortunate for the Negro laborers in this district that there was then a demand for labor in the North when this condition began to obtain.

This demand was made possible by the cutting off of European immigration by the World War, which thereby rendered this hitherto uncongenial section an inviting field for the Negro. The Negroes have made some progress in the North during the last fifty years, but despite their achievements they have been so handicapped by race prejudice and proscribed by trades unions that the uplift of the race by economic methods has been impossible. The European immigrants have hitherto excluded the Negroes even from the menial positions. In the midst of the drudgery left for them, the blacks have often heretofore been debased to the status of dependents and paupers. Scattered through the North too in such small numbers, they have been unable to unite for social betterment and mutual improvement and naturally too weak to force the community to respect their wishes as could be done by a large group with some political or economic power. At present, however, Negro laborers, who once went from city to city, seeking such employment as trades unions left to them, can work even as skilled laborers throughout the North. Women of color formerly excluded from domestic service by foreign maids are now in demand. Many mills and factories which Negroes were prohibited from entering a few years ago are now bidding for their labor. Railroads cannot find help to keep their property in repair, contractors fall short of their plans for failure to hold mechanics drawn into the industrial boom and the United States Government has had to advertise for men to hasten the preparation for war.

Men from afar went south to tell the Negroes of a way of escape to a more congenial place. Blacks long since unaccustomed to venture a few miles from home, at once had visions of a promised land just a few hundred miles away.

Some were told of the chance to amass fabulous riches, some of the opportunities for education and some of the hospitality of the places of amusement and recreation in the North. The migrants then were soon on the way. Railway stations became conspicuous with the presence of Negro tourists, the trains were crowded to full capacity and the streets of northern cities were soon congested with black laborers seeking to realize their dreams in the land of unusual opportunity.

Employment agencies, recently multiplied to meet the demand for labor, find themselves unable to cope with the situation and agents sent into the South to induce the blacks by offers of free transportation and high wages to go north, have found it impossible to supply the demand in centers where once toiled the Poles, Italians and the Greeks formerly preferred to the Negroes. In other words, the present migration differs from others in that the Negro has opportunity awaiting him in the North whereas formerly it was necessary for him to make a place for himself upon arriving among enemies. The proportion of those returning to the South, therefore, will be inconsiderable.

Becoming alarmed at the immensity of this movement the South has undertaken to check it. To frighten Negroes from the North, Southern newspapers are carefully circulating reports that many of them are returning to their native land because of unexpected hardships. But having failed in this, Southerners have compelled employment agents to cease operations there, arrested suspected employers and, to prevent the departure of the Negroes, imprisoned on false charges those who appear at stations to leave for the North. This procedure could not long be effective, for by the more legal and clandestine methods of railway passenger agents the work has gone forward. Some Southern communities have, therefore, advocated drastic legislation against labor agents, as was suggested in Louisiana in 1914, when by operation of the Underwood Tariff Law the Negroes thrown out of employment in the sugar district migrated to the cotton plantations.

One should not, however, get the impression that the majority of the Negroes are leaving the South. Eager as these Negroes seem to go, there is no unanimity of opinion as to whether migration is the best policy. The sycophant, toady class of Negroes naturally advise the blacks to remain in the South to serve their white neighbors. The radical protagonists of the equal-rights-for-all element urge them to come north by all means. Then there are the thinking Negroes, who are still further divided. Both divisions of this element have the interests of the race at heart, but they are unable to agree as to exactly what the blacks should now do. Thinking that the present war will soon be over and that consequently the immigration of foreigners into this country will again set in and force out of employment thousands of Negroes who have migrated to the North, some of the most representative Negroes are advising their fellows to remain where they are. The most serious objection to this transplantation is that it means for the Negroes a loss of land, the rapid acquisition of which has long been pointed to as the best evidence of the ability of the blacks to rise in the economic world. So many Negroes who have by dint of energy purchased small farms yielding an increasing income from year to year, are now disposing of them at nominal prices to come north to work for wages. Looking beyond the war, however, and thinking too that the depopulation of Europe during this upheaval will render immigration from that quarter for some years an impossibility, other thinkers urge the Negroes to continue the migration to the North, where the race may be found in sufficiently large numbers to wield economic and political power.

Great as is the dearth of labor in the South, moreover, the Negro exodus has not as yet caused such a depression as to unite the whites in inducing the blacks to remain in that section. In the first place, the South has not yet felt the worst effects of this economic upheaval as that part of the country has been unusually aided by the millions which the United States Government is daily spending there. Furthermore, the poor whites are anxious to see the exodus of their competitors in the field of labor. This leaves the capitalists at their mercy, and in keeping with their domineering attitude, they will be able to handle the labor situation as they desire. As an evidence of this fact we need but note the continuation of mob rule and lynching in the South despite the preachings against it of the organs of thought which heretofore winked at it. This terrorism has gone to an unexpected extent. Negro farmers have been threatened with bodily injury, unless they leave certain parts.

The Southerner of aristocratic bearing will say that only the shiftless poor whites terrorize the Negroes. This may be so, but the truth offers little consolation when we observe that most white people in the South are of this class; and the tendency of this element to put their children to work before they secure much education does not indicate that the South will soon experience that general enlightenment necessary to exterminate these survivals of barbarism. Unless the upper classes of the whites can bring the mob around to their way of thinking that the persecution of the Negro is prejudicial to the interests of all, it is not likely that mob rule will soon cease and the migration to this extent will be promoted rather than retarded.

Looking beyond the war, however, and thinking too that the depopulation of Europe during this upheaval will render immigration from that quarter for some years an impossibility, other thinkers urge the Negroes to continue the migration to the North, where the race may be found in sufficiently large numbers to wield economic and political power.

Great as is the dearth of labor in the South, moreover, the Negro exodus has not as yet caused such a depression as to unite the whites in inducing the blacks to remain in that section. In the first place, the South has not yet felt the worst effects of this economic upheaval as that part of the country has been unusually aided by the millions which the United States Government is daily spending there. Furthermore, the poor whites are anxious to see the exodus of their competitors in the field of labor. This leaves the capitalists at their mercy, and in keeping with their domineering attitude, they will be able to handle the labor situation as they desire. As an evidence of this fact we need but note the continuation of mob rule and lynching in the South despite the preachings against it of the organs of thought which heretofore winked at it. This terrorism has gone to an unexpected extent. Negro farmers have been threatened with bodily injury, unless they leave certain parts.

The Southerner of aristocratic bearing will say that only the shiftless poor whites terrorize the Negroes. This may be so, but the truth offers little consolation when we observe that most white people in the South are of this class; and the tendency of this element to put their children to work before they secure much education does not indicate that the South will soon experience that general enlightenment necessary to exterminate these survivals of barbarism. Unless the upper classes of the whites can bring the mob around to their way of thinking that the persecution of the Negro is prejudicial to the interests of all, it is not likely that mob rule will soon cease and the migration to this extent will be promoted. . . .

INDEX

A

abolitionists and abolitionism, 26, 43, 70, 87, 92, 93, 208, 119, 122, 123–26, 134, 137, 141, 144, 146, 147, 165, 169, 173, 179, fn180, 200, 209, 218, 227, fn231, 241, 253, 263, 268, 281, 282, 331–32, 412, 418, 429; black abolitionists, 213 16, 292; educated fugitives, 146; gradual abolition, 95; through evangelism, 265
"Abolitionists, The . . ." (John Greenleaf Whittier), 122
Academy for Negro Youth, 218
Adams, John, 188
Addams, Jane, 384, 446, 452
"Addams of the Liberty Party . . ." (Henry Highland Garnet), 148
"Address on Colonization to a Deputation of Colored Men" (Abraham Lincoln), 258–62
"Address to Miss Phillis Wheatley, Ethiopian Poetess in Boston, An" (Jupiter Hammon), 50
"Address to the Negroes in The State of New York, An" (Jupiter Hammon), 51, 52
"Address to the Slaves, An" (Henry Highland Garnet), 147, 148–54
Adventures of Huckleberry Finn (Mark Twain), 358

Adventures of Tom Sawyer, The (Mark Twain), 358
Advocate, the, 420
Africa, 40, 60–62, 66, 81, 84, 98, 99, 129, 260, 288, 431, 440; as paradise, 121; not contributing to world culture, 435; return to, 91, 155, 160–61, 343, 380, 465
Africa and America . . . (A. Crummell), 293
Afric-American Female Intelligence Society, 96, 97
African Background Outlined, The (Carter G. Woodson), 466
African Civilization Society, 147, fn260
African Colonization Society, 147, fn260,
African Methodist Episcopal (A.M.E.) Church, 72, fn91, 281, 445
Africa diaspora, 60, 87, 175, 192, 202, 292, 343
African Heroes and Heroines (Carter G. Woodson), 466
African Methodist Episcopal Zion church, 264, 420
African tribes, 73, 202
Africans as slaves, 25, 34, 40, 254
Afro-American newspaper, 454
Afro-American. See Fortune. T. Thomas
Afro-Americans—expatriates, 224; family of, 129; hair, 436; identity, 397–411; inferiority, 410; passing, 397; self-

Afro-Americans *(cont'd)*
  sufficiency of, 155; skin color, 39–40,
  232, 393, 436; uniqueness, 440; *See also*
  African diaspora; Africans as slaves; mu-
  latto; race in America; slavery in
  America
Age of Reason, The (Thomas Paine), 30
"Ain't I a Woman" (Sojourner Truth), 264
Aldrich, Ira, fn224
Alexander, Charles, 420
Alexander's magazine, 420
Alger, Horatio, 419
Allen, Richard, 72–73, fn91
Along This Way (J. W. Johnson), 324, 326
American Antislavery Society, 119, 122,
  123, 227, 228; *See* Purvis, Robert
American Colonization Society, 77–78,
  128, 186
American Crisis, The (Thomas Paine), 30
American Democrat, The (James Fenimore
  Cooper), 83
American Equal Rights Association, 265
American Freedman's Aid Association, 141
American Missionary Association, 317, 458
American Negro Academy (ANA) (1897–
  1928), 294, 426, 430; women banned,
  426
American Slavery as It Is . . . (Weld and
  Grimké sisters), 138, 139–40
Amistad, 153
A.M.E. Christian Recorder, 282
Anderson, Charles, 324
Anderson, Osborne P., 208
Anglo-American, the, 148
Anthony, Aaron, 157,
Anthony, Susan B., 93, 265, 283, 443
antiabolitionist, 130
Anti-Slavery Declaration (1833), 122
antislavery movement, 24, 31–34, 37, 41–
  42, 43, fn51, 92, 93, 134, 158, 173, 223,
  272; economic aspects, 99
*Appeal in Favor of That Class of Americans
  Called Africans, An* (L. M. F. Child),
  119, 120–21
"Appeal to Caesar, An," (A. W. Tourgée),
  303, 305–7
*Appeal to the Christian Women of the
  Southern States* (Angela Grimké), 134,
  135–36
*Appeal to the Women of the Nominally Free
  States, An* (Angelina Grimké), 134

"Appeal to Woman, An" (S. Forten), 268
Armstrong Manual Training School, 465
Armstrong, Samuel Chapman, 317
Army Life in a Black Regiment (Thomas
  Wentworth Higginson), 272, 273,
  274–78; bravery of Afro-Americans, 278
Arthur, Chester A., 148, 304
Associated Publishers (Carter G. Wood-
  son), 466
Association for the Study of Negro Life
  and History (ASNLH—Carter G.
  Woodson), 465, 466
"As the Lord Lives, He Is One of Our
  Mother's Children" (P. E. Hopkins),
  416–17
"As to the Leopard's Spots: An Open Let-
  ter to Thomas Dixon" (Kelly Miller),
  432–42
Atlanta Compromise, 295, 317, 318, 430
Atlanta Constitution, 287, 308, 395
Atlantic Monthly, 253, 264, 332, 333, 342,
  360, 395, 396
Attucks, Crispus, 185, 186–89, 231
Auld, Sophia, 157
"Author's Acount of His Country, The"
  (Olaudah Equiano), 60
Autobiography of an Ex-Colored Man
  (J. W. Johnson), 325
Avary, Myrta L., 241

B

Baker, Ray Stannard, 453
Baltimore Afro-American, 452
Banneker, Benjamin, fn38, 45–46
Banta, Martha, fn334
"Barbarism of Civilization, The" (C. H.
  Pemberton), 385
Barber, Jesse Max, 459
Barlow, Joel, fn38, fn45
Barnett, Ferdinand, 445, 446
Barnier, Ella D., 348
Beecher, Edward, 161
Bendixen, Alfred, fn384
Benson, Helen, 92
Bentley, Dr. Charles, 454
Berry, Theodore M., 16
"Best Methods of Removing the Disabili-

ties of Caste from the Negro" (J. W. Johnson), 327–30

Bibb, Henry, 205

Bible, 32, 55, 56–57, 58, 96, 100, 104–7, 120, 151, 211, 214, 215, 245, 257, 262, 315, 338, 364, 367, 375, 417, 442, 450, 457, 459; and crucifixion, 106–7; and slavery, 32, 243; David and Goliath, 366; Ezekiel, 29; Genesis, 23; Jacob, 24; Jeremiah, 28–29, 432; Joseph, 23; Rachel, 24; Sodom, 235

Bible Argument against Slavery (Theodore Dwight Weld), 137–38

Birth of a Nation, The, 422, 430, 465; *See also* Dixon, Thomas, Jr.

"Black Abolitionist in Defense of John Brown, A" (C. H. Langston), 213–16

Black and White: Life, Labor, and Politics in the South (T. Thomas Fortune), 295, 296, 297–301

Black History Month (1976 to present—formerly Negro History Week, 1926–75), 465

black laws, 144

Black Manhattan (J. W. Johnson), 326

black nationalism, 175, 176

"Black Woman of the South: Her Neglects and Her Needs, The" (Alexander Crummell), 293, 343

Blaine, James, fn424

Blake . . . (M. R. Delany), 174

Blow, John, fn190

Bomefree, Isabella. *See* Sojourner Truth

Bonaparte, Napoleon, 152, 274

Booker T. Washington Papers, The, 318

Boston Evening Record, 423

Boston Female Anti-Slavery Society, 119

Boston Literary and Historical Association, 419

Boston Transcript, 431

Boyd, Julian P., fn39

Brantley, Etheldred T., 106

Brawley, Benjamin, 372

B'rer Rabbit. *See* Harris, Joel Chandler; Uncle Remus folklore

Brooklyn Daily Eagle, 201

Brown, John, 93, 147, 156, 208–9, 213, 214, 216, 217, 218, 219, 221, fn231, 272, 282, 426; craziness of, 220

Brown v. Board of Education, 304

Brown, William Wells, 179–81, 185 233, 270, 412

Bryant, William Cullen, 122

Building Our Own . . . (Sutton Griggs), 380

"Burden of Black Women, The" (W. E. B. Du Bois), 426

burnings, 447–48

Bursting Bonds (William Pickens), 458

Butler, Samuel, fn440

C

Cable, George Washington, 308–10, 342, 395; and Booker T. Washington, 316; and Charles W. Chesnutt, 395; and Kate Chopin, 310; and Mark Twain, 310; as reformer, 308, 316

Call, The (O. G. Villard), 451, 452, 453, 454, 455

Canada. *See* Chatham; West Canada

Caribbean, 60, 146, 157, 176, 180, 203, 276, 324, 419, 436, 445, 458–59, 464; *See also* West Indies

Carlyle, Thomas, 166, 292; *Discourse on the Nigger Question*, 292

Carnegie, Andrew, 431

carpetbagger, 302, 390

Carse, George B., 267

Carver, George Washington, 317

Century magazine, 308

Cary, Mary Ann Shadd, 205

"Celebrated Jumping Frog of Calaveras County" ["Jim Smiley and His Jumping Frog"] (Mark Twain), 358, 359, 361

Century magazine, 308

Century of Negro Migration, A (Carter G. Woodson), 466, 467–72

Chapman, Maria Weston, 96

Chatham (West Canada: Ontario), 174

Cheatham, Henry, 391

Cheerful Days (T. W. Higginson), 273

Chesnut, James, Jr., 242

Chesnut, James, Sr., 241

Chesnut, Mary Boykin, 241–42, 247

Chesnutt, Andrew Jackson, 393

Chesnutt, Ann Maria, 393

Chesnutt, Charles W., 331, 333, 380, 393–

Chesnutt, Charles W. *(cont'd)*
97, 412, 413; literary accomplishments,
394, 412, 413
Chicago Conservator, 446
Chicago Haymarket Square riot, 333
Chicago World's Fair (1893), 346, 358; no
black representation, 346
"Chiefly about War Matters" (N. Haw-
thorne), 253, 254
Child, David, 119
Child, Lydia Maria Francis, 96, 119–20,
123, 247, 269
Children's Aid Society, 384
Chopin, Kate, 310
Cinque, Joseph, 153
Citizen's Trade Association, 459
"Civil Disobedience" (H. D. Thoreau),
217
civil rights, 80, 144, 148, 295, 309, 421,
427, 430, 443, 444, 458
Civil Rights Law (1875), 444
Civil War, 93, 111, 136, 137, 144, 148, 156,
170, 186, 192, 202, 205, 228. 233. 238,
241, 252, 255, 257, 265, 270, 272, 273,
282, 288, 291, 292, 294, 302, 306, 308,
315, 316, 332 342, 359, 371, 382, 385,
393, 418, 419, 420, 430, 433, 440; Con-
federacy, 241, 242
Clansman, The . . . (Thomas Dixon), 430
Clapperton, Hugh, 82
Clayton, Eva M., fn391
Clemens, Samuel L. *See* Mark Twain
Cleveland, Grover, 304, 419, 424
Clotel . . . (W. W. Brown), 180–81
Clotelle . . . (W. W. Brown), 181
Cole, Bob, 325, 326
Coleman, Elihu, fn26
Collins, Robert, 232
Colman, Lucy N., fn263, fn266
Colonization Scheme Considered, The . . .
(Samuel E. Cornish and Theodore
Wright), 78
Colonel's Dream, The (C. W. Chesnutt),
396
"colored," 343
Colored American magazine, 144, 145, 413,
414, 415, 416, 432; versus *Colored Amer-
ican* newspaper, fn413
Colored Aristocracy (P. E. Hopkins), 413
Colored Citizen, 420

Colored Co-operative Publishing Com-
pany, 412, 413
*Colored Patriots of the American Revolu-
tion* (W. C. Nell), 185, 186–89
Colored Reading Society for Mental Im-
provement (William Whipper), 144
Committee of Twelve for the Advance-
ment of Interests of the Negro Race, 431
Common Sense (Thomas Paine), 30
Communist Manifesto, The (Marx and
Engels), 166
Complete Works of Abraham Lincoln, The,
257
Complete Writings of Thomas Paine, The,
30
"Concerning Father" (C. W. Chesnutt),
397
"Confessions of Nat Turner, The" (Nat
Turner), 103
Conjure Woman, The (C. W. Chesnutt),
395, 397
Contending Forces . . . (P. E. Hopkins), 414
Continental Congress, 35
"coon songs," 326
Cooper, Anna Julia (Annie Haywood),
fn270, 342–44, 346; and feminist
thought, 342, 343; "womanhood . . . ,"
343
Cooper, Rev. George, 343
Cooper, James Fenimore, 83–84
Copeland, John, 212
Cornish, Samuel E., 77–79
*Cotton Kingdom, The . . . [A Journey of the
Seaboard Slave States; A Journey through
Texas; A Journey in the Back Country]*
(Frederick Law Olmstead), 237, 238–40
Craft, Ellen, 232–33
Craft, William, 232–33
Creole, 309, 310
Creoles of Louisiana, The (G. W. Cable),
310
Creole revolt, 156
Crisis, The, 415, 422, 453, 461
Cromwell, John Wesley, 295
Crum,, William, 233
Crummell, Alexander, 146, 291–93, 294
343, fn427; and feminist thought, 343
*Crusade for Justice: The Autobiography of
Ida B. Wells,* 446, 455

D

Daily Worker, 461
David Walker's Appeal in Four Articles . . . (David Walker), 87, 93, 147
Davis, Isaac, 189
Davis, Jefferson, 242, 439
de Beaumont, Gustave, 127
de Buffon, Georges-Louis Leclare, 36, 43
de Chastellux, Marquis François-Jean, 36, 43
Declaration of Independence, 30, 35, 37, 70, 94, 184, 188, 195, 196, 198
de Condorcat, Antoine Nicolas, 45
Deism, 69
De la Littérature de négres (Abbe Henri Grégoire), 38
Delany, Martin Robison, 173–75, 179
de Marbois, François, 35
Democracy in America (Alexis de Tocqueville), 127
Denham, Dixon, 82
de Tocqueville, Alexis-Henri-Charles-Maurice Clerel, 127–28, 180
DeVoto, Bernard, 358
Dial, The, 218, 432
Diary (Samuel Sewall), 23
Diary from Dixie, A (Mary Boykin Chesnut), 241, 243–46
Dickinson, Emily, 273
Dixon, Thomas, Jr., 286, 380, 430, 432, 434, 438, 439, 442; See also *The Clansman; The Birth of a Nation*
Domestic Manners of the Americans (Frances Milton Trollope), 108, 109–10
Douglass, Frederick (Frederick Augustus Washington Bailey), 18, fn146, 147, 155–58, 160, 161, 174, 180, 185, 265, 292, 295, 317, 328, 331, 342, 346, 372, 396, 419, 439, 444, 445; and women's rights, 156, 158–59
Douglass, Grace, 141, 142, 143
Douglass, Sarah Mapps, 141–42, 143 265
Douglas, Stephen A., 256
Dred Scott decision. *See* Scott, Dred
Dr. Sevier (G. W. Cable), 309
Du Bois, W. E. B., 175, 255, 291, 292, 318, 343, 415, 421, 425, 426, 431, 432, 452, 453, 454, 455, 459, 460, 461

Dumont, John, 264
Dunbar, Alice, 413; *The Goodness of St. Rocque*, 413
Dunbar, Paul Laurence, 326, 331, 370–73, 379, 394, 413; reprints of new poetry collections, 373
Dupree, William, 420
Duster, Alfreda M., 446
Dyer Antilynching Bill, 446
Dyer, Leonidas, 446

E

Eddy, Mary Baker, 360
Education of the Negro Prior to 1861, The (Carter G. Woodson), 466
Edwards, Jonathan, 50
Ellicott, Andrew, 45, 48
emancipation, 71, 110, 117, 149, 173, 316, 390
Emancipation Proclamation, 175, 202, 204, 253, 256, 299, 324, 456
Emerson, Ralph Waldo, 122, 217, 218, 349
Engels, Frederick, 166
Enterprise, the, 420
Epistle to the clergy of the South, An (Sarah Grimké), 134
epileptic seizures, 240
Equiano, Olaudah (Gustavas Vassa), 60–61, 68
Essay on Slavery and Abolitionism (Catherine Stowe), 161
Eulogium on the Life and Character of Thomas Clarkson (A. Crummell), 292
Everlasting Stain, The (Kelly Miller), 432

F

Farm Book (Thomas Jefferson), 37
Female Anti-Slavery Society. *See* Purvis, Harriet Forten
feminist thought, 97, 120, 134, 135, 156, 158–59, 247, 248, 263, 268, 281, 342, 343, 346, 426, 443, 445; *See also* women's rights
Fighting Years: Memoirs of a Liberal Editor (O. G. Villard), 451, 454
Fitzhugh, George, 177–67, 169

Folks from Dixie (P. L. Dunbar), 373, 374–78

Following the Color Line: American Negro Citizenship in the Progressive Era (R. S. Baker), 453

Foner, Philip S., 30, fn385

Fool's Errand, A (A. W. Tourgée), 302, 369

Forbes, George, 420

Forest Leaves (F. E. W. Harper), 281

Forten, Charlotte (Grimké), fn122, 268–70, 272; and Afro-American élite, 268

Forten, James, 122, 227, 265, 268; daughters of, fn122

Forten James, Jr., 268

Forten, Mary Virginia Wood, 268

Forten, Robert Bridges, 268

Forten, Sarah ("Ada"), 268

Fortune, Emanuel, 294

Fortune, T. Thomas (Timothy Thomas; Gustafus Bert), 294–96, 297, 302, 308, 318, 325, 348, 420, 425, 427, 444, 445; Afro-American, 294; and Booker T. Washington, 295; *See also* "poor white trash"

Franklin, Benjamin, 27, 69–70, 72

Franklin Evans. . . . See Whitman, Walt

Frederick Douglass' Paper, 155, 282

Free African Society, 141

Freedman's Bureau, 173, 393

"Freedman's Case in Equity, The" (George Washington Cable), 308, 310, 311–15

Freedom's Journal (Samuel E. Cornish and John B. Russwurm), 77, 79, 81, 82, 87

Free Negro Owners of Slaves . . . (Carter G. Woodson), 466

Free-Soiler, 237

Free Speech and Headlight (later *Free Speech*), 444

From the Virginia Plantation to the National Capitol (J. M. Langston), 213

From Truth Stranger Than Fiction (Josiah Henson), 205, 206–7

Fugitive Slave Act (Law), 180, 186, 205, 218, 222, 230, 233, 237, 248, 256, 272

Future of the Negro, The (B. T. Washington), 316

G

Gage, Frances Dana, 264

Gandhi, Mohandas K., 218

Garfield, James, 303–4

Garnet ("Garnett"), Henry Highland, 146–48, 155, 266; physical disability, 146

Garrison, William Lloyd, 92–93, 95, 97, 100, 102, 119, 135, 138, 142, fn146, 147, 155, 180, 185, 186, 223, 227, 233, 265, 270, 277, 418, 422, 452; grandson: Oswald Garrison Villard, 452

Garvey, Marcus, 296, 461

General Coloured Association of Massachusetts, 87

Genius of Universal Emancipation, 92, 94

George III, 37

"ghetto" as social term, 422

Giddings, Joshua R., fn214

Gilbert, Olive, fn263

Gilded Age, 295, 394

God's Trombones (J. W. Johnson), 324

Gone with the Wind (M. Mitchell), 241

Gottesman, Ronald, fn334

Grady, Henry W., 308

Grandissimes, Les (G. W. Cable), 309

Grant, Ulysses S., 156, 173, 303, 385

Gray, Thomas R., 102, fn103

Great Depression, 422, 467

Great Migration, 348, 422

Greeley, Horace, 248

Greener, Richard T., 294–95

Greene, Lorenzo, 466

Grégoire, Abbe Henri, 38

Griffiths, D. W., 422, 430

Griggs, Rev. Allen, 379

Griggs, Sutton, 379–81; "New Negro," 379; Orion Publishing, 379; *See also Imperium in Imperio*

Grimké, Angelina Emily (Weld), 96, 134–35, 137, 141, 161, 241, 268, 418

Grimké, Archibald Henry, fn137, fn255, 419, 452

Grimké, Francis J., 270, 452, 466

Grimké, Sarah, 96, 134, 141, 161, 241

Guardian, the, 418, 420, 421, 422, 423, 452, 459

H

Hagar's Daughter . . . (P. E. Hopkins), 414

Hale, John P., fn214

Half a Man: The Status of the Negro in New York (M. W. Ovington), 452
Hall, David, 27
Hall, Robert, 152
Hammon, Jupiter, 50–51
Harlan, Louis R., 318
Harlem Renaissance, 16, 279, 461, 467
Harlow, Ralph, fn214
Harmon, John H., 466
Harper, Fenton, 282
Harper, Frances Ellen Watkins, 281–83
Harper's, 331, 333, 342, 371
Harper's Ferry raid, 93, 147, 156, 208, 209, 212, 213, 223, 282, 426, 454; *See also* Brown, John
Harris, Joel Chandler, 286–88, 291, 361, 370, 395
Harris, Mary, 287
Harvard Memorial Biographies (T. W. Higginson), 273
"Has the Race the Element of Self-Salvation in It?" (William Monroe Trotter), 423
"Haunted Oak" (P. L. Dunbar), 371
Hawthorne (Henry James), 252
Hawthorne, Nathaniel, 252–53; and Civil War, 252
Hayes, Rutherford B., 156
Hay, John, 257
Heir of Slaves (William Pickens). See *Bursting Bonds*
Hemings, Eston, 418
Hemings, Sally, 36–37, 418
Henry, Patrick, 156
Henson, Josiah, 161, 204–5
Hepburn, John, fn26
Heroic Slave, The (Frederick Douglass), 156
Hesiod, fn440
Higginson, Thomas Wentworth, 272–73; opposed Fugitive Slave Law, 272; Travellers and Outlaws series, 272
History of the Negro Church, The (Carter G. Woodson), 466
History of Wall Street, The (E. G. Villard), 451
Hobomok (L. M. F. Child), 119
Holmes, Oliver Wendell, Sr., 332
Holmes, Rev. John Haynes, 455

Hope, John, 460
Hopkins, Pauline Elizabeth (Sarah A. Allen, pseud.), 412–16
Horizon: A Journal of the Color Line, 426
House behind the Cedars, The ("Rena Walden") (C. W. Chesnutt), 396
House Committee on Un-American Activities, 461
Howard, Otis Oliver, fn294
Howard University, 294, 430, 431, 465
Howells, William Dean, 331–34, 342, 344–45, 360, 371, 373, 393, 453; and Afro-Americans, 331; indifference, 332; See also *An Imperative Duty*
Hughes, Langston, 213
Hyers sisters, 413

I

"Immediate Emancipation" (H. B. Stowe), 161
Imperative Duty, An ["The Letters of Olney"] (William Dean Howells), 331, 333, 334–41, 342, 344, 371; and miscegenation theme, 333
Imperium in Imperio (Sutton Griggs), 379, 380–83
Incidents in the Life of a Slave Girl (Harriet Jacobs), 247, 248, 249–51
Innocents Abroad (Mark Twain), 359
"Intellectual Progress of the Colored Women . . ." (F. G. Williams), 346
Interesting Narrative of the Life of Olaudah Equiano, The . . . , 60
International Labor Defense, 461
Inter Ocean newspaper, 446
"Intervention of Peter, The" (P. L. Dunbar), 374–78
Invisible Empire, The (A. W. Tourgée), 302
Iola. See Ida B. Wells-Barnett
Iola Leroy . . . (F. E. W. Harper), 283
Irving, Washington, 130
Isaacs, Virginia, 418
Ivins, Barclay, 233

J

Jackson, Andrew, 83, 191
Jacobs, Harriet (Linda Brent), 119, 247–48

James, Henry, 252, 333, 386, 458

Jefferson, Thomas, 35–38, 45, 46, 84, 88, fn101, 180, 418; and Abraham Lincoln on race, 256; *Autobiography*, 37; miscegenation, 36, 38

Jews, 68, 73, 74, 75–76, 460

Jim Crow, 370–71, 420, 426, 428; *See also* Rice, Thomas Dartmouth

Joan of Arc, 443

John Brown: A Biography of Fifty Years (O. G. Villard), 451

Johnny March, Southerner (G. W. Cable), 310

Johnson, Andrew, 173, 284

Johnson, Charles S., fn412, 414; "The Rise of the Negro Magazine," 414

Johnson, James Weldon (William), 324–26 460; *See also* "Lift Every Voice and Sing"

Johnson, Rosamond, 324

Jones, Absalom, 72–73

Journal of Charlotte L. Forten, The, 269, 270–71

Journal of Negro History, 414, 465, 466, 467

Journal of the Life and Travels of John Woolman in the Service of the Gospel, 27

Journal of the Times (Wiliam Lloyd Garrison), 92

Journals of Charlotte Forten Grimké, The (enlarged ed. by Brenda Stevenson), 270

"Justice and Expediency" (John Greenleaf Whittier), 122, 123–26

"Justice and Impolicy of the Slave Trade, and the Slavery of Africans, The" (Jonathan Edwards), 50

K

Kelley, Florence, 452

Kennedy, John Pendleton (Mark Littleton), 111–12, 130

Key to Uncle Tom's Cabin (Harriet Beecher Stowe), 139, 161, 162–65

"Kind Master and Dutiful Servant, The" (Jupiter Hammond), 50

King, Martin Luther, Jr., 218

Kipling, Rudyard, 441

Knapp, Isaac, fn92

Knickerbocker History of New York (Washington Irving), 130

"Knights of the Golden Circle," 447

Ku Klux Klan, 233, 294, 298, 302, 304, 447; *See also* lynching; "poor white trash"

L

Langston, Charles Howard, 212–13, 216

Langston, John Mercer, 212, 294, 295

Langston, Lucy, 213

Last of the Mohicans (James Fenimore Cooper), 83

"Last Speech to the Virginia Court" (John Brown), 210–11

"L'Attitude de la France . . ." (A. J. Cooper) 344

Lay, Benjamin, fn26

Leary, Lewis Sheridan, 212

Leatherstocking Tales (James Fenimore Cooper), 83

Leaves of Grass (Walt Whitman), 200, 201, 202

Lee, Robert E., 299, 439

Leopard's Spots, The . . . (Thomas Dixon), 430, 441

Letters from the South . . . (James Kirke Paulding), 130

Letters of a Northern Man (James Kirke Paulding), 130

Letters to Catherine E. Beecher (Angelina Grimké), 134

Liberator, the (William Lloyd Garrison and Isaac Knapp), 92, 93, 94, 103, 186, 231, 233, 268, 270, 282, 418

Liberty Party, 147

Library of Congress, 455

Life and Times of Frederick Douglass (F. Douglass), 156

"Life of Josiah Henson, The . . . ," 205

"Life without Principle" (H. D. Thoreau), 218

"Lift Every Voice and Sing" ("Negro National Anthem"—J. W. Johnson), 324

Lincoln, Abraham, 18, 93, 156, 192, 202, fn231, 253, 255–57, 261. 263, 265, 266, 324, 332, 360, 451, 456; and Sojourner Truth, 263, 266–67; and Thomas Jefferson on race, 256; as Great Emancipator,

255, 257; inaugural address (1861), 255; *See also* Emancipation Proclamation
Lincoln, Mary Todd, 257
Lincoln, Robert Todd, 257
Living Way, 444
Logan, Rayford W., fn326
Longfellow, Henry Wadsworth, 138
Louisiana Black Code, fn315
Love, John, 343
Lovejoy, Elijah P., 179, 422
Lukor, Ralph E., fn454
Lundy, Benjamin, 92, fn94
lynching, 444, 446–50, 463, 468; *See also* George Henry White
Lyrics of Lowly Life (P. L. Dunbar), 372

M

Madame Delphina (G. W. Cable), 309
Majors and Minors (P. L. Dunbar), 371
Marie; or, Slavery in the United States . . . (Gustave de Beaumont; tr. Barbara Chapman), 127
Mark Twain, 17, 310, 333, 358–61, 370; as Southerner, 360; *Autobiography*, 359, 360; black caricatures, 361; condemnation of slavery, 360; for slaveocracy, 359; *Tragedy of Puddn'head Wilson, The*, 360, 361–69
Mark Twain's America, 358
Marrow of Tradition, The (C. W. Chesnutt), 393, 396
Marshall, John, 192
Martineau, Harriet, 169
Martin, Isabella D., 241
Marx, Karl, 166
Mary Chesnut's Civil War, 242
Massachusetts Antislavery Society, 119, 142, 155
Massachusetts Institute of Technology, 415
Matthews, Robert ("Matthias"), 264
Mayflower, 254
"Meditation on the Divine Will" (Abraham Lincoln), 262
Methodists Freedman's Aid Society, 443
"Midnight Raiders," 447
Miller, Kelly, fn427, 430–32, 442, 466; and Howard University, 431

Miller, Mary Boykin, 241
Miller, Stephen Decatur, 241, 242
Mind of the Negro . . . (Carter G. Woodson), 466
miscegenation, 36, 38, 131, 132, 133, 295, 303, 333, 396, 409, 411, 414, 419, 439
Mis-Education of the Negro, The (Carter G. Woodson), 466
"Mob Rule in New Orleans" (I. B. Wells Barnett), 446
Modern Instance, A (William Dean Howells), 333
Moon, 426
Moore, Fred R., 414
Moorland, Jesse E., 431
"Morals of Slavery, The" (W. G. Simms), 169
Moran, Benjamin, 225
Morris, William, 333
Moskowitz, Henry, 451
Moss, Alfred A., Jr., fn426
Mott Lucretia, 96
Muhlenfeld, Elisabeth, fn241, fn242
mulatto, 127, 131, 243, 246, 275, 294, 314, 335, 337, 347, 361, 393–94, 395, 397, 418; *See also* Afro-Americans (passing; skin color)
Murphy, Gardner, 438
Murray, Anna, 156
Murray, Margaret, 348
Mysterious Stranger, The (Mark Twain), 360
"Mystery within Us, The" (P. E. Hopkins), 413

N

NAACP (1909), 318, 326, 331, 379, 392, 396, 397, 415, 422, 426, 446, 447, 451, 453, 454, 455, 458, 459, 460, 461; See also *The Crisis*; National Negro Committee Conference (1909)
Narrative: My Bondage . . . (Frederick Douglass), 156
Narrative of Her Life (Sojourner Truth with Olive Gilbert), 263, 264
Narrative of the Black People during the Late Awful Calamity in Philadelphia, A (Richard Allen and Absalom Jones), 72

Narrative of the Life of Frederick Douglass . . . , 155, 157

Narrative of William W. Brown, 180

Nashoba Commune, 108

National Antislavery Standard (L. M. F. Child), 119, 270, 282

National Association of Colored Women (NACW—National League of Colored Women [originally]), 347, 348, 452

National Citizens Rights Association A. W. Tourgée), 304

National Independent Equal Rights League, 422

National Independent League, 422

National Negro Business League, 324

National Negro Committee Conference (1909), 447, 451, 453, 455; *See also* NAACP

National Watchman, the, 148

Nation, The, 332

Native Americans, 23, 26, 36, 41, 83, 90, 129, 130, 213, 275, 294, fn309, 390, fn424

Nat Turner Rebellion, 102

Negro, 343, 358, 383, 391, 424, 427, 429, 433, 435, 438–39, 442, 454; as "problem," 392; inferiority, 428; in South, 463, 467–68; "question," 416

Negro–American Political League, 422

Negro as Businessman, The (Carter G. Woodson and John H. Harmon), 466

"Negro as Presented in American Literature" (William Dean Howells), 344

"Negro as the South Sees Him, The" (J. C. Harris), 286

Negro Business League, 454

"Negroes' Temporary Farewell to Congress, The" (G. H. White), 391, 392

Negro History Bulletin (1937—Carter G. Woodson), 467

Negro in Our History, The (Carter G. Woodson), 466

"Negro in Politics, The" (T. Thomas fortune), 295

Negro Orators and Their Orations (Carter G. Woodson), 466

Negro Professional Man and the Community, The (Carter G. Woodson), 466

Negro Question, The (G. W. Cable), 310

Negro Wage Earner, The (Carter G. Woodson and Lorenzo Greene), 466

Nell, William Cooper, 161, 185–86, 187

New England Anti-Slavery Society, 93, 119

New Heaven and Earth, The (Samuel Sewall), 23

New Negro for a New Century (ed. B. T. Washington[?]), 347

New Negro, The (William Pickens), 461, 462–64

New Testament, 219; *See also* The Bible

New York African Free School, 146

New York Age, 325, 348, 424, 445

New York Antislavery Society, 138

New York Emancipation Act (1827), 263

New York Evening Post, 451, 453, 454

Niagara Movement, fn296, 421, 422, 425–29, 430, 453, 454, 459, 460; as men's movement, 426

Nicolay, John G., 257

Nordau, Max, 441, 442

Norldloh, David, fn334

North Star, the (Frederick Douglass), 155, 157, 159

Notes on the State of Virginia (Thomas Jefferson), 35, 36, 37, 38, 39–44, 88

Notions of the Americans (James Fenimore Cooper), 83

November Boughs (Walt Whitman), 20

Nullification, 241

O

Oak and Ivy (J. W. Riley), 371

Oberlin College, 208, 212, 426, 452

"Observations Concerning the Increase of Mankind and the Peopling of Countries" (Benjamin Franklin), 69

Official Report of the Niger Valley Exploring Poetry (M. R. Delany), 174

Of One Blood (P. E. Hopkins), 414

Ogden, Robert C., 437

Ohio Anti-Slavery Society, 212

"Old Plantation, The" (J. C. Harris), 288–90

Olmstead, Frederick Law, 237–38; free-soiler, 237; landscape architect, 237

Ordinance of Secession, 242

Out of the House of Bondage (Kelly Miller), 432

Ovington, Mary White, 451, 452, 453, 454,

455; "Reminiscences," 454; *The Walls Came Tumbling Down*, 451

P

Page, Thomas Nelson, 286, 370
Page, Walter Hines, 396
Paine, Thomas, 30
Parker, Theodore, 185
Park, Robert E., 318
"Past and Present Condition . . . (Henry Highland Garnet), 148
Patriotic Gore (Edmund Wilson), 302
Paul Marchant, F. M. C. (Free Man of Color) (C. W. Chesnutt), 397
Paulding, James Kirke, 130–31; pro-slavery advocacy, 130
Paul, Thomas, Sr., 412
Peabody, Sophia, 252
Pearl Harbor, 461
Peculiar Sam . . . (P. E. Hopkins), 413
Peden., William, fn39
Pemberton, Caroline Hollingsworth, 384–86
Pemberton, Henry, 385
Pemberton, John Clifford, 385
Penn, I. Garland, 445
Pennington, James W. C., 156
Pennsylvania Anti-Slavery Society, 227
Pennsylvania Society for Promoting the Abolition of Slavery . . . (Benjamin Franklin), 69, 227, 282
Penn, William, 385
People's Advocate, 295
People's Savings Bank, 392
Peterson, Jerome, 295
Philadelphia Female Antislavery Society, 141
Phillips, Wendell, 138, 180, 185, 187, 265, 277
Piatt, John J., 332
Pickens, William, 458–62; and House Committee on Un-American Activities, 461; See also *The New Negro*
Pierce, Franklin, 253
Pierson, Robert, 264
Pillsbury, A. E., 449
Pindell, Geraldine, 419
Pitts, Helen, 157
"Plan for the Gradual Abolition of Slavery

in the United States . . ." (Frances Milton Trollope), 108
Plea for John Brown, A (H. D. Thoreau), 219–22
Plessy, Homer Adolph, 304
Plessy v Ferguson, 304, 317, 444
Plumb, Ralph, fn214
Poems of Two Friends (William Dean Howells), 332
Poems on Miscellaneous Subjects (F. E. W. Harper), 281
Political Destiny of the Colored Race (M. R. Delany), 174, 175–78
Poor Richard's Almanack (Benjamin Franklin), 69
"poor white trash," 297–98, 302; and the Ku Klux Klan, 298
Porter, Dorothy B., fn224
"Post-Bellum-Pre-Harlem" (C. W. Chesnutt), 397
prejudice, 81, 114–15, 116, 117, 145, 328, 414, 418, 461, 463; See also race; slavery in America
"Present Status and Intellectual Progress of Colored Women, The" (Fannie Barrier Williams), 348–57
Primer of Facts, A . . . (P. E. Hopkins), 415
Principia of Ethnology . . . (M. R. Delany), 174
"Private History of a Campaign That Failed, The" (Mark Twain), 359
Proceedings of the Massachusetts Historical Society, 1863–1864, 24
"Progressive Era" (1890–1920), 446
Pro-Slavery Argument . . . (W. G. Simms), 169
Puritan ethic, 23
Puritans, 24, 26, 254, 345, fn440
Purvis, Harriet Forten, 227; cofounder Female anti-Slavery Society, 227
Purvis, Robert, fn122, 183, 227–28, 233, 268; as integrationist, 228
Purvis, William, 227

Q

Quakers (Society of friends), 26–27, 30, 60, 88, fn94, 134, 141, 142, 179, fn183, 204, 233, 248, 264, 265, 331, 385
Quarles, Ralph, 213

Quarry, The (C. W. Chesnutt), 396
"Quick and the Dead, The" (T. Thomas Fortune), 295

R

race in the United States, 15, 36, 47, 128–29, 145, 197, 198, 283, 322, 323, 333, 342, 374–78, 380, 381, 385, 413, 432, 438, 441, 447–48, 451, 453, 456; accommodationist policy, 425; criminality of blacks, 463; economic caste, 327, 328, 329–30, 388, 472; ignorance of white population, 462–63, 464, 468–69; inferiority of Afro-Americans, 40, 88, 131–33, 325, 330, 331, 335, 345, 428, 433–34, 435; oppression, 468–69; purity, 430
"Race War in the North, The" (William English Walling), 451
Radical Reconstruction, 174, 279, 304
Raleigh News and Observer, 390
"Reason Why the Colored American Is Not in the World's Columbian Exposition, The" (I. B. Wells-Barnett), 445
Reconstruction, 144, 241, 248, 257, 279, 283, 286, 292, 302, 310, 393, 396, 430
Reconstruction Act (1867), 443
Redmond, Charles Lenox, 223, 269
Redmond, Sarah Parker, 223–24, 225, 226, 227, 233, 269; expatriate, 224
"Red Record, A . . ." (I. B. Wells-Barnett), 446
Reeve, Henry, 128
Religion and Pure Principles of Morality. . . . (Maria W. Stewart), 97
"Rena Walden." See *The House behind the Cedars*
Render, Sylvia Lyons, 397
"Resistance to Civil Government." See "Civil Disobedience"
Revels, Hiram, 444
Revolutionary War, 35, 169, 230, 259, 412, 420
Rice, Howard J., fn43
Rice, Thomas Dartmouth, 370
Richmond Examiner, 166
"Rights of Colored Persons while Travelling" (C. L. Redmond), 223
Rights of Man, The (Thomas Paine), 30

Riley, James Whitcomb, 372
Rise of Silas Lapham, The (William Dean Howells), 333
Roberts, Joseph Jenkins, 260
Rochester Female Antislavery Society, 157
Roosevelt, Theodore, 304, 318, 324, 348
Running of a Thousand Miles for Freedom . . . (William Craft), 233, 234–36
Rural Negro, The (Carter G. Woodson), 466
Russell, Charles Edward, 452
Russwurm, John B., 77–79

S

Sachs, Walter, 455
Salem witchcraft trials. *See* witchcraft trials, Salem
Sandiford, Ralph, fn26
Sanford, (Sandford), John F. A., 190
Saturday Evening Post, fn241m 286, 373, 432
Saxton, Rufus, 272, fn274, 276
Scott, Dred, 186, 190, 191, 192–99, 200, 229
Scott, Emmet J., 318
Scottsboro Boys, 461
Scroggs, William O., 468
secessionists, 170
Selling of Joseph (Samuel Sewall), 23, 24–25
separate but equal doctrine, 304
Septimius Felton (N. Hawthorne), 252
Serafin, Steven R., fn384
"Services of Colored Americans in the Wars of 1776 and 1812" (W. C. Nell), 185
Sewall, Samuel, 23–24, 26
Shakespeare, William, 234, 257, 360
Shaw, Robert Gould, fn270, 271, 273
Sherman, General W. T., 170, 173
Shockley, Ann Allen, fn412
Short Fiction of Charles W. Chesnutt (Sylvia Lyons Render, ed.), 397
"Sieur George" (G. W. Cable), 309
Silent South, The (G. W. Cable), 310
"Significance of the Frontier in American

History, The" (Frederick Jackson Turner), 358
Silent South, The (G. W. Cable), 310
Simms, William Gilmore, 169, 173
Slavery Abolition Act (Great Britain, 1833), 204
"Slavery Justified" (George Fitzhugh), 166
Sherman, Roger, 163, 273
Sketches of Places and People Abroad (W. W. Brown), 181–84
"Slavery" (Walt Whitman), 202–3
"Slavery in Massachusetts . . . (H. D. Thoreau), 218
slavery in the United States, 31–34, 37, 48, 50, 52–53, 83, 84–86, 112, 118, 130, 150, 192, 196, 197, 234, 241, 337, 359, 360, 430; and Uncle Remus folkore, 286; and women's rights, 159; and socialism, 166; bravery of, 126; condition of slaves, 110, 142, 164, 314; conforming to, 50; contradictions of in a democracy, 35; economic aspects, 167–68, 312, 319–20; effects on white population, 259, 314, 433; escape, 156, 275; evils of, 71, 88–89, 116, 117, 124, 129, 149, 152, 162, 169–70, 243, 249–51, 300, 311; feeble-mindedness, 114; obsequiousness, 170–72; opposition, 122, 123–26; plantation life, 288–90, 370; resistance, 154; slaves as animals, 340; violent conditions, 139, 378
Slavery in the United States (James Kirke Paulding), 130, 131–33
"Slavery Justified" (George Fitzhugh), 166
slave trade, 31, 37, 66, 75, 76, 120–21, 126, 202–3, 311, 312, 313
Slave Trade Act (1807), 72
Smets, Alexander, 238
Smith, James, 232
Smith, James McCune, 291
Smith, Maria, 232
Smith, Stephen, 144
Sociology of the South (George Fitzhugh), 166, 167–68
Sojourner Truth, 263–65, 268
Some Considerations on the Keeping of Negroes, 27
"Song of Myself" (Walt Whitman), 202
Souls of Black Folk, The (W. E. B. Du Bois), 291, 454

Southampton Insurrection. *See* Nat Turner Rebellion
"South as an Opening for a Career" (Booker T. Washington), 319–23
"Southern Horrors: Lynch Law in All Its Phases": a.k.a. "United States Atrocities: Lynch Law" (I. B. Wells-Barnett), 445
Souther, Simeon, fn164
Spingarn, Joel, 326, 460
Stanton, Elizabeth Cady, 157, 265, 283
states' rights, 241
Stephen the Black (C. H. Pemberton), 384, 385, 386–89
Stevenson, Brenda, 270
Steward, Maria W. (Maria Miller), 96–97, 265
Still, William, 282
Stokes, J. G. Phelps, 452
Storey, Moorfield, 452
Story, Joseph, 191
Story of My Life and Word (B. T. Washington), 348
Story of the Negro Retold, The (Carter G. Woodson), 466
Stowe, Catharine, 161
Stowe, Harriet Beecher, 17, 139, 204–5, 263–64, 292; ambivalence toward emancipation, 160–61
Styron, William, fn103
Sumner, Charles, 167, 422
Swallow Barn; or, A Sojourn in the Old Dominion (John Pendleton Kennedy), 111, 112–18
Swisshelm, Jane, fn266
Sword and the Distaff. See Woodcraft

T

"Talented Tenth, The" (W. E. B. Du Bois), 292
Taney, Roger Brooke, 190–92, 215, fn228, 229
Terrell, Mary Church, 347, 452
Terrell, Robert J., 343, fn347
Terry, Lucy, fn50
Thomas, Edward, fn262
Thoreau, Henry David, 217–19, 273
Thrasher, Max B., 318

Titus, Frances, fn263
Tobey, Henry A., 371
Toinette (A. W. Tourgée), 303
Tolstoy, Lev, 333
Tom Sawyer Abroad (Mark Twain), 361
"To the Daughters of James Forten"
    (James Greenleaf Whittier), 122
Tourgée, Albion Winegar, 302–5, 342, 396;
    separate but equal doctrine, 304
Tragedy of Puddn'head Wilson, The. See
    Mark Twain
Traitor, The (Thomas Dixon), 430
Trollope, Anthony, 108
Trollope, Frances Milton, 108
Trotter, Geraldine, 420
Trotter, James Monroe, 418, 419, 453, 455
Trotter, Monroe, 318, 418–23, 425, 426,
    452, 459; and "Boston Riot," 425
Truth, Sojourner. *See* Sojourner Truth
Turner, Arlin, fn308
Turner, Frederick Jackson, 358
Turner, Henry MacNeal, 380
Turner, Nat, 102–3, 108, 153, 216
Tuskegee, 317, 347, 454
Twain, Mark. *See* Mark Twain

U

Ulloa, Don Antonio de, fn36
"Ulrich Case," 317–18
Uncle Remus folklore (J. C. Harris), 286,
    287, 291, 395
*Uncle Tom's Cabin; or, The Man That Was
    a Thing* (Harriet Beecher Stowe), 139,
    160, 166, 205, 275, 292
Underground Railroad, 180
Underground Railroad, The (William
    Still), 282
"United States Atrocities . . ." *See* "South-
    ern Horrors . . ."
Up from Slavery (B. T. Washington), 316

V

Van Buren, Martin, 131
Vassa, Gustavas. *See* Equiano, Olaudah
"*Vengeance of the Gods, The*" . . . (William
    Pickens), 461
Vesey, Denmark, 87, 102, 153, 169

Views of Society and Manners in America
    (Frances Milton Trollope), 108
Villard, Oswald Garrison, fn422, 451–55;
    grandson of William Lloyd Garrison,
    452; *Yachting* magazine, 452
Voice from Harper's Ferry, A (O. P. Ander-
    son), 208
Voice from the South, A (A. J. Cooper),
    342, 344–45
Voice of the Fugitive, 205
Voice of the Negro, 414, 415, 459

W

Wagenen, Isabella Van [Van Wagener],
    264. *See* Sojourner Truth
Walden Pond, 219
Walden Pond; or, Life in the Woods (H. D.
    Thoreau), 217, 218
Wald, Lillian, 452
Walker, David, 77, 87–88, 92, 96
Walker, Edward Garrison, 88
Walker. Robert J., fn221
Walks and Tracks . . . (Frederick Law Olm-
    stead), 237
Walling, William English, 451, 452
Walls Came Tumbling Down, The (Mary
    White Ovington), 451, 452–53
Washington, Booker T. ("Wizard of
    Tuskegee"), 288, 292, 296, 316–20, 324,
    326, 331 342, 343, 347, 348, 370, 371,
    373, 414, 415, 420, 422, 423, 425, 430,
    431, 434, 437, 438 446, 453, 454, 458,
    459, 460; adoption of name, 316; and
    "Ulrich Case," 317–18; as successor to
    Frederick Douglass, 317; *See also* At-
    lanta Compromise; Tuskegee
Washington, George, 45, 259
Washington, Madison, 154, 156
Watkins, William, 281
Watson, Thomas, 434, 435
Wayles, John, 37
Webb, Frank J., 161
Webster, Daniel, 163
*Week on the Concord and Merrimack Riv-
    ers, A* (H. D. Thoreau), 217
Weld, Theodore Dwight, 135, 137, 142,
    418, fn419
Wells-Barnett, Ida B. ("Iola"), 318, 346,

443–47, 451, 452, 453, 454, 455; civil rights activism, 444; club, 446; muckraker, 446; state senate candidate, 446

Wells, Jim, 443

West Canada (Ontario), 174, 204, 206–7, 208

West Indies, 60, 65, 67, 74, 77, 90; *See also* Caribbean

"We Wear the Mask" (P. L. Dunbar), 372

"What Is a White Man?" (C. W. Chesnutt), 395

What Is Man? (Mark Twain), 360

"What to the Slave Is the Fourth of July?" (Frederick Douglass), 155

Wheatley, Phillis, 41, 51

Whipper, William, 144, 145, 228

White, George Henry, 390–92, 393; H. R. Bill 6963, outlawing mob lynching, 391; last former slave in Congress, 390

White, Walter, 461

"White Weeds" (C. W. Chesnutt), 397–411

Whitman, Walt, 200–202; and Abraham Lincoln, 202; *Democratic Vistas*, 201; *Eighteenth Presidency, The . . .* , 201; *Franklin Evans* ("Fortunes of a Country Boy . . ."), 200; on slavery, 200, 202–3; "Slavery," 202–3; *Specimen Days*, 201; See *Leaves of Grass*; "Song of Myself"

Whittier, John Greenleaf, 122–23, 138, 269, 332; opposition to slavery, 122

"Wife of His Youth, The . . ." (C. W. Chesnutt), 395

Williams, Ben Ames, fn241, 242

Williams, Dr. Daniel Hale, 347

Williams, Fannie Barrier, 346–48, 445, 446, fn461

Williams, George Washington, fn255

Williams, Peter, 291

Williams, F. Laing, 347, fn461

Willis, Nathaniel P., 248

Wilson, Edmund, 302

Wilson, Harriet E., fn180

Wilson, Woodrow, 326, 422

Winona . . . (P. E. Hopkins), 414

witchcraft trials, Salem, 1692–93, 23; (1691–92), 253

"Womanhood . . ." (A. J. Cooper), 343

women's rights, 158–59, 263, 283–85, 293, 295; black women, 293, 349–50, 351, 352, 354, 357; *See also* feminist thought

Woodcraft . . . (W. G. Simms), 169, 170–72

Woodson, Carter G., 16, 432, 464–67; and ASNLH, 465, 466; as popularizer, 466; "Father of Negro History," 16, 465

Woodward, C. Vann, fn241

Woolman, John, 26–27

Works of Francis J. Grimké, The (Carter G. Woodson), 466

World Anti-Slavery Convention (London, 1840), 223

World Congress of Representative Women, 346, 445, 446

World War I, 15, 469, 471

Wright, Frances, 108

Wright, Orville and Wilbur, 371

Wright, Theodore, 78

Y

Yellin, Jean Fagin, fn247

Young, John, 179

Your Little Brother James (C. H. Pemberton), 384